✳Child Psychology:

Behavior and Development

Ronald C. Johnson

University of Hawaii

Gene R. Medinnus

San Jose State College

✳ Child Psychology:

Behavior and Development

John Wiley and Sons, Inc., New York · London · Sydney

to John E. Anderson
whose ideas influenced this book and

to Carol and Colleen
whose patience and goodness
smoothed our way,
and to
Roni, Mark, Steven, Lisa, Laura, and David
young people whose behavior
is a spur to research,
since it is only minimally predictable
in the light of our present knowledge.

✳ PREFACE

Child psychology is inextricably linked with other psychological fields, such as experimental psychology, the psychology of individual differences, social psychology, learning, and personality. It is also multidisciplinary, since it draws on data gathered in such diverse fields as sociology, anthropology, behavioral genetics, pediatrics, and some areas of home economics. From these different areas of specialization we have gathered data dealing with two major aspects: first, those ways in which all humans are similar to one another in their potentialities, patterns of development, and behavior; and, second, the differences between human beings in capabilities and in behavior as these differences are manifested within this core of similarity.

We see two forces operating to produce similarity. The first is our biological nature, which makes humans the moderately large, omnivorous, tough, stimulation-seeking, problem-solving, symbol-using organisms that we are. The second is that necessary core of culture based on such aspects of the human condition as a long period of dependency which in turn demands a stable family structure, considerable instruction, and considerable psychological support if the highly immature organism is to survive. Within the limits imposed by these two forces, individual differences in behavior occur as a result of hereditary and environmental variability.

We have attempted to present a sound body of facts within the context of those ideas and theories that influence our view of development. We can discuss and raise questions, but the reader must interact with real children to understand the reasons for our interest, our discussion, and our questions.

The basic motivation of any science is to understand fully and accurately those natural phenomena that are the object of study within that science. We have tried to present data that will help the individual in the task of understanding the processes involved in human development. We have tried as best we could to weight the evidence in our interpretations and explanations of psychological phenomena. There are points where our position is not the only one available, and future research may demonstrate that we are clearly wrong, but, at this time, we believe our view to be supported by the preponderance of the evidence. Perhaps some reader will provide the crucial experimental data that will resolve some of the still unanswered questions concerning the psychology of human development.

We wish to express our gratitude to our teachers, John E. Anderson, Gene Gollin, Bryng Bryngelson, Dale B. Harris, Arnold Rose, George Strother, and Donald M. Johnson; to our colleagues, especially Harold Keely, James L. McGaugh, and Karl Mueller, who provided aid; and to our students. We wish to thank the authors whose research makes up this volume, and the publishers who granted us permission to quote some of these research findings. And finally, our thanks go to Henry Angelino, University of Oklahoma, and Aubrey Roden, University of Alberta, Calgary, for their invaluable criticisms. The task of writing has been evenly divided (there is no "first" or "second" author except in an alphabetical sense), and we are grateful to each other for the comments and encouragement that shaped the structure of this book and brought it to completion.

RONALD C. JOHNSON
GENE R. MEDINNUS

October 1964

�֍ CONTENTS

❋Child Psychology:

Behavior and Development

SECTION I ✳ INTRODUCTION

All sciences attempt to understand the phenomena with which they deal. Some of them control these phenomena. All of them make predictions. Whether physics, biochemistry, psychology, or any other of the sciences, the aims and methods of procedure are basically alike. Some sciences may have progressed further than others in achieving these aims. However, it is believed that all of them can ultimately reach the same level of accuracy in explanation and prediction if they employ what is universally known as the scientific method.

This opening section of the book, consisting of a single chapter, considers the scientific method and how child psychologists have developed techniques for observation and experimentation which have yielded a clearer, less biased, and more systematic understanding of human behavior and have enhanced predictive powers. A review of these processes also discloses the historical development of child psychology as a scientific discipline. It is to that review that the next several pages pay close attention.

chapter 1 ✳ Scientific Method and Child Psychology

One of the many reasons a person seeks knowledge is to understand the world around him. By knowing the *why* of what he sees, he acquires some proficiency at discerning orderly sequences of events and predicting the future from the present. Through understanding the causes of events, an individual may at times change the sequence and produce a different end result. Understanding leads to prediction and often, ultimately, to control of the environment. But there is a great difference between common, ordinary, everyday understanding and scientific understanding. The latter is achieved by application of what is widely known as the scientific method. Let us therefore explore this method to learn how scientific understanding, prediction, and control develop, in distinction to the more personal, day-to-day understanding of the universe which is shared by all manner of men. And then let us see how scientific techniques develop valuable findings in child development.

SCIENTIFIC METHOD

Observation

The raw data of scientific knowledge are facts, and scientific undertakings usually begin with their observation. Astronomy, the first of the sciences, grew out of the keen observations of Egyptian and Babylonian priests. To them, the orderly sequences of day and night and of the seasons might have suggested an orderliness, that is, a predictability, in the physical world. Careful observation led to knowledge of planetary movement and of fixed stars; and this knowledge enabled these priestly astronomers to make practical predictions, such as the time at which the Nile would flood. Since they also believed in astrology, they made less valid predictions too—such as "Beware of a dark-haired man next Tuesday." In all probability, the science of astronomy resulted from false notions about the influence of celestial bodies on human behavior as much as from a belief in an orderly universe. Yet the information collected by these early observers was substantially correct, even when their interpretations fell short of the mark.

Since these initial probings of the unknown, knowledge of the world has progressed a long way to its present state. In this advance, observation has played a major role: *knowledge, in fact, has depended on observation.* Although the ability to observe is widespread, scientific observation differs from ordinary observation in several respects. Scientific observation is systematic; it dwells on a particular phenomenon. This phenomenon may be the movement of the planets as observed by the ancients, or it may be the social relations of two-year-olds as observed by child psychologists. In either instance, as in any scientific undertaking, the observation is restricted to one or, at the most, a few kinds of objects or events; it does not extend to everything. Moreover, this kind of observation concentrates on *all* aspects of the particular kinds of events, whereas everyday observation may take in only part of many events.

Take the bias found in the casual observation of the relation between physical characteristics and behavior. Redheads have hot tempers, we hear; people with big ears are generous; long fingers denote the artist. If these views were valid, we could easily predict appropriate behavior toward redheads, whom to approach for a loan, and which child would perform in Carnegie Hall. This is hazardous terrain. It leads from fallacies concerning the most observable characteristics of people with big ears to the quicksand of characteristics believed to be evident among members of racial or religious groups. These questionable beliefs result from the human tendency *not* to observe negative manifestations. People prefer to notice only those things that confirm their beliefs. If an event runs counter to a belief, they are more likely to forget or distort the event than change the belief. This tendency may be seen in a vast number of studies cited by Rapaport (1942), and more recently in the work of Festinger (1957), centered in his theory of cognitive dissonance. Scientific method, in contrast, is aimed at insuring complete, accurate observation and inclusion of even negative findings. The observation of these instances—the cases that do not fit the expectation—is the very essence of science.

Observation leads to the formation of hypotheses, which may be considered "educated guesses" or suppositions. If these hypotheses are so linked that a test of any one of them yields information not only about itself but also about the other hypotheses dependent in whole or in part upon it, a theory exists. Sometimes the information bears no essential relation to any specific hypothesis and hence to the theory. For example, the difference in average sentence length in the speech of two-year-olds and three-year-olds may have some value for other purposes, but it suggests no new ideas or leads no further to basic understanding of the child. Other data, however, may help to find out whether an hypothesis conforms to reality; such data permit new predictions which in turn provide new insights about the world. Scientific procedure benefits greatly from findings of this kind and the experimental processes uncovering them, but all scientific investigations must start with the accumulation of facts from observation and then test their hypotheses against these facts.

If a theory or an hypothesis does not fit the observed facts, it must be discarded, whether it concerns a folk belief like the temper of redheads or a cosmological issue such as the question of whether the universe is expanding or standing still. The rejection of a theory generally results from systematic, close observation of *all* cases. Sometimes the facts fit the theory fairly well, but not well enough. Here, the negating instances indicate where a theory is weak and must be revised promptly to improve its accuracy. The next result is a fuller, clearer understanding of the world, which sharpens the skill of being able to predict the future more precisely.

Prediction

All scientific endeavor is concerned with making observations that do lead to accurate prediction—predictions ranging from what to anticipate from a change in the structure of a molecule to what new attitudes to expect to develop among race-prejudiced persons exposed to close contact with another race, as in an integrated teen-aged boys' camp.

Prediction, however, is never certain. It is merely a statement of probability. The form in which it is used in all sciences is often called *actuarial prediction*. This term is borrowed from insurance, whose actuaries can tell—barring great, unexpected catastrophes such as wars—the number of individuals in a given age group who will die in a particular year. An actuarial statement sets forth the odds, the chances that a specific thing will happen. In child psychology, for example, an actuarial statement might hold that "a child of IQ 70 at age 12 has less than one chance in 100 of completing a conventional high school course curriculum by age 20." The chance is there (Baller, 1936), but it is a long shot.

This form of prediction is also known as *nomothetic prediction*— that is, arising from or based on law—a distinction noted by Allport (1937). A nomothetic statement like an actuarial statement asserts the odds; it is a statement of probability. A statement like "Republicans worry more about a balanced budget than do Democrats" is a nomothetic statement. It may very well be true, based on a theory of budgeting which has influenced many Democrats, but it is only a matter of probability for any individual member of either party. Even though the odds in its favor are excellent, the statement is still not a certainty.

A second type of prediction, limited almost entirely to the social sciences, applies to the individual case. This is *idiographic prediction*, roughly a "drawing or graphing an individual," and it is aimed at understanding a particular individual. Idiographic prediction makes use of nomothetic knowledge, but is concerned only with one individual. To the applied psychologist, it is the predictive technique *par excellence:* "Mr. X will not commit suicide"; "Miss A will do better in group therapy than in analysis"; "Mr. K is not a good parole risk." Such predictions are often wrong. They are based on knowledge acquired by nomothetic means which only imply the odds. Nevertheless, the social scientist must make these predictions, since though they often prove inaccurate, they are frequently more precise than the predictions made by others. Indeed, considering the present state of knowledge and the complexity of subject matter, the proportion of accuracy in prediction is remarkable.

Whether nomothetic or idiographic, the accuracy of a prediction supplies cues to the truth of a belief. The most wonderful thing about science, believed M. R. Cohen (1949), is that built into it is the notion that unless ideas accurately portray reality, they must be changed. If of two theories, for example, one makes more accurate predictions about the phenomena with which both deal, this theory is accepted and the other is rejected. If the two predict equally well, the more *parsimonious* theory, the one making fewer assumptions, takes precedence. Should a new theory be developed that outshines either of the other two, both prior theories are discarded. No truth is sacred, universal, or immutable to science or the scientist. This attitude of disrespect for any authority other than nature, when observed systematically and without bias, is what has enabled science to change rapidly and relinquish old ideas for better—that is, more accurate or more truthful—new ones. Certainly this applies to many of the ideas discussed in this book; they are likely to be superseded in time by more reliable interpretations.

If the goal of psychology is highly accurate prediction, how closely has this been approached? Not very closely, but progress is being made. There are several reasons why success in psychological prediction has only been moderate. First, the subject matter of psychology is more complex than the subject matter of many other sciences; at least the psychologists claim this to be so. Second, psychology is a comparatively young science. One of the early American students of Wilhelm Wundt, a founder of modern psychology, died only recently. This makes one realize, as does nothing else, how young this science is. The youth of psychology cannot be changed until hundreds of years have passed and it has suffered the problems of growing up. But there are aspects of the young science that can be changed, aspects which at present contribute to a deficiency in skill.

One change desired by most psychologists and toward which they are working is an increase in the reliability and validity of measuring devices. In its simplest form, reliability means that a device used to measure a stable characteristic, such as the height of an adult, will give the same information on every occasion. If a yardstick expanded or contracted capriciously, what would measure five feet, ten inches today might measure three feet, six inches or nine feet, eight inches at some future date. Obviously this yardstick would be unreliable as a measuring device, and because of its unreliability, growth trends could not be predicted with any accuracy over intervals of time. The reliability of many measuring instruments is indeed low, especially the tests for measuring personality. Perhaps personality characteristics are basically unstable and individual personality varies greatly at different points in time. If this lack of reliability is largely the fault of inadequate tests rather than of actual personality change, the continued efforts to increase the reliability of psychological tests should make their results more dependable and therefore better instruments for predicting behavior.

A test is valid if it measures what it set out to measure. It is invalid if it measures other things and not what it was designed to test.

Suppose we measured the height of members of a psychology class and graded them on the basis of height. The measurements would be highly reliable on the subject of height, but they would not be valid for achievement, since tallness is hardly a good measure of ability. Whereas a reliable measure may not be valid, as in the foregoing example, a measure cannot be highly valid unless it is highly reliable. As better testing methods are used and reliability grows, the validity of measurements increases. But more important, the validity of the measuring device can be checked by comparing its findings with reality. Does the person who does well in a test of creativity, for example, actually behave creatively? Only when behavior in the real world is predictable from test results does a test become a valid predictive device. Development of tests at once reliable and valid increases the power to predict.

Phenotype and Genotype. Psychology also stands to gain in both understanding and predictability from an increasing awareness of *genotypic* variation as opposed to *phenotypic* variation between individuals. *Genotype* refers to the similarity in background forces that produce behavior. One young man steals an automobile. Another holds down two jobs to pay for an automobile. Both are motivated chiefly by a desire to impress some young woman. They are genotypically alike in this specific aspect of their motivation even though their outward behavior differs. *Phenotype,* on the other hand, concerns the phenomenal or observable world. Phenotypically, or observably, these young men differ greatly.

Psychologists, and social scientists in general, have dwelt on phenotypes rather than genotypes and, further, have not done as good a job as they might on distinguishing between phenotypes. Consider the problem as it relates to the diagnosis and treatment of physical and psychological disorders. A physical disorder entailing an increase in temperature is called a fever. Although various fevers differ in a number of secondary aspects, their major phenotypical or observable feature is the heightened temperature they all share. If physicians paid attention only to the temperature, no effective methods of treatment would have been developed, since a therapeutic aid for reducing one fever, such as quinine for malarial fever, is utterly useless in the treatment of many other fevers. Astute physicians managed, however, through keen observation to distinguish several *sub*phenotypes within the general phenotype *fever.* These subphenotypes differed in genotype—or cause—and, once separated from one another, also differed in the treatment effective for each of them. This knowledge enabled

development of individual treatments. By carefully examining subjects manifesting a common genotype, one can often discern systematic
variations in their observable characteristics. Though superficially
resembling one another, subjects in each group actually fall into
distinct subgroups, each a result of another genotype. This distinction
will be discussed at some length in Chapter 16.

How successful is this approach in psychology? Individuals with
severe mental defects—say, below IQ 50—are phenotypically alike in
being defective. Yet there are several rather easily observable distinctions among them. Some of these individuals have clearly suffered
brain damage during prenatal development, in a difficult birth process,
or after birth itself. Others form the low end of the normal distribution of intelligence. For every IQ of 160, presumably, there is another
of 40, and its possessor is defective as a result of multiple genetic
variation. Still others are defective from the effects of a single gene
rather than the multiple-genetic deficiency responsible for the IQ of
40. More careful scrutiny divides these individuals into additional
subphenotypes, suggesting the existence of still more genotypes than
are casually perceived. One variety of defectiveness resembles any
other *until* the individual's urine is subjected to chemical analysis.
This particular disorder with the formidable name of *phenylpyruvic
oligophrenia* or *phenylketonuria* has an observable symptom in the
excretion of phenylpyruvic acid in the urine when *phenylalanine,* an
amino acid, is incompletely oxidized. When this acid is found in the
urine, the individual is nearly always defective, presumably because
of this unmetabolized amino acid in the system. The condition results
from a double recessive genetic characteristic. Anyone may be a
carrier of the disorder, though the probabilities are slight. The carrier who transmits the disorder has one recessive and one dominant
gene, whereas the victim has a double recessive pair of genes. If
married, by chance, to another carrier, the original carrier has one
chance in four of having a child with this affliction, two chances in
four of having children who do not have it but who are carriers,
and one chance in four of having a child who is neither defective nor
a carrier.

Here is an instance in which careful phenotypical observation led
to the discovery of a specific genotype. Once the genotype was
found, effective treatment was soon developed. With a phenylalanine-
free diet, especially during the first year of life, a child could overcome the hereditary disposition toward idiocy (Armstrong & Tyler,
1955; Woolf, Griffiths, & Moncrieff, 1955). Without doubt, there are
probably a number of genotypes of this sort hidden within the larger

phenotypical category, "severely mentally defective," as there are in such widely inclusive phenotypes as juvenile delinquency, schizophrenia, or even "shyness." But as long as psychologists continue to study individuals on the basis of broad phenotypes, there is scant likelihood for additional success in diagnosis, prediction of outcome, and treatment. A shift in interest to genotypes may very well improve the predictive powers of the child psychologist.

Control

A basic purpose of prediction is control. However, prediction and control are separate aspects of science. In fact, control is not a necessary part of science, since some sciences exist for which control is clearly impossible. Many sciences such as astronomy, cosmology, volcanology, and seismology, for example, are reasonably adequate at predicting events, but they obviously have no control over the phenomena to which they attend. Predicting an eclipse is a simple matter for an astronomer, whereas causing or controlling one is indeed beyond human capability.

One might contend that ability to predict without ability to control is essentially useless. The argument depends on the definition of utility. If immediate, demonstrable usefulness is necessary, then, as Bugelski (1960, p. 20) said, "Such a viewpoint might limit the work of astronomers to observations of the moon and the navigational stars since outside of these might be little of an immediately practical nature in astronomy." Most scientists, however, are unconcerned with practical utility. For them, knowledge is an end in itself. More cogently and more practically, knowledge that does not have immediate utility might be of value in the future. Bugelski (1960) noted that Faraday once demonstrated an elementary form of a dynamo to Disraeli. "What good is it?" Disraeli asked. Faraday retorted, "Someday you may tax it." The practical and concrete fact often arises from the impractical and abstract theory. From an interesting set of ideas proposed by a young man named Einstein evolved the atomic bomb. The justification for seeking knowledge clearly does not depend on the practical utility of the knowledge for controlling the surrounding world.

In certain areas of psychology, notably clinical psychology, control of behavior is often considered to be a major aim. As used in this sense, control does not mean forcing the individual to act in a desired manner. It rather means increasing the frequency of certain behaviors and decreasing the frequency of other behaviors through a manipulation of the environment. Suppose it is believed that a boy who sets fires does so because of neurotic difficulties stemming from his acceptance of the masculine sex role. The clinical psychologist, using some form of therapy, tries to bring these problems into the open where they can be treated. If given some insight into the roots of his problems plus, perhaps, some form of training and support, the boy may indeed cease his arsonous activities. If successful, the clinician has controlled behavior. Certain behaviors, such as setting fires, decrease in frequency whereas other behaviors, such as dating, increase. Even if the boy now starts stealing cars to provide himself and his young lady friend with transportation, the therapy quite likely has been successful. It has discovered the sources of the arsonous conduct, and certain hypotheses have been formed regarding the efficacy of various treatment techniques. Behavior has been controlled.

Very often the child psychologist is asked questions pertaining to control. How does one increase a behavior, such as eating everything on the plate, or decrease a behavior, such as having temper tantrums? Psychology has some answers to these questions, and this book will attempt to deal with them. The scientist may not be sure that control should be attempted because he is not certain that control is desirable for human beings. The parent, on the other hand, controls his children's present and attempts to control their future through manipulating the environment. Good or bad, this is parenthood. All any parent can do is to try to increase those behaviors that he values as "good" in a child and decrease those deemed "bad." Like the clinician and the parent, the teacher, too, must act. Since these acts have far-reaching consequences, parent and teacher, again like the clinician, should use what scientific understanding is available. Although much remains to be known, this book will endeavor to discuss what is understood, what is predictable, and what forms control may take.

RESEARCH METHODS IN CHILD PSYCHOLOGY

There are several reasons why knowledge of research methods is important for the beginning student in child development. Like other areas of the social sciences, child psychology is quite imprecise as compared with the more exact physical sciences. Yet in a relatively brief interval of time, the precision of research and, hence, the reliability and validity of conclusions have shown a remarkable advance.

Moreover, the studying of research methods tends to foster a critical faculty in the student; he is better able to judge the value of research data and the conclusions by examining the methods that produce them. This ability is perhaps more necessary in the field of child psychology than in any other scientific area. Here every layman considers himself an expert and is quite willing to proffer advice in such matters as child discipline, juvenile delinquency, and child growth. It is therefore of particular importance that the student of child psychology be well grounded in scientific methods. Only then can he judge, not on the basis of apparent meaningfulness and plausibility of statements, but by examining the source of the data, the correctness and appropriateness of the techniques employed, and the justifiability of the conclusion drawn.

Four main questions will guide the inquiry into research methods in child psychology: (1) Where is the particular method applicable? (2) What are its advantages? (3) What are its disadvantages? (4) What does the method tell, and what kinds of information can it not provide?

Naturalistic Observation

The scientist, like the novelist, can gain his raw data from observing organisms in nature—that is, in their natural habitat, and not in any controlled or experimentally manipulated environment. Many psychologists believe that such naturalistic observation, which is relatively objective, will ultimately yield more information than better controlled but more limited techniques—limited in the sense of the amount of behavior observed—such as experimentation.

Baby Biographies. Among the types of naturalistic observation the early diary accounts describing child behavior have been of both historical and methodological importance. The biographer, usually an interested parent or relative, has observed the behavior of a single child and recorded the observations in diary style. Often the biographers have been scientists in fields other than child behavior. Charles Darwin, for example, was a biologist. Thus, an individual of scientific bent, curious, yearning to know, to understand, to find out, approaches each new, unexplored area with a desire to observe and record the phenomena under study. Many criticisms may be voiced over the "trustworthiness" of the information contained in these early biographies. The following excerpt from Darwin's biography of his infant son illustrates several points.

It was difficult to decide at how early an age anger was felt; on his eighth day he frowned and wrinkled the skin round his eyes before a crying fit, but this may have been due to pain or distress, and not to anger. When about ten weeks old, he was given some rather cold milk and he kept a slight frown on his forehead all the time that he was sucking, so that he looked like a grown-up person made cross from being compelled to do something which he did not like. When nearly four months old, and perhaps much earlier, there could be no doubt, from the manner in which the blood gushed into his whole face and scalp, that he easily got into a violent passion. A small cause sufficed; thus, when a little over seven months old, he screamed with rage because a lemon slipped away and he could not seize it with his hands. When eleven months old, if a wrong plaything was given him, he would push it away and beat it; I presume that the beating was an instinctive sign of anger, like the snapping of the jaws by a young crocodile just out of the egg, and not that he imagined he could hurt the plaything. When two years and three months old, he became a great adept at throwing books and sticks, and the like at anyone who offended him; and so it was with some of my other sons. On the other hand, I could never see a trace of such aptitude in my infant daughters (in Dennis, 1951, p. 57).

Darwin's attempts to separate the facts of observation from an interpretation of them were not always successful. A common weakness of such observations is the tendency to project onto the child the emotions, motives, and attitudes of the adult. Besides, there are other disadvantages and limitations to the biographical approach. First, the relevance of the observations depends in part on the adequacy of the observer's background and training. Since such observations are highly subjective, the biases of the observer may very well influence the types of behavior recorded and the interpretations of these behaviors. Second, it is immediately apparent that the child cannot be considered truly representative of all children of his age and sex. This limits the extent to which the data can apply to other children. Third, the type of parent who would engage in such painstaking observation and recording would not be likely to represent parents in general.

So much for the observer and the observed. Several things may also be said about the information itself. Since the baby biographies were usually initiated with no specific purpose in mind, no single type of behavior was examined systematically. How representative any of these sampled behaviors might be is a matter for debate. Representativeness is imperative in research if the investigator attempts to conclude from his observations that a certain behavior is typical or characteristic of a particular child. As a final caution, the observer must remain alert to the danger of the observation itself interfering with the behavior of the child under observation. More recent research, to be discussed in a moment, has dealt with this problem through a similar observational method.

Case-Study Method. A modern approach that shows much similarity to the baby biography is the case study. This technique collects a great variety of information about a single child usually to help a professional person understand the child's behavior. Delinquency, school failure, problem behavior are common subjects studied through the case method. School records, accounts obtained from parents, relatives, other interested adults, and the child himself, as well as the results of psychological examinations are among the sources of information consulted. The following case study was undertaken to obtain clinical evaluation of one child's behavior problems.

CASE-STUDY REPORT

Name: ANDREWS, James
Age: 10 years, 6 months   *Examined by:* L. S. Martin, Ph.D.

Reason for Referral

Mr. and Mrs. Andrews requested an evaluation of their son, James, because they have become increasingly upset by his behavior and have been unable to handle him at times. They are especially frightened of his rage reactions and are concerned about his lack of self-discipline and his inability to accept limits.

Interview with Parents

The parents described Jim as an intelligent boy who is overweight, has a quick temper, and is a chronic "tease." They believe that he is sensitive about his obesity and that this prevents him from taking an active part in sports. They also noted that his rudeness, his unwillingness to cooperate, and his inability to accept criticism help to prevent his participation in organized sports.

The Andrews feel that Jim hates to be frustrated, is rebellious, disorderly, and that he refuses to dress up. He likes to work with mechanical things and is very interested in "hot rods." Jim shows a great deal of animosity toward his eight-year-old sister. He becomes profane when angry and constantly threatens to leave home.

The parents remember Jim to have been a relaxed and happy baby. They are rather vague about developmental history, but believe that he did everything early. Mrs. Andrews holds certain beliefs about food which do not have their basis in religious ideas. Hence, she has raised Jim as a vegetarian and he was fed soy-bean milk for approximately the first three years of life.

Mrs. Andrews could not recall when he stopped taking the bottle, nor could she describe how weaning occurred. She thought that Jim walked at nine months and talked at one year, but she could not recall his first words. She thought she began toilet training at about a year and a half and that Jim was easy to train.

Jim fell out of a crib before age two, fell off a tricycle and hurt his chin at age four or five and he fell out of a car when he was four or five years old. His ears bother him; he feels as if there is wax in them and has had X-ray treatment for this irritation. He does not report hearing difficulties, however, nor does he hear peculiar sounds.

Jim never sucked his fingers or showed evidence of masturbatory activity. Nightmares, sleepwalking, or enuresis were not present according to the parents. Sexual information has been obtained largely from other boys, although he is able to talk with his father about sexual matters.

The Andrews have moved around a good deal; hence, Jim has attended a variety of schools. There were no apparent difficulties about starting to school and no academic problems until recently. He attended Broadhurst Elementary School, beginning two years ago, but was about to be expelled when his parent contacted the clinic. They transferred him to Edgewater Elementary School but Jim does not like this school. His recent school history indicates that he constantly disrupts the classroom with various kinds of attention-getting behavior.

The parents also described Jim as being somewhat belligerent toward younger children and as somewhat blustering in his approach to other children. He has to have his own way, and at times it seems that he deliberately antagonizes his playmates.

Mr. Andrews feels that he has always been "too indulgent" toward Jim. He has always found it difficult to set limits on Jim's behavior or to attempt to discipline him. Mrs. Andrews, on the other hand, feels that Jim should be made to conform to certain standards; she keeps after him to see that he does.

Psychological Evaluation

TESTS ADMINISTERED. (1) Wechsler Intelligence Scale for Children; (2) Rorschach Inkblot Test; (3) Thematic Apperception Test.

BEHAVIOR AND APPEARANCE. Jim is an obese ten-and-a-half-year-old boy who was quite belligerent toward the interviewer when first seen. At the same time, he seemed frightened about coming. On his first visit, he ran out of the building and across the street, and on his second visit, he sat in the car refusing to come into the building. On the third and last visit, however, he was able to talk about his anger toward the clinician, including his feelings that "what he was like was his business," and that he couldn't be helped anyway. He denied any fears about coming to the clinic, although he was able to talk about his concern with what his friends would think if they knew he was coming to see a "head shrinker." Initially, he denied having any problems, but as the session progressed, he was able to admit that he was not very satisfied with his family. He claimed that his mother always nags him, especially about eating and about getting his hair cut. He said he likes his father and that they get along fine together when they are away from the rest of the family. He describes his sister as a pest who always gets her own way.

In general, Jim's behavior was quite ambivalent. He vacillated between ingratiation and direct criticism and between joviality and hostility. He seemed to utilize blandness and denial in attempts to handle his anger and fear.

TEST RESULTS AND IMPRESSIONS. On the Wechsler Intelligence Scale for Children, Jim attained the following scores:

Verbal Scale IQ   = 123 (Superior)
Performance Scale IQ = 114 (Bright-Normal)
Full Scale IQ   = 120 (Superior)

Despite Jim's superior intellectual abilities, he frequently does not function at this level because of his negativistic approach to tasks and his tendencies to put forth minimally adequate efforts. Such tendencies reflect a lack of stamina and of enduring goals and are sufficient to prevent constructive planning for the future.

Jim is able to see things as most people do; he is aware of conventionally approved standards of behavior. However, he maintains an active independence of thought and a stubborn insistence on the right to make up his own mind. Hence he finds it difficult to accept many conventional standards as being the appropriate ones for him to follow. Instead, his behavior is most apt to be governed by his needs for immediate gratification.

Jim has a great deal of anxiety about dealing with people and is unable to satisfy his needs by manipulating his environment in a socially acceptable manner. Hence he tends to avoid situations which require social conformity, despite his interest in achieving social adequacy. Furthermore, he has difficulties in forming close emotional relationships, and seems to vacillate between superficial emotional responsiveness and uncontrolled explosive outbursts.

The test protocols suggest rather intense feelings of hostility which are not very well defended. It appears that Jim's hostility stems largely from concerns about frustration of impulse gratification and particularly about frustration of oral-dependent needs. He is resentful of restrictions in general, and feels that social rules and regulations are unfair for the most part. For example, he told TAT stories about people who were put in jail or kicked out of school because they did not conform to certain standards, e.g., getting a license for a bicycle or getting a haircut.

These attitudes appear to be related to Jim's attitudes toward parental figures. He sees mother figures as depriving, restricting, and making demands upon their children. He sees father figures as intervening in such situations, siding with the child and talking the mother into giving in to the child's wishes. At the same time, he maintains strong underlying feelings of hostility toward father figures. For example, to TAT Card 8BM he told a story about a "foolish" boy who shot a man accidentally and the man died; then the boy wasn't foolish anymore and lived happily ever after. Then, too, in the story to Card 12M, the Lilliputians kill the giant. Jim's ambivalent feelings toward father figures as well as his apprehensiveness toward them is probably best illustrated in his story to TAT Card 13MF: "This guy came in drunk, and he's wipin' his eyes, 'cause he can't see. And he's an alcoholic and a dope fiend. And he's a teacher (laughs), and well—he started all his pupils out on the dope and the alcohol and the principal found that out, so he shot him and then he shot himself and everybody laughed—no—that's not a good ending. They died happily ever after." It appears that Jim is confused about the motivations of father figures and views them as destructive.

Jim's sexual identification is primarily a passive, feminine one. However, he struggles diligently to maintain a façade of masculine assertiveness and becomes very anxious if others think of him as feminine or refer to him as a "sissy."

Summary Impression

Jim is an emotionally disturbed boy who is currently functioning at a superior level of intelligence. However, his motivation for achievement is sporadic and his behavior is governed strongly by his needs for immediate gratification and his apprehensiveness about forming close attachments to others. Hence consistent intellectual efforts and effective achievement are minimal. The test records contain evidence of a passive, dependent orientation with hostility stemming largely from feelings of frustration. Ambivalent feelings toward parental figures are pronounced. Although reality awareness is adequate, there appears to be a lack of integration of conventional standards as guides for his own behavior.

Diagnostic Impression

This appears to be the record of a primary behavior disorder, passive-aggressive type. Although the test record is not suggestive of brain damage, in view of the history of falls, etc., as well as the uncontrolled outbursts of rage, neurological and electroencephalographic studies would seem warranted.

Some branches of child psychology have used the case study more frequently than others. Clinically oriented child psychologists employ it to a great extent. Although the case study helps to understand a single child, the method unfortunately suffers from some of the same defects as the early baby biographies. For example, the reliability of the information gained from informants may be questioned. Does the informant's relationship to the child color his report? Do biases and emotional involvement cloud his memory of past events? Furthermore, how reliable are the test results in the case study? Often the very factors contributing to a child's failure at school also prevent him from scoring at his *true* level in an intellectual examination. The IQ score on the test tells very little about his intellectual potential; it does not contribute to an understanding of the child's school difficulty. Perhaps an even more important consideration in evaluating the case study is the professional who interprets and assesses the data. His experience, theoretical biases, knowledge of research findings, and psychological understanding and skill all influence the value of the study.

Finally, caution has to be exercised whenever one attempts to identify causes and effects. Was a child's rejection by his father the reason for his delinquent behavior? Is rivalry with a year-older sister the basis for a young girl's underachievement in school? Sweeping generalizations and explanations are often made and conclusions drawn from unreliable, sketchy information. *A child's past can never be completely reconstructed.* Rigorous safeguards are required in interpretation, and the person using case-study material must view his conclusions as *tentative* and subject to modification. Since the case study lacks many of the controls present in the experimental method (to be discussed shortly), generalization of the data tends to be hazardous. No child's heredity or environment is identical to another child's. For this reason, factors causing a certain type of behavior in one case may or may not produce the same result in others.

Psychological Ecology. Two psychologists, Robert Barker and Herbert Wright, have organized a Midwest Field Station in a small Kansas community, which they liken to a weather outpost or a biological field station. It has the purpose of collecting data about children and their daily lives, where they go, what they do, what they say, and with whom they interact. These two men argue that psychology, unlike many other sciences, began early and perhaps somewhat prematurely to gather data in laboratory situations. Psychologists manipulate and experiment with small isolated units of behavior and with specific behavior variables without first describing in detail some of the basic information of human life. They ignore such things as the frequency with which certain behaviors occur and the settings in which these take place.

> It is different in other sciences. Geologists, biologists, chemists, and physicists know in considerable detail about the distribution in nature of the materials and processes with which they deal. Chemists know something about the laws governing the interaction of oxygen and hydrogen, and they also know how the elements are distributed in nature. Entomologists know the biological vectors of malaria, and they also know about the occurrence of these vectors over the earth. In contrast, psy-

chologists know little more than laymen about the frequency and degree of occurrence of their basic phenomena in the lives of men—of deprivation, of hostility, of freedom, of friendliness, of social pressure, of rewards and punishments. Although we have daily records of the behavior of volcanoes, of the tides, of sun spots, and of rats and monkeys, there have been few scientific records of how a human mother cared for her young, how a particular teacher behaved in the classroom and how the children responded, what a family actually did and said during a mealtime, or how any boy lived his life from the time he awoke in the morning until he went to sleep at night (Barker & Wright, 1954, p. 2).

The study of behavior in natural situations is given the name *psychological ecology*. This distinguishes it, say Barker and Wright, from experimental psychology which studies behavior in artificially planned situations. The Kansas work involves primarily observation and recording of everyday behavior. To maintain some scientific precision and give some purpose to the observations, the psychological ecologists developed several categories. They call the stable parts of the physical and social milieu of a community, which by their very nature lead to standard and distinctive patterns of behavior, *behavior settings*. In their community, Midwest, U.S.A., these settings include the drug store, second-grade classroom, tavern, Methodist Regular Worship Service, cemetery, library, and Brownie's Regular Meeting (Wright & Barker, 1949). They designate the part of a stream of behavior that describes a separate action and the situation in which it occurs a *behavior episode*. Such episodes might include "painting the lips," "wiping paint off face," "moving crate across pit" (Wright & Barker, 1949, 1954). A third category, the *specimen record,* is a collection of behavior episodes. It is "a detailed, sequential, narrative account by skilled observers of an individual child's behavior through a more or less extended time" (Wright & Barker, 1949). A book entitled *One Boy's Day* describes a day in the life of seven-year-old Raymond Birch. Eight observers took turns throughout the day observing and recording the boy's activities. Their objective was to include everything he did. The following paragraphs typify their report.

> *Some cars were resting on a ledge part way up the sloping side of the pit. The ledge consisted of an old shingle and resembled a bridge, supported at each end by dirt. Stewart started undermining the ledge to make the cars fall into the pit. It seemed to me that his action copied Raymond's very closely, although his purpose differed.*

Raymond suddenly stood up and brushed off the dirt which he had carelessly flipped upon his legs and lap.

He knelt down and smoothed the dirt from the rock.

Then he started chopping rhythmically. Time after time he shoved the stick into the damp dirt, and pulled sideways, flipping the dirt away. The stick bent under his vigorous efforts.

Inadvertently and unnoticed by Raymond, one of the flying clods of dirt happened to hit Clifford. Clifford didn't complain; he was too busy watching what Stewart was doing.

Finally a car fell off the ledge which Stewart was tearing down. Stewart shouted, "Look at it roll on down below in the canyon."

Raymond looked over and watched the rolling car with mild interest.

He returned immediately to his own digging, not even looking up to see the second car roll down (Barker & Wright, 1951, pp. 356–357).

With some exceptions, the advantages, disadvantages, and usefulness of psychological ecology are the same as those of the baby biographies. One is impressed by the ability of a specimen record to capture the richness and complexity of the environment, the multitude of interactions which influence and shape a child's approach to people and situations, and the repetitiveness but yet apparent randomness of child behavior. Moreover, the psychological ecologists seem to have avoided some of the shortcomings of the baby biographies. Well trained in observation and well grounded in the basic notions of psychology, they have deliberately attempted to separate the content of observation from interpretation; in fact, interpretation is indented and set off from observed data in a specimen record. There is also the question of the extent to which the observer, as a result of his observation, changes or influences the individual being observed. Wright and Barker hold that children under the age of nine show neither sensitivity nor self-consciousness when being observed and soon adjust or adapt to the presence of an observer. This view seems to be supported by the relatively small effect an observer has on those being observed, especially when the observation continues over an extended period. Children tend not to act very long in ways differing from their usual behavior. Finally, how representative is the group of children investigated? Although the community chosen was small enough to include all its children in the study, and its environment was undoubtedly less complex than that of a large urban area, it remains to be shown whether environmental complexity has psychological significance in the lives of children.

Controlled Approaches to Observation

Although observation lies at the base of all scientific research, "uncontrolled" observation, as we have seen, has many disadvantages. There is clearly a need for "controlled" observation of phenomena if meaningful comparisons and determinations are to be made. Scientists have developed many techniques for a controlled approach to observation, and in the following several pages we shall examine some of them.

Time Sampling. Arrington (1943) has defined time sampling as a method of observing the behavior of human beings "under the ordinary conditions of everyday life in which observations are made in a series of short time periods so distributed as to afford a representative sampling of the behavior under observation." The method was developed in order to overcome many of the weaknesses in the anecdotal descriptions of child behavior. It was first used by Willard Olson (1929) to record the incidence of "nervous habits" in school children. Briefly, Olson marked off a record blank into five-minute intervals and entered a check whenever a designated behavior occurred within each time interval among a classroom of children he was observing. As originally conceived, time sampling yielded a score indicating *the number of time intervals* in which a specific behavior manifested itself.

Over the years the technique has undergone a great number of modifications. Most of them have resulted from a desire for finer precision in the sampling and recording of behavior. The time interval has been shortened, often consisting of periods from 30 seconds to one minute. Only one child is observed at a time, with the observations distributed at random throughout the day as well as over a term of a week to several months. Symbols have been developed to record continuous behavior instead of the occurrence or nonoccurrence of specific acts. For example, an elaborate set of such symbols has been devised to facilitate the objective description and recording of interaction between adults and children (Moustakas, Sigel, & Schalock, 1956). This set uses five-second time intervals and enters a series of category code letters on a prepared scoring sheet covering 16 minutes of continuous recording. Each square on the sheet represents five seconds of time, and the main categories symbolized by the code letters in this particular recording system include: nonattention, attentive observation, recognition, statement of condition or action, joint participation in activity, offering information, giving help, reassurance, seeking information, restricting, forbidding, disciplinary action, affection, compliance.

Most of the time-sampling studies have been concerned with the social behavior and social interactions of the young child. Among the specific behaviors studied have been language frequency or content, ascendant behavior, physical contacts, quarrels, conflict, resistance, friendship patterns, cooperative and competitive behavior, rivalry, and aggression. The principal advantages of this technique are the reliability and objectivity of recording. Attention is centered on a specific well-defined behavior so that agreement about it among different observers can be achieved. Since scores are obtained usually in terms of frequency, the results can be treated statistically. For example, the frequency of quarrels can be related to age, sex, IQ, ratings of adjustment, and many similar factors.

Time sampling will not work when the behavior under study is neither overt nor readily observable. It is not feasible, either, for observing infrequent behavior, such as the display of sympathy, compliance, or rare, private child behaviors like fire setting. Because time-sampling studies are restricted to the investigation of a specific behavior, much of the richness and meaningfulness of child interaction goes unrecorded. Precision may be obtained at the cost of understanding. Moreover, data thus obtained can never of themselves yield information about cause and effect. If it were found that one child quarreled more frequently than others, it would be necessary to draw on methods other than time sampling to determine the cause.

Psychometric Instruments. Although intelligence and personality tests are not customarily considered as vehicles for observation, they are, in fact, very short samples of behavior and are extremely important in terms of their ability to disclose useful information. Knowledge of the results of an intelligence test provides insights into a child's ability in comparison with other children and into his level of intellectual performance. It also permits one to make predictions about how the child will cope with other tasks and other situations. The usefulness of a score on such *psychometric* tests—tests that measure the speed and precision of mental processes—depends on the meaningfulness of the theory on which the test is based, on the rigor of the procedure, and on the appropriateness of what is measured.

The object of a psychometric test is to provide in a brief interval of time information that would otherwise require hours of intimate contact to obtain. Tests, therefore, are "shorthand observational techniques" which enable us to make inferences about a larger body of data. For example, in administering a standard intelligence test to a five-year-old, we are not interested in his ability to answer the specific questions as such but in how these questions sample his general intelligence. Specific intelligence and personality tests will be discussed in subsequent chapters.

Questionnaires. Like the intelligence and personality tests, the questionnaire is a shorthand method for gaining a considerable amount of information on a specific problem in a brief interval of time. Its use, either written or oral, to obtain information about children has a long history. G. Stanley Hall is often credited with being the first to use this approach in child psychology. Under his supervision school teachers in the Boston area administered a general information questionnaire to beginning first-grade children. Although such a procedure seems commonplace today, it was a marked contribution at a time when unscientific speculation often substituted for the collection of data.

One result of Hall's study was the realization that children's thinking did indeed differ from that of adults in terms not only of the quantity of information but also of its quality. The following excerpt from Hall's original paper gives the content of the children's responses to certain questions included in the questionnaire.

The chief field for such fond and often secret childish fancies is the sky. About three fourths of all questioned thought the world a plain, and many described it as round like a dollar, while the sky is like a flattened bowl turned over it. The sky is often thin, one might easily break through; half the moon may be seen through it, while the other half is this side; it may be made of snow, but is so large that there is much floor-sweeping to be done in heaven. Some thought the sun went down at night into the ground or just behind certain houses, and went across on or under the ground to go up out of or off the water in the morning, but 48 per cent of all thought that at night it goes or rolls or flies, is blown or walks, or God pulls it up higher out of sight. He takes it into heaven, and perhaps puts it to bed, and even takes off its clothes and puts them on in the morning, or again it lies under the trees where the angels mind it, or goes through and shines on the upper side of the sky, or goes into or behind the moon, as the moon is behind it in the day. It may stay where it is, only we cannot see it, for it is dark, or the dark rains down so, and it comes out when it gets light so it can see. More than half the children questioned conceived the sun as never more than 40 degrees from the zenith, and, naturally enough, city children knew little of the horizon. So the moon comes around when it is a bright night and people want to walk, or forget to light some lamps; it follows us about and has nose and eyes, while it calls the stars into, under, or behind it at night, and they may be made of bits of it. Sometimes the moon is round a month or two, then it is a rim, or a piece is cut off, or it is half stuck or half buttoned into the sky. The stars may be sparks from fire-engines or houses, or, with higher intelligence, they are silver, or God lights them with matches and blows them out or opens the door and calls them in in the morning. Only in a single case were any of the heavenly bodies conceived as openings in the sky to let light or glory through, or as eyes of supernatural beings—a fancy so often ascribed to children and so often found in juvenile literature. Thunder, which anthropologists tell us is or represents the highest God to most savage races, was apperceived as God groaning or kicking, or rolling barrels about, or turning a big handle, or grinding snow, walking loud, breaking something, throwing logs, having coal run in, pounding about with a big hammer, rattling houses, hitting the clouds, or clouds bumping or clapping together or bursting, or else it was merely ice sliding off lots of houses or cannon in the city or sky, hard rain down the chimney, or big rocks pounding, or piles of boards falling down, or very hard rain, hail, or wind. Lightning is God putting out his finger or opening a door, or turning on gas quick, or (very common) striking many matches at once, throwing stones and iron for sparks, setting paper afire, or it is light going outside and inside the sky, or stars falling. God keeps rain in heaven in a big sink, rows of buckets, a big tub or barrels, and they run over or he lets it down with a water hose through a sieve, a dipper with holes, or sprinkles or tips it down or turns a faucet. God makes it in heaven out of nothing or out of water, or it gets up by splashing up, or he dips it up off the roof, or it rains up off the ground when we don't see it. The clouds are close to the sky; they move because the earth moves and makes them. They are dirty, muddy things, or blankets, or doors of heaven, and are made of fog, of steam that makes the sun go, of smoke, of white wool or feathers and birds, or lace or cloth. In their changing forms very many children, whose very life is fancy, think they see veritable men, or more commonly, because they have so many more forms, animals, faces, and very often God, Santa Claus, angels, etc., are also seen. Closely connected with the above are the religious concepts so common with children. God is a big, perhaps blue, man, very often seen in the sky on or in clouds, in the church, or even street. He came in our gate, comes to see us sometimes. He lives in a big palace or a big brick or stone house on the sky. He makes lamps, babies, dogs, trees, money, etc., and the angels work for him. He looks like the priest, Frobel, papa, etc., and they like to look at him, and a few would like to be God. He lights the stars so he can see to go on the sidewalk or into the church. Birds, children, Santa Claus, live with him, and most but not all like him better than they do the latter. When people die they just go, or are put in a hole, or a box or a black wagon that goes to heaven, or they fly up or are drawn or slung up into the sky where God catches them. They never can get out of the hole, and yet all good people somehow get where God is. He lifts them up, they go up on a ladder or rope, or they carry them up, but keep their eyes shut so they do not know the way, or they are shoved up through a hole. When children get there they have candy, rocking-horses, guns, and everything in the toy-shop or picture-book, play marbles, top, ball, cards, hookey, hear brass bands, have nice clothes, gold watches, and pets, ice-cream and soda-water, and no school. There are men there who died in the war made into angels, and dolls with broken heads go there. Some think they must go through the church to get there, a few thought the horse-cars run there, and one said that the birds that grow on apple-trees are drawn up there by the moon. The bad place is like an oven or a police-station, where it burns, yet is all dark, and folks want to get back, and God kills people or beats them with a cane. God makes babies in heaven, tho the holy mother and even Santa Claus makes some. He lets them down or drops them, and the women or doctors catch them, or he leaves them on the sidewalk, or brings them down a wooden ladder back-wards and pulls it up again, or mamma or the doctor or the nurse go up and fetch them sometimes in a balloon, or they fly down and lose off their wings in some place or other and forget it, or jump down to Jesus, who gives them around. They were also often said to be found in flour-barrels, and the flour sticks ever so long, you know, or they grow in cabbages, or God puts them in water, perhaps in the sewer, and the doctor gets them out and takes them to sick folks that want them, or the milkman brings them early in the morning, they are dug out of the ground, or bought at the baby-store. Sometimes God puts on a few things or else sends them along if he don't forget it; this shows that no one since Basedow believes in telling children the truth in all things (Hall, in Dennis, 1948, pp. 267–269).

The questionnaire has several methodological advantages over the earlier baby biographies. Since questionnaires are designed to obtain information for specific purposes, their questions concentrate on a well-defined area. Besides, the researcher who uses them can obtain data from a large and representative sample in a relatively short time as compared with the baby biographies which were concerned with an individual child. These data can be related to several vari-ables. For example, several researchers have administered Hall's questionnaire, with modifications, to children of various ages and related the subjects' scores to chronological age, mental age, IQ, socio-economic class, and sex, noting the differences in total scores as well as in answers to specific questions.

A wide variety of questionnaires has been employed with children and their parents, but one further example will suffice. This question-naire is directed to parents because knowledge of their attitudes and values is often essential to understanding the child's behavior and personality. Questionnaires of this type may deal with statements of fact, such as the age of weaning the child, or with statements that tap attitudes and values that often relate to child-rearing procedures. In the following items excerpted from the Parent Attitude Research Instrument developed at the National Institute of Mental Health, the parent is asked to check the response that best represents his point of view for each statement.

	Strongly Agree	Mildly Agree	Mildly Disagree	Strongly Disagree
Children should be allowed to disagree with their parents if they feel their own ideas are better.	A	a	d	D
It is frequently necessary to drive the mischief out of a child before he will behave.	A	a	d	D
A wise parent knows better than to pick up the baby whenever he cries.	A	a	d	D
The experience of being on their own is often good for children.	A	a	d	D
Most parents prefer a quiet child to a "scrappy" one.	A	a	d	D

(Schaefer & Bell, 1958)

Complete reliance on questionnaire responses has its weaknesses. Both "truthfulness" and unconscious falsification have to be considered. Some questionnaires contain a "lie scale" designed to assess the respondent's willingness to falsify his replies. And there are researchers who believe that in assessing a parent's attitude toward certain topics, falsification as such becomes unimportant. Moreover, parents differ in willingness to divulge various kinds of information. Whether the parent comprehends the question as it was intended by the creator of the questionnaire is another matter of concern. In evaluating the findings emerging from a questionnaire, critical note must be taken of all these points.

Experimental Method. One of the outstanding characteristics of this method is its control over the phenomena under investigation and the variables being observed. Scientific experiments are often called "questions put to nature," and the more precisely the questions are stated—that is, the more carefully the experiment is designed—the more exact and unambiguous the answers will be. Tracing a hypothetical problem of the kind a child-development researcher might face may clarify various points.

Shortly before the Second World War the effect of nursery-school experience on intelligence provoked an important controversy. Some say that more heat than light was generated over the issue; if so, the fault lay with the methods used to examine it. Suppose we consider this problem. To begin with, the problem must be stated clearly and precisely or else the research will be neither well defined nor definitive. The problem is usually presented in the form of an hypothesis: nursery-school experience raises the IQ. Now the hypothesis needs to be tested.

First, the IQs are tested of a group of children who have had a year of nursery school. If their IQs are above 100 (average) the hypothesis would seem confirmed. But the group chosen might have been well above average intelligence before going to nursery school. It might have been a *biased sample*. Therefore, the above-average IQs cannot be attributed to the nursery-school experience. Something has been learned, but it is necessary to test again.

This time the children to be tested are selected at random from a large group of five-year-olds to ensure an *un*biased sample. The children are tested for intelligence and then retested after a year of nursery school. If the measure of intelligence increases after the second test, the hypothesis would again seem confirmed. However, other factors than nursery-school experience might have improved the children's intelligence; in other words, the effects of other variables have not been controlled. The need is apparent for testing a similar group of children who are *not* exposed to nursery school.

This leads to selection of a *control group* which does not undergo special treatment; the group accorded it is called the *experimental group*. Subjects for both groups are drawn from a large pool of children and assigned at random to either one. Often, to ensure the presence of no features that differentiate the two groups, both are matched on relevant variables, that is, other factors that might influence the results. These might include such things as initial level of ability, sex of the child, or occupational status of the parent. Thus, only the one variable under investigation, the *independent variable* (in this illustration, nursery-school experience), is left to be systematically altered. Its effect on the *dependent variable* (intelligence scores) is then measured.

To return to the problem at hand, the intellectual level of both control and experimental groups is measured by administration of a standard intelligence test. The experimental group is then given nursery-school training while the control group is not. Once again, intelligence tests are administered after a period of time. If the scores in the experimental group are significantly higher than those in the control group, the hypothesis is accepted. If no difference in scores exists, the hypothesis is obviously invalid.

This method, then, holds all possibly relevant variables constant while identifying *the effects of the systematic manipulation of the single variable* under investigation. Although it is the most valuable method for research, this technique does not always apply in child development. In many important problems the researcher cannot manipulate the independent variable. For example, rejection or acceptance by parents is thought to have important bearing on child personality and adjustment. Yet it is manifestly impossible to manipulate this variable for research purposes. Under the circumstances, researchers turn to "experiments in nature." They assess the adjustment of children who are thought to have suffered from parental rejection in the past and contrast this with the adjustment of a group of children thought to be accepted. Even so, they can never be sure that the two groups do not differ in other variables which perhaps helps to account for the difference in adjustments. Nor can they ever be sure that parental rejection or acceptance does, in fact, affect adjustment, because they are unable to set up an "experimental control," that is, a control group in distinction to an experimental group. The same criticism may be made of any studies that attempt to tie parental attitudes to a type of behavior in the child when the parental attitudes are sought *after* the behavior has appeared.

Interview Method. Although the interview has been used most frequently as a clinical tool for understanding an individual case, it is now being employed increasingly as a research device for gaining information about a specific question under investigation. An interview is composed of several questions designed to elicit certain kinds of information. Often the questions are tested beforehand to find out if they do, in fact, obtain the information desired. Frequently the interview is tape recorded so that the interviewer need not rely on memory or sketchily written notes. The information acquired from the interview is evaluated in various ways on a rating scale, with ratings usually made independently by two persons to check on inter-rater agreement. In the following replies of two mothers to the question: "Some people feel that it is very important for a child to learn not to fight with other children; and others feel that there are times when a child has to learn to fight. How do you feel about this?" the first reply was rated as indicating no demand for the child to be aggressive toward her peers, whereas the second reply was considered a high demand to have the child fight.

A

Mother. I go out and ask other mothers what happened and when I find out, I say "All right come in the house now." Sooner than go to their mothers and fight with them, I bring her in the house and keep her in for a while and talk it all over with her and tell her where she's wrong or where the other child is wrong and then after a while I let her out again and tell her to go—either, she'll end up probably playing with the same child again, anyway—to go play with somebody else.

B

Mother. Well, I believe that a child has to fight and to stick up for his own rights. I hate to see a kid that is always—well—I think if they don't they are whining babies and are always home with their mothers; and we have always taught Bill to hit them right back and to give them one better than what he got. And there are a few children, in this neighborhood, that Bill is afraid of and he will come home and tell me what they have done to him—but the only satifaction that he has ever got was that, "We have told you if he hits you to hit him back, and until then don't tell me your stories" (Sears, Maccoby, & Levin, 1957, pp. 246–247).

Some of the disadvantages of the questionnaire pervade the interview, but others are eliminated. A mother's need to portray herself in a certain way affects her report. Moreover, the success of the interview depends on her willingness to divulge various sorts of information and on her memory. Several studies have found many inaccuracies in mothers' recall of earlier events related to child-rearing attitudes and practices. One investigation compared information obtained in three interviews with mothers with data from a final interview (Haggard, Brekstad, & Skard, 1960). The interviews spread over a period beginning about a month before delivery and ending when the child was between seven and eight years of age. As a rule, the final interviews were more a reflection of the mother's current recollections of the past than of accurate accounts of past events themselves. The accuracy of recall was related to the type of information requested. Specific facts, such as the length of the child at birth, were recalled best, whereas information on general wishes and attitudes was recalled next best. Data based on earlier anxieties of mothers were recalled least accurately. Furthermore, the lack of independence of the data poses another problem in interviews, especially when the person interviewed is a mother or someone else who is not the actual subject of the investigation. The information so gathered may reflect the personality of the mother rather than the actual facts.

On the other side of the ledger, the face-to-face relationship between interviewer and interviewee enables a skilled interviewer to gauge the earnestness and sincerity of the respondent. This is not possible in a questionnaire. One well-known scale for rating parents, Fels Parent Behavior Rating Scale, which is based on interviews with mothers, contains this additional rating for each interview: "Certainty: Do you feel that your rating is based on adequate evidence?"

Longitudinal vs. Cross-sectional Approaches

Although there is a multitude of "facts" one might wish to learn about child behavior, probably one of the most persistent objectives of child research is the study of development. This is the emphasis in child psychology; it is on the changes that take place over time in the behavior and characteristics of children. Thus, if we know enough about development in general and about a particular child's past development, we can predict his future development, his adult personality, his adult adjustment, and the values and purpose he will have as an adult.

Since child psychology is concerned with development, much research has been devoted to the description of children at various ages. Data are available in the areas of motor development, language development, intellectual development, social development, emotional development, and physical development. These have been acquired through two approaches, the longitudinal and the cross-sectional.

Longitudinal Method. This approach is best suited to the study of development since the same children are studied over a period of time. Munn (1955, p. 8) has likened it to time-lapse photography where a single object is photographed at periodic intervals providing a picture of continuous growth. Longitudinal study provides a knowledge of the patterns and processes of change over the long run; thus, individual growth curves can be plotted in such areas as language and physical development. With this knowledge of changes in a single individual, one can relate them to the presence or absence of other factors. For example, the changes in IQ in an individual case can be shown to relate to various environmental circumstances (Honzik, Marfarlane, & Allen, 1958). But this does not necessarily mean there is a cause-and-effect relationship.

Some research topics require use of the longitudinal approach. It is essential in investigating the effects on development of instituted procedures when remeasurement is necessary at a later time. It is also useful for gathering data on generational differences and consistency in child-rearing practices. Several longitudinal studies have been conducted; for a report of them to 1954, see Stone and Onque (1959). Before considering some of the obstacles to this kind of research, let us briefly examine two longitudinal studies.

One of the first of its kind was the short-term longitudinal study by Shirley (1931, 1933a, b) of motor, intellectual, and personality development, which followed 25 infants from birth to two years of age.

During the first week in the hospital, the infants were examined daily. During the second week they were examined every other day. For the remainder of their first year, they were seen at weekly intervals in their homes, and throughout their second year at biweekly intervals. All this time the infants' responses to simple tests were recorded in descriptive, qualitative terms, and mothers' records supplemented the examination data. With respect to motor development, Shirley concentrated on the sequence of development and concluded: (*a*) there is a consistency in the sequence, with few reversals in the appearance of such items as chest up, sit alone, stand with help, and creep; and (*b*) motor development is in line with the anatomical law of the direction of growth which states that growth proceeds from the head to the feet (*cephalocaudal*). The data collected in the intensive study of the 25 infants have been of considerable interest and value in laying the basis for certain areas of developmental research and in providing information obtained by careful, scientific methods.

The second study deals with the long-term prediction of adjustment. In 1950 a wide variety of information was obtained from the entire school population—3200 children—in the fourth grade and above in Nobles County, Minnesota.

> There were scales measuring the child's attitudes toward his family, his sense of responsibility, his work and attitudes toward work based on his experience in home duties and chores, his interests and play activities, and his favorable attitudes toward experience. There was also a scale made up of items that in previous studies had been answered differently by delinquent and by nondelinquent children. The items had to do with personal-social attitudes, and with the child's fears and worries. From school records, we obtained the Intelligence Quotients of the children. In addition to information about the education and occupation of each parent, we also had several measures of socio-economic or cultural status. On the basis of a check against the current adjustment of the children, five scores were selected from the inventories given the children to be combined into a Pupil Index, which is used as a general score to predict future adjustment.
>
> Because we wished to see how well ratings made by teachers would predict future adjustment of children, three rating forms were filled out by the teachers in 1950. These ratings concerned the child's responsibility, his personality traits, and his adjustment in the classroom or home room. Scores on these were combined to form the 1950 Teacher Index (Anderson, 1959, pp. 8–9).

Several follow-up studies were conducted and the final assessment of adjustment was made seven years later, in 1957. Again various kinds of information were obtained to measure the adjustment.

In designing measures of outcomes in terms of later adjustment, the type of information that can be secured about a person's relation to the demands of life must be considered. There is first the record made by the person in school, community, and on the job, which is the most obvious sign of his success. Such information may be regarded as the objective aspect of the person's life and can be obtained from various records. Next, there are the person's own feelings about himself and his view of his relation to others. Does he feel happy and satisfied with his life? Does he think he gets along well? Such information may be regarded as more subjective evidence of the person's life adjustment and is obtained from the person himself. Last, there are the impressions made by the person upon other people. How is he seen by others who know him? Some who know him very well are likely to balance his traits and feelings against his objective record. Finally, an interview with the person himself secures information about his accomplishments and feelings. The psychologically trained interviewer may thus balance the objective and the subjective aspects of the process of adjustment. In our follow-up studies we attempted to secure information about the person for each aspect of his life, such as work, recreation, education, and family life, from each of the sources, that is, from the records, the person's own statement about himself, the impressions others had of him, and the judgment of skilled psychological interviewers with psychological training (Anderson, 1959, pp. 9–10).

In general, the investigators predicted good adjustment more readily and more accurately than poor adjustment. Although separate criteria proved useful for predicting adjustment by sex, IQ predicted equally well for boys and girls. The investigators concluded that "it seems unlikely that a very short screening instrument that will predict well into the future can be developed from our personality measures on the children" (Anderson, 1959, p. 36).

Several characteristics of the longitudinal approach make it costly in terms of time and effort as well as difficult to carry out. First is the matter of turnover in research personnel. Much time is lost if it becomes necessary to change research directors or other personnel during the investigation. Next is the problem of dropping out among subjects. Often the data cannot be analyzed until the very end of the investigation; consequently, if a subject drops out during the study, considerable information involving many hours of research effort is lost. Moreover, the final sample may depart from the original group of subjects so markedly that it may affect the results of the research. Often, too, new insights are achieved and new measuring instruments are developed in the course of a longitudinal study, yet it is never possible to "go back" and obtain previously unsolicited information. For once the plan of research has been established and the subjects and procedure have been selected it is difficult if not hazardous to attempt to alter them without jeopardizing the entire investigation.

Cross-sectional Method. Because of the foregoing disadvantages of the longitudinal approach, researchers have predominantly used the cross-sectional method in child-development research. This method consists of studying children of different ages. For example, to study language development in the young child, Templin (1957) selected 60 children at each of the following age levels: three, three-and-a-half, four, four-and-a-half, five, six, seven, and eight. This selection furnished norms for four measures of language: speech sound articulation, sound discrimination ability, sentence structure, and vocabulary. Obviously this approach is easier to pursue and saves more time than the longitudinal. The investigator does not have to wait for subjects to pass through various age periods; eight-year-olds, nine-year-olds, and ten-year-olds can all be studied simultaneously. A large number of subjects representative of the population is readily available in the public schools. Furthermore, the plan of research can be modified without a necessary loss of time.

Yet there are some types of information that cross-sectional studies, by their very nature, cannot provide. They teach very little about causation: why does a certain behavior appear at a certain age level? Why are there individual differences at every level? These cross-sectional data do not explain. Nor do they reveal the effect on personality of deviations in development: what effect does retardation in language development have on a child's social adjustment at school? How does an infant's accelerated motor development influence his father's attitude toward him? Finally, the cross-sectional approach does not illuminate the patterning of behavior over the long run for any single child because it studies different children at different age levels at one time.

Some of the advantages of both longitudinal and cross-sectional methods are incorporated in the accelerated longitudinal or convergence approach (Bell, 1953, 1954). Subjects of different ages are re-tested with some overlapping of age level for younger and older children. For example, four groups of children, aged six, eight, ten, and twelve, are each measured over a three-year term. This provides data for 12 points in time rather than only three, and since there is an overlapping of ages tested during the three-year interval, information is obtained which permits the comparison of different groups at the same ages. Note the overlaps in the following illustration.

Group	Ages Tested
A	6, 7, 8
B	8, 9, 10
C	10, 11, 12
D	12, 13, 14

Normative Studies

A brief mention of normative studies or surveys should be made. Although these may be longitudinal, normative data are usually obtained from cross-sectional investigations. In this sense norms are stages related to the age at which various skills or characteristics "normally" appear, or the ages at which they appear among "normal" children. *Norms do not, however, tell what is "normal" for an individual child.* Many aspects of development are related only loosely to chronological age. For example, at one time only norms of weight were listed for various ages. Then, as the importance of other variables affecting weight was recognized, weight norms began taking height into account also; and more recently, body build and structure have been added.

However, there has been an overemphasis on norms, especially in books and periodicals available to laymen. Such norms are misunderstood and have been the source of much unnecessary worry and concern, on the part of mothers particularly. Arnold Gesell, an early worker in child growth and development, has published norms for many aspects of development. Table 1-1 contains schedules describing the behavior characteristic of an 18-month-old child. Many of these items are presented pictorially in Figure 1-1. Such books by Gesell as *Infant and Child in the Culture of Today* (Gesell & Ilg, 1943), *The Child from Five to Ten* (Gesell & Ilg, 1946), and *Youth: the Years from Ten to Sixteen* (Gesell, Ilg, & Ames, 1956) have been criticized for stressing ages and stages of normal development. Entire chapters of these books are devoted to descriptions of the "one-year-old," "two-year-old," and so forth. Perhaps the fault lies not so much with the books as with those who seek too eagerly for early indications of normality or precocity in their children.

Misconceptions about norms have also arisen because of the emphasis on the mean or "average" time of appearance of a certain skill or behavior. Too often, however, the age *range* at which the skill appears in the subjects sampled has not been described. Although

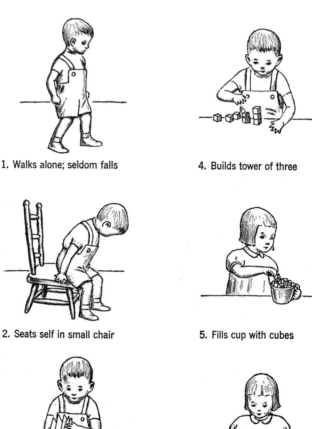

1. Walks alone; seldom falls

4. Builds tower of three

2. Seats self in small chair

5. Fills cup with cubes

3. Turns pages two or three at a time

6. Dumps pellet from bottle

FIGURE 1-1 (Adapted from Gesell & Amatruda, 1941.)

the norm for walking alone may be 59 weeks, the *normal range* may be from eight to eighteen months. Few if any developmental skills can be considered to suggest a pathological condition if they do not appear at a *precise* age. Norms do provide some basis for comparison, however, and aid in understanding normal behavior and development.

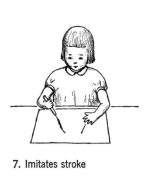

7. Imitates stroke

10. On command puts ball on chair

8. Identifies one picture

11. Walks into ball

9. Hurls ball

12. Pulls toy

SUMMARY

In this chapter we have explored techniques of observation, prediction, and control and have described various ways for obtaining information about children. Noting some of the advantages and disadvantages of each, we have seen the research areas in which each method of gaining information is most appropriate. In addition, we have stressed the cautions one must observe in making statements

TABLE 1-1   Developmental Schedules

	15 Months	KEY AGE: 18 Months	21 Months
Motor	Walks: few steps, starts, stops Walks: falls by collapse (*18m) Walks: creeping discarded Stairs: creeps up (*18m) M. Cubes: tower of 2 Pellets: (no dem.) places in bottle Book: helps turn pages (*18m)	Walks: seldom falls Walks: fast, runs stiffly (*24m) Stairs: walks up, 1 hand held (*21m) Small chair: seats self Adult chair: climbs into (*. . .) Ball: hurls (*48m) Large ball: walks into (*21m) Book: turns pages, 2–3 at once (*24m)	Walks: squats in play (*. . .) Stairs: walks down, 1 hand held (*24m) Stairs: walks up, holds rail (*24m) Large ball: (dem.) kicks (*24m) M. Cubes: tower of 5–6
Adaptive	M. Cubes: tower of 2 Cup-cu: 6 in & out cup (*18m) Drawing: incip. imitation stroke (*18m) Formbd: (no dem.) places round block Formbd: adapts round block promptly	M. Cubes: tower of 3–4 Cup-cu: 10 into cup Pellet & bo: dumps responsively Drawing: scribbles spontan. (*36m) Drawing: makes stroke imitatively Formbd: piles 3 blocks (*24m)	M. Cubes: tower of 5–6 M. Cubes: imitates pushing train (*24m) Formbd: places 2–3 blocks Perf. box: inserts corner of sq. (*24m) Perf. box: retrieves ball
Language	Vo: 4–5 words includ. names Vo: uses jargon (*24m) Book: pats pictures (*18m)	Book: looks selectively Vo: 10 words includ. names Picture cd: names or points 1 Test obj: names ball Ball: 2 directions	Vo: 20 words Speech: combines 2–3 words spontan. (*24m) Ball: 3 directions
Personal-Social	Feeding: bottle discarded Feeding: inhib. grasp of dish Toilet: partial regulation (*24m) Toilet: bowel control Toilet: indicates wet pants (*18m) Commun: says "ta-ta" or equiv. Commun: points, voc. wants (*21m) Play: shows or offers toy (*21m) Play: casts obj. in play or refus. (*18m)	Feeding: hands empty dish (*. . .) Feeding: feeds self in part, spills (*36m) Toilet: regulated daytime (*24m) Play: pulls a toy (*30m) Play: carries or hugs doll (*24m)	Feeding: handles cup well Commun: asks for food, toilet, drink Commun: echoes 2 or more last words (*24m) Commun: pulls person to show (*24m)

about cause and effect. The identification of cause-and-effect relationships is most valuable for it permits predictions about behavior, and predictability is the aim of all scientific research. Only through carefully designed and carefully controlled scientific experiments can safe statements about causation perhaps be made. Yet the basis for formulating "fruitful" experimental hypotheses—that is, hypotheses leading to new hypotheses—may be the use of other research methods. Much has been learned and much else remains to be learned from use of case studies, questionnaires, broad observational techniques, and psychometric tests. And some research requires the judicious combination of several of these methods. Only when students and researchers recognize the safeguards that must be taken and the shortcomings and weaknesses of a given research method can they show adequate caution in accepting the findings and claims of research. How information is obtained determines the extent to which one can rely on its validity.

REFERENCES

Allport, G. W. *Personality; a psychological interpretation.* New York: Holt, 1937.

Anderson, J. E. *A survey of children's adjustment over time.* Minneapolis: Inst. Child Develpm. and Welf., 1959.

Armstrong, M. D., & Tyler, F. H. Studies in phenylketonuria. I. Restricted phenylalanine intake in phenylketonuria. *J. Clin. Invest.,* 1955, **34**, 565–580.

Arrington, Ruth E. Time sampling in studies of social behavior: a critical review of techniques and results with research suggestions. *Psychol. Bull.,* 1943, **40**, 81–124.

Baller, W. R. A study of the present social status of a group of adults who, when they were in elementary schools, were classified as mentally deficient. *Genet. Psychol. Monogr.,* 1936, **18**, No. 3.

Barker, R. G., & Wright, H. F. *One boy's day.* New York: Harper, 1951.

Barker, R. G., & Wright, H. F. *Midwest and its children.* Evanston, Ill.: Row, Peterson, 1954.

Bell, R. Q. Convergence: an accelerated longitudinal approach. *Child Develpm.,* 1953, **24**, 145–152.

Bell, R. Q. An experimental test of the accelerated longitudinal approach. *Child Develpm.,* 1954, **25**, 281–286.

Bugelski, B. R. *An introduction to the principles of psychology.* New York: Rinehart, 1960.

Cohen, M. R. *Studies in philosophy and science.* New York: Holt, 1949.

Darwin, C. A biographical sketch of an infant. *Mind,* 1881, **6**, 104–107.

Festinger, L. *A theory of cognitive dissonance.* Evanston, Ill.: Row, Peterson, 1957.

Gesell, A., & Amatruda, Catherine S. *Developmental diagnosis.* New York: Hoeber, 1941.

Gesell, A., & Ilg, F. L. *Infant and child in the culture of today.* New York: Harper, 1943.

Gesell, A., & Ilg, F. L. *The child from five to ten.* New York: Harper, 1946.

Gesell, A., Ilg, F. L., & Ames, Louise B. *Youth: the years from ten to sixteen.* New York: Harper, 1956.

Haggard, E. A., Brekstad, A., & Skard, A. On the reliability of the anamnestic interview. *J. abnorm. soc. Psychol.*, 1960, **61**, 311–318.

Hall, G. S. The contents of children's minds. *Princeton Rev.*, 1883, 249–272. Reprinted in W. Dennis, *Readings in the history of psychology.* New York: Appleton, 1948. Pp. 255–276.

Honzik, Marjorie P., Macfarlane, J. W., & Allen, L. The stability of mental test performance between two and eighteen years. *J. exp. Educ.*, 1948, **17**, 320.

Moustakas, C. E., Sigel, I. E., & Schalock, H. D. An objective method for the measurement and analysis of child-adult interaction. *Child Develpm.*, 1956, **27**, 109–134.

Munn, N. L. *The evolution and growth of human behavior.* Cambridge, Mass.: Riverside, 1955.

Olson, W. C. The measurement of nervous habits in normal children. Minneapolis: Univer. Minn. Press, 1929.

Rapaport, D. *Emotions and memory.* Baltimore: Williams & Wilkins, 1942.

Schaefer, E. S., & Bell, R. Q. Development of a parental attitude research instrument. *Child Develpm.*, 1958, **29**, 339–361.

Sears, R. R., Maccoby, Eleanor E., & Levin, H. *Patterns of child rearing.* Evanston, Ill.: Row, Peterson, 1957.

Shirley, M. M. *The first two years: a study of twenty-five babies, Vol. I. Postural and locomotor development.* Inst. Child Welf. Monogr. Series, No. 6. Minneapolis: Univer. Minn. Press, 1931.

Shirley, M. M. *The first two years: a study of twenty-five babies, Vol. II. Intellectual development.* Inst. Child Welf. Monogr. Series, No. 7. Minneapolis: Univer. Minn. Press, 1933. (a)

Shirley, M. M. *The first two years: a study of twenty-five babies, Vol. III. Personality manifestations.* Inst. Child Welf. Monogr. Series, No. 8. Minneapolis: Univer. Minn. Press, 1933. (b)

Stone, A. A., & Onque, Gloria C. *Longitudinal studies of child personality.* Cambridge, Mass.: Harvard Univer. Press, 1959.

Templin, Mildred C. *Certain language skills in children.* Inst. Child Welf. Monogr. Series, No. 26. Minneapolis: Univer. Minn. Press, 1957.

Woolf, L. I., Griffiths, R., & Moncrieff, A. Treatment of phenylketonuria with a diet low in phenylalanine. *Brit. Med. J.*, 1955 (*4905*), 57–64.

Wright, H. Psychological development in Midwest. *Child Develpm.*, 1956, **27**, 265–286.

Wright, H., & Barker, R. Psychological ecology and the problem of psychosocial development. *Child Develpm.*, 1949, **20**, 131–143.

Wright, H., & Barker, R. *Methods in psychological ecology.* Lawrence, Kan.: Dept. of Psychology, Univer. Kansas, 1950.

SECTION II ✳ BASIC FACTORS IN DEVELOPMENT

For the most part, five areas of development provide a basis for the common qualities of human beings. These five—heredity, growth and maturation, learning and motivation, language, and intelligence—each explored in an individual chapter, form the substance of this section.

Heredity serves all species in the same way, providing human beings with a basic similarity. Regardless of individual differences, all human beings are moderately large primates who manipulate the environment with well-developed hands, who show much curiosity, and who seek experience and variation in their surroundings. All human beings follow a similar pattern of growth and maturation. Although human learning capacities and responses to various motivating forces in the environment in many ways resemble those of all other animals, in some forms of learning, especially those involving formation of concepts, solving of problems, and creativity, man excels. This is because of man's high intellectual capacity as a species; and although individual differences are marked, these differences conceal the basic similarity of one human being to another as compared with other species.

Superiority in learning ability and in retaining information appears largely to result from the fact that man is unique in being able to communicate symbolically. Mediated by common capacities, individual differences, whether hereditary or based on environmental forces, come into being. The hereditary forces producing these differences occupy attention in this section, whereas the environmental influences will be discussed later in the book.

chapter 2 ✸ Heredity

How mutable, or changeable, is human nature? This question is implicit in any study of the influence of heredity, or biological inheritance, on growth and behavior. Anyone who believes that only a minor portion of an organism's capacities and patterns of response are inherited must also believe that the organism can be molded in large part by its surroundings—its environment. Subscribers to this view are called environmentalists. To paraphrase a distinguished exponent of environmentalism, John B. Watson (1919), "Give me a dozen children and full control of the environment, and I will make of them what I wish—atomic scientists, commissars, professors, or beatniks." If this assertion is correct, human nature is indeed changeable and future generations of mankind can be made to differ in basic character from the present generation. Yet the hereditarian insists that man is what he is, and that no amount of manipulation of the environment, unless it is accompanied by some form of selective breeding, can change him significantly.

Only recently the science of genetics—the study of heredity—received a setback in the U.S.S.R. The Soviets felt that a belief in genetics implied that human character was determined, in part, by biological inheritance; to that extent, human nature was immutable (Zirkle, 1949). Legislating out of existence one set of views about the nature of the world, the Soviets supported another (Lysenkoism-Michurianism), which holds that changes in the environment of an organism alter the genetic characteristics transmitted to the organism's offspring. This belief, known to the Western world long ago as Lamarckianism, was accepted in the West as a means of explaining variation among offspring (see Darwin, 1890), but was fairly well disproved by the 1920's. As a scientific theory it has little to recommend it, although it is most useful as a scientific rationalization for those who believe they can change the basic character of mankind. Yet even now, Soviet scientists are attempting to restore Soviet genetics to a Western point of view.

The belief espoused by the Soviets in the inheritance of acquired characteristics may seem, at first sight, an optimistic one. It holds that any efforts at self-improvement live on in one's offspring. But Herman Muller (1948), America's Nobel Prize-winning geneticist, suggested that this concept might not be as optimistic as it first seemed. If it were true, he noted, then individuals in a backward environment —an environment that allowed little growth in intellect or development of potentialities—should become *genetically inferior*. As Muller pointed out, this is not so. It certainly is not true, for example, of Chinese peasants. Assuming the same form of breeding in two differing environments, individuals from environments that have been depressed for generations display, as a group, when placed in an adequate setting, the same level of abilities as any other group. Those who stress that heredity—as defined in Western culture—is the significant determinant of human capacities would maintain that just as a fine environment cannot make men into angels so a degraded one cannot make them like beasts.

These, then, are the issues involved in the study of heredity and environment as they affect human nature. Although a lengthy discussion of the mechanisms of heredity may belong, more appropriately, in a course in genetics, the foregoing philosophical considerations are clearly a part of child psychology. How they are regarded determines to a considerable degree the way the child is viewed.

THE HEREDITARY PROCESS

The mechanisms of heredity are essentially the same for all species of plants and animals, although they may be more easily investigated in an ear of corn or the fruit fly than in humans. What is discovered about hereditary transmission in one species can apply, with few qualifications, to all others.

Among humans a sperm cell of the male penetrates the ovum (egg) of the female and thus fertilizes the ovum. Each normal male and female cell has 46 chromosomes. As a result of cell division, any single sperm or ovum contains approximately half the number of chromosomes of its parent cell—usually one-half of 46, or 23. In the fertilized egg known as a *zygote* the chromosomes of sperm and ovum combine to give the fertile egg 23 *pairs* of chromosomes; this restores the normal complement of 46, with half inherited from each parent. Each of these chromosomes is composed, in turn, of many genes.

The sperm and the ovum are *germ cells*. Their substance, the chains of genes formed into chromosomes, is called *germ plasm,* which is quite distinct from the plasm of the body, called *somatoplasm.* Through the germ plasm parents transmit their genes to their children. The offspring in turn pass on these genes to their progeny. In a sense, germ plasm, transmitting characteristics as it does across generations and generally unaltered by environmental influences, is immortal. Genetic inheritance determines in large part the physical structure and behavioral potentialities of human organisms. The exception occurs in the case of mutations caused by factors in the environment. These mutations are sudden changes in the gene structure which result from X-ray, cosmic ray, or fallout irradiation or from exposure to mustard gas.

What any individual is genetically is determined largely by chance. Half of his genes come from the one sperm cell, among millions of possible sperm cells, that penetrates one of the hundreds of egg cells produced by a female during her reproductive life. Each parent contributes one member of each pair of the many thousands of pairs of genes that affect human inheritance. Each sperm cell and each egg cell differs in the genes it contains from all other sperm and egg cells produced by the same individual. By the random combination of the genes from a particular sperm with the genes of a particular ovum, a human is formed. This human is unique from other humans and yet like fellow men in many respects.

Every individual, as we now know, contains thousands of genes. In some cases one gene is dominant and another is recessive. Those who receive one of each kind from their parents manifest the dominant characteristic, but stand an even chance of passing along the recessive gene to their offspring. Since genes are acquired from parents, it is very likely that individuals are more like their parents genetically and, hence, in observable characteristics than like people in general. However, many characteristics, which are recessive in both of one's parents and therefore not visible, may turn up in the individual. This is one

TABLE 2-1   A Hypothetical Case of Multiple Gene Determination of a Trait *

Gene Pair	Father's Genes	Mother's Genes
1	bright-bright	bright-dull
2	bright-bright	bright-bright
3	bright-dull	dull-dull
4	bright-dull	dull-dull
5	bright-dull	bright-dull
6	dull-dull	bright-bright
7	bright-dull	dull-dull
8	dull-dull	bright-dull
9	dull-dull	bright-dull

Each parent can contribute only one gene out of any gene pair. Possible contributions include the following combinations.

Offspring #1

Offspring Gene Pair	Father-Mother
1	bright-dull
2	bright-bright
3	bright-dull
4	bright-dull
5	bright-bright
6	dull-bright
7	bright-dull
8	dull-bright
9	dull-bright

This offspring has 9 of 9 pairs of genes with one or more bright genes in the pair. The offspring, then, is brighter than either parent.

Offspring #2

Offspring Gene Pair	Father-Mother
1	bright-dull
2	bright-bright
3	dull-dull
4	dull-dull
5	dull-dull
6	dull-bright
7	dull-dull
8	dull-dull
9	dull-dull

This offspring, on the other hand, has only three genes disposing toward brightness and six double recessive pairs of genes disposing him toward dullness. He is less able than his parents.

* We have decided to call bright genes dominant.

reason why children do not always resemble their parents as closely as might be expected.

Although some characteristics are determined by a single pair of genes, many more characteristics result from the interactive effect of a large number of gene pairs. Suppose that intellectual ability were determined by nine pairs of genes, which is likely to be less than the actual number. Suppose further that there could be only two possible genes in each pair—one that disposed toward "brightness" and the other toward "dullness." Now suppose that the genes disposing toward brightness were dominant in two particular parents, whereas those disposing toward dullness were recessive. Since brightness is dominant in this case any of the nine pairs of genes containing one or both bright genes would dispose the offspring toward being intelligent. Table 2-1 presents several possibilities. Because of the many potential combinations, numerous differences may result. A pair of morons, for example, might produce a genius, and vice versa; this is not impossible but highly improbable.

INHERITED SIMILARITIES

Most psychological research into the influence of heredity has been directed toward determining its role in producing differences among humans. But the overwhelming significance of heredity is not really in this area; rather it is in the area of achieving similarities between individuals.

Humanness is the result of a number of genetically determined characteristics which, interacting with one another, produce that portion of behavior that is not common with other species. La Barre (1954) argued that the characteristics that made humans unique, except for resemblance to other higher primates, were bipedal locomotion, stereoptic vision, hands, and a fairly high capacity for learning.

When man, heir of four limbs, uses only two of them for walking, his clever primate hands are then finally freed from use in any kind of locomotion whatever. They can now be used for purely exploratory grasping. The advantages of this are not to be underestimated.

Emancipated hands are not enough: many dinosaurs had them, but they lacked sufficient brains. Intelligence is not enough: elephants have a great deal of intelligence behind their trunks, but they do not have stereoscopic sight; the prehensile-tailed monkeys are intelligent too, and they have stereoscopic vision as well, but they do not ordinarily see their tails. Stereoscopic eyes are not enough either: for the intelligent, tree-living apes have them, with color vision and the yellow spot in the retina to boot. It is the combination that counts. Man has paired grasping organs, fully in his field of vision and wholly freed from locomotor duties, in a stereoscopic-sighted, big-brained mammal—and these add up to the answer.

Anaxagoras claimed that man had brains because he had hands, but Aristotle argued that man had hands because he had brains. When the implications of these statements are better understood and the dust of battle has settled a bit, modern anthropologists are inclined to give the decision to Anaxagoras rather than to Aristotle. But hands, brains, and eyes are a case, really, of hens-and-eggs causality; nor did it all begin, strictly speaking, with man. For in all primate evolution they influence each other mutually and develop progressively together; and the ability to "monkey with things" that man got from his primate ancestors is still one of the keystones of human nature. Certainly such hands and eyes and brains put an animal into closer object-relationship with reality and enlarge the animal ego in the technical sense of increasing awareness and testing of reality. Very literally, such an animal as man has more contacts with reality (La Barre, 1954, pp. 86–87).

La Barre's views were supported by Butler (1953, 1954) and others working with Harlow at the University of Wisconsin on experiments dealing with curiosity drive. Butler described his work as follows.

. . . I was testing monkeys on a food-rewarded problem. The monkey worked behind a screen where it could not see the experimenter. By the same token, the experimenter could not see the monkey, and there was a great temptation to peek to find out what the animal was doing. I first made a small peephole in the panel, but the monkey quickly discovered it and thereafter spied on me as often as I did on him. I next tried placing a small mirror in a position that enabled me to watch the animal constantly. The monkey turned the tables by dropping its work and watching me through the mirror!

Taking advantage of this lead, we designed an experiment to investigate monkey's visual exploratory behavior. The apparatus was essentially an enclosure with a built-in color discrimination problem. Monkeys were rewarded by a view of the surroundings outside the enclosure, provided they responded correctly on the problem.

The results of the experiment left no doubt about the strength of the monkey's curiosity or its power in promoting learning. Throughout the 20 days of testing the animals worked away eagerly at the problem. . . . Without tiring of the game, they went on pushing the doors enthusiastically to get a look at the people working in the laboratory outside the box. In a second study that ran for 57 days and presented various color-discrimination problems, the subjects worked just as unflaggingly.

These data strongly suggest that the drive to explore visually is indeed a fundamental drive in monkeys. To measure its strength and persistence further, two monkeys were tested for four continuous hours each day for five days. The animals worked as fast on Day Five as they did on Day One. A second experiment yielded still more surprising results.

Three monkeys were put to the door-opening test hour after hour, with 30 seconds between trials, until they quit. One monkey performed for nine continuous hours, another worked for 11 and the third for more than 19 hours! The response time of this marathon performer was actually shortest during the final hour of the test. That the monkeys would work as long and as persistently for a food reward is highly unlikely . . . (Butler, 1954).

Through producing a better understanding of the environment, this primate trait, curiosity, has so much value for survival that natural selection has made it a human characteristic inherited in much the same manner as the opposable thumb. The existence of the curiosity drive and the need it may arouse for stimulation probably produces fundamental differences in learning between primates and nonprimates. This is shown, for example, in the work of Harlow and others who have found that primates attack problems involving manipulation, such as unlocking doors and solving problems, without any special reward. If such a reward is introduced, the primate does *less* well in these tasks (Harlow, 1950). Yet there seems to be little doubt that intrinsic reward hastens learning. Since all responses that satisfy curiosity are rewarding to primates, it seems reasonable to believe that the primate will learn a wide variety of behaviors, some of which will have survival value. In contrast, the learning of nonprimates seems largely restricted to techniques to reduce such drives as hunger and thirst.

Through an interplay of environment and biological inheritance, the primate—and especially man—has developed physical characteristics that enable an active, manipulative approach to the environment. As a consequence, genetically determined structure and behavior produce a basic similarity among all men. Within this similarity heredity helps to establish variations, or individual differences.

INHERITANCE OF INDIVIDUAL DIFFERENCES

All humans differ from one another. How much of these differences may be imputed to heredity? Although this is not an entirely valid question, since heredity and environment interact, some answers to it can tell something about the relative contribution of each to human variability.

The idea that abilities are inherited certainly is not new. Long before there was a science of behavior, the belief in the inheritance of traits formed the basis for class distinction. The knight, no matter how impoverished, could not marry the merchant's daughter, no matter how substantial the dowry. During the late Middle Ages people believed that there were vast differences between the nobility and the merchant class and between the merchant class and the peasantry. Those in superior positions considered themselves, somehow, transcendentally different, and held that this superiority was transmitted to their progeny. Even though such ideas, like subsequent notions of racial purity, rested on value judgments about the relative worth of individuals and on rather dubious genetic principles, they do indicate that man has long believed in heredity as a determinant of personality.

The first scientific study of the inheritance of ability was undertaken by Sir Francis Galton in *English Men of Science* (1874). A cousin of Darwin and a member of the brilliant but eccentric Darwin-Wedgewood-Galton family, Sir Francis may have been drawn to this area of research by his ponderings over his extensive family and its rich contribution to English science and industry. His discovery that a relatively small number of English families produced most of England's scientists suggested to him that genius was inherited. The difficulty in interpreting his work is the same one encountered in interpreting much of the research into the inheritance of characteristics conducted since his time. Some English families certainly produced many scientific geniuses—but can this be attributed to heredity? The child of a genius may inherit genius or, just as likely, may acquire it through association with a dedicated, brilliant parent—or both. This same contamination of heredity by environment pervades several recent studies which nevertheless have some bearing on the inheritance of individual differences.

The United States has an open class society. Individuals of great ability may rise and those of slight ability may descend in occupational level. Although there is considerable variation in ability within any social class, IQ differences are still found to exist among members of various classes when large samples of individuals are measured in each. If intelligence were inherited, these differences, though attenuated, should also appear in the children of these individuals. Table 2-2 shows results of studies aimed at testing this hypothesis.

Individual differences do exist. Although superior environment in upper occupational levels may play a part in producing them, the similarity in the size of the gaps over a 20-year span during which class distinctions have markedly decreased suggests that heredity figures strongly.

Many studies have measured family resemblances in intelligence.

TABLE 2-2   Mean IQs of Preschool Children Classified by Father's Occupation
According to the Minnesota Occupational Scale (Goodenough & Anderson, 1931)

	Study		
Father's Occupation	Goodenough (1928)	Terman & Merrill (1937)	Johnson (1948)
Professional	116	116	116
Semiprofessional and managerial	112	112	112
Clerical and skilled trades	108	108	107
Rural owners, farmers		99	95
Semiskilled, minor clerical	105	104	105
Slightly skilled	104	95	98
Unskilled	96	94	96

Table 2-3 presents typical results of such studies.   Even though higher
correlations among identical than fraternal twins suggest the impact
of heredity on resemblance, the correlation of fraternal twins in contrast to ordinary siblings or to parents and children implies that similarity of environment increases the degree of resemblance, since fraternal twins are no more similar, genetically, than the other two
groups.

The closer resemblance in intelligence between identical than fraternal twins is of particular interest, because pairs of fraternal twins
should be expected to share the same environment just about as much
as do pairs of identical twins.   However, this closer resemblance between identical than between fraternal twins in intelligence-test scores

TABLE 2-3   Intrafamily Resemblances
in Intelligence

Relationship	Correlation of Intelligence
Identical twins *	.88
Fraternal (like sex) twins *	.63
Siblings †	.53
Parents and children †	.49

* Newman, Freeman, & Holzinger (1937).
† Burt & Howard (1956).

has also been demonstrated in several more recent studies (Blewett, 1954; Strandskov, 1954; Vanderberg, 1956).

Jost and Sontag (1944) presented evidence on the inheritance of autonomic nervous-system responsiveness. The autonomic nervous system is basically a network of nerves which regulates the body's involuntary functions, such as digestion or breathing. Jost and Sontag based their findings on measurements of heart and respiratory patterns, electrical skin response, pulse, and other indicators of autonomic performance. Differences in autonomic performance, they found, were less for identical twins than for siblings and less for siblings than for persons not related to each other. Since emotionality is controlled by autonomic functions, their findings detected some inheritance of this characteristic.

Freedman and Keller (1963) compared sets of identical and fraternal twins. Occasionally the suggestion has been made that identical twins show a greater resemblance than do fraternal twins because the former are treated more alike. Using the Mental and Motor Scales of the Bayley Infant Behavior Profile, Freedman and Keller compared twins within the first year of life when the effects of differential treat-

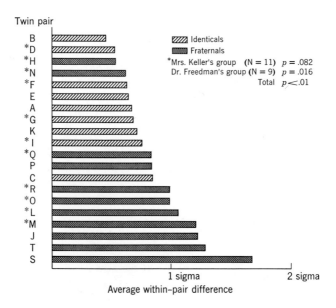

FIGURE 2-1 The Bayley Mental and Motor Scales averaged to form a single distribution. Average within-pair differences in the first year, based on 8 to 12 monthly administrations (Freedman & Keller, 1963, p. 197).

ment between types of twins could be expected to be minimal, if not nonexistent. The differences in scores were found to be significantly smaller between members of identical twins as compared with members of fraternal twins. This closer resemblance at such an early age supports the notion that hereditary influences have been at work.

The foregoing studies all shed some light on the inheritance of characteristics. However, except for the Freedman and Keller investigation, these studies, like Sir Francis Galton's experiments in the last century, do not provide adequate controls for testing similarity of the environment. Other experimental procedures are needed if one wishes to identify more accurately the relative contributions of heredity and environment. Three kinds of procedures employed to accomplish this task have been selective breeding, studies of identical twins, and investigations of adopted children.

What evidence about human characteristics has been produced by each of these three approaches? Most research by psychologists into the role of heredity has concentrated on the influence of heredity and environment on scores in intelligence tests. This is partly the result of an historical accident. Soon after the turn of the century psychologists had developed an adequate test of intelligence, but there is still no comparable measure of personality. Moreover, an older generation of psychologists believed that intelligence was a central factor in personality. By knowing the intelligence of an individual, they held, one could also know many other things about him—his honesty, his leadership ability, his values. Today's psychologists are much less certain that a high IQ automatically makes an individual trustworthy, loyal, obedient, God fearing, and kind. Thus, studies of intelligence seem to have less bearing on personality structure than they once had. And although psychologists should like to know more about hereditary influences on personality characteristics, this is an area in which they are least knowledgeable.

Evidence from Selective Breeding

Selective breeding is the breeding of organisms for the presence or absence of some particular trait. If the breeding can be achieved, the trait must necessarily have some hereditary base. The speed at which selective breeding progresses indicates, in part, the importance of heredity in determining how much of the trait is present in any organism.

Galton's study persuaded him that humans should engage in selective breeding. The able person should seek an equally able mate in order to improve the human race. This process of selective breeding Galton called *eugenics*. Although eugenics societies still exist, human beings have not taken Galton's ideas very seriously. They continue to fall in love without giving the slightest consideration to what the eugenicist might think of their choice. Yet even if people turned about and suddenly adhered to Galton's formula, problems would remain. What should be the goal of the breeders—vigor, beauty, intelligence? Often these are not found in the same individual, as the well-known story about George Bernard Shaw, the playwright, and Ellen Terry, the beautiful actress, illustrates. Miss Terry suggested to Shaw that they could produce a true *wunderkind* with her beauty and his brains. Shaw rejected the proposal, replying things might turn out the other way around; the child might inherit *his* beauty and *her* brains. The difficulty in any sort of selective breeding is thus the matter of choosing the objective of the process.

The few situations in which humans have bred selectively are indeed odd, since only eccentric people could and would indulge in such experiments. Frederick the Great is said to have married off a large number of his tallest guards to a group of strapping peasant girls and provided them with villages in which to live so as to ensure future rulers of Prussia a ready source of tall soldiers for honor-guard usage. Hitler attempted to breed "Aryan Supermen." The most interesting example of selective breeding among humans stemmed from the ideas of an American religious sect. John Noyes (see Holbrook, 1957) believed that the violent, antisocial emotions, such as jealousy and anger, resulted primarily from the existence of the *nuclear* family —the family composed of father, mother, and children formed into a tightly knit unit. Doing away with this family, Noyes held, also does away with possessiveness and, hence, with greed, jealousy, and anger. In its place he advocated a utopian scheme as part of a religion he called *Perfectionism*.

At Oneida, New York, Noyes and his followers maintained themselves for years in a communistic community. They practiced what outsiders called "free love" but what they themselves considered "multiple marriage." Although sexual behavior was, in a sense, free, Noyes and other leaders of the Oneida community decided who could have children, how many they could have, and who would be the partner of a particular individual in conceiving a child. Noyes desired only the brightest, most capable adults to reproduce. Long before Galton he practiced eugenics, though he called it *stirpiculture*.

The community flourished long enough for two generations, in some cases, to be bred selectively. Then federal prosecution of Mormon polygamy in the 1880's spilled over into Oneida, forcing the end of the experiment, the only one in which humans were bred for general physical and intellectual excellence. Although there have been assertions (Noyes, 1937) that children of the community have demonstrated high levels of ability, only an empirical study of the group's descendants can truly assess the success of the venture.

Among lower organisms it is easier to observe the results of selective breeding. Physical size and structure, ability, and emotionality are among the variations between organisms that can be genetically determined. By selecting and breeding dogs for smallness, as well as for other characteristics, one obtains the Chihuahua, whereas for largeness, one obtains the Great Dane. Moreover, dogs of different breeds vary in temperament and in ability almost as widely as they do in size. Since the ancestry of pedigreed dogs is known for generations, the researcher has purer strains at his disposal than he can obtain among humans.

Scott (1958, pp. 117–125) has reported studies conducted by Fuller and himself which disclose the effect on temperament of hereditary differences produced by selective breeding. In several of these studies, they compared cocker spaniels with *basenjis* (African barkless dogs). Basenjis proved considerably shier and more fearful than cockers, even when they were reared by cocker mothers. As a result of breeding cockers to basenjis, the hybrid progeny were as shy as fullblooded basenjis, suggesting that shyness was a dominant genetic trait in dogs. Breeds of dogs, which differ in parental stock and in the traits for which they are bred, also differ widely in other respects. Figure 2-2, for example, illustrates another hereditary trait of cockers.

By shifting from dogs to rats, we move from the domain generally inhabited by the animal fancier to the domain of the animal scientist. Many rats have been bred by investigators to study the influence of genetic inheritance on a variety of animal characteristics. The most famous rat-breeding experiment was conducted by Tryon (1940). Krech and Crutchfield (1958) have succinctly summarized Tryon's work.

> Tryon started with "parental" generation of 142 male and female rats. Each animal was run for 19 trials through a 17-unit maze. The brightest animals made a total of approximately 14 errors in learning the maze, the dullest, about 174. The bright females were then mated with the bright males, the dull females with the dull males—the other animals being discarded. Then the offspring of these matings were tested on the same maze. On the basis of their performance, the brightest rats within each of the bright litters were mated, and the dullest within each of the dullest litters were mated. This testing and selective breed-

FIGURE 2-2 Setting birds for the net. *Above,* having found the birds, the spaniel was trained to drop flat on the ground while men came up behind him and threw a net over both birds and dog. (Drawn after Blome, *The Gentleman's Recreation,* London, 1688.) *Below,* spaniels were selected for their ability to crouch. This tendency still survives in many modern cocker spaniels which will drop flat at a threatening gesture. (Adapted from Scott, 1958, p. 121.)

ing procedure was followed for 18 generations. The results are summarized in the distribution curves of (Figure 2-3) showing the errors made by the parental group, the third generation (F_2), the seventh generation (F_6) and the ninth generation (F_8). With successive generations the two strains of rats pull apart, until by the F_8 generations the dullest of the bright rats are about as bright or brighter than the brightest of the dulls (p. 572).

The Tryon experiment is itself of considerable significance and has led to further work in the biochemical aspects of brightness and dullness (see Chapter 6, pp. 159–160). Conceivably, this might be a key to the treatment of certain kinds of mental defect.

If, in eight generations, one can produce differences so great that strains of organisms do not overlap in a trait such as brightness or emotionality, then genetic factors are indeed powerful in establishing individual differences. The many studies in selective breeding, although dealing for the most part with lower organisms, strongly sup-

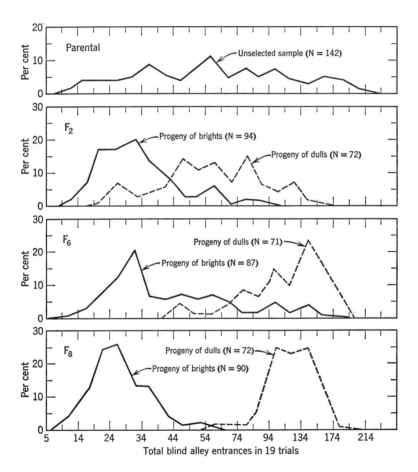

FIGURE 2-3 Error scores made by animals of successive generations. On the vertical axis is indicated the per cent of the total group of rats of any one generation making the number of errors indicated on the horizontal axis (Krech & Crutchfield, 1958, p. 572).

port the notion that human beings do not enter the world as a *tabula rasa*—a blank tablet. Instead they are born with certain abilities and propensities which are further accentuated by the environment. In fact, it might be said that any characteristic that has a structural base, such as activity level, tendency toward schizophrenia, emotionality, or intelligence, is inheritable.

Identical-Twin Studies

This single approach is perhaps the best available technique for evaluating the effect of heredity on human capacities. Genetically, identical twins are exactly alike. They result from the division of a fertilized egg after it has been penetrated by a single sperm; this division produces two individuals identical in heredity. By separating identical twins and raising them in quite disparate environments, and by holding heredity constant while varying the environment, the relative influences of each became discernible.

The group of twins discussed most intensively were those studied by Newman, Freeman, and Holzinger (1937). These men investigated 50 sets of fraternal twins, a like number of sets of identical twins raised together, and 19 sets of identical twins raised apart from one another. The 19 pairs of identical twins raised separately are of present concern. Some rather startling resemblances were discovered among them. For example, consider these findings about Ed and Fred.

> The most interesting feature of this story is the remarkable parallelism in the lives of these twins in spite of the fact that they lived without knowledge of each other's existence for twenty-five years. They were both reared as only children by childless foster-parents, both being led to understand that they were own children. Though they lived a thousand miles apart, they had about the same educational experience, and both found employment as repair men in branches of the same great telephone company. They were married in the same year and each had a baby son. Each owned a fox terrier dog named Trixie. According to their statements, both of them from early boyhood on were obsessed with the idea that they had a brother who died and often stated this to their playmates.
>
> The story of their discovery of each other's existence is almost stranger than fiction. When Ed was twenty-two he was accosted by a jovial fellow who had just come from a distant city to work at Ed's department. "Hello, Fred! How's tricks?" he inquired. Ed explained that he was not Fred and denied that he knew the newcomer, but the latter was hard to convince, declaring that Ed was trying to cover up his identity. Soon afterward another man accosted him as "Fred" and stated that if he was not Fred Blank he was exactly like a fellow of that name with whom he

had recently worked in a distant city. Ed was by this time rather disturbed about the matter and told his parents about it. Reluctantly, the parents were forced to admit that Ed was an adopted son and that he was one of a pair of twins; the other of them had been adopted by a couple who lived in their home town but with whom they were not acquainted. They also revealed the fact that when the twins were small boys they had attended school together for a short time and that the other children often noticed their close resemblance. It occurs to us that this early association of the twins may have led to the above-mentioned mutual feeling about a brother who had died.

Needless to say, Ed lost no time in getting in touch with Fred. The latter was out of work at the time and came to visit Ed. It was during this time that we succeeded in inducing them to come to Chicago to see the Fair and, incidentally, to be examined. Their visit with us was made even more interesting to them and to us by reason of a confusion of dates which resulted in their coming to us at the same time as a pair of young women twins, Ethel and Esther, whose story comes next in this series. The two pairs of twins became great friends and were much impressed by similarity in the circumstances that led to their discovery that they were twins. The visits to the Fair were made together, each young man taking one of the young women. When they walked about, people were startled to see one couple walking ahead and a duplicate couple following behind. Everywhere they went they attracted attention and enjoyed the sensation they created. On one occasion they attended a side show featuring a pair of Siamese twins and, according to their statement, stole the show, attracting more attention than the exhibits (pp. 147–148).

The 19 pairs of separated identical twins were studied at maturity. Members of each pair showed a close resemblance in physical size and in other phases of growth. They resembled one another closely in IQ and less closely in personality. Perhaps the degree to which heredity determines development diminishes from size to IQ to personality. Or perhaps the correlations were highest on concrete physical growth because here is where the best, most exact, and most reliable measuring instruments are available. Devices for measuring intelligence are less precise and reliable than devices used to check physical dimensions. The reliability of measures for personality is low even at the present time and was certainly a good deal lower at the time of the Newman et al. study in the 1930's. Actually, the reliability of most tests was so low in the 1930's that it was surprising to find any resemblance at all between twins.

Since the measures of intelligence were most central to the matters that concerned psychologists at the time, these tests have been the most widely discussed. Woodworth (1941) offered both IQ and environmental data for the 19 sets of twins studied by Newman and his associates, and for three other sets as well. As he noted:

Taken without regard to sign, the average IQ difference between separated identicals is 7.6 points. Correction for chance errors of observation would bring this difference down to 6 points net, a figure to be compared with the estimated net difference of 3 points between identicals reared together, and of 15 points or more between children paired at random from the same community. It is probable, then, that environment did make these separated twins differ in tested intelligence, though not to any such extent as obtains among the children of a community (Woodworth, 1941, p. 357).

The correlation obtained between identical twins reared in *separate* environments was +.767. This was a more substantial relation than was obtained between fraternal twins raised in the *same* environment. Although Newman, Freeman, and Holzinger considered their data to support an environmentalist view, heredity seemed to have played an important part in determining the level of intelligence. A more recent study of variations in intelligence among a comparable sample of identical twins who were raised separately (Burt & Howard, 1956) has turned up similar results. In this case it seems clear that some variability can be attributed to environmental circumstances, even though the heredity factor is quite strong.

One other intensive study of a single pair of identical twins (Burks, in McNemar & Merrill, 1942) supplies considerable information about the interests and personalities of the twins, as well as the more customary measurements of intelligence and physical size. The twins were girls, who had been separated before they were two weeks old. At the age of 12, personality ratings showed them to be quite similar to one another, despite a variability in certain areas of adjustment, which was produced by familial and environmental influences. The girls differed markedly in Strong Interest Test scores. At 18 they seemed even more similar to each other than at 12 and their interest profiles showed a distinct increase in comparability. Moreover, Rorschach tests at 18 indicated a high degree of likeness; the patterns of response were more alike than might have been anticipated even from previous studies of identical twins who had been reared together. The greater likeness at 18 suggested that as one grew older and, hence, freer from parental dominance, innate predispositions became more apparent. This study, the only known one to have measured separately raised identical twins with adequate devices for assessing personality, suggested that the extent to which individuals displayed *certain* personality traits was in large part the consequence of genetic inheritance.

Studies of identical twins who have been separated also have bearing for one particular aspect of the subject of heredity and environment.

This is the aspect of how "enrichment" affects intelligence-test scores and, presumably, innate ability. Wellman (1943) maintained that kindergarten experience increased the ability of the child. Goodenough (1940), on the other hand, held that it did not. More recently, Bowlby (1952), Goldfarb (1945), and Spitz (1945, 1946) asserted that a child's level of intellectual performance was largely determined by the closeness and richness of the mothering it received. However, Pinneau (1955) and others, among them Dennis and Najarian (1957), have taken a contrary position.

The latest phase of enrichment to be explored is that of very early enrichment. This is the area of enrichment that is most relevant to the study of identical twins. Thus far, most of the experimental work has been conducted with laboratory rats. Hebb (1949, pp. 298–299) reported that rats from an ordinary strain of laboratory species who were reared as home "pets" performed in significantly superior manner on a learning task to rats from the same strain who were reared in a normal laboratory environment. Other well-controlled experiments have extended these findings. In a representative study of this sort conducted by Forgus (1956), infant rats were exposed to visual forms from the time they first opened their eyes at the age of 16 days until they reached 41 days of age. A second group of rats was exposed to these same forms during the interval from 41 to 66 days of age. In both cases control groups of littermates were reared without the visual experience. Tests of both enriched and both control groups showed that the two enriched groups learned more rapidly than the control groups, and that the group that had been enriched early learned more rapidly than the late-enrichment group. Several similar studies (Cooper & Zubek, 1958; Gibson & Walk, 1956; and Luchins & Forgus, 1955) concurred in this finding. These indicate that deprivation retards later learning, whereas early enrichment increases the rate of learning.

Studies in the early enrichment of lower organisms contain implications for problems of human development. This has been suggested by Hunt (1961), McCandless (1961, pp. 261–262), Smith and Stone (1962, pp. 6–7), and Thompson (1959, p. 33). Perhaps, for example, the enrichment or deprivation of problem-solving experience to which a human is exposed before the age of two or three may be related to later ability.

If early enrichment or deprivation bears on the intellectual ability of humans, then identical twins who are exposed to a common early environment and share the stimulation it offers should resemble each other more closely on IQ tests than identical twins who have not shared a common environment for any length of time. The 19 pairs of separated identical twins studied by Newman et al., plus one pair each studied by Burks (1942), Gardner and Newman (1940), Muller (1925), and Saudek (1934) constitute 23 pairs. Of these 23 pairs of identical twins, 11 were separated before the age of six months and 12 were separated after their first year. The mean age of separation was two months for the younger group and 24 months for the other. The respective medians were one month and 18 months. If early environmental stimulation influences later ability, those twins who shared a common environment for a longer period of time should show a greater resemblance in intelligence than those separated at an earlier age. Table 2-4 contains such a comparison.

The results were quite the contrary from what some might have expected. The mean difference in IQ among those pairs separated before six months of age was 4.7, and for those separated after one year, 9.4. Thus, the similarity in IQ between identical twins significantly is *inversely* related to the time spent in the same environment. Since the two groups did not differ significantly in the age at which they were tested, in duration of separation, or in degree of environmental difference, it is hard to explain why the twins in the early-

TABLE 2-4   IQ Differences between Separated Identical Twins

Early Separation Group		*Later Separation Group*	
Age of Separation	*IQ Difference, in points*	*Age of Separation*	*IQ Difference, in points*
9 days (Burks) *	1	1 yr.	19
½ mo. (Muller)	1	1 yr.	5
1 mo. (Saudek)	4	1 yr.	1
1 mo. (Gardner & Newman)	3	14 mo.	4
1 mo.	1	18 mo.	12
1 mo.	6	18 mo.	12
1 mo.	1	18 mo.	24
2 mo.	2	18 mo.	7
3 mo.	15	2 yr.	10
5 mo.	17	2½ yr.	2
6 mo.	1	3 yr.	8
		6 yr.	9

* Unless otherwise noted, the pairs are from the Newman, Freeman, and Holzinger study.

separation group were more similar. The fact that the twins in the late-separation group were not more similar, despite the more equal environment for a longer period of time, rebuts the widespread idea, obtained from animal research, that early enrichment has a direct influence on later intelligence-test scores.

Adopted-Child Studies

Something about the influence of heredity and environment may also be learned by investigating the intelligence of a number of adopted children, of their true parents, and of their foster parents. Inferences may be drawn about the role played by heredity (true parent) and by environment (foster parent) in shaping the child's ability level from correlations between true parent and child ability and between foster parent and child ability. Yet for several reasons the results of this kind of investigation are not as clear-cut as those of the studies of identical twins. Even when children are raised by their true parents, the correlation of parent-child IQ is only about +.50. Moreover, as a result of the placement policies of adoption agencies, foster parents are somewhat similar to the true parents in ability and in appearance.

The most widely cited studies on adopted children were done years ago. They were conducted by Burks (1928), Leahy (1935), Skodak (1939), and Skeels (1936, 1941). Burks's and Leahy's studies argued for the hereditarian point of view. The opposite position was taken by Skodak and Skeels.

Together, Skodak and Skeels (1945, 1949) followed up 154 children, their true mothers, and foster parents after having independently studied the true mothers and the children some years earlier. They found that according to test results the true mothers were retarded in mental ability, whereas the foster parents were above average. Examining 100 of these children longitudinally, they discovered that they did not resemble their true mothers in test scores, but instead resembled the foster parents in tests given over a period of years. At various test ages their mean IQs ranged from 104 to 118 (Skodak & Skeels, 1949). These means were more than 20 points higher than the true mother mean. Although mean scores resembled the foster parents, the correlation between the IQ of the child and the ability of the true mother, estimated from amount of education, ranged from +.33 to +.38 (see Goodenough, 1940), whereas correlations with the ability of foster parents, estimated from their education, were only +.16 to +.19. How can this be explained? These children, separated from their true mothers soon after birth, obtained mean IQs 20 points higher than their mothers, yet resembled them almost as closely in a correlational sense as children raised by their own mothers. Quite likely the IQs obtained from the true mothers were not truly representative of ability. Many of them were tested shortly after having given birth, a rather inopportune time to test any woman—and especially a woman who had given birth to an illegitimate child in Iowa in the 1930's!

As a group, therefore, the adopted-child studies again point to the importance of heredity as a producer of individual differences.

SUMMARY AND CONCLUSIONS

In many ways humans resemble lower organisms. In many ways humans resemble one another. These basic resemblances result from the hereditary process. The effects of biological inheritance, although of great significance, are often overlooked, since they are universal. Besides similarities, heredity produces individual differences in such matters as size, intelligence, and temperament. The role of heredity is more apparent in shaping these differences than in determining similarities. People who differ genetically in some way, such as intelligence, are also treated differently; thus, environmental forces magnify the original hereditary distinctions.

The study of genetic similarities helps to develop a point of view about how far human character can be modified. The human is a medium-sized omnivorous animal. He lacks specialized weapons of offense or defense, but possesses native curiosity, hands free for exploring and manipulating the environment and for carrying weapons, moderately high aggressiveness, and communicative skills which make cooperation possible. It is doubtful whether a tendency to respond bred in by thousands of years of natural selection—for example, a quick and aggressive response to threats from the environment—can be eliminated unless natural selection takes a new course. This is what Veblen (1911) maintained happened starting at the time of the industrial revolution. Actually, there is hope for humanity, since built-in responses are susceptible to some modification as the social-environment shifts.

It may seem pessimistic to hold that much of the variation between human beings in physique, intelligence, and some aspects of personality results from genetic factors. Yet this is not a pessimistic view for various reasons. First, if this view is correct, humans are what they are and no environment, however deprived or depraved, can wipe out those aspects of human beings which are most endearing: the forming of close attachments, the need for one another, curiosity, and the sense of wonder. Second, although heredity imposes limits on individual achievement, one cannot tell whether the limit has been reached for any individual unless he has been exposed to the best possible social and intellectual environment. Each child and each adult differs from all others. Unless opportunities for expression are made available, potential abilities cannot be judged. However, one should not be surprised to find that some individuals gain more than others from any single environmental opportunity.

Through the study of individual differences in general and genetically determined individual differences in particular, people become aware of the vast range of these distinctions. We humans are even more different from each other than we seem and in more ways than was once realized. Although these differences at times impede communication between individuals and make the human being a baffling subject for scientific study, they do add richness to human interaction.

One specific result of the study of individual difference is apparent in child psychology. As we shall see in later chapters, child psychology was once "formula happy"—if you do *this* to the child, you will get *that* result. This approach to child rearing, however, has never proved effective, because humans vary so much from one another in their reactions to any treatment. Through increased awareness of the fact that individual differences exist, that they are of great magnitude, and that, to a fair degree, they are hereditary in nature, child psychology has progressed beyond oversimplified approaches to child-rearing practices and philosophies. This is the most important way that the study of individual differences has influenced child development.

REFERENCES

Blewett, D. B. An experimental study of the inheritance of intelligence. *J. ment. Sci.*, 1954, **100**, 922–933.

Bowlby, J. *Maternal care and mental health,* World Health Organization Monogr. Ser., Geneva, Switzerland, 1952.

Burks, Barbara S. The relative influence of nature and nurture on mental development: A comparative study of foster parent–foster child resemblance and true parent–true child resemblance. *Yearb. nat. Soc. Stud. Educ.*, 1928, **27** (I), 219–316.

Burks, Barbara S. A study of identical twins reared apart under differing types of family relationships. In Q. McNemar & Maud A. Merrill, *Studies in Personality*. New York: McGraw-Hill, 1942.

Burt, C., & Howard, M. A multiple factorial theory of inheritance and its application to intelligence. *Brit. J. statist. Psychol.*, 1956, **9**, 95–131.

Butler, R. A. Discrimination learning by rhesus monkeys to visual-exploration motivation. *J. comp. physiol. Psychol.*, 1953, **46**, 95–98.

Butler, R. A. Curiosity in monkeys, *Sci. Am.*, 1954, **190**, 70–75.

Cooper, R. M., & Zubek, J. P. Effects of enriched and restricted early environments on the learning ability of bright and dull rats. *Canad. J. Psychol.*, 1958, **12**, 159–164.

Darwin, C. R. *The variation of animals and plants under domestication.* New York: D. Appleton, 1890.

Dennis, W., & Najarian, P. Infant development under environmental handicap. *Psychol. Monogr.*, 1957, **71**, No. 436.

Forgus, R. H. Advantage of early over late perceptual experience in improving form discrimination. *Canad. J. Psychol.*, 1956, **10**, 147–155.

Freedman, D. G., & Keller, Barbara. Inheritance of behavior in infants. *Science*, 1963, **140**, 196–198.

Galton, F. *English men of science: their nature and nurture.* London: Macmillan, 1874.

Gardner, I. C., & Newman, H. H. Mental and physical traits of identical twins reared apart, Case XX. *J. Hered.*, 1940, **31**, 119–126.

Gibson, Eleanor J., & Walk, R. D. The effect of prolonged exposure to visually presented patterns on learning to discriminate them. *J. comp. physiol. Psychol.*, 1956, **49**, 239–242.

Goldfarb, W. Effects of psychological privation in infancy and subsequent development. *Amer. J. Psychiat.*, 1945, **102**, 18–33.

Goodenough, Florence L. The Kuhlman-Binet tests for children of preschool age: a critical study and evaluation. *Inst. Child Welf. Monogr.*, Minneapolis: Univer. Minn. Press, 1928, No. 2.

Goodenough, Florence L. New evidence on environmental influence on intelligence. *Yearb. nat. Soc. Stud. Educ.*, 1940, **39** (I), 367–384.

Goodenough, Florence L., & Anderson, J. E. *Experimental child study.* New York: Century, 1931.

Hall, C. S. Emotional behavior in the rat. *J. comp. Psychol.*, 1937, **24**, 369–375.

Harlow, H. Learning motivated by a manipulative drive. *J. exp. Psychol.*, 1950, **40**, 228–234.

Hebb, D. O. *The organization of behavior.* Wiley: New York, 1949.

Holbrook, S. H. *Dreamers of the American dream.* Garden City, N. Y.: Doubleday, 1957.

Hunt, J. McV. *Intelligence and experience.* New York: Ronald, 1961.

Johnson, D. M. Application of the standard score IQ to social statistics. *J. soc. Psychol.*, 1948, **27**, 217–227.

Johnson, R. C. Similarity in IQ of separated identical twins as related to amount of time spent in the same environment. *Child Develpm.*, 1963, **34**, 745–749.

Jost, H., & Sontag, L. W. The genetic factor in autonomic nervous system function. *Psychosom. Med.*, 1944, **6**, 308–310.

Krech, D., & Crutchfield, R. S. *Elements of psychology.* New York: Knopf, 1958.

La Barre, W. *The human animal.* Chicago: Univer. of Chicago Press, 1954. Pp. 86–87.

Leahy, A. M. Nature-nurture and intelligence. *Genet. Psychol. Monogr.,* 1935, **17**, 236–308.

Luchins, A. S., & Forgus, R. H. The effect of differential post-weaning environments on the rigidity of an animal's behavior. *J. genet. Psychol.,* 1955, **86**, 51–58.

McCandless, B. R. *Children and adolescents: behavior and development.* New York: Holt, Rinehart & Winston, 1961.

Muller, H. J. The crushing of genetics in the U.S.S.R. *Bull. atom. Sci.,* 1948, **12**, 369–371.

Muller, H. J. Mental traits and heredity. *J. Hered.,* 1925, **16**, 433–448.

Newman, H. H., Freeman, F. N., & Holzinger, K. J. *Twins: a study of heredity and environment.* Chicago: Univer. Chicago Press, 1937.

Noyes, P. B. *My father's house: an Oneida boyhood.* New York: Farrar & Rinehart, 1937.

Pinneau, S. R. The infantile disorders of hospitalism and anaclitic depression. *Psychol. Bull.,* 1955, **52**, 429–452.

Saudek, R. A British pair of identical twins reared apart. *Char. & Pers.,* 1934, **3**, 17–39.

Scott, J. P. *Animal behavior.* Chicago: Univer. of Chicago Press, 1958.

Skeels, H. M. Mental development of children in foster homes. *J. genet. Psychol.,* 1936, **49**, 91–106.

Skodak, M. Children in foster homes: a study of mental development. *Univer. Iowa Stud. Child Welf.,* 1939, **16**, No. 1.

Skodak, M., & Skeels, H. M. A follow-up study of children in adoptive homes. *J. genet. Psychol.,* 1945, **66**, 21–58.

Skodak, M., & Skeels, H. M. A final follow-up study of one hundred adopted children. *J. genet. Psychol.,* 1949, **75**, 85–125.

Smith, H. T., & Stone, L. J. Developmental psychology. In *Annual review of psychology,* 1962, Vol. 13. Palo Alto, Calif.: Annual Reviews, Inc.

Spitz, R. A. Hospitalism: An inquiry into the genesis of psychiatric conditions in early childhood. In O. Fenichel et al. (Eds.), *The psychoanalytic study of the child, Vol. I.* New York: International Univer. Press, 1945.

Spitz, R. A. Hospitalism: A follow-up report on investigation described in Vol. I, 1945. In O. Fenichel et al. (Eds.), *The psychoanalytic study of the child, Vol. II.* New York: International Univer. Press, 1946.

Strandskov, H. H. A twin study pertaining to the genetics of intelligence. *Carylogia Suppl., Att. 9th Internat. Cong. Genet.,* 1954. Pp. 811–813.

Terman, L. M., & Merrill, Maud A. *Measuring intelligence.* Boston: Houghton Mifflin, 1937.

Thompson, G. G. Developmental psychology. In *Annual review of psychology,* 1958, Vol. 10. Palo Alto, Calif.: Annual Reviews, Inc.

Tryon, R. C. Genetic differences in maze learning in rats. *Yearb. nat. Soc. Stud. Educ.,* 1940, **39** (I), 111–119.

Vanderberg, S. G. The hereditary abilities study. *Eugen. Quart.,* 1956, **3**, 94–96.

Veblen, T. *The theory of the leisure class.* New York: Macmillan, 1911.

Watson, J. B. *Psychology from the standpoint of a behaviorist.* Philadelphia: Lippincott, 1919.

Wellman, Beth. The effects of preschool attendance upon intellectual development. In R. G. Barker, J. S. Kounin, & H. F. Wright (Eds.), *Child behavior and development*. New York: McGraw-Hill, 1943.

Woodworth, R. S. *Heredity and environment*. New York: Soc. Sci. Res. Council, 1941.

Zirkle, C. *Death of a science in Russia*. Philadelphia: Univer. of Penn. Press, 1949.

chapter 3 ✳ Growth and Maturation

Anything that lives grows. Among the higher species, growth proceeds along specific lines producing physical changes in the organism. At the same time changes in behavior occur, which are believed to be direct consequences of growth. These behaviors, attributable principally or entirely to structural development, are called *maturational*. Many such behaviors occur in orderly fashion in young organisms, often appearing for the first time during the prenatal period. Their sequence of development is similar among widely divergent species. By their origins they illustrate the substantial role played by biological inheritance in the development of behavior.

PRENATAL GROWTH AND BEHAVIOR

After the egg is fertilized, it receives nurture from surrounding tissues and starts to grow. The mass of the cell increases more rapidly than its surface area, thus limiting the size of any cell while permitting sufficient nourishment to penetrate its walls. Perhaps because of the pressure of the bulkier mass on the cell's surface, the cell divides. This division continues as cells grow and split, until a ball-like cluster of cells emerges.

Up to this point in development, all cells are presumably the same and interchangeable. Now the cells begin to separate into layers according to their position in the cluster. The outer layer—*ectoderm* —becomes, for the most part, the sense organs and nervous system of the growing new organism. The middle layer—*mesoderm*—is the primary source of the skeleton and muscles, and the inner layer— *endoderm*—leads to the viscera and glands of later development.

Once these three layers have formed, specialized development overtakes the new organism. Development advances faster in the head than in the tail region of the embryo and in the central areas before the peripheral areas. These courses of development are called *cephalocaudal*—from head to tail—and *proximodistal*—from central to peripheral. In the embryo, and later in the newborn infant, many of the early behaviors are massive in approach because of this uneven nature of growth, whereas later movement becomes more specific. The young child, owing to less adequate distal development, uses his whole body in reaching and grasping, employing many distant muscle groups. As he ages and as distal development improves, he is eventually able to use his fingers alone; this is a change from mass to specific movement.

Many behaviors become apparent prior to birth. These include a large number of reflexes, such as breathing, swimming, or sucking as well as behaviors like flexing the leg which occur as a direct response to stimulation. As a result, the infant is born with a large repertoire of unlearned behaviors in addition to some that may have been acquired through learning.

POSTNATAL MATURATIONAL GROWTH

Since many prenatal behaviors develop at a time and in a sequence that do not vary from child to child, occurring as the result of the growth of the embryo, we may naturally wonder about the development of postnatal behaviors. Are these, too, the result of growth?

Developmental Norms

Sequences of postnatal development common to all members of a species are readily observable. If any of these sequences is orderly, it may possibly stem from physiological maturation. Table 3-1 contains three sets of norms for stages of development, each obtained from a different sample of children. Figure 3-1 illustrates one of these sets. As both Table 3-1 and Figure 3-1 indicate, postnatal develop-

TABLE 3-1   Three Sets of Developmental Norms

Mean Age in Months
(to nearest full month)

Test Items	Shirley (1933)	Bayley (1935)	Aldrich & Norval (1946)
Fetal position	0		
Chin up (can raise chin when prone)	1		
Head erect		2	
Chest up (can raise chest when prone)	2		
Head control when sitting			3
Head erect and steady		3	
Sits with support	4	4	
Sits alone	7	6	6
Sits alone with good coordination		9	
Crawls	9		7
Creeps	10		
Walks with help	11	12	10
Stands alone	14	13	11
Walks alone	15	13	12

ment is essentially cephalocaudal and proximodistal, thus suggesting that prenatal growth trends continue into the postnatal period. Reisen and Kinder (1952) believe that an increasingly large number of muscle groups is engaged in each successive behavior and that the pattern progresses from simple to more complex responses. Perhaps it is this passage from simplicity to complexity rather than gradients of inner growth that accounts for the apparent continuation of pre-natal growth sequences. Either way, the order of development seems similar to all three studies cited in the table; the sequences of behavioral change are lawful and predictable even though the mean ages at which any behavior occurs vary somewhat among the three sets of norms.

Learning and Maturation

Psychologists have often asked whether vast collections of human behavior are learned or maturational. In a sense this is another version of the question: heredity or environment? Maturation is hereditary; it is an orderly sequence of events determined by changing

FIGURE 3-1 The motor sequence (Shirley, 1933, frontispiece).

physical structure which, in turn, is governed by heredity. Learning, on the other hand, results from environmental stimulation. If the behaviors of the young child, whether they be physical, emotional, or social, are largely the result of maturation, then the role of parents is largely to let children grow by themselves, since development and change come from within rather than from without. Under these circumstances, whatever adults do to children, whether good or bad, will not change children drastically. If, however, early behaviors are learned, what children are taught, how they are taught, and when they are taught is of prime significance. To revert to the question posed at the outset of the last chapter: how mutable is the human organism?

If humans actually vary through changes in the environment, the study of learning and maturation may shed some light on the extent to which they do. For example, by selecting two similar groups of subjects and exposing one of them to environmental stimulation while withholding it from the other, the two groups should differ in behavior if learning, a product of such stimulation, really influences the development of that behavior. On the other hand, if innate maturational mechanisms occasion the behavior, then the environmental difference between the two groups should be of no consequence. Another way of going about this is to stimulate the experimental group excessively while limiting the control group to the ordinary amount of environmental stimulation. This may be done by using identical twins; it is called the *co-twin* method. From studies of this kind, it becomes possible to establish roughly the relative influences of hereditary, maturational factors, on the one hand, and of learning, which is dependent on the environment, on the other.

The first area of maturation studied was that of physical maturation. One repeatedly hears the assertion, "We are teaching Johnny to walk." Is this true, or will the child learn without training—in fact, without having much opportunity to attempt to perfect his walking? Since withholding the opportunity to walk from a control group of children merely to test an idea would hardly be ethical, researchers turn to "experiments in nature" in the hope of finding the information they desire. Among the various cultures, for example, there are several that restrict—sometimes quite severely—the movement of the child. The practice of *swaddling*—that is, wrapping and binding an infant in long, narrow bands of cloth—was and is an accepted cultural practice in the Near East, the Balkans, Poland, and Russia, as this description shows.

In the great Russian peasant population, and to a varying degree in all the regions and classes which shared and continue to share the common cultural heritage of the great central plains of Russia, the item of child care called swaddling was developed to an extreme. While the custom of bandaging newborn infants is widespread, the ancient Russian extreme insists that the baby be swaddled up to the neck, tightly enough to make a handy "log of wood" out of the whole bundle, and that swaddling be continued for nine months, for the greater part of the day and throughout the night (Erikson, 1950, p. 344).

When asked why babies must be swaddled, simple Russians have answered with astonishment: What other way was there to carry a baby and to keep him warm through a Russian winter? And besides, how could one otherwise keep him from scratching and harming himself, and of scaring himself with the sight of his own hands? Now it is probably true that a swaddled baby, especially when just unswaddled, has not sufficient mastery over his own movements to keep from scratching and hitting himself. The further assumption that *therefore* he has to be swaddled again is a favorite trick of cultural rationalization. It makes a particular pattern of infant-restraint culturally self-supporting. You must swaddle the infant to protect him against himself; this causes violent vasomotor needs in him; he must remain emotionally swaddled in order not to fall victim to wild emotion. This, in turn, helps to establish a basic, a preverbal, indoctrination, according to which people, for their own good, must be rigidly restrained, while being offered, now and then, ways of discharging compressed emotion. Economically and politically seen, swaddling, then, is part of a system of stubborn institutions which support and prolong the Russian combination of serfdom and "soul" (pp. 346–347).

More important to the present discussion than the Russian "soul" is something much simpler—the effect of deprivation of motor experience on the rate of motor development. Danziger and Frankl, as reported in Orlansky (1949), ventured into Albania to test swaddled children and compare their development with that of Viennese infants. This is what they found:

> Until they are one year old, the Albanian children are bound securely to a wooden cradle customarily placed in the darkest corner of the room, often with a cloth thrown over their heads so that no light is visible. These children displayed poor muscular coordination, but once given an opportunity to practice, their performance improved rapidly so that it was clear no permanent retardation had been effected. Their social behavior, as measured by response to the experimenters in a series of standardized tests, was equal or superior to the norms for Viennese children of the same age. Identical observations could undoubtedly be made on the children of many primitive peoples who, tied securely to cradleboards during their first year of life, may experience comparatively little bodily contact or fondling by the mother (Orlansky, 1949, p. 16).

Most American Indian tribes believe—or once believed—that infants should be reared on some type of cradleboard. A cradleboard usually consists of a straight board for a back. The child, covered with skins or blankets, is bound to the board so that its posture, the Indians maintain, will be good. Indians in southern Alaska, for example, have been seen with heads sloping upward as a result of having spent their infancy in cradleboards with their soft, growing heads pressed against the top. According to their tribe, this was the proper shape for a human head.

Dennis and Dennis (1940), in studying various groups of Hopi Indians, noted that in most villages infants were placed on a cradleboard shortly after birth and remained on it almost continuously for the first three months of their lives. Then they spent less time on the board but were attached to it at least for a while until reaching about 14 months of age. By comparison with other Hopi infants reared in the same general fashion but without cradleboards, there was no difference in the age of walking.

Turning to another study by Dennis and Dennis (1935, 1938, & 1941), a pair of fraternal female twins was raised under restricted opportunities to practice motor or social responses. These conditions prevailed from the thirty-sixth day to the fourteenth month in the lives of the twins. Writing years later to summarize their research, the Dennises gave the following description of the environmental background.

> Throughout the experiment the twins lived in our home but they were confined to the nursery. This was a second-floor room, so situated that from the infants' position only sky and tree tops were visible through the windows. The room itself contained only the subjects' cribs, a bureau, a table, two chairs, and a screen near the door. No picture or decoration of any sort was permitted in the nursery. The door of the room was kept closed, and we entered the room only to care for the subjects, to observe them, and to experiment with them. . . .
>
> The subjects were placed in individual cribs, of the trade name "Kiddie Koop." The cribs were placed side by side with a screen equal in height to the cribs between the two, so that the twins could see each other only when taken from their beds. During the first nine months the subjects were taken from the cribs only for feeding and bathing or when removal from the cribs was demanded for the purposes of experimentation.
>
> With the exception of a few occasions during the latter part of the experiment the sole care of the twins was supplied by the experimenters. This means that we bathed and fed the infants, changed the diapers and bed clothing, and cleaned the room. The infants seldom saw other people, and when they did it was with our knowledge and supervision. Visitors were required to adhere to the same practices which we imposed upon ourselves. . . .
>
> With a few exceptions, we never encouraged or discouraged any act of the twins. The exceptions to this rule, and to other such general

rules, occurred in the last month of the investigation, when the experimental conditions were partially suspended. . . .

We not only avoided reward and punishment but we avoided acts which might have provided examples for imitation. With certain exceptions to be noted later our behavior in the nursery was limited to changing diapers, bathing, feeding, etc. We carefully refrained from baby talk and from babbling, as we wanted to know whether such vocalizations would occur without example. Likewise, we never performed for the twins such acts as patting their hands or playing with their toes.

Thus far we have spoken only of the conditions which remained relatively constant until the last few weeks of the experiment. We turn now to more stringent restrictions in the environment of the subjects which, in the main, were applied only for the first half-year. The conditions to be described were designed to provide answers to specific questions and were abandoned when the answers were obtained.

We wished to determine whether or not the infants would smile upon hearing the voice of the adult, if speech were not associated with the care and attention which the adult supplied. For this reason, until the twins were 26 weeks of age, we never announced our entry into the nursery and never spoke to the subjects. We were not totally silent, for we occasionally commented to each other while in the nursery, but we were careful not to make comments while we were feeding or otherwise caring for the twins. Our speech when we were outside the nursery could be heard by the infants, but it had no more relation to their behavior than did traffic noises or other common sounds (Dennis & Dennis, 1951, pp. 106–109).

From this description, it is clear that the twins were raised in an environment as cold and as unstimulating as the Dennises could make it. Yet is was the Dennises and not the children who found the routine trying, so trying that they ended it before they had planned in order to respond in a normal way to the infants. Figure 3-2 illustrates the age at which certain behaviors appeared in each of the twins as compared with a normally raised sample of children also studied by the Dennises. In the figure the symbol 0 represents one of the twins and the symbol Δ the other. Although somewhat retarded in motor skills but less retarded in social responses, the twins' sequences of development seemed normal and their retardation slight. It should be noted, however, that the twin symbolized by Δ suffered from moderate brain injury during birth and that some, if not all, of her slowness can be attributed to this.

Another method of testing whether walking is inherent or taught is to compare the performances of a set of identical twins in which one twin T is trained and the other C is not. In presumably the first experiment to use this approach (Gesell & Thompson, 1929) the experimental twin T was trained to climb stairs while the control twin C was given no such training. Once T had learned to climb stairs

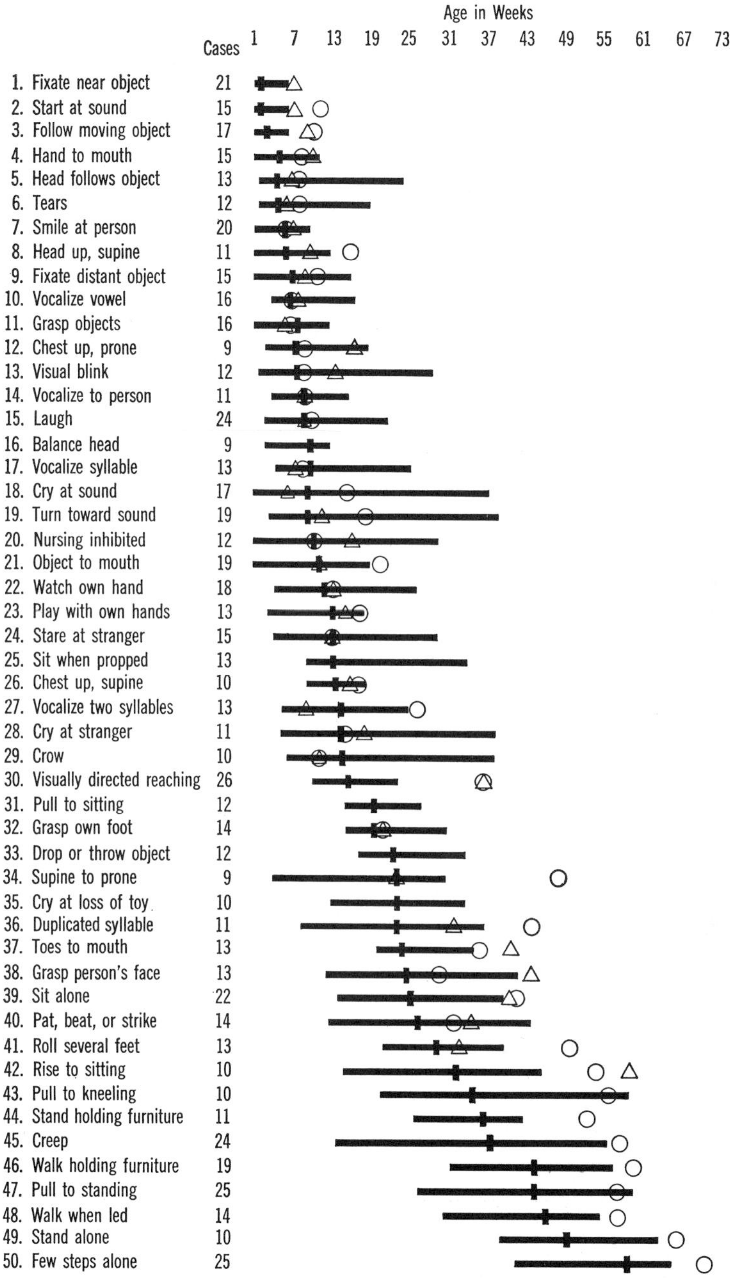

Age in Weeks

	Cases	1	7	13	19	25	31	37	43	49	55	61	67	73

1. Fixate near object 21
2. Start at sound 15
3. Follow moving object 17
4. Hand to mouth 15
5. Head follows object 13
6. Tears 12
7. Smile at person 20
8. Head up, supine 11
9. Fixate distant object 15
10. Vocalize vowel 16
11. Grasp objects 16
12. Chest up, prone 9
13. Visual blink 12
14. Vocalize to person 11
15. Laugh 24
16. Balance head 9
17. Vocalize syllable 13
18. Cry at sound 17
19. Turn toward sound 19
20. Nursing inhibited 12
21. Object to mouth 19
22. Watch own hand 18
23. Play with own hands 13
24. Stare at stranger 15
25. Sit when propped 13
26. Chest up, supine 10
27. Vocalize two syllables 13
28. Cry at stranger 11
29. Crow 10
30. Visually directed reaching 26
31. Pull to sitting 12
32. Grasp own foot 14
33. Drop or throw object 12
34. Supine to prone 9
35. Cry at loss of toy 10
36. Duplicated syllable 11
37. Toes to mouth 13
38. Grasp person's face 13
39. Sit alone 22
40. Pat, beat, or strike 14
41. Roll several feet 13
42. Rise to sitting 10
43. Pull to kneeling 10
44. Stand holding furniture 11
45. Creep 24
46. Walk holding furniture 19
47. Pull to standing 25
48. Walk when led 14
49. Stand alone 10
50. Few steps alone 25

FIGURE 3-2 (Dennis & Dennis, 1951, p. 112.)

both twins were tested on stair-climbing ability. In several studies of essentially maturational phenomena, it was found that C, merely by growing older and becoming more developed—as well as receiving normal environmental stimulation—was immediately the equal of T as soon as confronted by a test of behavior—in this case, stair climbing. Yet other studies of the same sort found C's ability inferior but "ready" for learning. Since C was now older than was T when trained, C could be trained to the same proficiency as T in far fewer sessions.

To move to another example, let us consider the McGraw (1940) study of bladder training. One twin, Hugh Putney, was initiated to the toilet at the age of 30 days and spent a large portion of his waking hours on it until the study ended when he was 800 days old. For his twin, Hilton, bladder training was begun at two years of age. Figure 3-3 shows the respective patterns of their success. Since hereditary differences in the development of bladder control presumably remain constant, any gain on Hugh's part may be attributed to training and to the learning resulting from it. Indeed, other children may vary in the age at which maturation has reached the point that permits bladder control, but this study suggested that training prior to the age of maturational readiness had little value.

Several similar studies all have led to the same conclusion. So far as *phylogenetic* skills are concerned—those abilities, such as walking

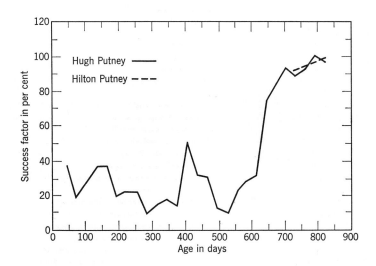

FIGURE 3-3 Achievement curves showing the percentages of successful responses to the toilet situation for twins whose training for bladder control was started at different times (McGraw, 1940, p. 586).

or toilet performance, that are common to all humans—early training consumes valuable time and does not often achieve more than a transitory improvement in skills. However, if one is willing to invest the enormous amount of time and effort required, one might find, as evidence suggests, that early training of motor behaviors results in increased expertness in such behaviors in later life. An earlier Mc-Graw (1935) study of maturation supports this view. In this study twin T was trained in various motor skills from the age of 21 days to 22 months. The training was extremely extensive and may be seen in the book or film *Growth: A Study of Johnny and Jimmy*. The control twin received no special training, except for regular tests of motor ability which might have, in themselves, constituted some training. The experimental twin, as a result of his training, advanced greatly in some ways; for example, he was an accomplished roller skater before he was two. His greatest superiority turned up in *ontogenetic* skills—that is, individual or uncommon skills—whereas he showed little superiority in phylogenetic skills, such as walking. Among skills like climbing which are probably phylogenetic but only slightly exercised in normal child development, the experimental twin also disclosed a considerable degree of superiority. The value of this experiment is decreased, however, by the fact that although these twins at first seemed identical, they were actually fraternal. Yet the great differences between them seem unlikely to result from genetic distinction. Of even greater interest is the knowledge that twin T, in tests conducted years after the differential training had ceased (McGraw, 1939), retained his motor advantages over twin C.

Mickey Mantle, the baseball player, is said by sportswriters to have been trained by his father in catching, throwing, and batting from the moment he could first respond. The McGraw study suggests that if someone wants badly enough to produce an expert and is prepared to spend the necessary amount of time, this is the right course to pursue. In the case of ontogenetic skills, the evidence points clearly to the efficacy of early training.

Readiness

Ontogenetic skills apparently can be acquired through training, as we have seen. Phylogenetic skills, in contrast, turn up in their own good time as a result of growth; neither training nor deprivation has any noticeable effect on their development. This suggests that an age of readiness exists for the appearance of many behaviors and that prior to this age these behaviors can be learned only with difficulty, if at all.

Readiness is discussed most frequently in relation to such academic skills as reading. The idea of reading readiness is of some utility; reading depends, for example, on the ability to discriminate symbols. This facility may be maturational. Nevertheless, some children learn to read much earlier than the age at which they are considered ready: according to Gates (1937) and others, this age is six-and-a-half years.[1]

If reading readiness is a common, maturational skill, the variation in the age at which it is reached is far wider than in other areas of maturational development. It would thus seem that a number of unique factors contribute to the ability to read. To the extent that these factors prevail, any belief in a minimal age of reading readiness would be open to question. One way to test this speculation, a way probably never tried to date, would be to obtain a large sample of children and then subject different random subsamples of them to instruction in reading beginning at various ages, such as five, six, and seven. It then becomes possible to measure the mean amount gained by each subsample during several intervals of time—six months, one year, two years. Insofar as ontogenetic skills bear on the process, the groups may be expected to gain about the same, whereas to the degree that phylogenetic skills are involved, the older group may be expected to benefit the most from such training. Those who believe that phylogenetic skills dominate in reading must suspect that the oldest group, quite apart from its advanced mental age, would benefit most from instruction in reading.

This is a rather unorthodox stand. Let us therefore consider some other research that seems to support this position. The length of time that a child will concentrate on a specific task is called the child's *attention span*. Attention span increases systematically with age. Van Alstyne (1932), for example, obtained mean attention spans of seven minutes for two-year-olds, 8.9 minutes for three-year-olds, 12.4 for four-year-olds, and 13.6 for five-year-olds. This increase might be assumed to be maturational. Perhaps it is. Highly relevant, however, are the findings of Moyer and Gilmer (1955), who used one simple toy, a red plastic automobile, and six carefully designed, relatively intricate toys as stimuli in a study of attention span. Some of their results appear in Table 3-2.

Two things may be noted. First, there is no age progression in

---

[1] For a discussion of children who learned to read at considerably earlier ages, see Fowler (1962).

TABLE 3-2   Mean Attention Span for Toys

	Mean Attention Span by Age						
Toy	1½	2	3	4	5	6	7
Red automobile			3.1	4.9	5.4		
Complex toy #1 *	24.3	26.5	21.2	22.7	18.5		
Complex toy #2		34.0	32.9	32.4	28.9		
Complex toy #3			30.3	33.0	30.7		
Complex toy #4			15.6	22.2	26.7	31.9	
Complex toy #5				29.0	29.4	33.0	
Complex toy #6				39.2	35.0	39.7	28.5

* Each complex toy was not presented at each age level since they were designed to arouse interest within a limited age range.

length of attention span among the complex toys. Second, all of the spans are very high compared with those of many previous studies of this sort, of which many are reviewed by Moyer and Gilmer, or as compared with the attention span evoked by the toy automobile. Attention span is governed primarily by the type of stimulus—in this case, the type of toy—not by age. The results make it clear that the cliché about young children having too short an attention span to tackle a specific task is so much nonsense. If the task can be made challenging and interesting enough, even very young children have extremely long attention spans.

How does attention span apply to reading? It applies both directly and indirectly. In a direct sense teaching a child to read requires continued attention; indirectly, attention span is similar to reading readiness, for it purportedly shows a progression of age produced by maturation. Like attention span, reading readiness seems conditioned more by the amount of interest stimulated by the reading materials than by any development of phylogenetic skills. That is, reading readiness is more a matter of stimulation than maturation.

Extreme Deprivation of Stimulation

Within a rather wide range, the deprivation of experience results in nothing more than temporary slowing down of development. Although moderate deprivation has no appreciable effect on the development of motor behaviors, severe deprivation has a profound influence. Moreover, there may be a *critical period* for the learning of certain common developmental skills. During this period any exposure to learning, however brief it may be, brings out behavior at a normal pace. Any exposure before this period has only a small, transient impact. But a lack of exposure, that is, a deprivation, until the period has passed results in permanent injury, leaving a lasting mark of inferiority.

In the first study pertaining to this area, von Senden (1932) examined medical reports written about people who were born nearly blind as a result of congenital cataracts. These individuals were often able to distinguish light from darkness but could not differentiate forms. Since some patients who have cataracts removed do achieve approximately normal vision (von Senden, 1932; London, 1960), these people presumably should have been capable of making adequate visual discriminations after undergoing appropriate surgery. Yet interestingly and surprisingly when their cataracts were removed some of them remained unable to make certain types of visual distinctions. They could tell that the visual field was quite varied, but could not identify objects or describe their shapes from visual cues. When allowed to feel the objects, they were able to identify them immediately. Colors were perceived and named accurately; color mazes were learned quickly. Nevertheless, it took many trials for an individual to learn even so simple a difference as that between a square and a triangle. After learning, if required to make this discrimination in a new setting or under new conditions of illumination, the individual was again unable to differentiate. Despite an apparently adequate, although perhaps somewhat abnormal, visual mechanism (see Riesen, 1960), many who were studied remained unable to distinguish between different persons on a purely visual basis even after years of visual experience. Furthermore, some of them could not learn to discriminate between objects on the basis of their shapes, despite seemingly normal vision. Others learned, but very slowly. Von Senden's findings suggested strongly that many aspects of vision were permanently impaired by lack of visual experience during a critical period ending somewhere above the age of four.

These data were based on individual patients, on one physician reporting on a single patient. Such accounts do not constitute the best scientific data. Besides, these patients had learned to cope with the world through other sensory means, such as touch, so that the motivation to make full use of their newly acquired vision might not have been great. However, other studies of humans who have not had early visual experience also support the critical period view. Dennis (1934), although finding the data to be equivocal, reached much the same conclusions as von Senden. London (1960), reporting on recent cataract patients in the U.S.S.R. whose cases were followed with more adequate scientific controls, fully supports von Senden. From all this, it seems likely that even innate behaviors cannot be at all adequate in later development unless they undergo at least some exercise during a critical period.

Maturation Related to Social and Emotional Behavior

Thus far, this chapter has dwelt entirely on the maturation of motor behaviors. More interesting and less well settled, however, is the influence of maturation on social and emotional behavior. One may well ask: to what extent are social and emotional responses maturational in character? How does deprivation affect these responses? Are there critical periods for learning them?

In an early and thorough investigation of emotion conducted by Darwin (1881; present reprint edition, 1955), the noted scientist presented several main arguments. If human emotional expressions evoked by a certain kind of stimulus were shared by animals lower than humans, he maintained, then evolutionary linkage to these lower orders would be proved. Second, if all humans, irrespective of age or culture, responded in the same way to specific emotional stimuli, one would have to concede that specific emotional expressions arose as a result of natural selection and were inherited and innate in the human.

The following quotation from Darwin's writings pertains to the first hypothesis.

> . . . Young chimpanzees make a kind of barking noise, when pleased by the return of any one to whom they are attached. When this noise, which the keepers call a laugh, is uttered, the lips are protruded; but so they are under various other emotions. Nevertheless I could perceive that when they were pleased the form of the lips differed a little from that assumed when they were angered. If a young chimpanzee be tickled—and the armpits are particularly sensitive to tickling, as in the case of our children,—a more decided chuckling or laughing sound is uttered; though the laughter is sometimes noiseless. The corners of the mouth are then drawn backwards; and this sometimes causes the lower eyelids to be slightly wrinkled. But this wrinkling, which is so characteristic of our own laughter, is more plainly seen in some other monkeys. The teeth in the upper jaw in the chimpanzee are not exposed when they utter their laughing noise, in which respect they differ from us (Darwin, 1955, p. 131).

In another quotation, Darwin deals with both hypotheses:

> . . . That the chief expressive actions, exhibited by man and by the lower animals, are now innate or inherited,—that is, have not been learnt by the individual,—is admitted by everyone. So little has learning or imitation to do with several of them that they are from the earliest days and throughout life quite beyond our control; for instance the relaxation of the arteries of the skin in blushing, and the increased action of the heart in anger. We may see children, only two or three years old, and even those born blind, blushing from shame; and the naked scalp of a very young infant reddens from passion. Infants scream from pain directly after birth, and all their features then assume the same form as during subsequent years. These facts alone suffice to show that many of our most important expressions have not been learnt; but it is remarkable that some, which are certainly innate, require practice in the individual, before they are performed in a full and perfect manner; for instance, weeping and laughing. The inheritance of most of our expressive actions explains the fact that those born blind display them, as I hear from Rev. R. H. Blair, equally well with those gifted with sight. We can thus also understand the fact that the young and the old of widely different races, both with man and animals, express the same state of mind by the same movements (Darwin, 1955, pp. 350–351).

Darwin concluded that specific emotional expressions in response to particular emotional stimuli showed so great a degree of commonness that they had to be innate, inherited, and unlearned. On the other hand, certain emotions required practice before they could appear in their fullest form. Darwin was referring here to changes occurring with age which seemed likely to be the result of maturation rather than learning.

With its emphasis on innate characteristics, Darwinism was one of the forces that brought forth, in psychology, an environmentalist reaction led by John B. Watson (1919). Watson and others who shared his point of view believed that little human behavior was innate or unlearned; to the contrary, they held that a vast majority of behavior was learned. These "behaviorists" did much to make psychology a science by causing it to concern itself with observable, measurable behavior. Let us note that it was against such presumably innate characteristics as *instinctive motives,* rather than against phenomena now called maturational, that Watson's main criticism was directed.

The first experimental study of emotions by Watson and Morgan (1917) was undertaken to test the hypothesis that a large number of human emotions, such as fear of snakes or darkness, were innate to the species. By studying infants during the first months of life, they concluded that three basic, innate emotions were discernible. These emotions were fear, rage, and love. Fear, they maintained, was aroused chiefly by loss of support and by loud noises; it was *not* occasioned by experiences previously thought to be innately productive of fear, such as exposure to snakes or darkness. Rage emerged from restriction of movement, and love was the response to fondling and stroking.

This investigation inspired other psychologists to study the emotional development of infants. Some of these found reason to question parts of the Watson and Morgan conclusions. For example, Sherman (1927), in studying the responses of infants less than 12 days of age, noted that judges were unable to agree on the character of specific infant reactions *unless they saw the stimulus that preceded the response.* This suggests that adults read into the responses of the young infant the emotion that they themselves would feel if stimulated in the same way. As Watson and Morgan knew the stimulus preceding the response of their subjects, their observations were contaminated by this knowledge. They, too, may have read into the infant's responses the way that they would have felt under the same circumstances.

Another study to refute a portion of the Watson and Morgan findings was Dennis's (1940). This showed that infants habituated to restricted movement as a result of being reared on a cradleboard did not manifest any signs of anger because of the restrictions on their movements. Thus, it is possible that learning might have been involved in the responses of rage observed by Watson and Morgan, or else that the responses were provoked by "rough handling" rather than by restriction itself.

Other studies indicate, however, that specific forms of emotional responses to particular stimuli are unlearned. Again we turn to the fraternal twins raised by the Dennises. These twins were restricted in physical movement and also in exposure to the emotional responses of others. The Dennises, for example, did not smile at them. Having had no experience at seeing others smile, did the twins nevertheless respond with smiles?

> We wished also to know whether positive responses toward us would develop if we refrained from smiling at the twins and from petting, cuddling, and fondling them. In order to determine the answer to this question we avoided these expressions during the first 26 weeks. Withholding of demonstration of affections of this sort was not an easy task to impose upon ourselves, particularly as the subjects themselves were very expressive. From the 15th week onward they almost invariably greeted us with a smile and a vocalization. After this fact was thoroughly established, we decided in Week 27 to return their smile of greeting, and to speak to them as we approached (Dennis & Dennis, 1951, p. 109).

Clearly, smiling is a response to pleasurable event or experience and is not the result of exposure to the smiling of others. As Figure 3-2 notes, even without social stimulation, emotional responses such as smiling still occur at a normal time.

Similarly, a blind and deaf girl, who obviously had no opportunity to see others express emotions (Goodenough, 1932), displayed essentially the same responses to various forms of stimulation as children not subjected to such environmental deprivation. In yet another study by Goodenough (1931) a number of judges watched pictures of a ten-month-old infant accompanied by captions describing various emotional states—dissatisfaction, astonishment, anger, pleasure, fear. The judges showed substantial agreement with the descriptions, indicating that the emotional expressions of a child of ten months can be categorized with a fair amount of success. This, of course, counters Sherman's findings and corroborates Watson's and Morgan's position.

One further study pulls together the apparently contradictory findings into a unified whole. This is the oft-cited study by Bridges (1930), which observed for periods up to four months groups of children ranging in age from birth to slightly over two years. As shown in Figure 3-4, during the interval shortly after birth the only differentiation that could be made was between quietude and excitement. By six months a number of emotions might be distinguished from one another, whereas by two years even more emotional patterns might be reliably noted. The contradictory findings of Watson, Sherman, and Goodenough become understandable since each studied infants of markedly different ages.

The Bridges study suggests that Darwin was right. What is observed as a response associated with a specific emotion, such as blushing with shame, appears to be innate, that is, a result of maturation. In other words, emotional behaviors appear in a rather stable sequence, very much like motor behaviors. However, the frequency and intensity of emotional expression is largely learned. The feeling or emotion evoked by a stimulus has an element that is learned, and this phase of emotional development will be explored in later chapters. But once an emotion is felt the physical demonstration of the feeling seems largely *un*learned and indeed, as in the case of blushing, almost entirely beyond conscious control.

Critical Periods. Several students of emotions have suggested that the response of love depends on having received love during infancy, especially in the last half of the first year of life (see, for example, Ribble, 1943; Bowlby, 1952). Perhaps there is also a critical period in

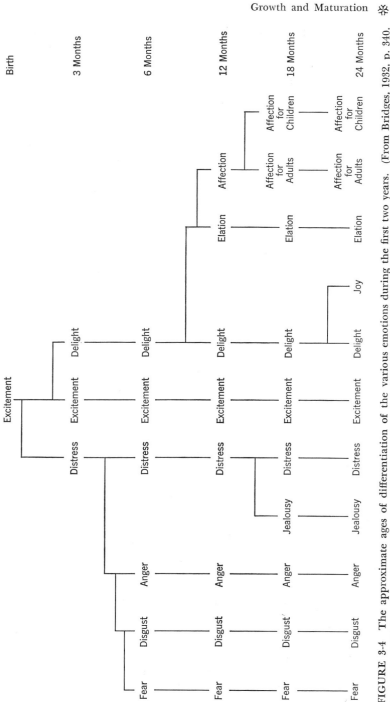

FIGURE 3-4 The approximate ages of differentiation of the various emotions during the first two years. (From Bridges, 1932, p. 340. Copyright 1932 by the Society for Research in Child Development; published with permission.)

social and emotional development. In Chapter 9 we shall consider at length studies relating to the deprivation in infancy of love and other forms of stimulation. Those who believe that deprivation of contact with a single mother symbol during infancy causes a lasting emotional deficit, especially in the area of being able to give love, are often called the *maternal deprivation school*. Although this school is open to many criticisms, certain experiments support its view. However, not many of these are easily conducted among humans. Researchers are therefore obliged to search for analogous findings in the animal kingdom.

The ability of dogs (Melzack & Scott, 1957) and chimpanzees (Nissen, Chow, & Semmes, 1951) to adapt to pain stimuli requires early exposure to pain. Later exposure produces apparently little or no learning. A dog lacking early experience of pain will do such things as putting his nose into the flame of a paper match, thus extinguishing the flame; he will repeat this behavior, as badly adaptive as it may be, over many days of testing. Here, then, is an emotional response that requires some exercise during a critical period if it is to develop at all.

In a most interesting book, *King Solomon's Ring* (1952), Lorenz presents much of the pioneering work on *imprinting* which he conducted concurrently with Tinbergen (see also Tinbergen, 1953). Imprinting is a type of learning which must occur within an innately determined period of time—within a critical period. It may be seen in the response of a young graylag gosling to objects in its environment, which was described by Heinroth whom Lorenz quoted.

I have often had to try and place an incubator gosling with a pair that was leading very young birds. In so doing, one meets all sorts of difficulties, which are typical for the whole psychological and instinctive behavior of our birds. When you open the lid of an incubator where young ducklings have just broken their shells and dried off, they will at first duck and sit quite motionless. Then, when you try to pick them up, they scoot away with lightning speed. Quite often they jump to the floor and hide beneath various objects, and one has a hard time getting hold of the tiny creatures. Not so young goslings. They look at you without betraying any sign of fear; and, if you handle them even briefly, you can hardly shake them off. They peep pitifully if you walk away, and soon follow you about religiously. I have known such a little creature to be content if it could just squat under the chair on which I sat, a few hours after I had taken it from the incubator! If you then take such a gosling to a goose family with young of the same age, the situation usually develops as follows. Goose and gander look suspiciously at the approaching person, and both try to get themselves and their young into the water as quickly as they can. If you walk toward them very rapidly, so that the young have no chance to escape, the parents, of course, put up a spirited defense. This is the time to place the small orphan among the brood and leave in a hurry. In the excitement, the parents at first regard the newcomer as their own, and show an inclination to defend it as soon they see and hear it in human hands. But the worst is yet to come. It doesn't even occur to the young gosling to treat the two old birds as geese. It runs away, peeping loudly, and, if a human being happens to pass by, it follows him: it simply looks upon humans as its parents (Lorenz, 1957, pp. 103–104).

The first object to enter the gosling's world during a fixed, quite short interval and which fits certain specifications, such as having movement, becomes "mother" to the bird. The gosling that does not have the opportunity to imprint during its critical period never identifies itself with a mother. It is unable to attach itself to a mother symbol and engage in the behavior of "following" which Heinroth described.

The length of time during which imprinting may occur varies for different species. Among jackdaws, the period for imprinting lasts up to 20 days of age (Lorenz, 1957, p. 106), whereas for certain types of ducks, it is successful only between 11 and 18 hours after hatching.

In a rigid, time-bound sense, imprinting seems likely to decrease in significance as the order of mammals ascends. Yet certain patterns of imprinting are evident in higher mammals; bottle-reared lambs, for example, identify with humans, not with sheep (Scott, 1958, p. 179). Even so, it is perhaps unsound to generalize too widely from the experiences of other species to humans because even such closely related species as the goose, duck, and jackdaw differ considerably from one another in length of critical periods and in the irreversibility of imprinting. Among humans, imprinting certainly seems possible but has never been shown to occur. Showing interesting parallels in the patterns of socialization of canine and human infants, Scott (1963) subscribes to the view of a critical period in human maturation during which something closely akin to imprinting presumably takes place.

Moreover, the work of Harlow (1958) on various types of mothering of monkeys and their aftereffects also bears on any discussion of this sort. Harlow reared young monkeys with artificial substitute (*surrogate*) mothers. His artificial mothers fell into two major groups, as may be seen from his description of them and from Figure 3-5.

   . . . In devising this surrogate mother we were dependent neither upon the capriciousness of evolutionary processes nor upon mutations produced by chance radioactive fallout. Instead, we designed the mother surrogate in terms of modern human-engineering principles. . . . We

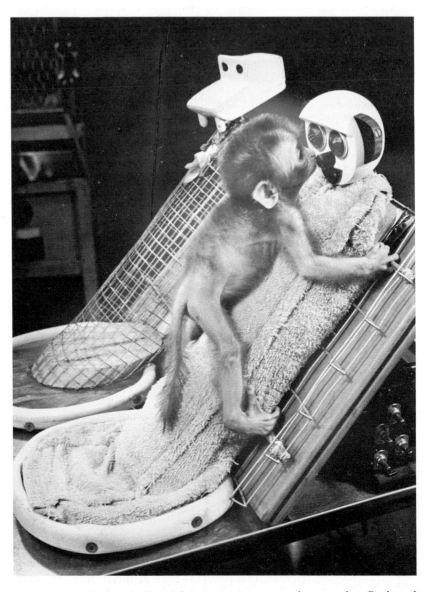

FIGURE 3-5   Cloth and wire mother surrogates were used to test the affection of infant monkeys.   The infants spent most of their time clinging to the soft cloth "mother" (foreground) even when nursing bottles were attached to the wire mother (background).   (From Harlow, *Scientific American*, 1959, **200**, p. 69; photograph by Gordon Coster.)

produced a perfectly proportioned, streamlined body stripped of unnecessary bulges and appendages. Redundancy in the surrogate mother's system was avoided by reducing the number of breasts from two to one and placing this unibreast in any upper-thoracic, sagittal position, thus maximizing the natural and known perceptual-motor capabilities of the infant operator. The surrogate was made from a block of wood, covered with sponge rubber, and sheathed in tan cotton terry cloth. A light bulb behind her radiated heat. The result was a mother, soft, warm, and tender, a mother with infinite patience, a mother available twenty-four hours a day, a mother that never scolded her infant and never struck or bit her baby in anger. Furthermore, we designed a mother-machine with maximal maintenance efficiency since failure of any system or function could be resolved by the simple substitution of black boxes and new component parts. It is our opinion that we engineered a very superior monkey mother, although this position is not held universally by the monkey fathers.

Before beginning our initial experiment we also designed and constructed a second mother surrogate, a surrogate in which we deliberately built less than the maximal capability for contact comfort. This surrogate mother . . . is made of wire-mesh, a substance entirely adequate to provide postural support and nursing capability, and she is warmed by radiant heat. Her body differs in no essential way from that of the cloth mother surrogate other than in the quality of the contact comfort which we can supply . . . (Harlow, 1958, pp. 675–676).

A feeding bottle was attached to one of the mothers of each pair of monkeys. Even when fed by the wire-mesh mother, the young monkey spent a majority of its time clinging to the terry-cloth mother (see Figure 3-5). This suggests that body contact, not the primary reward of food when hungry, is the dominant factor that produces the young mammal's affection for its mother; terry-cloth mothers were good mothers, always there, never rejecting. The young monkey was not harmed by being reared by a terry-cloth mother; it was, in fact, more secure and emotionally stable than infant monkeys reared by their biological mothers (Harlow, 1958). *However,* monkeys reared by artificial mothers have been generally unable to mate (Harlow & Harlow, 1961).

The majority of cloth-mothered animals are sexually mature. Yet none of the males has achieved any semblance of normal sex behavior, even though they show sexual excitement during mating opportunities. The females have been slightly more responsive, no doubt because their role is relatively passive compared with the male's, although success has been achieved only with three and only after numerous exposures to selected breeding males. . . .

At the present time, we have very limited data on the effect of early mothering experience on the child's maternal affectional pattern, but we have discovered enough to present some fairly suggestive findings. As already stated through the use of patient measures, one cage-raised and three cloth-mothered females were successfully bred. All are now raising their babies in a playpen situation. . . .

The first mother paid no attention whatsoever to her baby after it was born but, instead, would sit in her cage staring vacantly into space. She gave no evidence of protective maternal responses either when her infant was threatened or when the experimenter took the baby away several times a day for artificial feeding. As soon as the baby could locomote, it struggled desperately to establish a normal contactual relationship with its mother. It would climb on its mother's back only to be brushed away by the mother as if she were brushing off flies. When the baby persisted, the mother would crush the baby's face or body down on the floor of the cage with her hand or foot while either looking at the infant or staring blankly into open space . . . (Harlow & Harlow, 1961, pp. 54–55).

The other three mothers, themselves reared without a real monkey mother, were also quite inadequate as mothers. Festinger (1961) has suggested "that rats and people come to love things for which they have suffered." Perhaps punishment as well as reward may be a necessary part of the mother-child relationship; hence, the young mammal that does not receive both during early immaturity—and conceivably within a specific critical period—may not make a normal social adjustment as an adult. Like the work of students of imprinting, the work of Harlow is merely suggestive with respect to human infancy. It may, however, provide the key to understanding the crucial elements of early socialization, the timing of the development of emotional responses, and the consequences of inadequate rearing among humans, in terms of when the stimulation should be applied or the type of stimulation to be used. In short, it may supply the clue to handling the critical period in the social and emotional development of children.

SUMMARY

Several human motor behaviors seem to result largely from genetically determined patterns of growth rather than from learning. Because of this, the sequence in which the behaviors occur does not differ appreciably between individuals. Neither special stimulation nor deprivation of experience, within fairly wide limits, appears to influence the development of those behaviors that are phylogenetic or common to all members of the species. However, special training of ontogenetic skills seems to benefit performance. Phylogenetic behaviors, although not affected by moderate deprivation, require at least some exercise during a critical period if permanent or near-permanent deficiencies are to be avoided. The motor accompaniments of many emotional states seem to be unlearned and innate, yet require the individual to have reached a certain level of maturation before they can appear. Certain social and emotional responses *may* also require exercise during critical periods if they are to be present in the individual's repertoire of behaviors. Least influential in the child's motor development and of only moderate importance in the development of emotional expression is the role of the parent. Quite clearly, he has relatively little to do in matters of growth and maturation.

REFERENCES

Aldrich, C. A., & Norval, Mildred A. A developmental graph for the first year. *J. Pediat.*, 1946, **29**, 304–308.

Bayley, Nancy. The development of motor abilities during the first three years. *Monogr. Soc. Res. Child Develpm.*, 1935, **1**, 1, 3.

Bowlby, J. *Maternal care and mental health.* Geneva: World Health Organization, 1952.

Bridges, Katharine H. B. Emotional development in early infancy. *Child Develpm.*, 1932, **3**, 324–341.

Darwin, C. R. *The expression of the emotions in man and animals.* New York: Philosophical Library, 1955.

Dennis, W. Congenital cataract and unlearned behavior. *J. genet. Psychol.*, 1934, **44**, 340–351.

Dennis, W. The effect of restricted practice upon the reaching, sitting and standing of two infants. *J. genet. Psychol.*, 1935, **47**, 17–32.

Dennis, W. Infant development under conditions of restricted practice and of minimal social stimulation: a preliminary report. *J. genet. Psychol.*, 1938, **53**, 149–157.

Dennis, W. Infant reactions to restraint. *Trans. N. Y. Acad. Sci.*, 1940, Series II, **2**, 202–217.

Dennis, W. Infant development under conditions of restricted practice and of minimal social stimulation. *Genet. Psychol. Monogr.*, 1941, **23**, 143–189.

Dennis, W., & Dennis, Marsena G. The effect of cradling practice upon the onset of walking in Hopi children. *J. genet. Psychol.*, 1940, **56**, 77–86.

Dennis, W., & Dennis, Marsena G. Development under controlled conditions. In W. Dennis (Ed.), *Readings in child psychology.* New York: Prentice-Hall, 1951.

Erikson, E. H. *Childhood and society.* New York: Norton, 1950.

Festinger, L. The psychological effects of insufficient rewards. *Amer. Psychol.*, 1961, **61**, 1–11.

Fowler, W. Cognitive learning in infancy and early childhood. *Psychol. Bull.*, 1962, **59**, 116–152.

Gates, A. I. The necessary mental age for beginning reading. *Elem. Sch. J.*, 1937, **37**, 497–508.

Gesell, A., & Thompson, H. Learning and growth in identical infant twins. *Genet. Psychol. Monogr.*, 1929, **6**, 1–124.

Goodenough, Florence L. The expression of emotions in infancy. *Child Develpm.*, 1931, **2**, 96–101.

Goodenough, Florence L. Expressions of the emotions in a blind-deaf child. *J. abnorm. soc. Psychol.*, 1932, **27**, 328–333.

Harlow, H. F. The nature of love. *Amer. Psychol.*, 1958, **13**, 673–685.

Harlow, H. F. Love in infant monkeys. *Sci. Am.*, 1959, **200**, 68–74.

Harlow, H. F., & Harlow, Margaret K. A study of animal affection. *Nat. Hist.*, 1961, **70**, 48–55.

London, I. D. A Russian report on the postoperative newly seeing. *Amer. J. Psychol.*, 1960, **73**, 478–482.

Lorenz, K. *King Solomon's ring; new light on animal ways.* New York: Crowell, 1952.

Lorenz, K. Companionship in bird life. In Claire H. Schiller (Ed.), *Instinctive behavior.* New York: International Univer. Press, 1957.

McGraw, Myrtle B. *Growth: a study of Johnny and Jimmy.* New York: Appleton, 1935.

McGraw, Myrtle B. Later development of children specially trained during infancy. Johnny and Jimmy at school age. *Child Develpm.*, 1939, **10**, 1–19.

McGraw, Myrtle B. Neural maturation as exemplified in achievement of bladder control. *J. Pediat.*, 1940, **16**, 580–590.

Melzack, R., & Scott, T. H. The effects of early experience on the response to pain. *J. comp. physiol. Psychol.*, 1957, **50**, 151–161.

Moyer, K. E., & Gilmer, B. von H. Attention spans of children for experimentally designed toys. *J. genet. Psychol.*, 1955, **87**, 187–201.

Nissen, H. W., Chow, K. L., & Semmes, J. Effects of restricted opportunity for tactual, kinesthetic and manipulative experience in the behavior of a chimpanzee. *Amer. J. Psychol.*, 1951, **64**, 485–507.

Orlansky, H. Infant care and personality. *Psychol. Bull.*, 1949, **46**, 1–48.

Ribble, Margaret A. *The rights of infants.* New York: Columbia Univer. Press, 1943.

Riesen, A. H. Effects of stimulus deprivation on the development and atrophy of the visual sensory system. *Am. J. Orthopsychiat.*, 1960, **30**, 23–36.

Riesen, A. H., & Kinder, Elaine F. *Postural development of infant chimpanzees: a comparative and normative study based on the Gesell Behavioral Examination.* New Haven, Conn.: Yale Univer. Press, 1952.

Scott, J. P. *Animal behavior.* Chicago: Univer. Chicago Press, 1958.

Scott, J. P. The process of primary socialization in canine and human infants. *Monogr. Soc. Res. Child Develpm.*, 1963, **28**, No. 1.

Sherman, M. The differentiation of emotional responses in infants: I. Judgments of emotional responses from motion picture views and from actual observation. *J. comp. Psychol.*, 1927, **7**, 265–284.

Shirley, Mary M. *The first two years of life* (Vol. II). Minneapolis: Univer. of Minn. Press, 1933.

Tinbergen, N. *Social behavior in animals.* New York: Wiley, 1953.

Van Alstyne, Dorothy. *Play behavior and choice of play materials of preschool children.* Chicago: Univer. Chicago Press, 1932.

Von Senden, M. Space and sight: the perception of space and shape in the con-
genitally blind before and after operation. (Transl. by P. Heath.) New York;
Free Press of Glencoe, 1960. (Original German edition: Leipzig, Barth, 1932.)

Watson, J. B. *Psychology from the standpoint of a behaviorist*. Philadelphia: Lippincott, 1919.

Watson, J. B., & Morgan, J. J. B. Emotional reactions and psychological experimentation. *Am. J. Psychol.*, 1917, **28**, 163–174.

chapter 4 ✳ Learning and Motivation

The human animal acquires much behavior through learning. The behaviors he learns come about through a pattern of reacting to stimuli and to the reward accompanying such reaction; the response may either be initiated by the human organism itself or copied from the responses of some other organism. Either way, the human differs in this respect from lower orders of the plant and animal worlds, which inherit their major patterns of response, even though these behaviors may be inspired by specific conditions in the environment. Learning, of course, takes many forms which gradually become more complex from childhood to adulthood or from simple to more intricate organisms. In this chapter we shall explore these various forms and then the forces that motivate learning.

LEARNING

Essentially, there are two kinds of learning—simple and complex. Setting aside for the present the latter category, let us consider the two techniques through which simple learning occurs. Simple learning is either *respondent* or *operant*. Respondent learning is the classical method of conditioning often called *Pavlovian* after the Russian physiologist I. P. Pavlov (1927). In this type of learning the organ-

94

ism remains relatively passive as it learns; all that is required of it is to respond. Operant learning, on the other hand, engages the active participation of the organism seeking to learn. It is a trial-and-error process, sometimes called *instrumental* learning, in which the organism acts and in so doing generates results.

Respondent Learning

Pavlov preferred to use dogs in his experiments. He had already won a Nobel Prize for his work on gastric secretions when he turned his attention to his now famous experiments on conditioned reflexes. Noting that dogs salivated before food entered their mouths, he saw that the mere presence of food or even the sound of the keeper's footsteps was enough to bring on salivation. Pavlov was so taken by this phenomenon that he dedicated the latter part of his life to pursuing it and its implications.

An organism instinctively responds to a stimulus in some concrete manner. The dog salivates, for example, on the presentation of food. This salivation is assumed to be innate and not learned. The dog is exposed to the sound of a bell and is then given food in the form of meat powder. After several repetitions of this pattern, the dog salivates at the sound of the bell even before the food arrives. The meat powder is called the *unconditioned stimulus* and the salivation it engenders, the unconditioned response or *unconditioned reflex*. The bell is the *conditioned stimulus* and the salivation occasioned by its sound, in the absence of the meat powder, is the conditioned response or *conditioned reflex*.

Besides the conditioned stimulus itself, other stimuli resembling it also produce the same effect. Thus, if an organism is conditioned to respond to a medium tone of bell, it will also react to a high or a low tone, although to a lesser degree. This phenomenon is known as *stimulus generalization* because it extends the power of the stimulus to other objects and events. As we shall see later in the chapter, when we consider complex learning, stimulus generalization contributes significantly to the concepts human organisms form.

The conditioned reflex diminishes and eventually ceases, however, if the conditioned stimulus is presented repeatedly without the accompanying unconditioned stimulus. The conditioned reflex is now said to have been "extinguished." Yet, curiously enough, this cessation may not be final. An environmental change can revive the reflex. Even a small change in the surroundings, such as slamming a door, is sometimes enough to reawaken an extinguished response for a time.

Several well-known examples of conditioning in humans illustrate the process. The first is the case of "Little Albert" who was conditioned by Watson and Rayner (1920). As remarked in the previous chapter, Watson believed that the young child was innately afraid of sudden, loud noises. In an experiment that demonstrated the fear of sudden loud noises, Watson and Morgan (1917) also found that infants showed no fear of darkness, snakes, or other stimuli which to that time had been thought to be innately or "instinctively" productive of fear. Watson therefore concluded that all fears, except for those involving sudden loud noises or loss of support, were learned —and further, were to be learned through conditioning. His experiment with Rayner around the nine-month-old boy, "Little Albert," demonstrated the conditioning of the fear response.

The infant was presented with a white rat. He was not afraid of it. Thereafter, whenever the rat was presented to the boy, a steel bar was struck, producing a sudden loud noise. Following a relatively few conditioning trials, Little Albert responded to the rat with reactions of fear. In addition, he was also afraid of a fur coat, a rabbit, a Santa Claus mask, and a wad of absorbent cotton. Rather wide stimulus generalization had occurred, apparently among soft, white, hairy substances.

The Watson and Rayner study of "Little Albert" may well have influenced the plot of Aldous Huxley's *Brave New World* (1932). In this imaginary society of the future, ability is determined by the amount of oxygen allowed to enter the bloodstream of a fetus, which is grown in an artificial uterus. Each intelligence group is so adapted as to be best able to perform a given level of job. Problems of overproduction are solved by conditioning individuals to consume, whereas such nonconsumptive behaviors as enjoying books or nature are extinguished. This conditioning process is described in the following passage from the book.

> Turned, the babies at once fell silent, then began to crawl towards those clusters of sleek colours, those shapes so gay and brilliant on the white pages. As they approached, the sun came out of a momentary eclipse behind a cloud. The roses flamed up as though with a sudden passion from within; a new and profound significance seemed to suffuse the shining pages of the books. From the ranks of the crawling babies came little squeals of excitement, gurgles and twitterings of pleasure.
>
> The Director rubbed his hands. "Excellent!" he said. "It might almost have been done on purpose."
>
> The swiftest crawlers were already at their goal. Small hands reached

out uncertainly, touched, grasped, unpetaling the transfigured roses, crumpling the illuminated pages of the books. The Director waited until all were happily busy. Then, "Watch carefully," he said. And, lifting his hand, he gave the signal.

The Head Nurse, who was standing by a switchboard at the other end of the room, pressed down a little lever.

There was a violent explosion. Shriller and even shriller, a siren shrieked. Alarm bells maddeningly sounded.

The children started, screamed, their faces were distorted with terror.

"And now," the Director shouted (for the noise was deafening), "now we proceed to rub in the lesson with a mild electric shock."

He waved his hand again, and the Head Nurse pressed a second lever. The screaming of the babies suddenly changed its tone. There was something desperate, almost insane, about the sharp spasmodic yelps to which they now gave utterance. Their little bodies twitched and stiffened; their limbs moved jerkily as if to the tug of unseen wires.

"We can electrify that whole strip of floor," bawled the Director in explanation. "But that's enough," he signalled to the nurse.

The explosions ceased, the bells stopped ringing, the shriek of the siren died down from tone to tone into silence. The stiffly twitching bodies relaxed, and what had become the sob and yelp of infant maniacs broadened out once more into a normal howl of ordinary terror.

"Offer them the flowers and the books again."

The nurses obeyed; but at the approach of the roses, at the mere sight of those gaily-coloured images of pussy and cock-a-doodle-doo and baa-baa black sheep, the infants shrank away in horror; the volume of their howling suddenly increased.

"Observe," said the Director triumphantly, "observe."

Books and loud noises, flowers and electric shocks—already in the infant mind these couples were compromisingly linked; and after two hundred repetitions of the same or a similar lesson would be wedded indissolubly. What man has joined, nature is powerless to put asunder.

"They'll grow up with what the psychologists used to call an instinctive hatred of books and flowers. Reflexes unalterably conditioned. They'll be safe from books and botany all their lives." The Director turned to his nurses. "Take them away again" (Huxley, 1932, pp. 21–22).

Not only emotional states but also motor responses are susceptible to conditioning. Spelt (1948) demonstrated that a fetus past six-and-a-half months of age could be conditioned while in the uterus. In his experiment a loud noise served as the unconditioned stimulus while the tactile vibration on the mother's abdomen was the conditioned stimulus. The movement of the fetus, originally an unconditioned response to noise, became a conditioned response to vibration. How infants may be conditioned is seen in the work of Marquis (1931) who, in seven out of eight instances, conditioned infants to associate a buzzer with food. Following a number of presentations of both

FIGURE 4-1 Conditioning in *Brave New World*.

buzzer and food, the infants began sucking and decreased crying and other manifestations of hunger upon sounding of the buzzer alone. Although both infants and fetuses seem open to conditioning, they are more likely to respond to changes in the environment than to a specific conditioned stimulus. Wickens and Wickens (1940) have called this "pseudoconditioning," but it appears to be a *bona fide* conditioning if different in type from the conditioning obtained with more mature organisms.

Many human behaviors result from classical conditioning, that is, from respondent learning. Simple enough in principle, it can be used to account for most, if not all, human learning. Watson (1919) thought so, and the Soviets continue to think so (see Razran, 1961). Russian acceptance of classical conditioning as the only form of learning, although quite foreign to American way of thinking, has, as Brackbill (1960) has noted, produced research of both practical and theoretical importance. However, most American psychologists, unlike their Soviet colleagues, believe also in a second way of learning —the operant way.

Operant Learning

One of the foremost early students of learning was E. L. Thorndike. Concentrating his investigations on lower organisms rather than on humans, he placed his subjects in mazes and puzzle boxes where they were neither required to show sudden understanding of a problem at hand nor called on to solve it. Instead they had to learn a set of motor responses that had essentially no pattern, that is, no right-left-right-left turns. Thorndike (1913) noted, not surprisingly, that much like illiterates learning to find their way about a strange city without assistance, his organisms decreased their errors of entering blind alleys only slowly. Correspondingly, the amount of time they required to get from the start of the maze to the goal decreased slowly. From this, Thorndike concluded that learning in lower organisms was slow and lacked insight. He further believed that human learning was also of this trial-and-error sort.

Consider the acquisition of the ability to ride a bicycle. Complex operant or trial-and-error behaviors, as Skinner (1958, 1960) has shown, can be learned by organisms. Such learning occurs most rapidly when the "method of approximations" is used in the training process and the learner tries to approximate or imitate the behavior of others. There is no magic way of learning to ride a bicycle; learning must take place by a simple, trial-and-error procedure. The beginner falls frequently, whenever he leans too far to one side to retain his balance at the speed at which he is then moving. But as he is highly impelled to ride, even crude approximations of bicycle-riding behavior bring him gratification; to be able to move even a few feet without falling is at first rewarding, indeed, a victory. Those behaviors that lead to this victory tend to be repeated; this is known as *positive reinforcement*. Meanwhile, the behaviors that precede falling begin to diminish in frequency. As the rewarding behaviors gradually increase, the child ultimately reaches the point at which he rides off alone, tipsy, insecure, and not really inspiring confidence in either himself or anyone watching. Eventually, of course, he makes it.

There is nothing intrinsically different between a child learning to ride a bicycle and a rat learning to run a maze. For both, learning is a slow, gradual, trial-and-error process in which rewarded responses are retained while those that do not bring reward are eliminated. Most likely, a substantial proportion of learning in infancy and childhood, such as the acquisition of motor skills or of speech, consists largely of simple operant activity, common to all organisms.

Learning Sets

It is a mark of progress to pass from the simple to the complex. But such transitions are not always easily made. Often they require some extra effort or some intermediate step. In learning, many believe that one connecting link is an understanding of *learning sets* which were developed by Harlow (1949) in the course of his experiments with monkeys. Learning sets, in substance, are groups of habits employed by organisms in the process of learning. In experiments concerning them, subjects are presented with a series of problems. Each of these problems has its own stimuli which are entirely different from those of the remaining problems, yet each must be solved by application of the same learning habits. If the organism learns the habits rather than the simple, operant solution to a particular problem, it can then apply them to any succeeding problem. The organism has learned to learn; it can extend its responses to other situations, transfer its habits of problem solving from one problem to the next. The organism has thus developed a *learning set,* which can cope with even unusual situations. Indeed, the learning set leads directly, as we shall soon see, to the formation of concepts, one of the principal forms of complex learning.

There are wide differences in the speed at which various species establish learning sets. Although it may take a hundred or more trials for a monkey to acquire a learning set (Harlow, 1949), very young humans (Koch & Meyer, 1959) or severely retarded humans of below 50 IQ (Fehmi, 1960) develop them quite rapidly, often in fewer than ten series of problems. As a rule primates are markedly superior to nonprimates in this form of learning, even when previous learning has been controlled. Moreover, there are great differences even between members of the primate order in the development of learning sets. That humans surpass other primates and primates excel nonprimates suggests a distinct superiority among primates—and especially humans—in the transfer of old learning to new problems. It is this ability to transfer that contributes substantially to the formation of concepts.

Concept Formation

In simple learning adults are not always superior to young children, nor do humans invariably surpass other organisms. But in complex learning, to which we now shift attention, wide chasms separate all these groups. Except in rare instances, the human adult excels all others in the various forms of complex learning—concept formation, thinking, and creativity.

It is quite possible that from coping with problems that develop in a learning situation, a subject may evolve a concept for solving them all. Yet this is not necessarily so. The subject might actually solve each problem independently without ever becoming aware of a common principle or concept applicable to the entire series. Concept formation requires an organism to develop an understanding, which can be measured by the organism's behavior, that certain objects, events, or characteristics of a stimulus have a common element. On the basis of this element phenomena may then be classed. The actual source of the concept lies in respondent or operant learning. It is the transfer—or generalization—of what is learned to other situations sharing common elements which constitutes the formation of a concept.

Humans generalize more adequately than other organisms. In large measure they succeed more widely than others in transferring learning because they have the facility of language. Take the matter of transposition in music. Subjects are exposed to two musical tones, *do* and *re*. Once they learn to respond to *re*, subjects are then exposed to succeeding pairs such as *re-mi, mi-fa, fa-sol,* and so forth. The lower organisms will respond to the higher of the two tones only when it is one step removed from the learned tone. However, human children able to use words to describe the learning principle involved seem capable of transposing and generalizing responses to new tones no matter how far removed these may be from the original learning stimuli (Alberts & Ehrenfreund, 1951; Kuenne, 1946).

The learning of both concrete and abstract concepts seems to gain from language. Words provide additional, constant cues for the distinguishing of different "concrete" objects. Spoons, for example, vary in size and shape; nevertheless, they have enough common elements to fall into a single perceptual grouping. Despite their variations, they are identical in name, which facilitates development of the concept spoon. The mere presence of a name imposes limits on the concept more simply and perhaps more accurately for the young child than would a variety of stimuli lacking a name. Language simplifies the formation of concepts and also reduces the differences between individuals in the content of their concepts.

Language also enables the adequate development of "abstract" concepts that are independent of specific concrete physical stimuli or physical reference. Since specific objects cannot serve as cues in these cases, learning tends to be slower than for concrete concepts. Those concepts with few or misleading—sometimes both—verbal designations are generally considered abstract and are learned slowly and often erroneously (Johnson, 1962; Voeks, 1954). This may be seen in the study of animism, the belief that all objects possess a natural life. Whether children (Piaget, 1930) or college students (Dennis, 1953), subjects have an inadequate concept of life, of what is alive. They attribute animacy to many nonliving things, such as the sun, the ocean, and a lighted match. The inadequacy of the concept appears to result from the sparseness and at times misleading nature of the verbal terms used to define life. The attribute of life most commonly mentioned is movement. But this is actually a characteristic shared by the animate and the inanimate, such as the railroad engine, the automobile, or the sun; hence, an accurate demarcation between living and nonliving, and therefore an adequate concept of life, is difficult to obtain as long as movement remains life's chief criterion.

Concept formation, then, rests on the bases of generalizing and transferring stimuli, which are common to man and lower organisms. Man's supremacy over other organisms stems from the ability to organize in a wide variety of ways, through the use of symbols, a greater amount of experience, only some of which is sensory. Although not unique to humans, concept formation is an area of learning in which human capacity far exceeds that of other organisms.

Thinking

The leading theories on children's thinking come from the European psychological tradition and are tied most intimately to theories of concept formation. Best represented in American circles by Werner (1957), they have also been given attention in several critiques published in the United States (Fowler, 1962; Johnson, 1962). These theories maintain that the thought processes of children differ in quality from those of adults.

The best known and most comprehensive of these theories was developed by the Swiss psychologist Jean Piaget. In his view a child passes through three stages of mental activity en route to maturity. First, there is a *sensorimotor* stage in which action is governed by sensations; simple learning occurs, but the child does not think. Next, the child moves into a phase of egocentricity; by *egocentricity* Piaget means neither selfishness nor self-centeredness, but more likely the inability to put oneself in the place of another. The major portion of this period lasts from the age of seven or eight to the age of eleven or twelve; during it, the child is concerned with concrete ideas. In this stage the formation of concepts is felt to involve "operational groupings concerning subjects that can be manipulated or known through the senses" (Piaget, 1952, p. 123). Finally, the child advances to the stage of abstract concepts; "from 11–12 years and during adolescence, formal thought is projected and its groupings characterize the completion of reflective thought" (Piaget, *ibid.*). By "reflective thought" Piaget refers to the ability to form adequate abstract concepts.

This theory says, then, that thought processes change with advances in age by sudden (*saltatory*) jumps. Thus, any given eight-year-old would differ qualitatively from any given 12-year-old in the way he thinks. This difference may be detected in the child's concept formations. How valid is this theory?

Piaget (1930b) investigated the concept of animism in an effort to measure developmental changes in children's thinking about the kinds of things believed to be alive. At first children consider anything active to be alive; a telephone, for example, is alive, at least when it is ringing. Later in the child's development, life is ascribed only to objects that move. Still later, life is attributed to objects that move without visible stimulation, such as the sun or wind. Eventually, at about age 12, children restrict consciousness—*life*—to plants and animals.

Most other researchers (e.g., Russell & Dennis, 1939; Russell, 1940) have found these same four periods but have varied considerably in their explanations of what happens at any age level. Dennis (1942) saw his daughter with an IQ of 150 pass through the four stages but reach an adult level of understanding the concept *life* at six years and two months. Later, he discovered (Dennis, 1953) a substantial portion of college students retaining some animistic beliefs at their age. And in one of the relatively few crosscultural studies of animism, as opposed to the great number of mere observations, Huang and Lee (1945) detected almost no evidence of animism among Chinese children. Although such findings often depend on the procedure followed in the research, studies both within a culture and across different cultures do not suggest a universal, sudden change in the content of animism as a result of changes of age.

Or take the concept of causality. One aspect of justice, or of moral judgment, is moral realism. This is the tendency to judge acts exclusively in terms of consequences without regard to motives or causes. The history of jurisprudence, it has been said, shows a gradually increasing concern for cause as cultures grow older (Maine, 1861). But even adults have not yet reached what Maine (1861) and Piaget (1932) would call complete moral maturity in this area. Certain changes in moral judgment relative to age fit both concrete and abstract explanations of changing mental life. Piaget (1932) found young children to be morally realistic, whereas older children were not, partly because of the concreteness of younger children's thought processes. At about 12, he held, the change toward a concern for motives becomes complete. Yet in the Chinese culture much younger children advance beyond this stage (Liu, 1950). The faster advancement of Chinese children than Caucasians of the same age results, Liu maintained, from having a culture and philosophy that require acts to be weighed in terms of cause or motive. On the other hand, high school students in American settings continue to show evidences of moral realism (Johnson, 1962).

In causality Piaget (1930a) asserted that children progressed by stages from magical explanations of natural phenomena and the imputation of lifelike characteristics to inanimate objects to an adult view of the concept. They said such things as "the candle in an airtight jar goes out because it is tired." From these beginnings, children passed through several different types of explanations until eventually reaching the mature conception. Once more, however, contrary evidence has shown that refinement of the content of the concept to a point of accuracy may not involve as neat a progression of age as Piaget suggested. As Deutsche (1937) saw it, all forms of explanation were present in children at about the age of eight.

More recently Piaget and his associates have turned to other aspects of children's thinking and conceptualizing. These studies have revolved around the understanding of such ideas as *conservation of quantity* and *spontaneous measurement*. Mature modes of response do not occur, Piaget held, before the age of nine in some cases and 11 or 12 in others. Nevertheless, a child of six (Johnson & Petit, 1964) responded maturely to all the tests of thinking discussed by Piaget (1953) as well as to those mentioned some years later by Inhelder and Matalon (1960) as appropriate for children at or above her age. These tests sought to ascertain whether a child would be aware that a quantity of beads which filled a small glass was the same when poured into a large glass which it only half filled; this was the principle of conservation of quantity. They also sought to test whether children were aware of the constancy of a measuring unit, such as a ruler or a stick, even when its position was changed; the principle of spontaneous measurement.

If maturity does indeed enter into stages of thought then it is quite astonishing that bright, American five- to six-year-olds match Swiss 11- to 12-year-olds. It is also astonishing that environmental factors, such as socioeconomic status (see Bronfenbrenner, 1962; Hoffman, 1962; Johnson, 1962), and race and religion (Liu, 1950), relate substantially to the maturity of children's responses to questions bearing on concepts presumably so bound up with age as moral judgment and animism. Although a shift in type of response does occur with age, as Piaget asserted, there is nothing to suggest that this change is sudden or that such shifts as do take place happen at the times mentioned by Piaget.

Opposed to the view that children's thinking differs in quality from that of adults is the position expressed less often that children think in the same way as adults, only on the basis of less adequate information. Presumably abstract concepts should be formed only after about 12 years of age. However, research on children shows clearly that such concepts are formed rather early, but with inaccurate or insufficient content. The three-year-old has a concept of life; others just happen to believe the content of his concept is wrong if he attributes life to a racing locomotive. All in all, not much is known about the physiological basis of thought, nor is there much information on the influence of such phenomena as imagery and language on the thought process. Yet what information is available does not support the belief in substantial differences between children and adults in world view or in approach to problems—that is, in thinking.

Creativity

From thinking we pass along to creativity, perhaps the highest form of problem solving. In the scale of learning it lies at the opposite end from respondent learning which began this discussion. Creativity has been described by Drevdahl as follows.

> Creativity is the capacity of persons to produce compositions, products, or ideas of any sort which are essentially new or novel, and previously unknown to the producer. It can be imaginative activity, or thought

synthesis, where the product is not a mere summation. It may involve the forming of new patterns and combinations of information derived from past experience, and the transplanting of old relationships to new situations and may involve the generation of new correlates. It must be purposeful or goal directed, not mere idle fantasy—although it need not have immediate practical application or be a perfect and complete product. It may take the form of an artistic, literary or scientific production or may be of a procedural or methodological nature (Drevdahl, 1956, p. 22).

Originality and creativity are probably present in all individuals—adults and children—but clearly in quite different degrees (Wilson, Guilford, & Christensen, 1953). The measures used most frequently to test creativity are those developed by Guilford and his colleagues.

The basic components of creativity, Guilford (1950) maintained, are a sensitivity to problems, an ability to produce many novel ideas or solutions, a flexible approach to solving problems, and the capacity to analyze and synthesize a complex collection of ideas. The tests he and his colleagues devised (see Wilson, Guilford, and Christensen, 1953) were aimed at measuring these qualities. On these tests, adult subjects are asked to do such things as describe how the United States might have developed if there had been no Mississippi-Missouri river system or think up a title for a movie scenario presented to them. Their responses can be rated on the basis of quantity and quality, since most studies show the two to be closely related, and then compared with criteria of creativity in real life. Responses to the Barron-Welsh Art Scale (Barron & Welsh, 1952) or the Welsh Figure Preference Test (Welsh, 1959) predict creativity in real life among both adults and children fairly well (MacKinnon, 1962). Creative individuals prefer complex and asymmetrical figures to the simple and symmetrical. They also produce a very high proportion of unusual word associations (MacKinnon, 1962); hence, tests of such associations also may help to judge creativity.

In following up these findings, Houston and Mednick (1963) discovered creative adults to be far less tolerant of the banal or the commonplace. And Jacobsen and Asher (1963) have remarkably predicted creativity in real life from the way individuals reacted to a perceptual task. The task in question consisted of a series of 21 pictures during which the silhouette of a dog gradually changed into one of a cat. The more flexible subjects caught the change early in the series; these individuals generally proved the most creative in the actual life task which, in this experiment, was to design a desk. Thus, these various tests in their different forms were able to measure the presence in an individual of the basic components of creativity.

Presumably these components relate to a manner of intellectual functioning, but they are apparently independent of intelligence as it is usually measured through IQ. In most creative endeavor, quite obviously, a minimal IQ may exist, below which an individual cannot function. However, above this level, IQ has no significance. If one compares, for example, the 150 least creative and productive males with the 150 most creative and productive from Terman's study of gifted children (Terman, 1954) there is little difference in ability between the two groups. Other studies (Drevdahl, 1956; MacKinnon, 1962; Torrance, 1960) contain similar findings. Among individuals selected to form an above-average group, the specific performance of any one of them on a conventional intelligence test is no indication of creativity.

Besides intellectual traits, such as a fluency of ideas and flexibility, certain personality characteristics differentiate the creative from the noncreative individual. There are those who say that creative persons are less anxious (Reid, King, & Wickwire, 1959), less defensive, and more willing to concede faults (MacKinnon, 1962). Creative individuals tend to be radical, unconventional, and sensitive to the feelings of others (Drevdahl, 1956). On tests of masculinity versus femininity they score more toward the feminine end of the scale (MacKinnon, 1962). This does not signify some sexual aberration, but merely indicates a higher number of cultural interests. Creative persons are also independent and self-sufficient, not overly concerned with maintaining close ties with social groups or with receiving the approval of others (MacKinnon, 1962).

Since highly creative individuals share all these traits which are believed to be shaped by environment, creative individuals should also have common elements in their backgrounds. Abundant evidence shows they tend to have close ties with parents. McCurdy (1957) demonstrated that historical geniuses had very little contact with their peers, but had intensive, generally warm relations with parents and siblings. Both Greenacre (1958) and MacKinnon (1962) found this to be true. The family of a genius is a tightly knit unit, often estranged from its neighbors because of different values or cultural aspirations, and the creative individual himself is often alienated from his mates during childhood (MacKinnon, 1962; Torrance, 1960). The family, therefore, has a more profound influence on him than most of his peers, since the latter, the neighborhood, and probably the school have less opportunity to inspire behavioral change.

This intimate, closely knit family relationship is marked by warmth and by mild discipline of a psychological rather than a physical turn. The child is presented with a clear set of parental standards but is given much freedom of expression which he is encouraged to exercise

(MacKinnon, 1962). Parental democracy also stimulates creativity and imaginativeness among children (Baldwin, 1949). Moreover, Terman's study of gifted children showed that the noncreative came from homes having more stress, more conflict, and less interest in achievement than the homes of the creative subjects among his sample.

These data indeed suggest that parents have a great deal of influence in developing the ability of their children to cope with tasks requiring the solution of problems and creativity. Possessed of the necessary formal intelligence (IQ), the creative individual benefits most by growing up in a home that is hospitable and sympathetic to creative interests. In such a home there is marital harmony. Parental standards are unambiguous. Discipline is neither severe nor physical. The emphasis is on achievement and independent action with parents establishing conditions that allow the child to meet these expectations. And finally, the family is the major agency of socialization, increasing its position at the expense of the child's peers, the neighborhood, and the school. If a parent wishes his child to be creative, to be a productive artist, scientist, or innovator, his parental behavior must follow directions that are fairly well marked. Yet it is quite possible that many parents are unwilling to accept these conditions for having a creative, self-directed child despite their lip service to the idea that creativity is a good and worthwhile aspiration.

So much for the way behavior and knowledge are acquired. Through these various techniques organisms learn the things they need to know in order to survive. Indeed learning is crucial to survival. But how does the necessity to survive make organisms learn? How do forces in the environment and in the organisms themselves activate the many techniques of learning? They do so by stimulating the organism, by supplying it with motivation to learn, and by reinforcing or not reinforcing the things that are learned. Because learning and motivation are almost two fitting pieces of the same jigsaw puzzle, the rest of this chapter deals with the second piece, motivation—including the effects of reinforcement and nonreinforcement on learning and behavior.

MOTIVATION

Motivation is the force or condition within the organism which impels it to act or respond. Presumably organisms are motivated by physiological needs, such as hunger or thirst. These needs generate drives, that is, tendencies to behave in a manner likely to reduce the needs. Indeed, there is widespread belief that behaviors will be learned only if they can reduce an organism's needs or tensions. The primary needs of an organism are biological—hunger, thirst, and, to a lesser degree, sex. In a society of plenty, such as American civilization, it is not often likely for drives engendered by primary needs to produce behavior among children or adults. Rather *secondary* drives, derived from primary drives, are considered to be more significant. The infant's affection for its mother comes from her feeding it; she reduces its primary drive of hunger. Not only is the feeding rewarding to the infant, but so is the mother, because she is always associated with reduction of the hunger. She becomes rewarding in her own right, if only on a secondary basis; this secondary reward, or *reinforcement,* is taken to be the basis for human socialization. The infant now needs the mother as well as the food and expands this need to encompass human beings in general. Although plausible, this explanation of the relationship between mother and child may not be correct. In the last chapter, it will be recalled, Harlow's data (1958) regarding monkeys indicated that the development of infantile affection had nothing to do with feeding.

Perhaps, then, the mainspring for human motivation, and especially the motivation of the very young human, lies in other needs not tied to immediate biological necessity. Because of their value for survival, these other needs have become, through natural selection, part of the human condition. In their specific forms, they have been described as constituting curiosity and manipulative drives which quite likely fit under the heading of "arousal" (see Hebb, 1955).

Arousal refers to the capacity of various sensory stimuli to excite the organism. It covers both primary and secondary drives, since all drives and all stimuli have the power to arouse. Actually, stimulation by the environment serves two purposes. The first of these, which is rather obvious, is to provide the organism with *cues* or hints on how to respond. The second, far less apparent, is highly significant: it is to *arouse* the organism and keep it actively engaged in dealing with the environment. This second function of stimulation may very well explain why primates seek stimulation for its own sake. Be that as it may, the amount of cueing supplied by a stimulus depends on when the organism is aroused. Figure 4-2 illustrates a cue-arousal curve, showing the quantity of cueing at various levels of arousal.

The validity of this curve is demonstrable. The organism that is overaroused because it is subjected to a large number of highly relevant stimuli receives very little cueing or information from the stimuli

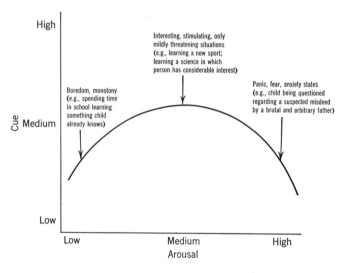

FIGURE 4-2 The amount of behavioral cue offered by a given stimulus at different levels of arousal.

and is thus often wrong in its responses. In extreme cases, this may bring on panic. More typically, several studies (e.g., Birch, 1945; Johnson & Thomson, 1962) disclose that both high and low motivation are less effective in producing learning than moderate amounts. In fact, there appears to be a point of diminishing return beyond which any increase in the amount of motivation results in a deterioration rather than an enhancement of learning. This point occurs at different places in different age groups and also varies among individuals within any given age bracket. Results of experiments in motivation indeed indicate the necessity for parent and teacher to show as much concern over learning situations in which motivation is very high as those in which motivation is very low.

In one study which appears to measure the effect of high arousal on children, Leitch and Escalona (1949) produced overstimulation in infants by presenting them with a succession of toys—all enjoyable, but much too many and for too long. Behavior deteriorated rapidly. Although the children were highly alert or aroused, their behavior began to resemble that of an earlier stage of development; in other words, the children regressed. In fact, the case, observed rather frequently, of the child who has too many toys, too many experiences, too much contact with an excessively directive mother, and who becomes "difficult" might be explained as an instance of overarousal.

At the opposite extreme, monotony develops (see McBain, 1961). In this condition so few stimuli are present in the environment that the organism does not respond accurately to those at hand. The most striking example of this among children is found in the institutional care of infants. Institutionalization during infancy is said by many to inflict permanent psychic damage on those involved. But as we shall see in Chapter 9, this is a dubious view. The effects that are found tend to be temporary. Generally they consist of an apparent mental retardation, frequent tics, and peculiarities in affect. According to Casler (1961) lack of variation in the environment is a major factor in the generation of these deviant behaviors. Some of them, such as head banging, stem from the maintenance of low arousal despite the child's own efforts to increase the environmental stimulation.

Although human behavior is motivated by the necessity to reduce tensions or arousal when biological needs grow too strong, far more behavior is engendered by the necessity to increase tension or arousal when the environment fails to provide enough variation. The most obvious thing about children, said Anderson (1948), is that they seek stimulation. There seems to be a need for maintaining arousal, and for increasing it when it falls too low. The optimal level of tension or arousal for any individual is likely to increase with maturation; this level lies somewhere in the middle, as Figure 4-2 shows, for that is where stimuli supply the most cues to guide behavior.

Rosenzweig (1945) found that if younger children were permitted to choose between easy and difficult—in this case, insoluble—tasks, they would, as a rule, choose the easy one. Older children, on the other hand, chose the difficult one. From this and other studies like it, one can conclude that young children, although they seek a wide variety of stimulation, are more easily overaroused than older children. Yet individual differences at any single level of maturation are probably influenced by inherited differences in emotional instability, emotionality, learned tolerance of frustration, capacity to reduce tensions, and a number of other variables.

The motivation to behave and to learn, then, may come from primary and secondary needs. The goal of the behavior may be the reduction of tensions produced by these needs. However, in primates, and particularly in young humans, such tension-*producing* behavior as curiosity or manipulation seems so marked that it may be sounder scientifically to accept the probable need to increase arousal and generate tension as well as to reduce both.

Reward, Punishment, and Nonreinforcement

The concept of arousal helps to account for the influence of three possible outcomes of any act on the probability of the act's recurring in the future. These possibilities are positive reinforcement—*reward;* negative reinforcement—*punishment;* and nonreinforcement—neither reward nor punishment. Thorndike (1913) in his "Law of Effect" stated that reward stamped in a behavior and punishment stamped it out. If things were this simple, life would also be simple, since most problem behaviors would vanish. The child who is a behavior problem has undergone considerable punishment through rejection by those around him, yet remains a problem. If punishment worked, then prisons—at least harsh prisons—should be 100 per cent effective. The matter of reward and punishment, and especially punishment, is much more complicated than might be expected from the original law of effect. Moreover, questions regarding the influence of reward, punishment, and nonreinforcement are, of course, closely related to the very practical subject of disciplining children.

Reward. Before we can consider the influence of reward or positive reinforcement on learning, we must decide what constitutes reinforcing. All behaviors that lead to the reduction of primary and secondary drives must be regarded as positively reinforcing. Any behavior that decreases the probability of overarousal or increases underarousal may also be included in this category. Since pain, for example, is usually overarousing, behaviors that lead to its avoidance are positively reinforcing. Even the painful consequences of behavior *can* be positively reinforcing. When they are, they increase the tendency for the behavior to recur. The head banging of institutionalized infants noted earlier may be viewed as positively reinforcing merely because it increases arousal. The daydreams and fantasies commonly reported by individuals in monotonous industrial, school, or prison situations are rewarding in the same sense.

There seems little doubt that positive reinforcement following a response increases the probability of the response's recurring. Thus, if a behavior is rewarded but does not increase in frequency, the positive value of the reinforcement may very well be open to question. On the other hand, if an act is rewarded every time it occurs—that is, if there is 100 per cent reinforcement—the organism ultimately ceases to perform it (Hovland, 1936; Calvin, Clifford, Clifford, Bolden, & Harvey, 1956). Although this process has been interpreted in various ways, it may merely indicate that 100 per cent reinforcement becomes monotonous. In other words, it decreases arousal, and the negative reinforcement associated with this decrease overtakes the positive reinforcement resulting from the reduction of specific needs.

Although full reinforcement may bring about the halting of a rewarded behavior, a program of reinforcement composed of smaller proportions of reward proves quite effective in impelling a behavior to recur. Skinner (1938, 1960) experimented with reinforcing organisms both at fixed intervals and at fixed ratios. In the first instance, he supplied reinforcement only once per time interval—once every five minutes in his original studies. In the other, he conferred a reward for every so many occurrences of behavior, such as one reward for every tenth appearance. Organisms learned better, he found, under either of these conditions—and especially under the fixed ratio—than under 100 per cent reinforcement. The organism actually learns best and performs most adequately when there is far less than full reinforcement.

Anyone working with children does not need to be too concerned about reinforcing a child excessively. Even those behaviors that adults most desire to inculcate are usually not rewarded at anywhere near the 100 per cent level, since children often perform them even when adults are not at hand. And often when present, the parent or teacher may be too busy with other things to provide reinforcement. Moreover, it is as important to make certain that the same behavior is not rewarded on some occasions and punished on others as it is natural and good from the standpoint of learning neither to reward desirable behaviors nor to punish undesirable ones all the time.

Behavior, then, is likely to recur when rewarded. That intermittent reward is more effective than constant reinforcement suggests that other factors, perhaps related to arousal, may be significant aspects of the reinforcement, quite apart from its specific capacities to reduce needs and drives.

Punishment. The effects of punishment seem to be more varied than those of reward. If it is severe enough, punishment effectively reduces the frequency of a behavior's occurrence. In research with animals, Masserman (1943) exposed cats to severe shock. A single, very painful exposure was often sufficient to bring about a permanent cessation of the behavior that led to the shock. Bettelheim (1943), in describing his own experiences in a Nazi concentration camp, reported an analogous situation among humans. The harsh punishment of the concentration camp, along with other features of camp life, successfully broke the wills of the inmates and made them innocuous. However, in such situations far more is changed than the behavior that originally occasioned the punishment. Severe punishment is capable of producing catatonic types of psychotic behavior, responses of extreme rage often directed toward the self, and a number of other bizarre symptoms in addition to extinguishing more commonly accepted behaviors.

Within normal limits, punishment may be effective, at times, in various ways. If an organism—rat, dog, child, or adult—strongly tends to respond in a particular way because of past reinforcements, it shows very slight variation in its responses. Suppose, now, that a new behavior is desired to replace the old one. The new behavior must be made to appear so that it can be rewarded. By punishing the original response, the organism gains variability in its behavior, and through this greater variability becomes able to make the desired response with sufficient frequency. In the wake of rewards, the new response grows stronger than the original, and eventually replaces it.

As used in this discussion punishment covers both itself and negative reinforcement. Actually the two terms are not always synonymous; a distinction is often made between them. Punishment refers to painful stimulation for performing an action, whereas negative reinforcement pertains to such stimulation for failing to do something. Thus, the child is punished by spanking for shooting a water pistol in the living room, but is negatively reinforced by spanking for having neglected to wash before eating.

Even relatively mild punishment produces a temporary decline in the frequency of a behavior's appearance. Skinner (1938) first demonstrated this phenomenon in an experiment with rats. Rewarded by food, the animals had learned to press a lever. Then the reward was withdrawn and the response ceased. Half of the rats were never punished; they were merely no longer rewarded. The remaining half were punished by having their paws slapped during the first ten extinction tests. For awhile, the lever-pressing responses of the punished rats stopped. However, by the time that the responses of the unpunished rats were extinguished, the punished rats had made as many lever-pressing responses as the unpunished; their responses were merely postponed. Not long after this study, Estes (1944) discovered that punishment continued for a sufficient time did produce some decrease in the frequency of a response, but that Skinner was essentially right in his belief that the main function of punishment was to delay the occurrence of undesired behaviors.

During the temporary period of inhibition, the organism is more variable in behavior. Thus, the chance of accidentally hitting upon the desired response and being rewarded for it increases. Clearly punishment is helpful in producing changes in behavior. It is effective among humans for another reason as well. Humans tend to "internalize" punishment; they accept it as valid and punish themselves by performing the response that has led to punishment in the past. The toddler who has been punished for turning on the TV set at full volume may be seen to slap himself when approaching the console. He has become self-punishing.

On a less overt level the same self-punishment occurs in the individual who feels guilt. Anthropologists distinguish between societies based on guilt and those based on shame, as we shall observe in Chapter 7. Guilt involves the development of a form of anxiety after performance of an act that is not approved or sometimes after considering the commission of an act that is "bad." Shame, on the other hand, is merely a sense of inferiority at being caught. The individual who experiences guilt engages in self-punishment whereas the person who feels only shame does not. Margaret Mead has suggested that the development of guilt depends on the individual's having loving, concerned, nurturing parents whose disciplinary techniques are based on love (1943, pp. 127–130). If the withdrawal of love is to be punishing, parental love must first be present. But once this withdrawal occurs and has been associated with deviant behavior, the child begins to link anxiety with the consideration or commission of such behaviors and to punish himself. Since the child now carries his own punishment around with him, the extinction of previously punished behaviors becomes relatively permanent. MacKinnon (1962) found that college students who had cheated in an experimental test of honesty had usually been physically punished as children whereas those who did not cheat had been psychologically punished. Similarly Glueck and Glueck (1950) noted that delinquents had been raised by parents who had used a high amount of physical punishment, whereas carefully matched nondelinquents had been raised by parents whose disciplinary techniques were based on love. These data corroborate Mead's ideas and show that the effects of psychological punishment are relatively lasting in their influence on human behavior. Physical punishment, to the contrary, seems to produce more often the psychological state of shame and to have the same temporary impact on behavior as observed by Skinner in his experiments.

Unless extremely severe or traumatic, the punishment of a response may not decrease the organism's tendency to perform it again. Sometimes, as we have seen, it is effective in achieving a temporary reduction in the frequency of a behavior. This reduction may be relatively permanent, of course, if the individual internalizes the punishment. Yet even these patterns are not inevitable. For example, in a study of parent practices and resultant child behavior, Sears, Maccoby, and Levin (1957) noted:

> The unhappy effects of punishment have run like a dismal thread through our findings. Mothers who punished aggressive behavior severely had more aggressive children than mothers who punished lightly. Mothers who punished toilet accidents severely ended up with bedwetting children. Mothers who punished dependency to get rid of it had more dependent children than mothers who did not punish. Harsh physical punishment was associated with high childhood aggressiveness and with the development of feeding problems. Our evaluation of punishment is that it is ineffectual over the long term as a technique for eliminating the kind of behavior toward which it is directed (Sears et al., p. 484).

Quite apparently the forms of punishment to which their findings allude were most often physical in character.

A specific form of punishment found to be extremely disruptive is the random reward and punishment of the same behavior. Pavlov, in his conditioning experiments, observed that requiring a dog to make a distinction between an ellipse and a circle, a task apparently beyond a dog's sensory capacities, produced a breakdown in behavior. In some of his animals this breakdown took the form of aggressive behavior in which the animal would indiscriminately bite himself, his harness, or the researcher. Other dogs would exhibit withdrawn behavior, and still others, stereotyped, compulsive behaviors.

Dogs subjected to this experience generally lost the ability to make simple discriminations that had previously been learned easily. On the basis of this discovery, Pavlov developed a theory of neurosis and spent his final decades working on it (Pavlov, 1941). In the United States Maier (1939) obtained the same results. Requiring organisms which had learned simple discriminations to make finer and finer ones, he rewarded the correct response and punished the other. The process of discriminating became so arduous that the organisms responded by chance. Since they had one chance in two of being right, they were rewarded half the time and punished the rest of the time for responses that, to them, seemed identical. Behaviors became extremely stereotyped and remained so even after discriminations were again made simple.

No doubt the effects of such random or seemingly random reward and punishment, in which the organism cannot distinguish between the rewarded and the punished response, are as detrimental to humans as they are to lower organisms. The analogy to Pavlov's dogs is probably the unfortunate child whose arbitrary parent rules with an iron whim—who punishes a behavior on one occasion and rewards it on another.

Sears, Maccoby, and Levin (1957) indicated that punishment did not eliminate the behavior toward which the punishment is directed. Others who have studied authoritarianism (e.g., Adorno, Frenkel-Brunswik, Levinson, & Sanford, 1950; Block, 1955) and creativity (e.g., MacKinnon, 1962) have suggested that an overly controlling parent reduces a child's curiosity, creative bent, and problem-solving ability. In many cases, the punished child is timider and less counteractive toward adults—although generally more aggressive toward peers. Thus, he may be easier for parents to deal with and control even further. Punishment also helps to establish conflicts of approach and avoidance. Although punishment does not reduce motivation, the fear of it throws the organism into conflict; it still desires the goal at which the punished behavior is aimed, yet is afraid of pursuing it. Conflict of this sort, of course, disrupts behavior.

From this varied evidence, it would seem that punishment has only limited utility in extinguishing a punished act and, on top of this, a number of undesirable side effects. Why, then, do parents, and for that matter why does society, continue to try to control behavior through punishment? First of all, punishment is effective *sometimes;* when it is, it serves as intermittent reinforcement to the punisher. Second, no matter what effect punishment has on the child, it usually makes the parent feel better, at least for awhile. Third, it is traditional to use punishment.

Nonreinforcement. "A response can be permanently weakened only by a sufficient number of unreinforced elicitations . . ." (Estes, 1944). If it is neither rewarded nor punished, it is not reinforced. Western culture, which is evaluative as a rule (Osgood, 1952), judges acts as good or bad and believes accordingly that they should be rewarded or punished. Other cultures are different. Their members merely note whether an act occurs, without taking the extra step of judging it. Perhaps because of this distinction, Westerners scarcely consider nonreinforcement as a possibility, whereas some other cultures make it a major mode of social control. Among Eskimos, for example, even the most permissive parent in American society would be considered quite punitive by their standards. Eskimo children have far wider latitude than American children in making decisions. Errors in judgment or in behavior are not punished. Neither are "bad" behaviors.

They are just not reinforced. They appear to fall into a vacuum since they are ignored and no response is made to them. (However, this ignoring of a behavior or an action may well constitute a punishment in the mind of a child seeking approval.) As both Skinner and Estes point out, the way to extinguish a behavior permanently is neither to punish nor reward it. Sometimes this is a slow technique, but it is more efficient than punishment, if one has the necessary patience and if the child is not killed through neglect in the process, as in the case of a toddler who might cross a busy highway.

Nonreinforcement seems a difficult technique for persons to use in Western culture. Even if a parent attempts to use it to control behavior, the whole Western culture opposes him. Yet both the effectiveness and some of the difficulties of nonreinforcement may be seen in Williams's (1959) succinct description of the elimination of tantrums in a toddler.

One area of psychology in which the effectiveness of this technique is demonstrated is "play therapy." In play therapy, a form of nondirective therapy described by Axline (1947) in which disturbed children spend their time at play, the child is permitted to engage in all behaviors—except hitting the therapist, although sometimes even this is not prohibited. Toys that call forth aggression predominate—water to throw about and flood the room, life-size dolls to punch, dolls which can be dismembered without permanent damage, and toys of a similar sort. The child, assumed to have a great deal of hostility but to be incapable of handling its expression, is placed in a setting where aggression is not only permitted but, in fact, is deliberately provoked. Since all children who are "behavior problems" have been punished in the past, this child, fearing a trap, is usually nonaggressive for a time. Gradually he becomes more aggressive. Upon discovering that aggression is no longer punished the child grows rapidly in aggressiveness, hostility, and destructiveness, both inside and outside the therapeutic situation. Although this increase is quite vexing to parents and others who have to deal with the child, he gradually becomes more manageable and very frequently better adjusted as therapy progresses, despite the unlikelihood of the outside environment changing markedly.

The reduction in problem behavior appears to occur for several reasons. The therapist interacts with the child and presumably provides him with insight and understanding. The child exhausts the vast store of hostility brought into therapy and at the same time learns to express anger in less explosive ways. Finally, the aggressive response is extinguished through nonreinforcement.

The work of Skinner and Estes with lower organisms on punishment and nonreinforcement is directly analogous to the play therapy situation. It may be impossible to use nonreinforcement very widely in Western culture, but play therapy suggests that where it can be applied, it does prove effective in the control of behavior.

SUMMARY

Simple learning may be either respondent or operant. Humans and lower organisms do not differ appreciably in the way they approach learning problems of this kind, nor do they show substantial differences in rates of learning. It is with the introduction of learning sets that wide distinctions may be noted across species, with humans showing considerable superiority. The learning set is a bridge to complex learning and in particular to concept formation at which humans excel. Humans are best at concept formation because of their wider experience, greater ability to transfer training, and language skills. Thinking is another form of complex learning which is considered unique to humans. Children think much the same way as adults although children's thought processes are handicapped chiefly by their smaller stores of information. Closely related to thinking is creativity. Both intellectual and personality traits are associated with creativity, whereas intelligence per se is not. Certain environments are more conducive than others to the development in the child of a problem-solving, creative approach to the world.

All these aspects of behavior, from simple respondent learning to complex creativity, are part of the learning functions of humans. After years of concentrating on those phases of learning common to all organisms and the motivations for learning, researchers are finally acquiring information about the phases that are uniquely human. Although much remains to be learned, psychology has begun to develop considerable understanding of the forces that motivate such higher levels of human functioning as creativity.

The learning of a response presumably depends on the reduction of a need and its related drive. Whereas nonprimates more often tend to act in order to reduce tension or arousal, primates need to maintain arousal. For this reason the latter engage in many learning experiences that are difficult to explain in terms of reducing the tensions produced by the more conventional primary biological needs or the secondary needs stemming from them.

A behavior may be either rewarded, punished, or nonreinforced.

In most cases reward causes behavior to increase. Punishment *sometimes* decreases the frequency of a response, but also has a number of side effects. Nonreinforcement seems most effective in reducing the probability of response but is not likely to be widely used in Western society.

REFERENCES

Adorno, T. W., Frenkel-Brunswik, Else, Levinson, D. J., & Sanford, R. W. *The authoritarian personality.* New York: Harper, 1950.

Alberts, E., & Ehrenfreund, D. Transposition in children as a function of age. *J. exp. Psychol.,* 1951, **41,** 30–38.

Anderson, J. E. Personality organization in children. *Amer. Psychologist,* 1948, **3,** 409–416.

Axline, Virginia. *Play therapy: the inner dynamics of childhood.* Boston: Houghton Mifflin, 1947.

Baldwin, A. L. The effect of home environment on nursery school behavior. *Child Develpm.,* 1949, **20,** 49–62.

Barron, F., & Welsh, G. S. Artistic perception as a possible in personality style: Its measurement by a figure preference test. *J. Psychol.,* 1952, **33,** 199–203.

Bettelheim, B. Individual and mass behavior in extreme situations. *J. abnorm. soc. Psychol.,* 1943, **38,** 417–452.

Birch, H. G. The role of motivational factors in insightful problem solving. *J. comp. Psychol.,* 1945, **43,** 259–278.

Block, J. Personality characteristics associated with fathers' attitudes toward child rearing. *Child Develpm.,* 1955, **26,** 41–48.

Brackbill, Yvonne. Experimental research with children in the Soviet Union. *Amer. Psychologist,* 1960, **15,** 226–233.

Bronfenbrenner, U. The role of age, sex, class, and culture in studies of moral development. *Relig. Educ.* (Research Supplement), 1962, **57,** S3–S17.

Calvin, A. D., Clifford, L. T., Clifford, B., Bolden, L., & Harvey, J. Experimental validation of conditioned inhibition. *Psychol. Rep.,* 1956, **2,** 51–56.

Casler, L. Maternal deprivation: a critical review of the literature. *Monogr. soc. Res. Child Develpm.,* 1961, **26,** Serial No. 80, No. 2.

Dennis, W. Piaget's questions applied to a child of known environment. *J. genet. Psychol.,* 1942, **60,** 307–320.

Dennis, W. Animistic thinking among college and university students. *Sci. Mo.,* 1953, **76,** 247–250.

Deutsche, Jean M. The development of children's concepts of causal relations. *Univer. Minn. Inst. Child Welf. Monogr.,* Minneapolis, Minn., 1937.

Drevdahl, J. E. Factors of importance for creativity. *J. clin. Psychol.,* 1956, **12,** 21–26.

Estes, W. K. An experimental study of punishment. *Psychol. Monogr.,* 1944, **57,** No. 263.

Fehmi, L. G. The formation of learning sets in severely retarded brain injured and familial children. *Proc. Spartan Psychol. Assn.,* San Jose, Calif., 1960.

Fowler, W. Cognitive learning in infancy and early childhood. *Psychol. Bull.*, 1962, **59**, 116–152.

Glueck, S., & Glueck, Eleanor. *Unraveling juvenile delinquency.* New York: Commonwealth Fund, 1950.

Greenacre, Phyllis. The family romance of the artist. *Psychoanal. Stud. Child,* 1958, **13**, 9–43.

Guilford, J. P. Creativity. *Amer. Psychologist,* 1950, **5**, 444–454.

Harlow, H. F. The formation of learning sets. *Psychol. Rev.,* 1949, **56**, 51–65.

Harlow, H. F. The nature of love. *Amer. Psychologist,* 1958, **13**, 673–685.

Hebb, D. O. Drives and the C.N.S. (conceptual nervous system). *Psychol. Rev.,* 1955, **62**, 243–253.

Hoffman, M. L. The role of the parent in the child's moral growth. *Relig. Educ.* (Research Supplement), 1962, **57**, S18–S33.

Houston, J. P., & Mednick, S. A. Creativity and the need for novelty. *J. abnorm. soc. Psychol.,* 1963, **66**, 137–141.

Hovland, C. I. "Inhibition of reinforcement" and phenomena of experimental extinction. *Proc. Nat. Acad. Sci.* (Washington, D. C.), 1936, **22**, 430–433.

Huang, I., & Lee, H. W. Experimental analysis of child animism. *J. genet. Psychol.,* 1945, **66**, 69–74.

Huxley, A. L. *Brave new world.* Garden City, N. Y.: Doubleday, Doran, 1932.

Inhelder, Barbel, & Matalon, B. The study of problem solving and thinking. In P. Mussen (Ed.), *Handbook of research methods in child development.* New York: Wiley, 1960. Pp. 421–455.

Jacobsen, T. L., & Asher, J. J. Validity of the concept constancy measure of creative problem solving. *J. genet. Psychol.,* 1963, **68**, 9–20.

Johnson, R. C. A study of children's moral judgments. *Child Develpm.,* 1962, **33**, 327–354.

Johnson, R. C. Linguistic structure as a variable in concept formation and concept content. *Psychol. Bull.,* 1962, **59**, 468–476.

Johnson, R. C., & Petit, L. Mathematical and other concepts of a child of known environment. Univer. of Hawaii, 1964, in preparation.

Johnson, R. C., & Thomson, C. W. Incidental and intentional learning under three conditions of motivation. *Amer. J. Psychol.,* 1962, **75**, 284–288.

Koch, Margaret B., & Meyer, D. R. A relationship of age to learning set formation in the preschool child. *J. comp. physiol. Psychol.,* 1959, **52**, 387–389.

Kuenne, Margaret R. Experimental investigation of the relation of language to transposition behavior in young children. *J. exp. Psychol.,* 1946, **36**, 471–490.

Leitch, Mary, & Escalona, Sybille. The reactions of infants to stress. *Psychoanal. Stud. Child,* Vol. 5. New York: International Univer. Press, 1949.

Liu, C. H., The influence of cultural background on the moral judgment of children. Unpublished Ph.D. dissertation, Columbia Univer., New York, 1950.

McBain, W. N. Noise, the "arousal hypothesis," and monotonous work. *J. appl. Psychol.,* 1961, **45**, 309–317.

McCurdy, H. G. The childhood pattern of genius. *J. Elisha Mitchell Sci. Society,* 1957, **73**, 448–462. (Also in R. A. King [Ed.], *Readings for an introduction to psychology.* New York: McGraw-Hill, 1961.)

MacKinnon, D. W. Violation of prohibitions. In H. A. Murray (Ed.), *Explorations in personality.* New York: Oxford Univer. Press, 1938. Pp. 491–501.

MacKinnon, D. W. The nature and nurture of creative talent. *Amer. Psychologist,* 1962, **17**, 484–495.

Maier, N. R. F. *Studies of abnormal behavior in the rat: the neurotic pattern and an analysis of the situation which produces it.* New York: Harper, 1939.

Maine, Sir H. S. *Ancient law.* London: Murray, 1861.

Marquis, Dorothy P. Can conditioned responses be established in the newborn infant? *J. genet. Psychol.*, 1931, 39, 479–492.

Masserman, T. H. *Behavior and neurosis.* Chicago: Univer. of Chicago Press, 1943.

Mead, Margaret. *And keep your powder dry.* New York: Morrow, 1943.

Osgood, C. E. The nature and measurement of meaning. *Psychol. Bull.*, 1952, 49, 197–237.

Pavlov, I. P. *Conditioned reflexes.* (Trans. by G. V. Anrep.) London: Oxford Univer. Press, 1927.

Pavlov, I. P. *Conditioned reflexes and psychiatry.* (Trans. by W. H. Gantt.) New York: International Publishers, 1941.

Piaget, J. *The child's conception of physical causality.* London: Routledge and K. Paul, 1930. (a)

Piaget, J. *The child's conception of the world.* New York: Harcourt, Brace, 1930. (b)

Piaget, J. *The moral judgment of the child.* London: K. Paul, Trench, Trubner, 1932.

Piaget, J. *The origins of intelligence in children.* New York: International Univer. Press, 1952.

Piaget, J. How children form mathematical concepts. *Sci. Amer.*, 1953, 189, 74–79.

Razran, G. The observable unconscious and the inferrible conscious in current Soviet psychophysiology: interoceptive conditioning, semantic conditioning, and the orienting reflex. *Psychol. Rev.*, 1961, 68, 81–147.

Reid, J. B., King, F. J., & Wickwire, P. Cognitive and other personality characteristics of creative children. *Psychol. Rep.*, 1959, 5, 729–737.

Rosenzweig, S. Further comparative data on repetition-choice after success and failure as related to frustration tolerance. *J. genet. Psychol.*, 1945, 66, 75–81.

Russell, R. W. Studies in animism. II. The development of animism. *J. genet. Psychol.*, 1940, 56, 353–366.

Russell, R. W., & Dennis, W. Studies of animism. I. A standardized procedure for the investigation of animism. *J. genet. Psychol.*, 1939, 55, 389–400.

Sears, R. R., Maccoby, Eleanor, & Levin, H. *Patterns of child rearing.* Evanston, Ill.: Row, Peterson, 1957.

Skinner, B. F. *The behavior of organisms.* New York: Appleton-Century-Crofts, 1938.

Skinner, B. F. Are theories of learning necessary? *Psychol. Rev.*, 1950, 57, 193–216.

Skinner, B. F. Reinforcement today. *Amer. Psychologist*, 1958, 13, 94–99.

Skinner, B. F. Pigeons in a pelican. *Amer. Psychologist*, 1960, 15, 28–37.

Spelt, D. K. The conditioning of the human fetus *in utero.* *J. exp. Psychol.*, 1948, 38, 338–346.

Terman, L. M. The discovery and encouragement of exceptional talent. *Amer. Psychologist*, 1954, 9, 221–230.

Thorndike, E. L. *Educational psychology.* New York: Teachers College, 1913.

Torrance, E. P. Explorations in creative thinking. *Education*, 1960, 81, 216–220.

Voeks, Virginia. Sources of apparent animism in students. *Sci. Mo.*, 1954, 79, 406–407.

Watson, J. B. *Psychology from the standpoint of a behaviorist.* Philadelphia: Lippincott, 1919.

Watson, J. B., & Morgan, J. J. B. Emotional reactions and psychological experimentation. *Amer. J. Psychol.*, 1917, **28**, 163–174.

Watson, J. B., & Rayner, Rosalie. Conditioned emotional reactions. *J. exp. Psychol.*, 1920, **3**, 1–14.

Welsh, G. S. *Welsh Figure Preference Test: Preliminary manual.* Palo Alto, Calif.: Consulting Psychologists Press, 1959.

Werner, H. *Comparative psychology of mental development.* (Rev. ed.) New York: International Univer. Press, 1957.

Wickens, D. D., & Wickens, Carol. A study of conditioning in the neonate. *J. exp. Psychol.*, 1940, **26**, 94–102.

Williams, C. C. The elimination of tantrum behavior by extinction procedures. *J. abnorm. soc. Psychol.*, 1959, **59**, 269.

Wilson, R. C., Guilford, J. P., & Christensen, P. R. The measurement of individual differences in originality. *Psychol. Bull.*, 1953, **50**, 362–370.

chapter 5 ✳ Language

The tools of communication are of two kinds. All organisms use signs and signals, but symbols are unique to humans. Symbolic communication, or language, is so closely related to learning that any attempt to separate them, even for purposes of discussion, is doomed to failure because of the tightness of their bond. Equally allied, as we shall see eventually, are language and memory. Since human achievement rests on both learning and memory, language, their common kin, is the central force in man's dominance over his environment.

Animals make a variety of sounds; in fact, a sound count published by Yerkes and Learned (1925) renders it possible to determine the relative frequency of different sounds uttered by chimpanzees. These utterances are specific and occur only in a single context. One cry may signify "food," another, "danger," but they cannot be used in a new sense. Nor are two sounds ever combined to form a third sound distinct from the original two. These vocalizations refer to immediate situations, to the present danger and not to the danger of five minutes ago nor to the danger yet to be discerned. Thus, only objects or events that have been sensed can give rise to utterances. These sounds and other sign or signal types of communication in lower organisms are often compelling, for the animal exposed to a stimulus *must* respond to it.

In contrast, human symbolic behavior is highly varied. Humans are capable of emitting many sounds, each of which can be used in any combination with a large number of other sounds. Any single sound or group of sounds may have several meanings that are based on mutual agreement rather than on some innate response mechanism. Human speech can deal with the abstract or nonphysical and, in the case of the physical, with the past and future as effectively as the present. It can also handle objects out of visual range as well as those sensed at the moment of vocalization. Although highly informative, human communication, unlike the communication of lower organisms, is not compelling.

Language permits the communication of information from one generation to the next. Since the wisdom as well as the errors of the past are thus available to the present generation without the necessity of having to learn by direct imitation, a fuller mastery of the environment is possible. Moreover, symbolic behavior through its intricacies enables individuals to understand one another better. With this understanding comes an increased prospect for cooperation and for the development of feelings. It is language that separates humans most clearly from all other organisms. In this chapter we shall first consider the normal development of language in childhood, then individual differences in language development, and finally, the impact of language on thought, learning, and memory.

THE COURSE OF LANGUAGE DEVELOPMENT

The first sound uttered by a child is its cry at birth. Most of its vocalizing of the next few months falls under the heading of crying. Early crying consists of vowel sounds, Lewis (1959) has pointed out, especially a-a-a-a as in *fat*. Some of the sounds of the English language are difficult, if not impossible, to make before one has teeth, since several of them depend on the action of the tongue against the teeth. Other sounds are difficult for other reasons. But soon after birth the change from vowel cries to consonant-vowel combinations commences. Some sounds involving oral movements like those occurring in sucking—for example, *ba-ba*—come to be associated with comfort whereas others—for example, *na-na* with a nasal *a*—are linked to states of discomfort (Lewis, 1959). Consonants then increase in proportion to vowels (Irwin & Chen, 1946). Within a few months after birth, the child makes a wide assortment of sounds and by about a year of age is capable of uttering most of the different sounds used in the various languages of mankind (Irwin, 1947a, 1947b, 1948).

Theories abound as to how humans progress from babbling to speaking meaningful words. Primates are noisy creatures as a rule, but it seems probable that the association of sounds with comfort, as in a mother's conversation when changing, feeding, and bathing an infant, causes sounds to become somewhat rewarding in themselves. The child receives pleasure through his own production of sounds. Sound making is thus reinforced and increases in frequency. In somewhat different ways both Mowrer (1950) and Miller and Dollard (1941) emphasize the emotive quality of early sound making. It is very pleasant for a parent to lie abed in the morning, soon after the sun comes up, and listen to a baby babbling in his crib. Although part of the pleasure comes from not having to get up, some of it reflects the apparent joy of the infant as he works through his storehouse of sounds. It is this joy that is considered the first step in meaningful communication (Mowrer, 1950; Miller & Dollard, 1941).

The English language does not contain all the sounds made by humans in communication. The French rolling *r*, the German umlauts, the Zulu or Bushman tongue-clicks, and some of the sounds the Swede must make to pronounce the name *Skjellbjörn* are foreign to the English-speaking adult. Yet infants in any culture can make them all, although those not found in English disappear quite rapidly in American and other English-speaking children. When the infant or young child in the English-speaking orbit utters foreign sounds, his parents more often look baffled and do not reinforce the sound-making behavior. The parents do, however, directly reinforce the sounds germane to English by parental attention and also by making the sounds themselves. This provides the sounds with an indirect or secondary rewarding quality. Through reward of sounds found in a language and nonreinforcement of others alien to it, the infant begins to utter more often those sounds to be used later by him in forming words.

Use of Words

Some sounds occur more frequently than others in infant vocalization, and it is to these that adults attach meaning. Since infants in all cultures often make the same sounds, the basic infant vocabulary of all languages is common, even though cultures differ in the association of specific sounds with specific meanings. In English-speaking homes, the child utters the sound *ma-ma* and the meaning *mother* is attached to it. But in other cultures *ama* is mother, and in still others, *da-da*. In some languages *ama* means grandmother; elsewhere it is nurse. To Americans *baba* signifies baby but to many Slavic peoples it means grandmother. And so on. Adults grasp at the sounds uttered frequently by children in babbling and invest them with meanings according to the cultures in which they live. This process hastens the learning of language, for the child now makes sounds denoted as words and reinforced as words.

From reiterated infant sounds, therefore, come the first words. Often they are recognized by the parents as words having specific meaning but not necessarily the same meaning they have for the child. A boy of six months said "da-da" on his father's return from work each day. Although this gratified the father, it later developed that the response was a rather low-level, conditioned reaction to a situation in which the father was present. The da-da was associated with him but did not mean father to the child. Much later, the child, upon acquiring an understanding that words denote physical things, began naming behavior and thus developed speech. Now he dropped the da-da altogether and referred to both parents as "ma-ma" for several months.

Although the young child may be capable of emitting sounds without knowing their denotations, it is more common for him, so far as adults can tell, to become aware first of a word's meaning and then attempt to approximate its sound in order to convey that meaning. Humans of all ages, of course, understand the meaning of words they do not articulate. The young child has an awareness of many word meanings even though he cannot yet emit them. Through the constant association of word with stimulus in a wide variety of settings, he recognizes that the sound combinations that man calls words have meaning. This is where speech begins.

Parents are famous (or fatuous) for their understanding of their children's utterances. Although they doubtless find meanings even where none is intended, they also understand the approximations employed by one- and two-year-olds which are incomprehensible to strangers. One little boy living in a wet climate, for example, said "Ne-Ne-Lah-Lah." This is a relatively difficult sound pattern to decipher; what the child meant was "Roni's (his sister's) umbrella." Actually, the syllables have a number of meanings. They can mean "It is raining," "Roni has her umbrella," "I want her umbrella," or "Here comes Roni with her umbrella," depending on the inflection of the sounds. From such slender roots, consisting of primitive sound groups that only in a very limited sense approximate the words they are intended to signify, yet that *have meaning for both speaker and listener*, stems symbolic communication.

Infants utter words such as da-da even before it is likely that they attribute sense to them or even know that words have meaning. Quite possibly infants may have their own meanings for words which adults cannot apprehend. Yet symbolic communication requires agreement in meaning between speaker and listener. Symbolic communication is a two-way affair; it cannot occur in a vacuum, nor can it take place unless the listener understands the speaker's utterances. Because understanding is essential, it is hard to ascertain when the first word appears in infant speech.

Available data suggest that a child's first word is uttered at about one year of age (McCarthy, 1946). Averages, however, are not always reliable. Gifted children are advanced in speech (Terman, 1925), whereas retarded children are slow in developing it. In fact, retarded children are infantile in speech, using fewer consonants and more vowels than normal children of the same age (Irwin, 1942). Nevertheless, although early speech is a reasonably good indication of general precocity, delayed speech is not, of itself, a portent of later deficiency. Some children are slow in developing speech merely because they have received little reinforcement and others because their mothers are so solicitous that their demands are met without having to speak. Some, of course, are behind in speech development owing to sensory or intellectual weaknesses, whereas others are retarded for no discernible reason at all.

Once a child has begun to speak, there are two ways to determine the number of words in his vocabulary. The first is to spend enough time with a child to hear every word he knows. Leopold (1937–1949) kept an accurate diary of the speech development of his daughter from the eighth week to the seventh year of her life. Although word counting was quite incidental to his major purpose, this diary is an excellent example of the approach in which *all* words the child says become part of a vocabulary score. The more common method for studying language growth is to select a sample of words and then present a child with pictures or other stimuli capable of leading him to say the word if he knows it. From the child's responses to this sample of words, his total vocabulary can be estimated. Table 5-1 presents data gathered through this technique by Smith (1926) in her study of vocabulary extensiveness.

Although these figures indicate the rapid increase in verbal comprehension, especially between two-and-a-half and three years, they do not say anything by themselves about the range of individual differences. Among the 25 children Shirley (1933) studied from birth to

TABLE 5-1 Number of Words
Known by Children of Different Ages

Age in Months	Number of Words	Gain
8	0	
10	1	1
12	3	2
15	10	16
18	22	8
21	118	96
24	272	154
30	446	174
36	896	450
42	1222	326
48	1540	318
54	1870	330
60	2072	202
66	2289	217
72	2562	273

two years of age, the number of words spoken in the presence of examiners just prior to their second birthdays varied from six to 126. This was a tremendous range for a normal population.

By about four the ordinary child has learned all the rules of the English language and has developed sufficient vocabulary for quite effective communication. His errors beyond this point generally result not from ignorance but from too much faith in the sensibility of language. The child says, "I wented," a usage not allowed in English. But why is "wented" any less correct than "wanted"? The suffix *ed* frequently denotes past tense. The child learns the rule only to discover that the English language does not always follow its rules too rigorously. As he grows older, language development consists of increasing the complexity and breadth of word usage and of learning the exceptions to the rules.

INDIVIDUAL DIFFERENCES IN LANGUAGE DEVELOPMENT

The high amount of variability among children in rates of language development has impelled psychologists to run down the sources of these individual differences. To a degree language skills depend on maturation. Language requires a highly accurate control of tongue and lip movements; like most motor behaviors, this control is largely maturational in its development.

Sex Difference

One would naturally expect girls to excel boys in language skills because females mature more rapidly than males. Most of the earlier studies of sex differences in language development show female superiority in vocabulary, articulation, length of sentences, complexity, and grammatical correctness up through the age of about ten (see McCarthy, 1946, pp. 551–555). As to sheer number of words spoken, girls again lead (Jersild & Ritzman, 1938). Reasonable as it may seem to attribute this feminine superiority to maturational factors, this may not entirely be the case. Several recent studies (Sampson, 1959; Templin, 1957; Winitz, 1959) have found few sex differences in verbal facility. Environmental considerations may be involved; forces that once favored girls may have become more equal in their influence. As we shall see, environmental changes over a period of time have reduced other areas of individual differences. These same shifts may well have reduced sex differences, too.

Family Size and Structure

The average three-year-old uses a vocabulary of about 500 words as compared to the average adult who uses at least 20,000. Clearly the more that a child associates with adults, the more words he is exposed to, and may learn. The only child is superior in nearly all forms of verbal ability to children with siblings, twins are more retarded than children with siblings (Davis, 1937), and triplets have less verbal facility than twins (Howard, 1934). The Dionne quintuplets were markedly slow in language development (Blatz, 1937). How could the five girls learn to speak at a normal rate since a great deal of their time was spent with one another? There is not much that a toddler can learn from four other, equally naive toddlers. Doubtless the amount of contact a child has with conversation of adult complexity is directly related to the rate of language growth.

Socioeconomic Factors. Family socioeconomic status also bears on the young child's scores on various measures of speech development (Davis, 1937). Children from lower economic homes display some impoverishment in vocabulary and less complex and accurate sentence structure. This may result from the smaller vocabulary used by their parents than by parents in the upper-income brackets. In addition, there is a relation between economic status and family size, the families on the lower rungs of the economic ladder having the larger families. Naturally this disposes the parent to have less contact with any one child. The more contact adults have with infants and young children, the greater is the youngster's likelihood of receiving reinforcement for vocalization, which has been shown to bring about an increase in the frequency of vocal expression (Rheingold, Gewirtz, & Ross, 1959).

The lower-class child, in contrast to the middle-class child, is exposed less often to adult conversation, and when so is probably exposed to a less adequate parental vocabulary. Further, it is likely that he receives less reinforcement for vocalizations. From a purely environmental standpoint, he is handicapped in developing language skills. Whereas IQ tests are heavily laden with verbal questions, Davis (1948) has argued that environmental, *not* genetic, factors which influence language development cause the differences between classes in mean IQ scores. Yet even "culture free" intelligence tests make a distinction between children of different classes (e.g., Haggard, 1954). Class differences in IQ, though partly a result of differences in language ability, are discernible apart from any direct bearing of vocabulary.

Deprived Children. Studies over the years of neglected children (Bühler, 1931; Pringle & Bossio, 1958) and of institutional children (Skeels, Updegraff, Wellman, & Williams, 1937; Haggerty, 1959) concur that the lack of adult contact and speech reinforcement occasions considerable retardation of speech among children thus deprived. These four studies found among the children they tested a greater backwardness in language than in any other area of development. To the extent that communication is limited, all other aspects of development are handicapped. Nevertheless, the effect of severe language retardation can be transitory. Tutoring and enrichment of the environment are capable of producing marked, rapid, and permanent language gains in previously retarded youngsters (Dawe, 1942; Luria & Yudovich, 1959; Skeels et al., 1938).

The Bilingual Child. Great numbers of Americans in the past grew up knowing the language of their immigrant parents as well as English. Now again as the nation's isolation dissolves in a shrinking, contemporary world, a growing proportion of young Americans are learning two languages. Working in Hawaii, Smith (1939) observed that bilingual children were distinctly retarded in speech development. The deficiency was so pronounced that at school-entrance age the bilingual child was about equal in language skills to a *haole* (how-lee = Caucasian) monoglot three years old. Smith noted that both bilingualism and pidgin English might be involved in this retardation. The bilingual children were probably not exposed to standard English to any marked degree, but instead learned pidgin, the *lingua franca* of the Pacific. This bogus tongue of 600 to 700 words that could be easily learned by all evolved from an admixture of many races and languages.

Except for a few individual cases, the Smith study did not compare true bilinguals. It compared people who spoke English with others who spoke a peculiar and primitive English dialect as well as a rather impoverished Oriental language. Small wonder that these Hawaiian "bilinguals" were retarded. It was not bilingualism per se that seemed likely to have caused their deficiency, but rather the poverty of the languages they used.

At the other extreme is the upper-class European tradition of ordering the environment in a manner that produces bilingual, trilingual, or even polylingual children. Although empirical data are largely lacking, the learning of several languages, when each of them is used at high level by adults in the environment, appears to have no harmful effects. In Leopold's four-volume description (1937–1949) of his daughter's language development, he told of how she was brought up as a bilingual in German and English. His account was an argument for the assertion that learning two languages need not retard language development.

Several factors enter into the successful rearing of a bilingual child who is fully competent in both tongues. The languages themselves must be bona fide languages, not simple dialects. Each language should be learned from a different source (Smith, 1939); for example, each parent might communicate with the child in only one of the two languages. It seems important for the child to become aware, as soon as possible, that the two languages are distinct from one another. Having separate speakers for each tongue is one way of handling this problem. Using the languages at different times or in different contexts might also serve this purpose. Finally, to produce a truly bilingual child, it would seem imperative to maintain situations in which each of the languages must be used. Most bilingual children have bilingual parents; if the parents respond to one language more than the other, the child will gradually cease using the less established one in the interest of communicating with as little effort as necessary.

Recent Changes

As we have seen, it was believed years ago that in language skills girls were superior to boys, children with many adult and few child associations excelled those with few adult and many child associations, and children from lower-economic backgrounds lagged behind children from upper-economic homes. This is no longer entirely so. Signs of decrease in the differences in some of these areas are evident. Templin (1957) noted that children in her study of language development were generally more talkative and used a more mature level and organization of speech than children studied 25 years earlier. Sex differences seemed substantially diminished, and although socioeconomic differences continued to be significant, they had apparently decreased in magnitude.

Television may be a very important factor in this change. It produces a general improvement in the language skill of young children at the same time that it narrows the variations between children exposed to different environmental circumstances. Two of the most intensive studies of television's impact on the child (Himmelweit, Oppenheim, & Vince, 1958; Schramm, Lyle, & Parker, 1961) agree that television increases the information—and presumably, the vocabulary —of all children, but that children of lesser ability and from lower economic backgrounds receive more benefit and for a longer time.

Take two hypothetical situations. Child A, five years old, comes from a lower economic group. Because of the pressures on them, his parents spend little time with the child, thus seldom serving as models and as reinforcers. Their vocabulary is relatively impoverished so that they are less adequate than others as models. Child A spends much time with siblings aged two, three, and six, who have a combined vocabulary of about 2500 words. The family purchases a television set and Child A spends 25 hours a week in front of it. The average vocabulary to which he is now exposed is probably well above 15,000 words since even comic strips and comic books have vocabularies of over 10,000 words (Thorndike, 1941). The television set is more stimulating for language development, so far as providing a model, than the pre-TV environment. Of course, it cannot completely overcome environmental handicaps, since it does not reinforce the child's vocalizations; as Rheingold et al. (1959) have noted, reinforcement of verbal behavior seems likely to determine its quantity—and quality.

Child B, also five years old, is the only child of a nonworking mother and a father who is a member of the medical profession. Both parents are college graduates. Each has a speaking vocabulary of approximately 30,000 words. They spend a good deal of time talking to the child and they read stories aloud to him every night before bedtime. The child has much exposure to adults, including visitors, grandparents, and neighbors as well as parents. Introduction of a television set into this child's life sharply reduces the amount of verbal stimulation he receives during every hour spent viewing.

Although television does narrow the differences in the way of life between families of separate regions and classes, it has not been able to eliminate individual differences between children in areas so influenced by environment as language because of its inability to provide the necessary reinforcement.

Stuttering

Even if stuttering, in its own right, might well be omitted from a text in child psychology, certain findings pertinent to its basis have wide implications for the whole area of problem behavior. Although other speech problems, such as the substitution of sounds, tend to vanish speedily as a function of age, stuttering is rather persistent. As such, it has evoked wide interest. Various theories have attempted to account for this phenomenon. A pleasant and chivalrous explanation of stuttering is the "dirty word" theory. This view elucidates stuttering by saying that children learn profane and obscene words among their playmates. They come home and in talking begin to say these words. They catch themselves in time and block their speech, so that instead of saying, "Pass the damn sugar," they say, "Pass the d-d-d-d sugar." Stammering and stuttering emerge from these dirty words, and the child becomes a stutterer. Since six to eight times as many boys stutter as do girls, this theory rests on the assumption that boys swear among their mates six to eight times as often as girls. This may be chivalry but it is hardly scientific.

A second, older theory involves cerebral dominance. For the right-handed individual, the left cerebral hemisphere dominates the control of motor responses, whereas the reverse holds true for left-handed persons. The theory of cerebral dominance got its start from the observable fact that there is a connection between handedness—and especially "changed handedness"—and stuttering. The left-handed child, forced into becoming right handed upon entering school, stutters more often than would be expected to occur by chance alone. This observation gave rise to the theory that exercising the right hand had made the cerebral hemispheres equal in dominance, so that neither had control, whereupon stuttering resulted. However, this explanation accounted neither for sex differences in stuttering nor for the fact that few stutterers stuttered equally in all situations. If a physiological mechanism is of prime significance, it is difficult to understand why most stutterers stutter with adults but not with animals, or babies, or when alone. More likely the adults who change children's handedness may also manipulate children in other ways, with the direct manipulation of speech producing the stuttering.

This "manipulation of speech" leads to a third explanation of stuttering, which is now most widely accepted. Johnson (1944) noted wide differences between groups in the incidence of stuttering. American Indians, despite an emphasis on excellence in speaking, had no stutterers—and, in fact, have no word in their languages to denote stuttering. Indians assume that all children will speak well if one merely waits. Johnson began to suspect that parent attitudes, more than child articulation, caused stuttering. Intensive studying demonstrated that this was indeed the case; that stuttering developed after diagnosis. This fact formed the basis of Johnson's semantic or diagnosogenic theory of stuttering (Johnson, 1946).

All human beings have nonfluencies in their speech—that is, stammering and stuttering. This is primary stuttering. Young children have more of it than adults. Within any age and either sex the individual variations in the proportions of nonfluency are considerable. Although a few children are so pronouncedly nonfluent that almost any parent would diagnose them as stutterers, the nonfluency of most children lies in a range that may or may not cause parents to show concern over their speech development. If a parent is concerned when a child blocks on a word or stutters and responds frequently with such comments as, "Start over again and talk more slowly" or "You'd better be careful and talk slowly—you're beginning to stutter," the child becomes anxious and thus has more nonfluencies. Some things are done best, however, when humans are not conscious of them. Speech is one of these. As a child's speech deteriorates, the parent is increasingly inclined to diagnose him as a stutterer. It is this diagnosis by parents, or teachers, or others, plus the child's acceptance of it that makes him a stutterer. He is now a secondary stutterer. Once an individual accepts this status and becomes aware of his nonfluencies, his stuttering worsens and he takes to using "tic-like" behaviors in the vain hope of reducing it. A considerable body of findings (e.g., see Johnson, 1955, 1959) supports this theory of stuttering.

Here is a clear case of the effect on behavior of the assignment and acceptance of a social role. Perhaps less fluent than most other children, very likely as a result of biological causes, the child is given the role of stutterer, accepts the role, and becomes a *secondary* stutterer rather than remaining a primary stutterer with a larger proportion of nonfluencies than usual. The point of all this is that if humans can make stutterers by diagnosis, perhaps they can produce other problem behaviors such as delinquency or illiteracy with the same techniques. The experience of Lecky (1945) with intellectually competent young people who could not learn to read certainly adds fuel to this fire.

THE IMPACT OF LANGUAGE ON THOUGHT, LEARNING, AND MEMORY

Language and Thought

Many of the early psychologists conceived of thought as a stream of mental images. To understand the thought process, they believed, one had to look inward, to *introspect,* to discern this flow of images. The "Würzburg school" of psychologists (see Humphrey, 1951, pp. 30–131) demonstrated, however, that thought could occur without any conscious awareness of imagery. As a result, the Würzburgers as well as the descendants of the imagery school of thought, led by Titchener, emphasized the relation of muscle tensions and other kinesthetic-proprioceptive responses to thought. This idea, that thought is primarily a set of motor behaviors, was brought to fruition by Watson (1914) who believed that human thought was nothing but subvocal speech. It was at this point that language reached its peak as an explanatory device: to many psychologists of this era language was not merely associated with thought, it *was* thought.

This view is not without support. Young children do speak without the intent of communicating to others and appear to be overtly verbalizing their thoughts, just as adults may covertly verbalize them. This observable phenomenon is the basis of Piaget's (1926) notion of children's egocentric speech—speech not based on the idea of social communication. Even as adults, people "think out loud," talking to themselves especially when confronted with complicated problems.

Further, lip, tongue, and laryngeal movement increases among individuals as they silently solve problems of an increasing challenge (Jacobson, 1932). Yet despite this supporting evidence, the notion that language and thought are synonymous is generally rejected. It seems more likely that the movement of lip, tongue, and larynx accompanying thought are incidental consequences having no more significance than the snapping of fingers or the scratching of the head has when attempting to recollect a forgotten event. Several studies, beginning with Thorson's (1925), suggest that the motor accompaniments of thought are a nervous discharge rather than necessary substrata of thought. Although not synonymous with thought, language seems to be intimately related to learning and memory, as we shall discover in the remainder of this chapter.

Language and Learning

The relation of language to learning was mentioned in the previous chapter. There it was said that language benefited learning by allowing a higher degree of—and more rapid—vicarious trial and error than occurred in other species. Language facilitates the formation of concrete concepts, providing a common name—for example, spoon—to link together a class of objects with a variety of physical characteristics despite their external variations. Because verbal terms are available, they govern the dimensions along which categories form and set the limits for the generalizing of stimuli. This leads to concept formation. Moreover, language enables the formation of abstract concepts as well.

Language not only facilitates learning. In many (e.g., Ervin, 1960; Kuenne, 1946) but not all (e.g., Kendler, Kendler, & Wells, 1960) studies, it also produces a more adequate transfer. Here are two examples of the effect of language on learning. The first is from the autobiography of Helen Keller, deaf and blind from infancy; at the age of seven her beloved teacher, Annie Sullivan, returned her to the world, by making her aware of symbolic communication. Miss Keller describes her awakening to an awareness of language in her book, *The Story of My Life.*

> . . . The morning after my teacher came she led me into her room and gave me a doll. The little blind children at the Perkins Institution had sent it and Laura Bridgman had dressed it; but I did not know this until afterward. When I had played with it a little while, Miss Sullivan slowly spelled into my hand the word "d-o-l-l." I was at once interested in this finger play and tried to imitate it. When I finally succeeded in making the letters correctly I was flushed with childish pleasure and

pride. Running downstairs to my mother I held up my hand and made the letters for doll. I did not know that I was spelling a word or even that words existed; I was simply making my fingers go in monkey-like imitation. In the days that followed I learned to spell in this uncomprehending way a great many words, among them *pin, hat, cup* and a few verbs like *sit, stand* and *walk*. But my teacher had been with me several weeks before I understood that everything has a name.

One day, while I was playing with my new doll, Miss Sullivan put my big rag doll into my lap also, spelled "d-o-l-l" applied to both. Earlier in the day we had had a tussle over the words "m-u-g" and "w-a-t-e-r." Miss Sullivan had tried to impress it upon me that "m-u-g" is *mug* and that "w-a-t-e-r" is *water*, but I persisted in confounding the two. In despair she had dropped the subject for the time, only to renew it at the first opportunity. I became impatient at her repeated attempts and, seizing the new doll, I dashed it upon the floor. I was keenly delighted when I felt the fragments of the broken doll at my feet. Neither sorrow nor regret followed my passionate outburst. I had not loved the doll. In the still, dark world in which I lived there was no strong sentiment or tenderness. I felt my teacher sweep the fragments to one side of the hearth, and I had a sense of satisfaction that the cause of my discomfort was removed. She brought me my hat, and I knew I was going out into the warm sunshine. This thought, if a wordless sensation may be called a thought, made me skip with pleasure.

We walked down the path to the well-house, attracted by the fragrance of the honeysuckle with which it was covered. Some one was drawing water and my teacher placed my hand under the spout. As the cool stream gushed over one hand she spelled into the other the word *water*, first slowly, then rapidly. I stood still, my whole attention fixed upon the motions of her fingers. Suddenly I felt a misty consciousness as of something forgotten—a thrill of returning thought; and somehow the mystery of language was revealed to me. I knew then that "w-a-t-e-r" meant the wonderful cool something that was flowing over my hand. That living word awakened my soul, gave it light, hope, joy, set it free! There were barriers still, it is true, but barriers that could in time be swept away.

I left the well-house eager to learn. Everything had a name, and each name gave birth to a new thought. As we returned to the house every object which I touched seemed to quiver with life. That was because I saw everything with the strange, new sight that had come to me. On entering the door I remembered the doll I had broken. I felt my way to the hearth and picked up the pieces. I tried vainly to put them together. Then my eyes filled with tears; for I realized what I had done, and for the first time I felt repentance and sorrow.

I learned a great many new words that day. I do not remember what they all were; but I do know that *mother, father, sister, teacher* were among them—words that were to make the world blossom for me, "like Aaron's rod, with flowers." It would have been difficult to find a happier child than I was as I lay in my crib at the close of that eventful day and lived over the joys it had brought me, and for the first time longed for a new day to come (Keller, 1917, pp. 22–24).

This is not only a testimonial to the role of language in learning, it is also a moving example of insightful learning.

The other illustration of the effect of language on learning is drawn from a study by Luria and Yudovich (1959) of a pair of twins who were retarded in speech development. Although both were defective in speech, one twin was more deficient than the other. The two were separated for a large part of their waking hours and the more retarded twin (Twin A) was given training in language development. Following this training, both twins were exposed to various test situations. This is a description of one of these tests:

> Both children are asked to play out several examples of a game which involves attaching conditional meanings to objects. They are told that the pencil is "mama"; the vase, "a tree"; the spoon, "a wolf," etc. The game, which comprises subject matter covering corresponding things, is played out with the aid of the objects.
>
> The differences between the twins are here very substantial.
>
> Twin A deciphers the meaning of the gesture game at once, during manipulation of objects; decoding does not present any difficulties to him and he immediately describes the whole game verbally; "The engine drives along, the mother wolf runs, the little wolf goes up the tree, mama comes out of the house, sits on the engine, takes the boy," etc.
>
> When asked to make up a game independently with the same objects, he does this easily; some of the conditional meanings are retained, others created anew. "Mama caught a hare, the wolf ran to look for the hare, the engine drove along, the hare was in the house with mama, it jumped through the window straight on to the fir-tree. . . ."
>
> The same operation was performed altogether differently by Twin B who had not undergone speech training.
>
> He could not decode the stories related by gestures immediately but was only able to do this in parts and then only in reply to questions put to him. When asked to repeat the game, he repeated it without any changes, as it had been shown to him by gestures, and when asked to give new meanings to the objects he refused (Luria & Yudovich, 1959, pp. 104–105).

Clearly, from these examples and from the studies cited in the previous chapter, language facility has a distinct influence on learning and knowledge.

Language and Memory

Although lower organisms and human infants are not capable of symbolic communication, they are certainly capable of remembering. Memory, as both Watson (1914, 1930) and Guthrie (1952) have held from different theoretical positions, may be at least partly motor. In a simple situation suggested by Tomkins (1961) a motor activity recalls events associated with the activity's original use. An individual is instructed to write his name in letters one inch high at the rate of one letter every five seconds. Not only does his signature look like that of many years ago, but also a flood of associations frequently accompanies the motor act. Similarly, visceral tensions, muscular states, and the like do at times evoke the behaviors tied to them in the past, so that in a sense they constitute a memory system.

Eidetic Imagery. More important, with regard to memory not dependent on symbolic skills, is eidetic imagery (EI). Eidetic imagery, first investigated by German psychologists, especially Jaensch (1931), is essentially synonymous with what is popularly called "photographic memory." EI consists of being able to evoke an extremely clear image or picture of an absent object or event. Upon being tested for ability to recall, the eidetic individual is sometimes 100 per cent accurate, because the visual image evoked has such clarity that every detail of the picture is available to him during the test. Eidetic imagery is not remarkably common at any age, but it seems to decline appreciably in incidence after about the age of nine. The most detailed review of the subject may be found in Klüver (1933). Actually, eidetic imagery has fallen from grace and has not been a live topic for research for many years, perhaps because Jaensch was an apologist for the Nazis.

However, while conducting psychological tests in the public schools, one of the authors of this book came across a boy who, in the course of testing, displayed eidetic talents. The child had been referred for testing because of his difficulty at learning to read. Nevertheless, further testing showed him to be a genuine *eidetiker*. Inspired by this experience, the researcher undertook a larger scale investigation of EI (Zelhart & Johnson, 1959). This study employed nonsense shapes like those shown in Figure 5-1; such shapes have been used with adult populations (Vanderplas & Garvin, 1959) to determine their associative value, that is, the extent to which individuals are reminded of something by sight of the shape.

In the study, the associative values of 48 nonsense shapes were first determined among a sample of third-grade children. These shapes were then classified into the 16 lowest, 16 medium, and 16 highest in associative value for the sample group of children and were presented in individual tests to other third graders who had not been part of the original group. The shapes, cut from masonite, were placed on a checkerboard of 16 squares, one to a square. Following a 30-second exposure, the board was swept clean and the child was told

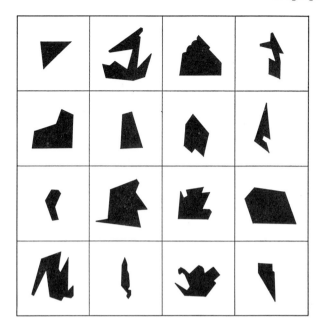

FIGURE 5-1   Nonsense shapes of differing association values (McBain & Johnson, 1963, p. 98; from Vanderplas & Garvin, 1959).

to restore the shapes to their proper places.   It was assumed that any eidetics among the third graders would be able to put back the shapes into the proper squares with a high degree of accuracy, that they would do as well with shapes in the center squares as in the peripheral ones, and that they would do equally well on the three classes of shapes, even though these differed in associative value.

The results were generally disappointing.   Children performed the task poorly, despite their evident relish for it.   There was one exception.   Eight children who were remedial readers—actually non-readers—did significantly better than the others and showed a high degree of accuracy in recall.   These findings suggest that eidetic imagery is rare, but that it does exist.   Interestingly enough, high eidetic talent may be related in some way to difficulty in dealing with the symbolic system of reading and writing.

Words and Memory.   Although memory exists without language, language evidently facilitates memory.   To use William James's term, language provides "fish hooks."   As James wrote before the turn of the century, "In mental terms, *the more facts a fact is associated with in the mind, the better possession of it our memory retains.* Each of its associates becomes a hook to which it hangs, a means to fish it up by when sunk beneath the surface. Together, they form a network of attachments by which it is woven into the entire tissue of our thought" (James, 1892, p. 294).

The more fish hooks or associations a word or an event has, the more likely it is to be recalled. Thus, as the child's vocabulary grows, learning and retention increase. In view of this, children's textbooks are written with a concern for word frequency. Words are selected from those most frequently used in the English language for two reasons. First, if they occur often enough it is assumed that they have many associations and can thus be learned more readily. Second, once learned, they will be met often in the future and have a greater positive transfer value. Although word frequency and the number of associations evoked by words are correlated, there are many low-frequency words, such as *zoo* or *circus,* with many associations and many high-frequency words, like *the, when,* or *where,* that awaken few associations. Johnson, Frincke, and Martin (1961) have suggested that the choice of words for textbooks might better be based on a large number of associations rather than on word frequency per se, as is now done.

Just as the number of associations evoked by a word seems related to the ease with which it is learned and remembered, so it appears likely that the greater the number of words and associations to words available to the individual, the more adequately will he learn and remember. Part of the variance in rates of learning and in memory between age groups may be due, basically, to differences in vocabulary. Thus, although language is not thought, as was once believed, it is closely linked with both learning and memory.

SUMMARY

Humans are a noisy bunch. Infants make many sounds and make them often. From their sound-making activity emerges language. Sound making becomes emotionally rewarding to the infant, thus increasing the amount of vocalization. Parents selectively reward or reinforce the sounds that are like those of words, thus causing the frequency of certain sounds to increase even more. Certain sounds come to have mutual meaning for the infant and the parent; at this point sound making has become symbolic communication.

Vocabulary growth is slow for a time, and then shows rapid increase at about age three to four. By preschool age the child has successfully learned the ground rules of communication. Henceforth, errors in word usage result from the failure of the English language to follow the rules very closely.

Wide individual differences in communicative skills, especially vocabulary, have been shown to exist between children. The sex of the child, his family's size, his parents' occupational and educational levels, the number of languages spoken in the home, and parental attitudes toward their children's speech are among the factors associated with individual differences. Since IQ, on most intelligence tests, depends largely on language ability, children from lower occupational groups and large families may be unfairly handicapped on such tests. Some presumed handicaps to adequate language development, such as bilingualism, may have been greatly exaggerated in their influence. Quite apparently, increasing homogeneity of the environment is decreasing the individual differences between children in rate of language development.

Although it was once held that the entire thought process was merely subvocal speech, this view is not supported by the majority of research findings. Language does seem to alter and enhance learning and to strengthen memory. All said and done, language is the uniquely human characteristic that sets humanity apart from all other organisms.

REFERENCES

Blatz, W. E., et al. *Collected studies on the Dionne quintuplets.* Toronto: Univer. of Toronto Press, 1937.

Bühler, Charlotte, *Kindheit und Jugend.* (3rd ed.) Leipzig: Hirzel, 1931.

Davis, A. *Social class influences upon learning.* Cambridge, Mass.: Harvard Univer. Press, 1948.

Davis, Edith A. The development of linguistic skill in twins, singletons with siblings, and only children from age five to ten years. Minneapolis: Univer. of Minn. Press, *Inst. Child Welf. Series,* No. 14, 1937.

Dawe, Helen C. A study of the effect of an educational program upon language development and related mental functions in young children. *J. exp. Educ.,* 1942, **11**, 200–209.

Ervin, Susan M. Training and a logical operation by children. *Child Develpm.,* 1960, **31**, 555–563.

Guthrie, E. R. *The psychology of learning.* (Rev. ed.) New York: Harper, 1952.

Haggard, E. A. Social status and intelligence: an experimental study of certain cultural determinants of measured intelligence. *Genet. Psychol. Monogr.,* 1954, **49**, 141–186.

Haggerty, A. D. The effects of long term hospitalization or institutionalization upon the language development of children. *J. genet. Psychol.,* 1959, **94,** 205–209.

Himmelweit, Hilde T., Oppenheim, A. N., & Vince, Pamela. *Television and the child.* London: Oxford Univer. Press, 1958.

Howard, R. *A developmental study of triplets.* Unpublished Ph.D. dissertation, Univer. of Minn., 1934.

Humphrey, G. *Thinking.* London: Methuen, 1951.

Irwin, O. C. The developmental status of speech sounds of ten feebleminded children. *Child Develpm.,* 1942, **13,** 29–39.

Irwin, O. C. Infant speech: consonantal sounds according to place of articulation. *J. Speech Hear. Dis.,* 1947, **12,** 391–401. (a)

Irwin, O. C. Infant speech: consonant sounds according to manner of articulation. *J. Speech Hear. Dis.,* 1947, **12,** 402–404. (b)

Irwin, O. C. Infant speech: development of vowel sounds. *J. Speech Hear. Dis.,* 1948, **13,** 31–34.

Irwin, O. C., & Chen, H. P. Infant speech: vowel and consonant frequency. *J. Speech Hear. Dis.,* 1946, **11,** 123–125.

Jacobson, E. Electrophysiology of mental activities. *Am. J. Psychol.,* 1932, **44,** 677–694.

Jaensch, E. R. *Eidetic imagery.* New York: Harcourt, Brace, 1930.

James, W. *Psychology: briefer course.* New York: Holt, 1892.

Jersild, A. T., & Ritzman, R. Aspects of language development: the growth of loquacity and vocabulary. *Child Develpm.,* 1938, **9,** 243–259.

Johnson, R. C., Frincke, G., & Martin, Lea. Meaningfulness, frequency, and affective character of words as related to visual duration threshold. *Canad. J. Psychol.,* 1961, **15,** 199–204.

Johnson, W. The Indians have no word for it: I. Stuttering in children. *Quart. J. Speech,* 1944, **30,** 330–337.

Johnson, W. *People in quandaries: the semantics of personal adjustment.* New York: Harper, 1946.

Johnson, W. (Ed.). *Stuttering in children and adults; thirty years of research at the University of Iowa.* Minneapolis: Univer. of Minn. Press, 1955.

Johnson, W., et al. *The onset of stuttering: research findings and implications.* Minneapolis: Univer. of Minn. Press, 1959.

Keller, Helen. *The story of my life.* New York: Doubleday, Page, 1917.

Kendler, Tracy S., Kendler, H. H., & Wells, Doris. Reversal and non-reversal shifts in nursery school children. *J. comp. physiol. Psychol.,* 1960, **53,** 83–88.

Klüver, H. Eidetic images. In C. Murchison (Ed.), *A handbook of child psychology.* (Rev. ed.) Worcester, Mass.: Clark Univer. Press, 1933.

Kuenne, Margaret R. Experimental investigation of the relation of language to transposition behavior in young children. *J. exp. Psychol.,* 1946, **36,** 479–489.

Lecky, P. *Self consistency, a theory of personality.* New York: Long Island Press, 1945.

Leopold, W. F. *Speech development of a bilingual child,* Vols. I–IV, Evanston, Ill.: Northwestern Univer. Press, 1937–1949.

Lewis, M. M. *How children learn to speak.* New York: Basic Books, 1959.

Luria, A. R., & Yudovich, F. *Speech and the development of mental processes in the child.* London: Staples Press, 1959.

McCarthy, Dorothea. Language development in children. In L. Carmichael (Ed.), *Manual of child psychology.* (2nd ed.) New York: Wiley, 1954. Pp. 492–630.

Miller, N. E., & Dollard, J. *Social learning and imitation.* New Haven: Yale Univer. Press, 1941.

Mowrer, O. H. *Learning theory and personality dynamics.* New York: Ronald Press, 1950. Pp. 688–726.

Piaget, J. *The language and thought of the child.* New York: Harcourt, Brace, 1936.

Pringle, M. L., & Bossion, Victoria. A study of deprived children. II. Language development and reading attainment. *Vita Humana,* 1958, **1,** 142–170.

Rheingold, Harriet L., Gewirtz, J. L., & Ross, Helen W. Social conditioning of vocalizations in the infant. *J. comp. physiol. Psychol.,* 1959, **52,** 68–73.

Sampson, O. C. The speech and language development of 5 year old children. *Brit. J. educ. Psychol.,* 1959, **29,** 217–222.

Schramm, W. L., Lyle, J., & Parker, E. B. *Television in the lives of our children.* Stanford, Calif.: Stanford Univer. Press, 1961.

Shirley, Mary M. *The first two years of life: A study of twenty-five babies,* Vols. I and II. Minneapolis: Univer. of Minn. Press, *Inst. Child Welf. Monogr. Series,* No. 7, 1933.

Skeels, H. M., Updegraff, Ruth, Wellman, Beth L., & Williams, H. M. A study of environmental stimulation: An orphanage preschool project. *Univer. Ia. Stud. Child Welf.,* 1938, **15,** No. 4.

Smith, Madorah E. An investigation of the development of the sentence and the extent of vocabulary in young children. *Univer. Ia. Stud. Child Welf.,* 1926, **3,** No. 5.

Smith, Madorah E. Some light on the problem of bilingualism as found from a study of the progress in mastery of English among preschool children of non-American ancestry in Hawaii. *Genet. Psychol. Monogr.,* 1939, **21,** 121–284.

Templin, Mildred C. *Certain language skills in children: their development and interrelationships.* Minneapolis: Univer. of Minn. Press, 1957.

Terman, L. M., et al. *Genetic studies of genius:* Vol. 1, *Mental and physical traits of a thousand gifted children.* Stanford, Calif.: Stanford Univer. Press, 1925.

Thorndike, E. L. Words and the comics. *J. exp. Educ.,* 1941, **17,** 110–113.

Thorson, A. M. The relation of tongue movements to internal speech. *J. exp. Psychol.,* 1925, **8,** 1–32.

Tomkins, S. S. Address, Spartan Psychological Assn. Meetings. San Jose, Calif., 1961.

Vanderplas, J. M., & Garvin, E. A. The association value of random shapes. *J. exp. Psychol.,* 1959, **57,** 147–154.

Watson, J. B. *Behavior: an introduction to comparative psychology.* New York: Holt, 1914.

Watson, J. B. *Behaviorism.* (Rev. ed.) New York: Norton, 1930.

Winitz, H. Language skills of male and female kindergarten children. *J. Speech Hear. Res.,* 1959, **2,** 377–386.

Yerkes, R. M., & Learned, B. *Chimpanzee intelligence and its vocal expression.* Baltimore: Williams & Wilkins, 1925.

Zelhart, P., & Johnson, R. C. An investigation of eidetic imagery. Spartan Psychological Assn. Paper, San Jose, Calif., 1959.

chapter 6 ✳ Intelligence

Certainly one of the most basic factors in human development is intelligence. Although intelligence is intimately related to both learning and language, psychologists are still of two minds as to whether it is a single trait of the individual or the sum of many abilities to cope with all sorts of situations. This chapter deals with intelligence from various vantage points. It begins with a review of various definitions of intelligence and ideas about its nature. Then it considers the growth of intellectual ability, the constancy of that ability, and the relation of individual differences in intelligence, as it is ordinarily measured, to learning capacities and social skills. Specific intelligence tests are noted here only as they pertain to the topics under examination. A more comprehensive discussion of them has been reserved for Chapter 14, which treats the subject of individual appraisal.

DEFINITIONS

In the first useful intelligence test (see Binet & Simon, 1916), Binet maintained that intelligence consisted of comprehension, invention, direction, and censorship. This definition contains several interesting elements. It surely seems reasonable to correlate inventiveness and intelligence, but as noted in Chapter 4 on learning and motivation, there is little relation between ability beyond minimal levels, as measured by conventional intelligence tests, and creative talent. Neither Binet's test nor those modeled after it meets Binet's own criteria, since none of them measures inventiveness. Another interesting aspect of Binet's definition is its inclusion of direction; this is really a measure of purposiveness and perseverance rather than ability. Finally, Binet includes censorship, that is, self-censorship; this is an aspect of intelligence not included in any other definition, yet is clearly one of considerable significance.

In designating invention as a mark of intellectual ability, Binet foreshadowed Guilford (1950) who emphasized creativity in his definition of intelligence. Because of this emphasis, Guilford expressed dissatisfaction with conventional intelligence tests. Another to attack such tests was Cattell (1957) who held there were two types of intelligence which he labeled *fluid* and *crystallized*. Fluid intelligence solves novel or "culture free" problems; it is the more general of the two types and is largely innate. Any decline in fluid ability from, say, brain injury will influence a wide variety of intelligence-test scores. Crystallized intelligence, on the other hand, is seen in acquired, complex, familiar cultural activities and skills—for example, reading or mathematics; it is composed of quite specific factors, such as verbal fluency and mechanical ability, and is dependent largely on environmental forces. For the most part, conventional intelligence tests measure crystallized intelligence while neglecting the fluid kind of ability most closely allied with the creative talent stressed by Guilford. A similar distinction to Cattell's was made earlier by Hebb (1949, pp. 294–303). In Hebb's view intelligence tests tapped far more than they should, namely, those aspects of intelligence influenced substantially by forces in the environment. Even if one does not agree completely with Hebb and Cattell on the role of environment in conventional intelligence-test scores, one has to concede that such tests leave much to be desired as instruments for measuring high levels of intellectual ability, such as skills in solving problems and creativity.

How one defines intelligence determines the kind of behavior one wishes to tap by intelligence tests and also one's satisfaction with the testing apparatuses available. Porteus (1941, 1959) waged a long and lonely fight to emphasize planfulness, the capacity to use a long-term perspective, as a measure of ability. Another view (Goddard, 1946) defined intelligence as the amount of experience available for the solution of immediate problems and the anticipation of future ones. Addressing a seminar, John E. Anderson once said he believed that intelligence could be defined as the ability to maintain a high level of response under stress. This definition may be synonymous with another based on the maintenance of an optimal level of arousal in the face of variations in the environment. Finally, there is the one definition of intelligence which has had the most influence on intelligence-test construction, although it may not be the most adequate definition. This was Terman's (1916), which said that intelligence was the individual's capacity to think abstractly and use abstract symbols.

Since Terman and his associates produced all of the more widely accepted revisions of the Binet test, which have received extensive use both as a test and as a criterion for other tests, Terman's definition has had a marked impact on test construction and on theories about the nature of intelligence. Perhaps most conventional intelligence tests measure too much verbal but too little performance ability, too much crystallized but too little fluid intelligence, and too much abstract material slanted to the middle class. This essentially results from the pervasive influence of Terman's belief that intelligence consists of the talent to deal with abstract symbols, which is another way of saying verbal skill. One thing that may be said on behalf of Terman's definition is that the sort of facility he wished to measure was apparently the kind of intelligence most closely correlated with success in formal academic undertakings. Although Terman's definition did not lead to the construction of a test that could measure with accuracy such personal characteristics as perseverance, planfulness, and creativity, it did give rise to a device apparently well suited to its most frequent task, that of predicting success in academic endeavors.

Nature of Intelligence

Quite special in their approach to the nature of intelligence are the factor analysts. Factor analysis is a technique for determining the number of basically unrelated capacities which, by their total impact, produce individual differences in some observable characteristic. For example, athletic ability seems to depend on three unrelated factors—weight, intelligence, and reaction time. The relation of each of these to athletic success differs with the sport concerned. Weight would be expected to count in success as a football tackle but would be negatively related to prowess at ping pong. However, a major part of the variance between individuals in any type of athletic competition could be explained if measures of each of these three factors were available for every competitor. The scientist seeking to measure the factors that constitute intelligence is in a much more difficult position. No simple, directly observable criterion exists for intelligence as for athletic success. In fact, if Cattell, Hebb, and others are correct in their analysis, there appears to be more than one kind of intelligence. In the view of Spearman (1904), there appeared to be a *g* or general factor present in all forms of intellectual behavior. His conclusions were based on students' examination scores in such things as classics and mathematics, on rated capacities—that is, on cleverness and common sense—and on responses in laboratory tasks such as weight discrimination. As he put it: "All branches of intellectual activity have in common one fundamental function." Yet promptly after this statement Spearman noted that the "one fundamental function" might actually consist of a group of functions. His data, discussed in both his 1904 and 1927 studies, suggested, in addition to the *g* factor, the presence of specific or *s* factors whose importance varied from subject area to subject area, with *s* factors being of least significance in the study of the classics and of highest significance in musical accomplishment.

The findings of other factor analysts who have studied intelligence have depended largely on the tests used to measure intelligence. The Binet test, a conglomeration of diverse test items with an emphasis on verbal skills, implies that intelligence is composed of a *g* factor plus certain *s* factors, especially *v* or verbal ability (McNemar, 1942). The Wechsler Intelligence Scale for Children (WISC) measures both verbal and performance capacity and consists of fewer and more disparate test items. Probably because of this difference in structure, a different set of factors emerges, with *g* having much less significance (Digman, 1962).

Since the results of factorial studies are conditioned, to a considerable extent, by the instruments used to acquire the raw data, current views may be outmoded by the emergence of a new and radically different test of ability. At the time of this writing, the long-term trend seems to depart clearly from the emphasis on *g* toward a belief that intelligence comprises a large number of distinct factors (Guilford, 1956; Humphreys, 1962; Thurstone, 1946). What Thurstone (1946) called the "primary mental abilities" are: S (space), N (number), V (verbal comprehension), W (word fluency), and M (memory), in addition to induction, deduction, flexibility, and speed of closure. Others have posited a different number of factors, perhaps designated by different names. Indeed, the great number of rather specific factors discovered since Spearman's time leads to a far different notion of intelligence than might be obtained from a thoroughgoing acceptance of his g.

Those who believe that intelligence is composed of many separate and unrelated specific factors should also believe that most individuals are good at *something* and can be greatly benefited vocationally if the area in which they manifest high ability is exploited. On the other hand, those who consider intelligence as consisting largely of a g factor would expect individuals to show a good deal of consistency in their level of functioning in many, widely diverse areas of behavior. They would look for "common level traits"—that is, the individual who is academically able should also score high in such other areas as social and mechanical intelligence. Since there seems to be evidence for believing in at least a moderate amount of similarity in trait level, the authors of this book are inclined to believe that a fairly strong g factor is present. Nevertheless, the variability in performance of different types of activity is certainly great enough to suggest that highly specific factors also exist. As Spearman held many years ago, the relative influence on behavior of g and s factors varies according to the activity. To straddle the issue, it may be said that general intelligence, as usually measured, consists of a moderately strong g factor and a number of specific factors. There may also be another g factor, not adequately measured at present, that taps fluid intelligence.

THE CURVE OF INTELLECTUAL GROWTH

Although the nonparent may not recognize it, a one-year-old child has gained tremendously in ability as compared to his capacity at birth. In any year of infancy or early childhood the changes in symbolic and problem-solving skills are profound. Yet one should not expect any marked gain in native wit to occur between the ages of 20 and 21. Casual observation leads to the belief that there are unequal increments in mental growth during various stages of development. This belief is reinforced by the postulation of several possible curves of mental growth.

Many intelligence tests are designed to show that the average person gains one year in mental age for each year of chronological age, usually up through the age of 15. In the 1937 Stanford-Binet test, this curve of mental growth—actually a straight-line function—is a built-in feature. Tests of this kind are constructed to display an equal gain in mentality for each year of gain in chronological age. In the Stanford-Binet, this holds through 15. At that point the growth curve breaks down because no items can be presented beyond 15 to indicate a significant increase with age in percentage of subjects able to pass them. From the structure of the test, therefore, it need not follow that any intellectual growth will take place beyond this age. This particular growth curve is represented by curve A in Figure 6-1.

Thurstone and Ackerson (1929) established statistically an absolute zero of intelligence shortly before birth, a point where there is no variation in ability between individuals. By equating mental growth units at various ages, they obtained curve B in Figure 6-1. From this curve, it may be seen that growth is slow at first, but then positively accelerates for about the first ten years of life. After ten it slows down and is negatively accelerated by 11. According to Thurstone and Ackerson growth continues at least through 18.

Using data from the Berkeley Growth Study, from studies by Owens (1953), and from Terman's work on intellectual growth during maturity, Bayley (1955) developed curve C. This curve shows intellectual growth to continue at least to age 50. Terman and Oden (1959) indicate this to be true for gifted individuals. Owens (1953) shows it applies to a bright, but not remarkably talented, sample of subjects. And Bradway, Thompson, and Cravens (1958) demonstrate that essentially the same growth curve exists for a random sample of the population.

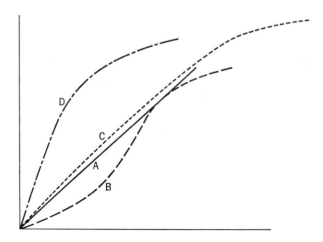

FIGURE 6-1 Hypothetical curves of intellectual growth.

The final type of mental growth curve is suggested by the work of Gesell (1928) and to an even greater degree by data provided by Goodenough (1954, p. 479). This kind of curve, represented by curve D, implies a far higher proportion of mental growth occurring very early in life than do any of the other curves. Consider the newborn infant, his conceptual skills and his ability to cope with his environment. Now consider an average adult in the same way. At what point in development does the individual come half way from the almost "absolute zero" intelligence of the newborn child to the capacities of the adult? Goodenough posed this general question to experts in the field of developmental psychology. The mean age of their responses was three. A fair amount of experience with young children tempts one to agree with Goodenough's view and to believe that curve D most accurately represents mental growth. Yet there is little empirical evidence to support this position, perhaps because researchers do not often attempt to measure ability below the age of two, and even when they do attempt it, they are handicapped by the general inadequacy of infant measures.

Individual Differences

The curves of mental growth contained in Figure 6-1 represent various hypotheses on general patterns of intellectual development. In charting the intellectual growth of any single individual, it becomes necessary to switch to his actual intelligence-test scores. For the Stanford-Binet test, the mental growth curve should resemble curve A (Figure 6-1), as the test is designed to show this type of development. However, the variations from this curve are numerous in individual cases, even when using the Stanford-Binet test. Figure 6-2 illustrates this variability.

The figure shows two kinds of variation. First, the differences in ability become increasingly apparent with age. Cases 5M and 13M differ enormously in facility and since 13M is not too capable, his growth is slow as compared with more intelligent individuals. This should not surprise anyone who believes that individuals vary in ability. Second, there is the irregularity found in the growth curves of specific individuals. For instance, Honzik, McFarlane, and Allen (1948) analyzed the data from the Berkeley Growth Study, from which Bayley also acquired her information, and found that many of the 252 individuals studied longitudinally from shortly after birth through the age of 18 varied widely in intelligence-test scores. Take the ex-

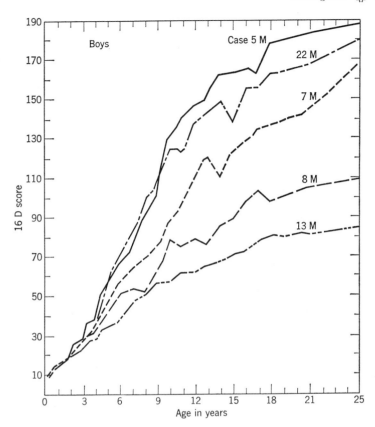

FIGURE 6-2 Individual curves of intelligence (16 D units) for 5 boys, one month to 25 years, Berkeley Growth Study (Bayley, 1955, p. 815).

treme case presented in Figure 6-3. Although few young people vary as greatly as this boy, several studies (Honzik et al., 1948; Sontag, Baker, & Nelson 1958) demonstrate that the *average* amount of deviation from the highest to the lowest scores among children followed from early childhood to early adulthood is at least 15 points. Thus, there could be a change in intellectual rank from being fiftieth among 100 to being one of the lowest 25 or the highest 25 in test score.

Table 6-1, adapted from Honzik et al. (1948), shows the amount of variation in individual test scores over a period of time. The table contains correlations between test scores of individuals at different ages. If individual scores remained constant, if each individual maintained the same position in the group from the first to the final test,

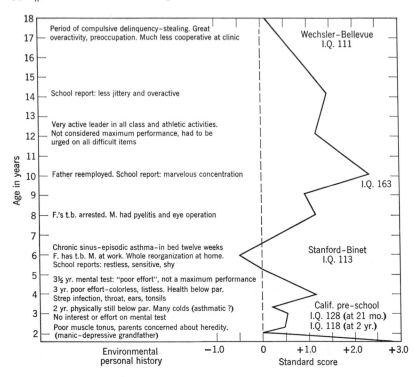

FIGURE 6-3 Variation over time in one subject's intelligence-test scores (Honzik et al., 1948, p. 320).

the correlations would all be +1.00. Were there no connection between an individual's score on one test and his score on any other test, the correlations would all be .00. As Table 1 indicates, the IQ at age 18 can be predicted from very early test scores no better than by chance, as, for example, by coin flipping: heads he is bright, tails he is dull. Indeed, test scores at two are not very good at predicting scores achieved at five or six. On the other hand, it is possible to predict more accurately over a period of time at a later age, say from 14 to 18. This greater reliability of prediction at later ages may signify that ability becomes more stable at later ages, or it simply may be an artifact of the test.

The data in the table disclose that intelligence-test scores vary much more than is commonly supposed. This may be explained in a number of ways. First, it may stem from the changing amounts of intellectual enrichment in the child's environment at various times. Differences in enrichment may indeed contribute to the variance, yet even

TABLE 6-1   Correlations* between Test Scores Obtained
at Different Ages

Age	5	7	10	14	18
2	.32	.46	.22	.07	.07
5		.73	.75	.61	.56
7			.77	.73	.71
10				.85	.70
14					.73

* The tests from which these correlations are derived are the
California Pre-School Schedule through age 5, the Stanford-
Binet (Form L) from 7 through 14, and the Wechsler-Bellevue at
age 18. (Data from Honzik et al., 1948.)

those who most believe that intelligence-test scores are influenced by
such enrichment would not hold that it produces so much deviation.
Second, Anderson (1939) argued that intelligence tests tapped quite
different abilities at different ages and therefore should not be expected
to yield identical scores, even if the actual level of ability remained
constant.   Early tests, for example, contain several sensorimotor items
and the Binet tests place greater emphasis on vocabulary and memory
as age increases.   Because there is far more overlap in the areas tested
among 14- to 18-year-olds than among two- to six-year-olds, this would
explain the increase in test reliability with age.   In dealing with the
same question, Bayley (1955) reached different conclusions.   Her explanation of the variation in IQ over a period of time was that the
component elements of intelligence changed with age: "The very fact
that the scores of mental growth in individual children tend to exhibit
gradual shifts in relative status supports the theory that a changing
organization of factors is in process."   Is change in intelligence-test
score due, then, largely to the changing character of the items in the
tests, as Anderson contended, or to the changing character of intelligence, as Bayley said?   Pinneau (1961), in analyzing the Berkeley
longitudinal data, noted some of both.   Part of the variation in test
scores results from the characteristics of the test, he concluded, and
part from actual changes in intelligence with age.

Honzik et al. (1948) imputed individual deviations in test scores to
persisting social and emotional factors.   Their findings showed that
these factors, when more than mere day-to-day fluctuations in feeling,
bore a substantial relation to test-score variation.   This position is

buttressed by the Fels studies (Baldwin, Kalhorn, & Breese, 1945), which demonstrated that children reared in warm, democratic homes gained eight points in mean IQ over a three-year interval, whereas the mean IQ of children from less emotionally gratifying, rejecting, and indulgent homes either fell or remained constant.

Although all these explanations of variation in tested intelligence have some merit, the one advanced by Honzik et al. apparently accounts for the largest proportion of the IQ changes found in longitudinal studies. Yet it has not been followed up by subsequent research. Certain hypotheses may, however, be derived from it. If, for example, this explanation is correct, changes in tested intelligence should occur in direct proportion to improvements in adjustment resulting from psychotherapy. Furthermore, class differences in tested ability may be narrowed by matching children in adjustment across class lines, since children from various social classes generally differ in adjustment, with those from lower economic groups manifesting a larger number of social and emotional problems.

Generational and Subcultural Differences

The differences in intellectual growth discussed thus far have concerned children of the same generation, all reared within the mainstream of American culture. There are also differences between generations as well as between members of the dominant culture and those who belong to divergent subcultures, such as Southern mountaineers or partially assimilated Mexican-Americans.

Nearly a hundred years ago, Galton was worried. He felt that human ability would decline because the least able members of the population produced the most children. This worry, supported by a fair amount of data (e.g., Maxwell, 1954), persists to the present day. Maxwell has shown that duller individuals have more children; the correlation between IQ and number of children is approximately −.30. But Maxwell's data may not be true of all levels of IQ; quite possibly males of low ability encounter greater difficuly in finding mates and therefore marry less often and later than the population at large. Nevertheless, average level of ability, as measured by conventional intelligence tests, is rising as time moves onward (Tuddenham, 1948; Wheeler, 1942), to judge from tests of succeeding generations. The most likely explanation of these conflicting findings is that many intelligence tests, assumed to be relatively "culture free," are heavily influenced by educational and cultural factors. American culture has grown so much richer and the term of formal education has been so greatly extended over the past several generations that these forces have more than wiped out the genetic deficit. Quite likely, however, the time will come when further increases in advantages across generations will fail to overcome the negatively selective breeding.

Once it was thought that intelligence-test scores were essentially free of cultural influences. Were this so, differences in opportunity would have little, if any, role in producing individual differences in tested ability. Operating on this assumption, many early students of mental retardation (e.g., Goddard, 1912) tested individuals living under extreme deprivation and concluded these people were mentally defective. It is quite true, of course, that brighter people tend to flee deprived environments and settle in more adequate ones (Maxwell, 1954). Because of this selective migration, with the duller members of each generation remaining behind, it is not surprising to find the stay-at-homes quite dull after several generations. Nevertheless, much of the dullness reported in the early studies appears to result from environmental considerations. This is borne out by intergenerational studies (e.g., Wheeler, 1942) and also by studies of the change in intelligence-test scores among children of different ages within the same generation, such as the one conducted by Sherman and Key (1932).

This latter study, later described in more detail by Sherman in his book, *Hollow Folk* (1933), dealt with the intelligence testing of children in a Southern country town and a number of mountain hollows. These hollows decreased in civilization the further one went into the mountains. In the most acculturated of these hollows, the local school was in session about seven months a year; the most isolated hollow had no school at all. Moving up through the hollows, one found the mean IQ of the children decreasing. This could be accounted for either by selective migration or by the influence of environment on test scores. Within each hollow, and especially the more remote ones, the average IQ decreased from very near average at six to a positively defective level by 14 to 16. If the scores of these children resulted from selective migration across generations, the six-year-olds should have been as retarded as the 16-year-olds. The vast difference in scores of children separated by only a ten-year span, during which few of them would be able to migrate of their own accord, strongly suggests that these hollows had something in common with the major American culture, in which the Stanford-Binet test was standardized: the mountain six-year-olds had been exposed to most of the test items at their level, but by adolescence the content was so foreign to the experience of these young people as to make the test no longer a fair measure of their ability. This study, and others like it, shows that groups not exposed to the common American culture are so handicapped that the mental growth curve flattens appreciably with advancing years, resulting in a mounting inferiority in score as the child ages. (For a highly graphic account of the changing life in these hills one can turn to Jesse Stuart's *God's Oddling* (1960). An American novelist reared in Appalachia, Stuart gives a vivid autobiographical report of his youth and manhood, and of the cultural and educational changes in the mountain country over the past generations.)

Yet this decline in tested ability among the culturally undernourished is not indicative of deficiencies in real ability. During the Second World War many young mountaineers learned to read and write to fifth-grade level within five weeks at the Navy's school for illiterates at Bainbridge, Maryland. They then underwent conventional training for recruits, received their orders, found their way across the continent, and joined their ship in California. Although most of them had never been more than a few miles from home, and had seen neither electric lights, flush toilets, nor shower baths, much less the ocean and warships, prior to their military service, they adapted well. Within a few months they were indistinguishable from fellow seamen. Ironically, if conventional intelligence tests had been administered to them upon first leaving their mountain haunts, their mean scores would almost certainly have fallen well within the mentally defective range.

Clearly the amount of education to which an individual is exposed and the closeness of his culture to the dominant American culture have a pronounced influence on intelligence-test scores. May this not also be true of variations with the prime cultural setting? If mountaineers are grossly handicapped because of educational and cultural shortcomings, and consequently score low on intelligence tests, perhaps the differences in IQ found between socioeconomic groups may similarly be attributed to this same cause. This thesis has been advanced most vigorously by Allison Davis (1948). Davis said that the higher mean IQ on tests of middle-class children than of lower-class children was caused by the bias of intelligence tests in favor of the former and certain class differences in motivation, not by any real differences in ability. If class differences produce biases in test construction, it should be possible to build a test that is unbiased or "culture free," which would not discriminate among social classes. Various individuals have attempted this. Davis and Eells (1953) constructed the Davis-Eells Games Test, an entirely new test. Haggard (1954) revised a conventional intelligence test in an effort to make it culture free. He also attempted to control class differences in motivation by using such techniques as offering concrete rewards, which are supposedly necessary to get the best performances from lower-class youngsters, for improvement in test scores.

Notwithstanding, there is a good deal of evidence that so-called culture-free tests do not erase class differences; these differences are as prominent on culture-free tests as on conventional intelligence tests (Angelina & Shedd, 1955; Knief & Stroud, 1959). Moreover, Haggard's endeavor to reduce class differences in ability through varying such factors as motivation was largely unsuccessful; several of his efforts actually increased these differences. Since American society is open and its members rise or fall in occupational level on the basis of ability, differences between occupational groups are not surprising, no matter which tests are used or which motivational techniques are tried.

From all this it would seem that cultural and educational factors affect conventional intelligence-test scores more than was once assumed, yet their influence is not very great among individuals of the same generation raised in the same cultural milieu.

THE CONSTANCY OF ABILITY

Although an individual's IQ does vary over the long run, the cause of the variance is not yet clear. Some of this may be due to test construction, some to the fact that intelligence tests are not entirely culture free, and some to long-term variations in the emotional healthfulness of the environments of those being tested. But how much can be attributed to a deliberate manipulation of the intellectual richness of the environment? This is the major question and its wide implications have yet to be satisfactorily resolved.

If a rich early environment produces lasting changes in ability, these changes must have some physiological base. Among lower organisms this has been shown to be so. Rats reared in an enriched environment differ in brain chemistry from rats not exposed to the same conditions (Krech, Rosenzweig, & Bennett, 1960). In addition, enrichment produces an increase in brain weight (Rosenzweig, Krech, Bennett, & Diamond, 1962). And as noted in an earlier chapter, enrichment or deprivation by the environment influences the later learning capacities of lower organisms, quite possibly because of the effects of these factors on brain structure and function.

Presumably these findings should apply across the species. If enrichment occasions lasting physiological and behavioral change in lower organisms, it should have the same impact on humans. Yet, paradoxically, the evidence suggests something else. An analysis of data pertaining to separated identical twins (Johnson, 1963), the slight and ephemeral effects of special nursery-school training (see Chapter 12) and the inability of Honzik et al. (1948) to find a discernible consistent relation between amount of environmental enrichment and IQ variation, as well as many other studies, all run counter to the hypothesis.

At least two explanations are possible for the differing results of research on humans and subhumans. To begin with, laboratory rats reared in cages are far more severely deprived than even the most deprived humans. Thus, by starting from a far lower base, the effects of enrichment may be much more apparent for subhumans. Put another way, the influence of enrichment among humans within the normal range of environmental variation may not be enough to produce an appreciable change in IQ.

The second explanation maintains that bright and dull organisms differ more pronouncedly in learning ability when learning is *massed,* that is, when learning events follow one another in rapid succession, than when learning is *distributed,* when there is a longer interval of time between them. This applies alike to rats (Jennings, 1960; McGaugh, 1961; McGaugh, Westbrook, & Burt, 1961) and children (Madsen, 1961). Among rats changes in the internal or external environment of the organisms effect a greater impact on massed than on distributed learning (Breen & McGaugh, 1961; McGaugh, 1961; McGaugh, Westbrook, & Thomson, 1962). Thus, massed learning appears to be far more susceptible to various hereditary and environmental forces. Perhaps humans, like rats, are greatly benefited by enrichment, but this has not been evident to researchers because they have tried to measure the influence of enrichment on tasks that are *not* highly responsive to such influence. Or it may be that enrichment has more impact if one moves away from the study of IQ change to investigate the influences of environment on proficiency at tasks that involve massed learning techniques, such as maze learning or the verbal learning of paired associates.

Data gathered to date imply that although IQ is far from constant, little of the variation results from enrichment or deprivation. Yet recent research on animals suggests that a large amount of influence may have escaped detection through use of the wrong measuring devices.

INTELLIGENCE DIFFERENCES AND BEHAVIOR

If intelligence tests have validity, knowledge of an individual's IQ should enable a prediction of his behavior to the extent that behavior depends on intellectual capacity. Through conventional laboratory measures of learning, such as mirror drawing or maze learning, IQ has been shown to be only minimally related to performance (Woodrow, 1946). On the other hand, as we have already seen, conventional measures of ability do not enable a prediction of creativity, except for establishing a floor below which an individual could engage in little creative endeavor. It is in the tasks falling between these two extremes that intelligence tests can most adequately predict performance. Conventional academic tasks—reading, writing, arithmetic, and other studies of the type—fit this specification and performance of them can be predicted with a reasonable degree of accuracy from individual intelligence-test scores. Scholastic achievement is what the Binet test sought to forecast, and in this area the Binet and other tests like it prove most effective. Children with high IQs generally perform well in the school setting (Anderson, Hughes, & Dixon, 1957; Terman, 1925), whereas children of low IQs do poorly from the beginning and become progressively more retarded in scholastic achievement with age (Johnson, 1950). These findings support the validity of the IQ test. It fulfills its major purpose of predicting success in school, even though it is not as adequate at predicting learning in tasks that are either less or more demanding intellectually than those encountered in the academic setting—namely, maze learning or creativity.

Individuals do vary from each other in ability. Figure 6-4 represents a graphic illustration of individual IQ scores. The score corresponding to a particular point on the curve depends, in part, on the test administered. One test administered to all children of the same age in a large school might yield IQs ranging from 50 to 150, whereas a second test might range in scores from 60 to 140. A child scoring 60 on the second test achieves the lowest score, whereas a 60 on the first test would be a low score, but not the lowest. Table 6-2, taken from Pintner, Dragositz, and Kushner (1944, p. 135), presents the percentile breakdown of individuals of varying IQs on the Stanford-Binet test or any other test having approximately the same mean and standard deviation.

As a rule, researchers concern themselves with the two extremes

Number of people making each score
(shown by height of curve above baseline)

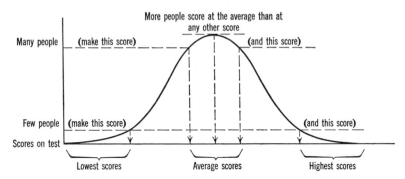

FIGURE 6-4 The curve of intelligence (McBain & Johnson, 1962, p. 151).

when considering the influence of IQ on behavior and adjustment. The general comparison of these extremes in a diversity of situations seems best to indicate the validity of intelligence tests. Let us, therefore, pay some attention to each of these extremes.

High Intellectual Ability

Once it was believed that highly able young people were physically weak, of questionable moral character, rejected by their agemates, antisocial, prone to psychotic or neurotic disturbances, and likely to become mentally defective in later years. Although unsupported by acceptable evidence, these notions were widely held. Possibly the reason for this acceptance is that it is only fair to have "compensatory traits." It would be manifestly unfair for one individual to have everything—brains and brawn, and beauty, too. If this latter idea were buttressed by empirical evidence, the gifted would certainly suffer.

Shortly after the First World War, Terman and his associates undertook their extensive study of gifted children in order to test currently prevalent ideas on the exceptional. Starting in 1921, Terman gathered data on 1000 children with IQs of more than 140, except for a few cases in which a sibling of an exceptional child, whose IQ fell between 135 and 140, was included. Thus, the children in Terman's sample constituted the top 1 per cent of the population as judged by tested ability. These youngsters differed completely from popular belief. They were physically superior, highly acceptable socially, of good character, and in excellent health—a superior group

TABLE 6-2   Percentile Values of Various IQ Scores

The Child Whose IQ Is:	*Is Equalled or Excelled by*
160	1 out of 10,000
156	3 out of 10,000
152	8 out of 10,000
148	2 out of 1,000
144	4 out of 1,000
140	7 out of 1,000

The Child Whose IQ Is:	*Equals or Exceeds*	*The Child Whose IQ Is:*	*Equals or Exceeds*
136	99 per cent	99	48 per cent
135	98	98	45
134	98	97	43
133	98	96	40
132	97	95	38
131	97	94	36
130	97	93	34
129	96	92	31
128	96	91	29
127	95	90	27
126	94	89	25
125	94	88	23
124	93	87	21
123	92	86	20
122	91	85	18
121	90	84	16
120	89	83	15
119	88	82	14
118	86	81	12
117	85	80	11
116	84	79	10
115	82	78	9
114	80	77	8
113	79	76	8
112	77	75	6
111	75	74	6
110	73	73	5
109	71	72	4
108	69	71	4
107	66	70	3
106	64	69	3
105	62	68	3
104	60	67	2
103	57	66	2
102	55	65	2
101	52	64	1
100	50	63	1
		62	1

164 ᠅ Basic Factors in Development

generally, most superior in intellectual pursuits but superior in other ways as well.

This group was followed from 1921, when its mean age was ten, to 1956 and a mean age of 45 (Terman et al., 1925; Burks, Jensen, & Terman, 1930; Terman & Oden, 1947, 1959). Almost all performed well in academic pursuits. Most entered college and received bachelor degrees. Many went on to obtain graduate degrees. Those who did not achieve as well as might have been expected from their IQ scores seemed handicapped by little emphasis on scholarly accomplishment and many tensions at home. These particular individuals, however, gained considerably over their young adult days. At last check (1959), many of them seemed to have finally managed to overcome the adverse effects of their childhood environment and to have begun at last to achieve. Far from "burning out" or becoming mentally defective, the entire group seemed to grow progressively more superior in accomplishment as well as in tested ability at least through the age of 45. During these 35 years, the group had a low death rate, low divorce rate, low crime rate, and a low rate of psychological disturbance. The findings about this group indeed demonstrated the falsity of many beliefs about the gifted.

However, the optimal level of IQ in relation to adjustment is believed to lie between 125 and 155 (Hollingworth, 1942). In her book, *Children Above 180 IQ,* Hollingworth described a number of children far above this level. These youngsters were prolific achievers to judge from a summary of the scholastic accomplishment of one of her subjects whose IQ was 187:

> In addition to his regular school work E, by the time he was 8 years old, had covered the following special work in language and mathematics, either with a tutor or with his mother:
> Mathematics: Algebra as far as equations; geometry.
> Latin: Partial knowledge of the four declensions (he has been taught by the direct, informal method, and reads easy Latin).
> Greek: Worked out the alphabet for himself from an astronomical chart, between the ages of 5 and 6 years.
> French: Equal to about two years in the ordinary school.
> German: Ordinary conversation.
> Spanish: Attended class with his mother—reads and understands.
> Italian: Reading knowledge and simple conversation.
> Portuguese: Asked his mother to take this course at the Columbia Summer School because he could not be registered himself.
> Hebrew: A beginning.
> Anglo-Saxon: A beginning.
> Astronomy: He has worked out all the constellations from MacCready, and displays a very great interest in this subject.

One evening this winter he noticed a new planet near the Twins. He said it was Saturn but his mother thought it was Mars. E went home, worked the position out from the chart and found it to be Saturn.

Miscellaneous: He has a great interest in nature, wherever found. . . . His writing is not equal to his other accomplishments. He is very slow at it and for this reason dictates most of his "home work" to a stenographer.

History is his chief and absorbing interest among school subjects (Hollingworth, 1942, p. 140).

Although high achievers, the young people studied by Hollingworth were not well adjusted members of the age group to which they belonged. They were neither antisocial nor actively maladjusted. Rather they were largely asocial, uninterested in their agemates and their activities, and apparently living in a quite different world from their classmates, teachers, and sometimes their parents. They did not interact easily with agemates; in fact, children of this high a level of ability might benefit from isolation from peers.

The adjustment of the gifted depends, to a large extent, on the criterion used for giftedness. With Terman's criterion of a 140 IQ, adjustment is indeed superior. With the criterion of Hollingsworth (1942) or of McCurdy (1957), adjustment most likely could not be considered optimal. In any case, with respect to intellectual performance, *achievement* is high.

The Mentally Deficient

At the other end of the intelligence curve are those individuals who are regarded as mentally deficient. It is not entirely fair, as is often done, to designate individuals below IQ 70 as "mentally defective." An IQ score alone is not enough to justify this diagnosis. Social competence is a better standard of measurement. If an individual with an IQ of 50 makes his own way in the world without supervision and manages to keep employed, out of trouble, and even marry and successfully raise a family, it would be quite unfair to label him defective.

The earliest studies of social competence, some of them undertaken long before the introduction of intelligence tests, were actually investigations of families that displayed social incompetence for several generations. The best known of these is probably Goddard's (1912) study of the "good" and the "bad" Kallikaks, in which one family line generally evinced social competence and the other social incompetence, presumably because of the inheritance of these characteristics.

Because of these studies and their findings, it was once believed that all mental defect, except for clear instances of anomalies of development, was hereditary. Nowadays, it seems apparent that although some defective individuals may inherit their handicaps, a large number of persons are *called* defective because of brain injury, biochemical factors such as cretinism or *phenylketonuria* (the incomplete oxidization of amino acids), deprived backgrounds, or a number of other reasons. There are many sources for a low IQ, and individuals of the same low level of ability differ substantially from one another, depending on the specific etiology (cause) of their low scores. Some of these persons will show considerable social competence and will benefit greatly from training, whereas others will not. In other words, only *some* individuals with low IQs are mentally defective within the customary definition.

Thus, most individuals with low IQs would seem to do poorly in school. A low intelligence-test score was once thought to be an almost certain indication of social and scholastic incompetence. This is not the case. During the depths of the Depression, Baller (1936) studied 206 individuals, most of whom were in their middle 20s, whose IQs fell below 70 and who, in grade school, had attended "opportunity classes" for extremely slow learners. Of these 206, thirty-three had completed elementary school, three had finished high school, and one had entered college. Despite the challenging economic conditions of the time, 84 per cent were partially or wholly self-supporting. Only 8 per cent were confined in institutions. Following up Baller's subjects in the late 1940's and early 1950's, Charles (1953, 1957) found 80 per cent of them to be employed and self-supporting. Their mean age at the time he began studying them was 42. Their types of homes and percentage of home ownership closely resembled the general population's. Those who had married did not have "herds of children" as is reputedly the case with persons of low ability; the average number of children was actually a little under the national norms. The children on the whole fell into the range of low-average ability. Finally, approximately two-thirds of these people, who had been below IQ 70 as children, now tested in the normal range of 80 and above.

These data are not isolated. Other studies have supplied similar results. Kennedy (1948) also demonstrated that most individuals who were below IQ 70 while in school did reasonably well on the job once they got out of school. Muench (1944), like Charles, showed that many who scored in the defective range in childhood and early adolescence scored within the normal range as adults.

From this, the Binet test seems to be a good forecaster of school success but not of subsequent success on the average job. After a period of frustration and low self-esteem during school years, many persons of low tested ability come into their own when finally employed. More important, these individuals not only perform well on the job, but also often do well as adults on intelligence tests. This may be explained in various ways. First, the low-ability individual has "regression toward the mean" operating on his side. If he scores low on his first test, he has nowhere to go but up on his second one. Second, many individuals with a low tested IQ may score low because of emotional problems (Honzik et al., 1948) or because of a deprived environment. Age and independence from parents may cure both these ills. In sum, since the diagnosis of mental deficiency depends on social competence, many persons with low IQs are not mentally defective as children but are merely academically inept—and even fewer can be legitimately termed mentally defective as adults.

SUMMARY

There are many definitions of intelligence. Different definitions accent such distinctive aspects of intelligence as comprehension, direction, invention or creativity, censorship, availability of past experience, ability to operate at a high level under stress, and ability to use abstract symbols. Terman emphasized the capacity to deal with abstract problems and to use abstract symbols. Since he devised the most widely used intelligence test and shaped the format of most others, his definition appears to have been most influential. As a result, intelligence tests provide an adequate measure of abstract symbolic skills, but are far from satisfactory at checking the kind of *fluid* intelligence involved in creativity or the abilities central to other definitions of intelligence. Factorial studies differ in their conclusions at least partly because different tests, or even the same test at different age levels, seem to measure other aspects of intelligence. The evidence suggests strongly that intelligence consists of a *g* factor of moderate strength plus a number of specific factors.

Various theories try to account for the shape of the curve of intellectual growth. It seems reasonable to believe that the average growth curve accelerates sharply during infancy and early childhood, slows down after this point, but continues to rise at least into middle maturity. Individual growth curves of persons reared in typical American environments show much irregularity. Differences in the kinds of material tapped by intelligence tests at various ages and differences in the emotional well-being or intellectual stimulation of those being tested might be responsible for this variation. A comparison of generations discloses that the present generation demonstrates greater intellectual growth than its forebears, as measured by scores on conventional group intelligence tests. The mental growth curves of individuals raised outside the mainstream of American culture indicate a deceleration that apparently results from the intellectual impoverishment of their environment.

Individual differences in intelligence-test scores do not relate substantially to most laboratory measures of learning, nor do they enable predictions of creative capacities. Intelligence-test scores, however, do permit prediction of academic success with a fairly high amount of accuracy. Individuals who score high on such tests, when compared to the general population, are not only superior in accomplishment, but also are better physical specimens and seem better able to withstand psychic stresses. Individuals found in the ranks of the genius category as children maintain their superiority at least through the mid-forties. Individuals on the low end of the intelligence curve do poorly in school but perform better on the job. In many cases they also test within the normal range of intelligence as adults.

Although measures of intelligence are far from perfect, thus preventing one's understanding of the nature of intelligence and of intellectual growth from being complete, psychologists have come a long way toward achieving accuracy in predicting performance in a highly complex area of behavior.

REFERENCES

Anderson, I. H., Hughes, B. O., & Dixon, W. R. The rate of reading development and its relation to age of learning to read, sex, and intelligence. *J. educ. Res.,* 1957, **50,** 481–494.
Anderson, J. E. The limitations of infant and preschool test in the measurement of intelligence. *J. Psychol.,* 1939, **8,** 351–379.
Angelina, H., & Shedd, C. L. An initial report of a validation study of the Davis-Eells tests of general intelligence or problem solving ability. *J. Psychol.,* 1955, **40,** 35–38.
Baldwin, A. L., Kalhorn, Joan, & Breese, F. H. Patterns of parent behavior. *Psychol. Monogr.,* 1945, **58,** No. 268.
Baller, W. R. A study of the present social status of a group of adults, who, when they were in the elementary schools, were classified as mentally deficient. *Genet. Psychol. Monogr.,* 1936, **18,** No. 3.
Bayley, Nancy. On the growth of intelligence. *Amer. Psychologist,* 1955, **10,** 805–818.

Binet, A., & Simon, T. *The development of intelligence in children.* (Trans. by Elizabeth S. Kite.) Training School, Vineland, N. J., 1916.

Bradway, Katherine P., Thompson, Clare W., & Cravens, R. B. Preschool IQs after twenty-five years. *J. educ. Psychol.,* 1958, **49,** 278–281.

Breen, R. A., & McGaugh, J. L. Facilitation of maze learning with posttrial injections of picrotoxin. *J. comp. physiol. Psychol.,* 1961, **54,** 498–501.

Burks, Barbara S., Jensen, D. W., & Terman, L. M. *Genetic studies of genius: III. The promise of youth: follow up studies of a thousand gifted children.* Stanford, Calif.: Stanford Univer. Press, 1930.

Cattell, R. B. *Personality and motivation structure and measurement.* New York: Harcourt, Brace & World, 1957.

Charles, D. C. Ability and accomplishment of persons earlier judged mentally deficient. *Genet. Psychol. Monogr.,* 1953, **47,** 3–71.

Charles, D. C. Adult adjustment of some deficient American children. *Am. J. ment. Def.,* 1957, **62,** 300–304.

Davis, A. *Social class influences upon learning.* Cambridge, Mass.: Harvard Univer. Press, 1948.

Davis, A., & Eells, K. *Davis-Eells Games: Davis-Eells test of general intelligence or problem solving ability.* Yonkers, N. Y.: World Book, 1953.

Digman, J. M. A factor analysis of WISC IQ test scores. Unpublished manuscript, Univer. of Hawaii, Honolulu, 1962.

Gesell, A. *Infancy and human growth.* New York: Macmillan, 1928.

Goddard, H. H. *The Kallikak family.* New York: Macmillan, 1912.

Goddard, H. H. What is intelligence? *J. soc. Psychol.,* 1946, **24,** 51–69.

Goodenough, Florence L. The measurement of mental growth in childhood. In L. Carmichael (Ed.), *Manual of child psychology.* (2nd ed.) New York: Wiley, 1954. Pp. 459–491.

Guilford, J. P. Creativity. *Amer. Psychologist,* 1950, **5,** 444–454.

Guilford, J. P. The structure of intelligence. *Psychol. Bull.,* 1956, **53,** 267–293.

Haggard, E. A. Social status and intelligence: an experimental study of certain cultural determinants of measured intelligence. *Genet. Psychol. Monogr.,* 1954, **49,** 141–186.

Hebb, D. O. *The organization of behavior.* New York: Wiley, 1949.

Hollingworth, Leta S. *Children above 180 IQ.* Yonkers, N. Y.: World Book, 1942.

Honzik, Marjorie P., McFarlane, Jean W., & Allen, Lucille. The stability of mental test performance between two and eighteen years. *J. exper. Educ.,* 1948, **17,** 309–324.

Humphreys, L. G. The organization of human abilities. *Amer. Psychologist,* 1962, **17,** 475–483.

Jennings, R. D. Strain differences in the effects of distribution of practice on maze learning. Unpublished M.A. thesis, San Jose State College, 1960.

Johnson, G. O. A study of the social position of mentally handicapped children in the regular grades. *Amer. J. ment. Def.,* 1950, **55,** 60–89.

Johnson, R. C. Similarity in IQ of separated identical twins as related to length of time spent in the same environment. *Child Develpm.,* 1963, **34,** 745–749.

Kennedy, R. J. R. *The social adjustment of morons in a Connecticut city.* Hartford, Conn., Mansfield-Southberry Training Schools, 1948.

Knief, Lotus M., & Stroud, J. B. Intercorrelations among various intelligence, achievement, and social class scores. *J. educ. Psychol.,* 1959, **50,** 117–120.

Krech, D., Rosenzweig, M. R., & Bennett, E. L. Effects of environmental complexity and training on brain chemistry. *J. comp. physiol. Psychol.,* 1960, 53, 509–519.

McBain, W. M., & Johnson, R. C. *The science of ourselves.* New York: Harper & Row, 1962.

McCurdy, H. G. The childhood pattern of genius. *J. Elisha Mitchell Sci. Soc.,* 1957, 73, 448–462. (Also in R. A. King (Ed.), *Readings for an introduction to psychology.* New York: McGraw-Hill, 1961. Pp. 269–278.)

McGaugh, J. L. Facilitative and disruptive effects of strychnine sulphate on maze learning. *Psychol. Rep.,* 1961, 8, 99–104.

McGaugh, J. L., Westbrook, W. H., & Burt, G. Strain differences in the facilitative effects of 5-7-diphenyl-1-3-diazadamantan-6-OL(1757I.S.) on maze learning. *J. comp. physiol. Psychol.,* 1961, 54, 502–505.

McGaugh, J. L., Westbrook, W. H., & Thomson, C. L. Facilitation of maze learning with posttrial injections of 5-7-diphenyl-1-e-diazadamantan-6-OL(1757I.S.). *J. comp. physiol. Psychol.,* 1962, 55, 710–713.

McNemar, Q. *The revision of the Stanford-Binet Scale: an analysis of the standardization data.* Boston: Houghton Mifflin, 1942.

Madsen, M. C. Massed and distributed practice at three levels of intelligence. Western Psychological Assn. Paper, Seattle, Wash., 1961.

Maxwell, J. Intelligence, fertility, and the future. *Eugen. Quart.,* 1954, 1, 244–247.

Muench, G. A. A follow-up of mental defectives after eighteen years. *J. abnorm. soc. Psychol.,* 1944, 39, 407–418.

Owens, W. A. Age and mental abilities: a longitudinal study. *Genet. Psychol. Monogr.,* 1953, 48, 3–54.

Pinneau, S. R. *Changes in intelligence quotient—infancy to maturity.* Boston: Houghton Mifflin, 1961.

Pintner, R., Dragositz, Anne, & Kushner, Rose. Supplementary guide for the Revised Stanford-Binet Scale (Form L). *Appl. Psychol. Monogr.,* 1944, No. 3.

Porteus, S. D. *The practice of clinical psychology.* New York: American Book Co., 1941.

Porteus, S. D. *The maze test and clinical psychology.* Palo Alto, Calif.: Pacific Books, 1959.

Rosenzweig, M. R., Krech, D., Bennett, E. L., & Diamond, M. C. Effects of environmental complexity and training on brain chemistry and anatomy: A replication and extension. *J. comp. physiol. Psychol.,* 1962, 55, 429–437.

Sherman, M. *Hollow folk.* New York: Crowell, 1933.

Sherman, M., & Key, Cora B. The intelligence of isolated mountain children. *Child Develpm.,* 1932, 3, 279–290.

Sontag, L. W., Baker, C. T., & Nelson, Virginia L. Mental growth and personality development: a longitudinal study. *Monogr. soc. Res. child Develpm.,* 1958, 23, No. 2.

Spearman, C. "General intelligence," objectively determined and measured. *Amer. J. Psychol.,* 1904, 15, 201–292.

Spearman, C. *The abilities of man.* London: Macmillan, 1927.

Stuart, J. *God's oddling.* New York: McGraw-Hill, 1960.

Terman, L. M. *The measurement of intelligence: An explanation of and a complete guide for the Stanford Revision and Extension of the Binet-Simon Intelligence Scale.* Boston: Houghton Mifflin, 1916.

Terman, L. M., et al. *Genetic studies of genius: I. Mental and physical traits of a thousand gifted children.* Stanford, Calif.: Stanford Univer. Press, 1925.

Terman, L. M., & Oden, Melita H. *Genetic studies of genius: IV. The gifted child grows up.* Stanford, Calif.: Stanford Univer. Press, 1947.

Terman, L. M., & Oden, Melita H. *The gifted group at mid-life: Thirty-five years' follow-up of the superior child.* Stanford Calif.: Stanford Univer. Press, 1959.

Thurstone, L. L. Theories of intelligence. *Sci. Mo.,* 1946, **62,** 101–112.

Thurstone, L. L., & Ackerson, L. The mental growth curve for the Binet tests. *J. educ. Psychol.,* 1929, **20,** 569–583.

Tuddenham, R. D. Soldier intelligence in World Wars I and II. *Amer. Psychologist,* 1948, **3,** 54–56.

Wheeler, L. R. A comparative study of the intelligence of East Tennessee mountain children. *J. educ. Psychol.,* 1942, **33,** 321–334.

Woodrow, H. The ability to learn. *Psychol. Rev.,* 1946, **53,** 147–158.

SECTION III ✳ THE FAMILY
AND ITS INFLUENCE
ON DEVELOPMENT

This section, composed of the next four chapters, concerns the child in his family setting. Such forces as heredity and maturation impose limits on the influence that parents and other social groups may bring to bear. At the present time this subject of the influence of family on the behavior and personality of the child is a matter of lively interest among researchers, and much effort is being expended in its investigation.

The first of the four chapters considers the anthropological, sociological, and historical forces that have made the family in America what it is today and that determine, in part, the way in which the family influences development. The succeeding chapter examines various aspects of the family and of the child's place within it. Such matters as "onliness," sibling position, physical or mental defects of siblings, maternal employment, and divorce are discussed.

The third chapter covers the interaction of the child with parents during infancy. Among the topics explored are Freudian concepts; the relation of early parent practices, such as toilet training and weaning, to personality and behavior; and the effects of maternal deprivation. The final chapter of the section pertains to parental influences during the period of childhood following infancy. It includes such matters as the impact of parent personality, parent attitudes, and parent behavior on child personality and behavior.

All told, the cultural, psychological, and social forces in the family situation, together with the personalities, attitudes, and behaviors of each parent and other members of the family affect the child. Born with certain characteristics that form the core of his uniqueness, the child finds this uniqueness increased by these many influences. Their interplay within the family renders accurate prediction of the effect of any single force on any single child difficult. As this section indicates, however, child psychology is developing predictive skills, notwithstanding the complexity of the problem.

chapter 7 ✳ The Influence of Culture on Child-Rearing Practices

Individuals who share a set of values, beliefs, practices, and information, and who pass these views from one generation to the next, constitute a culture. Americans are part of Western culture, a broad grouping of individuals in North America, Europe, the British Commonwealth, and other areas of the earth. Western culture, an amalgam of Judeo-Christian, Greco-Roman, and other influences, differs from other cultures in the "world view" it builds into people. Although philosophers since Hume may argue that it is improper to talk of "cause" and "effect," Westerners at a very early age accept the ideas that present conditions have their roots in the past, that the future can be predicted from the present, and that the future, moreover, can be changed. Yet the implied notion that there is lawfulness and predictability in the world, based on orderly cause and effect, is far from universally held.

Other ideas common to the West also are not accepted by all cultures. Such value judgments as that life in this world is "good," that progress is possible and desirable, that individuality should be developed to as high a degree as it can, or that the individual human is of considerable worth are not necessarily shared by others. Nor are the values prized by others always acceptable to the West. One cannot imagine many Americans believing that the goal of existence is to lead such a good life that once dead, reincarnation is no longer necessary and instead one again becomes nothing. Few within Western culture take the position that if an individual develops a skill more than do others, he is disturbing the equilibrium of the group and thus making supernatural beings unhappy. Americans do not believe that the old way is necessarily the best way. Instead they welcome change for its own sake.

One's beliefs shape patterns of child rearing in various subtle ways. But since all are subjected to the same influences, these factors and their effect of making people similar to one another in basic approach are often overlooked. Frequently it is necessary to be thrown suddenly into another culture to recognize the essential oneness underlying the apparent diversity of the West. Although part of the same Western culture, Americans have produced within it their own adaptation of it, the *American* culture. This chapter begins with an examination of various cultural considerations that bear on the social environment of the child. This will be followed by discussion of the forces, both past and present, that have produced current child-rearing practices, and by an attempt to show the impact of these forces on various groups in their approaches to child rearing.

DIMENSIONS OF CULTURE

Cultures can be variously divided into two distinct groups, but all such dichotomies have a certain inherent falsity. Things seldom are "either-or." More likely they are blends of various sorts, shading toward one or the other of the types that form the dichotomy. Such is the case with the dimensions of culture to be discussed. Cultures probably do not differ from one another in kind, but rather in the degree to which certain characteristics are present.

Child-Rearing Practices of Primary vs. Secondary Groups

This distinction is mentioned first for several reasons. It is the earliest distinction that we shall discuss. Having formed an important aspect of sociological theory since the 1860's, it has a certain historical priority. More important, considerable evidence suggests that the development of the *self concept*—one's attitudes and beliefs about oneself—is an extremely significant phenomenon. The concept of self comes largely from one's ideas about one's social roles; and the type, consistency, and clarity of the roles played seem to depend on whether one grows up in a primary- or a secondary-group society. Primary groups are characterized by intimate, face-to-face contact, by the mutual social support of the individuals who belong, and by the group's ability to proscribe, constrain, or order a considerable proportion of the behavior of its individual members. Family and peers, two such primary groups, have considerable influence in American society. Such groups as the typical urban community or neighborhood, or one's trade union or professional association are secondary groups. These are not characterized by close or continual contact or by a concern in any but a limited segment of a member's behavior. They do not offer any great deal of support nor generally can they exert any great degree of pressure, except perhaps within rigidly limited areas, toward conformity to group standards of behavior.

Historically, according to many social theorists (Durkheim, 1947; Tonnies, 1940; Becker, 1948), societies composed solely of primary groups reigned supreme. In a primitive culture or even in a contemporary rural one, all individuals know one another. Although not much happens, everyone knows everything that does happen. These social groups are primary groups; little conflict of value systems occurs among them, since everyone holds much the same values. A high proportion of behaviors are "public" behaviors, known to all members of the group and judged by them in terms of propriety.

One of the authors of this book recalls, for example, coming home to the rural community in which he grew up in a newly acquired 1939 Buick phaeton. Everyone in the community asked him, at first encounter, how much he paid for it. They told him that going to college must have made him foolish—that no one in northern Minnesota should buy a convertible. Had they been reprimanded, "None of your business," they would have been surprised as well as hurt. In their opinion it *was* their business to pass judgment on the behavior of members of the group, just as it was to take up a collection and have a building bee if someone's house or barn burned down, or to do the farm chores for a neighbor with a broken leg. It is their business to help members of the group. This combination of inquisitiveness and psychological support found in a primary-group society makes the majority of people escape as soon as possible and then remember the society with nostalgia for the rest of their lives.

The city, on the other hand, is largely a secondary-group society. The individual is exposed to a wide variety of groups, most of which are not characterized by intimate, face-to-face contact across a broad range of behavioral settings. Multiple group membership is the rule. Since urban groupings, such as trade unions, church organizations, P.T.A.'s, and fraternal organizations, differ in composition and often in values and goals, an individual can easily encounter conflict between two antagonistic social roles. Further, the roles prescribed by any one group generally do not deal with wide varieties of behavior, but only with that narrow range of public behaviors of concern to the group. Because no universal consensus exists regarding the "goodness" or "badness" of a given behavior, all values are relative, and none is held as strongly as in a primary-group society (Durkheim, 1915).

Some segments of American culture are still dominated by primary-group associations. This is true of isolated farm groups, members of pietist religious sects (see Francis, 1955; also Kaplan & Plaut, 1956), and probably the very rich. An ever-increasing proportion of Americans, however, lives in urban areas. U. S. Census figures show that well over two-thirds of the population now as opposed to one-half in 1890 are city dwellers. This majority does not often have such ties as those of religious zealots or of the very rich and thus is not as subject to the influence of primary codes.

Children reared in these two types of environment are subjected to discernibly different forms of parental training. The parent within that part of society still composed largely of primary groups takes a stand toward behavior based on the one traditional set of values to which he has been exposed. There is only one acceptable way for him to respond to any given situation; his whole group agrees on this matter. Once he *knows* what is right, it becomes his duty to teach this to his children and to extirpate any tendencies they may disclose to respond in other manners. Social roles are clearly defined and strengthened by the views of the group. If the child learns to play his allotted share of roles correctly so that they do not conflict with the group and so that he fulfills its expectations, the parent's task is essentially complete. If none of the few available roles seems desirable to the child, he must be induced to make do with them. The function of the parent is to hammer home "self-evident, universally held truths" and to defend the group against the youngster's tendency toward change. Small wonder that parents in primary-group societies are believed to be highly conservative (Spencer, 1912; Durkheim, 1951) and authoritarian (Jaensch, 1938).

The child-rearing practices of a secondary-group society vary to an ever-increasing degree from those of a primary-group environment. An urban culture is dynamic and rapidly changing. Traditional behaviors are of little utility in preparing a child for adulthood, since the adulthood of any child will differ greatly from that of his parents. As a result the parent is quite uncertain as to what to teach the child (Riesman, 1953; Boehm, 1957). Despite the desire to rear children with values consonant with their own, parents often must grant their children autonomy in a number of decision-making areas quite early in the developmental process. This is because the differences in experiences are so great between generations. Moreover, because the parent is less certain that he knows the correct course of action, he delegates authority to other groups. The peer group and the schools take over and thus influence the development of conscience, as shall be discussed presently. The American urban child as opposed to the Swiss, Boehm (1957) has shown, is far more autonomous and far less guilt ridden, presumably because of this weakened parental and increased peer influence.

Owing to economic changes accompanying the development of an industrial, urban, secondary-group society, the parent is warmer and more permissive. Equalitarian treatment of the child follows both from the viewing of the child primarily as a love object and from the parent's own lack of certainty as to what the child should be like. The child is exposed to many differing social groups with diverse values; none of these groups has a high degree of dominance in its influence. No group, not even the family, can keep a constant check on the child in all areas of activity as in a less complex social setting. The child, as a result, knows many sets of conflicting values and probably accepts none of them wholeheartedly until he must select from them as well as from diverse social roles those that he finds best. Then he must adapt them to form a self-consistent set of roles, often referred to as the *self concept*.

The historical changes in child-rearing practices apparent in American culture may result largely from the continuing shift from a relatively uniform, rural, agrarian society to a variegated, urban, industrial one.

Child-Rearing Techniques in Cultures of Want and of Plenty

Urbanization requires the development of technology and the division of labor. These, in turn, are necessary for a materially rich culture. The American culture is presumably the richest the world has yet known. Certain aspects of child rearing within it appear to relate to economic circumstances.

Because of advanced scientific technology, the death rate among children is very low. A grandmother stressed the significance of this fact, with respect to child rearing. In discussing the changes that occurred in the 80 years she could remember, she commented on one quite noticeable development that seemed to have escaped everyone's attention—the greater amount of love that parents lavish nowadays on children. "Back in the old days," she said, "parents couldn't get involved with younger children as greatly. They were afraid that deep love would lead only to deep sorrow, for so many children died before reaching maturity." Although other factors undoubtedly enter into this increased parental involvement and love, mortality figures indicate that a parent at the turn of the century could not *assume* that his children would live to maturity.

Advanced technical achievements appear likely to have contributed in other ways to increased parental love and involvement. Children of a few generations ago were viewed primarily as economic assets. The farmer with a crop of growing boys knew that if he could only hold on for a few more years, he would have plenty of help. Moreover, this help would be of the very best sort, since neither were wages required nor would there be any complaints about a 12-hour day, seven-day work week. No longer can children be viewed in this fashion. There are fewer and fewer things a child is useful for, even on the farm. It is easier, cheaper, quicker, and more efficient to buy a new hay baler or harvesting machine than to breed a crop of farm hands. Since another function of children is that of receiving and giving love, this role has come to the fore, no longer overshadowed by economic necessity. Children are to be loved.

Not only are children loved more, but they are also loved as children far longer. The closer a culture is to a subsistence economy, the shorter the period of childhood, one writer has suggested (Landis, 1945). Hunting or fishing cultures, nearly always only a few days away from starvation, have the shortest childhoods, whereas agrarian cultures are intermediate, and industrial societies are longest in the period they term childhood.

Nearly a century ago, the grandfather of one of the authors sailed from a fishing village on the island of Gotland in Sweden at the age of ten and was a ship's officer on a windjammer at 17. How the world has changed in less than 100 years! Most segments of Western culture are now sufficiently affluent that children are no longer needed on the labor market. Besides, most occupations demand a relatively high degree of formal training. The young person must now remain dependent on the family for a considerable period of time after having reached physical maturity in order to receive this training. Although the influence of the family on children's values may not be as it once was at any time during the early years, the family does have many more years in which to shape the child.

Continuous vs. Discontinuous Cultures

Anthropologists such as Ruth Benedict make a distinction between continuous and discontinuous cultures. In a continuous culture, the child begins learning adult roles as soon as he begins to understand the world about him, as the following examples indicate.

> . . . The gravity of a Cheyenne Indian family ceremoniously making a feast out of the little boy's first snowbird is at the furthest remove from our behavior. At birth the little boy was presented with a toy bow, and from the time he could run about serviceable bows suited to his stature were specially made for him by the man of the family. Animals and birds were taught him in a graded series beginning with those most easily taken, and as he brought in his first of each species his family duly made a feast of it, accepting his contribution as gravely as the buffalo his father brought. When he finally killed a buffalo, it was only the last step of his childhood conditioning, not a new adult role with which his childhood experience had been at variance.
>
> The Canadian Ojibwa show clearly what results can be achieved. This tribe gains its livelihood by winter trapping and the small family of father, mother and children live during the long winter alone on their great frozen hunting grounds. The boy accompanies his father and brings in his catch to his sister as his father does to his mother; the girl prepares the meat and skins for him just as his mother does for her husband. By the time the boy is 12, he may have set his own line of traps on a hunting territory of his own and return to his parent's house only once in several months—still bringing the meat and skins to his sister. The young child is taught consistently that it has only itself to rely upon in life, and this is as true in the dealings it will have with the supernatural as in the business of getting a livelihood . . . (Benedict, 1949, pp. 300–301).

A discontinuous culture, on the other hand, does not prepare the young child for adulthood through a continuous inculcation of social roles. Discontinuous cultures teach children roles that are in opposition to those they will assume later. For example, like the American Indians, the mainstream of the culture desires a bold and courageous child—in fact, it desires these attributes more than any others (Haimowitz, 1960, p. 2). The Indians are continuous in their training for these characteristics. A bold act, such as that of a two-year-old boy physically attacking his father, is applauded. The prevailing American culture, on the contrary, is truly discontinuous; it expects the individual to be submissive while young and then magically to become dominant at maturity.

American society is clearly discontinuous—not only in failing to provide training for certain adult functions but also in establishing childhood roles that are antagonistic to the roles demanded by adulthood. It may not be as discontinuous, however, as is believed by many anthropologists. Nor is it certain that discontinuity is undesirable. Perhaps in a complex, rapidly changing, secondary-group society, a certain facility in taking new roles is necessary. Conceivably the ease in making these shifts and adjustments comes from the discontinuity of roles and from the conflicts among those roles faced and mastered during the growing-up process.

Guilt vs. Shame Cultures

A traditional aim of a parent in urban industrial culture is to produce a child with what used to be called a well-developed conscience but is now more often termed a strong superego—in any case, a child who feels guilt following wrongdoing. Guilt comes from within. If cultural conditioning has been successful, many humans are self-regulating organisms who punish themselves without being caught. This is an explicitly stated goal in Western culture. It is not common to all cultures. Anthropologists say that the very notion of guilt is lacking in some cultures, and that social controls are based on shame. Shame results from an act being found out by others; as long as one is not caught, any action is acceptable.

It should be noted that there is no one-to-one relation between primary versus secondary groups and the guilt-shame dichotomy. Many primary groups use shame as a means of control, but others base social controls on guilt. Some secondary-group societies emphasize guilt; others shame.

Many clinical psychologists believe that Americans have succeeded only too well at building in the guilt response. The basis of neurotic symptoms, they hold, frequently lies in the patient's strong, often unjustified, feelings of guilt. A certain type of training is necessary to produce a child who feels guilt. A child must be reared in such a fashion that its parents are primarily responsible for the inculcation of values—not other groups of individuals, such as peers, hired caretakers, or the community at large. The parents must be convinced that they are correct and must be willing to reject the child, and even risk rejection by the child, when the child's behavior deviates. A withholding of love, rather than physical punishment, must be the chief means of discipline (Mead, 1943).

Let us suppose that a child is found to be engaging in childhood sex play in a culture in which sex play is prohibited. Guilt-oriented parents might admonish the child in this way: "We love you so much and now you have disobeyed us and done something *bad*. We feel so hurt we don't want you to be near us for a while. How can parents love a child who does things like that? You go to your room and think about how *bad* you are and when you're ready, come out and say that you're sorry and won't ever do that again." The response of a shame-oriented parent would follow a different form. Physical punishment would be likely to occur and be followed by statements of this kind: "No little child is supposed to do this. If someone saw you he would tell others and everyone would laugh at you or be disgusted with you. Then wouldn't you feel like a fool? You must remember that you would have to hang your head in shame if you were caught."

Shame, as a technique for controlling behavior, is probably quite effective when used by a primary-group society, since most behaviors are public. Many primary-group societies do use shame as a major technique. For an urban industrial culture shame does not appear to be an effective technique, since it is so simple to maintain anonymity. Few group ties are strong enough to cause concern about the opinion of the group. Even if one belonged to groups before which one would feel shame, one would first have to be caught and then forced to remain in the group that would be aware of the misdeed. Persons in urban societies are less likely to be caught, and if caught, can probably join another group that either does not know of the shameful deed or else does not care. Here guilt has the greater influence. Although irrational and excessive guilt may dispose one toward neurosis, members of a mass society may need at least a moderate sense of guilt to maintain the society.

It is believed, however, that urbanites are moving away from a guilt toward a shame orientation (Riesman, 1953). This may result, in part, from the influence of psychoanalysis, as has recently been claimed (LaPiere, 1959). Other forces probably have contributed far more greatly to this shift. American culture is changing at so rapid a rate that parents are unsure of their own values, and as a result, abandon much of their function to other groups such as the school and the peers. The peers, unlike the usual parent, use shame as a major disciplinary technique. Parents also do a less adequate job of building a sense of guilt since, as already noted, children are more precious these days. Hence, the parent is unwilling to withhold love for fear that it may lead to his own rejection by the child. Lessened parental influence, differing to some degree in type from that of a generation ago, appears to have resulted in a shift away from guilt and toward shame as a means of social control. If the clinicians are right, this shift may result in a lowered proportion of neurosis and "withdrawn" behavior problems. On the other hand, there may be more "acting out" or delinquent behavior problems. As society moves from guilt toward shame, the change, resulting at least in part from parental practices, is likely to have considerable social consequence.

THE CHILD IN AMERICA

So much for cultural factors. Historical influences also appear to be significant in modes of child rearing. Some of these influences, such as the *Protestant Ethic,* operate in Europe as well as America. The effects of other influences, such as that of the frontier, are uniquely America's own.

The Frontier and American Child-Rearing Practices

The settler of the Atlantic seaboard was a transplanted European, generally an Englishman, still tied to Old World behavior patterns. Clad in homespun, he bowed to the squire and deacons, and still "knew his betters." Entering the Allegheny Mountains, he fought it out with the Indians. A generation later, clothed in the skins of wild animals, swinging strings of scalps, and refusing to admit any man to be their equal, much less their better, some of his descendants emerged on the western side of the Alleghenies. The frontiersmen were called, with considerable justice, "White Indians" by those who remained on the seaboard. They moved on to master the continent.

The frontier did much to shape American attitudes toward the world. Since the pervasive attitudes of a culture shape its child-rearing practices, the experience of the frontier necessarily contributed markedly to the differences in child rearing between the American and the European branches of Western culture.[1] Frederick Jackson Turner in his classic study, *The Frontier in American History* (1921), described some of the changes in American attitudes and character wrought by the frontier. The frontiersman was optimistic: the promised land was always just over the next hill. Today may be bad but tomorrow will be better. Even now, in Alaska, as the season closes and winter nears, one frequently hears the statement, "Well, I didn't make it this year, but next year—well, watch me go." This hopeful

---

[1] Like the American branch of Western culture, the Australian branch underwent the same experiences and, similarly, differed from the Europeans.

attitude, resulting from the fluidity of social position on the frontier, may have much to do with high levels of aspiration for oneself and one's children. The hope and belief, so widespread in America, that one's children can and should surpass oneself in accomplishment may well stem from this basically optimistic world view of the frontier.

Most European visitors to America such as the Trollopes, the mother in the 1830's and the son 30 years later, have remarked on the wilfulness, independence, and general orneriness of American children. This general feeling persists to the present time and probably has a certain basis in fact; it is attested to by anyone who has spent much time in Europe. Equalitarian treatment of children—equalitarian by European standards—was and is at least partially the result of the frontier experience.

The frontiersman, as a member of a relatively anarchistic hunting society, may have desired independence in his children in order to improve their chances of survival. Further, the frontiersman apparently believed, with a fervor not understandable today, in the idea of equality in social relations. The frontiersman also may have been exposed sufficiently to American Indian child-rearing practices to have received social reinforcement for his beliefs from them; the Indians valued a fairly high degree of self-assertion on the part of children, especially male children, because they believed this to be indicative of later strength and determination. Whatever the relative influences of specific underlying causes may have been, American experience has resulted in the American parent granting to the child a greater degree of freedom and equality than is granted by his European counterpart at any given period of time. As the content of the American experience has changed, it is not surprising that different modes of child rearing have appeared, such as was evidenced in shifts associated with the decline of the *Protestant Ethic* and the rise of the *Social Ethic*.

Protestant Ethic, Social Ethic, Self-Reliance, and Child-Rearing Practices

Max Weber (1930) introduced the term *Protestant Ethic* to denote a set of ideas about man's relation to the natural and supernatural which gained prominence during the period of the Reformation. This new "world view" emphasized the development of the individual. The individual, within this framework, was without a mediator in his church and had to find salvation for himself. Self-reliance was emphasized as opposed to reliance on the social group. Further, the Protestant Ethic contained within itself the doctrine of "stewardship," the belief that God had made us the stewards or caretakers of His material world. The amount of possessions one had was a good predictor of whether one would fall among the sheep or the goats, the elect or the damned. Thus, hard work, self-sacrifice, and thrift, leading to the acquisition of funds, indirectly served as a measure of one's probability of being saved. Within the Protestant Ethic man became steward not only of his possessions, but of his time; God granted humans only a brief time to serve Him and this was not to be wasted on frivolous activities. The Protestant Ethic, in pure form, had as an ideal a pleasureless, hard-driven, and independent individual, ultimately responsible for his own affairs in both this and the next world.

It has been argued that the Protestant Ethic is being replaced in contemporary American society by the Social Ethic, an ethic that emphasizes adjustment to and dependence on others at the cost of independence and self-reliance; an ethic in which "other-direction," a concern for group approval, takes precedence over "inner-direction," the satisfaction of one's own standards and values (Riesman, 1953; LaPiere, 1959; Whyte, 1956). Adherents of this position believe that we have:

> . . . On the one hand, "the man of enterprise" of The Protestant Ethic, self-confident that through reason, integrity, industry, initiative, and faith in God he can bring into being the perfect social order, and, on the other hand, the delicate, womb-yearning individual of The Freudian Ethic, lacking self-reliance, at odds with "pathological society" from birth to death, chafing under its restraints, socially irresponsible, needing to be constantly nourished with love and pampered through such consideration as condones his offenses, delinquencies, and crimes, no matter what his age or status (Wescott, 1960).

This is an extreme view (not held, by the way, by the author of the foregoing quotation). The changing structure of society forces people in some ways, as in decreased reliance on the support of primary groups, to be *more* independent. Yet, it seems likely that dependency relations are increasing within the family at one extreme and toward the federal government at the other. This results from the weakening of extrafamilial primary group ties that used to sustain individuals.

With regard to child rearing, it has been demonstrated that child-training practices differ between hunting and fishing as opposed to agricultural societies (Barry, Child, & Bacon, 1959). Achievement and independence are more highly prized by hunters and fishers than by agriculturalists, whereas the reverse holds true for obedience and responsibility. The aims of child rearing differ according to the manner in which food is acquired. It may be that forces equally strong as those differentiating hunting and fishing from agricultural societies produce differences in child-rearing patterns in entrepreneurial, industrial societies, in contrast to bureaucratic, welfare-state societies. The independence, inner-directedness, and self-reliance that were the goals of the Protestant Ethic might have been a result of an adaptation to the industrial revolution, whereas the supposedly increasing emphasis on other-direction and reliance on, and conformity to, larger social groups may be a necessary adjustment to the new and growing welfare-state bureaucracy.[2]

This explanation of the shift from Protestant Ethic to Social Ethic finds considerable support in contemporary psychological research. In a most interesting and important book entitled *The Changing American Parent,* Miller and Swanson (1958) differentiate between entrepreneurial and bureaucratic parents. They use a number of criteria, such as calling all foreign-born and rural-born individuals entrepreneurial in orientation, which have been subject to considerable criticism. The basic difference between the two groups appears in the area of risk taking, and their differentiation should be made in these terms. Such representative entrepreneurial occupations as physician or clinical psychologist in private practice, small businessman, door-to-door salesman on straight commission, or contract fruit picker, though differing widely in status and required skills, have in common the fact that they do require the older ethic of self-reliance and independence. Income depends on hard work, individual initiative, and a fair degree of risk taking. In bureaucratic occupations, on the contrary, job security is high and risk taking minimal. A "womb-to-tomb" security is available to anyone who accepts the system and represses the once necessary trait of independence. Adjustment to the group and its norms becomes an important aspect of employment. Small wonder that bureaucrats and entrepreneurs differ in their attitudes toward the world, in what they believe their children should be like, and in how they go about obtaining the kind of behavior they seek from their children.

Entrepreneurs, as a group, believe the world to be harsher than do bureaucrats. They believe that children should be trained early to cope with this hostile environment. At least so far as early parent

---

[2] We should note that the words *welfare state* and *bureaucracy* have acquired negative connotations. We do not intend to use the words in either a positive or a negative sense, but merely to describe an existing phenomenon.

practices are concerned, the entrepreneur is more severe. Toilet training, weaning, and the completion of many other developmental tasks are demanded earlier of children by entrepreneurs than by bureaucrats (Miller & Swanson, 1958). As compared with bureaucrats, entrepreneurs are more authoritarian and lean toward a more rigid delineation of sex roles and a more traditionalistic orientation to family life (Johnson, Johnson, & Martin, 1961). These differences may result in part from the higher educational achievements of bureaucrats than of entrepreneurs of comparable social-class level.

Results of studies of occupational types, bureaucrat and entrepreneur, show considerable agreement in finding entrepreneurs to be more closely tied to the values of the Protestant Ethic. As a consequence, their goal is to produce independent children. To do so, they are more inclined to reject the child's impulse life—his responding to impulses rather than to reason—and to allow less variability in role playing than are bureaucrats. The bureaucrat, probably because his life is less demanding and his world more secure, is more optimistic. He appears to emphasize adjustment—the Social Ethic—rather than independence. The child is given wider areas of freedom, since mistakes, when made, do not bear as dire consequences. The bureaucrat generally is more permissive.

In the view of William H. Whyte (1956), the independent entrepreneur has abdicated in favor of the "organization man." Although the Protestant Ethic, and the parent attitudes and behaviors that went along with it, might have been admirably suited to an earlier economic era, the milder, more socially oriented Social Ethic has supplanted it, and parents have adapted their demands on children to newer circumstances. For better or worse, change has occurred in the basic orientation of Americans toward the world, and with it, changes in child-rearing practices. As the proportion of bureaucrats continues to increase in the future, present trends should become even more pronounced.

Is the Child Basically Good or Bad?

Until the middle of the 1950's it was often assumed that before the advent of psychology parents led a relatively untroubled life in which each generation was reared in the same fashion as the one before. The father was a bearded, stern but fair judge, and the mother, a subordinate, warm, loving, motherly, house-bound woman. Research has since shown that even this era of comparative calm was rocked with such controversies as those having to do with the morality of bottle feeding and with "breaking the will of the child" (Sunley, 1955). The golden age was less golden than had been believed. One historical analysis of child rearing in America demonstrated that religious orientation prompted certain assumptions about the nature of children. The major orthodox Christian point of view is that man is depraved. Adherents of the Calvinistic point of view, for example, believed the newborn to be damned as a result of Original Sin, and to be full of "the Old Adam." From this point of view, the young child was both evil and rebellious. The child's will had to be broken so that he would submit to parents and to God's will. This Calvinistic tradition was very strong in America in the 1800's, leading to episodes like the following:

> . . . One mother, writing in the Mother's Magazine in 1834, described how her sixteen-month-old girl refused to say "dear mama" upon the father's order. She was led into a room alone, where she screamed wildly for ten minutes; then she was commanded again, and again refused. She was then whipped, and asked again. This kept up for four hours until the child finally obeyed. Parents commonly reported that after one such trial the child became permanently submissive. But not all parents resorted to beatings to gain this end. One mother spoke of "constant though gentle drilling," which consisted partly of refusing to give the child an object just out of its reach, however much it cried. Another mother taught submission and self-denial at one and the same time by taking objects away from the child. Strictness in diet and daily routine was apparently frequently an accompaniment to obedience training. However, many mothers seemed to find it hard to follow out such prescriptions, and the Mother's Magazine carried many exhortations to mothers to do their duty toward their child (Sunley, 1955, p. 160).

This point of view was not without opposition, even in the early 1800's. Jean Jacques Rousseau taught that natural man—man before he was socialized—was good, and that society produced evil. Rousseau's ideas about child rearing are described in his book *Émile*. They consist, in part, of advocating that the child be let alone so that natural goodness can become manifest and, in part, of hardening the child, through vigorous exercise, for a difficult and harsh world. A third point of view, held most fully and defended most ably by Froebel (1898), also was present in this early era. This maintained that the child was like an unfolding flower and needed love and nurture. It is this last set of beliefs which appears to have gained ascendancy, but only after a long and bitter struggle.

Sunley (1955) suggested that the view of the child as evil had prevailed for a long time, and still had some adherents. This attitude has decreased in strength, as shown in analyses of the changes in the child-rearing practices advocated over the years by the U. S. Children's Bureau pamphlet, *Infant Care* (see Wolfenstein, 1951). One of these analyses compared the attitudes about the nature of children which served as bases for practices recommended in the 1914 edition with the attitudes reflected in the 1942–1945 editions of this guide. It concluded that, in 1914:

> . . . The infant appeared to be endowed with strong and dangerous impulses. These were notably autoerotic, masturbatory and thumb-sucking. This child is described as "rebelling fiercely" if these impulses are interfered with. The impulses "easily grow beyond control" and are harmful in the extreme: "children are sometimes wrecked for life." The baby may achieve the dangerous pleasures to which his nature disposes him by his own movements or may be seduced into them by being given pacifiers to suck or having his genitals stroked by the nurse. The mother must be ceaselessly vigilant; she must wage a relentless battle against the child's sinful nature. She is told that masturbation "must be eradicated . . . treatment consists of mechanical restraints." The child should have his feet tied to opposite sides of the crib so that he cannot rub his thighs together; his nightgown sleeves should be pinned to the bed so that he cannot touch himself. Similarly for thumb-sucking "the sleeve may be pinned or sewed down over the fingers of the offending hand for several days and nights," or a patent cuff may be used which holds the elbow stiff. The mother's zeal against thumb-sucking is assumed to be so great that she is reminded to allow the child to have his hands free some of the time so that he may develop legitimate manual skills; "but with the approach of sleeping time the hand must be covered . . . (Wolfenstein, 1951, p. 16).

In the 1942–1945 editions of *Infant Care,* it was noted that:

> . . . the baby has been transformed into almost complete harmlessness. The intense and concentrated impulses of the past have disappeared. Drives toward erotic pleasure (and also toward domination, which was stressed in the 1929–1938 editions) have become weak and incidental. Instead we find impulses of more diffuse and moderate character. The baby is interested in exploring his world. If he happens to put his thumb in his mouth, or to touch his genitals, these are merely incidents, and unimportant ones at that, in his over-all exploratory progress. The erogenous zones do not have the focal attraction which they did in 1914, and the baby easily passes beyond them to other areas of presumably equal interest. "The baby will not spend much time handling his genitals if he has other interesting things to do." . . . Everything amuses him, nothing is excessively exciting.
>
> The mother in this recent period is told how to regard autoerotic incidents: "Babies want to handle and investigate everything that they can see and reach. When a baby discovers his genital organs he will play with them. . . . A wise mother will not be concerned about this. . . . See that he. . . . Similarly with thumb-sucking: "A baby explores every-

thing within his reach. He looks at a new object, feels it, squeezes it, and almost always puts it in his mouth." Thus again that that was formerly a "fierce" pleasure has become an unimportant incident in the exploration of the world. . . . "As he grows older other interests will take the place of sucking" . . . (Wolfenstein, 1951, p. 17).

Early assumptions that the infant finds "fierce pleasure" in his world and that this pleasure is "bad" are being questioned. We are getting warmer and more lenient, largely as a result of the shifts occurring in the culture. Some of these shifts are material, such as greater wealth and higher technical level, but others have to do with the changing view of man—the increasing conviction that humans are not, by their nature, depraved.

Influence of "Experts" on Child-Rearing Practices

Evidence indicates that there have been two "revolutions" during the twentieth century in the definition of parental roles and practices. These definitions have been made by experts and accepted by individuals who advise parents in the mass media of communication. Actually parents have not shifted in behavior as much as might have been expected from the written media, but the experts have influenced parental practices, with the amounts of any particular influence differing among social classes at various times.

Table 7-1 contains data on child-rearing topics discussed and methods advocated in three women's magazines from 1890 through 1948, providing a view of the changes and continuities over the period (Stendler, 1950, pp. 122–134). Although the ladies' magazines are not the most accurate reflection of reality, their writers have concerned themselves with reader problems and expert opinion. The reader problems have been resolved according to the expert opinion then prevalent, thus disseminating these opinions to the reading public. Table 7-1A shows that parent problems do not vary greatly over the years. Opinions on how to deal with children and their problems, however, change materially, especially with regard to the care of infants, as is indicated in Table 7-1B. Clearly, the women's magazines have shifted the ground rules for being "a good parent."

From Table 7-1 it is apparent that tight scheduling of infant feeding was beginning to be advocated by 1900. The trends toward early weaning and toilet training, toward rigid scheduling, toward a rejection of play, rocking, fondling, and other forms of bodily contact between parent and child, and toward a prohibition of such devices as pacifiers that gave the child passive pleasure increased in force.

TABLE 7-1

A. Percentage of Topics Dealing with Various Aspects of Child Training as They
Appeared in Three Women's Magazines Analyzed in 10-Year Intervals

Aspect of Child Training	1890	1900	1910	1920	1930	1940	1948
Physical development	38%	19%	24%	30%	49%	22%	27%
Specific behavior problems	11	20	13	22	15	18	10
Infant disciplines	11	10	17	8	12	15	12
Character and/or personality development	35	31	39	3	24	23	21
Development stages	1	3	7	1	5	10	9
Sex education	0	6	0	1	1	4	0
Place of father	0	4	3	1	5	0	2
Miscellaneous	3	4	10	31	3	6	17
Total topics	63	95	75	82	65	76	80
Total articles	53	78	62	65	49	59	66

B. Percentage of Methods Recommended for Two Aspects of Child Training as
They Appeared in Three Women's Magazines Analyzed in 10-Year Intervals

Method Recommended	1890	1900	1910	1920	1930	1940	1948
Guiding Character or Personality Development:							
Discipline	18%	14%	34%	34%	38%	28%	2%
Provide a good home influence	61	53	30	12	14	5	3
Ignore undesirable behavior	12	5	9	0	12	18	4
Look for cause and plan accordingly	0	0	0	1	14	48	84
Invoke divine aid	15	20	15	0	0	0	0
Feed properly	0	0	0	50	0	0	0
Miscellaneous	4	8	12	3	21	2	8
Infant Disciplines:							
Tightly schedule	0	22	77	100	75	33	0
Loosely schedule	100	78	23	0	0	0	0
Self-regulate, "mother"	0	0	0	0	25	66	100

This often is called Watsonianism, since John B. Watson culminated these trends in his book, *Psychological Care of Infant and Child,* published in 1928. From the data in Table 7-1 and the aforementioned analysis of *Infant Care,* it seems clear that Watson was merely riding the tide and did not himself produce the trends. Yet his book did add weight to the idea of how child rearing should be conducted. Here are some of the typical passages from it.

The behaviorists believe that there is nothing from within to develop. If you start with a healthy body, the right number of fingers and toes, eyes, and the few elementary movements that are present at birth, you do not need anything else in the way of raw material to make a man, be that man a genius, a cultured gentleman, a rowdy or a thug (p. 41).

There is a sensible way of treating children. Treat them as though they were young adults. Dress them, bathe them with care and circumspection. Let your behavior always be objective and kindly firm. Never hug and kiss them, never let them sit in your lap. If you must, kiss them once on the forehead when they say good night. Shake hands with them in the morning. Give them a pat on the head if they have made an extraordinarily good job of a difficult task. Try it out. In a week's time you will find how easy it is to be perfectly objective with your child and at the same time kindly. You will be utterly ashamed of the mawkish, sentimental way you have been handling it (pp. 81–82).

The aims of this system of child rearing are described by Watson as follows.

We have tried to sketch in the foregoing chapters a child as free as possible of sensitivities to people and one who, almost from birth, is relatively independent of the family situation. . . . Above all, we have tried to create a problem-solving child. We believe that a problem-solving technique (which can be trained) plus boundless absorption in activity (which can also be trained) are behavioristic factors which have worked in many civilizations of the past and which, so far as we can judge, will work equally well in most types of civilizations that are likely to confront us in the future (pp. 186–187).

Watson valued independence, a controlled impulse life, and an active manipulative, striving posture toward the world. He wished to rear children in a way consonant with the Protestant Ethic, not the Social Ethic. Watsonianism, most fashionable in the entrepreneurial 1920's, may have begun losing its influence partially as a result of the accelerated growth of bureaucracy in the 1930's.

There are other reasons why Watsonianism was not destined for a long life. Its child-rearing technique appeared to be full of stress to parents. One still finds, occasionally, a Watsonian mother rearing her infant on a rigid, four-hour schedule. Three hours and 55 minutes since the last feeding, the baby is howling as it has been for 15 minutes, and has turned red with rage. The mother's eye is on her wristwatch. The remaining five minutes seem like hours. The psychic wear-and-tear alone of such aspects of Watsonianism seemed sufficient to turn parents away from this philosophy of child rearing. Besides, as has been noted, the role of children is more and more that of being a love object. It is difficult to express this love when every kiss leads to future neurosis, and even such relatively innocuous activities as bouncing the baby on one's knee may produce sexual feelings in the young child and lead to later sexual abnormality.

Certain ideas ran counter to Watsonianism and helped its decline. Although Watson apparently accepted the reality and significance of the Oedipus complex, and for this reason advocated a "distant" relation with the child in order to reduce the Oedipal conflict, other interpreters of Freud used the same theory to defend the gratification of the child's impulse life. More important in bringing about the eventual decline of Watsonianism was the idea of _homeostasis, or in-_ ternal equilibrium, originated by Walter B. Cannon in the early 1920's, and fully developed in his book, _The Wisdom of the Body_ (1932). Cannon's thesis, in brief, was that the body adapted to environmental stresses and among other adaptive mechanisms often "told" the indi- vidual through cravings what the body needed. The tendency of pregnant women in some parts of the world to eat earth as the result of an "irresistible urge" really occurred because the women suffered mineral deficiencies that could be reduced through the eating of cer- tain kinds of earth. Cannon's theory, buttressed with facts, suggested that if individuals craved something, the craving might be the result of actual physiological needs. Clara Davis (1931) operating from this same general point of view, allowed infants to self-select their diets. They chose the nourishment they desired from a rather wide variety of foods. Although any infant might go on short "food jags" during which he ate only one type of food, each infant over a long time inter- val chose a perfectly balanced diet. This fact demonstrated Cannon's correctness and also ran counter to Watson's view that children almost necessarily liked what was bad for them.

People began to think that if infants thrived on self-selected diets, they also might thrive on self-regulated schedules, and also might "need," in a physical sense, the contact and cuddling they seemed to enjoy, despite Watson's belief that these behaviors led to later maladjustment. It was probably because they needed it and not because of perversity.

The first complete reversal of the Watsonian trend was that of

Margaret A. Ribble in her book, *The Rights of Infants* (1943).[3] From the earlier position that fondling, hugging, kissing, rocking, and other forms of body contact between parent and child was *bad,* she demurred, maintaining that these activities were all important, and that the child denied them was deprived as significantly as one denied nourishment or sunshine. She held that the complex of treatments often lumped together as "tender loving care" was necessary for the physical, intellectual, and emotional growth and well-being of any child. Research data (Harlow, 1958) suggest that she might be basically correct regarding the need for body contact, even though certain of her hypotheses have been shown to be incorrect (Hopper & Pinneau, 1957; Pinneau, 1951).

Support for Ribble's position came fast. A new, "easier," warmer approach gained ascendancy. Yet there have been suggestions that the field is being reversed again—that society is moving back to the tough approach (Wolfenstein, 1951). It seems doubtful, however, that parent practices will swing back completely to Watsonianism. If they should, they will be bucking a strong current of forces, such as increasing bureaucracy and greater involvement with children, which dispose parents toward increased mildness.

There is not much probability that expert opinion will intensify future changes in child-rearing practices. Naive acceptance of expert opinion has dwindled. The higher level of general education and the several rapid about-faces in advocated techniques have made the public wary about experts. Parents wonder whether the experts really know what they are talking about. Besides, the experts themselves are less likely to be certain of having *the* formula for perfect child rearing as they grow aware of the wide range of innate individual differences in temperament and ability among humans. Watson and his followers explicitly rejected the notion of innate individual differences, and the "tender loving care" school has largely ignored them. If individual differences are great, then no single method of rearing can be expected to work for all. Nevertheless, there are ways to increase the probability of rearing children with the virtues prized most highly by parents and the defects they find least offensive.

Variation in Child-Rearing Practices

Social class has continued to attract the interest of child psychologists. This variable drawn from sociology has had considerable signifi-

---

[3] Other prominent adherents of this orientation were Spitz (1945) and Bowlby (1952).

cance in child-psychology research because of the wide belief that parental practices vary among classes, which results in discernible differences in the personality and behavior of children in these classes. Education, occupation, area of residence, and income play major roles in the definition of social class. To the extent that children are reared differently by parents who vary in these respects and who respond in diverse ways to social institutions, class differences may be expected in their upbringing.

Researchers once found that social classes differed substantially, but races only slightly, in child-rearing practices. The middle class showed greater harshness and an earlier and more general curbing of the child's impulse life than the lower class (Davis & Havighurst, 1946). These observations may have been entirely correct in describing the child-rearing patterns of the 1940's. But apparently what was true of the 1940's no longer applies. A study conducted, for example, in the Boston area in the early 1950's (Maccoby & Gibbs, 1954) obtained results markedly opposed to the Davis-Havighurst study. Although both studies found the middle class to have higher educational and occupational aspirations for its children, the Maccoby-Gibbs study noted that the middle, not the lower, class was more tolerant of aggression, sex play, and other expressions of impulse life. It was less demanding in toilet and cleanliness training, and it used less severe punishment. This reversal is probably due, in part, to the latter researchers' inclusion in their lower-class sample of individuals who by other criteria of social class would perhaps fall in the lower-middle class. The shift in the opinion of experts, whose influence is likely to be greater among the middle class, as a result of its wider exposure to the mass media, may also have been a contributing factor. In addition, the reversal may have been prompted by other forces.

Still more recent and more psychologically important data (Miller & Swanson, 1958; Klatskin, 1952) lead to the conclusion that differences in classes decreased appreciably in the postwar years.

> As of 1957, there are suggestions that the cultural gap may be narrowing. Spock has joined the Bible on the working-class shelf. . . . Apparently "love" and "limits" are both watchwords for the coming generation of parents. As Mrs. Johnson, down in the flats, puts away the hairbrush and decides to have a talk with her unruly youngster "like the book says," Mrs. Thomas, on the hill, is dutifully striving to overcome her guilt at the thought of giving John the punishment she now admits he deserves (Bronfenbrenner, 1958, p. 423).

The differences in world view that once existed among classes must have had some basis in sociological, anthropological, and historical influences. Doubtless the differences in child rearing and in child personality have dwindled substantially as a result of the increased homogeneity of the culture. One distinction often noted—the willingness of the middle, but not the lower, class to delay gratification—has been attributed to the uncertainty of lower-class life (Davis, 1946). This uncertainty led individuals to seize gratifications immediately; otherwise, the opportunity would very likely vanish. As members of the lower class acquired the greater security of low but relatively certain income, resulting from union protection on the job, unemployment compensation, and other features of the welfare state, their lives were likely to become more predictable. Hence, they became more willing to postpone reward and develop long-range goals.

The reduction of income disparities within the population also seems to have narrowed the differences in the styles of living among classes. Today's society in America has fewer extreme poor and fewer extreme rich. The greater availability of the appurtenances of the culture as a result of credit has reduced the differences still further. Moreover, a lower-income family no longer has to live under crowded slum conditions; Federal Housing Administration loans, as well as government-owned housing, make better quarters possible. Although these homes have often been called the slums of tomorrow, one can expect a family of two parents and five children to change in attitude when moving from a cramped, run-down, one-bedroom tenement apartment to a clean, new home which has so much room that no more than two persons have to occupy any single bedroom. Most families do change under these circumstances. Many of the parents are now property owners and must train their children and themselves, too, to respect property and to be neat and less aggressive. Accompanying this kind of change comes what the sociologists call "upward mobility." There is an increased interest in education as a means of self-improvement, and a greater acceptance of the Protestant Ethic at a time that it appears to be losing its appeal for the middle class.

A final force narrowing the differences between the classes is the mass media of communication. Middle-class patterns of democracy, consultation, and arbitration; of paternal involvement in household chores and child care; of parental permissiveness; and of delayed gratification, long-range planning, and high aspirations for children— all these are grist for the mills of the producers of television family series. Exposure to any set of values should cause some rubbing off on the exposed individual. Although television and other mass media may present a distorted image of middle-class life, their picture is an intimate one which allows social learning to occur and which causes identification to take place. Thus, the mass media also help to diminish class, race, religious, and regional differences in child-rearing practices and in attitudes toward children.

Entrepreneur vs. Bureaucrat. As previously noted, on top of the more conventional social-class differences, considerable variation exists between entrepreneurial and bureaucratic individuals in the upper occupational brackets, probably as a result of conflicting social demands. The entrepreneur, an independent individual, as a means of controlling behavior accepts the Protestant Ethic and feelings of guilt more than does the more socially minded bureaucrat. This difference is less discernible than the one concerning the classes. Yet entrepreneurs and bureaucrats are faced with different sets of social pressures; this occasions a variance between them in their attitudes toward the world. Because they view the world differently, they raise their children differently; and the children have to adjust to the world as perceived by their parents.

Perhaps many conflicts regarding child-rearing practices, such as the question of the school being overly concerned with adjustment at the expense of achievement, may have their roots in the entrepreneurial-bureaucratic antithesis. The bureaucratic orientation of educators, for example, may be at odds with the entrepreneurial orientation of school boards dominated by businessmen. The differences between these groups are substantial and, unlike variations in class, may retain their significance for some time.

Race, Religion, Region. Racial, religious, and regional differences in child-rearing practices persist, too. Data are scant in this area because social scientists have paid little attention to it. Some studies do exist, however, such as the book, *Children of Bondage* (1940), which described what it was like to grow up as a Southern Negro. Data on the child rearing of such "unworldly" groups as the Hutterites (Kaplan & Plaut, 1956) and the Amish (Francis, 1955) are also available. Far more information may be found, however, in autobiographical form. Several anthropological studies, described in the 1960 Proceedings of the Society for Research in Child Development, have been undertaken to determine subcultural differences within the United States. Beneath the homogeneity of growing up in America, there is much heterogeneity, these studies show. Among five groups of settlers living, for example, in the same locality in the American Southwest, three are non-Indian; these are Spanish-Americans, Texans, and Mormons.

Two of them are fully within the limits of Western culture, and yet even these two vary in values and behavior (Vogt & Roberts, 1956). Parallel with differing attitudes toward the world go individual modes of child rearing. Further studies in which subgroups within a culture are compared with one another will undoubtedly provide useful information about the impact of specific parental practices on variability in human behavior.

CONCLUSION

Benjamin Lee Whorf (1956), whose studies of language have played a significant role in contemporary psychology, concluded from a study of Indo-European tongues that the differences among them are very minor—so minor, in fact, that he lumped them all together as "Standard Average European." This may be small consolation to a student learning a language. Yet German, Classic Greek, French, Latin, and Latvian resemble one another so closely that the differences among them are slight in comparison with the distinction between all of .hem and non-Indo-European languages. The same might be said about variability within the Western culture. Although Westerners differ from each other, they nevertheless have been subjected to sufficiently similar experiences to show a strong resemblance. Since experiences within American society disclose a common quality even greater than that of its ties with Western culture, variability among Americans is reduced still further.

To draw another analogy from language, Americans speak a number of dialects. The differences among Down East Yankee, "Brooklynese," the dialects of the Midwest and Far West, and the drawl of the Southerner are easily discerned, but all Americans can understand each other without strain. So, too, with differences in child-rearing patterns. Differences certainly exist, but within a larger pattern of homogeneity.

This common bond in the socialization process is strong enough to produce an "American type," an individual different from all others yet patently similar to fellow Americans in basic orientation. Since all individuals are exposed to the various influences described in this chapter, if in somewhat varying degrees, the differences between parents in child-rearing practices and between children in personality and behavior are markedly narrowed. It is within this cultural homogeneity that the specific life situation of an individual child produces a unique person.

REFERENCES

Barry, III, H., Child, I. L., & Bacon, Margaret K. Relation of child training to subsistency economy. *Amer. Anthropologist,* 1959, **61,** 51–63.

Becker, H., & Meyers, R. C. Sacred and secular aspects of human socialization. *Sociometry,* 1948, **5,** Nos. 4 and 5.

Benedict, Ruth. Continuities and discontinuities in cultural conditioning. In P. Mullahy (Ed.), *A study of interpersonal relations.* New York: Hermitage Press, 1949. Pp. 297–308.

Boehm, Leonore. The development of independence: a comparative study. *Child Develpm.,* 1957, **28,** 85–92.

Bronfenbrenner, U. Socialization and social class through time and space. In Eleanor E. Maccoby, T. M. Newcomb, & E. L. Hartley (Eds.), *Readings in social psychology.* (3rd ed.) New York: Holt, 1958. Pp. 400–425.

Cannon, W. B. *The wisdom of the body.* New York: Norton, 1932.

Davis, A. The motivation of the underprivileged worker. In W. F. Whyte (Ed.), *Industry and society.* New York: McGraw-Hill, 1946. Pp. 84–106.

Davis, A., & Dollard, J. *Children of bondage.* Washington, D. C.: Amer. Council of Educ., 1940.

Davis, A., & Havighurst, R. J. Social class and color differences in child rearing. *Am. sociol. Rev.,* 1946, **11,** 698–710.

Davis, Clara M. Self-selection of diets: an experiment with infants. *The Trained Nurse and Hosp. Rev.,* 1931, **86,** 629–634.

Durkheim, Émile. *The elementary forms of religious life.* (Trans. by J. W. Swain.) New York: Macmillan, 1915.

Durkheim, Émile. *The division of labor in society.* (Trans. by G. Simpson.) Glencoe, Ill.: Free Press, 1947 (orig. publ. 1902).

Durkheim, Émile. *Suicide.* (Trans. by J. A. Spaulding and G. Simpson.) Glencoe, Ill.: Free Press, 1951 (orig. publ. 1897).

Francis, E. K. *In search of utopia.* Glencoe, Ill.: Free Press, 1955.

Froebel, F. *Mother play.* (Trans. by Henrietta R. Eliot and Susan E. Blow.) New York: Appleton, 1898.

Haimowitz, M. L. What price virtue. In M. L. Haimowitz & Natalie R. Haimowitz (Eds.), *Human development: selected readings.* New York: Crowell, 1960.

Harlow, H. The nature of love. *Amer. Psychologist,* 1958, **13,** 673–685.

Hopper, H. E., & Pinneau, S. R. Frequency of regurgitation as related to the amount of stimulation received from the mother. *Child Develpm.,* 1957, **28,** 229–235.

Jaensch, E. R. *Der gegentypus.* Leipzig: Barth, 1938.

Johnson, R. C., Johnson, Carol M., & Martin, Lea. Authoritarianism, occupation, and sex role differentiation of children. *Child Develpm.,* 1961, **32,** 271–276.

Kaplan, B., & Plaut, T. *Personality in a communal society; an analysis of the mental health of the Hutterites.* Lawrence, Kan.: Univer. Kan. Publications, 1956.

Klatskin, E. H. Shifts in child care practices in three social classes under an infant care program of flexible methodology. *Amer. J. Orthopsychiat.,* 1952, **22,** 52–61.

Landis, P. H. *Adolescence and youth.* New York: McGraw-Hill, 1945.

LaPiere, R. *The Freudian ethic: an analysis of the subversion of American character.* New York: Duell, Sloan & Pearce, 1959.

Maccoby, Eleanor E., & Gibbs, Patricia K. Methods of child rearing in two social classes. In W. E. Martin & Celia B. Stendler (Eds.), *Readings in child development.* New York: Harcourt Brace, 1954.

Mead, Margaret. *And keep your powder dry.* New York: Morrow, 1943.

Miller, D. R., & Swanson, G. E. *The changing American parent.* New York: Wiley, 1958.

Pinneau, S. R. A critique on the articles by Margaret Ribble. *Child Develpm.,* 1951, **21**, 203–228.

Riesman, D. (with Glazer, N., & Denny, R.). *The lonely crowd: a study of the changing American character.* New Haven: Yale Univer. Press, 1953.

Ribble, Margaret A. *The rights of infants.* New York: Columbia Univer. Press, 1943.

Society for Research in Child Development. Proceedings Twenty-fifth Anniversary Meeting. *Child Develpm.,* 1960, **31**, 187–239.

Spencer, Herbert. *The study of sociology.* New York: Appleton, 1912.

Spitz, R. Hospitalism. In O. Fenichel et al. (Eds.), *The psychoanalytic study of the child,* Vol. 1, New York: International Univer. Press, 1945.

Stendler, Celia B. Sixty years of child training practices. *J. Pediat.,* 1950, **36**, 122–134.

Sunley, R. Early nineteenth century American literature on child rearing. In Margaret Mead & Martha Wolfenstein (Eds.), *Childhood in contemporary cultures.* Chicago: Univer. Chicago Press, 1955. Pp. 150–167.

Tonnies, Ferdinand. *Fundamental concepts of sociology: Gemeinschaft and Gesellschaft.* (Trans. by C. P. Loomis.) New York: American Book Co., 1940.

Trollope, A. *North America.* New York: Harper, 1862.

Trollope, Frances. *Domestic manners of the Americans.* New York: Knopf, 1949 (orig. publ. 1832).

Turner, F. J. *The frontier in American history.* New York: Holt, 1921.

Vogt, E. Z., & Roberts, J. M. A study of values. *Sci. Amer.,* 1956, **195**, 25–31.

Watson, J. B. *Psychological care of infant and child.* New York: Norton, 1928.

Weber, M. *The Protestant ethic and the spirit of capitalism.* (Trans. by Talcott Parsons.) London: Allen & Unwin, 1930.

Westcott, Regina H. Man of enterprise: whether bound, a review of La Piere's "the Freudian ethic . . . ," *Contemp. Psychol.,* 1960, **5**, 258–259.

Whorf, B. L. *Language, thought and reality.* Cambridge, Mass.: Technology Press, 1956.

Whyte, W. H. *The organization man.* New York: Simon & Schuster, 1956.

Wolfenstein, Martha. The emergence of fun morality. *J. soc. Issues,* 1951, **7**, 15–25.

chapter 8 ✳ Psychosocial Aspects
of the Family Setting

What a child learns in the home is conditioned by a number of diverse influences. Such things as order of birth, position of siblings, family size, marital relations of parents, the presence of a handicapped child, whether the mother works, and whether the family belongs to a minority group all affect the social learning experiences of the child in his home. These factors, which, of course, are accidental, might be called, as Sears (1950) designated them, "sociological variables." How much, if any, psychological bearing they have can be judged only through examining the research in existence, sparse as this may be in several of these areas. In some instances, little more than reports of clinical impressions are available; in others, the research undertaking has not been designed adequately enough, having neglected many controls. Thus, the precise *psychological* import of these *sociological* variables remains to be uncovered through research. At that, there is sufficient evidence of some psychological content in these factors to warrant their close examination in order to understand the psychosocial nature of the family environment.

Later in this book we shall encounter some of the major psychological forces prevalent in the home, such as democracy and acceptance. As they affect the child these forces may outweigh the sociological variables to be considered here, even though the latter may well diminish the significance of the psychological influences. Often omitted in a psychological treatment of childhood, the accidental variables so contaminate and interact with the psychological that the result of their interaction, the child's behavior, is the product of both. The exact impact of each set of variables, however, is not easy to assess. For example, one might believe that democracy in the home is a pervasive influence on the child's behavior, yet it would be misleading to ignore the presence of one or more of the accidental variables. How does divorce, to cite one of them, affect parental use of democratic policy?

Psychology has been relatively unconcerned with the accidental variables. *Ex post facto* study based on retrospective reports has been the main source for investigating such matters as the effects of divorce on the child. Although some other procedure may pose greater difficulty, the pursuit of it may be worthwhile, if only because of the greater conclusiveness of the results likely to be obtained. The Koch investigation, as we shall see presently, which dealt with sibling position, exemplifies both the complexity of a well-designed study and the richness of findings yielded by a well-planned empirical exercise.

FAMILY COMPOSITION

Early in this century an unusual amount of time and effort was invested in discovering the effects of order of birth and ordinal position in the family—that is, family composition—on personality. Nearly every phase of behavior of any psychological import was studied in relation to the order in which the child was born. Many publications contained studies on the ties between birth order and "(a) genius and feeble-mindedness, (b) suggestibility and aggressiveness, (c) dominance-feeling and sensitivity to pain, (d) sociability and ascendancy, (e) religious attitudes and political attitudes, (f) emotionality and stability, (g) neurotic make-up and psychotic trend, (h) happiness and jealousy, (i) school failure and fame" (Krout, 1939, pp. 5–6). In a handbook on child psychology, Murchison (1931) devoted an entire chapter to the "Order of Birth in Relation to the Development of the Child," mentioning 78 references.

Onliness

Before discussing birth order and sibling position, let us view the narrower topic of "onliness." Largely refuted by research findings, statements regarding the effect on personality of being an only child provide a lesson for child psychologists. Students of child psychology know that statements unsupported by research, even if made by so-called experts, are to be taken with caution. Scientific thinking differs from nonscientific thinking, as we saw in Chapter 1, in that ideas, hypotheses, or theories are abandoned whenever research proves them wrong. One can be truly critical of statements in the area of scientific endeavor only when aware of the research findings. In child psychology, the literature on onliness illustrates the point.

"Being an only child," said G. Stanley Hall, "is a disease in itself." In an early book on child guidance, the Blantons (1927) asserted: "The only child is greatly handicapped. He cannot be expected to go through life with the same capacity for adjustment that the child reared in the family with other children has" (p. 175). And a book concerned with abnormal psychology (Maslow & Mittleman, 1951) maintained: "The only child is likely to be overprotected, and he is never dethroned by any later children. His parents may spoil him, make him dominating, egotistical, and, at the same time, essentially weak in his character structure. In that case he tends to be deeply hurt when he is not the center of interest and attention" (p. 147). All three statements were made in textbooks written by reputable practitioners of psychology.

But what does research show on the bearing of onliness on development and personality? Several studies have compared only with non-only college students on standard behavior and adjustment tests as well as on achievement (Fenton, 1928; Campbell, 1933; Dyer, 1945), whereas other studies have employed teacher ratings of elementary school children (Fenton, 1928; Guilford & Worcester, 1930). In general, the findings have indicated no essential differences between only and other children. One researcher (Campbell, 1933) felt that his results suggested a more pronounced effect of onliness among girls than among boys. He attributed this to the fact that boys are given more freedom in the home than are girls. This enables boys more than girls to associate with other children outside the home, which compensates for the absence of siblings at home.

Consistently in language development, as noted in Chapter 5, only children advance more rapidly than children with siblings (Davis, 1931). The superiority of only children in language facility is significant because it leads to the real psychological importance of onliness—the effect on the child of the undeniably greater contact he enjoys with his parents. What are the results of a comparatively intensive parent-child relationship? How does a greater amount of interaction with adults affect development and personality as compared with interaction with children of one's own age?

As we have seen, a child with adults as his primary speech models is advanced in language development. There are also indications that relative isolation from peers, including siblings, contributes to intellectual achievement and scientific eminence (Faris, 1940; McCurdy, 1957; West, 1960). Two related explanations support this hypothesis. One holds that an individual who finds great satisfaction in his social relationships has little motivation to partake of the intense effort required for high achievement. The other point of view, which is more attune with this discussion, emphasizes the influence of close contact with interested adults who stimulate the child in intellectual spheres. Combined with isolation from children of one's own age, this influence encourages a rich fantasy life, independence, and originality.

As to the effects of onliness on personality, the research is inconclusive, and with good reason. Undoubtedly the significant factor is the quality of the relationship between child and parent. The adjustment, personality, child-rearing attitudes, and behavior of the parent need investigation before one can make assumptions about the impact of onliness on a child. When research lumps together all only children and investigates various aspects of personality, small wonder that the findings show few differences between only and nononly children. Important as onliness may be in directing attention to the crucial importance of the parent-child relationship, the fact of wide differences among parents of only children suggests that onliness is phenotypical. Too often, as mentioned in Chapter 1, research in child psychology has investigated phenotypes with inconclusive results. It has failed to account for really important psychological characteristics and for wide differences among children and parents within any single group, differences which cancel each other out when subjects are bunched together for research purposes.

Birth Order and Sibling Position

For both topics the literature and findings are as contradictory as they are voluminous. This results, of course, from the importance of a child's "psychological position" in the family, which may bear no relation whatsoever to his order of birth. "The question whether the child feels accepted and loved; his emotional relation with his parents; the competition or support which brothers and sisters bring to him; and the specific pressures or areas of freedom and stimulus that come along with one position in the family or another are probably more important than the objective fact of ordinal position"

(Murphy, Murphy, & Newcomb, 1937, p. 363). No one would argue that the child's psychological environment is not significant, nor that siblings are an unimportant part of this environment. Siblings, interacting with each other, create an ever-changing psychological environment in the family. Jealousies and hostilities, favoritism, the extent to which the child meets the unconscious needs of the parent—all these arise early in the family situation and may have intense emotional bearing on the child's personality and development.

It may be useful to note what Adler (1928) had to say on this subject.

> The oldest child feels dethroned by the coming of his brother and wants to restore his place by fighting. Unless he can overcome in the struggle for supremacy in his universe he is apt to become depressed, peevish, more or less hopeless, and will show his hopelessness later in life if confronted by problems. He is very likely to be conservative, to understand power and to agree with it. If he is strong enough he becomes a fighting child.
>
> As for the second child he is never alone, but is always confronted by the older child. This constant picture before him of an older and bigger child begets in him a sense of rivalry. If successful, he is an excellent type, but if defeated, for instance, if he is not able to compete successfully with the older child in word and in play, he loses hope, becomes depressed and has a bad time of it.
>
> The third child has to fight for a place in the sun, but he has no successor. This gives him a great sense of power, and if he is capable he often overcomes the older children in the family by his sense of importance. If he is not capable, he perhaps hides behind the fact of being spoiled, and becomes lazy, escaping from tasks, wasting time and making excuses.

First-born and early-born children have been found to be inferior in size and weight to children born later. First-borns also show higher percentages of premature births and stillbirths. Findings regarding intelligence are contradictory but generally there seems to be no connection between order of birth and intelligence. Some evidence shows, as Table 8-1 indicates, that gifted children and American men of science come disproportionately from first-borns.

Although first-borns are sometimes thought to be handicapped in emotional adjustment, conclusive research is lacking. One early study found that first-borns were more likely than children born later to be given ratings of undesirable traits by their teachers (Goodenough & Leahy, 1927). It cited the comparative inexperience of parents in the case of first-borns, the imposition of tasks on the eldest child, and the difficulty of changing from only child to nononly child as possible explanations for its findings. Another study (Sears, 1951) noted less doll-play aggression among older than among younger siblings. This

TABLE 8-1   Percentages of Gifted Children and of American Men of Science
in Each Birth Order for Each Size of Family

Size of Family	Birth Order			
	First	Second	Third	Fourth
2	56.1 * (57.4) †	43.9 (42.6)		
3	36.9 (44.0)	31.9 (31.2)	31.2 (24.8)	
4	33.0 (36.1)	26.8 (22.4)	15.4 (21.8)	24.7 (19.7)

* Terman, L. M., et al. *Genetic studies of genius, Vol. 1: The mental and physical traits of a thousand gifted children.* Stanford, Calif.: Stanford Univer. Press, 1925.
† Cattell, J. McK. *American men of science.* (4th ed.) Garrison, N. Y.: Science Press, 1927.

would indicate that, at least in the family setting, the older sibling experiences fewer frustrations than the younger sibling. The older sibling has fewer more powerful frustrating agents in his environment. Moreover, in the doll play there was stronger identification with the mother among older brothers than among their younger siblings. These several findings accent the psychological importance of sibling position and point to some of the pertinent areas which might be examined for insights into the influence of sibling position on the unfolding of personality.

The Koch Study.   The extensive study by Helen Koch (1956e, 1960) deserves special mention.   It is one of the few relatively recent investigations of sibling influence on a child's psychological development.   Its rarity and extensiveness both stress the great complexity of this zone of research, especially if a study is to be designed adequately, employing most of the necessary controls.   This study covered 360 five- and six-year-old children from two-child, urban, native-born, white, intact families (Koch, 1956e, 1960).   Investigated as the independent variables were the sex of the child under study, the sex of the sibling, ordinal position, and three spacings between siblings —less than two years, two to four years, and four to six years.   Each of 24 subgroups contained 15 children.   Through analyzing the ratings assigned by teachers for a variety of traits, the impact of these variables on the characteristics of child behavior was discerned. The following are samples of Koch's findings.

1. In language development (Koch, 1956a), first-born children consistently spoke more articulately than second-born. The greater the gap in age between siblings, the better the articulation tended to be. In addition, there were indications that stuttering might be related to the sex of the sibling and the difference in age between the two children. The amount of stuttering was thought to stem from how much jealousy and conflict there was as a result of the sibling's sex and difference in age. Similarly, the degree to which the child was frustrated by its sibling as well as the extent to which the child was allowed to express these frustrations was felt to have some bearing on the amount of stuttering.

2. Identification with a sex role was studied through ratings of sissiness in boys and tomboyishness in girls (Koch, 1956b). Boys with a slightly older sister were rated as relatively sissified. This characteristic tended to decrease as the age differential between siblings widened. In parallel manner, girls with older brothers were considered more tomboyish than girls with sisters. Such findings provided evidence for the psychological impact of having a sibling.

3. In intellectual development, children with male siblings scored higher than those with female siblings on both verbal subtests and total scores of the Primary Mental Abilities Test (Koch, 1954). Possibly the broader experience of boys, a result of a higher level of activity, might have had some relevance. The greater competitiveness and aggressiveness associated with boys may create a more stimulating environment for the sibling.

4. Both ordinal position and spacing of siblings influenced range of interest. The wider the spacing, or age difference, the greater was the number of interests held by the child under study. Indeed, second-borns were noted to have more numerous interests than first-borns. Again, familiarity with an older sibling's preoccupations and association with his companions proved important influences on the later-born child.

5. Even when the gap in age was minimal, first-born children seemed better planners than second-born. To Koch this implied a greater responsibility as the lot of the first-born as well as a necessity to plan carefully in order to maintain his superior position.

In her findings, Koch proceeded beyond mere description to offer valuable clues and insights concerning the motivations for various traits and behaviors of children (Koch, 1956c). Her analysis of ratings of several emotional factors pointed to the existence of greater stimulation or strain when siblings belonged to opposite sexes than when they were of the same sex (Koch, 1956d). Perhaps this may be explained by sex rivalry, preference for one parental sex over the other, or other subtle factors in the family and sibling relationship.

Largely the data indicated that as spacing between siblings increased the tendency grew for each to go his own way. It might be said that the narrower the spacing, the more easily various emotional characteristics of the child could be imputed to sibling interaction, whereas the wider the gap, the greater were the influences of the child's interaction with his parents (Koch, 1956d, 1957).

Without doubt these findings illustrate the enormous complexity of both the research on sibling influence and the influence itself. As a research matter, the topic may easily remain quiescent for many years. But as a clinical item, sibling influence should continue to play an important part in understanding and interpreting individual behavior.

Other Studies. Two studies, in particular, have probed the crucial area of maternal attitude. In the first of these Dean (1947) asked 20 mothers of pairs of children of the same sex to compare their youngsters' with regard to a number of traits. The mothers reported their older child to be more fearful, dependent, worrisome, and anxious, whereas they described their younger one as more physically aggressive, negativistic, stubborn, affectionate, happy, and good-natured. Whether these children actually possessed the characteristics is less important than the fact that the differences in how the mothers perceived their first as compared with their second child were consistent. If expectations as to the behavior of first and second children are uniform, they could well exert an influence on the outcome.

In the second study, Lasko (1954) compared the behavior of mothers toward first and second children. Mothers of 46 pairs of children were rated on the Fels Parent Behavior Rating Scales, based on interviews with the women and observations of mother and child interaction in the home. Whereas the families considered in this project had been participants in a longitudinal investigation lasting a number of years, ratings of the mother's behavior toward her two children at the same chronological age could be matched. In general, the mothers behaved less warm emotionally and were more restrictive and coercive toward their first child than toward their second. Moreover, they tended to baby and protect the second child more than the first. Analyzing the shifts in parent behavior as the two children grew older, Lasko concluded that the most important trend for the first child was a lessening of parent-child interaction. There seemed to be no parallel change for the second child. The first child was subjected to much verbal stimulation and attempts to speed up its development during the first two years of life, whereas no such regimen was imposed on the second child. There was also a tendency for disciplinary frictions to be exacerbated in dealing with the oldest child. As women had more children, they seemed to develop warmth combined with a sense of strictness.

An experimental study among college students implied that first-borns were more suggestible than later-borns in social situations and more apprehensive in surroundings that aroused anxiety (Staples & Walters, 1961). This could be ascribed to the greater needs of first-born children for some kind of affiliation because of the inconsistent rearing received in childhood.

That the differences in maternal attitudes and behavior pointed out by Lasko could produce distinctions in the personalities of children is indeed plausible. The reduction in babying and protectiveness, the decreased contact with the mother, less parental solicitude, and the less child-centered home experienced by the first child could well influence his perception of the extent to which he is accepted by his parents. The first child, upon the birth of a sibling, must adjust to a change in the quality of his interaction and relationship with parents. The second child, on the other hand, enjoys a greater stability of parental policies. From all these considerations, one can see how position in the family may very well explain differences in personality and behavior among children.

FAMILY SIZE

Like family composition, the size of the family is a sociological variable. This is an area scarcely touched by psychologists because of the problems of designing properly controlled studies of the effect of family size on personality and development. However, sociologists have dealt at length with the changing trends over the years in size of American families.

The Small Family

Bossard (Bossard & Sanger, 1952) has contrasted the large and small family with respect to impact on the child. In the small family, most issues such as family size, spacing of children, and the main objectives of education and child rearing are matters of general agreement. Parenthood is intensive rather than extensive. For the child the implications are many. Considerable emphasis is placed on individual development. Because of the parents' tremendous investment, emotional and otherwise, in each of the few children, the child is under relentless pressure to measure up to family expectations. His development and achievements are weighed against others in his neighborhood and social class. The primary disciplinarian is the mother, with little discipline issuing from siblings. In view of the identification of intimate relations with only a few people, mostly adults, the child's resentments, said Bossard, tend to be directed toward the same person or persons. The small family group enables a greater degree of democratic participation by all the children, something not possible in larger families.

> In summary, the small family rests upon the ideas of planning, individualization, democratic cooperation, social isolation and intensive pressures. The small family system is a quality system, chiefly at the middle class level. Its driving force is one of ambition, in an open class system; its social justification, if one may thus speak of it, is that it represents an 'adjustment to a rapidly changing society, with its train of attendant insecurities (Bossard & Sanger, 1952, p. 6).

The Large Family

Large families are different. They take many crises in stride, partly because so many of them, large and small, occur. In a large family one has to learn to make adjustments to all sorts of changes—changes in status, in responsibilities, in role. Emphasis on the group rather than on the individual is encouraged. Often economic necessity makes cooperation mandatory. Moreover, one's own actions and behavior inevitably depend on the conduct and attitudes of others. Because a large number of persons reside within a limited space, a greater degree of administration, organization, and authoritarian control is needed (Bossard & Sanger, 1952). This suggests that the authoritarian control exercised several generations back may have stemmed from the larger family size of that day. Although this authority usually rests with the dominant member of the family—one of the parents or an older sibling—it is often wielded by the siblings toward one another. Furthermore, there is less intimate contact in a large family between the parent and any individual child. Overprotectiveness, overindulgence, and intrusiveness seldom occur. And by the very nature of the family's size, problems of internal stress and strain are manifold.

Conditions in large families have been described in a book by Bossard and Boll (1956) covering a study of 100 families with at least six children. The data were obtained from interviews and questionnaires in which at least one member of each family responded. In evaluating the findings one must bear in mind the limitations and disadvantages of the interview and case-study techniques as these were explained in Chapter 1. Although several aspects of the Bossard and Boll study were beyond the pale of psychological significance, many of its points are worthy of consideration.

Through necessity, sibling sacrifice was often inevitable. Where death befell one of the parents, the burden of caring for the rest of the family descended generally on the older children.

> My sister was the oldest of a large family. After my father's death and my mother's remarriage, the entire responsibility of the large house became hers. Instead of going to dances, parties, and playing basketball, as her friends were doing, she was at home, keeping house, doing the laundry, and watching over her younger brothers and sisters. When mother went to the hospital, she and I were left in charge altogether. The baby cried routinely every night, but still we got up and saw that the family had breakfast and were ready for school. Often my sister would miss school (Bossard & Boll, 1956, p. 121).

The responsibilities assigned to the older children were mentioned frequently.

> "From the time that I was five," writes the oldest of eight, "I can remember taking care of the children. I used to lie on my mother's bed and push my little brother back and forth in his carriage until he fell asleep. Mother kept on having babies. Many problems beset us. By the time I was in the third grade, I was always helping mother while the others played with the neighboring children. This made me old beyond my years, serious, and quite responsible for all that went on in the household. . . . Each Saturday, my mother went into the city six miles away for the groceries and stayed for the day. In the evening she and dad visited friends and came home at about midnight. From age fifteen to nineteen, I found myself responsible for seeing that the housework was finished, cooking lunch and dinner for the children, and caring for the newest baby. At night, I bathed six children, washed their heads, and tucked them into bed. Saturday nights continued like this until I rebelled. I wanted to have time for dates like other girls had" (Bossard & Boll, 1956, pp. 159–160).

Discipline was often administered by siblings. Many of the responses received during the study considered this to be perhaps more satisfactory and effective than parental discipline. For one thing, children might understand each other and each other's problems better than parents do. Besides, the respondents felt that children were often better judges than parents of what constituted misbehavior. Finally, sibling discipline might be more effective because ostracism or disapproval by one's brothers and sisters might be more meaningful than a parental spanking.

Most of the respondents believed that a large family produced a sense of security in the individual. Support by siblings and cooperation helped to foster this belief. It would be interesting to see what carefully controlled research which compared large and small families might turn up here.

Bossard and Boll (1955, 1956) also discussed the various roles played by the members of a large family. To them specialization of role, specifically personality role, was characteristic of life in the large family unit. The following eight personality types were described.

1. The *responsible* type. This was most often the oldest child, especially the older or oldest daughter because of her responsibility of rearing the young children.
2. The *popular, sociable, well-liked* type. Frequently this was the second-born, or the one following the responsible sibling in order of birth.
3. The *socially ambitious* type, or "social butterfly." Most of these were usually third, fourth, or fifth in order of birth.
4. The *studious* type. This child withdrew from sibling activities to find satisfaction in books.
5. The *self-centered isolate*. This was the child affected by the pairing off of other siblings or the child who staged a general rebellion because of a rebellion against one of the parents.
6. The *irresponsible* type. This child withdrew from family life and family responsibility.
7. The *physically ill* child. In some cases, this child suffered from chronic illness, in others, he seemed hypochondriacal.
8. The *spoiled* sibling. Often this was the youngest child.

Since each child strives for recognition in the large family, as Bossard and Boll have emphasized, he adopts a specialized role for this purpose. Quite naturally, the older children pre-empt a number of these roles leaving the younger ones to scramble for those that are left.

Certainly these data pertaining to the size of the family suggest interesting and fruitful hypotheses about whether size is actually a psychological as well as a sociological variable. Nevertheless, on the basis of available evidence, one must side with Bonney (1942) who held that family size neither explained nor described adequately the personality of any particular child.

MARITAL RELATIONS OF PARENTS

Based on the conclusions of clinical studies that marital conflict and divorce affect the adjustment of children, many writers have attributed a number of child behaviors to domestic discord. Delinquency, stealing, truancy, lying, disciplinary difficulties, jealousy, hyperactivity, problems of speech, reading problems, poor social adjustment, and homosexuality are all said to result from marital strife. This list is far from inclusive. Yet not much adequately designed research is at hand to help in sorting out the effects of a variety of factors and in identifying true cause-and-effect relationships. It may seem "obvious," for example, that divorce in an adolescent's background is *the* cause of current poor social adjustment. When quizzed, in fact, an adolescent will recall a vast number of traumatic feelings associated with the divorce (Landis, 1960). However, one cannot be sure from after-the-fact recollections what the experience was like at the time of occurrence. A child's past can never be fully reconstructed, as was noted in Chapter 1. Motivated by all kinds of conscious and unconscious needs and feelings, one may falsify in retrospect the memory of circumstances and events. Besides, it is impossible to single out one particular event as *the* source of all future behavior. Finally, the independent variable, in this case marital conflict or divorce, has not been systematically controlled: there is no control group matched with an experimental group on a number of variables, with only the factor of divorce or strife differentiating the two. With these limitations in mind, let us review the meager literature in existence on research into the effects of marital adjustment on the child.

Marital Adjustment and the Child

Several investigations have resulted in negative findings. One of these (Burchinal, Hawkes, & Gardner, 1957) analyzed the relation of parental scores on a marital adjustment inventory to scores of fifth graders on the Rogers Test of Personality Adjustment. Only in one of ten cases did the correlations seem significant, and the magnitude of this was so small that no support was found for the expected connection between marital adjustment and the personality adjustment scores of children. However, the measures of both types of adjustment were so unreliable that it is difficult to tell whether any relation, even if one existed, could have been detected from these test results.

Another study (Stroup, 1956) found no relationship between the mother's marital adjustment and the child's score on a standard personality test. Medinnus (1963) observed slight bond between interparent agreement on three measures of attitude and the adjustment and popularity of the child in first grade. However, Leton (1958) noted a greater discrepancy between attitude scores of parents of poorly adjusted children than between parents of well-adjusted children. In Medinnus's study interparent agreement was found to be fairly specific, with little general consistency among the various measures. Because of this, one could hardly expect to discover a relationship between parental disagreement on a specific matter or in a specific area and so ambiguous a measure of child behavior as general adjustment. More fruitful results are likely to emerge from an examination of the effects of particular areas of disagreement between parents on particular aspects of child behavior.

A number of studies have sought to identify the marital factors in the home which have contributed to the behavior of the young child in school (Hattwick, 1936; Baruch, 1937). Children from "happy, calm" homes tend to be less negative than youngsters from the opposite type of home (Hattwick, 1936). The latter showed more signs of emotional disturbance, such as jealousy, fear, grumbling, nervousness and sulking, and tenseness. Baruch and Wilcox (1944) named the following five main tensions in the home as influencing poor adjustment among preschool children: tension over sex satisfaction, tension over lack of consideration, tension over insufficient expression of affection, tension over inability to talk things through, and tension over ascendance-submission relations. The first three were interpreted as indicating a lack of security in the marriage relationship. The fifth reflected on the child's feelings of adequacy. No doubt both parent security and adequacy exert important psychological influences on the adjustment and personality growth of the young child. But the primary significance of marital adjustment seems to be its reflection of a more basic adaptation of the two people involved in the relationship.

Divorce

That divorce hampers child adjustment cannot be denied. However, its precise effects are not easy to determine because most of the data come from clinical case studies. How much of a child's maladjustment may be charged to the divorce as such, or how much results from the long period of conflict, tension, and discord leading to divorce is hard to say. Then, too, how much may be attributed to the poor personality adjustments of the partners in the particular marriage? Whatever the case, many child behaviors stem from parental divorce as several research studies have indicated.

As a group, adolescents from broken homes showed less psychosomatic illness, less delinquent behavior, and better adjustment to parents than those from unhappy, unbroken homes (Nye, 1957). This would suggest that in some cases separation and disruption of the home is desirable. Perhaps this might follow from the additional finding that the adjustments of parents individually and to their spouses were superior in broken homes than in the unhappy homes that remained intact.

To Landis (1960) the grouping together for research purposes all children of divorce and treating them as if they were a homogeneous group with respect to the effects of divorce seemed unsound. He found differences between adolescents who, prior to learning of the divorce, remembered their homes as happy and those who considered their homes as unhappy and full of conflict. The former were especially likely to feel that their first knowledge of the divorce was a traumatic experience; they had been caught by surprise and had been unable to accept the fact. Asked to state how they believed the divorce had affected their feelings of security and personal happiness, they replied that they had experienced little change in these areas. Those who, on the other hand, had conceived of their homes as unhappy said they felt greater security and happiness after the divorce. The children from homes regarded as happy, however, reported greater difficulty in adjusting to their peers as the children of divorced parents. One must remember, however, that all these responses bear the disadvantages of any retrospective account.

Landis divided the respondents into three groups according to age at the time of divorce—five to eight years, nine to twelve, and 13 to 16. Fewer among the younger children said they felt a loss of security and were less happy because of the divorce. Memory may play tricks here or this finding may suggest that divorce is less damaging to a young child's security than to the security of an older child. Landis thought there were certain potentially traumatic situations awaiting the child of divorcing parents.

> First, there is the necessity to adjust to the knowledge that divorce will probably take place; (2) there is the necessity to adjust to the fact of divorce; (3) there is the possibility that in the predivorce or postdivorce

years one or both parents may "use" the child as a weapon against the other, with traumatic effects upon the child; (4) there is the necessity for a redefining of relationships with parents; (5) the new status of being the child of divorced parents may necessitate new adjustments with the peer group; (6) some trauma may result for children who recognize the implications of their parents' failure in marriage; and (7) there may be problems of adjustment for the child if the parents remarry (Landis, 1960, p. 7).

To gather data on the effects of divorce, Goode (1956, p. 317) interviewed 425 divorcées. That these mothers did worry about the possible impact of their divorces on their children was evident from comments made throughout the interviews. Table 8-2 reports the replies to a question on this matter.

The women were questioned as to the extent to which they believed that the divorce experience had been a traumatic one for them. A link clearly related the severity of this trauma to the women's reports of how "hard to handle" were the children. The greater the trauma, the higher was the proportion of mothers who stated that their children at some time had been difficult to manage. Although

TABLE 8-2 Replies of Divorcées Regarding Impact of Divorce on Their Children

Question: Now that the divorce is all over, would you try to tell me, in your own words, how you felt about the divorce and the children. What went through your mind when you thought of the possible effects of the divorce upon him/her/them?

Coded Answers	Per Cent of Respondents Giving Answer* (N = 425)
Better for them; I was right	31
Worried about lack of parent; clear ambivalence with no explanation (child needs father, but not this one)	27
No effect, child too young, didn't worry	10
Didn't worry then, but negative items appeared later	3
Worried about possible effects of remarriage on child	2
Worried about social stigma for child	6
Religious difficulties: child in Catholic school; child might be rejected by congregation	1
Finances (other than education): support, clothes, etc.	8
Bad for child (answer not elaborated)	9
Miscellaneous, never thought of it, not sure	6

* Some respondents gave more than one answer.

half the women considered the children no harder to handle after the father's visits, 25 per cent of them believed that the child became more of a problem in management following these occasions. It would seem clear that the whole matter of custody and visiting privileges might well prove a source of anxiety for the child.

Subtle Factors. In Western culture parents feel a responsibility to the child, not only for his physical welfare but also for his emotional welfare. Since divorce threatens the child's emotional stability, the parent contemplating such action often experiences strong feelings of guilt. These feelings may also arise from resenting the child who renders the divorce situation more difficult. To compensate for them, the parent may attempt to be overprotective of the child and to show excessive concern for its welfare. Yet just as divorce may foster feelings of guilt in the parent, it may arouse similar sentiments in the child. To the youngster's mind, the separation may seem punishment for his own past "naughtiness" or for unconscious, hostile feelings toward his parent. More obvious, however, are the occasions when the child overhears parental controversy in which such statements as the following may be hurled at one another: "If it weren't for Jimmy we wouldn't have had all this trouble; I would have divorced you long ago." It is not too challenging to discern how the child may feel himself the cause of this discord, nor how he may view the subsequent divorce and loss of one parent as punishment (Despert, 1953).

Whereas parents themselves in a predivorce situation are not sure of the course to be followed, their uncertainty and anxiety are communicated readily to the children. The tension and vague threat of change are hard for the child to cope with psychologically. Although the statement "the emotional stability of the child is dependent upon the emotional stability of the parent" lacks confirmation through research, it is quite evident that an unstable home environment for whatever cause may have harmful implications for the child's psychological adjustment.

Following divorce moving often becomes necessary. This adds to the adjustment problems facing the child, especially if he is of school age. Furthermore, arrangements for substitute care for him may be required if the mother returns to employment outside the home.

In a later chapter we shall discuss the process of identification whereby the child patterns his behavior after that of the parent of his own sex. This process is impaired in many ways when there is only one parent present in the home. In approximately 90 per cent of divorce cases the mother receives custody of the child. This certainly affects a boy's identification with a father figure, and a gap in learning certain aspects of future adult roles may well occur when there is one parent lacking in the home. The oft-heard phrase "I am marrying again because Johnny needs a father" may be another way of expressing the need for a male figure with whom a young boy can identify. Additional complications may aggravate the divorce situation when the mother deliberately endeavors to subvert the child's loyalties to the father by derogatory comments.

In the family, in general, the parents tend to serve as buffers or neutralizers in their mutual influences on the child. This is familiar in fiction and folk literature where the mother often is pictured as the intercessor between father and son, attempting to temper the severity of the father's punishment. Where there is but a single parent in the home, the child's relation with that parent is unmitigated by the presence of another. Any conflicts and antagonisms already in existence may become accentuated.

Thus, even though research has yet to separate the effects of divorce from those of the marital strife that might have preceded it, factors present in the divorce situation are known to exert harmful influences on the child's psychological adjustment. Tensions, instabilities, lack of proper figures for identification, hostilities, guilt feelings —all these come to the fore when divorce occurs. To understand and identify the precise impact of divorce on any child one needs to know how much love and understanding will continue after the action and how much real concern and affection exists for the youngster. In other words, does the child perceive the divorce as punishment and rejection or has the situation been approached with maturity and insight so that the child's love for and confidence in the parents are not shaken?

HANDICAPPED CHILD IN THE FAMILY

Much has been written about the handicapped child, but the material is predominantly clinical in character. Few carefully designed research studies can be found, understandably. It is not easy to impose the controls necessary for effective research on investigations into the influence of a handicapped child on siblings. Left largely with clinical reports, therefore, one must beware of the pitfalls of acquiring information through these channels. Undoubtedly a host of considerations colors the parent's account. Certainly the extent of his own emotional involvement and his own needs and motivations, as noted in Chapter 1, affect his report. In addition, as we have already seen, caution must be exercised in seeking to attribute effects to specific causes. For example, many parents have ascribed marital discord to the presence in the family of a retarded child. However, one careful study (Farber, 1959) found a similarity between marital integration *before* the arrival of the handicapped child and marital integration some years after. Moreover, it may be easier for a parent to blame the presence of a handicapped child for sibling maladjustments than to impute these to disruptive factors within the parent-child relationship and within the family structure.

Although a few studies supply direct evidence of the influence on siblings of a handicapped child in the family, most of the literature has dealt with the impact on parents and the whole family unit. Any upset such as mental illness, depression, or unemployment which affects the family structure or parental personality and adjustment may be said to concern the personalities, adjustments, and attitudes of that family's children. For this reason, we shall consider briefly some of the repercussions of the presence of a handicapped child.

Nonclinical Impact

Before examining the clinical aspects of having a handicapped child in the family, let us consider some of the other problems. First comes the obvious additional financial burden which specialized medical attention imposes. For both diagnosis and treatment, parents of a handicapped child often spend a considerable amount of money. Such outlays may directly affect the siblings and work more subtly through the worries and tensions they produce in the parents.

Family activity and the pattern of living may be curtailed which may influence the siblings in a number of ways. Frequently parents of a mentally retarded child mention a gradual social isolation. Neighbors and the community do not understand mental retardation. They do not know its causes, or what can be expected from such a child, or how to handle the youngster. This ignorance leads to unfounded fears and apprehensions. One parent would not permit his child to play with a neighbor's mentally retarded youngster because of a fear that his child might be led "into all sorts of perversions." The isolations and withdrawals that occur certainly affect the social adjustment of the siblings. Adolescents often hesitate to invite friends into the home because of their feelings of shame and embarrassment over the appearance and behavior of the retarded child.

The extra toll levied on the parents of a retarded or handicapped child by the necessity to provide physical care and to plan for the youngster, together with the responsibility they assume, may easily produce an undue amount of anxiety and tension. The very nature of the child's limitations places more demands on a parent than would a normal child—and it is no secret that the demands of even the normal child often exhaust the parent! Any such increase in tension and anxiety in the household is likely to have profound influences on the siblings.

The possible theological conflicts (Murray, 1959) confronting the parent of a handicapped child could perhaps affect his outlook and philosophy of life. Although such problems may be resolved either with bitterness and disillusionment or with acceptance and constructive effort, the normal siblings cannot escape unscathed.

Clinical Findings

Parents of handicapped children vary considerably in the adequacy of their own personality adjustments on which the birth of such a child may impose a great strain. Many aspects and decisions stemming from the presence of a handicapped child in the family prove threatening to the parent and are capable of arousing anxiety within him. The question of whether to place the child in an institution, for example, may stir unconscious feelings in the parent; these may be repressed feelings of wishing to be rid of the child or feelings of rejection which he cannot resolve. Then, too, since the child is his own biological offspring, the parent may regard any injury, impairment, or disability in the child as an injury to himself. More important, perhaps, the parent may view the birth of a handicapped child as a reflection of his own inadequacy and incompetence. The parent may find it difficult to adjust to "this blow to the psychological self."

Often the presence of a handicapped child arouses a tremendous amount of guilt in the parent. He may interpret the birth of such a child as a punishment for real or imagined sins. Or perhaps the feeling of ambivalence, or often rejection, toward the handicapped child may generate strong sentiments of guilt. This can have unfortunate consequences of overconcern and of overprotection of the child. Such overprotection may result in neglect of the siblings as well as an intrusive behavior by the parent in the relationship between the handicapped child and his siblings.

All in all, self-blame is sometimes the outcome of guilt feelings. One mother, for example, expressed excessive concern that her handicapped child might fall into the family swimming pool. It developed from therapeutic consultation that her concern arose from a time when she deliberately tried to push the child into the water. The satisfactory solution of these various types of problems hinges upon the parent's own adjustment to himself and to life. How he succeeds or fails may indeed affect the personality growth of the siblings. Some parents, of course, use the handicapped child as a psychological scapegoat for their own shortcomings and inadequacies. Those who do are prevented from dealing realistically with their own problems.

A parent's disappointment at the birth of a handicapped child may have far-reaching implications for the siblings. Some children have reported increased parental pressure to achieve in academic and nonacademic pursuits—for example, athletics—to compensate for the nonachievement of the handicapped sibling. One study (Zuk, 1959), in fact, found mothers more willing to accept a younger mentally retarded child than an older one. This might be taken to mean that dissatisfaction with the nonperformance and nonachievement of the child increases over the years.

What, then, do research studies have to say about all this? What do they find about the effects on families of the presence of a retarded child? In a study of the adjustment of parents and siblings of institutionalized and noninstitutionalized retarded children (Caldwell & Guze, 1960), which combined psychiatric interviews with several objective measures, including a family attitude scale and a children's anxiety scale, few differences were generally found between the two groups of siblings. Yet the study discovered that although most siblings of the institutionalized mentally retarded thought institutionalization worked best, most of the siblings of the retarded who were not institutionalized felt that home care was preferable. Perhaps the demands of a handicapped child in the household produce a sense of responsibility and a certain amount of resourcefulness among the siblings. That such a situation may also result in increased sensitivity to the needs, misfortunes, and problems of others is a matter for speculation.

Farber's large-scale, well-designed study (Farber, 1959), which covered 240 families with a severely mentally retarded child, was based on interviews with both husband and wife and on results of a variety of measures. The study sought to check the effects on family integration of such a handicapped child in the home. These were the results obtained from two of the indices, an index of marital integration and another of sibling role tension: in general it was noted that the marital integration of parents of mentally retarded boys at home was lower than that of mentally retarded girls similarly at home. One possible explanation for this is the usually more disruptive effect of the boy; another is the thwarting of greater parental expectation for the boy than for the girl. Although the sex of the retarded child did not affect the integration of its siblings, a high degree of dependence on the part of the deficient youngster did do so adversely. The pressures on the mother of caring for the retarded child and the added responsibilities falling to the siblings had relevance here. Supporting this interpretation was a finding that the younger the retarded child was the more he influenced the adjustment of his siblings.

Thus, as we have seen, there is evidence for the belief that a handicapped child in the family may affect the siblings in various ways. This seems to be fairly well established even though research in this area has been sparse. To recapitulate, a handicapped child in the family affects parental personality and adjustment. It also causes financial strain, curtailment of family activity, possible social isolation and withdrawal, anxiety and tension in the parents, and an increase of expectations and pressures among normal siblings.

MATERNAL EMPLOYMENT

Since the Second World War when women entered the labor force on an unprecedented scale, there has been an increasing interest shown in the influence of a working mother on child adjustment. In fact, a large number of wartime and postwar juvenile problems have been charged to the absence of the mother from the home. But here, too, as with other portions of this chapter, early claims regarding the harmful consequences of maternal employment have not been confirmed by subsequent research.

The 1961 census estimated that 13.3 million married women were employed or were in search of employment in March of that year. These women represented approximately one-fifth of the nation's labor force. An increase of 4.2 million married women in the work force between April 1951 and March 1961 had accounted for almost half—45 per cent—of the total force growth during that decade. Approximately 53 per cent, that is, seven million, of the employed married women in March 1961 had children under 18 years of age; more specifically, 33 per cent had youngsters between the ages of six and 17, whereas 20 per cent had children under six.

By tradition, "the mother's place is in the home." She seeks outside work only if the family economic situation demands it. The position taken by a group of psychologists, that the child's eventual personality adjustment depends on a close relationship with his mother during his early years, has lent support to this point of view. Unless there is a "continuous mother figure" present, harmful consequences are likely to ensue.

Despite these assertions, the authors of this book regard maternal employment as a sociological variable which may or may not exert a significant psychological influence. A variety of other factors actually may be more crucial than maternal employment in governing the child's adjustment. Some of these include the age of the child, provisions for substitute care, the consistency between mother and substitute in attitudes and behavior, the basic affectional relationship between mother and child, the personality and personality needs of the particular child, the reasons for maternal employment, and the mother's attitude toward working and child care. Research investigations that group together children of working mothers and those of nonworking mothers ignore important variables that cut across this division. It is not surprising, therefore, that research findings have been largely negative. Only if maternal employment were more pertinent than these other factors would one expect to find significant distinctions between the two groups of children.

Research Findings

In an effort to discover differences between the attitudes and adjustment of employed and nonemployed mothers toward children, Nye (1959) detected few significant ones between the two groups of women. The nonemployed were more likely to say that "children make me nervous," but this was the only distinction noted between the two groups on five items examined. From the finding that "adjustment to children" improved the longer the mother worked, Nye concluded that although her employed status at first produced some conflict, these contentions began to disappear as the mother became reconciled to her new role in the family structure.

To test the adjustment of the child of a working mother several measures have been applied. These include ratings by teachers, check lists of problems exhibited, personality inventories, and observational methods. In general the studies can be separated according to the age of the children under investigation—infants, preschool youngsters, elementary school children, adolescents. Having scrutinized these studies, Stolz (1960) indicated that not many basic differences were observed between the children of employed and nonemployed mothers at any of these age levels. The few undertakings that have attempted to relate the child's achievement in school to the employment status of the mother have also produced negative findings, counter to the popular opinion of teachers that children of employed mothers perform less well than those of mothers who do not work outside the home.

Often listed as causes of delinquency are neglect and lack of supervision by the working mother. Yet some investigations have failed to set up controls for the socioeconomic status of the family. Since both the employment status of the mother and juvenile delinquency are offshoots of the economic level of the home, the variable of socioeconomic status clearly must be controlled before valid comparisons may be made. In a study of 500 delinquent boys matched with an equal number of nondelinquents for age, ethnic and racial derivation, and general intelligence, the Gluecks (1957) observed no difference in the proportions of delinquents and nondelinquents whose mothers were regularly employed. However, a larger number of delinquents than nondelinquents had mothers who worked irregularly. Still it does not follow that irregularity of employment is the cause of delinquency; the irregular worker may be the kind of mother who works to escape household tasks and maternal obligations. In other words, both the sporadic employment of the mother and the child's delinquency may be products of a more basic emotional maladjustment of the parents. Nevertheless, the Glueck data do relate lack of supervision to tendencies toward delinquency.

Other studies have substantiated the view that maternal employment outside the home may influence the children's perception of the feminine role. In Hartley's study (1960) more daughters of nonworking mothers said "housewife" when asked what they expected to do when they grew up, whereas more daughters of working mothers mentioned various professional aspirations. Furthermore, more daughters of working mothers said they would continue to work after marriage.

The extent to which the mother viewed her work positively or negatively was studied by Hoffman (1959). As a rule, the mothers whose attitudes toward their work was positive also experienced a more positive relationship with their children and used milder discipline.

It would appear, then, the maternal employment has not been found to play a decisive part in influencing the child's adjustment or achievement. Despite the inadequacy of research, measuring devices, and control of pertinent variables, no gross distinctions have been discerned between children of employed and nonemployed mothers.

Quite likely it is the quality and not the quantity of interaction between mother and child which is of psychological significance. Consequently maternal employment per se does not seem to affect child adjustment adversely.

MINORITY GROUP MEMBERSHIP

Finally, there is the impact on the child of membership in a minority group. Although the country abounds with racial, religious, and political minorities, the present discussion deals largely with the Negro minority group. To a large extent what is said about Negroes applies equally to other minority groups. The Negro group is distinguishable from other minorities for several reasons. To cite two of them, it is more readily identifiable by the color of its skin and it constitutes the country's largest minority.

Awareness and Identification

At what age do racial awareness and accurate racial identification develop? The typical procedure for finding this out involves individual interviews with young children in which they are presented with dolls or drawings which include white and colored figures. The children are asked questions to elicit information concerning racial identification and racial preference. This is the set used by Clark and Clark (1947, p. 169):

1. Give me the doll that you like best.
2. Give me the doll that is a nice doll.
3. Give me the doll that looks bad.
4. Give me the doll that is a nice color.
5. Give me the doll that looks like a white child.
6. Give me the doll that looks like a colored child.
7. Give me the doll that looks like a Negro child.
8. Give me the doll that looks like you.

Table 8-3 (from data by Clark & Clark, 1947) lists the results obtained from 253 Negro children divided according to age levels. It is evident that in general there was an increase with age in the percentage of children who identified themselves accurately with the colored doll. There was also a marked tendency for the children to show a preference for the white doll. This tendency decreased with age although most children at each level preferred the white to the colored doll.

In attempts to identify various aspects of the self concept investi-

TABLE 8-3   Choices of Subjects at Each Age Level

	Age 3	Age 4	Age 5	Age 6	Age 7
Request 1 (play with)					
colored doll	42	24	26	29	40
white doll	55	76	74	71	60
Request 2 (nice doll)					
colored doll	36	24	28	46	44
white doll	58	76	72	53	52
Request 3 (looks bad)					
colored doll	68	52	78	63	43
white doll	19	24	11	15	17
Request 4 (nice color)					
colored doll	39	28	20	43	48
white doll	58	72	78	56	48
Request 5 (for white)					
colored doll	13	14	7	3	0
white doll	77	86	94	97	100
Request 6 (for colored)					
colored doll	77	83	94	96	100
white doll	13	17	7	4	0
Request 7 (for Negro)					
colored doll	55	59	61	78	85
white doll	29	35	30	17	7
Request 8 (for you)					
colored doll	36	66	48	68	87
white doll	61	31	52	32	13

gators have posed the question "What are you?" to young children. As children increase in age, they shift from describing themselves by their own names or with reference to individuals in their specific environment to the use of ethnic designations (Hartley, Rosenbaum, & Schwartz, 1948). This vividly illustrates the increasingly important role played by ethnic membership in one's feelings and attitudes about oneself.

Accurate racial identification, of course, does not necessarily imply full awareness of racial prejudice and of the significance of racial membership. Yet several investigators have reported great emotionality among some of the Negro children asked to make a racial self-identification. That racial awareness itself has certain psychological implications is borne out by its earlier occurrence among Negro children than white children (Horowitz, 1939). Actually psychological factors such as the effect of minority group membership on parents produce this earlier awareness in Negro youngsters.

Studying racial awareness in four-year-olds, Goodman (1952) discovered strong evidence for its presence among these children. The recognition of racial differences exceeded their capacity to express their feelings about them. One of the children interpreted the significance of membership in a minority group in these succinct terms: "The people that are white, they can go up. The people that are brown, they have to go down" (Goodman, 1952, p. 28). This is cut from the same cloth as the statement by a Negro adult: "You live in a city all your life, but you're never home. Maybe that's what it means to be a Negro" (Karon, 1958, p. 1). Goodman further noted a strong inclination for Negro children to refuse to identify, or to resent identification, with their own group.

> [Dianne] is a dark brown child, even darker than her mother, and she likes whiteness to a rather extreme degree. There are only a few colored children in her nursery school. She is conspicuous among the assorted whites, and conscious of the fact. She went home one day and asked her mother "am I colored?" The affirmative answer was followed by the explanation that "some people are black and some are white." Dianne, like most of our four-year-olds, was most concerned about herself. "I don't *want* to be colored," she declared. Back at nursery school again one day, Carol (w) took a good look at Dianne and asked her if she were colored. "Yes, I am. Don't touch me! Don't sit near me!" And Dianne sat away by herself looking unhappily at her arms. Then there were days when she vigorously lathered her arms and face with soap. After one of these efforts, she said triumphantly to Peter: "This morning I scrubbed and scrubbed and it came almost white." But she knew it had not really done so . . . (Goodman, 1952, pp. 37–38).

> There is a kind of desperation in Tony's cry of "Brown—brown—brown!!" as he throws down the picture about which we have been talking, and talking too long for his peace of mind. The matter is becoming more and more personal and personally threatening. He and others must have felt like Barbara, who was obviously unhappy. She did not enjoy being asked to tell which doll or picture looked most like herself, and her parents. And finally she said so, with intensity and exasperation: "Don't ask too many questions!—*I can't stand it*" (p. 42).

> Tony A. admits that his parents look like the pictured Negro couple, but finds it necessary to add, about his father and mother, "they're *good* people." Viola likes the white doll better " 'cause it's cuter than the other one" (the brown doll to which she has given scarcely a glance). Tony R. evades self-identification, as a good many of these children do occasionally. He says that he was like neither of the baby dolls, when he was a baby. But he adds wistfully: "I was called 'Butch' when I was a baby. Is that one (white) 'Butch'?" Joan G. says of the matching boy dolls that the brown one is nicer because "the white one is too heavy."

But her resolution to like brown fails her when we come to the girl dolls. She fondles the white one, and then—briefly—the brown one. "This one," she says, "this one I'm holding (brown)—*it just gets on my nerves*" (p. 43).

. . . "Then one night when he wasn't yet seven he did a queer thing. After he'd had his bath he put powder all over himself—he loves to do that—and he came out of the bathroom with this powder all over his face. I said to him 'you look awful—go wipe that stuff off your face.' He looked at himself in the mirror and said: 'No, I don't mummy. I look just like a little white boy now' " (p. 124).

Using ratings by the nursery-school teacher, Goodman unearthed evidence indicating that the personalities of the Negro children were affected by minority group membership even by the age of four. These youngsters were rated higher in activity, emotionality, sensitiveness, competitiveness, and aggressiveness than their white schoolmates. Greater aggressiveness among Negro children also showed in other studies. In a study by Hammer (1953), for example, the drawings of Negro children in a projective-type drawing test received higher ratings for the amount of hostility and aggression expressed.

Over half of the Negro youngsters in the Goodman study conveyed a sense of inferiority to whites through an assertion that whites were "nicer," "prettier," and "more desirable as playmates." This kind of acceptance of white standards leads not only to a depreciation of one's own group but also to a deprecation of oneself. "Though living in a democracy, many Negro citizens apparently learn by three years of age that skin color is important, that white is to be desired, dark to be regretted" (Landreth & Johnson, 1953). This same feeling is shared by members of other minority groups. At a Mexican baptismal party, the father was heard to utter the shocking imprecation, *"negro, negro; malo, malo"* (black, black; bad, bad). This was a terrible verdict to pronounce on one's own son at his baptism and seemed to be prophetic of the later life experiences of an unusually dark child (a "Black Mexican") in a light-skinned family. It pointed out the potentially dreadful consequences for self-acceptance in the minority group member's surrender to the majority group dictum that light is good and dark is bad.

Thus, the foremost effect of minority group membership apparently is its influence on the individual's concept of himself. Negative images of the self and even self-rejection flower early and serve as pervasive forces in shaping personality. But these, of course, are not the only penalties of minority group membership; the others simply are not relevant to this discussion.

Problems of Later Life

Although much psychological theory relating to the development of personality has stressed the critical nature of the early years, it would be misleading to overlook forces which impinge on the individual during his growing-up years as well. In fact, particularly with reference to the Negro in the South, Davis (1943) suggested that the full impact of belonging to a minority group was not felt until the individual sought a job; at that time he became fully aware of the educational, social, and economic barriers in his path. Frustration, disillusion, and cynicism followed.

The responses of 150 preadolescent Negroes concerning their feelings and impulses when placed in unfortunate situations illustrated some of the emotional difficulties of Negro children because of their race (Goff, 1950). Disparagement, rude treatment, direct ridicule, and physical ill-treatment were some of the things they suffered.

> "One day the teacher told us she wouldn't take us on no trips because it would be a disgrace to be seen on the street with a bunch of monkeys and laughing hyenas. She said, 'What would my friends say?' "
>
> "I went to get on the street-car and a white man jerked me off, and let a white woman on and then he got on."
>
> "One day I was swinging in the park, and a white girl stuck out her tongue at me and wouldn't use the swing when I got through using it. She waited for a white girl to get through."
>
> "I was riding my bicycle and got a flat. I took it in the station to get it fixed. The man wouldn't let me have no air, and he said he couldn't fix things for colored people" (Goff, 1950, pp. 154–155).

Material from the interviews indicated that ridicule alone had a marked effect on development of personality. There seemed to be a sex difference in reaction to the kinds of treatment related in the responses. More resentment was found among boys whereas girls were more likely to express feelings of inferiority.

The discrepancies between the impulses of the Negro youngsters in response to mistreatment by whites and what actually occurred dramatically demonstrates the psychological impact of such mistreatment. Although a desire to fight or to argue was reported in 57 per cent of the instances, withdrawal followed 82 per cent of the time. No wonder that frustration and ill-concealed hostility are psychological earmarks among the personalities of many minority group members.

The full significance of membership in the Negro minority, of course, cannot be discussed apart from factors of social class. A spate of circumstances has relegated most Negroes to the lower socioeconomic group. Thus, they are members not only of the lower *caste* but also of the lower *class*. In this country lower-class families are characterized by two things: material deprivation and low standards of conduct (Dai, 1956). Broken homes, dominance of maternal authority, residence in impoverished and deteriorating neighborhoods, parent-child friction and antagonism accompanied by harsh and severe parental treatment, encouragement of delinquency by the environment—all these are the lot of Negro lower-class, lower-caste membership.

In a study of 25 Negroes through psychoanalytic interviews, Rorschach tests, and Thematic Apperception Tests, Kardiner and Ovesey (1951) maintained that the direct effects of discrimination were low self-esteem and anger. Low self-esteem might be manifested in unrealistically high aspirations, or in apathy, in living for the moment, in hedonism, or in criminal behavior. Denial of aggression and of hostility together with the anxiety-provoking feeling of being angry lead the Negro adult to contradictory behavior; he is good humored, affable, irritable, fearful, submissive, capable of explosive outbursts, and generally constricted in his emotional life. In the opinion of Kardiner and Ovesey, the failure of the Negro subjects to use their potential intelligence might be attributable to inner conflicts which rendered them incapable of focusing their attention.

Similar findings were reported by Karon (1958) who compared the personality characteristics of Southern Negroes with those of Northern Whites and Negroes. Eleven characteristics differentiated the Southern Negro from the latter two groups. Six of these were related to aggression, either with its denial or with the suppression of anger. The Southern Negro was characterized also by "weakened affect," which may be interpreted as a "deadening of one's emotions" through stifling one's anger and hostility and through inability to express feelings of aggression and solve frustrations.

Accounts of how membership in the Negro minority conditions personality can be found in the autobiographical writings of such celebrated individuals as Marian Anderson (1956), Billie Holiday (1956), and Richard Wright (1950). Wright had this to say:

> These fantasies were no longer a reflection of my reaction to the white people, they were a part of my living, of my emotional life; they were a culture, a creed, a religion. The hostility of the whites had become so deeply implanted in my mind and feelings that it had lost direct connection with the daily environment in which I lived; and my reactions to this hostility fed upon itself, grew or diminished according to the news that reached me about the whites, according to what I aspired or hoped for. Tension would set in at the mere mention of whites and a vast

complex of emotions, involving the whole of my personality, would be aroused. It was as though I was continuously reacting to the threat of some natural force whose hostile behavior could not be predicted. I had never in my life been abused by whites, but I had already become as conditioned to their existence as though I had been the victim of a thousand lynchings (Wright, 1950, p. 90).

Of course, much variation exists among individuals in their reactions to membership in a minority group. This variation may be ascribed to psychological factors in the home. How does the parent respond to the situation: positively and constructively, or negatively and self-defeatingly? More important, to what extent is the child accepted by the parents? How far does the child, in consequence, develop feelings of self-worth, self-esteem, and self-acceptance? It has been noted that Negro children who are most self-accepting also tend to disclose more positive attitudes toward other Negro and white children (Trent, 1953). Unquestionably, the greater the child's sense of adequacy and security, the less need has he for counteraggression and the less stinging will be, as a rule, the detrimental blows of prejudice and intolerance.

SUMMARY

In this chapter we have examined the psychological consequences of six sociological variables: family composition, family size, marital adjustment and divorce, handicapped child in the family, maternal employment, and minority group membership. Conclusions are difficult to draw because of the problems of conducting adequate research. Although most researchers would agree that these variables are of potential significance to personality development of the child, they would have to concede that the precise influence remains to be clearly established.

Unfortunately, research follows the easiest course. Consider maternal employment. The research suggests that the quality of the interaction between mother and child is more pertinent to the child's behavior and adjustment than whether the mother is employed outside the home. But it is much easier to ascertain the employment status of the mother than to evaluate the psychological relation between mother and child. So it goes for the other variables considered in this chapter. Yet since the psychological factors in the home stem from a variety of circumstances, it would be unwise to ignore the possible influence on the parents and, in turn, on the child of the variables discussed in these pages.

REFERENCES

Adler, A. Characteristics of the first, second, third child. *Children,* 1928, **3,** 14 and 52. Quoted in H. E. Jones, Order of birth in relation to the development of the child, in C. Murchison (Ed.), *A handbook of child psychology.* Worcester, Mass.: Clark Univer. Press, 1931. Pp. 204–241.

Anderson, Marian. *My Lord, what a morning.* New York: Viking, 1956.

Baruch, Dorothy W. A study of reported tension in interparental relationship as co-existent with behavior adjustment in young children. *J. exp. Educ.,* 1937, **6,** 187–204.

Baruch, Dorothy W., & Wilcox, J. A. A study of sex differences in preschool children's adjustment co-existent with interparental tensions. *J. genet. Psychol.,* 1944, **64,** 281–303.

Blanton, S., & Blanton, Margaret G. *Child guidance.* New York: Century, 1927.

Bonney, M. E. A study of the relation of intelligence, family size, and sex differences with mutual friendships in the primary grades. *Child Develpm.,* 1942, **13,** 79–100.

Bossard, J. H. S., & Boll, Eleanor S. Personality roles in the large family. *Child Develpm.,* 1955, **26,** 71–78.

Bossard, J. H. S., & Boll, Eleanor S. *The large family system.* Philadelphia: Univer. Pa. Press, 1956.

Bossard, J. H. S., & Sanger, Winogene P. The large family system—a research report. *Amer. sociol. Rev.,* 1952, **17,** 3–9.

Burchinal, L. G., Hawkes, G. R., & Gardner, B. Marriage adjustment, personality characteristics of parents and the personality adjustment of their children. *Marriage fam. Liv.,* 1957, **19,** 366–373.

Caldwell, Bettye M., & Guze, Samuel B. A study of the adjustment of parents and siblings of institutionalized and non-institutionalized retarded children. *Am. J. ment. Def.,* 1960, **64,** 845–861.

Campbell, A. A. Personality adjustment of only and intermediate children. *J. genet. Psychol.,* 1933, **43,** 197–205.

Cattell, J. McK. *American men of science.* (4th ed.) Garrison, N. Y.: Science Press, 1927.

Clark, K. B., & Clark, M. P. Racial identification and preference in Negro children. In T. M. Newcomb & E. L. Hartley (Eds.), *Readings in social psychology.* New York: Holt, 1947. Pp. 169–178.

Dai, B. Some problems of personality development among Negro children. In C. Kluckhohn & H. A. Murray (Eds.), *Personality in nature, society, and culture.* New York: Knopf, 1956. Pp. 545–566.

Davis, A. Racial status and personality development. *Sci. Mo.,* 1943, **57,** 354–362.

Davis, Ella A. The mental and linguistic superiority of only girls. *Child Develpm.,* 1931, **8,** 139–143.

Dean, D. A. The relation of ordinal position to personality in young children. M. A. thesis, State Univer. of Iowa, 1947.

Despert, J. Louise. *Children of divorce.* Garden City, N. Y.: Country Life Press, 1953.

Dyer, Dorothy T. Are only children different? *J. educ. Psychol.,* 1945, **36,** 297–302.

Farber, B. Effects of a severely mentally retarded child on family integration. *Monogr. Soc. Res. Child Develpm.,* 1959, **24,** No. 2 (Serial No. 71).

Farber, B., & McHale, Julia L. Marital integration and parents' agreement on satisfaction with their child's behavior. *Marriage fam. Liv.*, 1959, **21**, 65–69.

Faris, R. E. L. Sociological causes of genius. *Am. sociol. Rev.*, 1940, **5**, 689–699.

Fenton, N. The only child. *J. genet. Psychol.*, 1928, **35**, 546–556.

Glueck, S., & Glueck, Eleanor. Working mothers and delinquency. *Ment. Hyg.*, 1957, **41**, 327–352.

Goff, R. M. Problems and emotional difficulties of Negro children due to race. *J. Negro Educ.*, 1950, **19**, 152–158.

Goode, W. J. *After divorce.* Glencoe, Ill.: Free Press, 1956.

Goodenough, Florence L., & Leahy, Alice M. The effect of certain family relationships upon the development of personality. *J. genet. Psychol.*, 1927, **34**, 45–71.

Goodman, M. E. *Race awareness in young children.* Cambridge, Mass.: Addison-Wesley, 1952.

Guilford, Ruth B., & Worcester, D. A. A comparative study of the only and non-only child. *J. genet. Psychol.*, 1930, **38**, 411–426.

Hammer, E. F. Frustration-aggression hypothesis extended to socio-racial areas: comparison of Negro and white children's H-T-P's. *Psychiat. Quart.*, 1953, **27**, 596–607.

Hartley, E. L., Rosenbaum, M., & Schwartz, S. Children's use of ethnic frames of reference: an exploratory study of children's conceptualization of multiple ethnic membership. *J. Psychol.*, 1948, **26**, 367–386.

Hartley, Ruth E. Children's concepts of male and female roles. *Merrill-Palmer Quart.*, 1960, **6**, 83–91.

Hattwick, B. W. Interrelations between the preschool child's behavior and certain factors in the home. *Child Develpm.*, 1936, **7**, 200–226.

Hoffman, Lois W. Effects of maternal employment on the child. Paper read at Natl. Council Fam. Relat., Ames, Iowa, 1959.

Holiday, Billie (with W. Dufty). *Lady sings the blues.* Garden City, N. Y.: Doubleday, 1956.

Horowitz, R. E. Racial aspects of self-identification in nursery school children. *J. Psychol.*, 1939, **7**, 91–99.

Jones, H. E. Order of birth in relation to the development of the child. In C. Murchison (Ed.), *A handbook of child psychology.* Worcester, Mass.: Clark Univer. Press, 1931.

Kardiner, A., & Ovesey, L. *The mark of oppression.* New York: Norton, 1951.

Karon, B. P. *The Negro personality.* New York: Springer, 1958.

Koch, Helen L. The relation of "Primary Mental Abilities" in five- and six-year-olds to sex of child and characteristics of his sibling. *Child Develpm.*, 1954, **25**, 209–223.

Koch, Helen L. Sibling influence on children's speech. *J. Speech Hear. Dis.*, 1956, **21**, 322–328. (a)

Koch, Helen L. Sissiness and tomboyishness in relation to sibling characteristics. *J. genet. Psychol.*, 1956, **88**, 231–244. (b)

Koch, Helen L. Children's work attitudes and sibling characteristics. *Child Develpm.*, 1956, **27**, 289–310. (c)

Koch, Helen L. Some emotional attitudes of the young child in relation to characteristics of his sibling. *Child Develpm.*, 1956, **27**, 393–426. (d)

Koch, Helen L. Attitudes of young children toward their peers as related to certain characteristics of their siblings. *Psychol. Monogr.*, 1956, **70**, No. 19 (Whole No. 323). (e)

Koch, Helen L. The relation of certain formal attributes of siblings to attitudes held toward each other and toward their parents. *Monogr. Soc. Res. Child Develpm.*, 1960, **25**, No. 4.

Krout, M. H. Typical behavior patterns in twenty-six ordinal positions. *J. genet. Psychol.*, 1939, **55**, 3–30.

Landis, J. T. The trauma of children when parents divorce. *Marriage fam. Liv.*, 1960, **22**, 7–13.

Landreth, C., & Johnson, B. C. Young children's responses to a picture and inset test designed to reveal reactions to persons of different skin color. *Child Develpm.*, 1953, **24**, 63–79.

Lasko, Joan K. Parent behavior toward first and second children. *Genet. Psychol. Monogr.*, 1954, **49**, 97–137.

Leton, D. A. A study of the validity of parent attitude measurement. *Child Develpm.*, 1958, **29**, 515–520.

Maslow, A. H., & Mittleman, B. *Principles of abnormal psychology.* (Rev. ed.) New York: Harper, 1951.

McCurdy, H. G. The childhood pattern of genius. *J. Elisha Mitchell Scientific Society*, 1957, **73**, 448–462.

Medinnus, G. R. The relation between inter-parent agreement and several child measures. *J. genet. Psychol.*, 1963, **102**, 139–144. (a)

Medinnus, G. R. The consistency of inter-parent agreement on several measures. *J. genet. Psychol.*, 1963, **102**, 145–150. (b)

Murphy, G., Murphy, Lois B., & Newcomb, T. M. *Experimental social psychology.* (Rev. ed.) New York: Harper, 1937.

Murray, Mrs. Max A. Needs of parents of mentally retarded children. *Am. J. ment. Def.*, 1959, **63**, 1078–1088.

Nye, F. I. Child adjustment in broken and in unhappy unbroken homes. *Marriage fam. Liv.*, 1957, **19**, 356–361.

Nye, F. I. Employment status and maternal adjustment to children. Paper read at Amer. Sociol. Soc., Chicago, 1959.

Sears, Pauline S. Doll play aggression in normal young children. Influence of sex, age, sibling status, father's absence. *Psychol. Monogr.*, 1951, **65**, No. 6 (Whole No. 323).

Sears, R. R. Ordinal position in the family as a psychological variable. *Amer. sociol. Rev.*, 1950, **15**, 397–401.

Staples, F. R., & Walters, R. H. Anxiety, birth order, and susceptibility to social influence. *J. abnorm. soc. Psychol.*, 1961, **62**, 716–719.

Stolz, Lois M. Effects of maternal employment on children: evidence from research. *Child Develpm.*, 1960, **31**, 749–782.

Stroup, A. L. Marital adjustment of the mother and the personality of the child. *Marriage fam. Liv.*, 1956, **18**, 109–113.

Terman, L. M., et al. *Genetic studies of genius:* Vol. 1. *The mental and physical traits of a thousand gifted children.* Stanford, Calif.: Stanford Univer. Press, 1925.

Trent, R. Analysis of expressed self-acceptance among Negro children. Unpubl. doctoral dissertation, Teachers College, Columbia Univer., 1953.

West, S. Sibling configurations of scientists. *Amer. J. Sociol.*, 1960, **66**, 268–274.

Wright, R. *Black boy.* New York: World, 1950.

Zuk, G. H. The religious factor and the role of guilt in parental acceptance of the retarded child. *Am. J. ment. Def.*, 1959, **64**, 139–147.

chapter 9 ❋ Family Influences in Infancy

Both sociologists and anthropologists have paid great attention to the family. Sociologists have dwelt at length on the functions served by the family in modern industrial society. Anthropologists have contrasted the role of the family in various cultures which differ widely in complexity and in their goals for socialization. Despite the vast differences in child-rearing practices from one culture to another, the family in most societies appears to serve three principal functions. First, it must be responsible for the physical care of the child, at least in infancy. Second, the parents must educate or train the child in certain areas that are essential to an adequate adjustment to the particular culture. Third, the family must accept the responsibility for the psychological and emotional welfare of the child. Although the first two functions have long been recognized, the third has been stressed only recently as a result of the growing body of psychological theory and research concerning the importance of the very early years and their influence on adult personality and adjustment.

The total physical helplessness of the human infant is immediately apparent. Although the newborn babe is capable of making a number of responses and enacting a number of behaviors, he is completely dependent on other human beings for his physical survival. Some of his responses actually elicit behaviors from the persons in his immediate environment; thus, from the very beginning the infant plays some part in the continuing interaction between himself and other individuals. Most of this interaction, however, is initiated by others for the purpose of meeting the infant's physical needs. Whether this early environmental pattern of physical care affects the infant's psychological development will be considered presently.

It is the second main function of the family, the training and education of the child for adjustment to the culture, which has received the most attention from psychologists interested in the socialization process. This function can be broken down into two broad categories. The first is the training in the methods whereby the child gratifies his physical needs such as feeding and excreting. He is also trained in the development of such skills as self-help in dressing and tidiness, which seem to be important in Western culture. The second category is the inculcation of various attitudes and values which, though varying greatly among subcultures within the culture, deal with uniform aspects of socialization. The attitudes toward siblings, adults, and other persons in authority, and toward such social institutions as the school and the law-enforcement agencies all fall into place here. The child is also made aware of various cultural prohibitions, ranging all the way from sanctions against biting another individual to the taboos associated with incest. Since cultural values filter down to the child from the parent who colors the transmission with his own particular sense of them, the values held by one child may indeed vary in some respect from those possessed by any other child.

The third function of the family, responsibility for the child's psychological and emotional welfare, emphasizes the importance of the early psychological relation between parent and child. Although few psychologists would contend that the early years have no psychological significance, two related controversial issues will be explored in this chapter. The first grows out of the notion that the child is most susceptible to psychological influences in the environment during the first year or two of life. The second concerns the extent to which very early experiences exert long-range influences on the child's personality.

MUTUAL INFLUENCE OF PARENT AND CHILD

Research into parent-child relations has by tradition viewed the parent as the independent variable and the child as the dependent one. In this light all of the child's characteristics, his behavior, his personality, and his adjustment, are seen as the direct product of

Parental characteristics ⟶ Child characteristics

(a) All of child's characteristics attributed to parental treatment and handling

Parental characteristics ⟷ Child characteristics:
physical appearance
health
sex of child
alertness
activity level

(b) Parent and child characteristics mutually interacting

FIGURE 9-1   Two conceptions of parent-child system.

various parental characteristics, namely, parental behavior, personality, and attitudes.   Figure 9-1a depicts this one-way relationship. Yet there are those who believe that, although parents exert a tremendous influence on a number of aspects of the child's development, the parent is affected reciprocally by various child characteristics which develop quite apart from parental actions.   This results in the two-way, circular interaction represented by Figure 9-1b.   Under this process come the several listed characteristics which vary from child to child and which appear so early in life that it would be misleading to attribute them to parental handling.

Psychological Environment at Birth

Although the principal concern of this chapter is the influences in infancy which affect personality development in later life, there are not many long-range studies capable of pinpointing them.   Therefore, let us consider the broader area of the environmental differences that are potentially significant in this regard.

Among 38 of 46 couples, LeMasters (1957) found "extensive" or "severe" crises in adjusting to their first child.   Most of them found the transition to parenthood hard to take.   In another study (Sears, Maccoby, & Levin, 1957), a number of factors were seen to affect the mother's attitude toward pregnancy.   Table 9-1 (Sears et al., p. 32) lists the attitudes of mothers covered in this investigation when they discovered they were with child.

By and large, the fewer the children the mother had, the more pleased she was to learn she was pregnant.   Thus, 64 per cent of the mothers were judged "delighted" to find themselves pregnant if the

TABLE 9-1   How Mother Felt When She Discovered She Was Pregnant

1. Delighted; very happy; had been waiting and hoping for this	50%
2. Pleased, but no evidence of enthusiasm (includes: "This was a planned baby," said matter-of-factly)	18
3. Pleased generally; some reservations	6
4. Mixed feelings; advantages and disadvantages weighed about equally	9
5. Generally displeased, although some bright spots seen	9
6. Displeased; no reservations	7
7. Not ascertained	1
Total	100%

child was their first, but only 34 per cent of those who already had children fitted this description. In addition, the favorable response to the news increased as the age gap between the expected child and the next older one widened. To some extent the mother's attitude was affected by the sex of the children already in the family. That mothers tended to be more pleased with their condition if their family consisted entirely of girls than if it was composed of only boys or of boys and girls may be interpreted in diverse ways. Either parents are more eager to have at least one boy than at least one girl, or they are more willing to take on the responsibility of another child if they have only girls, assuming that girls are easier to raise in the early years; having only boys a mother may quickly become discouraged from inviting further burdens. Age did not seem to be an important factor affecting the mother's attitude toward her pregnancy. Clearly the psychological atmospheres into which children are born vary quite a bit. The child may have been anticipated with some eagerness, with numerous favorable parental attitudes accompanying the birth. Or the pregnancy may have been unwanted, in which case the newborn infant is considered an unbearable burden. The harmful long-range impact of these early negative attitudes on eventual personality and adjustment has been pursued in clinical case studies, but regrettably these undertakings have lacked control groups. And since clinical reports are not the most reliable source of data for scientific endeavor, one must be careful in attributing long-term influences to experiences in early life, though differences in attitudes among parents with respect to a newborn infant must indeed exist.

Is there a kind of communion between mother and infant so that the child is able to perceive various emotional states of the mother and respond to them (Escalona, 1945, 1953)? Sullivan (1940) maintained there was and gave to this emotional linkage the term *empathy*. Disturbances in the mother are often reflected in feeding upsets in the infant. At birth the child was seen as possessing innate tendencies that permitted him to "sense" disturbances in his relationship with his mother (Ribble, 1944). Since most of the literature regarding such emotional linkage has been based on clinical observation, there is little research to illuminate the situation. It becomes necessary to examine developmental characteristics of the newborn and infant as established through observational research. In the opinion of William James the world to the newborn was a "blooming, buzzing confusion." The newborn's perceptual and intellectual faculties are only immaturely developed. He can neither focus on nor follow a moving object until four weeks of age, and he does not smile in response to the human face until three months. The infant cannot distinguish between strange and familiar faces until he is 24 weeks old. And only at the age of four does the child begin to understand the meaning of sarcasm. From these various considerations it is difficult to conceive of the infant as able to interpret and fathom the significance of nuances or subtleties in its mother's feelings and moods. True, the infant responds with crying and restlessness to bodily tensions induced by unmet biological needs. But it is probably unscientific to regard this behavior as the infant's response to insensitivity on the part of its mother.

Although it may be interesting to speculate on how orderliness and lawfulness in the universe produced by varying degrees of regularity and sensitivity in maternal care affect the child's developing awareness, it remains no more than speculation at the present time. Should evidence be gathered to make a case, it would indicate a connection between these factors only after infancy when the child's intellectual capacities have developed to the necessary level.

EFFECTS OF EARLY EXPERIENCE ON LATER BEHAVIOR

In one form or another the rest of this chapter pertains to the relationship between experiences in infancy and early childhood and subsequent behavior. For example, consider this passage:

"That's not the point," replied Mrs. Overmeyer. "Did you see The Snake Pit?"
"Yes."
"Lady in the Dark? Spellbound? All those other psychological things?"
"Yes."

"In every single one of those pictures, people go nuts because of something their parents did to them when they were kids."

"But what has that to do with you?" I asked, "You and George would never treat a child unkindly or cruelly."

"You don't get the idea at all," answered Mrs. Overmeyer. "In those movies the parents weren't unkind or cruel. They were perfect bricks to their children. And yet they did some mild little thing—something so unimportant they didn't notice it—and twenty years later the kids end up in the laughing academy. Remember Lady in the Dark? Remember what knocked the heroine off her trolley? When she was a little girl, her mother was all dressed up to go to a party. The girl wanted to kiss the mother good night, but the mother wouldn't let her because she was afraid the girl would muss her hair. The next thing you know, the girl's got a neurosis as big as the Ritz."

Mrs. Overmeyer poured herself another brandy and continued. "Who knows what goes on in their goddam subconsciouses? Anything can be traumatic, and it's always the parents' fault. It doesn't matter what you do for a kid—you buy him toys and candy and clothes; you send him to camps, take him to shows, bring him on trips; you never say a hard word to him—and then one day you happen accidentally to scowl at him and —wham!—he thinks he's Napoleon."

She sighed mightily. "How do you cope with something like that? Take our daughter Linda—a mean little bastard if you ever saw one. A good clout in the chops is what she needs. But how can we risk it? We're scared even to raise our voices to her. How do we know what would happen? We yell at her today and ten years later she's exposing herself on streetcars" (Shulman, 1959, pp. 91–92).

One of the hazards arising from the emphasis on the long-term effects of early childhood experiences, a point so prevalent in recent and current psychological research among children, is depicted stunningly in this excerpt from a popular work of fiction. Modern parents are confronted by the problem in their handling of the child. "Common sense," a term grossly misapplied in parent-child relations, and child-rearing practices and attitudes learned from their own parents conflict with the idea that each and every childhood experience leaves an indelible mark on the child. Current points of view, however, argue against this notion. Since research here, as in many other phases of parent-child associations, is both sparse and inconclusive, how one regards the contribution of early experience to subsequent behavior depends inevitably on one's view of the infant and the young child.

Conceptions of Infancy and Early Childhood

Oversimplified, inaccurate, and unjust as it may be to separate points of view and writers into two camps, suppose we do so for purposes of discussion. On the one hand there is the *clinical* point of view, probably traceable back to Freud but given impetus more recently by Ribble. This view holds that infantile experiences are of primary importance because of the earliness at which they occur and the impressionability of the infant at this time. The other point of view is the *developmental;* from it, the infant is seen as having tremendous capacity for adjustment, flexibility, and modifiability.

First, the Ribble position (Ribble, 1943, 1944): her main thesis is the importance of mothering for the infant. This arises from her conception of the infant as inadequately developed at birth. Because of an immature nervous system, Ribble believed, the infant is dependent on maternal stimulation for the development of proper physiological functioning.

> All good science begins by defining its terms, so that it is essential to make clear first of all just what we mean by mothering. It is really a continuance of the closeness of the prenatal state, and the more clearly it imitates certain of the conditions before birth the more successful it is in the first weeks. The newborn baby still needs to be carried about at regular intervals until he can move and coordinate his own body. This helps to strengthen his sense of equilibrium and to give him reassurance. Contact takes the place of equilibrium and to give him a feeling of security. Also he must have frequent periods of actual contact with the mother because the warmth and the holding give him reassurance. Contact takes the place of the physical connection before birth when the child was like an organ of the mother's body. In addition, mothering includes the whole gamut of small acts by means of which an emotionally healthy mother consistently shows her love for her child, thus instinctively stimulating his psychic development. Obviously, feeding, bathing, and all the details of physical care come in, but in addition to these duties, which can easily become routine and perfunctory, we mean all of the small evidences of tender feeling—fondling, caressing, rocking, and singing or speaking to the baby. These activities have a deep significance (Ribble, 1943, p. 9).

From physiological functioning Ribble moved to psychological functioning. Lacking consistent mothering, she held, the infant felt tense, insecure, and frustrated. The infant's development of personality depended on this early relationship with one consistent mother figure.

> It is difficult to draw a clear line between the infant's physical and psychological needs, for the very act of making him more comfortable physically, if done by a kindly hand, may at the same time stimulate his sense of aliveness and his consciousness of personal contacts. Certainly we know now that the capacity for mature emotional relationships in adult life is a direct outgrowth of the parental care, more specifically the mothering, which an infant receives. It is the first relationship of

life which activates the feelings of the baby and primes his dormant nervous system into full functional activity, giving to each individual personality its original slant. Social impulses are part of our primary equipment; emotional hunger is an urge as definite and compelling as the need for food. When we deny an infant fulfillment of these needs, we stifle his emotional and social life (Ribble, 1943, p. 13).

Ribble believed that deprivation of mothering not only definitely produced permanent psychological ill effects but also could bring on physical deterioration. Consistent mothering, on the other hand, facilitated speech development, intellectual development, and emotional development. Danger lurked in thwarting the infant's needs or desires. "The human infant in the first year of life should not have to meet frustration or privation, for these factors immediately cause exaggerated tension and stimulate latent defense activities" (Ribble, 1943, p. 72).

As Ribble saw the infant, then, it was characterized by immaturity and incompleteness, dependent on consistent maternal administrations for physiological and psychological welfare. The early relationship with the mother sets the pattern for all future emotional involvements. Thus, any disturbance even in the early months of life has far-reaching implications for the child's development of personality.

Now to the other view, the developmental, which was represented most clearly by Anderson (1948). As the developmentalists see the infant, it is an active energy system which seeks stimulation, is able to withstand a variety of stresses and strains, and has a great capacity for self-repair and readjustment. Both as infant and young child, the youngster reacts to a large number of stimuli each day, of which only a few are retained in memory to affect later behavior. When trauma occurs it does not result from a single instance but from the repetition and reiteration of events in the child's life. This keeps the events alive to achieve their traumatic effect. Thus, sexual assault may have a long-range traumatic significance for the child only if his parents react to it in a highly emotional manner and continue to talk about it.

In this view the child is a persistent and consistent personality system which maintains its integrity and resists "deformation, stress, and trauma." Out of his environment the infant selects those stimuli or events that are congruent with his personality structure. He is not subject, willy-nilly, to all of the influences surrounding him, nor does he respond passively to the many stimuli in his environment. Instead, he is at least somewhat selective and reacts to the stimuli in a manner determined by his goals and attitudes toward himself. To Anderson, the child is a tough, resilient organism, capable of adapting to different environments and environmental pressures, and of responding actively to the world around him.

Evaluation of these two views is difficult. To begin with, research in the area is really not definitive. Once more, the controls required for clear-cut results are almost impossible to impose. For example, Anderson took the position that in order to have traumatic consequences for a child an event had to be repeated or reiterated in the child's experience. Quite obviously, it is not very easy to control a child's subsequent experiences so that the long-term impact of single traumatic events can be tested.

Yet somewhat stronger evidence seems to support the developmental rather than the clinical position. Take this case report which typifies the kind of data used to justify Ribble's "clinical" conception of the child.

> A man suffered from a phobia of being grasped from behind, the disturbance appearing early in childhood and persisting to his fifty-fifth year. When walking on the street he was under a compulsion to look back over his shoulder at intervals to see if he was closely followed. In social gatherings he arranged to have his chair against the wall. It was impossible for him to enter crowded places or to attend the theater.
>
> In his fifty-fifth year he returned to the town in which he had spent his childhood. After inspecting his old home, he went to the corner grocery and found that his old boyhood friend was still behind the counter. He introduced himself and they began to reminisce. Finally the grocerman said this, "I want to tell you something that occurred when you were a boy. You used to go by this store on errands, and when you passed you often took a handful of peanuts from the stand in front. One day I saw you coming and hid behind a barrel. Just as you put your hand in the pile of peanuts, I jumped out and grabbed you from behind. You screamed and fell fainting on the sidewalk."
>
> The episode was remembered and the phobia, after a period of readjustment, disappeared (Bagby, 1922, p. 17).

The issue is not whether experiences and relationships in childhood are important in shaping future attitudes and personalities. Rather, it revolves around the susceptibility of the infant to effects of single specific events and the extent to which these events in the long run are powerful determinants of personality. The balance hangs on how one approaches the subject and regards the emotional and mental nature of the infant.

A common weakness of the clinical view is its interpretation of the child's feelings in terms of adult attitudes, feelings, and responses. Thus, holding the infant tightly is said to give him feelings of security. It may do so for the adult, but can we validly project such feelings into the infant? Stevenson (1957) stressed the fact that experiences have one meaning for the infant and the child and another for the adult; this results from differences in memories, in the meaningfulness of the contexts of events, and in the nature of thought processes. "If you take a toy away from a child, he will probably cry, but if you tell him the mortgage has been foreclosed he will probably go on playing with the toy. We have no proof that within the world as he sees it, a stress is any harder to bear in infancy than in adulthood" (Stevenson, 1957, p. 158). Anderson similarly discussed the fallacy of interpreting children's feelings on the basis of adult behaviors.

> At a recent panel discussion another error was made. A participant talking on jealousy described the situation of the jealous child as like that in which a husband tells his wife that he is bringing a new wife into the home, expatiates on her desirability and asks his wife to assist in preparing for the new wife's coming. While this analogy has obvious dramatic qualities, it is far from a good description of child behavior. There is little evidence that marked jealousy on the arrival of a new member of the family is frequent. However, the evidence available has been played up in the practical writings and jealousy quite appropriately ascribed to an unwise distribution of affection.
> But a young child is not like an old wife who has a whole series of attitudes reinforced by memory and by experiences tied in with the moral, social, and institutional systems of a monogamous society. Nor are the neighbors' valuations of conduct—so essential in the situation faced by the wife—present in the young child who reacts more specifically to the situation and less to the complex of background factors. Which, then, is the more tender, the wife who has been socially sensitized or the young child who has not (Anderson, 1948, p. 478)?

Turning more directly to the developmental view of the child, the data support the idea that the child is resilient, adaptable, and flexible. Reports from the concentration camps of the Second World War (Kral, 1951) showed that children and adolescents adjusted to the inhumane regimen far more quickly and completely than adults. Moreover, one must agree with Anderson that, in view of the host of events and experiences impinging on the child, the crucial significance of any one of them seems doubtful. Just the same, the pattern of experiences in childhood does contribute to the determination of a variety of attitudes toward others and oneself. As illustrated in the Bagby excerpt, specific incidents exert long-range influences in individual cases. However, one may question the pervasiveness of such incidents on the individual's personality. In other words, particular events of childhood may affect only isolated aspects of a person's later personality unless intervening experiences embellish, generalize, and magnify the import of the original event.

Since infants evince wide differences in their responses to environmental stimuli and in their spontaneous behavior, it would be erroneous to impute all of an adult's personality characteristics to the manner in which he was treated by his parents in the very early years, or to his original relationship with his mother. Although this admittedly exaggerates the clinical view, there is a disposition to ignore those infant characteristics that play a part in molding his psychological environment and that cause him, in a sense, to cull from the environment those aspects to which he will respond. As Anderson asserted, the infant does not respond passively "to all the stimulation to which he is exposed without action or selection on his part" (p. 488).

The impression that individual personality is fixed or jelled permanently in childhood, Stevenson (1957) felt, stems from the fact that one's range of experience ordinarily becomes channelized and constricted. Because both infant and child depend on parents for their experiences, they are relatively unable to extend their own range; "their personalities fail to change, not because they have permanently jelled, but because they never have the new experiences which seem essential for any change."

Early parent-child relationships are indeed important. Their repetitiveness and the lack of corrective experiences to alter the attitudes, impressions, and conceptions gained from repeated parent-child contacts make them so. They do not, as some have held, gain their significance from the view of the child as a particularly impressionable individual during these early years. Later on, as we shall see when discussing the relationships of peers, one of the principal functions of interacting with one's own playmates becomes to balance out or normalize any deviant experience undergone in the home before entrance into the peer set. Thus, the consequences of early parental rejection, for instance, may be countered to some extent for the child by acceptance among his agemates.

Freudian Influence

Turning now to the examination of specific maternal child-rearing practices, let us dwell on the part they play in the socialization process and on their long-range influence on adult personality. The practices that might be surveyed are legion. Those for which the most research is available, however, can be labeled the *Freudian variables,* namely, feeding, weaning, and toilet training. With these let us deal primarily. To fit the research findings into a suitable framework and understand why investigators have paid so much attention to these variables, it becomes necessary to review briefly the notions in Freud's "psychoanalytic" theory relevant to the discussion.[1]

To Freud it seemed apparent that many adult problems were traceable to parental frustration of the young child's basic biological drives. Because of this frustration, infantile strivings were repressed at the moment only to reappear in disguised form or as sources of unresolved conflicts which caused stress and anxiety in the adult. Thus, one is able to understand the child-rearing advice emerging from psychoanalytic theory which emphasizes the dangers of frustrating the infant's biological needs; immediate gratification is desirable in a sense —although Freud believed that the child had to and should ultimately come to terms with society and abandon immediate gratification.

Freud observed a basic energy, termed _libido,_ in every individual at birth. This energy supplies the sexual drive; the goal of that drive is to gain pleasure for the organism. To Freud, therefore, any pleasurable impulse was an expression of sexuality. In various areas of the body are tissues which provide pleasurable feelings when stimulated; these areas, the mouth and lips, the anal region, and the genital organs, are called _erogenous zones._ In the course of psychosexual development, each of these zones becomes in turn the center of erotic pleasure. Frustration results if erotic impulses are denied gratification.

Sexuality in the infant, although not the same as adult sexuality, is a forerunner of it and is continuous with it. This is the case because the same libidinal energy is released through the different erogenous zones throughout development. What are the stages of psychosexual activity related to these zones?

Oral Stage. Anyone who has observed an infant knows that much of its activity centers in the region of the mouth. Sucking, mouthing, and crying are important infantile behaviors. Fatty pads in the cheeks are present at birth to help the infant suck. A head turning reflex also causes the infant to pivot toward sources of stimulation whereupon stimulation of the oral region elicits a response of sucking. No doubt the act of sucking to receive nutrients serves a survival function. Freud maintained that sucking was also a source of pleasure.

Two psychological phenomena are said to emerge during the oral stage, _fixation_ and _regression._ These are the two most frequently used

---

[1] For clear expositions of Freud's theories, see: Munroe, Ruth, _Schools of Psychoanalytic Thought,_ New York: Dryden, 1955. Hall, C., & Lindzey, G., _Theories of Personality,_ New York: Wiley, 1957.

to explain child behavior. Should excessive frustration occur in any of the psychosexual stages, fixation may then develop. That is, the libidinal energy may remain locked in the erogenous zone from which the child obtained pleasure in that particular stage. In like manner, too much gratification, especially if it helps to relieve anxiety or tension, may also bring on fixation. This may be seen, for example, in giving an infant the breast or a bottle every time he shows signs of extreme upset or disturbance.

Regression refers to the tendency to return to an earlier mode of obtaining satisfaction when frustrated or anxious. A child of seven who has long since relinquished thumb sucking may resort to this behavior when faced with a new or strange situation or when tense and fatigued. Regression may occur in adults as well, according to Freudian psychology, but the method of gratification may appear in camouflage. Instead of thumb sucking, the adult may smoke excessively or overeat. From the gratification comes momentary relief from tension and frustration.

The oral stage continues until some time in the second year of life as a rule and then the seat of libidinal energy shifts to the anal region. The various psychosexual stages, of course, are not distinct, nor do they inevitably occur at a fixed age in every child. Although they overlap, the sequence remains constant.

Anal Stage. The young child now obtains his pleasure from expelling feces and urine. However, since toilet activity receives much attention in regard to the socialization process, conflict arises between the child's yearnings for satisfaction and parental sanctions. Parents teach the child to abhor feces, to view them with repulsion, and to eliminate at the proper time and place. These demands run counter to the child's desires; they impose limits on his impulse gratification.

Because the child learns ultimately to regulate elimination, he feels some sense of mastery over his environment. Nevertheless, too severe parental demands in toilet training may develop a fixation in the youngster at this point.

Phallic Stage. Sometime near the end of the third year the genital region displaces the anal as the center of libidinal energy. Erotic pleasure is obtained from stimulation of the genital organs. At this stage, both boys and girls show concern for the genitals; as a result, the beginnings of identification with the appropriate sex appear.

The phallic stage culminates in the Oedipal situation, a notion accorded a vast amount of attention by the Freudians. Drawing on the Greek tragedy in which Oedipus murders his father and marries his mother, Freud described the Oedipus complex as one in which the son experiences a sexual attachment to his mother although an emotional or affectional relationship has already existed between them, since it is the mother who is the principal caretaker for both sexes.

The Oedipal situation creates tensions and antagonisms between father and son which are resolved because of several pressures. First, of course, there is the strong social taboo against incest; consequently, the mother rebuffs any sexual behavior directed toward her by the son. Second, because the father is superior to the boy in strength and authority, the son gives up or represses his desires for his mother in order to avoid retaliation by the father and to relieve the anxiety which develops from fear of loss of love of both parents. Identification with the father takes place; the child wants to be like him and models his behavior after his father's.

Latency Period. At about the age of six the child represses erotic impulses toward the parent of the opposite sex, thus resolving the Oedipus complex. This is the start of the latency period. The findings of the famed Kinsey survey show, however, that there is not a cessation of sexuality in this interval. Parental inhibiting of sexual behavior and the child's growing *superego*—his conscience—merely play a part in swinging his attention to the development of social relations with his peers. Interests stimulated by intellectual curiosity now assume importance. This state of affairs continues until just before adolescence when a sharp rise in the production of hormones strongly reactivates the sexual impulses.

Genital Stage. At this stage increased sexual interests appear. The adolescent must now make adjustments to the opposite sex as well as to sexuality itself because of the prohibitions and sanctions relating to the sex drive in Western society. Satisfactory progress through the several psychosexual stages culminates in adequate adult heterosexual adaptation.

Feeding and Weaning

Having outlined Freud's ideas, we may now move along to the significance for personality of variation in maternal behavior in relation to the "Freudian variables"—first of all, to feeding and weaning. The earliest pressures of socialization are applied to the infant in the area of feeding. Regularity in gratifying the hunger drive is thought to be important, even when no rigid schedule is required; the method of acquiring sustenance changes from sucking to eating and chewing;

and the nature of the diet shifts from a liquid base to one of solid foods. In each of these aspects of feeding, the mother intervenes to a greater or lesser degree.

As a consequence of Freud's emphasis on the dangers inherent in frustrating the infant, much attention has been paid to the implications for personality of self-demand versus rigid feeding schedules and gradual versus abrupt weaning practices. In the latter case the criteria for measurement have been the age at which weaning has occurred and the severity of the weaning process. There has also been interest in the mother's initial decision of whether to breast or bottle feed the infant. Somehow breast feeding is seen as the more desirable, perhaps because of Ribble's emphasis on the importance of close contact between mother and infant and on the need for "mothering."

Breast vs. Bottle Feeding. The mother who breast feeds her infant is thought to be desirous and capable of establishing a warm, affectional relationship with her infant. In contrast, the mother who bottle feeds the infant is seen as a woman who shrugs off the psychological aspects of maternal responsibility. However, studies of differences between mothers who breast feed and those who bottle feed their infants have concluded that the principal difference revolves around attitudes concerning the psychosexual area (Adams, 1959; Sears, Maccoby, & Levin, 1957). Mothers showing strong feelings of discomfort toward sexual matters are more likely to bottle feed. Nevertheless, it would be a mistake to overlook the fact that a decision to breast feed may be governed by a variety of reasons, some having slight psychological relevance. These may include pressures of time, scheduling convenience, and physical factors, to mention but a few. Moreover, as noted in an earlier chapter, many aspects of child care in Western culture are subject to cyclical fads which have no relation whatsoever to the personality pattern or attitudes of any particular mother. In rating mothers' feeding behavior, Brody (1956) concentrated on the sensitivity of the mother to the infant. Not all mothers who fed by the breast were rated as disclosing completely satisfactory responsiveness to the infant.

The findings of research into the effects of breast versus bottle feeding on the child's personality have been generally negative. In the Pattern Study, as the Sears, Maccoby, and Levin (1957) study is familiarly known, six aspects of child behavior, such as aggressiveness, dependency, and development of conscience, were examined in relation to whether the child was breast or bottle fed, and no broad links were found. Sewell and Mussen (1952), in an extensive study of some phases of infantile feeding, detected no tie between the type of feeding in infancy and various oral symptoms of general adjustment, such as thumb sucking, nail biting, and stuttering, among five- and six-year-olds. Evidently, the container from which the infant obtains his milk, whether breast or bottle, has no psychological import. Despite speculation that the quality of the child's feeding experience is significant, scientific data on the subject is meager and equivocal.

Duration of Breast Feeding. The duration of breast feeding has also been given weight as a factor affecting the child's later personality. Moreover, Levy (1943) suggested that the length of breast feeding related to maternal attitudes. "In general, all factors favoring rejection of the child tend to shorten, all factors favoring overprotection tend to lengthen, the breast feeding act" (Levy, p. 59). Although this may be true in individual cases, especially in certain ones seen in clinical settings, there is not much evidence to support the generalization among a normal population. In fact, one investigation found no relation between length of breast feeding and maternal rejection (Peterson & Spano, 1941). Likewise, no relation has been established between length of breast feeding and personality ratings of nursery-school children.

Schedule vs. Self-demand Feeding. Over the years there have been many variations in expert advice on this topic. Thus, it seems fruitless to examine in detail the research that has endeavored to relate this aspect of early infant care to factors of maternal or child personality. In the Pattern Study an inverse relationship was noted between a mother's confidence in her ability to employ correct child-rearing procedures and the fidelity with which she followed her pediatrician's advice. The less confident the mother, the more she was likely to accept her doctor's recommendation of feeding techniques. This finding suggested once more that although a mother's methods of child rearing might be related to other aspects of her general attitudes and personality, her procedures might not reflect her feelings toward the child or toward child rearing itself.

Sucking and Thumb Sucking. Psychoanalytic theory contends that if an infant lacks sufficient oral gratification through his sucking to obtain food, he will indulge in sucking behavior unrelated to the feeding process. Learning theory, on the other hand, maintains that the greater the reinforcement received by the infant from sucking, the stronger his sucking drive will be. Each of these theories thus predicts different consequences for the infant's early sucking experience.

Psychoanalytic theory would hold that an infant who is cup fed from birth or whose breast- or bottle-feeding experience is brief would exhibit more "nonnutritional" sucking than an infant who received much oral gratification through sucking. If it could be shown that sucking the thumb were caused by lack of oral gratification, a mother could be advised with some assurance as to the appropriate method for preventing this behavior. The controversy is indeed an interesting one.

Although here, too, the research findings are contradictory, one must conclude that there are a variety of reasons for prolonged thumb sucking, some of which bear absolutely no relation to gratification or deprivation in early sucking. For example, Simsarian (1947) observed five thumb suckers among a group of 26 children who had been breast fed on self-demand schedules and who had been permitted to nurse as long as they wished. In another study, Traisman and Traisman (1958), who interviewed mothers of more than 2000 infants and children, noted little difference in the occurrence of thumb sucking between children fed by bottle and those partially or completely fed by breast. They also found only slight differences of types of psychological problems between those who did and those who did not suck their thumbs.

As a clinical matter, thumb sucking is taken as one sign of maladjustment or personality disturbance in a child. The seriousness of thumb sucking would depend, of course, on the frequency and extent of the behavior and the age of the child. In a three- or four-year-old such conduct would not be considered unusual in the face of a new, strange, or challenging situation. In an elementary-school child it may, however, require prompt investigation by a person trained in psychology. Even if one does not adhere strictly to psychoanalytic explanations of behavior, sucking the thumb may be regarded as regression, in the broad psychological sense of the term; the child reverts to an earlier form of behavior which assured gratification. In an older child, therefore, thumb sucking is sometimes interpreted as indicating strong feelings of insecurity.

Not much is known through definitive medical research about the effects of such behavior on the teeth. Current thinking generally holds that prolonged thumb sucking after the child's permanent teeth have appeared may very well affect the bite, especially where there is some tendency toward irregularity. Prior to this time, there is not much likelihood that sucking of the thumb would harm the dental structures. Nor is there any knowledge to speak of about the thumbs themselves becoming deformed through such activity!

Weaning. In the Pattern Study both the age at which weaning occurred and the severity of the process, that is, the amount of pressure exerted on the infant, were linked to a rating of the child's emotional upset during the procedure. Although nearly twice as many youngsters were rated as having shown some upset when weaning was initiated after 11 months of age than when it was started before five months, the children weaned in the intervening period showed the fewest emotional reactions. Then, too, the less severe the procedure was, the fewer the emotional upsets. What was learned about the relation of age of weaning to the emotional reaction to it contradicted the idea implied in psychoanalytic theory that the longer the infant remained breast or bottle fed, the more emotionally healthful this would be. The Sewell and Mussen study detected no connection between the personality adjustment ratings of its five- and six-year-olds and the age at which they were weaned or the character of the weaning process, whether sharp or gradual.

More than one writer (Fries, 1941; Escalona, 1945) has stressed the importance of the feeding area as a particularly sensitive indicator of both the child's relationship with its mother and its general adjustment. However true this may be, the point of concern here is the difference between short- and long-range effects of various maternal practices. Conceivably the mother's behavior toward her infant with respect to feeding may influence the infant's responses during the infancy period. But there is little support for the view that her conduct in this one aspect of child rearing exerts long-range impacts on the child's personality. To anticipate the beginning of the next chapter, there may be shifts in maternal behavior and attitudes toward child rearing over a period of time. Although a mother may employ a rigid, insensitive approach toward the young infant, she may revise her methods and attitudes as a result of both the child's changing developmental characteristics and capabilities and of her own learning about child care.

Another consideration is the interrelationships among the various practices a mother employs. One study (Klatskin, Jackson, & Wilkin, 1956) explored the tie between the flexibility of the mother's practices in feeding, sleeping, toilet training, and socialization, and evidences of disturbance in the child. Among its findings appeared a tendency for the relation between maternal flexibility and problem behavior in the child to be a discrete one; specific deviation from optimal handling by the mother led to problems in the child only in the one particular area. Thus, extreme rigidity in toilet training might lead to disturbances in toilet habits but leave unaffected the child's sleeping and eating behaviors. Second, the study uncovered no link between the mother's behavior in areas of feeding and socialization in the child's first year and his behavior then or in the year which followed.

In a study by Sewell, Mussen, and Harris (1955) mothers of a group of five- and six-year-olds were interviewed to try to ascertain the relationships among child-rearing practices during infancy and the years immediately following. Obtaining information on 38 items bearing on infant care, child-training procedures, and the handling of disciplinary problems, the study generally obtained low and insignificant correlations among the several practices. Apparently, a mother's attitude in one area of child training was germane to that area alone and did not affect her behavior in others. Inconsistency *as to the favorableness of the practice* was the rule.

What, then, are the effects of feeding practices on the child? First, regarding the significance of the mother's decision to breast or bottle feed, a host of factors, some without much psychological relevance, influence it. Several studies even propose that breast feeding may have some sexual implications for the mother, which may be more important than her attitude toward the infant, in deciding whether to breast feed. Second, no permanent effects of weaning activities on the child have been noted, although there is some evidence for a curvilinear relationship between age of weaning and emotional upset. Third, despite support for both deprivation and reinforcement as causes for thumb sucking, actually several causes exist. Finally, a child-rearing technique may exert immediate or short-range influence on child behavior but have no long-term significance; and the links among the various child-training practices employed by a mother are slight, so that it would seem hardly likely for one specific practice to have a general bearing on the child's development of personality.

Toilet Training

Every culture regulates toilet behavior. Cultures vary widely, however, in how much control and restrictiveness they impose. Present-day American society is relatively strict in this phase of child training. Quite likely, the urban, crowded conditions of American life which create an almost fanatical consciousness of germs and dirt contribute to this strictness. Be that as it may, mothers express great amounts of concern over the toilet habits of their young children, frequently mentioning the development of bladder and bowel control as a "problem" area.

Notwithstanding Freud's heavy emphasis on the crucial importance of toilet training to the child's subsequent development of personality, research offers little corroborating evidence for a relationship between the two. Abundant clinical reports, however, indicate the harmful consequences of overly severe toilet training. Examining case histories of children referred to a child-guidance clinic, for example, Huschka (1942) observed that in more than half the number bladder and bowel training was started prematurely. The list of child behaviors seen to derive from coercive toilet training includes negativism, aggressiveness, fearfulness, compulsiveness, rigid behavior, rage, guilt, excessive cleanliness, and defiance. But as we shall presently see, the relationship between toilet training and behavior or personality is by no means simple. More influential than the mother's practices are her own personality and the factors prompting her behavior. Moreover, the greater permissiveness of child-rearing practices in America suggests that coercive toilet-training procedures are much less common today than formerly. The practices of most mothers in this respect, therefore, fall within the normal range and do not contribute to aberration.

Although there are some similarities between weaning and toilet training, the differences are more significant. In both procedures built-in reflexes help the child to perform these behaviors. The basic mechanisms involved exist and operate efficiently at birth. Toilet training differs from feeding behavior, however, by requiring the child to control the built-in reflexes and prevent their operation except at certain approved times and places.

At first the child has no desire to control the process of elimination. To develop control he must learn to recognize signs that indicate the imminent relaxation of the anal sphincter muscles. Besides inhibiting action, voluntary control also involves the ability to "let go." Such a relatively complicated process requires much learning. If anxiety, resulting from punishment, is introduced into the situation, learning becomes more difficult and the process prolonged. Take the analogy of the impatient husband who attempts to teach a hopeful but unsure wife to drive a car. Punishment takes the form of disapproval which causes the wife to give up in despair. In both cases, toilet training and learning to drive, pressure and its resulting frustration so complicate and retard the learning process that negative attitudes may affect the whole "teacher-learner" relationship, whether between husband and wife or mother and child.

When does toilet training customarily begin? It should not begin before the child is ready to undertake the necessary learning. Because some amount of physiological maturation is probably required and children mature at different rates, it becomes impossible to state a precise age at which toilet training should be initiated. In the Pattern Study 87 per cent of the mothers started bowel training before the child was 20 months old. Eleven months represented the average age. In 80 per cent of the cases the training was completed by the time the child reached 24 months of age, the average age of completion being 18 months. The data showed that the later the training was undertaken, the quicker it succeeded.

A wide variety of reasons prompt a mother to undertake toilet training at a particular age, but the Pattern Study noted that maternal anxiety about the sexual sphere was an important element in her decision to begin training early and complete it as rapidly as possible. And this anxiety may indeed influence the restrictiveness with which she regards manifestations of sexuality in the child.

Severity of Training. From descriptions by mothers of their practices, ratings were made of the severity of toilet training. More important than the percentages listed in Table 9-2 (Sears, Maccoby, & Levin, 1957, p. 119) are the details of each of the five rating categories. As might be expected, the severity of the training was an influential factor in causing emotional upset in the child. But severity alone was not the full story. The attitudes of the mother also bore on the amount of upset. Severe toilet-training procedures became far more emotionally disturbing if accompanied by maternal coldness and

TABLE 9-2 Severity of Toilet Training

1. Not at all severe. Child more or less trained himself. Not his fault when he has accidents; they are considered natural. No punishment or scolding.	10%
2. Slight pressure. Mild disapproval for some late accidents. Mother makes some efforts to show child where, when, and how to go to toilet.	42
3. Moderate pressure. Scolding for some late deviations; fairly frequent toileting.	29
4. Fairly severe training. Child scolded fairly often; mother clearly shows disapproval. Child may be left on toilet for fairly lengthy periods.	16
5. Very severe training. Child punished severely for deviations; mother angry and emotional over them.	2
Not ascertained	1
Total	100%

undemonstrativeness than if presented in an atmosphere of maternal warmth which made the child feel emotionally secure. Thus, the entire emotional context within which day-to-day child-rearing methods occur must be evaluated to ascertain the effect of child-care techniques on child development.

Many writers have said that coercive and insensitive toilet training damages the parent-child relationship, perhaps with long-range consequences. If so, this assertion is entirely speculative. No doubt, coercive techniques are unwise for several reasons, yet other considerations are worth restatement. That no over-all favorableness or unfavorableness characterizes child-rearing methods implies that although a mother may use ill-advised techniques in toilet training, some of her other procedures may be perfectly acceptable. Moreover, the basic attitudes of the mother may be more significant for the child's development than any single child-rearing practice.

Taken together, these points suggest the need to assess the pervasiveness of a mother's attitudes toward her child before trying to predict their bearing on his future personality. Then there is the possibility that maternal attitudes may change in time. A mother may pressure her child into early toilet control and may not seem to accept him until he has achieved it, but once he has attained this goal, she may grow relaxed and accepting in her relationship with him.

To summarize, various explanations may account for the failure of the Freudian variables—feeding, weaning, and toilet training—to yield many clues to the personality development of the child. First, the range of practice for mothers in Western culture is limited, with few mothers at either extreme. Part of this situation may be charged to the widespread expert advice available and the general trend toward permissive child rearing. Second, the fact that a mother's child-training methods are often shaped by pediatric counsel or by current fads rather than by her own attitudes and personality makes them less pertinent psychologically than might otherwise be the case. Finally, since there is little connection among a mother's various child-rearing techniques, the general quality of the relationship between parents and child is more predictive of future personality than are the clearly observable effects of specific, short-term practices.

Brody's Analysis

While investigating infant behavior and personality development, Brody (1956) and her associates studied the conduct of mothers during a four-hour period in which they performed their normal functions of caring for the infant's needs. Their study had a great methodological advantage over the investigations dealing with feeding and toilet training. It actually observed the mothers caring for their infants, whereas the information acquired in the other studies came from retrospective verbal reports by the mothers.

The Brody team concentrated on 32 infants, four males and four females at each of four levels of age, four, 12, 20, and 28 weeks. The mothers brought their children to a central location where rooms were expressly equipped with the supplies needed to care for infants. Although the ostensible purpose was to observe infant patterns of behavior, two researchers kept detailed records of each mother's behavior in relation to her child. They particularly attended to six maternal activities: feeding, cleaning, moving, touching, offering objects, and speaking. In each of these areas they rated behavior on a five-degree scale in terms of the sensitivity with which the mother responded to the needs or wishes of her infant. Three indices, each describing a particular quality of maternal behavior, were computed for each of the six activities. The first, *frequency,* measured the absolute amount of a mother's sensitivity in the specific activity. The second, *mean,* measured the average amount of her sensitivity. The third, *standard deviation,* measured the consistency of the sensitivity.

Judged by these measures, the mothers fell into four main groups or types.

The mothers of group A were conspicuous for their ability to accommodate to the needs of their infants. By virtue of the kind of physical and emotional support they provided and the steadiness of their interest in and communicativeness toward their infants, they gave them freedom to move about, to vocalize, feed, rest or play with a minimum of interference. More regularly and with more ease than all the other mothers they recognized and tried to relieve passing discomforts in the infants. The mothers themselves were not without tension, but most of the time that tension appeared to heighten their intimacy with the infants.

The mothers of group B were conspicuous for their conscious willingness to accommodate to their infants. At first glance some of their behavior resembled that of the A mothers, but on the whole they were more tense, less communicative and less steadily attentive. At times they tried more actively to stimulate their infants and at other times they were mildly distant or insensitive to the infants' immediate needs. The quality of satisfaction with the infant and of enjoyment of their mothering tasks, outstanding in the A mothers, was much less evident, although B mothers were generally positive toward their infants.

The mothers of group C were conspicuous for their lack of spontaneity and their intentions to be efficient above all else. Physically and socially they were detached from their infants. Some reduced their attention to the carrying out of a minimum of essential details of infant care, and showed a low degree of interest in any activity with the infant of a non-physical nature. The mothers in group D were conspicuously active but also erratic in their attentiveness, efficiency and sensitivity. They quite sedulously governed their infants' actions by stimulating, restricting or instructing them, apparently hardly aware of the possible effects of their behavior on the infants' condition (pp. 265–266).

Thus, group A mothers were sensitive, consistent, and attentive. Group B mothers, as a rule, closely followed the group A pattern but fell short of the mark on each index; they were less sensitive, less consistent, and somewhat overactive or overattentive. Group C mothers were insufficiently sensitive, moderately inconsistent, but adequately attentive, whereas the mothers in group D were hypersensitive, very inconsistent, and hyperactive.

Besides probing aspects of maternal behavior, the study sought to relate the behavior and activity patterns of the infants to it. Few differences were found, generally speaking, among the four groups of infants either in level of activity or on scores obtained on Gesell Development Schedules. Although some correlation appeared between maternal behavior and the developmental status of the infant, Brody concluded that the relationship might not be causal. Innate differences among infants might easily have influenced the behaviors of the mothers.

Brody's study demonstrated, of course, that differences did exist among mothers in their behavior toward the infant. If these differences are based on or are related to fundamental characteristics of attitude and personality in the mother which persist over the years, they may actually affect the child's development in ways as yet unknown.

Maternal Deprivation

This is a subject that has aroused much current interest and much controversy.[2] Essentially maternal deprivation is illustrated by the infant or young child who does not enjoy a relationship with his mother as indicated by his separation from her. If its importance were to be judged by the number of infants suffering from maternal deprivation, the issue would be relegated to oblivion. However, both the issue it-

---

[2] For comprehensive reviews of the subject, see: Casler, L., Maternal deprivation: a critical review of the literature, *Monogr. soc. Res. Child Develpm.*, 1961, **26**, No. 2; and Yarrow, L. J., Maternal deprivation: toward an empirical and conceptual re-evaluation, *Psychol. Bull.*, 1961, **58**, 459–490.

self and the findings on the effects of such deprivation on the child are relevant to many basic aspects of child development and the mother-child relationship.

Although few psychologists would argue against the useful and necessary functions performed by the mother in the infant's early years, the issue of maternal deprivation revolves about the long-range, debilitative repercussions on the infant separated from his mother. Granted that every infant may need tender loving care, will deprivation of it scar him permanently?

The appearance of Ribble's *The Rights of Infants* in 1943, together with an essay by the same author (1944) heralded a new conception of the mother-infant relationship. As was evident in the excerpts from Ribble's book quoted earlier in the chapter, she conceived of the infant as incomplete and immature physiologically at birth and totally dependent on the mother's ministrations for survival.

> When the umbilical cord is cut at birth, the child, as we have said, is far from being a complete and independent individual. The infant is peculiarly helpless, and it is not until after the faculties of speech and locomotion have developed that he can cope with any separation from the mother without danger. Mother and child after birth are psychologically still a unit, and close relationship is as important for early mental development as was the more primitive connection with the fetus for physiological development. As we have seen in the study of marasmus, interference with this nature relationship means that the infant starves for mothering, and as a result the vital activities, first of alimentation, then of breathing and circulation, get out of order, and we find the small body functioning much as it did before birth (Ribble, 1943, p. 12).

Having observed 600 infants, Ribble (1944) concluded that tension was seen to disappear when the infant was in physical contact with the mother, whereas separation produced anxiety. Ribble imputed a wide variety of infant reactions to inadequate mothering: negativism, refusal to suck, hypertension, vomiting, wild screaming, a stuporous sleep, diarrhea, and finally, marasmus.[3]

Much interest was stimulated by Ribble's contentions. Her position was strengthened in a series of articles by Spitz (1945, 1946) which described the deleterious effects of institutionalization on infants separated from their mothers. A sharp drop in developmental quotient, a high mortality rate, and the appearance of disturbed behavior occurred in a group of foundling-home infants in the final third of their

---

[3] A disease, characterized by apathy and deterioration, said to be caused by an infant's separation from its mother.

first year (Spitz, 1945). These phenomena were ascribed to the absence of a mother-child relationship; in the foundling home the ratio of nurses to infants was one to eight. Spitz asserted that impairment of the mother-child relation for more than a three-month interval during the first year of life inflicted irreparable damage on the infant.

The terms used to describe infant reaction to the loss of maternal love and maternal stimulation are *hospitalism* and *anaclitic depression*. The principal symptoms of these syndromes are weepiness, withdrawal and lack of contact with the environment, refusal to act, and stupor. Take this case reported by Spitz:

> White female. Intelligent, friendly child who smiles easily and ecstatically at the approaching observer. No notable event in the course of the first 7 months. At this time a change occurred in the child. The observers got the feeling that the child was apprehensive. A week or two later the change was accentuated. The temper of the child had become unequal. She still was mostly friendly to the observer, but as often as not broke out crying when the observer approached closer. After another two weeks she could no longer be approached. No amount of persuasion helped. Whenever approached she sat up and wailed. Two weeks later, she would lie on her face, indifferent to the outside world, not interested in the other children living in the same room. Only strong stimulation could get her out of her apathy. She would then sit up and stare at the observer wide-eyed, a tragic expression on her face, silent. She would not accept toys, in fact she withdrew from them into the farthest corner of her bed. If the approach was pressed she would break into tears. This went on until the child was 9 months old (Spitz & Wolf, 1946, p. 315).

Sharp criticism by Pinneau (1950, 1955) of the efforts of Ribble and Spitz induces one to question many of the effects of maternal deprivation which they postulated. To cite one example of this criticism, Pinneau pointed out that the drop in development quotient described by Spitz occurred before, not after, the infants were separated completely from their mothers; thus, it could not possibly be charged to this circumstance.

It is not within the scope of this book to examine at length all the studies that have confirmed or invalidated the Ribble-Spitz belief. Yet certain lines of evidence of several key ideas help to clarify some of the basic matters at issue, of which the four main ones are consequences of institutionalization, the need for a single mother figure, deprivation of stimulation, and the contrast between long-range and short-range effects.

Institutionalization. Unfortunately, many of the investigations into the impact of institutionalization are weak methodologically. A number of important variables have not been controlled. Some of those that must be considered are the age at which separation occurs, the nature of the mother-child relation prior to separation, the reason for the separation, and the quality and atmosphere of the institution. If the separation occurs after the infant's first six months of life, any ill effects upon the child may result from the separation itself and the breaking of an affectional relationship rather than from the subsequent deprivation of a mother. Thus, a distinction must be made between separation and deprivation. To which of these are the ill effects being specifically attributed? Besides, if the child is separated at the mother's own instigation, the possibility must not be overlooked that the later harmful effects may stem from the mother's earlier rejection and neglect, and not from the actual separation and consequent deprivation.

Although the ratio of adults to children is low in most institutions, the percentage can vary widely. However, in addition to the sheer number of children assigned to each adult for care, one must also assess the quality of the care. Is affection shown by the nurse or attendant? How much stimulation do the infants receive from the caretakers? How much consistency exists in the handling of the infants? Then there are the physical characteristics of the surroundings. Are they drab and colorless? Are the infants deprived of visual and aural stimulation as well as the social and emotional stimulation of an adult? Nor can the length of institutionalization nor the ages at which it occurs be ignored in investigating the consequences.

In sum, the effects of being institutionalized may result as much from a lack of emotional involvement in relations with other persons as from an insufficient amount of sensory stimulation. Having conducted research among lower organisms, Scott (1962) argued that "the speed of formation of a social board is dependent upon the degree of emotional arousal, irrespective of that arousal" (p. 951). The emotional chill that often pervades the general psychological atmosphere of institutions as well as the relationship between caretaker and child may hinder the development of normal social, affectional ties.

Single Mother Figure. Various kinds of "multiple mothering" would certainly argue against Ribble's belief in the need for an infant to enjoy a relationship with a single mother figure. As Margaret Mead (1935) has reported, the extended family is the prevailing pattern in many South Seas cultures. The responsibilities of child rearing are shared by many members of the community. Brothers, sisters, and other members of the larger family may assume several of the maternal functions. Yet no effects on personality adjustment and development comparable to those noted by Ribble and Spitz have been attributed to this type of child care.

In the communal nurseries established in many Israeli settlements today the children are cared for by more than one significant adult. Although the child spends most of his day in the nursery he often sees his parents for several hours each evening as well as on weekends. This is an example of what might be called "intermittent mothering." The *metapelet*, the trained caretaker of the children, performs most of the traditional functions of motherhood related to routine care and training of the child. Accounts of the daily contacts between the children and their natural mothers indicate a warm, permissive, and affectionate relationship. Perhaps such a separation of care and training from the "affectional" functions of the maternal role might reduce some of the ambivalent feelings of parents and children characteristic of traditional parent-child relationships.

Compared with Israeli children raised in their own homes, these children reared in the settlements, or *kibbutzim*, show few differences in personality and intellectual development. Either this sort of multiple mothering does not exert any deleterious influence on the development of personality or experiences occurring after early childhood nullify any potentially harmful effects. Possibly both are true.

One study (Rabin, 1958) found that ten-year-old boys reared in the *kibbutzim* showed less intense feelings of sibling rivalry than boys reared in another fashion. Although the topic at hand is maternal deprivation, this finding suggests that some of an individual's most intense, destructive emotional feelings emanate from the traditional family arrangement of Western culture. Sibling jealousies, parent-child hostilities, and other long-lasting conditions of like kind may emerge from this scheme. Support for this point comes from a fascinating report (Freud & Burlingame, 1943) on the nurseries provided for the children evacuated from war-gutted London. At one point artificial families were created in which four children were assigned to one nurse, or mother substitute, investing the relationship with some continuity and stability. Out of this arrangement flowered violent attachments, possessiveness, and anxiety resulting from fear of loss of the mother figure, and jealousies resembling sibling rivalry. There were also positive consequences in evidence. Thus, the small family group, somewhat isolated, heavy on contact between its members, which symbolizes the family arrangement in Western society, may exert either negative or positive influence on the child's development of personality.

Stimulus Deprivation. Few controlled experiments pertaining to lack of sensory stimulation have been conducted among children. Several have used adults as subjects, and even more have involved lower organisms. A kinesthetic need or drive in infancy has been postulated by Kulka, Fry, and Goldstein (1960). It is a need for incoming stimulation through a variety of modalities related to the senses: light, touch, pressure, and temperature. The infant obtains gratification of this kinesthetic need when an adult cuddles him, rocks him, or supplies similar soothing services. Severe early deprivation of this need may lead to apathy and inactivity, or rocking, banging of the head, and other rhythmic movements by the infant which may represent an attempt to satisfy this yearning for stimulation. Could it be that the infant often stops crying when rocked because his need for such stimulation is fulfilled?

In a typical experiment involving adults (Goldberger & Holt, 1958), volunteer college students were placed in isolation in a specially designed chamber which admitted only a minimum amount of stimulation, whether visual, aural, or tactile. During an eight-hour period, or less, in the chamber, these students manifested anxiety, decreases in complex reasoning, and hallucinations. They reported disturbances in their awareness of time, unpleasant emotional feelings, and a sense of intellectual disorganization. Clearly, a certain level of sensory stimulation appears to be necessary for adequate intellectual performance. This notion is supported by the isolation included in the brainwashing of American prisoners by the Chinese communists, which has apparently resulted in a variety of psychological repercussions.

Long-Range vs. Short-Range Effects. Most of a series of papers by Goldfarb (1943a, b, c; 1945a, b; 1947; 1949) on the harmful long-range effects of early institutionalization dealt with a set of 15 children who entered an institution at about four-and-a-half months of age and remained there a little more than three years before placement in foster homes. These children were compared with a control group reared wholly in foster homes. When tested, they ranged from 10 to 14 years of age. Subjected to a number of personality and intelligence measures, the group that had experienced institutionalization showed itself to be inferior to the control children in many respects. Its members were apathetic, passive, fearful, apprehensive, less persistent, withdrawn, retarded in social maturity, and inferior in intelligence, language, vocabulary, and in concept formation. Goldfarb concluded that the poorer adjustment of this group was caused by its early privation during institutionalization.

Although Goldfarb's studies have been criticized for their methodology, the possibility of some inferiority in language and on intelligence tests, insofar as the latter depend on language ability, seems reasonable. As observed in the chapter on language, the superiority of only children in this area stems from their extensive contact with adults. Whether the limited association of Goldfarb's institutionalized group with adults during the first three years of life could exert so long-range an effect on language development remains a matter of speculation. There is little in the literature to substantiate this view.

Two other studies take an opposite position. They suggest that any deleterious effects institutionalization may produce in children do not persist. Dennis and Najarian (1957) examined the development of infants and children in a Beirut, Lebanon, foundling home. At the institution a ratio of one to ten prevailed between the caretaking staff and the children. Swaddling was employed until the infants reached about four months of age. Except for feeding and bathing the infant had very little contact with adults and was seldom taken out of his crib. From one to three years, the children spent most of the day in play groups of about 20 youngsters, with play equipment quite limited. At four kindergarten was provided.

Through tests administered to infants between two and 12 months of age and children between four-and-a-half and six years old as well as to comparable control groups of noninstitutionalized Lebanese children, the investigators found the experimental infants markedly inferior to the control infants in the two to 12 month period. However, among the four-and-a-half- to six-year-olds the institutionalized children were only slightly retarded in abilities measured. For the infants, the Cattell Infant Scale was used; for the children, the Goodenough Draw-A-Man Test, the Knox Cube Test, and the Porteus Maze Test were employed.

To lack of learning opportunities resulting from environmental restriction these investigators attribute the early retardation. But such privation did not seem to have lasting effects. It may be that the child gains from his peers the minimal amount of stimulation required for adequate development once he is able to behave actively toward his environment.

Experimental modification of the social environment of a group of institutionalized infants was tried by Rheingold (1956). For the typical institutional "multiple mothering" type of care, she substituted care by a single mother figure for a term of eight weeks, five days a week, seven-and-a-half hours per day. Both the control and experimental groups consisted of eight infants apiece, each about six months old. Before the experiment, at weekly intervals during it, and for four weeks thereafter, a battery of tests including a test of social responsiveness, tests of postural development and of cube manipulation, and the Cattell Infant Intelligence Scale was administered to the infants. Because the experimental group of infants did become more socially responsive than the control group, Rheingold concluded that the social behavior of infants could be modified by changes in their environment. Contrary to predictions, however, the experimental group did not perform significantly higher on the postural, cube, and Cattell tests.

A year later 14 of the original 16 children were subjected to a similar set of tests (Rheingold & Bayley, 1959). Apart from the fact that more members of the experimental group engaged in vocal expression during the social tests, there were no statistically significant differences between the two groups. Although attentive mothering produced some differences in behavior during infancy, the differences did not endure except perhaps in the area of verbal performance. One can only guess as to the effects of a longer period of "single mothering," in view of the failure of this study to show long-range consequences of a brief period during which social surroundings were modified.

In retrospect, then, it is difficult to distinguish the effects of sensory deprivation from those of separation from the mother. Several writers have mentioned that taking a child away from its mother is most harmful in the second half of its first year, although the effects of such separation diminish over the years. This makes sense. During the first six months of life the infant has not developed sufficiently in intellect to differentiate between strange and familiar faces and to be aware of changes of environment. Later, by the second or third year, reasons for separation can be comprehended to some extent by the child and his dependency needs have lessened somewhat, thanks to his association with his peers. Maternal deprivation after the first six months on the other hand, may be a matter of *separation* after an emotional bond has been established and as a result, harmful effects of perhaps long duration may appear in the emotional area.

SUMMARY

There are differences in the psychological environments into which infants are born. That such differences may not have long-range effects is due to the possibility that early parental attitudes toward the child may change in time and also to the subsequent experiences of the child. From birth the various characteristics of the infant affect the mother's attitude toward him so that from the very beginning the infant plays a part in creating his psychological environment. There is mutual interaction between parent and child.

The position one takes on the long-range effects of early experiences is determined in part by one's conception of the infant. Is he a passive recipient of environmental stimulation, impressionable, irreversibly affected by early events? Or does he react actively toward his environment, capable of resisting the long-term effects of traumatic experiences? Are single events crucial or is the repetitive pattern of events most influential?

Since Freudian theory emphasizes the importance of feeding and toilet training in affecting the child's development of personality, maternal practices in these areas were surveyed. The literature suggests that no long-range effects on the child's personality have resulted from the wide variation in maternal behavior in these two areas of early socialization. Since much maternal concern in the early years revolves about feeding and toilet training, these are important areas at the time, but their effects are of short-run significance for the child.

Maternal deprivation was examined at some length because of the light it casts on important elements in the early mother-child relation. Sensory deprivation seems to explain many of the harmful consequences of maternal deprivation. Attention from the mother is important because it provides the infant with a variety of stimuli.

REFERENCES

Adams, Abby B. Choice of infant feeding technique as a function of maternal personality. *J. consult. Psychol.*, 1959, **23**, 143–146.

Anderson, J. E. Personality organization in children. *Amer. Psychologist*, 1948, **3**, 409–416.

Bagby, E. The etiology of phobias. *J. abnorm. soc. Psychol.*, 1922, **17**, 16–18.

Brody, Sylvia. *Patterns of mothering: maternal influences during infancy.* New York: International Univer. Press, 1956.

Dennis, W., & Najarian, P. Infant development under environmental handicap. *Psychol. Monogr.*, 1957, **71**, No. 7.

Escalona, Sibylle K. Feeding disturbances in very young children. *Amer. J. Orthopsychiat.*, 1945, **15**, 76–80.

Freud, Anna, & Burlingame, Dorothy T. *War and children.* New York: Willard, 1943.

Fries, M. E. Mental hygiene in pregnancy, delivery, and the puerperium. *Ment. Hyg.*, 1941, **25**, 221–236.

Goldberger, L., & Holt, R. R. Experimental interferences with reality contact (perceptual isolation): method and group results. *J. nerv. ment. Dis.*, 1958, **127**, 99–112.

Goldfarb, W. The effects of early institutional care on adolescent personality (graphic Rorschach data). *Child Develpm.*, 1943, **14**, 213–223. (a)

Goldfarb, W. The effects of early institutional care on adolescent personality. *J. exp. Educ.*, 1943, **12**, 106–129. (b)

Goldfarb, W. Infant rearing and problem behavior. *Amer. J. Orthopsychiat.*, 1943, **13**, 249–265. (c)

Goldfarb, W. Effects of psychological deprivation in infancy and subsequent stimulation. *Amer. J. Psychiat.*, 1945, **102**, 18–33. (a)

Goldfarb, W. Psychological privation in infancy and subsequent adjustment. *Amer. J. Orthopsychiat.*, 1945, **15**, 247–255. (b)

Goldfarb, W. Variations in adolescent adjustment of institutionally-reared children. *Amer. J. Orthopsychiat.*, 1947, **17**, 449–457.

Goldfarb, W. Rorschach test differences between family-reared, institution-reared, and schizophrenic children. *Amer. J. Orthopsychiat.*, 1949, **19**, 624–633.

Huschka, Mabel. The child's response to coercive bowel training. *Psychosom. Med.*, 1942, **4**, 301–308.

Klatskin, Ethelyn H., Jackson, Edith B., & Wilkin, Louise C. The influence of degree of flexibility in maternal child care practices on early child behavior. *Amer. J. Orthopsychiat.*, 1956, **26**, 79–93.

Kral, V. A. Psychiatric observations under severe chronic stress. *Am. J. Psychiat.*, 1951, **108**, 185–192.

Kulka, A., Fry, C., & Goldstein, F. J. Kinesthetic needs in infancy. *Am. J. Orthopsychiat.*, 1960, **30**, 562–571.

LeMasters, E. E. Parenthood as crisis. *Marriage fam. Liv.*, 1957, **19**, 352–355.

Levy, D. M. *Maternal overprotection.* New York: Columbia Univer. Press, 1943.

Mead, Margaret. *Sex and temperament in three primitive societies.* New York: Mentor, 1935.

Peterson, C. H., & Spano, F. L. Breast feeding, maternal rejection, and child personality. *Char. & Pers.*, 1941, **10**, 62–66.

Pinneau, S. A critique on the articles by Margaret Ribble. *Child Develpm.*, 1950, **21**, 203–228.

Pinneau, S. The infantile disorders of hospitalism and anaclitic depression. *Psychol. Bull.*, 1955, **52**, 429–452.

Rabin, A. I. Some psychosexual differences between kibbutz and non-kibbutz Israeli boys. *J. proj. Tech.*, 1958, **22**, 328–332.

Rheingold, Harriet L. The modification of social responsiveness in institutional babies. *Monogr. soc. Res. Child Develpm.*, 1956, **21**, No. 2.

Rheingold, Harriet L., & Bayley, Nancy. The later effects of an experimental modification of mothering. *Child Develpm.*, 1959, **31**, 363–372.

Ribble, Margaret. *The rights of infants.* New York: Columbia Univer. Press, 1943.

Ribble, Margaret. Infantile experience in relation to personality development. In J. McV. Hunt (Ed.), *Personality and behavior disorders.* New York: Ronald, 1944. Pp. 621–651.

Scott, J. P. Critical periods in behavioral development. *Science*, 1962, **138**, 949–958.

Sears, R. R., Maccoby, Eleanor E., & Levin, H. *Patterns of childrearing.* Evanston, Ill.: Row, Peterson, 1957.

Sewell, W. H., & Mussen, P. H. The effect of feeding, weaning, and scheduling procedures on childhood adjustment and the formation of oral symptoms. *Child Develpm.*, 1952, 23, 185–191.

Sewell, W. H., Mussen, P. H., & Harris, C. W. Relationship among child training practices. *Amer. sociol. Rev.*, 1955, 20, 137–148.

Shulman, M. *Sleep till noon.* New York: Bantam Books, 1959.

Simsarian, F. P. Case histories of five thumbsucking children breast fed on unscheduled regimes, without limitation of nursing time. *Child Develpm.*, 1947, 18, 180–184.

Spitz, R. A. Hospitalism: an inquiry into the genesis of psychiatric conditions in early childhood. *Psychoanal. Stud. Child*, 1945, 1, 53–74; 1946, 2, 113–117.

Spitz, R. A., & Wolf, Katherine. Anaclitic depression. *Psychoanal. Stud. Child*, 1946, 2, 313–342.

Stevenson, I. Is the human personality more plastic in infancy and childhood. *Am. J. Psychiat.*, 1957, 114, 152–161.

Sullivan, H. S. Conceptions of modern psychiatry. *Psychiatry*, 1940, 3, 1–117.

Traisman, A. S., & Traisman, H. S. Thumb- and finger-sucking: a study of 2,650 infants and children. *J. Pediat.*, 1958, 53, 566–572.

chapter 10 ✽ Family Influences
on the Growing Child

The adult fills a variety of roles—father or mother, husband or wife, son or daughter, brother or sister, teacher, colleague, friend. For each of these roles, certain sets of behavior seem particularly appropriate. Thus, the behaviors that characterize or typify any individual permit him to fulfill one role more suitably and more adequately than another. Similarly, an individual's personality fits him better for one role than for some other. To paraphrase Abraham Lincoln, all people can play some of these roles, some people can play all of these roles, but all people cannot play all these roles with equal facility. How successfully any individual fills any one of them depends on the sum total of his characteristics and the requirements of the particular role.

Take parenthood. Western culture prescribes general requirements for the role of parent. The father must provide food, clothing, and shelter for his children—that is, economic support. He is also responsible for the children's behavior in public. Increasingly it is thought that the role of father includes emotional and psychological support for the children, too. What are some of the specific behaviors demanded of the modern, urban father beyond his occupational pursuits? He may accompany his son to the weekly cub scout meeting, mend a broken bat, punish his daughter for misbehavior, change the baby's diapers while the mother is shopping, attend a meeting of the

P.T.A. to hear another daughter recite some verse, watch a two-year-old try to catch a bird, rush a child to the doctor to set a broken arm, arbitrate a battle between siblings, teach a four-year-old the proper form for cartwheels, and drive the baby sitter home at two o'clock in the morning. This is merely a smattering of the behaviors performed by the typical father.

What of the mother? Society dictates that she provide physical care for the children—feed them, keep them healthy and, if possible, clean. She must comfort and console them when necessary and in general nurture them and provide emotional support. Long extolled by novelist and bard, the role of mother has been made almost impossible of fulfillment by the ordinary woman. Her feelings of inadequacy are matched only by her undying efforts. What, then, are some of the day-to-day behaviors demanded of her? A mother's typical day might begin—or end—with waking to give her infant a two o'clock feeding. Later she urges a son to the breakfast table to spoonfeed him cereal and hurry him off to school, cleans up the spilled orange juice, diapers and bathes the baby, wipes a daughter's running nose, tends to another child's chicken pox, listens to the five-year-old's account of his day, drives another daughter to a music lesson, enjoys the two-year-old's mimicry of the mother's household activities, and soothes a seven-year-old's broken heart because her best friend pushed her into the mud.

The young child depends totally on these parents who must be capable of meeting his needs. As the child grows older, the dependency on the parent lessens. Now father and mother must be able to relinquish some of the earlier control. Different behaviors and attitudes are required at different times. This is the price of parenthood. To say that some adults find the parental role more satisfying than others is to belabor the obvious. But how acceptable a woman finds the maternal role may indeed influence how adequately she performs it. As individuals, parents possess many psychological needs, most of which must be met if the particular person is to be moderately well adjusted. However, if the demands of the parental role conflict or are incompatible with the needs of the parent as an individual, difficulties almost invariably ensue.

HOW THE PARENT BECOMES AS HE IS

Does parenthood require a certain kind of person? Perhaps to some extent it does. Parenthood involves a number of demands and behaviors: sacrifice, relating emotionally to a child, intense emotional rewards and perhaps disappointments, willingness to let a child be a child—all these and more.

At the human level there is little evidence for the existence of a "parental instinct" or even a "maternal instinct." Although there is a connection between hormonal secretion and lactation, for example, this in no way implies that maternal behavior and the various activities and functions it involves are a direct outgrowth of hormonal activity. A mother cannot rely on innate, "built-in" mechanisms to guide her maternal behavior. How, then, does she become the kind of mother she is? To what sources may we attribute her maternal behavior and attitudes? As noted in the previous chapter, current fads and fashions in child rearing and her individual personality structure influence her behavior as a parent. There is also _generational continuity_, the relationship between parent and offspring in the way in which each, in due turn, fills the parental role. One's own parents are probably the only persons one observes intimately in the parental role. Like it or not, they serve as the models for one's own behavior as a parent, in addition to their wielding an enormous influence on one's personality development and adult character.

Several studies have looked into the similarity between parent and offspring in their handling of the parental role and into the influence of one's own childhood and early attitudes toward parents on one's own performance as a parent. In a study of four groups of parents —accepting, rejecting, dominating, and submissive—Symonds (1939) observed that the accepting type grew up in homes marked by good adjustment and acceptance. Dominating parents were dominated by their parents, whereas submissive parents enjoyed much freedom in their own childhood. A parent behaved just like his own parents and established a similar relation with his children; he repeated his early experiences in the home. More specifically, Symonds held, parents adopted an attitude toward their children that resembled the attitude taken toward them by the parent of the same sex.

Radke (1946) noted a tendency for parents to use disciplinary techniques similar to those remembered from their own childhood. And in Bronson, Kalten, and Livson's study (1959), mothers inclined to exercise strong authority in their homes if they remembered their own mothers as having done so. A similar pattern was found among fathers; they emulated their paternal parent, but rather in the area of affectional relationship than of authority. Why in one area and not in others is a matter for speculation. Methodologically both studies involved an individual's memory of his parents' practices and behaviors. Although an individual's perception and memory of parental treatment in childhood may have significance for his own behavior as a parent, it would be useful to have actual information of what happened years ago.

Attempting to trace the transmission of authority in the home from one generation to the next, Ingersoll (1948) defined the patterns in terms of leading or controlling the family activities. Four main patterns were discerned: _matricentric_—a pattern of authority in which the mother had the greater control; _patricentric_—the father exercised the greater control; _balanced_—fairly equal husband-wife control; and _intermediate_—lying midway between balance and control by either husband or wife. The parental backgrounds of second-generation couples were _homogamous_ or _heterogamous_. In the former, husband and wife were reared in homes having the same prevailing pattern of authority, whether matricentric, patricentric, or balanced. In the heterogamous situation, husband and wife came from homes of opposing authority patterns. Among homogamous marriages, the patterns of parental authority tended to be reproduced. In heterogamous marriages, the patterns were modified to form a balanced compromise. Nevertheless, in all cases, the Ingersoll study found deviations from the dominant trends.

In a study of the backgrounds of a group of normal children, Harris (1959) noted that what had happened to the mothers "as children was happening to their own children; what happened to their parents was happening to them as parents" (p. 39). Four factors influenced this continuity. The first was the degree to which the mothers were aware of it: "Joan is just like I was at that age—flighty and unconcerned." The second was the degree to which they wished to see repeated the experiences of their own youth: "I want our children to enjoy the kind of summer outings which I loved as a child." The third was the degree to which the mothers were involved in the continuity of their childhood, wishing to assume similar roles of dependence or independence as adults, and the fourth was concern with their own unfulfilled childhood expectations: "I want to be a better mother to my children than my mother was to me."

The kind of continuity experienced by a mother with her own childhood affected the adjustment she made to the maternal role. Too rigid an adherence to the past or too much conflict with it created problems of dependability and understanding between a mother and her children. Three types of mothers were discerned: traditional mothers, rebellious mothers, and dependent mothers. The traditional mother was satisfied with her own mother's child-rearing tactics and attitudes, and used them as a reference point in raising her own family. The rebellious mother sought to be less controlling than her own mother with whom she was dissatisfied because of excessive control, strictness, and interference. The children of such mothers tended to rebel against any rule interfering with their quest for pleasure. Indeed, there was some evidence that these mothers were endeavoring to work out their rebellious feelings against their own parent through their children. The third type, the dependent mother, was dissatisfied with her own mother because she thought she had not been accorded proper attention, love, or interest. Children of such mothers seemed to search for interpersonal warmth.

Not all the factors of continuity may operate at the conscious level, nor do they necessarily work directly on the child. Moreover, how a woman regards her husband may, in subtle ways, affect her children's attitude toward him. Thus, although parental behavior may not be inherited in a biological sense through the genes, it may be transmitted through the mechanisms of personality. Observations of mothers of problem children seen in clinics substantiate the notion that the "sins of the fathers are visited on the sons."

THREE PRINCIPAL PARENT VARIABLES

More important than how individuals model their behavior after perceptions of their parents' behavior is the influence parents exert on the adjustment and personality of their children which determines the kind of adults and, in turn, the kind of parents they will be. A mother spanks her five-year-old son if he flaunts her command to obey instantly when an order is given. Her choice of disciplinary tactic may be related to her belief or attitude that physical punishment is necessary when children do not submit readily to parental authority. This belief may emanate from her authoritarian personality structure, a vestige from her parents. It is one of three main parent variables— parent behavior, parent attitudes, and parent personality. Although it may seem obvious that the three variables are closely related—that is, a parent behaves toward his child in accord with his attitudes toward child rearing, which are an aspect of his personality structure—little research has been undertaken to find the nature of their relationships. Further research should endeavor to unravel the entwined strands of the three (Medinnus, 1959). Such investigations might employ personality tests to assess the dominant personality trends, needs, and goals among a group of mothers. They might also administer a standard parent attitude test and conduct interviews to acquire information about the mothers' actual child-rearing practices in numerous areas.

Parent Personality

If personality is the sum of an individual's character traits, attitudes, and values, the personality of a parent may be expected to influence the personality development of his child. Although not much is known about the precise operation of this influence, one can get some idea of how the parent's personality affects the atmosphere and emotional tone of the home and the child's development by categorizing parental personality as either healthy or neurotic. In addition, there are many other aspects of personality which psychologists have described.

Behrens (1954) assessed the adjustment of a small group of children and related their ratings to the feeding, weaning, and toilet-training practices of their mothers. Also, she rated each mother as a "total mother person" which signified the woman's character structure as reflected in how she fulfilled the maternal role. Behrens found little consistency among the three child-rearing practices and no tie between ratings of children's behavior and their mothers' procedures. There was, however, a close relation between child adjustment and "total mother person" ratings. Apparently what a mother *is* bears more on child adjustment than what she *does*. Actually, the Behrens study noted that the majority of mothers in the particular sample functioned reasonably well in specific child-rearing tasks, even though poorly adjusted themselves.

Various studies have sought to learn whether parental attitudes and parental behavior are tied in with parent personality. One factor analytic study (Becker, Peterson, Hellmer, Shoemaker, & Quay, 1959) found no close connection between parental behavior and personality as these affected problem behavior in children. But inspired by publication of the book, *The Authoritarian Personality* (Adorno, Frenkel-Brunswik, Levinson, & Sanford, 1950), considerable research has been undertaken to uncover the relation between authoritarian attitudes and personality structure. In the original investigation, the research team found persons having authoritarian attitudes to be rigid, inflexible, and concrete in their thinking, conforming and conventional in their values, excessive in their respect for authority, and prejudiced or ethnocentric in their view toward others who differed from them racially or in national origin.

Zuckerman and Oltean (1959), while studying maternal attitudes and characteristics of maternal personality, observed a correlation between scores of authoritarian-control on a standard parent attitude test and scores on the California F Scale which measures authoritarian social attitudes. Presumably both authoritarian social and child-rearing attitudes reflect a basic tendency of personality. Significantly, these investigators found a relationship between the scores of mothers on a hostility-rejection scale and three measures of personality. Mothers who tended to be hostile and rejecting as parents as a rule had a high need for achievement, a similar one for aggression, but a low need to provide nurture. The study also indicated that hostility and rejection were related to psychopathological symptoms in the mother.

Another study (Block, 1955) endeavored to describe permissive and restrictive fathers from their scores on a child-rearing attitude scale. Assessment of 20 fathers in each group characterized those with permissive attitudes as self-reliant, ascendant, and rebellious toward persons in authority, whereas the restrictive set was seen as submissive, suggestible, conforming, indecisive, ineffectual, and overcontrolled. The latter group clearly possessed traits denoting an authoritarian personality. Generally, the permissive fathers were stable but flexible, demonstrating an optimal degree of integrated personality.

Finally, several studies (Morris & Nicholas, 1950; Phillips, 1951; Hanvik & Byrum, 1959) have noted similarities between parents and children in the nature of personality disturbances. One can only speculate about the origin of these similarities. Are they the result of the child's modeling his behavior after his parent's? Or is the parent's behavior toward the child dictated in part by his own unresolved psychological needs which, in turn, produce like disturbances in the child? Parents, of course, are people whose own childhoods influence their adult personalities and behavior. Perhaps they project unmet needs and unsolved childhood problems onto their own children, as the following example illustrates.

> "Tom," age six, was referred because of enuresis, and this was the behavior which concerned the mother most. The interviews finally brought out that the mother had been enuretic until she began to menstruate, that ". . . people used to kid me about it." The mother recalled in this context that as a child she had been so afraid that she would wet the bed that she refused to go to bed at night, or when she did go to bed she would lie awake for long periods of time disturbed over possible bed-wetting (Phillips, 1951, p. 189).

Perhaps the personality of the parent may be more influential than his child-rearing practices in shaping the personality development of the child. The challenge for research is to ferret out the exact mechanisms through which parental personality affects the personality of the child.

Parent Attitudes

How the adult conceives of the parental role in relation to the child influences his attitudes as a parent. Does he see the parent's primary function as one of restricting and controlling child behavior? Does he view the socialization process as essentially a taming of the young child's uncivilized nature? Or does he regard the parental role as mainly one of guidance and setting the proper example for the child to emulate? The conception of the responsibilities, functions, and obligations of a role mold the individual's attitudes in the role which, in turn, presumably engender his behavior in it. The interest of the child psychologist in parental attitudes stems, therefore, from the notion that a basic, underlying attitude influences many behaviors of parenthood which are assumed to affect the personality development of the child.

"The essence of parent-child relations, it must be emphasized, lies more in how a parent *feels* than in what a parent *does*," Symonds (1949, p. xiii) remarked. In this respect Symonds's concern lay with parental attitudes *toward the child*. Subsequent research has also been concerned with attitudes *toward child rearing*.

The assessment of parent attitude poses a number of problems (Bell, 1958), most of them arising from attempts of psychologists to find a cause-and-effect relationship between these attitudes and child behavior. The first problem results from changes in parental attitudes. It is extremely hazardous to maintain in the assessment of parent attitudes that certain ones *cause* particular child behaviors when the measurement is made *after* the appearance of the behavior. One cannot know the attitude of the parent *before* the onset of the behavior, whether it be schizophrenia, stuttering, delinquency, or anything else. More importantly, one must be aware of the possibility of changes in parent attitudes. For example, a large percentage of parents can readily name the age level of children that they prefer and the level that they regard least endurable. Since one age level is more satisfying and rewarding than another, it might be assumed that the parent-child relationship is most conducive at that period to healthy personality development in the child. The following case study illuminates the point.

Billy was born after a labor of six and a half hours which Mrs. A. experienced as being much less painful than she had anticipated from the stories she had heard from her older sisters and friends. From the very beginning in her handling of the baby—a boy—she was not only surprisingly technically skillful and competent but she seemed particularly responsive to clues from him related to his needs and had great success in making him comfortable and happy. For example, by the time he was four days of age she was noting that he had particular objections to being wet, was able to change his diaper competently and was exceedingly pleased that she was able to comfort him. In the first visit of the pediatrician to the home when Billy was three weeks of age a note was made that Mrs. A.'s way of comforting him, once she picked him up and once when she patted him in his bassinet seemed to be "all he needed and not more."

During the first nine to ten months she was described by all members of the research team who saw her as a particularly warm and skillful mother and the impression of unity and understanding between her and Billy was repeatedly commented upon. This came up not only in relation to her ability to persuade Billy to respond as she wished him to in the areas of eating, sleeping and toileting, but also in the definite but indirect and subtle ways of prohibiting things of which she did not approve. It was noted, for example, that she interrupted the thumb sucking which she did not like not by pulling his thumb out, but by enticing him to become busy with something else—i.e., playing with her or with a toy. . . . She seemed to set limits in a way that aroused a minimum of protest from the baby. She anticipated no difficulty and seemed to feel perfectly sure that everything would go well between them. . . .

Some time must here be given to a description of Billy who showed surprising adaptability and smoothness in many of his physiological and maturational patterns from the beginning. As a newborn he was described as well developed, moderately active and mature. There was a specificity about his way of expressing this discomfort or wishes which seemed to make comforting him quite easy (i.e., not just by his mother but by others as well). One might say he gave clues which could easily be interpreted. His parents found him attractive, entertaining and easy to live with.

Thus those first nine to ten months gave us the impression of such an untroubled, conflict-free, mutually satisfying and stimulating mother-child relationship that the period of the "crisis" which became apparent during the tenth month was impossible to overlook. The first indication of this came on the occasion of Mrs. A.'s and Billy's visit to the clinic for his regularly scheduled checkup. It was both reported by Mrs. A. and observed that Billy was more difficult to dress. He did not "co-operate" in this as he had before and it looked as if his mother's usual ways of restraining him by distraction or touch could no longer control his drive toward activity. At this time he was creeping and cruising. He walked with two hands held. When his mother tried to hold him on her lap, he tried to get down. He was reaching out and scratching at her neck or face in a now provocative way and she was scolding him with a new sharpness in her tone. She looked more harassed and tired at that visit than the pediatrician had ever seen her and said about Billy, "I really work up a sweat trying to figure out what he wants now." She reported that Billy was now so active that he seemed to want to be down on the floor, out of his crib, or chair, or the previously satisfactory laps of his elders. She spoke with much more feeling than ever before about how much she wanted a "place of our own"—and added, "big families are nice in a way, but I'm tired of crowds." Such a move seemed impossible at that time as they had just bought a car which Mr. A. had to have for his work. At that point Billy would permit no one except his mother to feed him his meals and she was both pleased and irritated by this behavior. He also was making persistent grabs for the spoon during feeding and she found this annoying.

During the next three months she indicated her irritation at certain continuing aspects of her environment which had previously seemed less important to her. She complained about her husband's doing things for his mother. There was distinct displeasure expressed for the first time at Billy's enjoyment of his paternal grandmother, and the need to say, "but she [paternal grandmother] can't *really* take care of him" and an ever increasing determination to have a place of her own as soon as possible. She talked about Billy's behavior in a different way. For example, his activity and impatience with the lap were often spoken of as though they were primarily aimed at irritating her. His wish for certain objects to play with was seen as "everything he shouldn't have he wants." She was bothered by the fact that Billy could no longer be so easily persuaded to comply with her wishes. She summarized her difficulty in saying: "I can't figure him out any more."

Under the pressure of the dissatisfaction Mrs. A. returned to work and left the part-time care of the child to her sister. This does not mean that her relationship to B. had deteriorated, that she had become a "rejecting mother." The relationship has remained close, but has lost one impressive component—the full unity of mother and child. The relationship between mother and child now bears more resemblance to her relationship with other people. She is a woman who tries gently but firmly to dominate every situation. This is apparent in her relationship with her husband, and could be studied in some detail in her relationship with interviewer and pediatrician.

Retrospectively we find from this material that her reaction to the child's growing independence might have been anticipated, but we missed an even more significant clue. When the pediatrician discussed with her the giving of solid foods and in enumerating mentioned that he might not like the taste of some of them, Mrs. A. quickly responded, "Oh, he'll like spinach; I like it." What we saw in this was the unity; what we missed was the germ of discord since what she implied was that Billy was not thought of as having a taste of his own (Coleman, Kris, & Provence, 1953, pp. 30–33).

The second problem relates to the first. It is the impact on the parent's attitudes of the feedback provided by a certain kind of child. That children at birth differ in many ways is obvious and that these differences affect the parent's attitudes toward a child must be considered. Since parental attitudes condition the child's further development of personality, the point is especially important in relation to the effect of such attitudes on the personality growth of the handicapped, the chronically ill, or the extremely sensitive child. This brings up the matter of the "vicious circle" phenomenon which has such dreadfully harmful consequences for the youngster. Two examples will suffice. That a child's intellectual capacities are below his parents' expectations may first come to parental attention when the youngster experiences some difficulty in learning to read in the first grade, or when he is placed in a reading group that the parents consider beneath his level. The child must thus face the frustrations flowing from reading difficulties as well as the equally bitter torment of parental rejection. At a time when the child most needs parental acceptance and reassurance to bolster his self-confidence and sense of security, he is met with criticism and disapproval. This change in parental attitude only serves to handicap the child further in his efforts to improve his reading. Or to cite the other example, perhaps for deep-seated reasons rooted in his own psychological past, a parent may find himself unable to accept fully one of his children. From this nonacceptance may emerge undesirable school behavior such as attention seeking. When the teacher or other school officer expresses concern over this behavior, the nonacceptance may increase. Here again the change in parental attitude may aggravate rather than ameliorate the child's disturbance.

Third among these problems is the necessity for identifying the attitudes of the parent toward a particular child. It is well known that an individual views each of his children differently. Not only does a parent's attitudes vary according to the age of the child but also, undoubtedly, on the basis of such factors as sex, intelligence, personality, and appearance.

The fourth problem is that the emphasis in psychological literature on the crucial significance of parental attitudes for child adjustment has made parents highly sensitive and defensive about revealing their attitudes. Tapping a parent's attitudes directly is no simple task. How difficult this may be through a paper-and-pencil test may be judged from the failure of the Parent Attitude Research Instrument (PARI) to distinguish among the attitudes of various groups of mothers. For example, the PARI cannot differentiate significantly between the attitudes of parents of well-adjusted and poorly adjusted first-grade children (Medinnus, 1961a), nor among the attitudes of mothers of children with speech articulation problems, delayed speech development, or lack of speech (Moll & Darley, 1960), nor among mothers of asthmatic, chronically ill, or healthy children (Margolis, 1961).

Parent attitude testing has an extensive history. The PARI scale consisting of 23 subscales which assess a variety of attitudes is the most recently devised vehicle. Developed at the National Institute of Mental Health (Schaefer & Bell, 1955, 1958), it contains these subscales:

Encouraging verbalization	Fostering dependency
Seclusion of the mother	Breaking the will
Martyrdom	Fearing of harming the baby
Marital conflict	Strictness
Irritability	Excluding outside influences
Deification	Suppression of aggression
Rejection of the homemaking role	Equalitarianism
Approval of activity	Avoidance of communication
Inconsiderateness of the husband	Suppression of sex
Ascendance of the mother	Intrusiveness
Comradeship and sharing	Acceleration of development
Dependency of the mother	

From the various attitude tests two dominant attitudes emerge. One is the pattern of authority in the home. The other is the acceptance of the child as an individual. This is what the findings of research have to say about each of them.

Authoritarian Attitudes. To understand fully the effects of a parent's authoritarian attitudes on the personality development of a child requires a knowledge of their source. Several possibilities have been raised: the personality structure of the individual, his own upbringing and his parents' pattern of authority, his conception of both parent and child roles. Regardless of the cause, an authoritarian attitude implies an emphasis on authority and a belief in the value and efficacy of an autocratic approach to child rearing. Control is preeminent. The parent is dominant, the child subordinate. Insufficient respect is shown for the youngster as an individual, for his rights, his wishes, and his individuality.

From this it would seem possible to predict that authoritarian parental attitudes would lead to a child who would be submissive, lacking in security and independence, and who would, therefore, be less popular with his companions. In general such predictions have been borne out by research (Read, 1945; Radke, 1946; Miles, 1942). Yet Radke discovered that children from autocratic homes were rated by preschool teachers as more likely to fight and quarrel with other children, as more inconsiderate of others, and as more insensitive to praise or blame than those from democratic homes. A child from a home in which the notion of power is highly important assumes a role similar to his parents' when he finds himself in a relatively permissive nursery-school environment. His behavior leads to belligerence, inconsiderateness, and consequently, to unpopularity.

In general, children of autocratic parents are seen as emotionally unstable. This may be ascribed to a number of reasons. The difference in approach between the autocratic parents and the more permissive teachers leads to uncertainty and confusion for the child. Having little opportunity for choice and decision in the home, the child finds the freedom of the nursery school fearsome. Harsh paternal attitudes have also been seen to relate to personality problems of shyness and withdrawal and to conduct problems of truancy and stealing among kindergarteners (Peterson, Becker, Shoemaker, Luria, & Hellmer, 1961). Such attitudes are reflected in demands for instant and unquestioning obedience, in inability to tolerate the "annoyance value" of children, and in the preference for a quiet, cautious child rather than a noisy, daring one.

Parental Acceptance-Rejection Attitudes. A 40-item scale specifically designed to measure parental acceptance of children (Porter, 1954) posited four traits in the accepting parent. He is a parent who (*a*) "Regards his child as a person with feelings and respects the child's right and need to express these feelings"; (*b*) "Values the unique makeup of his child and does what he can to foster that uniqueness within the limits of healthy personal and social adjustment"; (*c*) "Recognizes the child's need to differentiate and separate himself from his parents to become an autonomous individual"; and (*d*) "Loves his child unconditionally." However, the results obtained from relating parents' scores on the Porter scale to the adjustment of children have been negative (Burchinal, Hawkes, & Gardner, 1957; Burchinal, 1958). No significant tie has been found between the two.

Because of the emphasis in Western culture on maternal love and the affectional obligations of motherhood, strong feelings of guilt arise in a parent who, for one reason or another, cannot fully accept his child. Any attempt to assess this sensitive area on an objective, paper-and-pencil level is therefore almost doomed to failure. What is needed is a subtle, disguised, projective-type instrument which does not arouse the parent's defense system. Psychologists have long shown concern over acceptance and rejection. Yet not much research has been directed toward creating an instrument for tapping these vital parental attitudes. Medinnus and Curtis (1963) defined maternal acceptance on the basis of the discrepancy between a mother's rating of her child on a series of traits and her description of how she wanted the child to measure up on them. A significant correlation was obtained between self-acceptance scores of a group of mothers and their acceptance of their children; this finding will be discussed in a subsequent chapter on "individual appraisal" (Chapter 14). Presumably the psychological adage that one can accept others only to the extent that one first accepts oneself applies to the mother-child relationship.

There is undoubtedly a wide margin of safety in parent attitudes (Ausubel, 1957, p. 362). Only when they deviate markedly from the typical do these attitudes perhaps exert harmful influences on child adjustment. In such cases, it is more likely the attitudes toward the child, relative to acceptance or rejection, than toward child rearing that are significant.

Parent Behavior

From what has been seen of parent behaviors in the previous chapter, it is apparent that an isolated examination of them is not likely to bear much fruit. At this point in man's knowledge more is to be learned from exploring the characteristics that describe the *general* behavioral atmosphere of the home. Table 10-1 contains some of the principal parent characteristics identified over several decades of research activity. Two recur throughout the studies; these are acceptance versus rejection and autonomy versus control.

The two characteristics that continually recur are depicted in Figure 10-1. In theory, the psychological atmosphere of a home may fall into any of the four quadrants, each of which represents one of four general combinations: acceptance-autonomy, acceptance-control, rejection-autonomy, rejection-control.

Acceptance vs. Rejection. The most significant aspect of the home is the warmth of the relationship between parent and child. Both the Pattern Study (Sears, Maccoby, & Levin, 1957) and the Fels research, to be considered presently, have maintained that warmth is the most crucial and pervasive factor affecting the child. After a careful review of the literature, however, Symonds (1939) concluded that the matter of

TABLE 10-1   Major Parent-Child Dimensions

Investigators	Psychological Dimensions	
Symonds (1939)	Dimensions:	Acceptance-rejection
		Dominance-submission
Baldwin, Kalhorn, & Breese (1945)	Syndromes:	Democracy in the home
		Acceptance of child
		Indulgence
Baldwin, Kalhorn, & Breese (1949)	Clusters:	Warmth
		Adjustment
		Restrictiveness
		Clarity
		Interference
Roff * (1949)	Factors:	Concern for child
		Democratic guidance
		Permissiveness
		Parent-child harmony
		Sociability-adjustment of parents
		Activeness of home
		Nonreadiness of suggestion
Lorr & Jenkins † (1953)	Factors:	Dependence-encouraging
		Democracy of child training
		Organization and effectiveness of control
Milton ‡ (1958)	Factors:	Strictness or nonpermissiveness of parent behavior
		General family interaction or adjustment
		Warmth of the mother-child relationship
		Responsible child-training orientation
		Parents' attitude toward aggressiveness and punitiveness
Schaefer (1959)	Dimensions:	Autonomy-control
		Love-hostility

* Based on the Baldwin, Kalhorn, & Breese (1945) data.
† Based on the Baldwin, Kalhorn, & Breese (1945) data and Roff's (1949) factor analysis.
‡ Based on the Pattern data (Sears, Maccoby, & Levin, 1957).

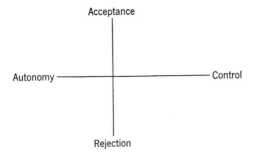

FIGURE 10-1 Two major psychological dimensions in the home.

acceptance or rejection was one of the two most significant considerations in the home, the other being autonomy as opposed to control. Despite leaving much to be desired methodologically, since its findings were based on case histories compiled by Symonds's former students, the study was fruitful enough to warrant examination. These were some of the parent behaviors that served as evidence for acceptance or rejection according to the study:

Evidence for Acceptance	*Evidence for Rejection*
Participates with child in games, sports, hobbies, takes trips together, special vacations together, pals	No interest in child
	No time for child—neglect
	Unfavorable comparison with siblings
	Verbal punishment—nagging, scolding
Parents make rearing child their main job—devoted	
Interested in child's plans and ambitions	Failure to support child
	Criticism or blame of child
Gives child loving care and protection	Physical punishment or cruelty
	Turned out of home or threaten to place in an institution
Interested in school progress	Does not speak well of child
Demonstrative in affection	Ridicule
Speaks well of child	Child unwanted at birth
Wanted at birth	Suspicious of child's behavior
Child encouraged to bring friends home	Too much supervision
	Neglect health, clothes, training, etc.
Parents worry when child is ill	(pp. 60–61)
Accepted as individual rather than as child	
Child trusted	
Parents talk over plans with child	
Parents do not expect too much of child	
Parents give wise counseling and encouragement	
(pp. 62–63)	

Symonds sought to find differences in behavior between accepted and rejected children in order to discover their causes in the marital relations of the parents and in the parents' own childhood. In general, he noted accepted children engaged predominantly in socially acceptable behavior, whereas rejected children manifested a number of unacceptable behaviors. Specifically, the behaviors characteristic of accepted children included good-naturedness, considerateness of others, cheerfulness, interest in work, friendliness, cooperativeness, and emotional stability. Among rejected children, on the other hand, attention-getting behavior, tendency toward delinquency, and problems in school were evident. More important, however, than descriptions of behavioral differences between accepted and rejected children is the need to understand how parental acceptance and rejection produce them.

Symonds (1949) observed that an individual's attitudes toward himself grew out of the attitudes displayed toward him by his parents during childhood. A child who was rejected developed feelings of insecurity and inferiority because it seemed to him that if he were unworthy of parental love, he was evidently worthless. A low conception of the self resulted from a low view of the child by his parents.

Such rejection brings on attempts by the child to win parental affection. These efforts may take the form of various attention-getting behaviors: refusal to eat, refusal to talk, temper tantrums, bed wetting, and whining. If these tactics prove futile, two general types of behavior often result; the child becomes hostile and aggressive or withdrawn and submissive. Symonds pointed out that whereas rejection might lead to good social adjustment outside the home and to close identification with and attachment to one's peers, it more frequently resulted in more negative consequences—feelings of insecurity, inferiority, inadequacy, worthlessness, isolation, humiliation, and anxiety. Even though a number of childhood experiences might not exert long-range influences on the child, a persistent pattern of rejection might very well prove pervasive in its effect on the child's adult personality and adjustment.

In his later study Symonds (1949) examined a number of factors, immediate and conscious as well as personality and unconscious, contributing to the parent's rejection of the child. Among the more obvious were the economic burden imposed by the youngster, the invasion of the parents' privacy and activities, the strain of childbirth and child care on the mother, the child's failure to meet parental expectations, and parental disappointment in the sex of the child. Symonds maintained that the child most likely to be accepted by his parents was the one easiest to accept. In this respect, the characteristics of the child definitely figure in the degree to which he receives parental acceptance.

Six elements, in particular, play an unconscious part in parental rejection, Symonds believed. First, the pattern of rejection adopted by a parent might be similar to the one experienced in his own childhood. Second, the parent might kindle in the child the hostility he felt toward his own parents. Third, one parent might show hostility toward the child as a means of injuring the other parent. Fourth, the parent might transfuse into the child the hostility he felt toward one of his own siblings. Fifth, he might implant in the child some of the feelings of hostility and rejection that he feels toward himself. Sixth, a mother—or a father, for that matter—might be so immature and narcissistic as to be unable to love another person wholeheartedly, and the resultant guilt might cause her to reject the child. Although verification of the presence of one or more of these six factors in the parent is difficult, short of extensive clinical interviews, a parent's attitudes and behaviors toward his child seem dictated as much by unconscious considerations as by those of which he is aware.

So much for Symonds. Let us now explore parental acceptance as seen in the Fels studies (Baldwin, Kalhorn, & Breese, 1945). The Fels Research Institute has dealt largely with the scientific collection of data on the home environment. To quantify these data obtained from direct obesrvation and interviews with mothers, the Institute devised a series of rating scales. The theory underlying the choice of areas for study and the rationale behind the assessment procedure have been described in detail by Champney (1941a, b). The Institute's directors assumed that the parent behaved consistently in certain ways toward the child from situation to situation. Thus, he provided the child with an environment for learning from which he could develop social habits and form his personality. Figure 10-2 represents one of the 30 scales in the Fels set.

One syndrome, or cluster of variables, to emerge in the Fels studies from examining the interrelationships among the 30 scales was labeled "Acceptance of the Child." Scales fitting into this cluster included rapport with child, affectionateness toward child, direction of criticism (approval), effectiveness of policy, acceptance of child, child-centeredness of the home, and nondisciplinary friction. Two other syndromes, "Democracy in the Home" and "Indulgence," also appeared. Thus, a home might be classified into one of a variety of possible combinations of the three. An acceptant home might be indulgent, democratic, or both.

FELS PARENT BEHAVIOR RATING SCALE NO. 7.2

Serial Sheet No.

Acceptance of Child
(Devotion—Rejection)

1	2	3	4	5	6	7	8	9	10	Number
										Period of observation
										Ratee
										Age in
										Months at End of Period
										Child

Rate the parent's acceptance of the child into his own inner circle of loyalty and devotion. Does the parent act in such a way as to indicate that the child is considered an intimate and inseparable partner? Or does the parent act as though he resents the child's intrusion and rejects the child's bid for a place in his primary area of devotion?

Consider all evidence which in any way may impinge upon the child as acceptance-rejection, however subtle, vague, or indirect. It is not the parent's true feeling, but his attitude, as a functioning unit in the child's environment, which we are rating.

Parent's behavior toward child connotes utter devotion and acceptance into his innermost self, without stint or suggestion of holding back in any phase of his life.

Parent clearly accepts child. Includes child in family councils, trips, affection, even when it is difficult or represents considerable sacrifice.

A "Charter member" of the family but "kept in his place". Parent accepts child in general, but excludes him from certain phases of parent's life.

Tacit acceptance. Excludes child so frequently that to the child the rejection attitude may seem to predominate even though parent takes acceptance for granted.

Parent's predominant tendency is to avoid, repulse, and exclude the child, but without open rejection.

Child openly resented and rejected by parent. Never admitted to inner circle. Made to feel unwanted, ostracized.

										Score	Rater:	Date of Rating:
										Tolerance		
										Range	Scored by:	Date:
1	2	3	4	5	6	7	8	9	10	Number	Checked by: Tabulated by:	Date: Date:

Rater's Remarks: (continue on back of sheet)

FIGURE 10-2

Generally, the studies found the acceptant home warm, granting unconditional acceptance of the child and characterized by a relatively noncoercive policy of child rearing. Rejecting homes, on the other hand, fell into two types: nonchalant and actively rejecting. In the nonchalant home, the child was largely ignored but punished severely for infractions or disturbances. In the actively rejecting home, auto-cratic control required the child's constant compliance, thus reducing the chance of disturbance. Aggressiveness typified the parent's relationship with his child in both types of rejection; he was expressing his hostility toward the child.

In these studies the investigators sought to establish a link between the atmosphere in the home and the child's behavior in nursery school and later in grade school. Children were observed both in preschool and school settings, and were rated on a variety of child behaviors. In emotional traits, the actively rejected preschool children were characterized by high emotionality and low emotional control (Baldwin, 1949). They showed a certain amount of resistance to adults, but were more active physically than accepted children. Indulged children were high in both friendliness and quarrelsomeness with other children. At school age, indulged children seemed shyer and less sociable than during preschool years, whereas rejected children showed a marked increase in quarrelsomeness and a great deal of sibling hostility. Although much of the difference between the two types had disappeared by the time all of them had reached school age, the rejected children still showed themselves to be more energetic.

Now for the Pattern Study. One of its scales used for rating extensive interviews with mothers was labeled "Mother's Rejection of the Child." From the mother's report, the investigators endeavored also to evaluate the father on his degree of acceptance or rejection of the child. Acceptance was defined as the giving of love without reservation, whereas rejection meant a withholding of love. Of the interviews assessed in this area, 220 mothers showed no rejection of the child and 101 were thought to indicate some rejection. The majority of these 101 instances, however, were closer to the acceptance end of the scale than the rejection end. As to the fathers only 47 were judged to evince some rejection.

Acceptance or rejection was seen to influence several child behaviors. First of all, children experiencing some rejection tended to show more dependent behavior than accepted youngsters. Acceptance, it would seem, promotes the wholesome development of independent behavior and of independence. The rejected child, far less secure in his relationship with his parents, needs their constant reassurance of willingness to nurture him. Thus, a continuing need for dependency in a child might very well reflect a lack of dependability on the part of his parents. Second, rejected children were slightly retarded in the development of conscience. Third, how much or how little a child adopted his parents' standards and values depended in part on the warmth and acceptance they accorded him.

Because indulgence and overprotection would seem to contain elements of both acceptance and rejection, they are pertinent to this discussion. Certainly these parental behaviors cannot be thought of as representing the extreme of acceptance. Yet their influence on the child suggests otherwise. In a classic study of maternal over-protection, in which he dwelt on 20 cases of "pure" overprotection of 19 boys and one girl, Levy (1943) pointed to four aspects of excessive maternal care in their mothers. One was *excessive contact;* "the mother is always there." Another was *infantilization;* "she still treats him like a baby." A third was *preventing independent behavior;* "she won't let him grow up" or "she won't take any risks." The fourth was *lack or excess of maternal control;* the mother may either dominate or be dominated by the child.

A number of factors in the personalities and backgrounds of the parents of these overprotected children seemed related to the over-protection. For some of the mothers there was a prolongd period of anticipation of childbearing. In other cases there were spontaneous abortions, stillbirths, and long periods of sterility. Still others experienced marital dissatisfaction and sexual incompatibility. Apparently many mothers sought to compensate for an unhappy marital relationship by establishing an intimate bond with their sons.

Incompatibility seemed to extend to social activities. The parents enjoyed little social life in common. Many of the mothers withdrew from nearly all outside social contact. Throughout the backgrounds of these overprotecting mothers ran a common thread of a lack of maternal love. The term used by Levy to describe the need in an individual which stemmed from lack of parental love involving affection, security, sympathy, and recognition was *"affect hunger."* It was as though these women attempted to satisfy their strong need for affection by maneuvering the child into an intimate affectional relationship in which he was somewhat isolated from other contacts. Yet these overprotecting mothers were, in general, responsible, stable, aggressive women who possessed strong maternal tendencies. Frequently their ambitions for education or for a career had been thwarted. The fathers of the children were seen as good providers, stable, but submissive, playing little or no authoritative role in relation to the child. They were ineffectual in counteracting the overprotective influence of the mother.

What about the children? How did they fare from overprotection? Those who, due to lack of maternal control, dominated their mothers were ill adapted to classroom discipline and reacted poorly to the authority of the teacher. However, the classroom behavior of over-protected children generally contrasted markedly with behavior at home. In achievement, they demonstrated relatively high success in language and showed special interest in reading, although they often fared poorly in arithmetic. Moreover, these children were restricted in contacts with agemates. Evidently because of the great impact of the overprotective relationship on their social life, they experienced difficulty in making friends or in having friendly relationships with peers.

Some overprotected children behaved rebelliously, aggressively, de-fiantly, and tyrannically toward mothers who were submissive toward them. They were disobedient, impudent, excessively demanding, and prone to temper tantrums. They were selfish and undisciplined. Others who were dominated by their mothers were, on the other hand, submissive and dependent.

Later, however, the behavior of both groups of overprotected chil-dren was better on the whole than might have been expected from their deviant early relationship with their mother. Attributable as this may be in part to the countering effect of peers and school, it may also indicate that overprotection is far less deleterious than rejection in the long run. At least the child develops a sense of self-worth when overprotected.

Erikson (1950) spoke of the necessity for the child to develop a sense of basic trust in his relationship with his parents; this is a require-ment for development of a healthy personality. From this basic trust in parents stems a basic trust in the world, in the universe, in other people, and, most of all, in oneself. With this comes a sense of secur-ity, of self-acceptance, and it all goes back to early acceptance by parents. Much of the behavior of rejected children probably can be charged to a lack of a secure feeling and a lack of self-acceptance. Such children are hostile and aggressive, striking out at an unfriendly world. Seeking the affection and acceptance they need, they are often unsuccessful in their quest; a rejected child fails to understand others because he has never been understood himself.

Parental rejection, then, may have pervasive, long-range, harmful implications for the child's personality. Lack of parental acceptance seemed to constitute an important factor in the poor adjustment of certain first-grade children (Medinnus, 1961), and Bandura and Wal-ters (1959) maintained that the failure to satisfy the child's needs for dependency in early years contributed significantly to the development of aggressive behavior in adolescence.

Autonomy vs. Control. The other important aspect of the psychological atmosphere in the home is the extent to which parents restrict the child's behavior or give him autonomy and freedom. Returning to Symonds's (1939) early study, these were some of the characteristics that described the behavior of dominant parents. They insisted on complete obedience. They supervised the child closely in the youngster's choice of activities. They provided too much supervision. They trained the child carefully. They expressed concern over trifles and criticized the child. Submissive parents, on the other hand, let the child have his own way. They could not control the child. They employed lax, inconsistent discipline and allowed the child to upset the home routine.

Although fathers satisfied many of their personality needs outside of the family, mothers were especially likely to fulfill their needs for dominance or submission by controlling or letting themselves be controlled by their children, Symonds noted. This finding supports the widespread notion that mothers exert a greater influence on the child than the father. The primary obligation of the mother's role is rearing the children, whereas occupational success and economic support of the family are important aspects of the father's role. Small wonder, therefore, that the mother may be more emotionally involved than the father in the end result of the child-rearing techniques used. Failure may cast a dark shadow over the mother's feelings of competence and adequacy. The father, however, can compensate for any deficiency as a parent with success in his job and the recognition it achieves. Whereas several recent investigations (Becker et al., 1959; Peterson et al., 1959) suggested that the father's attitudes and behaviors were as intimately connected as those of the mother to the development of problem behavior in the child, this finding might reflect an increased paternal participation and involvement in child rearing. It further signifies that the father's role is an important one in contemporary urban, somewhat isolated psychologically, small-sized, child-oriented families.

Symonds found differentiation in a number of behaviors between children of dominating parents and those of submissive parents. The former were better socialized as a rule; their behavior was more acceptable, more conforming to the group. They seemed to be more interested in school work. Yet they tended to be sensitive, shy, self-conscious, seclusive, retiring, and submissive as compared with children who were given more freedom by their parents. The children of submissive parents inclined toward disobedience, irresponsibility, lack of interest in school, stubbornness, and defiance of authority. They were able, however, to express themselves effectively.

As to personality, the dominated children were more likely to be courteous, loyal, honest, polite, and dependable albeit submissive and docile. The children of submissive parents were aggressive, disrespectful, and antagonistic, although independent and self-confident.

In the Fels projects the scales fitting the syndrome "Democracy in the Home" included justification of policy, democracy of policy, noncoerciveness of suggestion, readiness of explanation, direction of criticism (approval), clarity of policy, understanding of the child, and nonrestrictiveness of regulation. Figure 10-3 contains the democracy of policy scale. From the scale's descriptive phrases it is apparent that the principal criterion of democracy is the practice of consulting the child in family decisions, giving him a voice in the policy of the home. In the autocratic or dictatorial home all decisions are made by the parents, with the child accorded little participation or choice.

Rejection often shows itself in an autocratic home, but this is not invariably the case. Some parents adopt an autocratic method because they feel this is the most desirable manner of training and rearing children. Undoubtedly the parent's personality and his conception of child nature both influence the choice of a nondemocratic approach. This choice may be a matter of expediency or of policy. Similarly, a democratic approach to child rearing may reflect an intellectual policy of the parent, who may be trying to follow the latest "expert" advice, or it may flow from a warm, accepting, understanding relation between parent and child. Thus, there is the scientific, intellectual democratic home and the warm democratic home. To the Fels researchers the latter type was the ideal home for the development of a healthy personality in the child.

The Fels group concluded that democratic parents were more likely to be better educated and more intelligent than autocratic ones. However, education was not the only element involved in producing democracy. Objectivity and emotional maturity in the parent were also involved. The parent unable to separate himself psychologically from his child could not, by the very nature of the relationship, be truly democratic.

Many child characteristics were found in the Fels studies to be linked to the presence of democracy in the home. First, as compared with other types of home atmosphere, the democratic seemed most conducive to intellectual growth. The children from such homes showed increases in IQ over a period of time (Baldwin, Kalhorn, & Breese, 1945). A democratic environment not only permitted greater

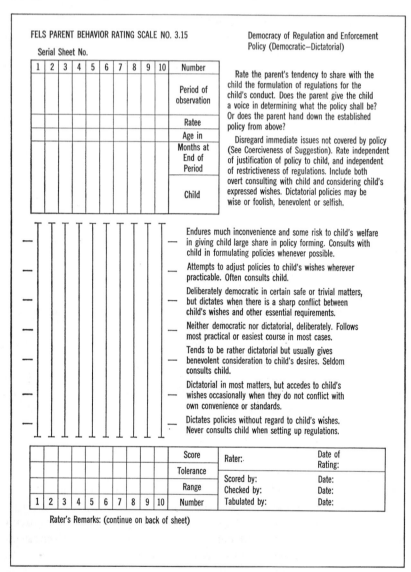

FIGURE 10-3

freedom but also often encouraged exploration and experimentation. Restriction was at a minimum.

On such intellectual variables as planfulness, curiosity, and originality the democratically raised children rated high. At the nursery school these youngsters were active, aggressive, fearless, likely to be leaders, somewhat cruel, nonconformist, and disobedient (Baldwin, 1948). Although strict control in the home tended to reduce disobedience, quarrelsomeness, and negativism, it also decreased fearlessness, planfulness, tenacity, and aggressiveness. Taken together, these qualities seemed to describe a well-behaved child but one subject to constricted personality.

Perhaps autonomy is not too different from acceptance in influencing child behavior. Both recognize the individuality of the child. Democracy, of course, the environmental condition for autonomy, takes special note of children's need for activity and exploration.

It is apparent from both the Fels data and the Symonds findings that a certain type of home atmosphere may produce both "good" and "bad"—that is, desirable and undesirable—behavior in the child. Should child psychology ever reach the point at which it could accurately predict the exact behaviors to be expected from any single type of home environment, the kind of child produced would still depend on personal preference and individual value judgment. Some parents prefer a well-behaved child at the price of originality and curiosity. Others would be willing to have a child who is somewhat rebellious and nonconformist but who shows inquisitiveness and inventiveness. Child psychology cannot make these decisions. Individuals must make them on the basis of the kind of society they want.

Finally, there is the question of permissiveness. Perhaps no other word is so misunderstood, so badly abused, and so maligned. Thus, it become difficult to formulate a clear definition of the term. Perhaps permissiveness might be considered as deriving from permit; if so, it implies that permissive parents allow their children to engage in a certain range of behaviors and make certain decisions appropriate to their capabilities. Permissiveness should not be understood to mean that a parent allows a child to do anything the child pleases. This is not permissiveness but license, a laissez-faire approach to child rearing.

Once this distinction has been made, the situation becomes more manageable. Complete abdication of parental control and responsibility suggests indifference, neglect, and rejection of the parent role. This is not permissiveness. In fact, a study comparing permissive and traditional households, all occupying small apartments, found that a permissive policy required a greater expenditure of energy by the parent (Blood, 1953). The permissive parents' livingrooms were more cluttered and their lives generally were more disrupted by the children's behavior. Besides, the permissive parents reported that their children's behavior was difficult to control when attempts were made to impose some restrictions. The children from restrictive homes, in contrast, accepted strict controls without question; they had no expectations of free play. Permissiveness would thus seem to be a deliberate policy, not shirking of parental responsibility.

The Pattern Study considered permissiveness versus strictness and used the following scales to describe maternal child-rearing practices in this area:

1. High restrictions on play in the house and with furniture.
2. High demands for good table manners.
3. High restriction on making noise.
4. High demands for being neat and orderly.
5. Severe toilet training.
6. High standards for strict obedience.
7. Strong emphasis on doing well in school.
8. Strict and rejective response to dependency.
9. High use of physical punishment.
10. Severe punishment for aggression toward parents.
11. Low permissiveness for aggression toward parents.
12. Low permissiveness for aggression among siblings.
13. Low permissiveness for aggression to other children.
14. Low permissiveness for nudity or immodesty.
15. Low permissiveness for masturbation.
16. Low permissiveness for sex play with other children.

(Sears, Maccoby, & Levin, 1957, p. 472)

The moderate interrelation of these scales suggests a consistency in a mother's behavior with respect to strictness or permissiveness. The authors of the Pattern Study spoke of a particular trait underlying a mother's use of permissive practices. One mother seemed to be fairly consistent in her tolerance of her child's *child* behavior—that is, his aggressiveness, his noisiness, his sex impulses—whereas another tended through punitive means to try to put an end to such behavior.

In an interesting study Watson (1957) compared the behavior of children from strict and permissive homes. Using a multiple-choice questionnaire entitled "How I Am Bringing Up My Child," he obtained parental reactions to 35 common situations of child behavior, such as toilet training, quarreling, and choice of television programs. Parents had a choice of three responses indicating permissiveness, strictness, or a middle-of-the-road approach to the situation. Then the children, divided into groups of those whose parents rated as strict and those whose parents seemed permissive, were exposed to a variety of psychological tests. Where possible, teacher ratings of behavior were acquired. Although there were no significant differences found between the two groups of children in some areas, youngsters from permissive homes showed greater independence, more cooperativeness, greater creativity, and more friendliness. Those from strict homes evinced greater hostility.

To sum up, any particular type of home atmosphere apparently gives rise to both desirable and undesirable child characteristics. Fearless, curious, and planful as may be the children from homes in which a psychological climate of democracy and autonomy prevails, they are also inclined toward cruelty, rebellion, and nonconformity. On the other hand, the well-behaved child of a home characterized by strict control may show signs of a constricted personality.

THREE FACTORS IN PARENT-CHILD RELATIONSHIPS

For an understanding of the psychology of parent-child relationships, three topics are significant. These are the child's perception of his parents, the matter of identification, and the question of discipline. We conclude this chapter with a consideration of each of these subjects.

Perception of Parents

How the child perceives the various aspects of his home is crucial to his behavior and adjustment. Notwithstanding what truth may lie in this assertion, it presents numerous problems for research in parent-child relations. First of all, the young child is not a very reliable informant, not through any desire to deceive, but through inability to express himself adequately in his early years. Besides, by its very nature the young child's thought forms conceptions on a very concrete basis, with little appreciation of some of the more subtle and abstract notions involved.

For example, in line with Piaget's notion (1932) that the young child felt that the harsher the punishment the "better" and more efficacious it was, one study (Radke, 1946) found that 74 per cent of preschool children interviewed mentioned spanking as the type of punishment they received, although parents said they used it rarely. In addition, 83 per cent said that spanking was the best punishment when they were naughty. Quite clearly the young child's response to the questions was not related to the actual quality or quantity of the punishment he received, but to his conception of what the most appropriate punishment was. Yet although the young child is not a very reliable informant, there is some evidence for relating a child's perception of his parents' behavior to ratings of the behavior itself by professional interviewers (Meyers, 1935; Bronson, Kalten, & Livson, 1959).

Many techniques have been employed to study children's perceptions of their parents. Directly, children have been interviewed about their parents. Indirectly, they have been asked general questions about parents, such as "What do parents do that boys and girls don't like?" Indirect methods also include drawings to obtain an idea of parental preference and pictures portraying a variety of child situations. The child may be asked, for example, who is absent, mother or father.

One consistent finding of such research is that children of most ages choose the mother as the preferred parent (Gardner, 1947; Harris & Tseng, 1957). Generally the mother is seen in a more favorable light than the father. She is considered friendlier, less strict, less punitive, less threatening, and more nurturing (Kagan, 1956; Kagan, Hosken, & Watson, 1961). The father and his role, in contrast, is regarded as more powerful, more interfering, more competent, and as the major source of punishment (Emmerich, 1959, 1961; Kagan & Lemkin, 1960). In addition, children usually ascribe "high power" to the adult role and "low power" to their own (Emmerich, 1961).

Although children ordinarily perceive their parents in positive terms, they are willing to criticize and voice dissatisfactions with them. Preschool children in the Radke (1946) study frequently mentioned punishment in this connection. The fifth and sixth graders studied by Gardner (1947) enumerated the following dissatisfactions with their fathers: scolding, general irritability, poor adjustment with the mother, and absence from home. These children's preference for their mother was based on her greater understanding, better nature, and less domineering behavior.

As children age a trend becomes discernible of preference for the parent of the same sex. Moreover, children incline to perceive themselves as more similar to the parent of the same sex (Gray, 1959). This will become more evident in the consideration presently of identification.

An interesting sex difference manifests itself in the perception of parents. As a rule, boys see their parents as stricter than do girls (Hawkes, Burchinal, & Gardner, 1957). Boys also seem to be more critical of their parents, especially of the father, and in general see them through their disciplinary function (Meltzer, 1943), with the father as a strong authority figure. Girls more than boys tend to perceive themselves as accepted by their parents (Ausubel, Balthazar, Rosenthal, Blackmore, Schpoont, & Welkowitz, 1954).

Although the data on differential treatment of boys and girls are inconclusive, the fact that boys more than girls believe there is disciplinary friction may account in part for the greater number of behavioral and disciplinary problems among sons than daughters. Possibly because of their higher level of activity and greater aggressiveness boys become more involved in situations requiring discipline both at home and at school. This view supports the *biosocial* explanation of human behavior that biological differences at birth accentuated by differential environmental, or social, treatment produces substantial variation among the individuals of a society.

As to the connection between perception of parents and child behavior, Serot and Teevan (1961) observed that well-adjusted fourth-grade children were more likely to perceive their relationship with their parents as happy and "ideal" than were poorly adjusted children. Gray (1959) discovered that elementary-school boys who perceived themselves as highly similar to the parent of their own sex were better adjusted than those who saw themselves less like father. Among girls the more they considered themselves similar to their mothers the better adjusted they were. To some extent, Gray further noted, older children who saw themselves as more distant from their parents were more socially acceptable to their peers than those who perceived themselves as closer to parents. As children approach adolescence independence from parents evidently becomes a highly prized characteristic among peers.

Thus far, most of the studies cited have dealt with young children. In addition, investigations among college students indicate that some aspects of their personalities relate to their perceptions of their parents. One of these (Mussen & Kagan, 1958) found that male students who manifested conformist behavior during an experiment were more likely than others to perceive their parents as harsh, restrictive, punitive, and rejecting. Thus, it is possible that conforming behavior as an adult might be traceable to parental demands for conformity in childhood. From the perceptions of college girls relative to the child-rearing attitudes of their mothers, Heilbrun and McKinley (1962) concluded that girls who disclosed some tendencies toward pathological personality were more likely than normal girls to see these attitudes as authoritarian, controlling, hostile, and rejecting. However, this finding must be regarded with caution. Conceivably the mere existence of some pathological tendency in personality will cause an individual to view many of his interpersonal relations as deviant in one way or another.

All told, the research is sparse in linking children's perceptions of parents with various child personality and behavior traits. Nevertheless, any information in this area serves a useful purpose when seeking to find relationships between particular parental and child characteristics.

Identification

Even though the concept of identification has been used in many ways with a host of meanings (see Sanford, 1955), let us define it as *the process by which an individual incorporates certain aspects of someone else's behavior, attitudes, and characteristics.* The terms copying, modeling, and imitating are sometimes used synonymously with identification. However, these connote a conscious process whereas identification may occur essentially at the unconscious level. Furthermore, these terms frequently are restricted to level of behavior whereas identification may encompass even more. The discussion of identification in the young child primarily concerns his identification with sex role, that is, the process whereby he develops characteristics similar to those of the parent of the same sex. However, numerous other behavioral traits seem to emerge from this process. Aggressive behavior, behavior and attitudes toward others, leisure-time pursuits, and a host of other characteristics may sprout from the child's identification with another person—usually, in early years, the parent.

Why the need for such a notion as identification? Are not the principles of learning sufficient to explain the reason for the child developing characteristics similar to those of the parent of the same sex (see Chapter 4)? Parental approval should be reward enough for behaviors valued by the parent and thus encourage their repetition. However, child behavior seems to go beyond what would be predictable from learning theory. A tremendous amount of learning occurs without any direct teaching as such. That children observe and are aware of their parents' behavior became evident to the father of a four-year-old when, after yelling at her, the child replied, "Don't yell at me. I'm not mommy."

The endless hours spent by a little girl playing house suggest some higher level of *patterning* of one's behavior after the behavior of someone else. But what is the motive for such behavior? One notion contends that the young child perceives himself as weak and inadequate in a superior world and in order to gain some sense of competence and ability to cope with the overwhelming environment identifies with the parent. Thus, the child gets some measure of security. Freud held, as we saw in the last chapter, that identification with the parent of the like sex occurred at the time of the resolution of the Oedipal conflict; the boy, for example, made such an identification with his father in order to avoid his punishment for incestuous desires toward the mother. Kagan (1958) postulated two major motivations for identification: love and mastery. Irrespective of theory, identification clearly serves an important function in the child's life. Gratification derives from behavior that emulates a significant adult's behavior; and in practicing the behavior of an adult, as in doll play, a child learns something of his future adult role and acquires some understanding of it.

At what age does identification begin? No specific age seems identifiable, although it would appear that it could not occur until the child was able to put himself in the place of someone else, as in taking the role of the parent in play, to pretend, to "assume the role of another." Certainly by ages two to three there is evidence for the beginning of such behavior in the child.

Turning to the literature on sex-role identification, Lynn (1961) has hypothesized that marked differences exist between boys and girls in several aspects of the identification process. As he saw it, both sexes in the very early years identify with the mother. Later, however, the boy has to shift his identification to the father and to a masculine role. No such shift is required of the girl. Several factors in the boy's environment facilitate the switch, however. There are numerous pressures for the boy to behave like a "little man." Moreover, in American society, at least, the male role is more desirable for many reasons. Males enjoy positions of dominance and authority. And in so material-minded a society the occupation of the father is the major source of prestige for the family.

For the girl, of course, although she continues in her identification with her mother, she discovers that the female role is devalued by society. She thus experiences some difficulty in identifying with the role appropriate to her sex. Moreover, her mother may feel some ambivalence about the female role because of society's downgrading of it. And there is less pressure on her to be girl-like in all behaviors than there is for boys to be manly. No punishment attaches to her wearing certain items of male apparel. Nor does tomboyishness in girls incur the stigma of sissified behavior in boys. Girls may play with boys without censure, but boys are ridiculed for playing with girls.

For these reasons, Lynn believed that with increasing age girls became less firmly tied to the female role, whereas boys who successfully make the transition from identifying with their mother to identifying with their father become more fully associated with the male role.

Because of the importance in Western culture of an appropriate sex identification, Lynn equated the failure to achieve this with psychological disturbance.

Some research evidence indicates that parents play a role in the identification process and that there are types of parent-child relationships which encourage an appropriate sex identification. Sears (1953) noted that sons of fathers who were warm, permissive, and easygoing tended to behave in a manner appropriate to their sex. In the doll-play situation, boys who chose the maternal role came from homes in which the mother, but not the father, was high in warmth. In an earlier study, Sears (1951) observed that boys from homes lacking a father showed less fantasied aggression than boys whose fathers were living with them. Although her finding implied that the father served as the son's model for aggression, it might also indicate that a boy whose father was absent experienced fewer frustrations.

Social class also influences sex identification. Rabban (1950) reported that lower-class children identified themselves with interests appropriate to their sex sooner than middle-class children. Perhaps there are stronger pressures brought at an earlier age in lower-class homes for behavior proper to the sex. Or it may be that a clearer distinction is made between the male and female roles in the lower class. This distinction, however, has been seen to blur on personality tests related to educational level. Possibly there may be less tolerance of any deviation from a stereotyped norm among lower-class parents. Whatever the case, there is likely to be more difficulty of a psychological nature for the lower-class child who, for one reason or another, cannot make a suitable sex-role identification.

As to other behaviors springing from a child's identification with his parent, the Pattern Study examined the subject as it bore upon the development of inner control or conscience. The greater the child's dependency on the mother, the study postulated, the greater would be the extent of identification. Indeed the kind of discipline chosen by the mother would stem from this mother-child dependency relation and would affect the development of conscience. The threat of a withdrawal of love would prove more effective in this regard than such techniques as physical punishment or deprivation of privileges. As has been seen, some support can be found for the notion that warmth between mother and child and maternal acceptance of the youngster both influence the development of conscience. Bandura and Huston (1961) provided further substantiation for it by discovering that a nurturing relation between a child and an adult encouraged the child's imitation of the adult's behavior.

Girls, as we know, experience a stronger and longer-lasting identification with the mother, although both boys and girls spend more time with her than with the father. Consequently, incorporation of the mother's demands and values plays the largest part in the child's early development of conscience. It would follow from these considerations that conscience develops more strongly in girls than in boys. The Pattern Study found this to be so. Identification led to the development of conscience.

Discipline

Quite likely no topic holds more interest and concern for parents than discipline. Yet relatively little research has been undertaken in this lively area. Thus, ideas and theories about discipline abound but scientific knowledge to back them up is conspicuously scarce. Why research on the subject is scant is easy to understand. The obstacles to experimental investigation are virtually insurmountable. One could hardly ask a group of mothers to administer a certain type of discipline at fixed intervals while another group employed a different kind of discipline or none at all. And even if this could be done, measurement of the effects of discipline (the independent variable) on the child's behavior and attitudes (the dependent variables) would be full of booby traps.

In current thinking, discipline is often equated with guidance. However, discipline might be more appropriately described as the methods used by parents to ensure their child's compliance with that guidance. The socialization process of getting the child to conform to what society expects of him creates conflicts between these social demands and the child's wishes and desires. Thus, discipline becomes an inevitable aspect of the parent-child relationship. That discipline may take a vast number of forms and vary widely in the frequency of its use from parent to parent is also true.

What are the functions of discipline? Most obviously, parents use disciplinary methods to obtain conformity to their demands. Discipline also provides the child with cues to behavior. For maximum effectiveness these cues should apprise the child of what constitutes approved or acceptable behavior. However, when it takes the form of punishment, discipline supplies only the cues to unacceptable behavior. This leads to a distinction between the short-term and long-range goals of discipline. Whereas the former is conformity to parental demands, the latter is the development of self-control or inner discipline. Some types of discipline are more conducive to accomplishment of the short-term objectives; others are better suited to achieving the long-range goals.

Which disciplinary techniques receive the more frequent use? Table 10-2 contains a ranking of the ten used most often at each of three age levels. The study from which the table is drawn (Clifford, 1959, p. 69) was based on records kept by mothers over a three-week period. With the increasing age of the child, the table implies, the parent comes to rely more on verbal techniques and less on physical methods. The Pattern Study divided training techniques into positive sanctions—praise and tangible reward—and negative sanctions—physical punishment, deprivation of privileges, withdrawal of love, and isolation. Generally those mothers who were above average in the group in the use of positive sanctions were also above average in ratings on warmth and affection shown to children, on satisfaction with their roles of wife and mother, and on esteem felt for their husbands. This would suggest that the use of praise and rewards reflected a mother's satisfactory adjustment to her life situation. Perhaps, then, there may be some relation between a woman's adjustment to the mother role and the reasonableness of her behavior in it.

Why is discipline used and when is it most frequent throughout the day? Clearly the most important single reason for discipline is disobedience—the child's noncompliance with parental demands. The

TABLE 10-2   The First Ten Methods of Control by Rank and Age of the Child

3-Year-Old Group		6-Year-Old Group		9-Year-Old Group	
Method	Rank	Method	Rank	Method	Rank
Reason	1	Reason	1	Reason	1
Scold	2	Scold	2	Scold	2
Coax	3	Coax	3	Take away privilege	3
Spank	4	Threaten	4	Coax	4
Divert	5	Ignore	5	Self-esteem	5.5
Threaten	6	Isolate	6	Threaten	5.5
Ignore	7	Spank	7	Ignore	7
Remove child forcibly	8	Divert	8	Remove difficulty	8
Isolate	9	Take away privilege	9		
Remove difficulty	10	Humor	10.5	Humor	10
		Order	10.5	Isolate	10
				Social disapproval	10

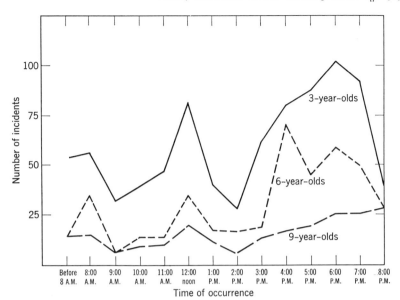

FIGURE 10-4   The frequency of discipline by the hour of occurrence and age (Clifford, 1959, p. 51).

Clifford study identified the following 11 categories as areas requiring discipline: *sibling relationships*—that is, quarreling, aggression, interference; *eating*—refusal to eat, making a mess, leaving the table during the meal; *sleep*—refusal to go to bed, noise in bed; *dressing*—refusal to get dressed, soiling clothing, changing clothes; *activities*—conflict over television, Sunday School; *school*—preparing to go to school, refusal to go to school; *health*—medication, general health protection; *inappropriate behavior*—irritability, boisterousness, destructiveness, forbidden behavior; *adult interaction*—refusing an adult request, interference with adult activity, persistent demand of adult attention; *home* —neatness of home, refusal to put things away; *social*—inappropriate social behavior, insistence on own rights, interference with activities of others.

As to frequency of discipline, Figure 10-4 represents the periods throughout the day at which discipline is most often required for each of three age levels. As the child grows older there is an apparent decrease in the frequency of situations requiring parental discipline. Perhaps this reflects a development of inner control with age; he is more aware of what is expected of him and is more able developmentally to conform to these expectations. Besides, as the child grows older, more of his time is spent interacting with others outside the home. The sheer quantity of his interaction with parents falls off. Now sanctions for inappropriate behavior spring increasingly from peers and from adults other than parents.

No discussion of discipline can ignore the effects of discipline on the child. Although discipline may achieve a behavioral goal, its accomplishment may be nullified by the emotional and attitudinal side effects it produces in the child. Several studies (Sperry & Hollenberg, 1951; Sears, 1950; Bandura & Walters, 1959) have shown a positive correlation between aggressive behavior in children and severity of discipline in the home. There is little doubt that harsh, arbitrary, and inconsistent discipline arouses resentment, hostility, and anxiety in the child. Anger and crying were reported by mothers as responses to discipline (Clifford, 1959); and 63 per cent of the preschool children interviewed in the Radke (1946) study said they were sad, unhappy, and pained by punishment, whereas only 14 per cent reported feelings of penitence or resolutions for better behavior.

From strong discipline a child builds up a store of hostility which he directs toward others. This is borne out by a study conducted by Hoffman (1960). Mothers were rated according to how they coerced the child to change his entire current pattern of behavior immediately. A significant positive relation was found between a mother's use of what Hoffman called "unqualified power assertion" and the child's hostility toward others, his power assertiveness, and his resistance to the attempts of others to influence him. Thus, the conforming, docile child at home may be a tiger on the outside.

Strict discipline by parents often leads to prejudiced, antidemocratic attitudes in the child (Harris, Gough, & Martin, 1950; Lyle & Levitt, 1955). This is another example of the displacement of aggression. Severe and punitive parental treatment awakens hostile and aggressive impulses in the child. Since these impulses cannot be directed toward the parent, they are leveled against others who are made into scapegoats and innocent victims.

The kind of discipline recalled by young adults as having been used by their parents is determined by their willingness to criticize their parents and by the favorableness of their attitudes toward them. College students who remembered their early discipline as primarily positive in nature were less critical of their parents than were those who recalled parental discipline as basically negative (Nakamura, 1959). Further, Itkin (1955) found positive correlations between the attitudes of college women toward their parents and their attitudes toward the discipline their parents had exercised. Both findings, although suffering from the weakness inherent in retrospective reports, suggest that the type of discipline employed is intimately related to a young adult's recollection of the earlier parent-child relationship as pleasant or unpleasant. These findings may also imply that rigorous, negative discipline leaves lasting emotional reactions in the child.

Let us round out this review with some general comments about discipline and child management. These are not oracular preachments to govern one's handling of children, but broad considerations which might profit a parent or a teacher to ponder.

Behavior is motivated. There is a reason, a cause for every behavior. Usually these causes are not apparent at the conscious level: the child does not know why he does the things he does. To pinch his arm and ask, "Why did you do it?" is preposterous. If he knew why, he probably would not have had to act as he did in the first place. Yet the adult must try to ascertain and understand the cause. What is the child trying to achieve? Is he trying to gain acceptance? Attention? Recognition? Affection? Meanness is not a cause but an interpretation.

Discipline is concerned too frequently with actions. Feelings are disregarded. The action or behavior may be stopped, but what happens to the feelings? These must be dealt with, too. The child needs the opportunity to express them. He will feel better if he can air his feelings and adults may learn something in the process. Since restrictions are frustrating, the child needs to give vent to his feelings. The young child usually does so; the older child learns not to, but this does him no good.

Because restrictions are frustrating, they should be kept to a minimum. The fewer there are the better. The simpler they are the better. And they should always be geared to the child's level of understanding.

Then, too, the adult might examine his own thoughts. What are his motives? Are his demands reasonable? Was the child's behavior truly not permissible, or was the adult's level of tolerance unusually low? Too great a price may be charged for conformity.

Finally, the parent-child relationship is unique; all authority, all the power, all the weight is invested in only one individual, the parent. The child must obey. For a parent to take advantage of such a relationship reflects little basic human understanding. Physical punishment is violence. It breeds a response detrimental to the individual and the society of which he is a part. Kindness, respect, and sensitivity, on the other hand, are qualities worth cultivating in a growing human being, and these may well develop out of the intimate relationship between parent and child. They flourish in a climate of mutual trust, and for mutual trust to be truly mutual, it takes the full cooperation of both parties.

SUMMARY

Parenthood involves a host of functions and duties, and imposes a variety of demands on those individuals who fill its role. Some parents are abler than others to meet these demands. Quite naturally these experience greater satisfaction in the parent role.

Many factors influence a parent's behavior: his childhood experiences and the behavior and attitudes of his own parents. Personality structure as well as current child-rearing fads also influence an individual's demeanor as a parent.

Three principal parent variables were explored, with the research relevant to the relation of each of these—parent personality, parent attitudes, and parent behavior—to the child's personality and adjustment presented.

Two main dimensions emerged from factor analytic studies of parent attitude scores and parent behavior ratings. One of them, acceptance versus rejection, assessed the parent's attitude toward the child. The other, autonomy versus control, related to parental attitudes toward child rearing.

In view of the present state of knowledge, it would seem that assessment of the broad psychological atmospheres in the home is more revealing of effects on the child than is information on specific child-rearing practices. However, the ultimate goal of parent-child research is the identification of specific aspects of the parents, the family, and the home which exert a significant psychological impact on the child.

The chapter also surveyed three factors of importance to understanding parent-child relationships: children's perceptions of their parents, identification, and discipline. The relationship between parent and child holds much in common with any relationship between two people. Mutual trust, mutual understanding, and mutual acceptance are imperative if the relationship is to be satisfying and rewarding to both.

REFERENCES

Adorno, T. W., Frenkel-Brunswik, Else, Levinson, D. J., & Sanford, R. N. *The authoritarian personality.* New York: Harper, 1950.

Ausubel, D. *Theory and problems of child development.* New York: Grune & Stratton, 1958.

Ausubel, D., Balthazar, E. E., Rosenthal, Irene, Blackmore, L. S., Schpoont, S. H., & Welkowitz, Joan. Perceived parent attitudes as determinants of children's ego structure. *Child Develpm.,* 1954, **25,** 173–183.

Baldwin, A. L. Socialization and the parent-child relationship. *Child Develpm.,* 1948, **19,** 127–136.

Baldwin, A. L. The effect of home environment on nursery school behavior. *Child Develpm.,* 1949, **20,** 49–61.

Baldwin, A. L., Kalhorn, Joan, & Breese, Fay H. Patterns of parent behavior. *Psychol. Monogr.,* 1945, **58,** No. 3.

Baldwin, A. L., Kalhorn, Joan, & Breese, Fay H. The appraisal of parent behavior. *Psychol. Monogr.,* 1949, **63,** No. 4 (Whole No. 299).

Bandura, A., & Huston, Aletha C. Identification as a process of incidental learning. *J. abnorm. soc. Psychol.,* 1961, **63,** 311–318.

Bandura, A., & Walters, R. *Adolescent aggression.* New York: Ronald, 1959.

Becker, W. C., Peterson, D. R., Hellmer, L. A., Shoemaker, D. J., & Quay, H. C. Factors in parental behavior and personality as related to problem behavior in children. *J. consult. Psychol.,* 1959, **23,** 107–118.

Behrens, Marjorie L. Child rearing and the character structure of the mother. *Child Develpm.,* 1954, **25,** 225–238.

Bell, R. Q. Retrospective attitude studies of parent-child relations. *Child Develpm.,* 1958, **29,** 323–338.

Block, J. Personality factors associated with fathers' attitudes toward child-rearing. *Child Develpm.,* 1955, **26,** 41–48.

Blood, R. Consequences of permissiveness for parents of young children. *Marriage fam. Liv.,* 1953, **15,** 209–212.

Bronson, Wanda C., Kalten, Edith S., & Livson, N. Patterns of authority and affection in two generations. *J. abnorm. soc. Psychol.,* 1959, **58,** 143–152.

Burchinal, L. G. Parents' attitudes and adjustment of children. *J. genet. Psychol.,* 1958, **92,** 69–79. (a)

Burchinal, L. G. Mothers' and fathers' differences in parental acceptance of children for controlled comparisons based on parental and family characteristics. *J. genet. Psychol.,* 1958, **92,** 103–110. (b)

Burchinal, L. G., Hawkes, G. R., & Gardner, B. The relationship between parental acceptance and adjustment of children. *Child Develpm.,* 1957, **28,** 65–77.

Champney, H. The measurement of parent behavior. *Child Develpm.,* 1941, **12,** 131–166. (a)

Champney, H. The variables of parent behavior. *J. abnorm. soc. Psychol.,* 1941, **36,** 525–542. (b)

Clifford, E. Discipline in the home: A controlled observational study of parental practices. *J. genet. Psychol.,* 1959, **95,** 45–82.

Coleman, R. W., Kris, E., & Provence, S. The study of variations of early parental attitudes. *Psychoanal. Stud. Child,* 1953, **8,** 20–47.

Emmerich, W. Young children's discrimination of parent and child roles. *Child Develpm.,* 1959, **30,** 403–419.

Emmerich, W. Family role concepts of children ages six to ten. *Child Develpm.,* 1961, **32,** 609–624.

Erikson, E. H. *Childhood and society.* New York: Norton, 1950.

Gardner, L. Pearl. An analysis of children's attitudes toward fathers. *J. genet. Psychol.*, 1947, **70**, 3–28.

Gray, Susan W. Perceived similarity to parents and adjustment. *Child Develpm.*, 1959, **30**, 91–107.

Hanvik, L. J., & Byrum, Mildred. MMPI profiles of parents of child psychiatric patients. *J. clin. Psychol.*, 1959, **15**, 427–431.

Harris, D. B., Gough, H. G., & Martin, W. E. Children's ethnic attitudes. II. Relationship to parental beliefs concerning child training. *Child Develpm.*, 1950, **21**, 169–181.

Harris, D. B., & Tseng, Seng Chu. Children's attitudes toward peers and parents as revealed by sentence completion. *Child Develpm.*, 1957, **28**, 401–411.

Harris, I. D. *Normal children and mothers.* Glencoe, Ill.: Free Press, 1959.

Hawkes, G. R., Burchinal, L. G., & Gardner, B. Pre-adolescents' views of some of their relations with their parents. *Child Develpm.*, 1957, **28**, 393–399.

Heilbrun, A. B., Jr., & McKinley, R. Perception of maternal child rearing attitudes, personality of the perceiver, and incipient psychopathology. *Child Develpm.*, 1962, **33**, 73–83.

Hoffman, M. L. Power assertion by the parent and its impact on the child. *Child Develpm.*, 1960, **31**, 129–143.

Hollenberg, Eleanor, & Sperry, Margaret. Some antecedents of aggression and effects of frustration in doll play. *Personality*, 1951, **1**, 32–43.

Ingersoll, H. L. A study of the transmission of authority patterns in the family. *Genet. Psychol. Monogr.*, 1949, **38**, 225–302.

Itkin, W. Relationships between attitudes toward parents and parents' attitudes toward children. *J. genet. Psychol.*, 1955, **86**, 339–352.

Kagan, J. Children's perception of parents. *J. abnorm. soc. Psychol.*, 1956, **53**, 257–259.

Kagan, J. The concept of identification. *Psychol. Rev.*, 1958, **65**, 296–305.

Kagan, J., Hosken, Barbara, & Watson, Sara. Child's symbolic conceptualization of parents. *Child Develpm.*, 1961, **32**, 625–636.

Kagan, J., & Lemkin, J. The child's differential perception of parental attributes. *J. abnorm. soc. Psychol.*, 1960, **61**, 440–447.

Levy, D. M. *Maternal overprotection.* New York: Columbia Univer. Press, 1943.

Lorr, M., & Jenkins, R. L. Three factors in parent behavior. *J. consult. Psychol.*, 1953, **17**, 306–308.

Lyle, W. H., & Levitt, E. E. Punitiveness, authoritarianism, and parental discipline of grade school children. *J. abnorm. soc. Psychol.*, 1955, **51**, 42–46.

Lynn, D. B. Sex differences in identification development. *Sociometry*, 1961, **24**, 372–383.

Margolis, M. The mother-child relationship in bronchial asthma. *J. abnorm. soc. Psychol.*, 1961, **63**, 360–367.

Medinnus, G. R. Research implications of several parent-child concepts. *Marriage fam. Liv.*, 1959, **21**, 329–333.

Medinnus, G. R. The relation between several parent measures and the child's early adjustment to school. *J. educ. Psychol.*, 1961, **52**, 153–156.

Medinnus, G. R., & Curtis, F. J. The relation between maternal self-acceptance and child acceptance. *J. consult. Psychol.*, 1963, **27**, 542–544.

Meltzer, H. Sex differences in children's attitudes to parents. *J. genet. Psychol.*, 1943, **62**, 311–326.

Meyers, R. R. Intrafamily relationships and pupil adjustment. *Teach. Coll. Contr. Educ.*, 1935, No. 651.

Miles, Katherine A. Relationship between certain factors in the home background and the quality of leadership shown by children. Reported by J. E. Anderson. Parents' attitudes on child behavior: a report of three studies. *Child Develpm.*, 1946, **17**, 91–97.

Milton, G. A. A factor analytic study of child-rearing behavior. *Child Develpm.*, 1958, **29**, 381–392.

Moll, K. L., & Darley, F. L. Attitudes of mothers of articulatory-impaired and speech-retarded children. *J. Speech Hear. Dis.*, 1960, **25**, 377–384.

Morris, W. W., & Nicholas, A. L. Intra-family personality configurations among children with primary behavior disorders and their parents: a Rorschach investigation. *J. clin. Psychol.*, 1950, **6**, 309–319.

Mussen, P. H., & Kagan, J. Group conformity and perceptions of parents. *Child Develpm.*, 1958, **29**, 57–60.

Nakamura, C. The relationship between children's expressions of hostility and methods of discipline exercised by dominant overprotective parents. *Child Develpm.*, 1959, **30**, 109–117.

Peterson, D. R., Becker, W. C., Hellmer, L. A., Shoemaker, D. J., & Quay, H. C. Parental attitudes and child adjustment. *Child Develpm.*, 1959, **30**, 119–130.

Peterson, D. R., Becker, W., Shoemaker, D., Luria, Z., & Hellmer, L. Child behavior problems and parental attitudes. *Child Develpm.*, 1961, **32**, 151–162.

Phillips, E. L. Parent-child similarities in personality disturbances. *J. clin. Psychol.*, 1951, **7**, 188–190.

Piaget, J. *The moral judgment of the child.* New York: Harcourt, Brace, 1932.

Porter, B. M. Measurement of parental acceptance of children. *J. Home Econ.*, 1954, **46**, 176–182.

Rabban, M. Sex-role identification in young children in two diverse social groups. *Genet. Psychol. Monogr.*, 1950, **42**, 81–158.

Radke, Marian J. *The relation of parental authority to children's behavior and attitudes.* Minneapolis: Univer. of Minn. Press, 1946.

Read, K. H. Parents' expressed attitudes and children's behavior. *J. consult. Psychol.*, 1945, **9**, 95–100.

Roff, M. A factorial study of the Fels Parent Behavior Scales. *Child Develpm.*, 1949, **20**, 29–45.

Sanford, N. The dynamics of identification. *Psychol. Rev.*, 1955, **62**, 106–118.

Schaefer, E. S. A circumplex model for maternal behavior. *J. abnorm. soc. Psychol.*, 1959, **59**, 226–235.

Schaefer, E. S., & Bell, R. Q. Parental Attitude Research Instrument (PARI). Normative data. Unpubl. mss. Library, National Institutes of Health, Bethesda, Md., 1955.

Schaefer, E. S., & Bell, R. Q. Development of a Parental Attitude Research Instrument. *Child Develpm.*, 1958, **29**, 339–361.

Sears, Pauline S. Doll-play aggression in normal young children: influence of sex, age, sibling status, father's absence. *Psychol. Monogr.*, 1951, **65**, No. 6 (Whole No. 323).

Sears, Pauline S. Child-rearing factors related to playing of sex-typed roles. *Amer. Psychologist*, 1953, **8**, 431. (Abstract)

Sears, R. R. Relation of fantasy aggression to interpersonal aggression. *Child Develpm.*, 1950, **21**, 5–6.

Sears, R. R., Maccoby, Eleanor E., & Levin, H. *Patterns of child rearing.* Evanston, Ill.: Row, Peterson, 1957.

Serot, Naomi M., & Teevan, R. C. Perception of the parent-child relationship and its relation to adjustment. *Child Develpm.,* 1961, **32,** 373–378.

Symonds, P. M. *The psychology of parent-child relationships.* New York: Appleton-Century-Crofts, 1939.

Symonds, P. M. *The dynamics of parent–child relationships.* New York: Appleton-Century-Crofts, 1949.

Watson, G. Some personality differences in children related to strict or permissive parental discipline. *J. Psychol.,* 1957, **44,** 227–249.

Zuckerman, M., & Oltean, Mary. Some relationships between maternal attitude factors and authoritarianism, personality needs, psychopathology, and self-acceptance. *Child Develpm.,* 1959, **30,** 27–36.

SECTION IV ❋ SOCIETAL INFLUENCES ON SOCIALIZATION

Although the family in Western culture imparts most of the society's values and beliefs and plays the largest role in molding personality and behavior, other social forces also make their impression on the child. The child's agemates, his school, and other outside influences including the community, religious experience, and exposure to the mass media all at times reinforce parental socialization. This is especially true of the school. At other times, the influence of these outside forces runs counter to that of the family. A child's peers, for example, often counter parental pressures, especially if the parents' behaviors and attitudes are deviant.

In this section, we shall consider these forces whose influence depends, to a large degree, on the adequacy of the parent-child relationship. Chapter 11 concerns the child and his agemates. Chapter 12 covers the school, and Chapter 13 is devoted to the community, the church, and the mass media. If parents are neglectful or so punitive that the child cannot have close relations with them, the influence of these social forces outside the home increases. How great an increase is determined by both the personality of the child and the behavior of the parents.

It seems reasonable to believe that the social influences forming the substance of this section are generally secondary in import to the family. Moreover, their effect is neither as deleterious as is sometimes maintained in the case of peers and the mass media nor as beneficial as is sometimes assumed in the case of school, school books, and religious instruction. More likely, these forces interacting with one another and with the family within the setting of the culture are each ambiguous in impact. Sometimes they conflict with each other, sometimes they reinforce each other. At times they dispose the child toward adaptive behavior, at other times toward maladaptive behavior.

chapter 11 ✳ The Child among His Peers

The society of children is clearly a primary group. As such, it features close, face-to-face contact, the ability to regulate or constrain the
behavior of its members, and psychological support for them. In most
cases, other than the family, it is the only primary group to which a
child belongs. Obviously this society is of great significance in shaping a child's beliefs and behaviors. Yet psychologists have not flooded
this important area with research. Indeed, far more is known about
parent-child relationships, however vague this knowledge may be, than
about the interaction of children with other children. Nevertheless,
let us look into three facets of children's groups: their change in degree of involvement and type of activity, the question of acceptance
by peers, and the functions such groups serve in the socialization
process.

CHANGES IN PEER INVOLVEMENT

The early "developmental tasks" of children are primarily phenomena of a maturational kind. Such things as the development of speech
and locomotion result from physical and motor maturation. As age
advances, the types of developmental tasks change, becoming essentially social in character. The socialization process moves in. Through

it, the infant, terribly egocentric in its demands and unable to suffer delay or interference, ultimately acquires concern for others and becomes able to postpone or even reject gratification if this occurs at the expense of someone else. How is this socialization reflected in the changing interactions of the child with his agemates, and how do these interactions contribute to the molding of the end product, the human adult?

The earliest contacts between agemates have been described by Maudry and Nekula (1939) who studied the social interactions of children under 25 months of age. Placing pairs of children matched in age in a play pen along with some toys, they found that at the earliest age level studied, six to eight months, children did not interact to any appreciable extent. Partners were treated as though they were play materials rather than individuals. Fighting over play occurred most frequently at the next level, nine to 13 months, but diminished from this point onward. At the final level studied, 19 to 25 months, children were chiefly interested in establishing social relations with one another, with the play materials being used to serve this end.

For many reasons, the young child does not interact too well with peers. Some of the more important ones are his rather greater distractability, his lower tolerance of frustration, his lesser ability to endure delay of gratification, and his inferior skill in communication. All these deficiencies may be related to the young child's inability to "take the role of the other." Because of a poorly developed capacity to discern the moods, motives, and feelings of others, the young child runs into the inevitable conflicts arising from social interaction. To put oneself in someone else's shoes or to empathize does much to reduce these difficulties.

Take this example. The mother is frantically attempting to cook dinner and at the same time cope with a two-year-old son with a cold who is lying on the kitchen floor, kicking his feet in the midst of a temper tantrum. The five-year-old daughter picks this moment to demand that her mother read a story, thus revealing her inability to "take the role of the other" and see the world at this juncture through the eyes of her mother. The two-year-old cannot be dealt with by arbitration; actually, as soon as he has been fed he will probably calm down anyway. But the five-year-old has come quite some way toward social maturity although this is not evident at the moment. If told, however, "I'm busy right now but I'll read you a story later; why don't you see if you can get your brother interested in something," she *may* respond maturely. The child is thus along the way to developing skills of empathy and in a few years may even be of some help to the mother in avoiding domestic crises of this sort.

From this, one can see that a pair of two-year-olds will engage in a fair amount of combat, since their personal needs generally cannot stand delay or compromise. But by the time they are five, compromise and arbitration become possible although usually these are not attempted until the efforts of either child to assert his rights have failed. While caring for a pair of five-year-olds, a baby sitter kept track of the number of times they fought, made up, and reached a compromise solution to the problem engendering the conflict. In the course of the afternoon, this sequence occurred 14 times, even though both children were bright and pleasant, loved one another dearly, and were both having a "good day." Such activity is doubtless hard on the parent, but is probably of considerable value to the child, since in the process, he learns several things—to take the role of the other and show concern for the other's wishes, to delay gratification, to arbitrate difficulties, and to achieve compromises.

As Barker (1955) and Anderson (1948) have emphasized, there is a tremendous amount of repetition of experience during childhood. Estimated quite conservatively, five-year-old children enter into conflict with their agemates at least 20 times a day and manage to resolve most of these clashes successfully. Multiplied by 365 days, these figures yield a total of 7300 annual conflicts between children of the same age. No wonder most of us learn something of the art of diplomacy over the years!

Through growth of conceptual power and social skill, partly as a result of interaction with age equals, the child is able to increase still further his participation with his peers. This has been demonstrated by Parten's study (1929) of children's play. Because it involved one of the first uses of time sampling, the Parten project is of methodological interest besides having provided valuable information on child behavior. Over many brief intervals, Parten observed the play behaviors of children ranging in age from slightly under two to four years and 11 months and saw that she could categorize this play according to amounts of social involvement. These were her categories (see also Figure 11-1):

Unoccupied Behavior—The child apparently is not playing at all, at least not in the usual sense, but occupies himself with watching anything which happens to be of momentary interest. When there is nothing exciting taking place, he plays with his own body, gets on and off chairs, just stands around, follows the teacher, or sits in one spot glancing around the room.

Solitary Play—The child plays alone and independently with toys that

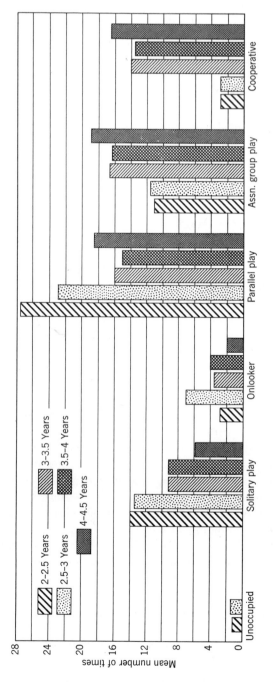

FIGURE 11-1   Mean number of times each activity was observed at different ages (Parten & Newhall, 1943, p. 517).

are different from those used by the children within speaking distance and makes no effort to get close to or speak to the other children. His interest is centered upon his own activity, and he pursues it without reference to what others are doing.

Onlooker Behavior—The child spends most of his time watching the others play. He often talks to the playing children, asks questions, or gives suggestions, but does not enter into the play himself. He stands or sits within speaking distance of the group so that he can see and hear all that is taking place. Thus he differs from the unoccupied child, who notices anything that happens to be exciting and is not especially interested in groups of children.

Parallel Play—The child plays independently, but the activity he chooses naturally brings him among other children. He plays with toys which are like those which the children around him are using, but he plays with the toys as he sees fit and does not try to influence the activity of the children near him. Thus he plays beside rather than with the other children (cf. solitary play above).

Associative Play—The child plays with other children. There are borrowing and lending of play material; following one another with trains and wagons; mild attempts to control which children may or may not play in the groups. All engage in similar if not identical activity; there is no division of labor and no organization of activity. Each child acts as he wishes, does not subordinate his interests to the group.

Cooperative or Organized Supplementary Play—The child plays in a group that is organized for the purpose of making some material product, of striving to attain some competitive goal, of dramatizing situations of adult or group life, or of playing formal games. There is a marked sense of belonging or not belonging to the group. The control of the group situation is in the hands of one or two members, who direct the activity of the others. The goal as well as the method of attaining it necessitates a division of labor, the taking of different roles by the various group members, and the organization of activity so that the efforts of one child are supplemented by those of another (Parten & Newhall, 1943).

Though increasingly interested in his peers, as seen in the development of parallel play, the young child does not have enough imaginative, role playing, arbitrational, or compromising skill to interact to any large degree at the more complex and intimate level of cooperative play. Interest in peers occurs early, but acquisition of the necessary skills requires time and practice. Developed largely through play, these skills open the door to future play and interaction of a more highly involved kind.

As interaction proliferates with age, the frequency of specific social responses changes. The number of quarrels children enter into diminishes as age and social skills increase (Jersild & Markey, 1935). However, the duration of any single quarrel becomes greater, perhaps because the child is less distractable. The use of language to resolve conflicts grows with age, whereas screaming, crying, and general tantrum decorum declines. Competition and rivalry rise sharply between two and five and less so between five and seven (Greenberg, 1932), although Parten's data suggested that cooperation also increased during this interval. Responses of both sympathy and aggressiveness among several groups of nursery children studied by Murphy (1937) manifested an increase with age. She found that highly aggressive children were often more sympathetic to others. These various patterns suggest that some children within a particular age group are generally more inclined than others toward social interaction, irrespective of type.

In the growing child, interest in peers awakens first and is followed by increasing interaction with them. From the greater interaction come improved social skills which, in turn, lead to even more interaction. Children who do not seek this interaction, who prefer adult company, are probably left behind more and more in their social learning, and are more often rejected by their peers (Marshall & MacCandless, 1957).

From the one-year-old, uninterested in other one-year-olds and unable to maintain friendly contact with them because of a deficiency in social skill, the child becomes a two-year-old, who is now more interested in his peers but is still incapable of compromising his own needs sufficiently to sustain friendly or cooperative relations for any length of time. By five the child has become fully involved in the world of agemates and has made great gains in acquiring social adeptness. Later on in childhood and adolescence, through combining a codification of rules and a genuine feeling for one another, the neighborhood band emerges as a remarkably cohesive and influential primary group which performs many functions in the socialization process.

That acceptance by one's peers is rewarding is demonstrated in the tremendous effort made by children to establish themselves when joining a new group of peers. Since the extent to which a child is involved with and accepted by his peers varies, the influence of the society of agemates also varies from child to child. It is to the personal qualities associated with such acceptance by peers that the discussion now moves.

ACCEPTANCE BY PEERS

The measure most often used to learn the degree to which an individual is accepted by others is the sociometric method devised by

Moreno (1934). The device is simple. One merely asks a group of individuals a question, of which the following are typical:

Whom would you like to have sit next to you in this classroom? This is asked of sixth-grade children.

Whom would you trust to fly at your wing position? This is asked of a group of fighter pilots.

Who is your best friend? This is asked of kindergarten children.

How often a particular individual is chosen may be considered a measure of how much esteem he has in the group. Questions might be phrased negatively, but generally are not. The mere posing of a negative question such as "Whom would you least like to have sit next to you?" might serve to increase the overt rejection of the child, once his classmates compared notes.

Where choices are not limited to a specific group, the sociometric method can turn up information on the group's cohesiveness. For example, if Sunday School children were asked to name their best friends, few choices might be within the Sunday School group. Thus, it is not a very significant social group in the eyes of its members. On the other hand, if members of an informal, neighborhood group of peers were requested to name their best friends, most choices would fall within the society, for groups of peers have a great amount of cohesiveness and solidarity.

Sociometric studies also provide some indication of group morale and single out children within the group in need of help to achieve a satisfactory adjustment. Figure 11-2 contains two sociograms of the same group of children. Note the change in the atmosphere of the group from October to March as the school year advanced. The number of isolates declined, the cliques disintegrated, and friendship choices increased.

A major reason for using measures of this sort is to ascertain the relative "healthiness" of a group. This healthiness is based on the satisfaction received by group members. What, then, happens to a group plagued by poor morale? If the group is a fighter squadron, it might be best to disband it and distribute its members among other groups, since their chances of physical survival would not be great if the original group remained intact. Dissolution of the group or removal of some members may also be the solution in children's groups. This applies especially to the younger child who suffers rejection or who is ignored.

Anderson (1956) said that one could not predict with any great amount of accuracy the adjustment or acceptance of a younger child,

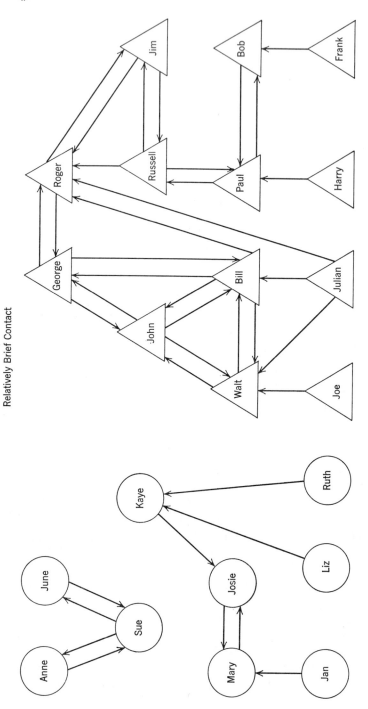

Relatively Brief Contact

FIGURE 11-2 Changes in sociometric structure as length of time in contact increases.

6 Months Later

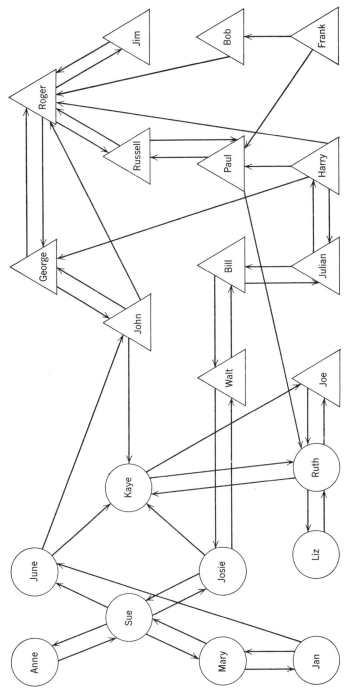

say one below the age of five. A child ignored within one group might be a highly accepted leader in another. However, this becomes less likely with increases in age. Accidental circumstances lose their importance, consistency in behavior gains, and the learning of social roles continues. The older rejected child is not likely to benefit greatly from transfer to another group, because he has developed certain roles and response tendencies which will probably persist in a new environment and lead to his rejection there. For this child, it might be preferable to teach him the skills valued by the original group, as was done by Jack (1934) and Page (1936), or to teach him mature responses, as was done by Keister and Updegraff (1937). In these areas social maturity is an important component of success.

Another rather widely employed measure of social acceptance is the "guess who" technique, first developed fully by Tryon (1939). To various classrooms of children aged 12 and 15, she put a number of questions such as, "Who always acts grown up?" By combining the "guess who" nominations with sociometric data on popularity, she discovered the traits and characteristics linked to popularity in boys and girls at the two age levels. In the eyes of the 12-year-olds, the ideal boy was aggressive, boisterous, unkempt, and most important skilled at games. The ideal girl, to the 12-year-olds, was friendly but demure and docile in social behavior, had quiet humor, and conformed to adult standards. At 15, the popular traits in boys did not change much from 12; the major emphasis was still on game skills. However, boisterousness and unkempt appearance were no longer positive virtues and some poise in dealing with girls became necessary. Meanwhile, the girl now had two highly acceptable new roles. First, she had to be a "girl's girl," a buoyant, rather aggressive pal of both boys and girls. The second was the role of the sophisticated and glamorous *femme fatale*. The demure conformist of 12 was now looked upon in a highly unfavorable light. Thus, girls may have greater problems than boys in developing a consistent concept of the self. The role most rewarded at 12 and therefore most likely to be emulated leads to social defeat at 15.

More recent research (Tuddenham, 1951) has indicated the same clusters of traits related to boy and girl popularity, but with the shifts away from the "little lady" and the unkempt, boisterous boy occurring roughly by the age of ten. The pattern of socialization apparently had not changed but the sequence had accelerated. The ten- to 12-year-old of midcentury resembled the 15-year-old of the 1930's in social responses.

Factors in Acceptance

Many personal characteristics of individuals affect their social acceptance or rejection. Discovery of these characteristics has various uses. First, it helps to solve the practical problem of enabling children to find some measure of acceptance. Second, it permits some inference about the values and orientation of a group from the personality traits it prizes.

The prime requisite for social acceptance in childhood—and adulthood, for that matter—is social maturity as defined by the groups to which the individual belongs. Childhood is a time of sharp gradations of age, perhaps because age alone tells so much about the social behavior of a child. The following dialogue is not unfamiliar among children. Here chronological age affects social maturity:

George: Hi. My name is George.
Bill: Hi. My name is Bill.
George: How old are you?
Bill: Eight, going on nine (he had his eighth birthday last week). How old are you?
George: Nine, going on ten.

Both George and Bill enjoy playing with older kids, say 12-year-olds, and hold younger kids, say six-year-olds, in kindly contempt. There may be a sound reason for this. Social maturity and game skills vary with age; thus, playing with older but not younger children connotes a learning situation.

Not long ago, Medinnus (1962) asked 25 elementary and junior high school teachers to describe the socially immature child in their respective grades. Table 11-1 lists those characteristics mentioned most often.

It is interesting to note that although most of these behaviors are child to child rather than child to adult in nature they closely parallel the factors found by Koch (1933) many years before to be predictive of unpopularity among preschool children. The following behavioral characteristics correlated negatively with popularity: the tendencies to play alone, to refuse or ignore the requests of other children, to attack other children or offer resistance to their attacks, to escape from undesirable situations, and to dawdle. Basically, social acceptance appears to be a reflection of social maturity.

Like chronological age, mental age is involved in social maturity. The diagnosis of mental deficiency stems from social competence. Thus, a person of IQ 50 who behaved in a socially acceptable man-

TABLE 11-1 Characteristics of Socially Immature Children

Grades 1–3:

Does not play with peers in a controlled manner when not directly supervised.
Wants to be "It" all the time; jealousy when playing; will not take turns.
Will not share readily.
Withdraws from the group.
Inconsiderate—pushes, shoves.
Lacks respect for others' property.
Does not cooperate in group activities; does not assume his share of the responsibility.
Interrupts; talks and bothers neighbors.
Plays with children younger than himself.

Grades 4–6:

Does not play or work well with others in his group:
(*a*) Picks fights; consistently employs pugilistic tactics rather than attempting to "talk it out."
(*b*) Uncooperative in planning games.
(*c*) Drops out of games when decisions are made against him (e.g., being called "out" in baseball).
(*d*) Wants his own way.
Tattles; tendency to report very slight infractions of rules and wrong behavior which is of little actual importance; judgment of wrong behavior corresponds to the evaluation of a younger child.
Rapid changes in friendship loyalties—i.e., a sudden turn against one's seemingly best friend.
Extreme shyness with marked tendency to hang his head or cover the face when asked questions.
Does not observe common courtesies:
(*a*) Walks in front of people.
(*b*) Interrupts when others are talking.
(*c*) Does not use "please" and "thank you."
Lacks respect for others.
Child feels that rules are made for everyone but him; consequently, makes own rules and does not follow the rules of the group.

Grades 7–9:

Plays with children younger than his group.
Interested in the opposite sex in the manner of a much younger person (e.g., would rather play tag than do something socially with a person of the opposite sex).
Child often ignored by peers, which leads to: showing off, giggling, grimaces, pushing or poking, slapping or tripping; or to withdrawal.
Hesitancy in responding when addressed or questioned.
Has difficulty in participating in more highly organized games.
Takes no responsibility for own conduct (must be reminded to be quiet, sit down, etc.).

ner would not ordinarily be termed mentally defective, whereas another of IQ 100 who disclosed gross social incompetence might very well be considered so by the most widely used criteria of mental deficiency (Doll, 1935, 1941). Then, too, as the Terman study of genius (Terman et al., 1925) indicated, the association of popularity with high IQ, irrespective of chronological age, could be quite conclusively demonstrated. But this relation has an end point. In the opinion of Hollingworth (1942), as we saw in Chapter 6, children above IQ 155 are neither social nor antisocial. Rather they are asocial in their adjustment to their peers, apparently because they live in another conceptual world.

But social maturity is not the only factor entering into acceptance by one's peers. One of the most potent determinants of how well one child is accepted by another during most of childhood is the sex of the children in question. In childhood sex cleavage in friendship is marked (Tuddenham, 1952). This cleavage is so readily observable that it becomes a defense and may actually have been the basis of Freud's idea of latency—that once a child rejected the parent of the opposite sex as a love object, it also rejected all members of that sex until reaching an adult level of sexuality. Girls initially reject boys who, after several years of rejection, finally retaliate by rejecting girls. By early high school years, girls again begin to accept boys, but boys, either because of social insensitivity or slower social maturity, continue to reject girls for several more years (Harris & Tseng, 1957). Generally, these data show, girls are more rejecting than boys, turning away from other girls and parents as well as from boys. Because of this, which also implies some rejection of themselves, girls are probably less satisfied by their roles and have lower morale, at least in Western culture at the present time.

Class and caste also play a part in acceptance by peers. They begin to have considerable effect during childhood (Bonney, 1944) and increase their influence as children become more accurate judges of social class position (Hollingshead, 1949). Both class and color play bigger roles in acceptance partly because propinquity or closeness is an important element in determining choice of friendship. Since the chance of any two children being neighbors results in part from class and race, it is not surprising to find that the more stable choices of friendship in later childhood and adolescence depend somewhat on these two factors.

Acceptance by peers is not all good, nor is rejection all bad. Achievement as an adult apparently depends to some extent on lack of involvement with peers (McCurdy, 1957). Yet a continuing rejection by one's peers seems to predict eventual maladjustment better than does an adult's diagnosis of "problem child" (Roff, 1961). The term *peer group* implies that one is being judged by one's equals. These judges are harsh but generally accurate, perhaps because they judge less from the prejudices of society and more from individual merit than does the adult world.

CHILDREN'S GROUPS AND THE SOCIALIZATION PROCESS

Far more than any other part of this book, this section is speculative in nature and has little basis in research findings. Nevertheless, its content is of great importance for the psychology of child development. Therefore, let us proceed with an examination of the functions served by children's groups in the socialization process. During childhood, the *peer group,* or group of equals, is remarkably cohesive. This cohesion or solidarity is voluntary. Clearly the group must provide something of value to hold its members in line. What do peers offer?

Normalizing or Leveling Influence

One of the most important contributions of the peer society is its normalizing influence. Adults differ from one another, but the astonishing fact is that they differ so little. As children they were reared with great variability. Yet as youngsters and later as adults they have not differed as much as might have been expected. So Levy's (1943) study of overprotected children, which was discussed in the last chapter, demonstrated. It is unlikely that any other group of children raised in their own homes and studied for any length of time was reared in as deviant a manner as this group. Nevertheless, in adulthood, these children were seen to be comparatively normal. They attributed their normality to school and, later, to the job—and to peers. No matter how deviantly an individual may be reared, he is generally exposed to essentially the same information as other individuals and has largely the same demands made of him by his peers. In return, he receives some psychological support from them.

The effect of other children on the development and adjustment of any one child is, first of all, to reduce the influence of parental idiosyncrasy in treatment. This normalizing or leveling influence, making children more similar to one another than might be expected, may prove detrimental to desirable goals. Children raised in homes free of racial prejudice, for example, learn quite quickly from their peers all the forms of bigotry to be found in the culture. Even if they also learn—perhaps more rapidly—to keep these ideas to themselves around home, certain damage has been done. They have been "normalized." A leveling process has occurred. To some moderate degree, they now hold the prejudices common to the culture.

Literature contains many illustrations of the shock of being removed from a tender and affectionate home into the rough and tumble society of peers. It seems equally clear that peers can moderate the influence of brutal, psychotic, neurotic, or otherwise deviant parents. Peer society provides a haven, at least for a time, from the unrealistic and arbitrary demands of the family. The child escapes temporarily into a world of agemates where he undergoes basically the same experiences as all other children of his age. He becomes a member of the "gang" for better or worse—depending on what homelife was like before initiation.

Following a lecture by Bruno Bettelheim, the noted psychotherapist, a member of the audience asked: "How do parents produce a schizophrenic child?" Bettelheim replied that this could not be done unless, perhaps, the parents kept the child locked up all the time. A child attending school and playing with other children, he said, was exposed to enough of the normal world to prevent parents from making it psychotic. He concluded by saying that even the Dachau or Buchenwald concentration camp would have been unable to destroy men's wills if only the inmates, of which he himself had been one, had been let out to play with each other for a few hours in the afternoon.

In a similar vein, Harlow (1963) found that infant monkeys deprived of mothering nevertheless developed normally as long as they were allowed considerable contact with agemates during their "childhood" and "adolescence." Apparently, the influence of peers has as normalizing an effect on monkeys as on humans.

Only children appear to be deviant more often in both positive and negative directions than are children with siblings. This may be because their parents' attentions, whether wholesome or harmful, are not diverted in any way. Similarly, children reared outside the world of agemates are more variable than other children, probably because they are more exclusively the products of parental pressures. Thus, although peers may teach prejudice to the unprejudiced and may divert genius, the "normalizing" effect of this society on child adjustment and behavior is generally good and ameliorative. Through it, the unjustly treated learns something of justice and the rejected finds acceptance among agemates.

Identification

To Freud, the infant in his first groping thoughts believed that he was all powerful and that the world was merely an extension of himself. Piaget demonstrated (1954) in remarkably well-thought-out experiments that Freud's speculations had observable and testable validity. The child learned at about six months that he and the external world were not one. This was the point at which, in Freudian psychology, the ego or concept of self developed. Once separating himself from the rest of the world, the child became aware of his not being omnipotent but rather impotent—a powerless creature in a threatening world.

Ausubel (1958) speculated that in response to this awareness of impotence the child sank roots of identification with his parents. To escape the fear associated with helplessness, the child identified with his parents, the all-powerful beings of his universe, and thus, vicariously, regained a feeling of power and control. Some parents did not allow the child to identify himself with them; then the child remained anxious and fearful. Although Ausubel did not suggest it, the child denied this vicarious control might, as he got older, show greater concern for compulsively ordering and thus controlling his small world than might the undenied child. Gaining some measure of power and control in this way seems possible, but the cost is likely to be steep in terms of psychic well-being. If parents deny a child vicarious power, Ausubel suggested, it may be obtained through identification with one's peers. Research conducted by Lesser and Abelson (1959) provided experimental support for the notion that a child who has not identified closely with parents will be more likely to identify strongly with peers.

Children identifying with peers should differ from others whose main identification is with parents. Such children should be lacking in inner controls, or conscience, which to a considerable degree depend for their development on the child's love relationship with his parents (Hoffman, 1962). These controls are unlikely to evolve if the parents reject the child's efforts to identify. To use Riesman's (1950) distinction, such children should be more "other directed" than "inner directed." In Freudian terminology, this type of individual should have an *externalized superego;* that is, his standards would vary with the standards of the group to which he belonged at any particular time. One might predict that children denied early identification with parents would associate more with their peers as well as adhere more rigidly to the codes of the peer culture.

Ausubel's theory fits the facts. Quite probably rejected children identify more closely with agemates and those who make this identification very close are likely to lack inner controls and become more delinquent. In everyday life one sees the gangs of juvenile delinquents composed of youths from broken homes or with no parent ties at all. Yet other, simpler explanations may account for these facts. Correct or not, Ausubel's ideas seem at present to be an interesting, if unproven, attempt to bridge the gap between psychoanalytic theory and observed differences in the degree to which children identify with parents and peers. If Ausubel's views are correct, a child would pay a price of lack of autonomy and of inner controls for identification with peers, yet would find the identification worthwhile, for without it the world would be too threatening to face with equanimity. It is an interesting sidelight that six orphaned Jewish children (Freud & Dann, 1951) who were denied any opportunity to identify with adults while forced to live in the most threatening of all environments, a Nazi concentration camp in which 30,000 Jews perished, developed peer ties that were remarkable in their strength.

Thus far, the emphasis in this discussion of identification with peers has been on the pathological, on the indications of disturbances in function. However, some degree of identification with one's agemates is a normal and useful part of child development. A major aim of child rearing in Western culture is to produce an autonomous or independent child. The child attempts to emancipate himself from parental control, while his parents gradually relinquish control in a rear-guard action to retain it. To borrow the language of Potter's *Gamesmanship* (1948), the child attempts to become one-up (dominant) with regard to parents, even when secretly desiring at times to remain one-down (submissive). The parents face the difficult task of teaching the child to be one-up by keeping him one-down until he has learned such "ploys" (maneuvers) that he bests them in the power struggle. At this point he is mature enough to be allowed to try out his ploys in the world at large: he is independent.

Identification with peers appears to be a prime force aiding in the emancipation from parents. It provides enough security for the child to risk the moderate parental rejection occasioned by each small victory in his development of independence. In the quest for emancipation, such identification forces the child to stick to the timetable used by agemates of the same sex. For example, a nine-year-old who is not allowed to go to Saturday movie matinees when other nine-year-olds are is made aware by his friends that his timetable lags. Pressing hard for this concession, he wins it after a few weeks and a number of encounters with his parents. He has thus taken one more step toward autonomy as a result of the combined coercion and support received from the peers with whom he identifies.

Boehm (1957) offered evidence to show that autonomy from adult control was attained a good deal earlier in the United States than in Europe (in her study, Switzerland). She believed that American parents were less secure, less sure that their way was the right way; therefore, they yielded more readily than European parents to pressure from their children. In the United States also the peer group was stronger than in Europe because most Europeans permitted far less interaction between agemates (see McKenney, 1953). Through its greater contact the American society of peers acquired more clearly articulated values and extra ability both to support and coerce members of the group. Under heavier peer pressure the American child encountered weaker parental resistance as he adapted to the demands of his friends. It is indeed possible that changes in the orientation of American culture over a period of time, as well as differences between American and European cultures, may result in part from the growing socializing role of peers in this country from generation to generation and from the greater function served by the peer society in the United States than in Europe.

Learning

A vast amount of learning occurs among peers. Although this group has neither the traditional authority of the family nor the legal authority of the schools for teaching information and values, it manages to convey a substantial body of material to its members. Robert Paul Smith (1958) in his evocative, poignant book, *"Where Did You Go?" "Out." "What Did You Do?" "Nothing."*, described the learning process in this way:

> I don't remember being taught how to play mumbly-peg. (I know, I know. In the books they write it "mumblety-peg," but we said, and it *was,* "mumbly-peg.") When you were a little kid, you stood around while a covey of ancients of nine or ten played mumbly-peg, shifting from foot to foot and wiping your nose on your sleeve and hitching up your knickerbockers, saying, "Lemme do it, aw come on, lemme have a turn," until one of them struck you in a soft spot and you went home to sit under the porch by yourself, or found a smaller kid to torture, or loused up your sister's rope-skipping, or made a collection of small round stones. The small round stones were not *for* anything, it was just to have a collection of small round stones.
>
> One day you said, "Lemme have a turn, lemme have a turn," and some

soft-hearted older brother, never your own, said, "Go-wan, let the kid have a turn," and there, by all that was holy, you were playing mumbly-peg . . . (Smith, 1958, pp. 4–5).

What Smith learned in a "house" he and his friends built he tells of as follows:

> It was a pitiful wreck of a tarpaper hut, and in it I learned the difference between boys and girls, I learned that all fathers did that, I learned to swear, to play with myself, to sleep in the afternoon, I learned that some people were Catholics and some people were Protestants and some people were Jews, that people came from different places. I learned that other kids wondered, too, who they would have been if their fathers had not married their mothers, wondered if you could dig a hole right to the center of the earth, wondered if you could kill yourself by holding your breath. (None of us could.)
>
> I learned that with three people assembled, it was only for the briefest interludes that all three liked each other. Mitch and I were leagued against Simon. And then Simon and I against Mitch. And then—but you remember. I didn't know then just how to handle that situation. I still don't. It is my coldly comforting feeling that nobody still does, including nations, and that's what the trouble with the world is. That's what the trouble with the world was then—when Mitch and Simon were the two and I was the one.
>
> What else did I learn in the hut? That if two nails will not hold a board in place, three will probably not either, but the third nail will split the board. I think kids still do that. I think objects made of wood by children, left to their own devices, if such there be, will assay ten percent wood, ninety percent nails.
>
> In the hut we looked and we learned. And drooled. I remember a picture of Clara Bow with one shoulder strap—and then there was Toby Wing—and look at Lily Damita—she's bending *way* over . . . (Smith, 1958, pp. 78–80).

Games and Social Learning

The chief voluntary occupation of children's groups is play. Yet children's games are among the most traditional and conservative of human institutions. It is difficult to establish the earliest historical mention of a game, but these are some of the macabre facts that have been found. *Hopscotch* seems to have originated in Greece or Crete, modeled after that most elaborate labyrinth of all, King Minos' (Spence, 1947). This mild game seems at one time to have been a method for selecting a sacrificial victim. Other games of the same original purpose abound. *London bridge* seems very likely to be a remnant of those older times when a person chosen by this method each year was flung from the Bridge to propitiate the gods. An identical "game" with the same purpose has been described in an Icelandic source, *The Vatnsdaela Saga*, dating from the eleventh century. *Blindman's bluff*, originally hoodman's blind, or executioner is blind, or Blind Harry, began as a northern European "game" in which a sacrificial "lamb" was selected at random. The game of *jacks* also seems innocuous enough, yet in its original form of knucklebones it was a fifth century B.C. device for foretelling the future (David, 1955). One throw, the "throw of Zeus," meant one could kill one's enemy and escape detection. From this bizarre form of soothsaying sprang both dice and jacks.

In her book of jump-rope rhymes, Patricia Evans (1955) wrote that rope jumping began as a form of sympathetic magic. Farmers would jump rope in the spring, believing that their small grains would grow as high as they jumped. Jump-rope rhymes are interesting in their continuity and in their geographical dispersion. Evans mentioned that the earliest rhyme she could find dated from medieval England and started with the words, "Andy pandy, sugardy candy." Coincidentally, in San Francisco in 1955, a popular rhyme began with "Amos and Andy, sugar and candy." She recorded another rhyme used in San Francisco that was almost identical to one recorded by Opie and Opie (1959) in England at approximately the same time.

Charlie Chaplin went to France
To teach the ladies how to dance
First he did the rhumba,
Then he did the kicks,
Then he did the samba,
Then he did the splits.
(Opie & Opie, 1959, p. 110)

Charlie Chaplin
Went to France
To teach the ladies
How to dance.
First the heel
And then the toe
Left foot forward
Out you go.
(Evans, 1955, p. 8)

Spence (1947) reported that *tag* at the time of its first reference in Germany involved touching iron, a medieval safeguard from witches and other supernatural beings, in order to be safe from the *it* who was called the devil.

Since adults do not pay much attention to the games of children, it is hard to find literary reference to them. However, Virgil in Volume VII of *Aeneid* described spinning tops. Shakespeare mentioned a number of games including *hide and seek (Hamlet, IV, ii, 32), leap frog (Henry V, ii, 141–144), blindman's bluff (All's Well That Ends Well, IV, iii, 137–138)*, and *prisoner's base (Cymbaline, V, iii, 19–20)*.

Several books on children's games show their amazing continuity. A curious volume called *A Little Pretty Pocket Book* was published by Isaiah Thomas in 1787. (The book actually dates back to 1744 when it was written and published by John Newberry in London. Thomas pirated the book and published it in the United States.) This book describes the games and sports popular with children of that era. Of the 24 activities listed, 21 are still popular today. Two studies of games appeared at the turn of the century. One by Newell (1899) described the games of American children, and the other by Gomme (1894, 1898) dealt with the games of English youngsters. There is a remarkable correspondence between the games contained in the two books. Moreover, most of them are still played today.

Change. Change does occur in children's games but only slowly. For example, both Newell and Gomme write of *Starlight, Moonlight,* a more complex version of hide and seek, which with the advent of traffic lights became known as *Red Light, Green Light.* Although Gomme stated her belief that traditional children's games would be forgotten with the increasing communication and urbanization of the English, these traditional games have shown an astonishing vitality. Despite modifications and changes, continuity is the rule. The Opies (1959) present an illustration of the continuity found in children's rhymes:

1725

Now he acts the *Grenadier,*
Calling for *a Pot of Beer:*
Where's his Money? He's
                    forgot:
Get him gone, a Drunken Sot.

1939

A frog walked into a public
                    house
And asked for a pint of beer.
Where's your money?
In my pocket.
Where's your pocket,
I forgot it.
Well, please walk out.

1907

Eenty, teenty, tuppenny bun,
Pitching tatties doon the lum;
Who's there? John Blair.
What does he want? A bottle of
  beer.
Where's your money I forgot.
Go downstairs, you drunken sot.

1950

Mickey Mouse
In a public house
Drinking pints of beer.
Where's your money?
In my pocket.
Where's your pocket?
I forgot it.
Please walk out.
                    (Opie & Opie, 1959, p. 11)

On the other hand, if something is provided to children from the adult world, children may seize on it, change it in various ways, and make it part of their oral tradition. Witness the various verses devised by English youngsters to the tune of *Davy Crockett:*

> Born on a roof top in Battersea,
> Joined the Teds when he was only three,
> Coshed a cop when he was only four
> And now he's in Dartmoor for evermore.
> Davy, Davy Crockett,
> King of the Teddy boys.
>
> Standing on the corner, swinging his chain,[1]
> Along came a policeman and took his name;
> He pulled out the razor and he slit the copper's throat,
> Now he's wiping up the blood with his Teddy boy's coat.
> Davy, Davy Crockett,
> King of the Teddy boys.

Once part of the oral tradition of children, a game or rhyme is transmitted across generations of children with little variation, perhaps because the older child of 11 or 12 insists that the younger child of six or seven learn it exactly. Frequently these games or rhymes are discarded aspects of the adult world. As Piaget (1932) showed, the young child was so impressed with the need for exactness that he often believed game rules were framed by God. Small wonder that child culture is conservative and allows little room for change. The question is why are games so tradition-bound and conservative?

Perhaps games and rhymes transmit certain values of importance to the peer society. Only one person has explicitly stated this to be the case. Froebel (1898), founder of the kindergarten movement, believed that the child acquired a set of values from those inherent in the games played. For this reason he invented a series of games which he felt would teach a *better* set of values, a set involving knowledge of temporal and spatial relationships, of causality, and of human social interaction.

Information Learned. Piaget (1932) noted that game functions appeared to have vital significance for the socialization process, yet this has not been explored further by anyone else. For him, as mentioned in Chapter 4, children were morally realistic, judging acts in terms of consequences, not motives. They also showed other signs of immature moral judgment. Such immaturity, Piaget believed, resulted from adult constraints as well as from the concreteness of children's own thought processes. This was countered, however, by the child's peers who, in part, helped him to achieve maturity in moral judg-

---

[1] Chain, i.e. bicycle chain, used as a weapon in street gang warfare (Opie & Opie, 1958, p. 119).

ment. Among peers one was judged by and judged others, exposing
the basic unfairness of moral realism. As Piaget saw it, one eventually learned from contact with peers that game rules were not immutable. Rather they could be changed by mutual consent, or reciprocity. Through this knowledge an awareness of democratic processes and of fairness developed. From games, one learned arbitration.

Time spent at games is about equally divided between playing and
arguing. Arguing over whether a pitched ball was a strike, over
whose turn it is, over whether one has been tagged out, over whether
one has been scalped by the Indians and must remain wounded for
an indeterminate interval—all these are among the most common
experiences of childhood. During these verbal battles, children
acquire an understanding of the spirit of rules and the law, in contrast to the understanding of the letter of the law manifested by the
young child. The child learns fairness and reciprocity, tact and
diplomacy.

Children's games are not highly organized and are usually based on
individual competition far more than on cooperative effort. If a
choice is involved, most children will choose a game where the *it*
role is made quite difficult and challenging (Sutton-Smith, 1955).
Games youngsters like best, in contrast to those liked best by teachers
and recreation leaders, are those in which a hierarchy of status on the
basis of ability is manifest. Children, and in particular those children
who find little chance for success at meeting adult demands, can find
a position of status among their peers through skill and daring.

Most games share another characteristic which might be referred
to as "manageable fear." Although adults undertake such sport,
children far more than their elders seem to relish frightening themselves as long as the fear is contained within bounds. Children's
games are frequently of this sort. They create a vicarious danger
which may provide the child with some of the information and
strength needed to deal with real perils.

Role Playing. The play activities of peers also open opportunities
for role playing and in so doing seem to fill a valuable function. The
ability to play a role is apparently related to intellectual ability
(Feffer & Gourevitch, 1960) and to adjustment. People differ in ability
to play social roles; excessively poor role players are less adequately
adjusted than individuals with some role-playing ability (Mann &
Mann, 1960). Certainly the dramatic play of childhood is concerned
chiefly with role playing. It provides the child with a rich variety
of roles to tackle. To be a cowboy is easy. To be a railroad engineer

or a parent is not much more difficult. But to be a sandbox, or something equally inanimate, may pose quite a challenge.

Most roles played offer some preparation for later roles in real life. Conceivably the play of girls with dolls, for example, provides a base for later care of real children both in attitudes toward infants and in knowledge of how to care for them. Even if a girl of four may leave her favorite "baby" out in the rain for a few days, the eight- or nine-year-old appears to have learned her maternal role quite adequately. For the boy, however, whose adult functions are not easily anticipated in play, unless he happens to become a cowboy as an adult, there is less to be gained from peer activities in this specific area, just as he probably benefits more than girls in learning arbitration, since his games are more complex and his rules more rigidly codified.

Peers as a Reality Check

A final form of learning to be discerned in the society of peers is that of growing more closely attuned to the reality about oneself. Parents may become so emotionally involved with the child that they cannot evaluate him in anything but the most favorable light. Or, they may be so caught up in their own problems that they cannot evaluate him at all, or can evaluate him only negatively. Teachers seem to be moving away from comparing children with other children. But the one group that can be relied on to evaluate and to compare is the society of peers.

Seldom is it enjoyable to have reality brought home to oneself— "to see ourselves as others see us." Yet only upon becoming aware of others' opinions does one consider change. Peers are harsh but relatively unbiased judges. Any undesirable trait is quickly spotted by them and they are quite frank to deride it, thus heightening the possibility for change. The accuracy of their assessment has been indicated by a study by Roff (1961) showing that among adults who were considered behavior problems in their own childhood, one of the best auguries of adult adjustment was acceptance by peers. If a child is judged to be a problem child by adults but is accepted by his peers his chances of making a normal adjustment are good. But if the peer society also considers him a problem his chances fall precipitously. Harsh as peer judgment and severe as its penalties may be, both seem relatively fair and accurate.

Psychologists have a vast, unexplored world to map, and the territory of peers is still largely unpenetrated. Yet it seems reasonable to believe from a brief sight of peer country that events occur to a child as a result of his interactions with other children of the same age which bear heavily on the process of growing up.

SUMMARY

Children are interested in other children early in life, yet their interactions are minimal because of their inadequate impulse control and their inability to have much feeling for the other person. With age, interaction increases, producing more quarrels and aggression as well as greater cooperation and sympathy. The degree of any child's involvement with agemates differs from age to age and also within any age group.

Children vary greatly in the degree to which they are accepted by mates of the same age and to which they become involved in peer activity. Measuring devices enable the social scientist to assess the acceptance of children by their mates and to determine the personality traits associated with acceptance or rejection by peers.

By elementary school age, sex division begins to occur among children of the same age. From this time onward during childhood the influence of the peer society is principally that of agemates of the same sex.

The peer society plays a vital role in socialization. Peers have a normalizing or leveling effect. They allow the child an opportunity for identification. Peer society conveys to its members a large body of information and values. It provides a wide opportunity for the learning and playing of social roles. It makes available to the child a reality check from which he can judge his own behavior more accurately. The world of peers is largely unexplored by psychologists, but seems to be a harsh though fair one which has great significance for the socialization process.

REFERENCES

Anderson, J. E. Personality organization in children. *Amer. Psychologist*, 1948, **3**, 409–416.

Anderson, J. E. Personal communication, 1956.

Ausubel, D. P. *Ego development and the personality disorders*. New York: Grune & Stratton, 1952.

Ausubel, D. P. *Theory and problems of child development.* New York: Grune & Stratton, 1958.

Barker, R. G., & Wright, H. F. *Midwest and its children: The psychological ecology of an American town.* New York: Row, Peterson, 1955.

Boehm, Leonore. The development of independence: a comparative study. *Child Develpm.,* 1957, **28,** 85–92.

Bonney, M. E. Relationships between social success, family size, socio-economic background, and intelligence among school children in grades III to V. *Sociometry,* 1944, **7,** 26–39.

David, F. N. Studies in the history of probability and statistics. *Biometrics,* 1955, **42,** 1–32.

Doll, E. A. *The Vineland social maturity scale. Manual of directions.* Vineland, N. J.: The Training School, 1935.

Doll, E. A. The essentials of an inclusive concept of mental deficiency. *Amer. J. ment. Defic.,* 1941, **46,** 214–219.

Evans, Patricia. *Jump rope rhymes.* San Francisco: Porpoise Book Shop, 1955.

Feffer, M. H., & Gourevitch, Vivian. Cognitive aspects of role playing in children. *J. Pers.,* 1960, **28,** 383–396.

Freud, Anna, and Dann, Sophie. An experiment in group upbringing. *The psychoanalytic study of the child.* Vol. 6. New York: International Univer. Press, 1951.

Freud, S. *The ego and the id.* London: Hogarth, 1935.

Froebel, F. *Mother play* (Trans. by Henrietta R. Eliot & Susan E. Blow.) New York: Appleton, 1898.

Gomme, Alice B. *Traditional games of England, Scotland, and Ireland* (Vols. 1 and 2). London: Methuen, 1894, 1898.

Gomme, Alice B. *Old English singing games.* New York: Dodd Merrill, 1900.

Greenberg, P. J. Competition in children; an experimental study. *Am. J. Psychol.,* 1932, **44,** 221–248.

Harlow, H. F. Effects of early experiences on personal–social, sexual, and maternal behavior. Paper read to the Society for Research in Child Development, Berkeley, Calif., April 11, 1963.

Harris, D. B., and Tseng, S. C. Children's attitudes toward peers and parents as revealed by sentence completions. *Child Develpm.,* 1957, **28,** 401–411.

Hoffman, M. L. The role of the parent in the child's moral growth. *Relig. Educ.,* 1962, **57** (Research Supplement), pp. S18–S33.

Hollingshead, A. deB. *Elmtown's youth: the impact of social classes on youth.* New York: Wiley, 1949.

Hollingworth, Leta S. *Children above IQ 180.* New York: World Book, 1942.

Jack, Lois M. An experimental study of ascendant behavior in preschool children. *Univer. Iowa Stud. Child Welf.,* 1934, **9,** No. 3.

Jersild, A. T., and Markey, F. V. Conflicts between preschool children. *Child Develpm. Monogr.,* No. 21, 1935.

Keister, Mary E., and Updegraff, Ruth. A study of children's reactions to failure and an experimental attempt to modify them. *Child Develpm.,* 1937, **8,** 241–248.

Koch, Helen L. Popularity in children: some related factors and a technique for its measurement. *Child Develpm.,* 1933, **5,** 164–175.

Lesser, G. S., & Abelson, R. P. Personality correlates of persuasibility in children.

In I. C. Javis & C. I. Hovland et al. (Eds.), *Personality and persuasibility.* New Haven: Yale Univer. Press, 1959. Pp. 187–206.

Levy, D. M. *Maternal overprotection.* New York: Columbia Univer. Press, 1943.

McCurdy, H. G. The childhood pattern of genius. *J. Elisha Mitchell Sci. Society,* 1957, **73,** 448–462. (Also in R. A. King (Ed.), *Readings for an introduction to psychology.* New York: McGraw-Hill, 1961, 269–278.)

McKenney, Ruth. Paris! City of children. *Holiday,* April 1953, 63–68. (Also in W. S. Martin & Celia B. Stendler (Eds.), *Readings in child development.* New York: Harcourt, Brace, 1954. Pp. 199–203.)

Mann, J. H., & Mann, Carola H. The relative effectiveness of role playing and task oriented group experience in producing personality and behavior change. *J. soc. Psychol.,* 1960, **51,** 313–317.

Marshall, Helen R., & MacCandless, B. R. Relationships between dependence on adults and social acceptance by peers. *Child Develpm.,* 1957, **28,** 413–419.

Maudry, M., and Nekula, M. Social relations between children of the same age during the first two years of life. *J. genet. Psychol.,* 1939, **54,** 193–215.

Medinnus, G. R. Behavioral indices of social immaturity. Unpublished mss., San Jose State College, San Jose, Calif., 1962.

Moreno, J. L. *Who shall survive?* Washington, D. C.: Nerv. & Ment. Dis. Publ. Co., 1934.

Murphy, Lois B. *Social behavior and child personality.* New York: Columbia Univer. Press, 1937.

Newell, W. *Games and songs of American children.* New York: Harper, 1899.

Opie, Ione, and Opie, P. *The lore and language of school children.* London: Oxford at the Clarenden Press, 1959.

Page, M. L. The modification of ascendant behavior in preschool children. *Univer. Iowa Stud. Child Welf.,* 1936, **11,** No. 3.

Parten, Mildred. An analysis of social participation, leadership, and other factors in pre-school play groups. Ph.D. dissertation, Univer. of Minn., Minneapolis, 1929.

Parten, Mildred. Social participation among pre-school children. *J. abnorm. soc. Psychol.,* 1932, **27,** 243–269.

Parten, Mildred, & Newhall, S. M. Social behavior of preschool children. In R. G. Barker, J. S. Kounin, & H. F. Wright (Eds.), *Child behavior and development.* New York: McGraw-Hill, 1943. Pp. 509–525.

Piaget, J. *The moral judgment of the child.* New York: Harcourt, Brace, 1932.

Piaget, J. *The construction of reality in the child.* New York: Basic Books, 1954.

Potter, S. *The theory and art of gamesmanship.* New York: Holt, 1948.

Riesman, D. (with N. Glazer & R. Denny). *The lonely crowd.* New Haven, Conn.: Yale Univer. Press, 1950.

Roff, M. Childhood social interactions and young adult bad conduct. *J. abnorm. soc. Psychol.,* 1961, **63,** 333–337.

Smith, R. P. *"Where did you go?" "Out." "What did you do?" "Nothing."* New York: Pocket Books, 1958. (First published by Norton, New York, 1957.)

Spence, L. J. *Myth and ritual in dance, game, and rhyme.* London: Watts, 1947.

Sutton-Smith, B. The "it" role in children's games. *The Group,* 1955, **17,** 123–128.

Terman, L. M., et al. *Genetic studies of genius.* Vol. 1. Mental and physical traits of a thousand gifted children. Stanford, Calif.: Stanford Univer. Press, 1925.

Thomas, Isiah. *A little pretty pocketbook.* Worcester, Mass., 1787.

Tryon, Caroline M. Evaluation of adolescent personality by adolescents. *Monogr. soc. Res. Child Develpm.*, 1939, 4, No. 4.

Tuddenham, R. D. Studies in reputation: III. Correlates of popularity among elementary school children. *J. educ. Psychol.*, 1951, 42, 257–276.

Tuddenham, R. D. Studies in reputation: I. Sex and grade differences in school children's evaluation of their peers. II. The diagnosis of social adjustment. *Psychol. Monogr.*, 1952, 66, No. 333.

chapter 12 ✳ The Child in the School

The school transmits the values of the society to each succeeding generation of children, thus perpetuating the basic facets of a culture. Its significance in the child's life becomes clear from the realization that it is the setting for much of his relationship with his peers. Because of the social interaction occurring within it, the school, through its personnel, attempts to guide and facilitate the personality development of its pupils. This list is far from complete; the school has many other functions. No longer the center of community life as it was in rural America, the school continues to play an important role in the lives of young people from five to eighteen.

The concern of the present chapter is essentially the various aspects of school experience that influence the child's development of personality. Nursery school, the beginning of formal schooling and what it means to the child, the teacher's role in the classroom, especially her part in establishing a psychological atmosphere, the factors involved in achievement, social-class membership, and competition—all these will be considered in turn. Educational methodologies and materials are better left to texts on educational practice. Besides, the teacher's fund of knowledge, her enthusiasm, and the kind of psychological and emotional relationship existing between her and her pupils are the really crucial matters in the classroom most significantly affecting the child.

NURSERY-SCHOOL EXPERIENCE

In the 1930's child psychologists spent inordinate amounts of effort endeavoring to discover the relative contributions of heredity and environment to a child's intellectual development. One aspect of this issue—or indeed, controversy—was the effect of nursery-school experience. According to one camp (see Wellman, 1932; Skeels, Updegraff, Wellman, & Williams, 1938), nursery school produced a gain in IQ; according to another (see Olson & Hughes, 1940; Goodenough & Maurer, 1940) this was not necessarily so. More likely, attendance at nursery school may increase IQ scores but most probably it does not exert any long-range influence on the functioning of the intellect. Actually any increase in IQ scores flowing from such exposure may result from a variety of nonintellective factors, such as increased familiarity with the materials and tasks contained in intelligence tests and greater adult-child rapport.

The enriched nursery-school environment might have a salutary effect on children from deprived or impoverished backgrounds, but it is doubtful whether nursery-school experience will improve the IQs of children from homes offering an adequate amount of intellectual stimulation. Yet even if one were to concede that nursery school stimulated intellectual development, it would be difficult to identify the specific factors in the nursery-school environment that accounted for this.

By the 1940's interest had shifted to the effect of nursery-school experience on the child's social and emotional adjustment. Even before that time Walsh (1931) had found a number of personality traits to be more pronounced in a group of children who had had six months of nursery-school training than in a similar group lacking such experience. The former group seemed more spontaneous in behavior and showed more independence, initiative, self-reliance, and curiosity than the control group. Other early studies noted similar differences (Hattwick, 1936; Van Alstyne & Hattwick, 1939). Later, Bonney and Nicholson (1958) saw some indications that elementary-school children who had had previous exposure to nursery school were more popular with their peers. However, this was not found to be the case in several earlier studies reviewed by them; these showed negative findings regarding the relation between preschool experience and pupil adjustment.

Notwithstanding the inconclusive nature of the research available, some comments seem to be in order. The very nature of the nursery-school situation in which relatively large numbers of children interact under the supervision of one or two adults would tend to encourage the development of independent behavior. In such a setting the child must learn to fend for himself. In addition, a certain amount of social learning inevitably occurs from participation in the group over a period of time. Some behaviors are discovered to be unacceptable to peers whereas other behaviors result in pleasant, favorable responses and are thus reinforced. However, a follow-up study of a number of elementary-school children who had previously attended nursery school found consistency in behavior from nursery school through the elementary years, thus implying that peer responses alone may not suffice to remedy behavior difficulties (Van Alstyne & Hattwick, 1939). Since the source of such problems often lies in the parent-child relationship, which is a continuing one, influences outside the home cannot always counter those within it.

Nursery schools vary widely in goals and procedures. So do the behavioral results they hope to achieve in children. Certainly the quality of the school and the characteristics of the teacher determine the effects of this experience on the child. The importance of the teacher is reflected in an experimental study (Thompson, 1944) which analyzed the impact on nursery-school children of two different types of teacher-child relations. In one group the teacher was instructed to develop a warm relationship with each child and to stimulate the children's activities by providing information and assistance. In the other group contact between teacher and children remained at a minimum and the teacher participated in the children's activities only upon request. At the end of the school year the children in the first group in contrast to those in the second were seen to be more ascendant as well as more constructive in the face of possible failure. Moreover, they showed greater social participation and leadership. No noteworthy difference was detected between the two groups in nervous habits or IQ.

Attendance at a nursery school for at least part of the day may have some bearing on the relationship between mother and child. The time spent away from home may benefit both. The mother may enjoy temporary relief from her child-care responsibilities; the child enters a situation in which he learns to accommodate to the demands of an adult other than his parent. Very much like the effect of maternal employment on the child, the quality not the quantity of the mother-child interaction is the important thing. Quite possibly a reduction in quantity raises the level of the quality, or so it would seem from the typical report of mothers whose youngsters attend nursery school.

The nursery-school setting through its equipment and type of supervision is designed to reduce the amount of restrictions placed on a child and to encourage physical activity and self-expression. Few homes are arranged like it either with respect to schedule or physical facilities. In consequence, frictions present in the home, such as sibling rivalries or mother-child antagonisms centering about certain areas of behavior, can be minimized or avoided in the nursery-school setting.

However, this does not mean that compulsory school attendance should be lowered to the preschool years. Early child rearing is a parental responsibility and should perhaps remain so. The value of the nursery-school experience is that it may enable the parent to gain some insight and understanding about the child-rearing process from a new perspective.

FORMAL SCHOOLING

The beginning of school marks the end of an era for the child, chronologically and psychologically. Before the age of five the child interacts more with parents and siblings than anyone else. They are the greatest influence on him. To be sure, he has playmates in the neighborhood but his parents are the only adults he knows intimately. They set much of the pattern of his daily life. It is their approval that is most important to him. With the beginning of school the child's world expands and becomes more complex. He spends more of his time away from home in the company of people other than his immediate family. The opinions, approval, and demands of these people now become of increasing importance. Yet he may now need his parents more than ever before—at least they wish this.

> Entrance into the conventional first grade marks a sharp break in the actual structure of the child's experience. For the first time in the case of many children, they are expected to conform to a group pattern imposed by an adult who is in charge of too many children to be constantly aware of each child as an individual. Flash cards are flashed at the group all at once. Stories are told and everybody must listen whether he will or no. Drawing paper and crayons are meted out whether you happen to feel like drawing at that moment or not. One child who found this shift quite beyond endurance remarked after his first day in school, "It's awful; all you do is mind all day long." And another day he added, "It really is awful. All you do is sit and sit and sit" (Murphy, Murphy, & Newcomb, 1937, p. 652).

School Readiness

Some children adapt to the new conditions imposed by the start of formal education, whereas others encounter difficulties. How can these differences be explained? Are they predictable prior to school entrance so that some ameliorative measures might be applied? What sort of preschool experiences facilitate successful adjustment in the first grade? Although, of course, there are no final answers to these questions, data are available which permit some fairly certain conclusions.

One investigation that made use of anthropometric assessments of physique (Simon, 1959) found that students who were failing in first grade were less mature physically than a group of successful students. Thus physical maturity would seem to pertain to school readiness.

To check school readiness and adjustment to the first grade, Medinnus (1961a) subjected a small group of five-year-olds to a series of tests in the year prior to their starting school. He also interviewed their mothers, made ratings of the psychological atmosphere of their homes, and had both parents complete a standard parent-attitude questionnaire. Upon the children's completion of the first grade, he correlated their scores on several criteria of achievement with their scores on academic skill-type tests. In addition, he related teacher ratings of general adjustment in the first grade to the scores obtained through assessment of the home psychological atmosphere. What he found was a moderate correlation of about +.50 between the children's IQ scores on a Stanford-Binet test administered before school entrance and their achievement scores at the end of the first grade. Thus, although intelligence is important in academic success in the first grade, other factors such as motivation, interest, and application also seem to have relevance. Further, Medinnus noted that the amount of information possessed by a child prior to entering school predicted reading achievement by the end of the first grade.

To discover how much children knew before their entrance into first grade, Medinnus confronted them with a questionnaire which modified one used by Templin (1958). These were some of its questions:

How many pennies in a nickel?
Friday, Saturday, Sunday—what day comes after Sunday?
What are the colors in the flag?
What is a helicopter?
What are clouds made of?
Whom was Red Riding Hood going to see?

What was the name of the boy who climbed the beanstalk?
What do we call a butterfly before it becomes a butterfly?
What is butter made from?
What is the brake on a car for?
In what game do you have a home run?

Among 40 five-year-olds quizzed, Medinnus found a wide range of total scores. Because of a substantial correlation between the children's mental ages and their scores, it was impossible to attribute higher performance on the information test to a richer home environment. Of course, innately more intelligent children turn up oftener in the better socioeconomic homes where parents provide a fuller, more stimulating environment than is supplied by lower-class parents. However, irrespective of socioeconomic status, the amount of time a parent spends reading to a child and the variety of experiences to which the youngster is exposed—trips, museums, zoos—serve to expand the quantity of his information.

Although IQ predicts academic success in the first grade better than any other measure, the importance of an intellectually stimulating home environment must not be underestimated. First-grade children who scored high on a standard measure of mental maturity, Milner (1951) learned, came from homes with more books available; these children were read to oftener by their parents and in general experienced a more positive emotional relationship with their parents than children who scored low. Time spent reading to a child accomplishes many things. It establishes a warm, friendly relationship between parent and child which increases the child's sense of security. The child's questions and comments inspired by the reading aids the parent's understanding of the child. And the influence of parent reading to child is certainly evident in the child's record of achievement.

From what the mothers told him in their interview, Medinnus rated their homes on a number of the Fels Parent Rating Behavior Scales. The differences in the ratings of homes of well-adjusted and poorly adjusted first graders showed a higher rating on a "Dependence-Encouraging factor" for those of the well-adjusted children (Medinnus, 1961b). This is borne out by Chance's (1961) study of academic achievement in the first grade. Mothers of the children who achieved above average in relation to intelligence favored later independence for them than mothers of children whose achievement on the basis of intelligence was low. Both findings seem to contradict the common notion that parents should stress early independence in their children to prepare them for school life. To Medinnus, great parental concern with the encouragement of independence perhaps reflected a basic rejection of the child. Parental clichés that children must learn to "stand on their own two feet," and "fight their own battles" may be attempts to justify an unwillingness to provide the child with emotional support, nurture, and acceptance. The teacher can teach the child to count but can never fully compensate for a lack of parental love and acceptance. Parents best prepare their children for school with affectional, accepting relationships.

Readiness Tests. A number of academic-readiness tests predict a child's capacity to master intellectual tasks and aid a teacher in identifying areas of strength and weakness in a particular child. Most of those tests at first-grade level assess reading readiness since reading is the primary preoccupation in the early elementary years. The principal element in most tests of reading readiness is the ability to discriminate word and letter forms. Comprehension and range of information are also included. Figure 12-1 illustrates the kind of things contained in a reading-readiness test.

Since the term *readiness* implies both level of maturity and prior experience, probably the best clues to academic achievement in first grade are scores of IQ tests and information tests. The former assesses mental maturity and the latter provides a measure of the range of the child's experiences. Correlations between certain tests administered to five-year-olds and the youngsters' achievement in reading at the end of first grade are presented in Table 12-1 (Medinnus, 1961a).

School Entrance and the Child

It is only natural to expect some changes in the child as a result of exposure to the formal school situation. Conformity to the demands of a new adult, intimate contact with a number of other children, separation from the mother for a substantial part of the day—all these must impinge on the child's behavior and his concept of the self. Information pertinent to this point was obtained by Stendler and Young (1950, 1959) in interviews with more than 200 mothers before their child began school, after he had been in school for approximately two months, and finally, after eight months of first-grade life.

An overwhelming majority reported that their child was looking forward to the beginning of school with some eagerness. The children's anticipations dealt with learning to read, write, and do numbers. Although middle-class parents are more likely than lower-class parents to teach the child various intellectual skills (Stendler, 1951),

Test 1:
Directions: Find a letter the same as this one. Draw a line from this letter to this one. You draw it now.

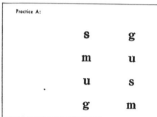

Practice A:

s	g
m	u
u	s
g	m

Test 2:
Directions: Look at these letters. Can you find the letter that is not the same as the others? Now draw a line through it to show that it does not belong there.

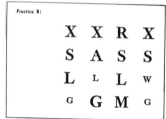

Practice B:

X	X	R	X
S	A	S	S
L	L	L	w
G	G	M	G

Test 3:
Directions: Put a mark on the cat. Now put a mark on the boy running.

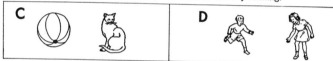

Test 4:
Directions: Look at the first large letter. Then find another which is just like it. Put a mark on it.

E O	M	O	R	S

FIGURE 12-1   Sample items from the Lee-Clark Reading Readiness Test (Lee & Clark, 1951).

the six-year-old generally knows the alphabet, some nursery rhymes and songs, and counting, and can usually write his name. Perhaps more important than these is the fact that the parents portray the school to the child as a socializing agent. Certain kinds of behaviors are required by the teacher and she has the authority to enforce them.

Most of the mothers said the child's behavior changed with school entrance, mainly in a positive way. The children took more responsibility, they helped more at home, and they showed greater self-control and more independent demeanor at the table, in dressing, and in

TABLE 12-1   Correlates of First-Grade Reading Achievement

SRA Achievement Test

	Language Perception	Verbal- Pictorial	Vocabulary	Comprehension
Stanford-Binet IQ	.51	.57	.41	.57
Gates Reading Readiness	.61	.57	.54	.64
Information test	.48	.51	.46	.42
Draw-A-Man IQ	.25	.36	.31	.22

going on errands. Two kinds of difficulties encountered by the child, both arising from social relations, were mentioned by the mothers. In more than half the interviews, they spoke of aggressiveness on the part of other children or of exclusion from a group. Thus, school attendance clearly involves much social learning. The child learns new behaviors, new ways of adjusting to other children, new roles to play.

No doubt some children are more successful initially at social interaction and some are more capable than others in meeting new social demands and in making the necessary social adjustments. For these reasons teachers must remain alert to children who run into difficulties in peer relations. Guidance and encouragement can be effective in aiding a child to build up self-confidence and confidence in others. If the wrong pattern is established early in the school career it may be difficult to modify.

Toward the end of the first year, a preponderant number of the mothers reported continued improvement among their children in such traits as maturity, self-control, helpfulness, responsibility, self-confidence, and getting along with playmates. Perhaps in consequence, more than half of them felt the first-grade year had been an easier one on them in their relationships with their children. Most of the children themselves continued to like school and the teacher, a liking that grew for many throughout the school year.

The beginning of school, then, is a significant moment for a child. Persons other than his immediate family begin to play an important role in the socialization process. His success in this new venture and his adjustment to its demands depend intimately on the skills and attitudes he brings to the new situation. However, the child's relation-

ship with his parents continues to exert its influence on his behavior—
and so it shall continue to be.

THE TEACHER

Throughout the child's days in school, especially during his early
years there, the teacher without doubt exercises the most significant
psychological influence on him. The physical plant of the school,
the teaching materials, the classroom schedule and routine all wane
in comparison with the potential impact of the teacher on the child—
on his adjustment to school, on his personality development, and on
his academic achievement. Interest and encouragement shown by a
teacher may determine the choice of a career or a decision about
values. Second only to the role of parent in its effect on the child,
the teacher role becomes costly if filled by any but the very best people.
It is the teacher more than the doctor, lawyer, journalist, or entertainer
who can inspire the leaders of tomorrow, the new generation, and
through these children influence the world of the future.

Teacher Functions

Both teachers and parents are concerned in Western culture with
the psychological and emotional welfare of the child. Both constrain
behavior. Both are in a position to enforce standards of conduct.
Yet the functions assigned to each differ. The teacher does not have
the responsibility for the child's physical welfare outside the school
setting—that is a parent function—but is charged with stimulating and
guiding the child's intellectual development. Moreover, because of
the nature of the school situation, the teacher is influential in determining the child's attitudes and values.

How does this influence work? Obviously the teacher's values are
communicated to the pupils directly through rules, comments, commands, and discussions. But perhaps what a teacher says is less important than what she does. The teacher serves as a model for the
children; they identify with her and try to emulate her. Teacher
approval is sought. Teacher disapproval is avoided. Indeed, the
parent may feel somewhat rejected when his first-grade child declares,
"I love my teacher more than anyone else in the world," or when a
second grader insists, "No, mother. My teacher wants me to do it
this way and she's right." Nor is it any accident when a third grader
calls the teacher "mother." She is, in fact, a mother surrogate—a

mother substitute—for the young, school-aged child. The child's attitudes toward his parents may extend to the teacher or the teacher may actually take the place of an absent or neglectful parent in a child's emotional life. At late as preadolescence, _hero worship_ of a teacher may still appear in a child.

However, the functions of a teacher are limited by the primary function of teaching. The teacher is not a therapist. She cannot practice individual therapy with certain children. She can, of course, create an atmosphere in the classroom which is conducive to the mental health of the pupils. In general, the teacher can alleviate or aggravate children's problems. But she can never substitute fully for a parent who is either physically absent or psychologically inadequate. Teachers function most efficiently and effectively when parents discharge their responsibility to the child. Frequently they are heard to remark that although they are aware of a particular child's emotional needs, their responsibility to the remaining 30 or 35 members of the class prevents their taking as much action toward this child as they might like. Their job is to teach certain academic skills; though responsible to an extent for the emotional and psychological well-being of their pupils, teachers can be neither psychotherapists nor parent substitutes.

Who Become Teachers?

A host of factors determine vocational choice. Among these are personality, attitudes and goals, social-class background, parental influences, and patterns of interest. Probably one or more of these differentiate the individuals in various occupations: teacher, engineer, plumber, carpenter, salesman, small businessman. Information on the backgrounds of teachers is slight, yet there certainly are factors favoring teaching over some other pursuit.

It has been emphasized many times that teachers come from middle-class backgrounds. Although this may be true, is it of any greater significance than personality factors which research has largely ignored? Table 12-2 contains the results of a survey of occupations of the fathers of a group of teachers (Stiles, 1957, p. 14). These figures would doubtless vary with a shift in geographical location. However, it is apparent that notwithstanding the underrepresentation of teachers from laboring-class backgrounds in relation to the proportion of laboring-class families in the population, such teachers do constitute a fair percentage of those surveyed.

Although data on trends showing changes in the social-class backgrounds of teachers over the years are scarce, several factors suggest

TABLE 12-2 Father's Occupations of a Sample
of Detroit Teachers

Occupational Grouping	Number	Per Cent
Professional	20	10.1
Business, managerial, etc.	31	15.6
Other white collar	25	12.6
Farmer	11	5.5
Skilled labor	27	13.6
Other labor	57	28.8
Retired, unemployed, dead	27	13.6

that present-day teachers are drawn in larger numbers from the lower class than was the case some decades back. The GI Bill, by giving financial aid to veterans of the Second World War who wished to attend college, made higher education available to numbers of young men who could not otherwise have afforded it. A rise in income among unskilled and skilled laborers during and since the war has enabled many a skilled worker to help his children through college. Then, too, decentralization of state colleges and universities has made these facilities accessible to more young people at lower cost. In 1962, for example, California had 70 junior and 16 state colleges. Indeed, Stiles (1957) reported that the teaching profession provided an opportunity for upward social mobility for at least 40 per cent of those who entered the field.

Numerous reasons have been advanced as the motive for choosing teaching as a profession. They include the desire for status in a respectable, middle-class pursuit, the need for security, an identification with a former teacher, a need for power and group leadership, family pressures, guaranteed superiority, and perhaps, inability to meet academic requisites of some other calling. From a survey of 150 Texas teachers (see Stiles, 1957) it was concluded that a large proportion of people entered teaching because they valued the security and predictability of behavior offered by the school system, and because doing so represented a continuance of close ties and strong identification with parent figures. Hopefully, there are teachers who are motivated to teach by the desire to make young people explore the unexplored, seek the unsought, and ponder the imponderable. Intellectual curiosity, yearning for the strange and new and novel, fearlessness in the face of unanswered questions cannot be aroused in children unless teachers themselves possess these qualities. It is not enough to be motivated to teach by a love for children. A love of their potentialities, their eagerness, their vision may be vastly more important.

Attitudes toward Child Behavior

If the teacher insists on a quiet, orderly classroom as an essential part of an efficient learning setting, anything that interferes with orderliness is of concern to her. Classroom behavior that prevents accomplishing the goal of producing academic achievement in pupils is viewed with disfavor. Certainly such achievement by the children contributes to the job satisfaction an individual finds in teaching. But are teachers overconcerned with behavior that disrupts management of the classroom and underconcerned with behavior that indicates possible maladjustment of individual personality? In a classic study of teacher attitudes toward children's behavior problems, Wickman (1928) observed appreciable differences between teachers and mental hygienists in their ratings of the seriousness of various behaviors in children. In general, the hygienists rated as most serious withdrawal, recessive behavior, and unsocial kinds of behavior. The teachers, on the other hand, regarded these particular behaviors as least serious, showing greatest concern over sex problems and behavior that transgressed authority and violated classroom rules. Wickman argued that teacher attitudes should move toward the direction of those held by the mental hygienists; they should display less concern for antisocial and deviant behaviors in violation of the rules and more concern for unsocial behavior indicative of emotional or social maladjustment.

Despite the many criticisms directed against the Wickman study, a number of subsequent investigations have supported his main thesis. Moreover, recent studies indicate some shift in teacher attitudes toward the mental hygienists' point of view. Table 12-3 (Hunter, 1957, pp. 8–9) ranks the seriousness of 50 child behavior problems as seen by teachers and mental hygienists in the 1920's and by teachers in the 1950's. Many reasons can be expressed for the differences between teachers and hygienists in the Wickman study and for the shift in the attitudes of teachers over the years (Beilin, 1959). The principal concern of the teacher is to teach academic skills whereas the main concern of the clinician is the emotional adjustment of the child.

TABLE 12-3   Comparison of Mean Ratings* by Teachers in 1955 and by Teachers and Mental Hygienists in 1926 of the Relative Seriousness of 50 Behavior Problems

Behavior Problems	Teachers (1955) N = 308	Teachers (1926) N = 511	Mental Hygienists (1926) N = 30
1. Stealing	14.9	17.0	12.5
2. Destroying school materials	13.7	14.3	5.1
3. Truancy	13.6	15.6	10.3
4. Cruelty, bullying	13.5	14.8	13.5
5. Unhappy, depressed	13.4	11.5	16.2
6. Impertinence, defiance	13.4	15.0	7.1
7. Untruthfulness	13.3	15.8	10.3
8. Unreliableness	13.1	13.9	10.4
9. Disobedience	13.0	14.1	6.4
10. Heterosexual activity	12.9	17.3	9.9
11. Resentfulness	12.5	10.8	14.1
12. Impudence, rudeness	12.4	12.2	7.6
13. Lack of interest in work	12.1	12.8	9.6
14. Quarrelsomeness	12.0	11.1	8.3
15. Easily discouraged	11.9	11.5	13.4
16. Cheating	11.9	14.7	10.3
17. Carelessness in work	11.8	11.3	7.1
18. Temper tantrums	11.7	13.0	11.7
19. Unsocial, withdrawing	11.6	8.3	17.3
20. Selfishness	11.6	11.3	11.8
21. Laziness	11.6	12.2	7.2
22. Disorderliness in class	11.5	11.7	3.4
23. Obscene notes, talk	11.5	16.6	8.8
24. Suggestible	11.4	11.0	13.3
25. Domineering	11.2	10.3	13.0
26. Inattention	11.1	11.2	7.3

* Rating chart: slight consequence, 5.0; considerable difficulty, 12.0; extremely grave problem, 20.0.

Yet over the years, the child psychologist has communicated to teachers his concern with the personality adjustment of children. He has done so through the psychology courses which have become a part of many teacher-training programs. Besides, the mental-hygiene point of view that adjustment problems themselves impede the learning process has been widely adopted by educational psychologists. Although teachers will continue to be irked by behaviors that disrupt

TABLE 12-3 (*Continued*)

Behavior Problems	Teachers (1955) N = 308	Teachers (1926) N = 511	Mental Hygienists (1926) N = 30
27. Nervousness	11.1	11.7	11.3
28. Masturbation	10.7	16.7	6.4
29. Profanity	10.5	12.3	2.9
30. Fearfulness	10.4	9.7	14.0
31. Sullenness	10.2	9.9	12.6
32. Attracting attention	10.2	8.5	8.5
33. Stubbornness	10.1	10.3	10.9
34. Over-critical of others	9.8	7.9	13.2
35. Physical cowardice	9.8	10.4	12.0
36. Thoughtlessness	9.7	8.7	6.8
37. Tardiness	9.7	10.5	5.6
38. Slovenly in appearance	9.7	10.1	7.2
39. Sensitiveness	9.6	7.0	13.1
40. Shyness	9.5	5.4	12.5
41. Suspiciousness	9.5	9.1	16.4
42. Enuresis	9.2	11.8	9.2
43. Interrupting	9.0	8.0	2.8
44. Inquisitiveness	8.8	8.0	5.3
45. Dreaminess	8.8	8.3	11.3
46. Restlessness	8.6	6.9	6.4
47. Tattling	8.1	7.5	8.8
48. Imaginative lying	8.0	8.1	7.5
49. Smoking	7.3	12.0	2.3
50. Whispering	6.3	7.5	0.8
Average	10.9	11.3	9.5

classroom routine—and to some extent this is a valid concern—a more thorough understanding of the place of adjustment in the learning process may lead to a true convergence of the teaching and clinical approaches to learning. Irritations caused by disruptive conduct in the classroom may interfere far less with a child's learning than emotional discomforts from within. Life during school hours can never be separated from those preceding or following them.

Teacher Adjustment

Just as the personality of the parent may be more significant than parent attitudes and behavior in affecting the child (see Chapter 10), so it is with teachers. Here again, as in parent-child research, there is little information to support the hypothesis. After reviewing numerous studies on this point, Snyder (1947) concluded that the evidence was overwhelming that the personal adjustment of the teacher had an influence on the pupils. Good adjustment in the teacher promoted favorable adjustment in the pupils; the converse was also true. However, reviewing the same studies, Gladstone (1948) maintained there was no strong confirmatory evidence. Gladstone even proposed that certain unfulfilled needs of some teachers might result in behavior beneficial to pupils. A strong need to display affection, for example, might cause the teacher to lavish affection on some child.

To Gladstone the teacher's adjustment *to the teaching role* in the classroom was potentially most significant in affecting the children. An individual might be an inspiring, beloved teacher, yet function far less effectively in the spouse, parent, or colleague role. Indeed far more knowledge is needed on this matter than is now available. In one study that trained teachers to appreciate the mental-health point of view of children and their problems (Baruch, 1945), those teachers who showed the greatest gains in personal adjustment disclosed the greatest acceptance of child behavior. In other words, self-acceptance apparently has to precede acceptance of others.

Teacher Problems

The teacher has suffered much criticism. She is a convenient target for parents frustrated or dissatisfied by their children. But what of the view from the teacher's rostrum? Teacher complaints are many. When asked to list the mental-health hazards facing them in the classroom, teachers point out that most of them deal with out-of-the-classroom phenomena. Conflicting personalities among colleagues, intraschool jealousies, fear of expression of honest opinions about schools, too many interruptions, undue amounts of needless paper work, too little time for parent conferences, inadequate pay, supplies, and equipment, conflicts with administrative policy, malfunctioning of the P.T.A., lack of recognition for work well done are some of the "rewards" of selecting a teaching career (Keliher, 1950; Kvaraceus, 1951).

To understand the teacher one must understand the entire school setting. Each classroom is not an isolated unit. Each teacher must interact with other teachers as well as with administrative personnel. Good relations among the entire school staff are essential for smooth functioning of the school. Although behavior problems posed by children in the classroom are of immediate concern to the teacher and must be handled, they seem to create fewer difficulties than other aspects of the teacher role.

Teacher-Pupil Interactions

The praise, reward, disapproval, and punishment administered by the teacher inevitably affect the emotional adjustment and self concept of some, if not all, pupils. Are these forms of encouragement or discipline dispensed in equal measure to all pupils? Or are certain ones more likely to be praised or punished? Clearly, the teacher receives the most satisfaction from children who learn rapidly and who without difficulty grasp the material presented. After all, the teacher's sense of adequacy as a teacher depends in large part on how well she accomplishes her primary mission of teaching the academic skills.

A study of the pattern of teacher approval and disapproval supports this notion (DeGroat & Thompson, 1949). To a sixth-grade class a Guess Who technique of a dozen statements of teacher approval and an equal number of statements of teacher disapproval was applied. Some of these statements were: "Here is someone whose work is often pointed out as being very neat"; "Here is someone on whom the teacher calls when she wants the right answer"; "Here is someone whom the teacher often asks to do errands for her or to be monitor while she is out of the room"; "Here is someone whom the teacher often scolds for disturbing the class in some way (shooting paper wads, chewing gum, etc.)"; "Here is someone who is often suspected by the teacher when something happens while she is out of the room"; "Here is someone who is often pointed out as not doing [his] best work." By and large, relatively few children were nominated for either teacher approval or disapproval. This suggested that certain pupils enjoyed a much higher level of interaction with the teacher than others.

Several characteristics differentiated the High Approval-Low Disapproval group from the Low Approval-Low Disapproval and High Disapproval-Low Approval groups. Those children of high approval were more intelligent; they rated higher in academic achievement and their scores on a personality-adjustment test were more favorable. Allowing for the tenuousness of cause-and-effect statements, this last point demonstrates the connection between teacher approval and pupil self-acceptance. This relationship may be viewed in various ways: those pupils who are more self-accepting elicit a favorable response in the teacher, or, the teacher's good reaction to the child's behavior is conducive to an attitude of self-acceptance in the child. In any case, it seems unfortunate that teacher approval is limited to relatively few pupils—at least as perceived by the children themselves. Perhaps those who most need overt signs of teacher approval are least likely to receive them.

One investigation (Hoehn, 1954) found that teachers had more favorable contacts with children of high economic status than with those from lower economic backgrounds. Conversely more conflict was seen between the teacher and the children of low economic status, especially among boys, than with youngsters of upper economic station. Hoehn concluded, however, that the basic factor in the contact between teacher and child was the latter's academic achievement. Quantitatively there was more contact between the teacher and low achievers but qualitatively the tie between teacher and high achievers was more favorable.

In a study by Meyer and Thompson (1956) involving both the Guess Who technique and classroom observations of teacher-pupil interaction, boys were seen to receive more teacher disapproval than girls. If this is true of the typical classroom situation, it is small wonder that boys more often than girls express dislike for school. The demands of school routine for orderliness and quiet are quite alien to the active, aggressive nature of boys. And when the resulting rebellious behavior brings forth blame and disapproval from the teacher, further hostility is generated. This is hardly likely to produce an atmosphere conducive to learning.

It has been shown that interaction between teacher and pupil relates to the pupil's acceptance by others as well as to his self-acceptance. Three studies, one at the first-grade level (Medinnus, 1962b), another at sixth-grade level (Gronlund, 1953), and a third at tenth-grade level (Flanders and Havumaki, 1960), have all found that pupils receiving praise from teachers and preferred by teachers were more likely to be chosen by peers in a sociometric exercise, thus indicating greater acceptance by peers. To Medinnus this suggested that at the first-grade level children so identified with the teacher that her values became theirs. Behaviors praised by the teacher acquired positive, favorable value whereas those viewed negatively by her were similarly devalued by the pupils. In like manner, the teacher is able to influence the attitudes of the pupils in a great number of areas—attitudes toward minority-group children, personal likes and dislikes in others, attitudes toward handicapped or less favorably endowed children, and the like.

CLASSROOM ATMOSPHERE

Drawn from another science, the terms *atmosphere* and *climate* denote the sociopsychological relationships existing among the group in the classroom setting. Though perhaps applied somewhat awkwardly to the classroom, the two terms accurately suggest the pervasiveness of the psychological tone present in any single schoolroom. To a large extent it is the teacher who establishes the relationships that determine the prevailing psychological atmosphere.

Types of Atmosphere

What are the principal types of relationships that create a particular atmosphere in the classroom? Many categories have been used to measure the relationship between teacher and pupils. These categories have then become indices of the over-all classroom atmosphere. They include dominating, integrating, learner-centered, teacher-centered, democratic, *laissez faire*, authoritarian, and more. In one study of the social and emotional climate of classrooms (Withall, 1949), teacher behavior fell into seven main classes, of which six fitted into the two categories, learner-centered and teacher-centered. The learner-centered behaviors were of three kinds: statements supporting the learner which reassured or commended him; statements accepting and clarifying the pupil which helped him refine his ideas and feelings and which gave him the sense of being understood; and statements or questions about the structure of problems which provided information or raised questions about a problem in a manner that facilitated its solution. The teacher-centered behaviors were also of three kinds: directive statements which outlined a recommended course of action for the pupil to follow; reproving or deprecatory statements intended to deter pupils from unacceptable behavior; and self-supporting statements designed to justify the teacher's position or actions.

A further study by the same investigator (Withall, 1952) dealing with four seventh-grade classes showed marked differences in the atmosphere under these four teachers. Yet from day to day there was a moderate amount of consistency for any one of them. Although knowledge is rather fragmentary on the effects of different classroom atmospheres on the emotional adjustment and academic accomplishments of pupils, certain kinds of psychological relations between teacher and children are far more conducive than others to the emotional and intellectual well-being of the youngsters in a school setting.

Anderson has distinguished between the dominating and socially integrating behavior. Integrating behavior was described as "flexible, dynamic, yielding, spontaneous." The individual who showed this behavior sought and found "common purposes with another; he expended energy with another, not against another." Dominating behavior, on the other hand, was "rigid, fixed, static." The dominating individual neither respected nor attempted to understand another's individuality. Energy was expended against another individual; the conflict of differences grew. Integrating behavior tended to elicit the same kind of behavior in someone else, whereas dominating behavior led to similar behavior in others (Anderson, 1939b). Some tie was found between integrative scores of children and chronological age, suggesting that perhaps in a developmental sense at least an integrating behavior was a sign of maturity (Anderson, 1937a). Although developed originally to assess the social interaction of preschool children (Anderson, 1937a, b; 1939b), the two categories of dominating and socially integrating behavior have been applied pertinently to the classroom interaction of teacher and pupils.

A group of kindergarten children were making May baskets. Terry had folded his basket on the lines which had been drawn on the material the night before by the teacher. He had pasted the flaps as he had been instructed and had the handle fastened in place. The teacher had cut out of other paper a handful of diamond-shaped pieces which she had distributed four to a child. These were to serve as decorations to be pasted horizontally on the basket. As she walked about the room she noticed Terry pasting his diamond decoration vertically.

"Oh, oh, Terry," she said. "The decorations are to be pasted on lying down and not standing up."

"But I want to paste mine this way," said Terry.

"Well, that isn't the way they are supposed to go. Here now, just paste it this way." And she turned the diamond horizontally and pasted it before Terry seemed to know what had happened. She remained while Terry at her instructions pasted two more shapes horizontally. Then she turned away, leaving Terry to paste the fourth.

At the end of the period Terry had only three decorations on his basket. When the teacher inquired about his basket, Terry, pointing to the undecorated side of his basket, said that he did not want one there.

"Oh, but every basket should have four. Here is one your color.

We'll just paste it on quickly." And with Terry speechless and trans-
fixed she pasted it on quickly.

Mary Lou had observed that at her table several handles did not
stick. "I guess I don't want a handle," she remarked to the boy seated
next to her. She cut up the handle of her basket and pasted the pieces
as decorations all over the basket. The teacher's remark to this *fait
accompli* was, "Oh, you've spoiled yours, Mary Lou; yours is all messy
and doesn't have a handle" (Anderson, 1943, p. 459).

Certainly the kind of teacher behavior described in the foregoing
excerpt fits Withall's teacher-centered category. Noncompliance with
goals defined by the teacher is castigated. No respect is shown for
either the child's wishes or his individuality.

Through observation and recording of the interaction between
teacher and pupils, Anderson (1939a, b) found teachers varying in
dominating and integrating classroom behavior. In contacts with
individual students, two teachers had twice as many dominating as
integrating relationships, whereas a third teacher had five times as
many dominating associations as integrating ones. In behavior toward
their whole class, the dominating characteristic in all three teachers
outdid the integrating by a ratio of five to one. Among pupils there
were wide differences in the extent and nature of their contact with
the teacher, as shown in Figure 12-2.

Teacher Influence

Because of the importance of the classroom teacher as a model for
the children, it might be wise to examine what happens to the child
whose contact with her is governed by dominating behavior. If he
develops antagonism or feelings of resentment these may impair his
capacity to learn.

The key role of the teacher in influencing classroom behavior and
establishing psychological atmosphere is illustrated in a classic study
of experimentally created social climates in boys' groups (Lewin, Lippitt, & White, 1939; see also Lippitt, 1940, and Lippitt & White, 1943).
Four groups, each composed of five ten-year-old boys, were exposed
in turn to three different social climates: democratic, autocratic, and
laissez faire. The four boys' clubs all participated in the same activity,
making masks, in a single physical setting. In the authoritarian
climate the leader set policy and made all major decisions, keeping
himself aloof from active participation with the group. Under the
democratic climate policies and decisions were determined and reached
through group discussion encouraged by the leader. The boys were

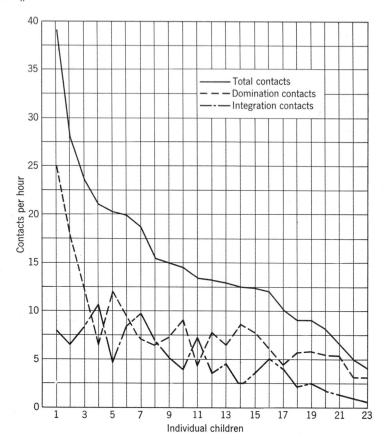

FIGURE 12-2 Mean number of contacts per hour which teacher *A* had with individual children enrolled in the morning session (Anderson, 1939b, p. 337).

free to select tasks and choose partners. In the *laissez faire* climate there was complete freedom, with a minimum of leader participation. The leader supplied information when requested but otherwise did not engage in the group's activities. Table 12-4 lists some of the behavioral consequences of the different social climates.

The autocratic approach limits and restricts the child's behavior, producing frustration. Although an autocratic leader may prevent the aggressive conduct engendered by frustration, tensions increase and aggressiveness arises when he is absent. Indeed, the orderliness and appearance of "control" in a classroom may actually camouflage the tensions created by too much restriction and too little freedom. Little group spirit and not much acceptance of a common goal develop

TABLE 12-4   Reaction to Three Social Climates

Autocratic			
Submissive Reaction	*Aggressive Reaction*	*Democratic*	*Laissez faire*
Low acceptance of group goal		High group morale	Low group morale
High dependence on leader		High acceptance of group goal	Quarrelsome
Low group morale			Bored
		Creative and	
Few friendly contacts among group members		constructive work products	Inefficient
			Disorganized
Group tension	Expression of aggression		
General apathy	Scapegoating		

in an autocratic climate because of the leader's usurpation of the decision-making process. Active interest in a task comes only from self-determination. Under *laissez faire*, at the other extreme from autocracy, children seem to benefit from some adult guidance and encouragement after they have reached a certain age level. Most of us can recall entire afternoons of early childhood bickering and haggling with parents in a futile attempt to reach some decision regarding how to spend the day. As in parent-child relations, democracy in the classroom does not signify a *laissez faire*, "hands off" policy. Through its tenets, democracy brings about creative effort, high morale, and an eagerness to accept the goals of the group.

Determining Factors

What are the personality factors and attitudes in the teacher which give rise to the psychological atmosphere established in the classroom? The autocratic teacher is inflexible and irresponsive to the needs of the children. For him autocracy is the easiest and most expedient atmosphere to maintain. It does not necessitate any consideration of the desires, personalities, or needs of each pupil. A democratic atmosphere, to the contrary, requires flexibility, sensitivity, and alertness to the individuality of the children. It makes far greater personality demands on the teacher. Because of its evident effect on the child, the democratic approach seems worth the effort involved. Control and discipline must come from within if they are to be effective; when both are self-imposed one can be sure that a major objective of socialization has been attained. The child's active participation in the setting of goals is always greater when encouraged by democratic leadership, when the teacher has a warm, cooperating, inspiring personality. And this applies equally to the accomplishment of a given task and the development of a specific behavior.

Children's Evaluation of Teachers

When asked to name reasons for disliking school, children mention the teacher more frequently than any other factor (Tenenbaum, 1940). Children hold positive opinions about their teachers and the qualities they prefer in them. The qualities they single out refer as often to characteristics of the teacher as an individual as to the characteristics of her teaching ability. One study, in fact, noted that a majority of the traits used by elementary-school children to describe well-liked teachers covered personality and disposition (Leeds & Cook, 1947).

Jersild (1940) found elementary-school children mentioning these qualities as typical of the teachers they liked best: *human qualities as a person*—sympathetic, cheerful, good tempered; *physical appearance, grooming, voice*—attractive, neat, nice manner of talking; *traits as a disciplinarian or director of class*—fair, consistent, did not scold or shout; *participation in activities*—joined in or permitted games or play; *performance as a teacher*—enthusiastic, resourceful, explained well, permitted expression of opinion. The age trend in the descriptions was worth noting; high-school students more frequently picked characteristics bearing on teaching ability whereas younger children singled out interesting projects introduced by the teacher. At all ages children valued highly the teacher who showed sensitivity and understanding toward them and who was effective and enthusiastic.

Through daily contact and interaction, the personality of the teacher affects the children and is basic in setting the emotional tone of the classroom. If the emotional relation between teacher and pupil affects the latter's learning experience, the child's perception of the teacher is of vital importance, especially when the teacher is a warm, helpful individual. This is perhaps truer in elementary school where the teacher indeed serves as a mother surrogate. An unsympathetic, ill-tempered, unfair, uninteresting teacher certainly cannot kindle children's interest in school and in the entire learning process.

SCHOOL ACHIEVEMENT

Since the primary goal of the school is the acquisition of academic skills by pupils, the extent to which this goal is attained reflects the success of the school's endeavor. It is not surprising, therefore, that great attention has been paid to academic achievement. Most research on the subject has sought to identify the factors responsible for differences in individual accomplishment. There are important reasons for this concern. Perhaps most significant is the obvious waste of human potentialities when children perform below their capacities. Furthermore, if the reason for a child's underachievement can be discovered, remedial measures might be undertaken.

Perhaps the single factor most related to academic achievement is intellectual capacity. The speed and level at which an individual acquires knowledge together with the facility to comprehend abstract concepts are key elements in learning ability. That intelligence bears on academic achievement is seen in the similarity of the tasks included in intelligence tests to those involved in school learning, at least after the early elementary school years. That is to say, the overlap helps to verify the tie. Yet other factors besides intellect influence achievement in school. This is born out by the clustering of correlations between intelligence-test scores and scores of academic achievement at about +.55.

Much of the discussion among educators about underachievement in the first grade and in the early elementary years has centered about the question of immaturity. The term needs definition. Few attempts have been made to define or evaluate emotional immaturity. Physiological and chronological immaturity are another matter. In a study comparing the scholastic achievement of 50 overage and 50 underage pupils in grades two through six, Carter (1956) found that 87 per cent of the underaged did not measure up to the classroom performance of children of normal age. Carter further noted that chronological age had a greater affect on boys than on girls. Simon (1959) observed failing students to be less mature than successful ones on several measures of physiological configuration even when the two were matched on IQ and chronological age. Among third-grade children, Klausmeier and Check (1959) detected a connection between physical development and reading and arithmetic achievement in boys, yet not in girls. Medinnus (1961c) proposed that although chronological age might shape a child's initial adjustment to first grade, it might be less important than other factors by the end of the year. This is seen in the low correlation of +.21 between chronological age and scores of adjustment after a year of schooling. Academic achievement, however, was only one of several factors entering into the assessment of general adjustment.

Parental Factors

A variety of parental factors influence a child's achievement in every school grade. These include the emotional relationship between parent and child, the attitudes of the parent toward school and school achievement, and parental concern for and interest in the child's performance. Psychologists have sought to find the forces behind a general drive for achievement, academic as well as other kinds (see McClelland, Atkinson, Clark, & Lowell, 1953; Atkinson, 1958). One of them (Winterbottom, 1953) established a relationship between a mother's encouragement of early independence and a child's motivation to achieve. The following questionnaire, presented to 29 women whose sons fell into two groups, high and low, with respect to achievement, deals with this matter (McClelland et al., 1953, pp. 298–299).

> Beside each statement there are two blanks. In the first one put a check mark if it is one of the things you want in your child by the time he is ten years old. In the second one put the approximate age by which you think your child should have learned this behavior. The sample below illustrates how to do this:
>
> <u> X </u>   <u> 10 </u>   To obey traffic signals and street lights when he is out `~~` alone
>
> This mother has checked this as one of the things she wants in her child and she expects him to learn this by the age of 10. Lots of books have been written on how a mother should treat her child but it's surprising how little information we have on what the people on the firing-line—the mothers—actually do. We would like you to answer these questions by telling us what you find works best with your child.
>
> _____   _____   To stand up for his own rights with other children
>
> _____   _____   To know his way around his part of the city so that he can play where he wants without getting lost
>
> _____   _____   To go outside to play when he wants to be noisy or boisterous
>
> _____   _____   To be willing to try new things on his own without depending on his mother for help

_____ _____ To be active and energetic in climbing, jumping and sports

_____ _____ To show pride in his own ability to do things well

_____ _____ To take part in his parents' interests and conversations

_____ _____ To try hard things for himself without asking for help

_____ _____ To be able to eat alone without help in cutting and handling food

_____ _____ To be able to lead other children and assert himself in children's groups

_____ _____ To make his own friends among children his own age

_____ _____ To hang up his own clothes and look after his own possessions

_____ _____ To do well in school on his own

_____ _____ To be able to undress and go to bed by himself

_____ _____ To have interests and hobbies of his own. To be able to entertain himself.

Mothers of boys who achieved high, Winterbottom discovered, demanded independence of their sons earlier than mothers of low achievers. The former required twice as many skills to be mastered before the age of eight than the latter. Thus, maternal stress on early independence seemed to be antecedent of high achievement. But the pattern was not so distinct. Another consideration blurred it. The mothers of boys who achieved high were more likely to demonstrate physical affection when a demand for achievement had been fulfilled. Hence, it was an early encouragement of independence coupled with a warm, affectionate mother-son relationship which produced the motivation for high achievement in the child.

Without this qualification, the Winterbottom findings would contradict the conclusion mentioned earlier in the chapter that children of parents who encourage early independence do less well in first grade than those of parents who defer demands for independence. Indeed, in the absence of an accepting relationship between parent and child, the promotion of early independence does not produce achievement. Identification is the factor of importance. As asserted in Chapter 10, a warm, accepting relationship is necessary between parent and child before the child will identify with the parent and take on his values and goals. Morrow and Wilson (1961) have provided support for this view in a study of the perceptions high-achieving and underachieving high-school boys have of their families. The former were more likely to see their family relationships in a positive light. They described their parents as approving, trusting, affectionate, relatively nonrestrictive, and encouraging—but not pressuring with respect to achievement. They said they accepted their parents' standards; in other words, they identified with them.

Clinical studies of learning difficulties have commented that underachievement may signify a rebellion against parents. Despite only slight research support for this position, it seems reasonable to believe that excessive pressure for achievement unaccompanied by a satisfactory and rewarding relationship with parents may engender anxiety and resentment in the child. The anxiety may inhibit the child from working to full capacity whereas the resentment may cause him to disappoint the parents by not meeting their expectations. Everyday observation of child behavior shows that rebellion may take a number of forms.

Personality and Emotional Factors

Notwithstanding the emotional and adjustment problems found in children who have difficulties in learning or achieving, the drawing of cause-and-effect conclusions is dangerous. In fact, a study of 34 children admitted for in-patient care to a psychiatric hospital observed none of them to be retarded in educational achievement (Tamkin, 1960). Conceivably, emotional problems and educational disabilities may be symptoms of the same underlying disturbance. Moreover, educational difficulties may be as frequent a cause of emotional problems as the other way around.

Within the limits of these precautions, several studies exemplify attempts to uncover emotional and personality factors as causes of scholastic underachievement. Among 20 high-school boys designated as underachievers, Kimball (1953) found the following significant things in their backgrounds. There was a poor relationship between father and son marked by an absence of strong identification with the father; there were passivity, strong needs for dependency, propensities toward aggression, and pronounced feelings of inferiority. These characteristics described a child with a low concept of self, low self-esteem, and a lack of the personal security necessary to permit a manipulation of the environment in order to achieve. Feelings of dependency and inferiority prevent an individual from realizing his potential.

Other studies (Conklin, 1940; Walsh, 1956) have implied that underachievers have a history of disturbed personal relations, especially with respect to their parents. In consequence, they feel rejection and an inability to express their hostile and negative reactions. In a longitudinal study by Haggard (1957), high achievers, in distinction to low achievers, tended to be more responsive to the socialization pressures of their parents; they accepted parental values and endeavored to live up to them and to the expectations of their elders. Yet this seemed to bring on anxiety. At the level of the third grade and more so by the seventh, there was evidence of hostility and antagonism toward adults among high-achieving children. By the seventh grade the anxiety apparent in these youngsters impeded their originality and creativity. By and large, they were aggressive, competitive, and persistent.

It would seem that the child who is relatively free from anxiety and other emotional upsets best concentrates on academic matters. This is more likely to apply in elementary school. In high school a host of factors, some of which may not be considered to reflect sound mental health or desirable personality traits, may occasion academic achievement.

Undoubtedly past experiences of success or failure in meeting the demands of a task together with the attitudes toward these experiences influence both an individual's performance and the level of achievement to which he aspires. Nothing fails so much as failure because of the sense of failing it provides. Sears (1940) has demonstrated the effect of past experiences on one's setting of goals. She experimented with two groups of fourth, fifth, and sixth graders, requiring them to select a series of goals for performance following respective successful and failing experiences. One group had successful records of achievement in reading and arithmetic, the other had been much less successful. In the experimental situation, the successful group attempted as a unit to improve performance but set realistic goals. The failing group was less consistent; some members chose goals of a very low level in the hope of attaining them whereas others selected goals of unrealistic challenge. Both goals were dictated by a desire to avoid failure.

A word is necessary about the effect of a series of repeated failures on the child's self-esteem. Demoralization sets in. One truly cannot condone any school curriculum in which certain children cannot avoid such failure. Perhaps teachers, because of the educational attainments demanded by their positions, are unable to understand the meaning of failure to a child and the impact it has on him. Naturally, every child does not have to be protected from failure, but success, in reality, is a relative term: it is relative to the goals set by the teacher, by the parent, and by the child himself. Although a sense of success certainly comes from achievement, it may derive also from having done a job to the best of one's ability. And ability varies in a classroom as much as height, weight, and color of one's eyes.

Miscellaneous Factors

Teachers affect the achievement of their pupils by the kind of contacts they have with them. Several investigations of high-school classrooms indicate that high achievers receive more motivation than low achievers from teacher approval (Battle, 1957), and that there is a closer kinship between the values held by the teacher and by high achievers than between those of the teacher and low achievers (McDavid, 1959). That is, the teacher tends to reward with approval those students most similar to himself in certain areas and this approval inspires them to strain for higher levels of performance.

Actually, the general psychological atmosphere established by some teachers is more appropriate to learning and achievement than the atmosphere set by others. Learning occurs best when there is understanding and acceptance between teacher and pupil. For example, Christensen (1960) noted a relationship between ratings of warmth for the teacher and the achievements in vocabulary and arithmetic among pupils of ten fifth-grade classes. Nevertheless, the level of teaching ability, a broad concept embracing a number of skills and attitudes, is the prime determinant of the quality of instruction in a classroom.

A child's attitudes also affect achievement in school. Great satisfaction with the school situation is likely to spur performance. In this regard, Malpass (1953) observed that eighth-grade children with the most positive attitudes toward the school evinced the higher achievement. Correspondingly, Briggs, Johnson, and Wirt (1962) found a close tie between susceptibility to delinquency and low achievement. In the same vein, a comparison of potential delinquents and nondelinquents in the sixth grade saw the former to be retarded in reading and arithmetic (Dinitz, Kay, & Reckless, 1957). This poorer achievement of potential delinquents was attributed to their negative attitudes toward school as well as toward other social institutions. Quite likely their resentment of the authority represented by the school reflected a general dislike of authority, an attitude stemming often from a child's relations with his parents.

Then there is socioeconomic status. The correlations between such status and achievement have been found to be consistent. Part of this result may be ascribed, as noted in Chapter 2, to differences in

IQ among social classes. Moreover, the attitudes of lower-class parents toward education, the school, and educational achievement as well as the attitudes of the typical college-educated teacher toward the values and behavior of the lower-class child cannot be ignored.

Many factors create different attitudes and motivations concerning achievement in school between children of the middle and lower classes. The press of economic problems on the lower-class family makes money earned today far more attractive than the acquisition of knowledge which may or may not prove an economic asset in the future. Additionally, the likelihood that the lower-class parent was not successful in school does not endear schooling to him. He probably believes that the years in school profited him little in terms of occupational advantage. He is not likely to urge academic achievement on his child. The middle-class parent, conversely, places great emphasis on education. He sees it as one of the few ways remaining for the maintenance and enhancement of social status. Told by a first-grade teacher that her son was intellectually "average," one middle-class mother responded, "I don't want him to be a ditchdigger. He's going to have to get a college education if he's going to support his family properly." Attitudes and values are not, however, the only factors in class differences regarding achievement. Living conditions and time and space available for study also bear heavily on the subject.

Finally, there is the matter of interest. Generally children—and adults too—do best those things in which they are most interested, and vice versa. School achievement is no exception. Girls prefer and do best in language and literature, boys in science and history. More important than sex differences is the interest value inhering in the academic materials. Children are not all interested in the same things, happily. It behooves the teacher, the builders of curriculum, and the authors of materials for academic use to ferret out the interests of pupils and also their *potential interests* in order to meet and stimulate these effectively in the classroom. There is little excuse for history, or for literature, or for science failing to hold the interest of pupils.

SOCIAL CLASS AND THE SCHOOL

To what extent does social-class membership affect the kind of child an individual is, his personality, his behavior? In addition, how does this affect the child's relationship with his teacher? The position to be taken here runs counter to the currently popular one placing great emphasis on a child's social-class background. Indeed, a recent text in child psychology (McCandless, 1961) devoted considerable space to a discussion of social-class differences in child behavior and in parental attitudes and values, as well as to the effect of these differences on school adjustment. In marked contrast, the authors of this book believe for a variety of reasons that social class is not only less significant than it once was but also is less important than numerous other factors in yielding a psychological understanding of the individual child. The reasoning takes the following form: in general differences in social class in the United States are less sharp now than ever. America is thus becoming a nation populated essentially by one broad middle class. Social-class differences in goals, values, and child-rearing practices are narrower now than they were in past decades. More teachers now come from lower-class and minority-group homes; misunderstandings arising from class differences in values are less frequent in classrooms. Clearly factors of social class account for a relatively small portion of the variation in personality and adjustment among children. Therefore, other factors of a psychological nature merit primary consideration.

The accent in educational circles on differences in social class grew out of a series of publications in the 1940's focusing attention on such differences (see Davis & Havighurst, 1946; Davis & Dollard, 1940; Havighurst & Taba, 1949; Hollingshead, 1949; Warner, Havighurst, & Loeb, 1944). The data cited in these studies buttressed the view that the school was largely a middle-class institution with personnel, curriculum materials, and advocated values and child behavior all presenting a middle-class bias. The result was that the middle-class child was rewarded with approval and support from the school, whereas the lower-class child, because of the very nature of the discrepancy between his behavior and attitudes and those of the school, was neglected, misunderstood, and punished.

On the basis of a careful review of social-class differences in child-rearing practices as they have historically affected the socialization process, Bronfenbrenner (1958) concluded that the gap may be narrowing. Moreover, Medinnus found no significant difference between scores of lower- and middle-class adults on an Attitude Toward Education Scale (Medinnus, 1962a). All people are becoming increasingly aware of the importance of education as a determinant of occupational status. The need for various skills and the demand for highly trained personnel in a technological society are apparent. The leveling effect of mass communication on values and attitudes is also being felt. Children and adults of all social classes, for example, are exposed to the same television programs.

Some differences in values remain among the classes but there is an overlap as well as wide variations within any single social class. Kohn (1959) discovered a broadly common set of values among working-class and middle-class mothers in parental ratings of child behavior. Both groups of mothers rate happiness, honesty, consideration, obedience, dependability, manners, and self-control as traits to be desired in children in the middle elementary-school years. Although the middle-class mothers were more likely to value self-control and the lower-class mothers emphasized obedience, *the similarities between the two groups were greater than the differences.*

Finally, the low relationship between a child's social-class background and various personality indices (Sewell, 1961) suggests that knowledge of the former is of little use in understanding the individual child. Insofar as social class tells anything about a child, the information should be obtained. But more important, what is the emotional relation between the child and his parents, and between the child and his siblings? How does he get along with his peers? What is the nature of the child's concept of himself?

Answers to such questions are necessary for understanding any child regardless of social class. These are important psychological considerations. The danger of emphasizing social class is that a teacher or any other adult may fall into the trap of believing that a child's behavior is explained and his personality is understood once information concerning his social-class background is known. The common elements among children of different social, racial, religious, and national backgrounds in motivation, fears, needs, and what makes them tick are greater than their differences. This must not be forgotten. The following excerpt well represents the position taken here.

> Many teachers have at last become aware of social class differences. It is not in vain that they have taken courses in sociology and the social foundations of education. Prior to this they tended to see each child as an individual, a being apart from his own background. But as a result of social class analysis they now have a new set of tags with which to classify children. They now recognize and shudder at the thought of that irreverent, undisciplined, non-motivated, and irrevocably handicapped lower-class youngster.
>
> What is this lower-class child like? An image has been created. He lives in a city slum or in tents and shacks for impoverished migrant families. His parents care nothing about education. His parents neglect him. He suffers from malnutrition, lack of affection, and general misunderstanding. His achievement level is low. His grades are poor. The intelligence tests are biased against him. The teachers do not speak

his language. And he fails dismally to meet the middle-class teacher's expectations. He swears. He comes to school dirty. He gets into fights. Sometimes he carries a razor or a switchblade. When he reaches high school he wears a black leather jacket and allows his hair to grow unusually long. Perhaps he smokes marijuana and hangs around the streets in the company of potential delinquents or races up and down the highways on motorcycles or souped-up jalopies.

A new stereotype has emerged. Teachers now recognize what their college professors are talking about when they use the term lower class. The image which this stereotype awakens both frightens and arouses pity, but how much basis is there for it?

A group of prospective teachers took a field trip to a lower-class school. They knew it was a lower-class school, because the children who attended were living in a run-down, temporary, government housing project, and the families were among the lowest income groups. The children were both white and colored and the faculty was integrated as well. They interviewed some of the teachers with questions designed to gain verification for the images which they held about lower-class children and their parents.

"Wasn't it true that these parents showed little interest in the school or their children's progress?"

"Oh, no," replied the teachers. "In fact, the parents turned out in large numbers to all school functions. The attendance at parent-teacher conferences was close to 100 per cent. They seemed to have high hopes for what the schools might do for the children."

"Were the children unruly or hard to handle?"

The teachers did not seem to think so. They agreed that they did have to modify some of their conceptions about acceptable behavior, but the teachers did not feel any more plagued by discipline problems than they had been in other classrooms.

"Did they find the achievement level rather low?"

The teachers recognized wide differences in levels of achievement, and could see no distinction between classes they were presently teaching and ones that they had taught in more favored neighborhoods.

The prospective teachers came back to class somewhat disillusioned. They had not received confirmation for their stereotypes. Why didn't these lower-class children behave like lower-class children are supposed to behave? One of the difficulties seems to be that a term used as an ideal-type construct designed primarily for anthropological or sociological research has deteriorated to a set of assumptions and descriptions which lend themselves easily to over-simplification.

There can be no doubt that studies do uncover class systems based upon a differential hierarchy of status. There is no doubt that statistically significant differences exist between social class categories of children in relation to school success. The evidence is fairly conclusive that commonly used intelligence tests do, indeed, discriminate against the vocabulary and motivation of children classified as lower class. But wherever statistically significant differences occur, they cover over the wide range of exceptional behavior within the groups being compared.

The argument here is not so much with the use of social class constructs in helping teachers to accept relevant differences. The real trouble comes with the realization that some teachers are swallowing whole the categories describing social class differences. This may well be doing more to place barriers in the way of better human relations than it does to overcome misconceptions.

It seems evident that our schools in many slum neighborhoods simply are not providing realistically for a large number of the children who attend. This does not mean that they fail with all of the children. They do offer the opportunity for many children to acquire some of the skills and attitudes which will enable them to use the schools as effectively as children in other parts of the city.

One trouble with stereotypes is that the lower-lower class child does not know that he is lower-lower class. He probably would not accept the classification if he did know it. He is just as apt to be insulted if someone thinks of him and treats him as if he were some kind of pariah.

Another trouble with the stereotype about slum children is that most people who live in slums would just as soon live elsewhere. The stereotypes about lower-class youth are applied by teachers to Negroes, Mexican-Americans, and Puerto Ricans whose families are frequently denied access to other neighborhoods. Members of groups who suffer from housing and employment discrimination frequently develop strong motivation to break out of the slums and to improve living conditions. Only when the avenues of escape are cut off by discrimination does apathy develop.

The parents of the children in the temporary housing development are not apathetic or hostile to the schools. As a matter of fact, they show great interest in the potential which the schools offer for their children and frequently hold unreasonable expectations of the hopes which education can fulfill.

In some ways the teacher who did not know about social class differences had better attitudes about the varying needs of individuals than the teacher who categorizes people too easily. It may come to the point where professors have to spend as much time breaking down stereotypes about lower-class groups as they now do about racial and religious groups. A stereotype obscures differences. The basic democratic value that differences be respected should lead teachers to be very careful about applying ideal-type constructs too indiscriminately. Teachers *do* need to know the social class background of the children they teach, but to know this is not enough. The next step must be to offer educational opportunities which will provide for the wide range of differences in abilities, interests, and goals which are found among *any* group of children (Fisher, 1961, pp. 309–311).

COMPETITION

"Children must learn early to compete and stand up for their own rights because, after all, ours is a competitive society." Is the stress on competition one of the foundations of the American philosophy of child rearing? Hopefully, it is not. Let us hope that cooperation is as much a part of the American way of life as competition.

Is competition among children a natural phenomenon or is it fostered by the culture? Both alternatives have their support. That competition and rivalry occur early in the home—by a year-and-a-half—and relatively early in the experimental situation imply an "inborn" nature to these traits. Perhaps competition is related to the urge for physical and psychological survival. Yet in some cultures little competitive behavior is evident in the older child. This would suggest that the course of competitiveness throughout the developmental span is charted largely by society's attitude toward competition. Whether it is fostered and encouraged or de-emphasized and discouraged by the particular society settles the role of competition in the social behavior of the child.

The first competition or rivalry, since it arises in the family setting, may invest this trait with an element of affection. It may represent. suit for a loved one's affection and esteem. In the classroom, the teacher must be aware of the possible effects on a child of failure to compete successfully. Feelings may be involved in addition to considerations related to the failed task. The child may feel rejected by the teacher and may resent what he perceives as favoritism shown by the teacher toward those children who succeed in the competitive situation.

Several experimental studies of children's behavior and performance in controlled competitive situations indicate that competition becomes pronounced in the four- to six-year-old child (Greenberg, 1932; Leuba, 1933). Parent handling of sibling rivalry and parental attitudes toward competition are important factors in the development of competitiveness in the child and in his position toward it. In the Greenberg study pairs of children were observed in a situation in which they were encouraged to build a block structure "prettier" and "bigger" than their companions'. The following percentages of competitive behavior were shown by the children at the various age levels:

2–3 years	0.0 per cent
3–4 years	42.6 per cent
4–5 years	69.2 per cent
5–6 years	75.4 per cent
6–7 years	86.5 per cent

These percentages may suggest that competitive behavior in children is unavoidable. This may or may not be the case. However, the concern here is with the psychological impacts of competition on the child.

The very nature of the school environment lends itself to competition. Children can readily compare their performance with others. Speed and accuracy are frequently emphasized and both of these rank pupils in an obvious manner. The child who hesitates and stumbles over words when his turn comes to read arouses the teacher's impatience and irritability; consequently, he is often followed by a child who reads with some fluency. Both teacher and children are aware of the difference between the two reading performances. It remains for the teacher to make sure that each child experiences some measure of success and competence. By its very existence competition creates differences among children with respect to success and failure.

But there may be advantages as well as disadvantages to a competitive situation. Some evidence (Stendler, Damrin, & Haines, 1951) implies that fewer negative social behaviors result from group competition than from individual competition. A competitive spirit in a group may promote a healthy interest in the activity. Feelings of personal worth and competence, of course, are less likely to be at stake than in a situation in which competition among individuals is encouraged.

It would seem most unfortunate, however, for a teacher to feel it necessary to introduce competition into the classroom in order to stimulate the children's interest in the subject matter. Reliance on such a crutch is harmful and unacceptable. The children may become more concerned with competing for the sake of competing than with learning or the content of the school work. Motivation to learn can be found in psychologically sounder methods. Indeed, the very purpose that competition is supposed to accomplish is often defeated, resulting in the opposite effect.

> Third-grade Johnny was relating to his mother some of the day's events at school. "We had a race in arithmetic to see who could get done first and get the most right. I worked hard but I came in last. You know, I wish I didn't have to take arithmetic any more."

Competition may be a part of the culture. Some parents may instill it in their children. But in the school setting the teacher decides when and how much competition to prescribe for the classroom or the playground. The value of competition and of a competitive attitude must be weighed against the disadvantages with respect to the psychological effects on the individual child.

SUMMARY

The teacher's role in the classroom drew the main emphasis in this chapter. The teacher stimulates and guides the intellectual development of pupils, affects their attitudes and values, and exerts a marked influence on their emotional adjustment through the kind of psychological atmosphere established in the classroom and through differential rewards and punishments.

Many factors relate to academic achievement: intellectual ability, level of maturity, relationship with parents, emotional and personality factors, past success and failure, attitude toward school, the teacher, socioeconomic status, and patterns of interest. Because the primary function of the school is the teaching of academic skills, the extent to which a child learns these skills reflects the effectiveness of the school's endeavor and also bears heavily on the child's concept of himself.

The years spent in school are important ones. Teachers and parents must work together to make certain that for each child these years are fruitful and well used.

REFERENCES

Anderson, H. H. An experimental study of dominative and integrative behavior in children of preschool age. *J. soc. Psychol.*, 1937, **8**, 335–345. (a)

Anderson, H. H. Domination and integration in the social behavior of young children in an experimental play situation. *Genet. Psychol. Monogr.*, 1937, **19**, 341–408. (b)

Anderson, H. H. The measurement of domination and of socially integrative behavior in teachers' contacts with children. *Child Develpm.*, 1939, **10**, 73–89. (a)

Anderson, H. H. Domination and social integration in the behavior of kindergarten children and teachers. *Genet. Psychol. Monogr.*, 1939, **21**, 287–385. (b)

Anderson, H. H. Domination and socially integrative behavior. In R. Barker, J. Kounin, & H. Wright (Eds.), *Child behavior and development*. New York: McGraw-Hill, 1943. Pp. 459–483.

Atkinson, J. W. (Ed.). *Motives in fantasy, action and society*. New York: Van Nostrand, 1958.

Baruch, Dorothy W. Procedures in training teachers to prevent and reduce mental hygiene problems. *J. genet. Psychol.*, 1945, **67**, 143–178.

Battle, H. Relation between personal values and scholastic achievement. *J. exp. Educ.*, 1957, **26**, 27–41.

Beilin, H. Teachers' and clinicians' attitudes toward the behavior problems of children: a reappraisal. *Child Develpm.*, 1959, **30**, 9–25.

Bonney, M. E., & Nicholson, Ertie Lou. Comparative social adjustments of elementary school pupils with and without preschool training. *Child Develpm.*, 1958, **29**, 125–133.

Briggs, P., Johnson, Rochelle, & Wirt, R. Achievement among delinquency-prone adolescents. *J. clin. Psychol.*, 1962, **18**, 305–309.

Bronfenbrenner, U. Socialization and social class through time and space. In Eleanor E. Maccoby, T. M. Newcomb, & E. L. Hartley (Eds.), *Readings in social psychology.* New York: Holt, 1958. Pp. 400–425.

Carter, L. B. The effect of early school entrance on the scholastic achievement of elementary school children in the Austin public schools. *J. educ. Res.*, 1956, **50**, 91–103.

Chance, June E. Independence training and first graders' achievement. *J. consult. Psychol.*, 1961, **25**, 149–154.

Christensen, C. M. Relationships between pupil achievement, pupil affect-need, teacher warmth, and teacher permissiveness. *J. educ. Psychol.*, 1960, **51**, 169–174.

Conklin, A. M. Failures of highly intelligent pupils. *Teach. Coll. Contr. Educ.*, 1940, No. 792.

Davis, A., & Dollard, J. *Children of bondage.* Washington, D. C.: Amer. Coun. on Educ., 1940.

Davis, A., & Havighurst, R. Social class and color differences in child-rearing. *Amer. sociol. Rev.*, 1946, **11**, 698–710.

deGroat, A. F., & Thompson, G. G. A study of the distribution of teacher approval and disapproval among sixth-grade children. *J. exp. Educ.*, 1949, **18**, 57–75.

Dinitz, S., Kay, Barbara, & Reckless, W. C. Delinquency proneness and school achievement. *Educ. Res. Bull.*, 1957, **36**, 131–136.

Fisher, R. J. Who is this lower-class child? *J. educ. Sociol.*, 1961, **34**, 309–311.

Flanders, N. A., & Havumaki, S. The effect of teacher-pupil contacts involving praise on the sociometric choices of students. *J. educ. Psychol.*, 1960, **51**, 65–68.

Gladstone, R. Do maladjusted teachers cause maladjustment? A re-review. *J. except. Child.*, 1948, **15**, 65–70.

Goodenough, Florence L., & Maurer, Katherine M. The mental development of nursery-school children compared with that of non-nursery school children. *Natl. soc. Stud. Educ., 39th Yrbk*, 1940, Part II, 161–178.

Greenberg, P. J. Competition in children: an experimental study. *Amer. J. Psychol.*, 1932, **44**, 221–248.

Gronlund, N. E. The accuracy of teachers' judgments concerning the sociometric status of sixth-grade pupils. *Sociometry*, 1950, **13**, 197–225, 329–357.

Haggard, E. A. Socialization, personality and achievement in gifted children. *Sch. Rev.*, 1957, **65**, 318–414.

Hattwick, LaBerta A. The influence of nursery school attendance upon the behavior and personality of the preschool child. *J. exp. Educ.*, 1936, **5**, 180–190.

Havighurst, R., & Taba, H. *Adolescent character and personality.* New York: Wiley, 1949.

Hoehn, A. J. A study of social class differentiation in the classroom behavior of nineteen third-grade teachers. *J. soc. Psychol.*, 1954, **39**, 269–292.

Hollingshead, A. *Elmtown's youth: the impact of social classes on youth.* New York: Wiley, 1949.

Hunter, E. C. Changes in teachers' attitudes toward children's behavior over the last thirty years. *Ment. Hyg.*, 1957, **41**, 3–11.

Jersild, A. T. Characteristics of teachers who are "liked best" and "disliked most." *J. exp. Educ.*, 1940, **9**, 139–151.

Keliher, Alice V. A day in the life of the teacher. *Ment. Hyg.*, 1950, **34**, 455–464.

Kimball, Barbara. Case studies in educational failure during adolescence. *Am. J. Orthopsychiat.*, 1953, **23**, 406–415.

Klausmeier, H. J., & Check, J. Relationships among physical, mental, achievement, and personality measures in children of low, average, and high intelligence. *Amer. J. ment. Def.*, 1959, **63**, 647–656.

Kohn, M. L. Social class and parental values. *Amer. J. Sociol.*, 1959, **64**, 337–351.

Kvaraceus, W. C. Mental health hazards facing teachers. *Phi Delta Kappan*, 1951, **32**, 349–350.

Lee, Murray J., & Clark, W. W. Lee-Clark Reading Readiness Test. Kdgn. and Grade 1. 1951 Rev. Los Angeles: Calif. Test Bur., 1951.

Leeds, C. H., & Cook, W. W. The construction and differential value of a scale for determining teacher-pupil attitudes. *J. exp. Educ.*, 1947, **16**, 149–159.

Leuba, C. An experimental study of rivalry in young children. *J. comp. Psychol.*, 1933, **16**, 367–378.

Lewin, K., Lippitt, R., & White, R. Patterns of aggressive behavior in experimentally created "social climates." *J. soc. Psychol.*, 1939, **10**, 271–299.

Lippitt, R. An experimental study of the effect of democratic and authoritarian group atmospheres. *Univ. Ia. Stud. Child Welf.*, 1940, **16**, No. 3, 43–195.

Lippitt, R., & White, R. The "social climate" of children's groups. In R. Barker, J. Kounin, & H. Wright (Eds.), *Child behavior and development*. New York: McGraw-Hill, 1943. Pp. 485–508.

McCandless, B. *Children and adolescence*. New York: Holt, Rinehart, & Winston, 1961.

McClelland, D. C., Atkinson, J. W., Clark, R. A., & Lowell, E. L. *The achievement motive*. New York: Appleton-Century-Crofts, 1953.

McDavid, J., Jr. Some relationships between social reinforcement and scholastic achievement. *J. consult. Psychol.*, 1959, **23**, 151–154.

Malpass, L. F. Some relationships between students' perceptions of school and their achievement. *J. educ. Psychol.*, 1953, **44**, 475–482.

Medinnus, G. R. An investigation of school readiness and first grade adjustment. Unpubl. manuscript, 1961. (a)

Medinnus, G. R. The relation between several parent measures and the child's early adjustment to school. *J. educ. Psychol.*, 1961, **52**, 153–156. (b)

Medinnus, G. R. The development of a First-Grade Adjustment Scale. *J. exp. Educ.*, 1961, **30**, 243–248. (c)

Medinnus, G. R. The development of a Parent Attitude Toward Education Scale. *J. educ. Res.*, 1962, **56**, 100–103. (a)

Medinnus, G. R. An examination of several correlates of sociometric status in a first grade group. *J. genet. Psychol.*, 1962, **101**, 3–13. (b)

Merrill, Barbara. A measurement of mother-child interaction. *J. abnorm. soc. Psychol.*, 1946, **41**, 37–49.

Meyer, W. J., & Thompson, G. G. Sex differences in the distribution of teacher approval and disapproval among sixth-grade children. *J. educ. Psychol.*, 1956, **47**, 385–396.

Milner, Esther. A study of the relationship between reading readiness in grade one school children and patterns of parent-child interaction. *Child Develpm.*, 1951, **22**, 95–112.

Morrow, W. R., & Wilson, R. C. Family relations of bright high-achieving and under-achieving high school boys. *Child Develpm.*, 1961, **32**, 501–510.

Murphy, G., Murphy, Lois B., & Newcomb, T. *Experimental social psychology.* New York: Harper, 1937.

Olson, W. C., & Hughes, B. O. Subsequent growth of children with and without nursery-school experience. *Natl. Soc. Stud. Educ., 39th Yrbk*, 1940, Part II, 237–244.

Sears, Pauline S. Levels of aspiration in academically successful and unsuccessful children. *J. abnorm. soc. Psychol.*, 1940, **35**, 498–536.

Sewell, W. Social class and childhood personality. *Sociometry*, 1961, **24**, 340–356.

Simon, Maria D. Body configuration and school readiness. *Child Develpm.*, 1959, **30**, 493–512.

Skeels, H. M., Updegraff, Ruth, Wellman, Beth L., & Williams, H. M. A study of environmental stimulation: an orphanage preschool project. *Univ. Ia. Stud. Child Welf.*, 1938, **15**, No. 4.

Snyder, W. U. Do teachers cause maladjustment? *J. except. Child.*, 1947, **14**, 40–46, 73–78.

Stendler, Celia B. Social class differences in parental attitudes toward school at Grade I level. *Child Develpm.*, 1951, **22**, 36–46.

Stendler, Celia B., Damrin, D., & Haines, A. C. Studies in cooperation and competition: I. The effects of working for groups and individual rewards on the social climates of children's groups. *J. genet. Psychol.*, 1951, **79**, 173–197.

Stendler, Celia B., & Young, N. Impact of first grade entrance upon the socialization of the child: changes after eight months of school. *Child Develpm.*, 1951, **22**, 113–122.

Stendler, Celia B., & Young, N. The impact of beginning first grade upon socialization as reported by mothers. *Child Develpm.*, 1959, **21**, 241–260.

Stiles, L. J. (Ed.). *The teacher's role in American society.* John Dewey Society. 14th Yrbk. New York: Harper, 1957.

Tamkin, A. S. A survey of educational disability in emotionally disturbed children. *J. educ. Res.*, 1960, **53**, 313–315.

Templin, Mildred C. General information of kindergarten children: a comparison with the Probst study after 26 years. *Child Develpm.*, 1958, **29**, 87–96.

Tenenbaum, S. Uncontrolled expressions of children's attitudes toward school. *Elem. Sch. J.*, 1940, **40**, 670–678.

Thompson, G. G. The social and emotional development of preschool children under two types of educational program. *Psychol. Monogr.*, 1944, **56**, No. 5.

Van Alstyne, Dorothy, & Hattwick, LaBerta A. A follow-up study of the behavior of nursery school children. *Child Develpm.*, 1939, **10**, 43–72.

Walsh, A. M. *Self-concepts of bright boys with learning difficulties.* New York: Bur. of Publ., Teachers Coll., Columbia Univer., 1956.

Walsh, Mary E. The relation of nursery school training to the development of certain personality traits. *Child Develpm.*, 1931, **2**, 72–73.

Warner, W., Havighurst, R., & Loeb, M. *Who shall be educated?* New York: Harper, 1944.

Wellman, Beth L. The effect of preschool attendance upon the I.Q. *J. exp. Educ.*, 1932, **1**, 48–69.

Wickman, E. K. *Children's behavior and teachers' attitudes.* New York: Commonwealth Fund, 1928.

Winterbottom, Marian. In D. C. McClelland, J. W. Atkinson, R. A. Clark, & E. L.

Lowell, *The achievement motive.* New York: Appleton-Century-Crofts, 1953. Pp. 297–306. (Also in) The relation of need for achievement in learning experiences in independence and mastery. In J. W. Atkinson (Ed.), *Motives in fantasy, action and society.* New York: Van Nostrand, 1958. Pp. 453–478.

Withall, J. The development of a technique for the measurement of social-emotional climates in classrooms. *J. exp. Educ.,* 1949, **17,** 347–361.

Withall, J. Assessment of the social-emotional climates experienced by a group of seventh graders as they moved from class to class. *Educ. psychol. Measmt.,* 1952, **12,** 440–451.

chapter 13 ✳ Other Socializing Influences

A growing child's family, his peers, and the school are not the only influences he encounters. A child grows up in a community. He is exposed to varying degrees of religious instruction. He takes cognizance of such organized groups as the Boy Scouts. He is confronted by the mass media of communication—books, comic books, movies, television. How much and in what way do these agencies of socialization affect his development?

THE COMMUNITY

The role of the community in the life of a young person depends largely on the child's parents. If they do not abdicate their responsibilities in the socialization process, the community oftener serves to reinforce parental values than as a source of values themselves (Peck & Havighurst, 1960). Even if a community is a deteriorated slum fraught with delinquency and crime, the child appears to be largely shielded against its criminal influences as long as his parents provide him with a positive concept of the self through close, effective family interaction and high expectations (Reckless, Dinitz, & Murray, 1956; Scarpitti, Murray, Simon, & Reckless, 1960). It is when parents abandon their function in socializing the child that the community assumes a more central role. If the parents fail to provide values, or if they are lacking in the techniques for implanting them, then the community, among other social forces, may take over by default. For children of this type of background the community has great importance.

Consider two types of communities. Observe their dominant values which might reinforce, replace, or rebut parental values. And note the effectiveness with which these community values are instilled and the type of reward offered for conforming to them.

The first community is a village with a population of approximately 250 located not far from a city of 10,000. The village homes are old and rambling. No major national or state highways pass through the village, and there is little local traffic. Two-year-olds can be turned loose to cross streets, since everyone drives slowly and carefully. By the age of three children have begun running about the village in small groups and at about six they begin playing around the creek, the gravel pit swimming hole, and in the forest that rings the village. The only supervision is the loose watch of the older children. There is always the hazard of drowning or of getting lost in the woods, but neither has occurred for several generations. Danger is present, though less so, and possibly more predictably, than in the city.

All but two of the families are Norwegian-American. All the original settlers came to the same place a few generations ago as a result of having been friends and relatives in Norway. Pressure is exerted on each generation of children to associate with one another and not with the people of the nearby countryside who are not Norwegian and Lutheran but predominantly Polish, French-Canadian, and American-Indian Catholics. Through intragroup marriages nearly everyone is related by blood, marriage, or both to everyone else.

The population is stable. Very few new families have moved into the village, but a fair—and probably the most enterprising—portion of the children of each generation move out. The men once worked in the woods and the sawmills of the nearby city. Now the timber is gone and the men have switched to the wood products factories of the city. These companies are paternalistic in the good sense of the term and usually have jobs available for the village's young people when they quit or graduate from high school. Net income among the families varies from about $3000 to $5000 a year, but this tends to be sufficient. Rent is below $50 a month, as a rule, and most families have a garden as well as some small livestock.

The one church is Norwegian Lutheran. The children are sent to

Sunday School with great regularity and to confirmation classes for two years during adolescence. At 15 they are confirmed as full members of the church, but do not attend church again, by and large, until middle or old aged. Because all members of an age group attend the same Sunday School and confirmation classes, there is an overlap between the lessons of the church and the practices among peers. Misdeeds often come to the attention of the minister who can exercise some pressure, such as refusal to confirm, a terrible disgrace, to induce a change of behavior.

The legendary wildness of one of the girls in the "roaring twenties" serves the present generation as the basis for a sermon. The girl was "wild" enough as an adolescent to run around with non-Norwegian boys. Even the contemporary generation knows of this. Behavior is judged by one's elders, one's peers, and even by future generations to come.

Children in this village are reared within the typical nuclear family structure but are the responsibility of everyone in the community. Grandparents, uncles, aunts, older siblings, even godparents are so intimately involved in the rearing of a child that they will take over completely if the parents are unwilling or unable to fulfill the function. The majority of adults in the community feel free to discipline, physically or verbally, any child who misbehaves. All adults believe it to be their duty to inform the child's parents of any misdeeds committed. The child is ruled by every adult. He is also defended by every adult—defended against "mean kids," outsiders, and strangers, and if need be, the forces of law and order.

The community is marked by the fact that a high proportion of behavior is *public* behavior. It is open, known by all, judged by all. Everyone agrees on most things; hence, the children are exposed to a single, well-defined set of values. Great pressure is brought to bear to enforce conformance. Defense is communitywide if needed. This is a clear-cut illustration of a *primary group* society.

The other community is described by a boy who grew up in it. The account is printed as he wrote it, including the misspellings.

> To begin with, the streets of Chicago in the naborhoods where I spent my early childhood were very poor and dirty like most of the slums are. The buildings are of wooden frame and most of them are in very poor condition. The alleys were unpaved and very sloppy and filled with trash. Junk yards and horse stables come out into the very heart of the naborhood, just a block away from my home were the railroads. They were always very smoky and dirty.
>
> In the naborhood there were jews, polocks and irish, mostly foreigners and a poor class of people that could hardly read or write but had a

flock of "kids." Some were very honest people and some were not, as you often find in such naborhoods. In many cases some were clean, but most of them were very dirty. Many of them were supported by charity societies like my people were. Others that found it hard to make a living sent their children out to earn and steal whatever they could, just to bring home the bacon as we say. Most of the boys that I knew in my early childhood had this sort of people. To go into further details their sisters and mothers sold their soules for bread and butter, not because they wanted to but for the family's sake. With so many babies to feed, the brothers and fathers went out to work and if it could not be found, they became gun men, not that they were looking for the so called "easy" ways to make a living, that often proves the hardest, but for the family's sake. Put yourself in their shoes. If the cairty society turned you down, with the excuse that you were young and healthy but too lazy to find work, then you found yourself in a helpless condition. Such were the nabors and the every day occurrences around my own naborhood.

You can just about judge for yourself how the adults in the naborhood thought about delinquency. The way they looked at it was "let him steal if he wishes to, so long as its not from me but for me." Times were always poor in the naborhood and I and other children had to steal coal off the tracks of the railroad and sometimes break seals on the box cars to get fruit or whatever the car contained. It seemed to me that many of the people encouraged young boys to crime by buying stolen articles. The junk yard dealers bought stolen junk from boys and often encouraged boys to steal so they could buy the junk. They never asked any questions. They didn't care how, what or when the goods were gotten just so they were able to buy them. Some of the money would go for the mothers and fathers of these children and so nine times out of ten they will encourage the child's mind to work for easy money.

Most of the games played by the younger boys were "craps," playing with toy pistols, fighting, junking, and stealing. So you see how a child can be brought up, not knowing himself what his first start in crime was. But as he grows older and looks back and sees just how and where he spent his early childhood the situation is solved. The older boys in the naborhood went in for big things, like stealing cars, holdups, burglary and shoplifting. The little fellows always mingled with these big guys and heard them talking about their stealing.

Most of the stealing done by little boys in the naborhood was fruit, clothing, coal, merchandise from the freight cars, junk, and sometimes breaking into some nabors houses. Maxwell Street, which was at the time the only market in the naborhood was a good place for the boys to steal from. The boys from sixteen to twenty use to hang around the corners and wait for some old drunkard whom they could beat and take from him whatever valuables he may have. People would stand by and stair and even laugh as the boys would rob the drunkard. This would happen during the day where everybody could see it and the older people only was amused by it. Wherever the older guys met they would talk about robbin. The older guys were called "big shots" for their ability to make money fast by picking pockets, snatching purses, and the use of a gun in holdups. They even had what is called "backers," a

lawyer or somebody with a pull. Just as soon as they got caught a lawyer would come and also a bondsman and out on the street the boy
went. The "backer" worked on a fifty-fifty basis.

During my time in the naborhood there was that notorious gang that
called itself the Valley Gang. Frankie Lake and Terry Druggan were
at the head of this gang. They were very active at that time in rob-
beries, stick-ups, and many of the murders in the naborhood were the
work of this gang. The boys, young and old, took part in this kind of
a living. They had many "backers" and also what they call "big shots."
This gang had mostly irish, and polish guys and very few jews. They
use to stickup trucks and sell the stuff on Maxwell Street. They also
stole cars and stripped cars of tires and broke into stores and raided
them of merchandise. Money was coming easy for these young guys.
Everything looked rosy for the mothers and fathers, sisters and brothers
who did not care how the one or many brothers were making all the
money that came into the family. The little fellows were impressed by
these big fellows and got the idea that stealing was an easy, rosy way to
make big money. This is something about the naborhood I lived in
during my childhood (Shaw, 1931, pp. 19–20).

This description is an old one, but it is graphic, portraying in a
slum child's own words his formative environment. Many social
changes have taken place since the 1930's, of course. And differences
in experiences and opportunity according to social class have markedly diminished, especially since the Second World War. Even so, at
least some contemporary children grow up in communities very much
like the two described. The plush Gold Coast of Chicago's near
North Side is still within walking distance of "Murder Corner," and
the child who matures in either of these areas remains exposed to
different experiences, values, and opportunities from those of the child
raised in the other. Yet both of them will see another aspect of life
from that seen by the rural youngster. Although the "distance" between rural and urban society has narrowed and differences of social
class have been virtually obliterated, these continue to exercise some
influence on differences between individuals.

As noted in Chapter 7, the pervasiveness and intensity of parental
impact on the child at any single time has decreased even though the
period of parental control and influence has grown longer. If parental influence has fallen off, what social forces have taken its place?
It is doubtful that the community has increased its influence. To
anticipate the rest of the chapter, it does not seem likely that the
other agencies to be considered here have gained much influence,
either. Perhaps the major legatee has been the child's peers. The
older primary group community is vanishing because of the greater
physical and social mobility and the increased urbanization of the

American people. The urban *secondary group* community does not teach values or reinforce existing values as adequately, even when these are not pathological, since the value system is not backed up by the consensus of a close-knit group. Only when filling a vacuum, only when providing values in the absence of any other source, does the community achieve any real significance in shaping behavior.

Sociologists have argued that the functions of the primary group community have been taken over, in part, by voluntary associations —interest groups such as the Boy Scouts, the Camp Fire Girls, the P.T.A., and the American Legion (see Rose, 1956). Like the community, these groups are probably most influential in molding the behavior of children when parents have neglected to do so. Young people are generally not too deeply involved in groups like the Boy Scouts and are interested in them for only a limited portion of the development cycle. Voluntary associations like the Scouts, which emphasize crafts and outdoor life, have a higher rate of drop-outs among youngsters once puberty has been reached and interest patterns change. Yet these groups do have well-defined values and have developed excellent techniques for instilling them (see Martin & Stendler, 1959, pp. 409–412).

The sheer number of organizations to which a child may belong is great. Fox (1952), in an undoubtedly incomplete count, found 5000 voluntary groups. Although the effect of any one of these may be slight, the cumulative impact of the organizations one joins while growing up may be very heavy. These "artificial" primary groups do much to supply the sort of extrafamilial influences once provided by the primary group type of community. The rehabilitation of urban slums like the second community described in the chapter depends, to a large extent, on the success of this new form of primary group, the voluntary association, in inculcating values as well as on the values inculcated.

THE INFLUENCE OF RELIGIOUS EXPERIENCE

Since the days of G. Stanley Hall and his disciples (Daniels, 1893; Starbuck, 1899), all of whom believed religious conversion to be an almost necessary part of adolescent experience, psychologists have shown intermittent interest in the impact of religion on development. Actually, relatively little is known of the direct influence of religion on behavior because the problem of setting up a criterion is a difficult one. How does one separate the religious from the nonreligious to determine whether the two differ in behavior and values? One criterion of a religious orientation is the individual's own statement: does he or does he not claim religious affiliation? In interviews and tests involving hundreds of delinquents, not one of them did not claim some religious tie. This surely cannot validate the hypothesis that delinquents would not be delinquent if only they had some religious experience. But a bit of probing discloses that most of these delinquents do not enter a church once a year. Their affiliation is verbal, not behavioral. Some criterion other than affiliation is necessary.

Nor will church attendance, as cited in many studies, do. Some persons attend church for nonreligious reasons—as a result of habit, of pressure, of social aspirations, or in order to acquire feelings of superiority. There are studies using test scores of religious knowledge (McDowell, 1952), but even this approach cannot uncover true religious commitment. Although Godin (1962) offered other suggestions for a criterion, the problem has not been adequately dealt with in any study of which one is aware. The data presented here, therefore, must be viewed as containing information on the relation between certain formal aspects of religion and behavior—for example, church going—rather than as presenting insights into the link between degree of religious involvement and behavior.

Religious experience might be expected to change both broad social attitudes, such as belief in the brotherhood of man, and specific behaviors, such as cheating on tests. Taking the social attitudes first, the case seems to be clear that church attendance does not increase acceptance of the Bill of Rights (Stouffer, 1955). In an unpublished study conducted in San Jose, California, Walter Morgan subjected members of an upper-lower and lower-middle class church congregation to measures of dogmatism, ethnocentrism, and fascism. He rated involvement in the church by asking subjects how frequently they attended Sunday services and the number of church-affiliated social activities they engaged in. The deeper the individual's involvement the higher was his score on each of the three measures.

Wilson (1960) found similar results in a study of religion and anti-Semitism. In another study (Kelly, Ferson, & Holtzman, 1958), subjects favorable toward religion were seen to view Negroes more negatively than did persons less religiously committed. Finally, Jones (1958) observed that adults high in authoritarianism showed higher religious training and values and lower interests in the theoretical and esthetic areas of personal experience than individuals of lesser authoritarian tendencies.

All these findings and more like them which have not been cited here imply that persons of active religious commitment are less tolerant of others, if these others differ in political affiliation and race. In the same light Johnson (1959) noted that children who had attended parochial schools were more punitive and severe in several areas of moral judgment than children of secular school backgrounds. Possibly these characteristics are associated with the "ideal" of Max Weber's Protestant Ethic (see Chapter 7)—the hard-driving, independent, entrepreneurial man, unwilling to accept weakness in himself or others.

Turning to the specific behaviors, the studies by Hartshorne and May in the late 1920's (1928, 1929) must be cited. In their first study (1928) they ascertained through a number of ingeniously designed test situations the amount of cheating done by children who attended Sunday School and by those who did not. One sampling disclosed cheating among respectively 31 per cent and 40 per cent of the two groups. A second sampling turned up respective findings of 38 per cent and 43 per cent. Although following the direction expected, the differences were negligible. In the subsequent experiment (1929) they observed that children who attended Sunday School regularly were more helpful than others whose attendance was irregular. Once again the difference was small. And even the minor positive results of these two studies might have been produced by inadequate matching.

To all those who believe in the positive value of religious instruction this may prove disappointing. That exposure to the teachings of religion is not efficacious in combatting intolerance or dishonesty is, however, not surprising. The young person, even if regularly attending church and Sunday School, is in contact with these religious institutions for less than one-fiftieth of his waking hours. Besides, there is an abundance of evidence dating back to Hall's original study that young children have an extremely low level and primitive conception of God and of other religious symbols such as heaven, hell, and angels. This makes it quite difficult for the young child to grasp the moral issues involved in religion and to be influenced in his behavior by the religious resolution of these questions. All these studies suffer, as we have remarked, because of the difficulty in establishing a criterion for religious involvement. But even though attending church or Sunday School does not appear to augur moral behavior too well, it may be that the deeper criteria of religious commitment may show this disposition to have considerable positive influence on behavior.

MASS MEDIA OF COMMUNICATION

Just as many consider religious experience a potent positive force in shaping behavior, so they look at most of the mass media of communication as a negative influence. As we shall see, the evidence against the mass media seems about as telling as the evidence supporting religious education or as convincing as an alcoholic's pledge of abstinence.

Books

The oldest of the mass media is the printed word—books, newspapers, magazines. Despite the aura of wisdom surrounding books, the tomes acceptable to adults are not all good, if examined at close range. In an informative study, Child, Potter, and Levine (1946) checked the values portrayed in children's textbooks. They examined the stories presented in all third-grade readers published since 1930. Stories were broken down according to *thema*. Each theme formed a unit composed of an individual confronted with a situation, behaving as a result of it, and feeling the consequences of the behavior. In the 914 stories reviewed there was a total of 3409 themes. In these themes, girls and women were depicted as being kind, sociable, inactive, unambitious, and uncreative. Boys, on the other hand, were oftener shown as being active, aggressive, and interested in achievement.

It is often proclaimed that the pre-eminence of men in all of the arts and sciences—excluding, perhaps, home economics—stems from the cliché belief that "it's a man's world." This argument is difficult to sustain when one views the arts in America. Girls are rewarded at every turn for developing talent in the graphic arts and in music. Conversely, boys who display such interests are compelled to battle relentlessly against being considered effeminate. Nevertheless, there are virtually no women composers, painters, or sculptors of first rank. Even in the playing of musical instruments, perhaps a lesser accomplishment than composing, there are very few highly able woman performers. Sex distinctions in creativity may very well result from what the culture does to girls and women.

If the analysis of the readers is any indication, society continually presents young women with a set of roles of being kindly, dependent, and passive, and should not be too surprised if women take these seriously. Amidst an outcry of need for scientists, the culture inad-

vertently may be losing a major portion of them through an influence that can, to a degree, be checked—and that, in fact, is apparently
shifting rather sharply. It may not be possible to change the way that
girls and women are portrayed in television, in novels, or in the other
mass media, but it is possible to modify the values depicted in the
books used in the public schools.

The themes of the children's textbooks are unrealistic in other ways.
They are inordinately pollyannaish. The hero never suffers defeat.
Moreover, children are rarely portrayed as aggressive and acquisitive.
Adults are oftener cast in antisocial roles. The general conclusion
inspired by the Child et al. study is that children's textbooks are—or
were—laden with pap, sugar-coated fare of which even the readers
must tire.

A recent study by deCharms and Moeller (1962) resembles the Child
et al. undertaking in that it, too, was based on an analysis of values
expressed in children's textbooks. This study covered sample pages
of readers used in the years 1800–1950. Striking changes in content
occurred. The use of religious or moral sanctions diminished substantially during the century and a half, while material stressing the
Social Ethic increasingly replaced them. Emphasis on achievement—
the Protestant Ethic—reached its apex about 1900, as did the number
of patents issued per million of persons, and has been on the decline
since. Although the rise of the Social Ethic continued over a longer
period of time than might have been expected, the conclusions
reached about it in Chapter 7 seem confirmed, for the most part, by
this analysis of children's reading materials (see Figure 13-1).

Comics and Comic Books

In every generation young people have insisted on reading trash—
penny dreadfuls, dime novels, big little-books, or comic books, each
in their own day—at the expense of the literature approved by the
school and their parents. A subcommittee of the California legislature issued a report in 1958 concluding that juvenile delinquency
stemmed from children's reading of comic books. Frederic Wertham,
a New York psychiatrist, presented the same view in his book, *Seduction of the Innocent* (1933). In an earlier era, Healy (1915) and Healy
and Bronner (1936) placed the onus of guilt on cheap novels and
magazines. If this were the case, the challenges to the imagination
would be great—think of how delinquency could be eliminated by
censorship, blinding the multitude, or forbidding everyone to learn
to read! Obviously it oversimplifies the issue to blame comic books

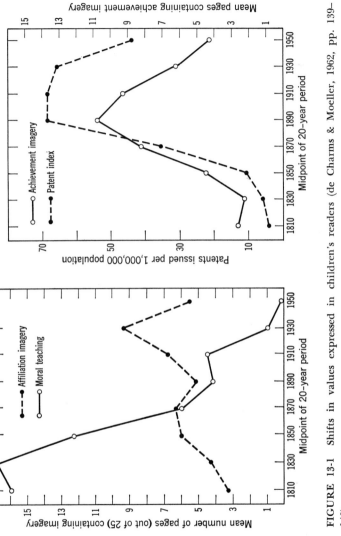

FIGURE 13-1 Shifts in values expressed in children's readers (de Charms & Moeller, 1962, pp. 139–140).

or other mass media for the existence of juvenile delinquency. Comics are a single, minor influence in the long sweep through which a child acquires a set of beliefs, values, and behaviors. What, then, is the real role that comics play?

To begin with, comic strips and comic books, as a rule, are neither funny nor amusing. They are exciting and contain a good deal of aggression. According to Bender and Lourie (1941) they fit the needs of children striving to understand the aggression of others and their own aggressive impulses. The comics and comic books share the characteristic of having justice prevail—the hero wins, the villain is punished. The vocabulary level of the typical comic book is high, about 10,000 words (Thorndike, 1941), and may be higher than the child is exposed to in conventional school texts.

Since the pictures provide cues to the words, and since the reader is highly motivated, many children unable to learn reading skills in a conventional classroom situation may gain from exposure to comic books. Although some of them and perhaps a few comic strips may center on sadism, masochism, or other pathological tendencies, and may at times provide an explicit blueprint for a specific crime, most comics for most children seem relatively harmless and, in some ways, beneficial. The question that arises is how much, if any, censorship of comic books or any other of the mass media should society impose on the majority in order to safeguard the suggestible minority. But this, more properly, is a point of interest for sociologists, philosophers, and political scientists than for psychologists.

Movies

The moral character of movies first came under attack as a result of the peepshow, "Dolorita in the Passion Dance," shown in Atlantic City in 1894 (Ramsaye, 1949). The attack intensified through the years until the late 1930's when other problems of an economic nature plus a gradual public adaptation to movies caused a slackening of interest. Like the other mass media, movies are not closely bound to reality; in fact, movie theaters were once known as "dream palaces," which certainly indicated an awareness of the movies' unreality. They portray a wide assortment of socially disapproved behaviors and at times present a master plan for criminal conduct. On the other hand, movies provide opportunities for other forms of social learning that are socially neutral or socially desirable.

In Denver, Colorado, for example, a city of about half a million people, the movies played a central role in changing the behavior of a large number of individuals. A substantial portion of the city's inhabitants are Spanish-Americans. Often they are called "Mexicans" even though some of their ancestors were living in Colorado and other parts of the Southwest at the time of the American Revolution. These people are frequently of low socioeconomic status. In the early 1950's prejudice against them ran high. Not only was there discrimination in housing and employment, but there were also numerous instances of vicious and gratuitous police brutality toward members of minority groups, especially Spanish-Americans.

The youths in this enclave were organized into loose neighborhood slum gangs. Most of them were out of school and unemployed except as agricultural laborers during the brief sugar-beet season. While idle they engaged in many delinquencies, most of them of a minor nature, and were subjected to a good deal of police investigation. Despite the justification of these investigations, they were often arbitrary and harsh.

Into this situation came a movie, *City Across the River,* based on a book by Irving Shulman, *The Amboy Dukes* (1947). The story concerning a delinquent gang in New York City presented a thorough description of the gang's structure and formal organization as well as of such specialized techniques as the construction of zip guns from automobile radio antennae. Every delinquent and predelinquent in Denver seems to have seen the film, many of them as many as three or four times. The most immediate consequence of the movie was the disappearance of radio antennae from automobiles at a tremendous rate. Working away in the metal and wood shops of the city's settlement houses, the delinquents, including the Spanish-American youths, became skilled craftsmen and developed a real ability at constructing zip guns.

With the Amboy Dukes as a model, the Denver gangs ceased to be loosely organized neighborhood groupings. The largest gang, composed almost exclusively of Spanish-Americans, was the Heads. The Heads had six branches, one of them at the State Industrial School at Golden, Colorado. Representatives of each of the branches met frequently. The gang elected officers, created a bail fund out of its monthly dues collection, and retained its own lawyer. One of the elected officers, the Minister of War, made treaties and declared war, following the vote of the representatives. The Minister of War was also in charge of the armory.

Like most delinquent gangs (see Thrasher, 1927; Whyte, 1943) the Heads indulged as a group in a wide selection of nondelinquent behaviors—camping, dancing, team sports, and legal—as well as illegal—drag racing. The formal structure of the gang caused it to form teams and, in some cases, enter organized competition. Its illegal activities included theft of automobiles, robbing of drunks, and other offenses. Committed by individual gang members, these offenses did not reflect decisions of the Heads' executive or legislative body, as did war with other gangs. However, if a gang member were apprehended, the gang's bail fund and lawyer were at his disposal. In a city where the concept of civil liberty was taken lightly, and individuals guilty or innocent might be held *incommunicado* for days or be treated roughly, the Heads gained legal rights through money and their attorney. Inspired by the movie, techniques of crime were learned that made the behavior of these delinquents more dangerous than had been the case when they belonged to neighborhood groups. Both in terms of frequency and seriousness of offense, crimes or delinquencies against persons and property increased sharply.

On the positive side, the movie produced an interest in organization and in a rough-and-ready kind of elected democracy. Many of the boys learned something of the fine art of administration and acquired executive skills. Because the gangs had power, both physical and monetary, they forced a change in the treatment of minority group members which is still apparent. The problems of minority group membership did not vanish, but were ameliorated. Thus, the film had certain positive effects, too. Moreover, its negative side was a result of an already existing situation. The movie did not create delinquents; these youths practiced delinquency long before the story was put before the cameras. Instead it converted existing delinquents into a more skilled and dangerous group.

As Blumer and Hauser (1934) said many years ago, movies can make a contribution to crime and delinquency.

> Through the display of crime techniques and criminal patterns of behavior; by arousing desires for easy money and luxury, and by suggesting questionable methods for their achievement; by inducing a spirit of bravado, thoroughness, and adventurousness; by arousing intense sexual desires; and by invoking daydreaming of criminal roles, motion pictures may create attitudes and furnish techniques conducive, quite unwittingly, to delinquent or criminal behavior (Blumer & Hauser, p. 198).

Whether or not an individual is swayed depends on other, more basic aspects of individual personality and of the environment. A high proportion of nondelinquent Denver youngsters saw *City Across the River* and were totally unaffected by it. But these were not slum children, fighting to maintain a favorable self concept in the face of harsh discrimination, economic deprivation, and a feeling of hopelessness.

Television

After years during which the public has worried about the effects of television, information needed for evaluation purposes has become available. Two extensive studies, one in England (Himmelweit, Oppenheim, & Vince, 1958) and one in the United States (Schramm, Lyle, & Parker, 1961), contain reliable information on the impact of television on children's personality and behavior. As with the other mass media, the chief fear expressed by the individuals concerned is that young persons become passive, anxious, or delinquent as a result of television viewing. The actual influence of television in these areas of adjustment together with its effect on aspects of cognitive functioning which are of less public concern, may be seen from the ensuing data.

It has been maintained that spectator activities promote passivity (e.g., Whyte, 1956). There is not much evidence for this contention as it relates to television. However, Glynn (1956), a psychotherapist, had this to say:

> Warmth, sound, constancy, availability, a steady giving without ever a demand for return, the encouragement to complete passive surrender and development all this and active fantasy besides. Watching these (viewers), one is deeply impressed by their acting out with the television set of their unconscious longings to be infants in their mothers' lap.
> These, then, are traits television can so easily satisfy in adults, or foster in children: traits of passivity, receptiveness, being fed, taking in and absorbing what is offered. Activity, self-reliance, and aggression are notably absent (Glynn, 1956, p. 178).

On the other hand, the Himmelweit group observed that television viewers were more curious about the world and showed a slightly wider variety of interests than either a group of nonviewers or they themselves before becoming viewers. These are the only bits of information available on the matter of passivity and television viewing —and they contradict each other.

Much more information is at hand on the capacity of television to produce anxiety. There is no doubt that a great amount of violence is portrayed on television. The National Association of Educational Broadcasters (Purdue Opinion Panel, 1954) had a team of viewers watch all the television broadcasts visible in New York City for one

400 ~~ Societal Influences on Socialization

week a year for four years. In the final year alone, 1954, during this one week 6868 incidents of a violent nature occurred on New York television screens. What is the general effect of this violence with respect to the production of anxiety among child viewers? The Himmelweit et al. study found one-fourth of the boys and one-third of the girls in a sample of more than 1000 young viewers aged ten to 14 to have been frightened by the events seen on television.

Violence that follows a conventional pattern with a foreseeable outcome is not frightening. Although dripping with gore, Westerns frightened only seven of the whole sample and of these five were below average in ability (Himmelweit et al., p. 194). It is the more complex pattern of aggression such as that shown in adult dramas which is mentioned most often as productive of fear. Particularly upsetting for children is the serious verbal expression of hostility on the part of adults (Himmelweit et al., p. 204; pp. 461–462). Children appear to be far more impressed by verbal than physical hostility, perhaps because *they* have observed their parents in verbal but not physical conflicts, and the television experience recalls the real-life conflict to them. It was also discovered that real violence, as shown in news programs, was far more capable of producing anxiety than fictional violence of the same sort.

Clearly some children are made anxious and fearful by at least some television programs. So, too, were some children of an earlier era and are some children of today by such traditional fairy tales as "Bluebeard" and by such fairy-tale figures as "Little One Eye," a girl created by the brothers Grimm with one eye, as big as a saucer, in the middle of her forehead. But as noted in Chapter 11, children seem to like and search for situations in which they can produce "manageable" fear. Consequently, there is no reason to believe that fear itself is necessarily bad or destructive.

Violence on television is also said to cause violence and delinquency in real life. "If the proverb is true that prison is a college of crime," said one psychiatrist, "then I believe that for young disturbed adolescents, T.V. is a preparatory school for delinquency" (Banay, 1955). As we have noted, comics and movies—and if we go farther back in time, for that matter, newspapers and stage productions—have also been blamed for delinquency. The lone large-scale study dealing with this issue failed to discover any more aggressive, maladjusted, or delinquent behavior among television viewers than among nonviewers (Himmelweit et al., p. 215).

Now to the positive aspects of commercial television. So far as social learning is concerned, Shayon (1951) noted that television "is the shortest cut yet devised, the most accessible back door to the grown-up world. Television is never too busy to talk to our children. It never shuts them off because it has to prepare dinner. Television plays with them, shares its work with them. Television wants their attention, needs it, goes to any length to get it." As the child's back door to the adult world, television would seem likely to produce a distorted view. Surprisingly, it does not. Himmelweit and his colleagues presented the following views. Viewers emphasized intelligence and bravery as important attributes for success in adulthood more often than did nonviewers (p. 468). There were no differences between the two groups in attitudes toward school, school work, or teachers (p. 246). Television viewing raised youngsters' levels of aspiration regarding employment (p. 258), and in older children of 13 to 14 it produced quite realistic worries and fears about the problems of being grown-up (p. 250).

Television has a leveling effect on class differences in general information and vocabulary, as was seen in Chapter 5. It also promotes a general elevation in vocabulary, with younger children gaining more than older ones, dull children more than bright ones, and heavy viewers more than light viewers (Schramm et al., 1961, pp. 75–97). Viewing does not decrease the reading of books and of most magazines but does reduce the reading of comic books and pulp magazines (Schramm et al., p. 15).

All told, the influence of television does not seem to be as great or as deleterious as commonly believed. There are differences between viewers and nonviewers but neither are they marked nor do the existing ones always favor the nonviewer.

Individual Susceptibility to the Media

The adverse effects of the mass media have been exaggerated, partly because most of the studies condemning them (Blumer & Hauser, 1934; Healy, 1915; Healy & Bronner, 1936; Wertham, 1953) have not used control groups and have dealt with small and deviant samples of the entire population. Wertham could hardly be expected not to have found all delinquency to be caused by comic books when he asked delinquent youngsters such leading questions that they could reply mainly in one way. If delinquents are asked whether reading comic books caused their delinquency, most of them will respond affirmatively. For that matter, if asked whether a phase of the moon caused their delinquency, most of them would also say yes, partly to be obliging, partly to shift the blame from themselves, and partly to avoid looking deeper into their own motivations.

Adequately designed studies do not show any considerable effect of the mass media on the behavior of most children, yet *some* youngsters are greatly influenced by them. Who are these children? These are the children who are addicted to the mass media. Those addicted to comic books showed marked tendencies toward neurosis as compared with nonaddicts; they were rather small and weak and identified with omnipotent heroism such as Superman (Wolf & Fiske, 1949). In television, Himmelweit et al. found addicts to have stronger feelings of rejection and insecurity than occasional viewers (pp. 390–391). In a parallel study, they noted these characteristics in ardent movie goers, implying that children who must withdraw from real situations find solace in all the media. These "findings suggest that these differences were there before television came to the home and explain why the addict views so much more than others of his age, intelligence and social background. The parallel analysis of cinema addicts showed them to be very similar kinds of children. Television meets a need which the child without television satisfies through the cinema or the radio" (Himmelweit et al., p. 390).

In a study of the same type, Bailyn (1959) confirmed the Himmelweit observations. Children subjected to considerable frustration in the home viewed television oftener than children not so greatly frustrated, at least in middle- and upper-class groups (Schramm et al., pp. 130–131; Maccoby, 1954, p. 303). Not only have frustrated children more contact with the mass media, but there is also some conflicting evidence that suggests that they may concentrate on and are better able to recall the acts of violence they have seen (Maccoby, Levin, & Selya, 1955, 1956).

One could argue that addicts are less social, more frustrated, and more beset by problems and neurotic tendencies than the nonaddicted *because* of their addiction, were it not for the fact that the Himmelweit study covered the same children before and after the introduction of television in their locale and showed the same problems to have existed *before* the advent of television. This type of pre- and postexposure investigation enables a very different interpretation from the typical one conducted after exposure to the mass medium, which serves as a basis for attacking the mass media. In short, addiction to the mass media is a symptom rather than a cause of social disorder.

In sum, the negative effects of the mass media are fewer than is commonly believed. The mass media have some positive effects, but these are obscured by the media's major task of convincing readers and viewers that humans are overfed, undernourished, suffering from vitamin deficiences, or, worst of all, prone to body odor.

SUMMARY

The influence of the community, voluntary associations, the church, and the mass media as agencies of socialization is secondary. If this conclusion seems to contradict the observations in Chapter 7 on the waning influence of parents on child behavior, the evidence seems to suggest that it is not the social forces discussed in this chapter that have gained ascendancy. Although the community, the voluntary associations, and the media may have acquired additional importance, the child's peers and his school have been the real beneficiaries of the parents' decline as a socializing influence.

Negative as may be the data on the influence of the social forces explored in this chapter, they are still worth knowing. Notwithstanding the array of pressures to which the child is exposed, the role of the family, though decreasing, remains primary in the socialization process. The community generally serves to reinforce parental values rather than as a source of values as long as parents meet their responsibility in child rearing. Only when parents abandon their role does community influence become more significant. As the community loses its influence through urbanization, voluntary associations fill the void, to a degree.

Religious experience does not seem to make much of an inroad on values or behavior, possibly because of the small portion of time spent by the average child in a religious setting or perhaps because researchers have not employed the proper criteria for religious commitment. Neither are the mass media, despite public outcry against them, of prime importance. However, continual influence in a fixed direction—such as women should be passive and noncreative, scientists are odd, or violence is permissible—may ultimately bear fruit. Some young people, because of existing personal problems, show much greater interest in the mass media and appear to be more susceptible to their influence.

REFERENCES

Bailyn, Lotte. Mass media and children: A study of exposure habits and cognitive effects. *Psychol. Monogr.*, 1959, **71**, 1–48.

Baney, R. S. Testimony before the Subcommittee to Investigate Juvenile Delinquency, of the Committee on the Judiciary, U. S. Senate, Eighty-fourth Congress. S. Res. 62. April 1955. Washington, D. C.: U. S. Government Printing Office, 1955.

Bender, Lauretta, & Lourie, R. S. The effect of comic books on the ideology of children. *Amer. J. Orthopsychiat.*, 1941, 11, 540–550.

Blumer, H., & Hauser, P. M. *Movies, delinquency, and crime.* New York: Macmillan, 1934.

Charms, R. de, & Moeller, G. H. Values expressed in American children's readers: 1800–1950. *J. abnorm. soc. Psychol.*, 1962, 64, 136–142.

Child, I., Potter, E. H., & Levine, E. M. Children's textbooks and personality development. *Psychol. Monogr.*, 1946, 60, No. 3.

Daniels, A. D. The new life: a study of regeneration. *Amer. J. Psychol.*, 1893, 6, 61–106.

Fox, S. D. Voluntary associations and social structure. Unpubl. Ph.D. dissertation, Harvard Univer., 1952.

Glynn, E. E. Television and the American character—a psychiatrist looks at television. In W. T. Elliot (Ed.), *Television's impact on American culture.* East Lansing, Mich.: Michigan State Univer. Press, 1956.

Godin, A. (S.J.). Importance and difficulty of scientific research in religious education: the problem of the "criterion." *Relig. Educ.*, 1962, 57, Supplement, pp. 166–174.

Hall, G. S. The moral and religious training of children. *Princeton Rev.*, 1882, 10, 26–48.

Hartshorne, H., & May M. A. *Studies in service and self control.* New York: Macmillan, 1928.

Hartshorne, H., & May, M. A. *Studies in service and self control.* New York: Macmillan, 1929.

Healy, W. *The individual delinquent: A textbook of diagnosis for all concerned in understanding offenders.* Boston: Little, Brown, 1915.

Healy, W., & Bronner, Augusta F. *New light on delinquency and its treatment.* New Haven, Conn.: Yale Univer. Press, 1936.

Himmelweit, Hilde T., Oppenheim, A. N., & Vince, Pamela. *Television and the child.* London and New York: Oxford Univer. Press, 1958.

Johnson, R. C. A study of children's moral judgments. Unpubl. Ph.D. dissertation, Univer. of Minnesota, 1959.

Jones, M. B. Religious values and authoritarian tendence. *J. soc. Psychol.*, 1958, 48, 83–89.

Kelly, J. G., Ferson, J. E., & Holtzman, W. H. The measurement of attitudes toward the Negro in the South. *J. soc. Psychol.*, 1958, 48, 305–517.

Maccoby, Eleanor E. Why do children watch television? *Pub. Opin. Quart.*, 1954, 18, 239–44.

Maccoby, Eleanor E., Levin, H., & Selya, B. V. The effect of emotional arousal on the retention of aggressive and nonaggressive movie content (abstract). *Amer. Psychologist*, 1955, 10, 359.

Maccoby, Eleanor E., Levin, H., & Selya, B. V. The effects of emotional arousal on the retention of film content: a failure to replicate. *J. abnorm. soc. Psychol.*, 1956, 53, 373–374.

McDowell, J. B. *The development of the idea of God in the Catholic child.* Washington, D. C.: Catholic Univer. of America Press, 1952.

Martin, W. E., & Stendler, Celia B. *Child behavior and development.* New York: Harcourt, Brace, 1959.

Morgan, W. Personality correlates of involvement in religious activities. Unpubl. study, San Jose State College, San Jose, Calif., 1958.

Peck, R. F., & Havighurst, R. J. *The psychology of character development.* New York: Wiley, 1960.

Purdue Opinion Panel, *Four years of New York television.* Urbana, Ill., National Assn. of Educational Broadcasters, 1954.

Ramsaye, T. The rise and place of the motion picture. In W. Schramm (Ed.), *Mass communications.* Urbana, Ill.: Univer. Ill. Press, 1949.

Reckless, W. C., Dinitz, S., & Murray, Ellen. Self concept as an insulation against delinquency. *Amer. sociol. Rev.,* 1956, **21,** 744–746.

Rose, A. M. *Sociology: The study of human relations.* New York: Knopf, 1956.

Scarpitti, R. R., Murray, Ellen, Simon, D., & Reckless, W. C. The "good" boy in a high delinquency area: four years later. *Amer. sociol. Rev.,* 1960, **25,** 555–558.

Schramm, W., Lyle, J., & Parker, E. G. *Television in the lives of our children.* Stanford, Calif.: Stanford Univer. Press, 1961.

Shaw, C. R. *The natural history of a criminal career.* Philadelphia: Saifer, 1931.

Shayon, R. L. *Television and our children.* New York: Longmans, Green, 1951.

Shulman, I. *The Amboy Dukes.* Garden City, N. Y.: Doubleday, 1947.

Starbuck, E. D. *Psychology of religion.* New York: Scribner's, 1899.

Stouffer, S. *Communism, conformity, and civil liberties.* New York: Doubleday, 1955.

Thorndike, E. L. Words and the comics. *J. exp. Educ.* 1941, **17,** 110–113.

Thrasher, F. L. *The gang.* Chicago: Univer. Chicago Press, 1927.

Wertham, F. *Seduction of the innocent.* New York: Rinehart, 1953.

Whyte, W. F. *Street corner society.* Chicago: Univer. Chicago Press, 1943.

Whyte, W. H. *The organization man.* New York: Simon & Schuster, 1956.

Wilson, W. C. Extrinsic religious values and prejudice, *J. abnorm. soc. Psychol.,* 1960, **60,** 286–288.

Wolf, Katherine, & Fiske, Marjorie. The children talk about comics. In P. F. Lazarsfeld & F. N. Stanton (Eds.), *Communications Research, 1948–1949.* New York: Harper, 1949.

SECTION V ✳

THE END PRODUCT

The previous sections of this book have investigated the forces affecting the human being—his inheritance, his growth and maturation, his learning and motivation, his language, his intelligence—and his unique pattern of response to the world around him: his personality. Now we approach the summing up. In this final section we shall take a deeper look into the child's personality. The first of the section's three chapters is devoted to a study of how the individual is appraised as an infant, as a young child, and in the elementary-school years. The second chapter, concerning personality development, covers two main facets of personality change occurring with age. These are an increasingly rich and diversified but consistent response to the world and the development of a self concept based on consistent attitudes toward the self and the world. The third chapter of the section, which, save for a summarizing concluding postscript, constitutes the final substantive portion of the book, deals with the psychological problems met in the course of the developmental process. It explores their causes, diagnosis, and probability of solution, either through therapy or the individual's own inner resources.

chapter 14 ✳ Individual Appraisal

Child psychologists and others concerned with the diagnosis of children's problems are often asked, "Is this child developing or progressing normally?" The question requires as accurate an answer as possible. To get at it psychologists have developed techniques for assessing the various aspects of child development. For early infancy, they have placed the accent on physical and motor development. For the period of early childhood, they have concerned themselves with intellectual functioning. And for the elementary-school years, they have shifted the attention to evaluation of the child's social, emotional, and personality adjustment. In this chapter, we shall consider each of these areas of individual appraisal in turn, commencing with assessment of infant procedures.

INFANT ASSESSMENT

In this country, Arnold Gesell played a major role in the devising of techniques to evaluate the growth and physical development of infants. Because of his training and dedication as a man of medicine, his methods stressed the diagnosis of deviation from normality rather than an evaluation of levels of normality. In addition, Gesell's emphasis tended toward the medical rather than the psychological aspects of development. Nevertheless, from his accent on the "lawfulness of growth" evolved the notion that growth and development were predictable.

The Gesell Developmental Schedules (Gesell, 1940; Gesell and Amatruda, 1947) are concerned with four major areas of behavior: motor characteristics, adaptive behavior, language, and personal-social behavior. In examining motor behavior the primary concern is the infant's increasing control of posture in the areas of locomotion and prehension. Head control comes first, followed by sitting posture and, later, upright posture. In prehension, the infant reaches out before it is able to grasp an object accurately. Through underlying neurological development he acquires coordination which permits increasing accuracy of arm and hand movements. How these motor behaviors are executed and the ages at which they appear supply clues to the maturity level of the infant. Deviation may signify an abnormality in development.

Adaptive behaviors involve some adjustment to the environment. Their presence is detected in the child's ability to manipulate blocks by arranging them in simple structures. Tests of simple number concepts and requiring a child to copy a circle and a cross appear at a later time.

In assessing language maturity, a number of aspects are taken into consideration. One observes the child's articulation, vocabulary, use in communication, and comprehension. Language development is reflected by an increase in the size of vocabulary, in the length and complexity of sentence structure, and by an increase in comprehension as revealed by the ability to respond to verbal directions and commands.

Personal-social behavior embraces such matters as feeding, dressing, toilet procedure, and play. In all of these maturity is judged by increased self-reliance and independence. Since environment plays a more influential part than maturation in these areas of behavior, deviations in development frequently furnish clues to the kind of psychological atmosphere in which the child is being raised.

Gesell devised the notion of a Developmental Quotient (DQ) which expresses the ratio between the child's *maturity age* and his actual age. Maturity age is based on a child's performance on a series of developmental tests which is then compared with the norms obtained from the administration of these tests to a number of children at various age levels. The DQ reflects the proportion of normal development attained at any given age level. By Gesell's own admission the DQ may be useful in predicting the course of future development only if no complicating factors arise. Since fluctuations in development are more common than not, maturity assessed at any one point in time may be more or less typical of any infant's developmental rate. All told, the DQ adequately assesses the infant's current rate of development taking into account its variability, complexity, and unevenness.

To Gesell, the developmental examination served not only to establish rate of development, as in the spotting of precocity and retardation, but also to diagnose neurological difficulties and other disturbances of development. Although not much information is available on the long-term predictive ability of the Gesell Developmental Schedules, they have achieved widespread use for the evaluation of the developmental status of infants. They have been used, for example, also as a measure for validation in a Developmental Questionnaire for infants of 40 weeks devised by Knoblock and Pasamanick (1956).

The very term *developmental diagnosis* suggests an attempt to assess level of development without considering mental growth or development as such. Yet child psychologists have chiefly directed their energies toward perfecting instruments for measuring infant intelligence and predicting later intelligence. The following items along with the age in months at when they should occur were included in one early infant mental test (Bayley, 1933a).

Age in Months	Item
(.5)	Postural adjustment when lifted
(.6)	Momentary regard of ring
(2.2)	Eyes follow pencil
(3.3)	Carries ring to mouth
(4.5)	Reaches for cube
(5.55)	Discriminates stranger
(9.3)	Fine prehension
(12.9)	Says two words

Tests administered before the age of five years have little value in predicting later ability. To begin with, a majority of the items at the earliest age levels tap the development of motor skills. As there is no relation between motor ability and abstract intelligence in adults, there is no reason to expect such a relation in infants. Furthermore, abstract ability may not be present in the infant prior to the development of language; and this ability to manipulate abstract symbols is frequently considered to be the ultimate criterion of intelligence at the adult level. As Goodenough (1949a) noted: "Attempting to measure infantile intelligence may be like trying to measure a boy's beard at the age of three" (p. 310). Anderson's comment that infant tests measure "little if at all the function which is called intelligence at later ages" (Anderson, 1939) was supported by a factor analysis of IQ scores obtained from a study in which successive tests were administered to a group of children from one month to 18 years of age (Hofstaetter, 1954). Three factors came to light. The first, called *sensorimotor alertness,* appeared prominently during the first two years. The second factor, *persistence,* reached its peak between two and four, declining and eventually vanishing in later childhood. The third factor, *abstraction and the manipulation of symbols,* began to emerge at about two and became a major consideration from four onward.

A second explanation for the low predictive value of infant tests relates to the difficulty of administering and scoring them; their reliability is uniformly low. Third, the rapid rate of development in infancy, coupled with fluctuations, increases the variability of test scores of any child from one test to the next. Fourth, motivation is well recognized as affecting test performance. However, attempts to encourage and motivate the infant are relatively fruitless. To secure his attention and cooperation alone is quite a task.

When precise scores have been obtained from infant tests and correlated with later scores, uniformly low coefficients have resulted. However, several studies (Escalona, 1950; MacRae, 1955) using somewhat broader categories of ability—mentally defective, below average, average, above average, and superior—have been more successful in predicting later ability from tests administered early. Illingworth (1960) maintained that infant assessment acquired greater predictive value through full understanding of infant development; this could be achieved by obtaining a medical-type history of the infant which included the relevant environmental factors. Because of the fluctuations in the rate of development data, a number of examinations had better predictive power than the findings of a single examination. Well-known infant intelligence scales include the California First-Year Mental Scale developed by Bayley (1933a, b), the Cattell Infant Intelligence Scale (Cattell, 1947), the Griffiths Mental Development Scale (1954), and the Northwestern Intelligence Tests constructed by Gilliland (1948).

INTELLIGENCE AND SCHOOL ACHIEVEMENT

Mental testing had many beginnings. However, the work of Alfred Binet in France represents the clearest and most direct forerunner of contemporary intelligence tests. In the closing decade of the nineteenth century, Binet together with Simon investigated a variety of measures to differentiate bright from dull school children. These early efforts came to a head soon after the turn of the century when, in 1904, the Minister of Public Instruction in Paris appointed a commission to study the advisability of establishing special schools for children incapable of profiting from instruction in the public-school classroom. Some means of identifying such children was clearly needed. Binet and Simon were consulted, with the result that a formal scale for testing the intelligence of children was constructed. The aim of this scale was to obtain an estimate of the child's level of mental development. Although a wide variety of tasks tapping different areas of ability was included in the scale, Binet and Simon did formulate a rather clear definition of intelligence: "To judge well, to comprehend well, to reason well, these are the essential activities of intelligence."

Binet Tests

The first scale, developed in 1905, consisted of 30 items arranged in order of increasing difficulty. It was revised by Binet and Simon three years later. New items were added and the method of arranging them by age level was employed, thus introducing the important notion of "mental age." Rather than denoting the number of items passed, the score now compared the child's performance with those of children of various chronological ages on whom the test items had been standardized. The following items appearing at three different age levels are drawn from the revised scale. Many of them have survived even the most recent revision of the original scale.

Three years:

Show eyes, nose, mouth
Name objects in a picture
Repeat two figures
Repeat a sentence of six syllables
Give last name

Six years:

Repeat a sentence of 16 syllables
Compare two figures from an esthetic point of view
Define, by use only, some simple objects
Execute three simultaneous commissions
Give one's age
Distinguish morning and evening

Nine years:

Give the date complete (day, month, day of the month, year)
Name the days of the week
Give definitions superior to use
Retain six memories after reading
Make change
Arrange five weights in order

The Binet-Simon scale made its debut in English at the Vineland Training School in New Jersey where Goddard put it to use as a diagnostic instrument for distinguishing between intellectually normal and subnormal children and for identifying various levels of subnormality. In 1916 Terman, at Stanford University, published a revision of the Binet-Simon scales. More than merely a translation, the Stanford revision included a number of new items and, as a result of a careful and thorough standardization procedure, changed the age placement of items. Moreover, scores were now expressed in terms of a ratio between mental and chronological ages. Although Terman was not the first to conceive of such a ratio, he popularized it by presenting tables in which mental age and chronological age figures were converted into Intelligence Quotients. Terman also interpreted the meaning of IQ levels through the percentage of people receiving the various scores. The following table contains Terman's original classification.

IQ range	Classification
Below 70	Definite feeble-mindedness
70–80	Borderline deficiency
80–90	Dullness
90–110	Normal or average intelligence
110–120	Superior intelligence
120–140	Very superior intelligence
140 and above	Genius or near genius

The Stanford-Binet test continues to retain its position as the most widely used individual test of intelligence for children. In the era in which intelligence testing of children probably reached its peak, the 1940's and 1950's, the 1937 revision of the Stanford-Binet was the test used. Although this was superseded by a 1960 revision, much of what follows applies to both.

Perhaps one of the most notable features of the Stanford-Binet is its precision of administration and of scoring. Clear instructions are provided for the examiner on the exact wording of his questions and the extent to which urging and further questioning are permissible.

The scoring manual is detailed, with numerous examples supplied to assist in scoring the child's responses. Both features tend to reduce as much as possible the effects on IQ scores of such factors as differences among examiners in the administration and scoring of tests. The kind of rapport etablished by the examiner with the child is important, however; for this and other reasons only a trained and experienced individual is qualified to administer an intelligence test.

The nature of the Stanford-Binet test items, especially at the younger age levels, is such that they are intrinsically interesting to children. Because of this it is usually possible to hold children's attention throughout the administration of the test which lasts approximately one hour. The 1960 revision consists of six test items at each half-year age level from two to five and six tests at each year level from five to 14.

Several points of importance in evaluating any intelligence test are worth noting. First, as to test reliability, Terman and Merrill (1937) reported reliability coefficients ranging from +.90 to +.98 for the children used to set up the standardization procedure. A median coefficient of +.91 resulted from correlating the two forms of the 1937 revision, Forms L and M, for each of the 21 groups involved in the standardization effort. It is quite apparent that the Stanford-Binet is a highly reliable measuring instrument. Nevertheless, individual performances on the test may show fluctuations over a period of time. IQ scores do change upon retesting. In Terman's 1916 standardization group half of the children deviated by five IQ points or more on retesting; 16 per cent deviated by ten points or more, 6.2 per cent by 15 points or more, and 1.85 per cent by 20 points or more. Thus, caution must be exercised in interpreting the meaning of a single assessment of a child's intelligence and in making predictions on the basis of a single score. Furthermore, as noted in Chapter 6, the later the age at which a test is administered, the more closely it correlates with an IQ score obtained at the age of 18. Scores of IQ tests show a sharp increase in long-term predictive power around five or six. Before then, they should be viewed with reserve.

The next important aspect of any test is its validity. Evaluating the validity of the Stanford-Binet is far more difficult than assessing its reliability. There is no definition of intelligence on which there is general agreement. In fact, there are as many views of intelligence as there are tests to measure it. This has led to the quip that intelligence is what intelligence tests measure. Such a belief is unduly pessimistic. IQ test scores have the ability to predict other things for groups of children such as school achievement and later intellectual functioning. Correlations between Stanford-Binet scores and achievement in first grade imply the moderate success of IQ scores in predicting school achievement. In this sense, the Stanford-Binet possesses *predictive validity*. The Stanford-Binet also possesses what is called *construct validity;* that is, it is constructed to contain items capable of measuring the kinds of abilities which Binet, and later Terman, termed as intelligence.

Finally, a number of cautions and criticisms should be noted. Although Binet attempted originally to assess a child's inborn or native capacity, an IQ is apparently only a measure of the child's *present level of functioning,* despite being moderately predictive of later functioning as well. A related point is that the Stanford-Binet assumes background experience similar to that of the children on whom the test was standardized. Many of its test materials presuppose a general familiarity with the American culture. Hence, scores of children whose backgrounds depart in any degree from the American norm should be viewed with suspicion. Although IQ scores of children of recently arrived Mexican laborers in California, for example, may fall below those of typical white, middle-class, urban youngsters, such results are not really valid indications of a difference between the two groups.

The Stanford-Binet has been charged with predicting neither social nor personality adjustment, nor success in life. Such criticisms lack validity. Binet, as we have seen, designed his test originally to identify levels of academic performance. In this respect, the test continues to do an adequate job. The intelligence test was never designed to assess personality factors, musical ability, or a host of other individual qualities. There are separate tests for these things.

Another criticism of the Stanford-Binet is its preponderance of items involving verbal ability. This is thought to penalize those children whose strengths lie in other areas of functioning. Although some children, such as those from bilingual homes or afflicted with hearing deficiencies, may be handicapped by the test's verbal biases, language facility remains a major factor in academic pursuits. To predict a child's success in such endeavors, an intelligence test must measure a child's potentialities in coping with their language demands. Besides, as noted in Chapter 5, the ability to deal with and to manipulate such abstract symbols as words is distinctly human and may be man's greatest glory. Thus, it is hardly inappropriate for intelligence tests to be weighted heavily in linguistic content. However, performance tests, as we shall see presently, have been developed to give a fair indication of the intellectual ability of children whose verbal facility may be limited.

One last caution. Although IQ tests and other tests differ in a number of ways, they also have many similarities. A child's performance on an IQ test, like his performance on any other test, depends, in part, on how he feels at the moment, on his mood, on his motivation, and on a score of similar incidental factors. An IQ result has maximal significance only if all conditions surrounding the test are optimal. It reveals no sacred, immutable truth about a child. It is only an index to one area of a child's functioning, an important area, to be sure, but one best interpreted when seen as the basis for a broad understanding of the child's behavior and personality.

Performance Tests

Although the term *performance* is something of a misnomer since performance tests require abstract abilities plus general knowledge and understanding, manipulation of objects has considerable importance in these tests. Verbal facility is a very important part of general intelligence, as has been observed, yet the evaluation of other skills uncovers valuable information regarding other areas of the child's capabilities. Studying the child's performance in the types of tasks usually contained in performance tests provides clinical insights into the techniques employed by the child in approaching a problem of the kind.

Appropriate for children between the ages of five and 15 is the Wechsler Intelligence Scale for Children (WISC) (Wechsler, 1949). The WISC includes both verbal and performance scales, of which the latter is probably the most widely used test of its kind at the present time. The performance scale comprises five subtests—picture arrangement, picture completion, block design, digit symbol, and object assembly. Figure 14-1 illustrates the administration of the WISC.

Because of the nature of the abilities measured by the WISC performance scale, it correlates less highly with the Stanford-Binet test than does the verbal scale. Similarly the IQs of the performance scale do not relate as well as the IQs of the verbal scale or the Stanford-Binet to school achievement. In view of the importance of verbal abilities in scholastic achievement this situation is quite understandable; even so, the lesser bearing of the performance IQs downgrades their predictive usefulness.

Another performance test, the Goodenough Draw-A-Man test (Goodenough, 1926), was one of the first such developed. The test requires

FIGURE 14-1

the child to draw "the best man he can." In the main the scoring is based on the number of details included in the drawing. The test is relatively simple to administer and score. Although Goodenough originally obtained rather high correlations between his Draw-A-Man IQs and those scored on the Stanford-Binet, Medinnus (1961a) found correlations ranging between +.26 and +.57 for a group of five-year-olds. Low correlations were also seen between Draw-A-Man IQs and subsequent first-grade achievement. Thus, though IQ scores obtained from children's drawings may be useful for gross estimates of ability and for general screening purposes, they do not serve the end for which intelligence tests were originally developed because they do not correlate highly with academic achievement. Samples of a child's Draw-A-Man products over a ten-month period appear in Figure 14-2.

Group Tests

Time is often a precious commodity. There is rarely enough of it to do what one wishes. To use time economically, tests have been developed to measure the ability of a large number of children simultaneously. Even if some of the advantages of individually ad-

FIGURE 14-2 Three-Draw-A-Man samples.

ministered tests are lost, group tests function as productive screening devices to single out those children who require further testing and observation. Indeed, a low score on a group test demands further testing because factors other than intelligence may intrude on the score. Misunderstood directions, anxiety over the test, and lack of motivation may affect a child's performance on a group test. In the administration of an individual test, an experienced examiner endeavors to eliminate such intrusions.

Commonly one hears that group tests are never as satisfactory as individual tests. Nevertheless, IQ scores obtained from group tests effectively predict school achievement. The closer similarity in the testing situation and nature of group IQ and achievement tests than of individual IQ and achievement tests may contribute to this predictability. Besides, in the day-to-day school situation the child does not enjoy the individual attention and encouragement that are present in the individual test situation. In school, the child's achievement rests in part on his capacity to follow directions, function independently, and apply himself to the task before him.

Figure 14-3 contains items extracted from a group test, the California Short-Form Test of Mental Maturity (Sullivan, Clark, & Tiegs, 1963).

Achievement Tests

The rapid increase in the testing of achievement during the 1950's stemmed partly from the self-critical, self-evaluative attitude of the nation's public schools. How effective are teaching techniques? How

Test 1 Opposites
Directions: In each row there is one picture that shows something which is opposite of the first picture. Find it and mark its number.

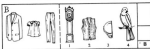

Test 2 Similarities
Directions: The first three pictures in each row are of things which are <u>alike</u> in some way. Decide how they are alike and then find the picture to the right of the dotted line that is most like them and mark its number.

Test 3 Analogies
Directions: In each row, the first picture is related to the second. The third picture goes with one of the four pictures to the right of the second dotted line in the same way. Find the related picture and mark its number.

Test 4 Numerical Values
Directions: Each problem tells you that a certain number of coins will add up to a certain amount of money. You are to find the correct number of coins of each kind—cents, nickels, dimes, quarters, and half-dollars.

D.   2 coins — 10 cents
     p   q   r   s   D

Test 5 Number Problems
Directions: Work these problems. Use scratch paper if necessary. Mark the letter of each correct answer.

E. There are 5 birds in a tree and 3 birds on a fence. How many birds are there in both places?
   a 2
   b 8
   c 15
   d 7   E

Test 6 Verbal Comprehension
Directions: Mark the number of the word that means the same or about the same as the first word.

F. blossom   1 tree   2 vine
             3 flower   4 garden   F

Test 7 Delayed Recall
Directions: Read the following items. Mark the number of each correct answer according to the story. (Story, The Life of a Fawn, read by examiner.)

G. The story read to you a while ago was about a
   1 fawn.
   2 dog.
   3 bear.
   4 wolf.   G

FIGURE 14-3   Sample items from the California Short-Form Test of Mental Maturity.

much have children learned from a particular course? Which areas of course content have pupils failed to assimilate? Such questions have spurred the drive to wider testing of achievement. In addition, knowledge of pupil achievement proves useful in counseling children and helps to make pertinent decisions about a child's academic strengths and weaknesses.

An indication of the importance attached to the assessment of achievement was a law passed by the California legislature in 1961 setting up a mandatory testing program throughout the state's public school system. California school districts are now required to administer standardized achievement tests in English and mathematics as well as intelligence tests at the fifth-, eighth-, and eleventh-grade levels. The State Board of Education has certified an approved list of tests from which school districts must select those to be used. Scores must be recorded in the pupils' cumulative records.

In the early elementary years achievement tests concentrate on the child's reading ability. One test commonly used at the primary level (Metropolitan Achievement Tests, 1959) isolates and measures four aspects of reading: word knowledge, word discrimination, sentence reading, and story reading. Later, achievement tests assess a number of fairly specific skills. A test considered appropriate for junior high-school students (Tiegs & Clark, 1957) covers three main areas: reading, arithmetic, and language, each of which is divided into the following subtests.

Reading
    Reading Vocabulary
        Mathematics
        Science
        Social Science
        General
    Reading Comprehension
        Following Directions
        Reference Skills
        Interpretations

Arithmetic
    Arithmetic Reasoning
        Meanings
        Symbols, Rules, and Equations
        Problems
    Arithmetic Fundamentals
        Addition
        Subtraction
        Multiplication
        Division

Language
    Mechanics of English
        Capitalization
        Punctuation
        Word Usage
    Spelling

Sample items drawn from two achievement tests are shown in Figure 14-4.

It may seem unnecessary to speak of the validity of achievement tests. Obviously they must be valid if they measure the amount of subject matter a child has learned from a course. Yet achievement

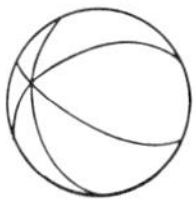

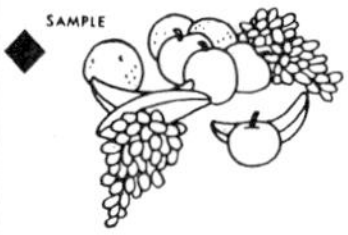

FIGURE 14-4   Items illustrating two school achievement tests.

tests have been criticized because too often they measure only a child's retention of isolated facts without concern for other possible goals of the course. How much, for example, has the course stimulated the child's interest and curiosity? To what extent has the child gained a broad understanding of the principles involved? To what extent is the child able to apply the information he has learned to the solving of problems in a specific area? Since all these are reasonable educational goals, an educational achievement test, to be valid, might well assess a child's proficiency in these regions. In all fairness, it must be pointed out that achievement tests have grown increasingly concerned with some of these matters. Another discernible trend is the measuring of a child's knowledge in such broad areas as natural science and social science rather than in fields of specific subject fare.

Achievement-test scores are typically interpreted on the basis of *grade norms*. The child's raw score is converted into one showing the grade level at which such a score is oftenest obtained. Despite the valid criticisms to which this method may be subjected, it has the advantage in the educational setting of denoting, at least approximately, a child's acceleration or retardation in a particular area of academic activity.

PERSONALITY APPRAISAL

The techniques devised to assess personality do not compare in effectiveness with those that appraise intellect. To begin with, personality is less clearly defined than intelligence; psychological theorists cannot agree on what constitutes personality. Furthermore, personality seems to be a subtler and more complex notion that intelligence, requiring more indirect methods of assessment (Goodenough, 1949b). Of the many appraisal techniques developed, each often assesses but one aspect of personality. They thus fall short of the mark because personality is the sum of several different traits in the individual.

The methods of personality appraisal also fail to measure up to the ideal for a historical reason. Many of them grew out of a clinical need for appraising or diagnosing children referred to child guidance or child clinical centers. However, a tool useful for clinical diagnosis of the nature of a child's psychological problems may not be equally productive for appraising the personality of nonproblem children. More recent research has gone beyond the applied nature of clinical diagnosis, looking to the development of more refined and precise instruments.

Finally, personality appraisal in children presents problems not found in the appraisal of adult personality. Yet many measures developed for the adult level have been adapted for use with children. Paper-and-pencil tests, for example, are inappropriate at the younger age levels. They limit the use of self-reporting techniques. And the problems of interpretation and validation are more numerous and more difficult at the child than at the adult level.

Many attempts have been made to classify the techniques of personality assessment. For purposes of classification various aspects of the techniques have been used—the type of response required of the individual, the nature of the test materials, and the interpretation of the responses. For the present discussion the appraisal techniques are divided into four main categories: observational method, projective measures, objective tests, and parental report. Although any single technique may easily be assigned to more than one category, the present scheme has been adopted for convenience. In actual practice, several techniques supplement the information gained through each.

Observational Method

At the outset of this book, the importance of observation as a scientific method for acquiring information was heavily emphasized. Indeed, insofar as personality is revealed in behavior, the observational approach is often the only way to validate a child's score or rating on a personality test. For example, to have validity, a child's score pointing toward maladjustment on an adjustment inventory must relate to his day-to-day behavior with his associates either in the home or outside of it. Extended observation of a single child seldom is feasible, however. For this reason short-cut methods are developed. But one should never forget that an instrument is no more uesful than its ability to yield information similar to that obtained by the more cumbersome approach of long-term observation of the individual.

Life Situations. Observation of the child's behavior in his day-to-day environment remains one of the most commonly used methods of personality appraisal. In fact, observation may be more productive in understanding the child's personality than complicated tests that are difficult to interpret. The child is spontaneous in his behavior, expressing himself less covertly and with fewer inhibitions than the adult. He represses little. Indeed he may reveal more in his overt behavior than in his responses to standard measures of personality assessment that may reflect some inhibition, anxiety, and shyness.

Methods of recording observations and the kinds of behaviors observed are showing increasing sophistication. Observational categories based on theory seem better at yielding information pertinent to the assessment of personality than random observations. In one study (Rafferty, Tyler, & Tyler, 1960), observational records of children's behavior were classified into six motivational categories (p. 693).

> recognition-status (concern with skill or competence in social, intellectual, or play activity), love and affection (concern with acceptance, warmth, liking or being liked by others), dominance (concern with direction or control of others), protection-dependence (concern with having others prevent frustration, make decisions), and independence (concern with self-mediated satisfactions including reliance on oneself)

Frequently impressions gained through observation are quantified through the use of check lists or rating scales designed to describe the child's behavior on the basis of a limited number of traits. The following is an illustration of a check list developed to find a child's position with respect to ascendant or submissive behavior.

1. Submits to any child who takes the initiative.
2. Even submits to younger children.
3. Dominates children more mature than himself.
4. Submits to a leader only after a struggle to dominate.
5. Usually leads a small group.
6. Decides who shall participate in the group activities.
7. Is a leader in any group.
8. Directs all activity about him.
9. Neither leads nor follows; plays alone.
10. Other children make many appeals to him for information.
11. Dominates other children through his ability to talk effectively.
12. Other children appeal to him to make decisions for the group.
13. Dominates other children through their love or admiration for him.
14. Dominates other children through his wealth of ideas.
15. Definitely schemes to get others to carry out his plans.
16. Gives commands with an air of finality.
17. Helpless unless someone organizes activity for him.
18. Hesitates to initiate activity.
19. Hesitates to make suggestions to other children.
20. Usually follows the ideas of others for activity.
21. Can take the initiative if it is absolutely necessary.
22. Usually takes the initiative.
23. Seeks the approval of the leader before he acts.
24. Does not push the issue in case of opposition.
25. Stands aside to let others participate.
26. Fights for his place as leader.
27. Opposition spurs him on to greater activity.
28. Insists that other children do as he wishes.
29. Does not defend his own rights with other children.
30. Gets willing cooperation easily.

(Stott & Ball, 1957, p. 261)

Ascendance-submission check-list data were available on 60 children over a ten-year interval from the age of two or three to over 13. Ascendant behavior increased throughout the three-year period of nursery-school attendance, with a very low frequency of interactive behavior at the age of three and under, increasing sharply up to the age of five. With the change from nursery school to kindergarten, ascendant behavior became less frequent. There were no consistent changes in the frequency of ascendant-submissive behavior after the age of five (Stott & Ball, 1957).

Observational rating scales are widely used in personality appraisal. Since the information obtained through them is purely descriptive in nature, the value of such scales is limited. Ratings of behavior do not interpret behavior in terms of its causes and the type of personality underlying it. Even so, note the following items drawn from a scale (Haggerty-Olson-Wickman Behavior Rating Schedules) designed to identify problem behavior in school children and to assess 35 physical, mental, social, and emotional characteristics (Haggerty, Olson, & Wickman, 1930).

How does he accept authority?

Defiant	Critical of authority	Ordinarily obedient	Respectful, complies by habit	Entirely resigned, accepts all authority

How does he react to frustrations or to unpleasant situations?

Very sub-missive, long-suffering	Tolerant, rarely blows up	Generally self-con-trolled	Impatient	Easily irritated, hot-headed, explosive

Is he suspicious or trustful?

Very suspicious, distrustful	Has to be assured	Generally unsuspicious and trustful	Somewhat gullible	Accepts everything without question

Does he act impulsively or cautiously?

Impulsive, bolts, acts on the spur of the moment	Frequently unreflective and imprudent	Acts with reasonable care	Deliberate	Very cautious and calculating

Miniature Life Situations. Although any interference with behavior in its natural setting introduces possible error in the accuracy of interpretation, control of a situation frequently increases the precision and significance of the data obtained. For this reason, real-life situations have been simulated in order to make appraisals of personality. The use of a miniature life situation assumes a relation between the individual's behavior in this experimental environment and his behavior outside of it. It is also argued that the child will reveal various personality characteristics by his manipulation of the materials at hand or by his solution of the problems presented.

In the Hartshorne and May (1928) study of deceit in children between the ages of eight and eleven, a variety of methods were employed. One of the measures of deception involved four athletic tests: the dynamometer test, the spirometer test, pull-ups, and standing broad jump. The children were led to believe that the tests were part of a real athletic contest in which badges were to be awarded to the winners of the four events. The directions for each test were given to the children individually and they were asked to try each procedure, the examiner taking mental note of their performance. Subsequently, the child was told to proceed alone, recording the best of several trials. The difference between the examiner's rating and the child's own was the measure of deception.

Selected general findings of the study indicated older children to be slightly more deceptive than younger ones. The sex differences were few. The more intelligent children cheated less. Children who showed symptoms of emotional instability were more likely to be deceitful than others, and children from lower socioeconomic backgrounds demonstrated less honesty than those from higher levels.

Observation of Play. This technique presents the child with a wide range of play materials including toys, paints, dough, and cold cream. Freedom is permitted in their use. If he so chooses, the child may arrange, build, destroy, or smear. The rationale for this freedom is that the natural language of children is behavior and that the child will disclose his needs, attitudes, feelings, and problems through the manner in which he approaches and deals with play materials. If a completely permissive and accepting atmosphere is established, the child will have no need to conceal his feelings; the restrictions in the world of reality will not be present.

What are some of the aspects of personality revealed in a child's play? An alert observer can identify differences among children in a great many personality areas. If a child is observed playing with toys representing real-life objects, such as a doll house with dolls suggesting the family unit, one can follow the enactment of situations and events, the treatment of the various dolls, the child's emotional expressions, and his verbal behavior. When manipulating such tactile materials as clay and finger paint, the child's attitude toward middle-class strictures against dirtiness and messiness may be disclosed through the spontaneity with which he approaches these materials. Is he inhibited, anxious, relaxed, aggressive? Is he secure enough to explore the possible artistic uses of such amorphous substances or is his behavior rigid and stereotyped?

The following excerpt describes a young child's reaction to playing with dough.

> Another little girl whispered "I can't" at first, and approached the dough almost tentatively. She ran her hand in a gingerly way through the mess, and did not squeeze the dough until the experimenter had done so. However, when she did, she squeezed *very* hard, with a kind of aggressive violence which no other child showed. After more play she volunteered, however, "I don't think it's nice." Yet when the experimenter started to put away the pan, she resisted: "I'm not all finished yet." She shook her hands through the mess saying, "Gooey, gooey, gooey!" She squeezed, made balls of the dough. But at the end, after she had washed her hands, she said, "I never want to do that again . . . why did you do this to me?" Her expressive face appeared "mildly horrified and puzzled," wanting rapport at the beginning; after being released by the experimenter's example she was definitely aggressive with the paste, in contrast to the other children, and then seemed to develop a sense of guilt as she went on, apparently feeling this was naughty. Among other comments made in the context of cleaning up after the dough, she said, "My mother spanks me if I'm naughty . . . I cry so the neighbors hear . . . sometimes I scratch her and she spanks me" (Murphy, 1956, p. 124).

Sometimes situations are provided which specifically encourage the release of aggressive, destructive feelings. The intensity in the child of these tendencies, his fear or anxiety over exhibiting such behavior, and the sequence of his behavior through which some control is achieved can be observed.

There is no question that the child reveals his personality through play. Problems arise, however, in the interpretation of such behavior. For example, a child who shows little aggression in his play either may have little need for aggressive outlets or he may be restrained from expressing aggression by anxiety or fear of punishment. Therefore, data obtained from observing a child's play must be used in conjunction with information from other sources, essentially from techniques that are more objective as to scoring and interpretation. To some of these the chapter now turns.

Projective Assessment Techniques

The idea that individuals will bring structure to ambiguous, diffuse stimuli on the basis of individual needs, feelings, and personality patterns is popular in psychology. The individual imposes on the environment his own psychological outlook, organization, and meanings. In a formless cloud the child sees the friendly face of a man and in the shadow on the wall a vicious animal about to pounce on its prey. This idea of projection is accepted widely as an approach to the assessment of personality because the individual is least willing or least able to reveal through interview or questionnaire those of his aspects that most adequately describe the uniqueness of his personality (Frank, 1939).

In the past few decades a tremendous growth has taken place in the development and use of projective techniques.[1] As a result, a great number and variety of projective instruments are now available. Taking the cue from Allport's (1961) classification, let us describe several examples of these techniques under three main headings: perceptive, apperceptive, and productive.

Perceptive Techniques. The child is confronted with ambiguous material and is asked to tell what it means to him. Either auditory or visual stimuli may be used; the latter is commoner. The most widely used instrument of this description is the Rorschach Ink Blot Test developed in 1921. The test consists of a series of ten cards, five colored and five achromatic. These are presented in sequence with the individual instructed to describe what he sees in the ink blots. Later, the child identifies on the card the location of what he saw and the clues used in his response. In scoring the child's responses, a variety of categories are employed, including the location and determinants of the response, its originality, and the time required for the individual to respond. From an interpretation of the record of the responses a full description of the individual's personality is constructed. The following account is a description of a nine-year-old boy referred to a child guidance clinic by his teacher because of his difficulties in the classroom.

---

[1] A fuller treatment of projective techniques appropriate at the child level may be found in the following source: Rabin, A. I., and Haworth, Mary R. (Eds.), *Projective Techniques with Children,* New York: Grune & Stratton, 1960.

Jim's thinking is fairly well organized and there is no evidence of bizarreness or morbidity in his fantasies. He is able to see things as most people do and there are indications of a very early inculcation of adult standards concerning propriety, right and wrong, and how one should behave.

Despite Jim's attempts to maintain a facade of happiness, willingness and compliance, he is rather vulnerable to emotional stimuli and is apt to react largely in terms of his feelings of the moment with immature expression of his emotions. However, when possible, Jim attempts to handle emotional impact in a superficial, behavioral way that is not essentially related to his own feelings. That is, he responds in terms of what he feels is demanded by the situation without a genuine integration of his own feelings with the realistic demands of the situation.

Jim is very concerned about handling sexual and aggressive impulses and a good deal of tension and anxiety is associated with such impulses. His great concern about aggression is reflected in Rorschach responses such as "Volcanoes," "Fire burning up the ground," and "Like they were in Africa and killed a bear." Jim is fearful of his own aggressive impulses and defends strongly against their direct expression. It appears that his fear of aggression has led to a generalized inhibition of most forms of assertiveness so that even socially acceptable strivings for attainment are inhibited. Hence, Jim's aggression is expressed primarily in indirect ways through passive resistance or passive negativism.

In part, Jim's fearfulness of aggression appears to stem from unresolved Oedipal conflicts in which castration anxiety plays a major role. While Jim would like to be able to compete aggressively against father figures, he is quite apprehensive about such wishes, fearing that his castration or destruction will be the outcome of such competition. He views father figures as quite dangerous. But despite his fearfulness of father figures, Jim seems to want father's permission (and probably father's encouragement and support) in expressing himself in a more masculine way.

Apperceptive Techniques. These techniques require the individual to respond to less amorphous material by contributing some interpretation of his own. Figure 14-5 shows a picture from a series intended to assess parent-child relations (Alexander, 1952). The subject is asked to develop a story about a picture, explaining what led up to the scene, what is occurring, and what will happen. The story is to include the thoughts and feelings of the characters. Stories are then evaluated for the approach used to solve their problems, the nature of the emotional expressions conveyed, whether positive or negative, and the way in which the characters in them are viewed—as friendly or hostile. The following is an Alexander summary about an 11-year-old boy.

Ronald found thinking about the stimuli in the cards a threatening experience. He used only the main stimuli (mainly the figures) in the

FIGURE 14-5   Sample picture from the Alexander Adult-Child Interaction Test.

cards and added few stimuli in an effort to account for the ones presented.   Emotional expressions were few in number and most of them
were negative.   Adults and parents are viewed as hostile and he has aggressive and hostile feelings in return.   He tries to solve his problems by
avoidance and escape (Alexander, 1952, p. 18).

Incomplete sentences have been used to elicit children's attitudes
and feelings toward people and toward other aspects of their environment.   Stems of sentences are provided, which the child is required to
complete.   The following list of stems represents a test intended to
assess parent-child relations (Hoeflin & Kell, 1959, p. 12).   The re-

sponses are scored on the bases of how the child conceives of the parent and child relationship, whether it promotes growth or is autocratic, and of the positiveness or negativeness of feeling.

1. Our family	11. Discipline
2. As a child I enjoyed	12. Teen-agers
3. My mother	13. My father
4. Being a child	14. Making high grades in school
5. Obedience	15. Punishment
6. Children should not	16. As a child I disliked
7. If my father	17. A democratic family
8. When I was in high school	18. If my mother
9. I wish my parents had	19. Being at home
10. Being a (boy) (girl)	20. Making decisions in the home

Productive Techniques. As the wording implies, the child produces something in these tests which the examiner then interprets. Long before the formal beginnings of psychology, interest was shown in analyzing people's handwriting. Yet not much progress has been made through the years toward developing an objective analysis and valid interpretation of handwriting. Similarly, numerous difficulties are met in attempting to construct a valid measure of personality from children's drawings although several drawing tests are in current use. The rationale for relying on these tests is that children divulge important aspects of their personalities through the way they express themselves artistically.

Most widely used among children is the Draw-A-Person Test (DAP), a descendant of Goodenough's original Draw-A-Man Test (1926) which, as we saw, was designed to assess intelligence in young children. This method for evaluating children's drawings on the basis of hints of several personality traits was devised by Machover (1949). To her, the child's drawing of the human figure represented his image of himself in relation to his environment. Things noted about the drawing include the kinds of lines employed, the part of the page covered, and the dimensions, proportions, and perspective of the figure. After the drawing has been completed, the examiner elicits from the child various associations he may have in connection with his picture. He is requested to describe the feelings and mood of the figure drawn and other such characteristics. There are no objective scoring norms for the DAP Test; its use is primarily as a clinical aid in understanding the individual child.

Several interesting findings emerged from a study which endeavored to develop a scale of sexual differentiation from the DAP Test

(Haworth & Normington, 1961). Pairs of drawings, male and female figures, were obtained from 312 children ranging in age from seven through 12. Four levels of sexual differentiation were detected, from the lowest level of "figures nearly the same, no apparent sex," to the highest level of "each figure well differentiated as to sex," with such items as mustache or pants fly for the male and breasts and jewelry for the female. With age an increase in sex differentiation was noted, girls consistently showing greater differentiation than boys and also placing greater emphasis on figures of their own sex.

Objective Tests

Objective paper-and-pencil tests are perhaps the oldest approach to the assessment of personality. Their development related to the early success in constructing tests to appraise intelligence. Because these tests presumably provided valid assessments of intelligence, it was only natural that psychologists should make the effort to apply their technique to personality measurement. However, the relative value of objective and projective tests has generated lively controversy. Adherents of the projective approach contend that measurement of separate traits does injustice to the complexity of personality and to the interaction among personality factors. The opposite position notes the difficulty of scoring and interpreting the projective material obtained; without objectivity, it holds, a scientific assessment of personality can never be attained. Both views contain strengths as well as limitations. For the present, at least, adequate evaluation of a child's personality involves the use of a wide variety of instruments.

Personality inventories are expected to uncover a specific number of elements considered to be important by the builder of the test. Two of the tests used most commonly with children, the California Test of Personality and the Rogers Test of Personality Adjustment, have some validity. There is evidence (Smith, 1958) that both are significantly, and at the least, moderately, related to teacher and peer nomination of well- and poorly adjusted children (see Chapter 12). Because of the nature of objective tests, they obviously cannot be used below the seven- or eight-year level, although in the California Test the questions can be read to children by the examiner.

The California Test of Personality has various forms appropriate for use from kindergarten through the adult level. Its organization has been described in the following way by its authors (Thorpe, Clark, & Tiegs, 1953):

1. Self Adjustment:
   Based on feelings
   of personal security

A. Self-reliance
B. Sense of personal worth
C. Sense of personal freedom
D. Feeling of belonging
E. Freedom from withdrawing tendencies
F. Freedom from nervous symptoms

Life Adjustment:
   A balance between
   self and social
   adjustment

A. Social standards
B. Social skills

2. Social Adjustment:
   Based on feelings
   of social security

C. Freedom from anti-social tendencies
D. Family relations
E. School relations
F. Community relations

The test comprises a series of questions which are answered by checking blanks marked "yes" or "no." The test's primary purpose, said its authors, is to indicate the extent to which a child is adjusting to the problems confronting him and to which he is developing a well-adjusted, socially effective personality. Fifteen raw scores, for which keys are provided, are converted into percentiles based on norms in order to be plotted on so-called *profile* sheets. Examination of a child's profile aids the teacher in ascertaining specifically where guidance or remedial effort is needed. The following items are typical of those contained in the primary series, kindergarten to grade three.

Is it hard for you to look out for yourself?	YES NO
Do the children forget to ask you to play with them?	YES NO
Do you feel bad because you can't do things well enough?	YES NO
Does your stomach ache often?	YES NO
Do you feel that some of the teachers have it in for you?	YES NO

The Rogers Test of Personality Adjustment (Rogers, 1931), designed for children from nine through 13, is one of the oldest personality tests available for youngsters. From it, four scores and a total score can be derived. A personal inferiority score indicates the degree to which the child perceives himself as physically or mentally less capable than his peers. The score of social maladjustment is an index to the child's feelings about his social relations with other children. The family-relations score represents the child's reports of conflict and dissatisfaction in his relations with his parents and siblings. The day-dreaming score reflects the child's indulgence in fantasies and unrealistic thinking. Composed of all of these, the total score indexes the seriousness of the child's maladjustment. As the intent of the items, as a rule, is rather concealed, the responses are probably more meaningful and valid than if the test simply required yes or no answers.

The Rogers Test of Personality Adjustment was administered to 256 fifth-graders drawn from small towns and rural areas in the Midwest. In general, children from higher social-class backgrounds showed fewer signs of personality maladjustment than children from lower-class homes. However, those children whose fathers had the highest educational achievement showed greater maladjustment than many of the children whose fathers were less well educated. Pressures for achievement exerted by high-achieving parents on their children may be detrimental to healthy personality development (Burchinal, Gardner, & Hawkes, 1958).

Self-ratings or check lists, while less objective than personality inventories, unveil the way the individual sees himself. Information thus obtained about the concept of the self helps the youngster to a better understanding of himself. The Mooney Problem Check List (Mooney & Gordon, 1950) represents an instrument designed for this purpose. Its form for junior high school consists of 30 items in each of seven problem areas: health and physical development; school; home and family; money, work, and the future; boy and girl relations; relations to people in general; and self-centered concerns. The youngster underlines items that he feels cause him some personal concern and circles the number of items that he considers as serious problems for himself.

Parental Report

Many of the more formal personality tests used with some success among adults are unsuitable for children, especially at the younger age levels, because of the young child's inability to read and write and respond in a relevant manner to the questions posed to him. However, information acquired from persons intimate with the behavior of children is frequently of great value in appraising a child's approach to people and to his environment in general. Clearly, parents are in a position to furnish such information. Although data of this type are obtained indirectly and parental impressions of a child may not be entirely unbiased or objective, a parent's perception of the young child exposes a great deal about the youngster's personality and about the kind of psychological environment in which the child's personality is formed. Parental report may vary from free-flowing discussions to the use of objective instruments.

Interview. As a technique for appraisal the interview can provide information about a child which is obtainable in no other way. The child's reaction to intimate interactions and situations within the family, the events that have been important in the shaping of his current level of adjustment, his characteristic mode of response to frustration and stress—all these and more may be discerned most directly from parental interviews. The alert interviewer will endeavor to separate facts from attitudes toward them. Both are valuable, perhaps equally so, but as the main interest is an appraisal of the child's personality, knowledge of a parent's attitude toward the child may help to explain rather than to assess his personality.

An interview may be totally unplanned in which the interviewee is free to pursue any topic he wishes or it may be confined to a predetermined list of questions. Each type has its advantages and disadvantages and, in actual practice, the interview is seldom completely one or the other. Frequently in the initial stages of an interview, rapport is established by letting the parent discuss those areas he selects; later the interviewer may wish to dig further into certain points or to obtain information where gaps exist.

Since the information gathered through interviews is not easily quantified, except through the tedious procedure of rating the transcript of the taped interview, examiners frequently employ more objective methods of assessing the child's personality as revealed through parental report. Two of these are the *semantic differential* and the *Q-sort* techniques. The semantic differential technique was designed originally as a device for measuring the meaning of various concepts (see Osgood, Suci, & Tannenbaum, 1957). As its name implies, the technique helps to discern the differences in meaning which an individual holds toward two concepts. The individual discloses his attitude toward a concept or the meaning the concept has for him by rating it on a number of polarized scales. The discrepancy between an individual's ratings of two separate concepts is taken as representative of the extent to which their meanings differ to him.

In a study of the relation between maternal self-acceptance and maternal acceptance of her child, Medinnus and Curtis (1963) asked 56 mothers of preschool children to describe "My child (as he is)" by rating him on 20 bipolar scales. Then the mothers were asked to repeat the procedure, now describing "My child (as I would like him to be)." The item by item discrepancy in their ratings of the two concepts was taken as a measure of maternal acceptance of the child. Moderate and statistically significant correlations were obtained between two measures of maternal self-acceptance and adjustment, and the "semantic differential" measure of child acceptance. As we have already seen, the mothers who were most accepting of their children were those who scored highest in self-acceptance. These were some of the bipolar scales used:

```
    friendly____:____:____:____:____:____:____hostile
     trustful____:____:____:____:____:____:____suspicious
   deliberate____:____:____:____:____:____:____impulsive
   submissive____:____:____:____:____:____:____assertive
     sociable____:____:____:____:____:____:____shy
       mature____:____:____:____:____:____:____infantile
   emotionally
```

The Q-sort of technique elicits an individual's view of himself or of others through a rating-type approach. Originally developed by Stephenson (1935), the technique requires the person to sort a large variety of descriptive phrases along a continuum from, say, "most like myself" to "least like myself." Rogers (1951) used this technique to obtain a picture of an individual's self-perceptions before and after therapy, as well as of his view of the "ideal self." The technique is particularly productive in collecting parental descriptions of their child and conceptions of the "ideal child." The latter sorting uncovers interesting information on the kinds of behavior and characteristics to which the parent attaches greatest significance. Moreover, discrepancy between two parents in their descriptions of their child and of the ideal child sheds some light on certain aspects of the psychological atmosphere in which the child is raised.

Thirty-eight sets of parents of five-year-olds sorted two pools of 42 items each to describe their own child and the ideal five-year-old (Medinnus, 1961b). Parental agreement was higher for the "real sort" describing their own child than for the "ideal sort," indicating that parents agree more in their perceptions of their children than in their expectations and goals for them. There was generally greater agreement between parents of boys than of girls. The item ranked as most important for the ideal five-year-old was: "is in good physical condition; is usually healthy."

OTHER APPRAISAL METHODS

Several further methods of gaining information about the child's behavioral development warrant brief mention, either because of general usefulness or because they attempt to appraise areas of behavior often overlooked in discussions of personality development.

Vineland Social Maturity Scale

Working with mentally retarded children, Doll observed great differences in the social competence of children of the same intellectual capacity. And since social competence is of particular importance to children of inferior intellectual ability, as we have seen, Doll recognized the need for a practical instrument to assess this area. First published in 1935, the Vineland Social Maturity Scale (Doll, 1935) consists of a series of items of growing difficulty representing progressive social independence in the following areas of behavior: self-help (eating, dressing), self-direction, locomotion, occupation, communication, and social relations.

Through interviews with parents, information about a child's behavior and development is obtained. The child is given a plus or minus for each item based on his ability to perform the task in question. The total score, representing the sum of the items passed, is translated into a Social Quotient (SQ) by converting the total score into a "social age" figure and dividing this by the chronological age of the child. The SQ, similar in computation to the IQ, compares the child's social competence with others of his chronological age. Thus, a child of average social maturity for his age level would receive an SQ of 100. These are items contained in the three- to five-year levels (Doll, 1953):

III–IV	IV–V
Walks downstairs one step per tread	Cares for self at toilet
	Washes face unassisted
Plays cooperatively at kindergarten level	Goes about neighborhood unattended
Buttons coat or dress	Dresses self except for tying
Helps at little household tasks	Uses pencil or crayon for drawing
"Performs" for others	Plays competitive exercise games
Washes hands unaided	

Sociometric Tests

A child's acceptance by and popularity among his agemates is an important part of his behavior and adjustment. Although adjustment to peers is only one facet of a child's personality, his relationship with others serves well as a measure of his general adjustment. Children who rank low in popularity frequently exhibit, as we have observed, a variety of maladaptive and maladjusted behaviors.

It would be rare, especially in elementary schools, for teachers to have no notion of how little or much a child is accepted by his peers.

However, data furnished by a sociometric measure specify quite clearly how any child is accepted by his peers. In addition, the Guess Who method discloses information about how a child is perceived by them. Is a particular child perceived as possessing primarily positive, acceptable qualities or characteristics? Or are the characteristics attributed to him by his peers largely negative?

Peer ratings spot areas of strength and weakness in any child's behavior as perceived by his agemates. This information assists a teacher in her efforts to manipulate a child's social environment so as to produce positive changes in his behavior. It also helps her to establish in the classroom a psychological atmosphere that is conducive to the development of healthy psychological adjustment in all the children. Among older children, the teacher or counselor may use the information gained from sociometric tests and Guess Who devices to aid the child in gaining insight into his behavior, especially with regard to those characteristics that impede his acceptance by his peers.

The Children's Manifest Anxiety Scale, the Children's Self-Concept Scale and a sociometric ranking were administered to 111 fourth, fifth, and sixth graders. The less popular children tended to be more anxious and they tended to hold poorer self-concepts. These findings were true for both sexes and for the three grade levels. However, the low magnitude of the correlations suggested that the interrelations are complex and that other variables are of considerable importance in affecting a child's sociometric standing (Horowitz, 1962).

School Anecdotal Records

As a trained person, the teacher is in a particularly advantageous position to observe a child's behavior in a variety of day-to-day situations. Both in the formal classroom setting and on the informal playground, the child displays his general response to his environment. Specifically, he demonstrates his response to frustration, his resourcefulness in meeting new situations, his level of persistence, his attitudes of independence, his sense of responsibility, and his social and emotional adjustment.

Anecdotal records keep track of these behaviors. They are diary-like accounts of crucial observations and impressions of a child's performance. Frequently the incidents entered into the record are highly significant in understanding the personality and adjustment of a particular child. The usefulness of these records depends, however, on the objectivity of the recorder and his observations, and on the rele-

vance of the incidents recorded. When anecdotal records are accumu-
lated over a period of time, they present a rich, factual, detailed picture of the child. Recurring patterns of behavior can be noted and
a broad understanding can be gained of a child's characteristic manner and level of functioning. The following entries in an anecdotal
record of a youngster kept by her third-grade teacher illustrate the
types of information generally included in such accounts.

March 1: Reading group three was in the front of the room having its
phonics lesson while the other two reading groups were working at their
desks. Debbie had volunteered to divide a word into syllables on the
chalkboard. Julie, seated in the reading circle behind Debbie, repeatedly swung her crossed leg, hitting Debbie's posterior. Julie's behavior
ceased when I remonstrated with her. (Julie's behavior was caused apparently by her jealousy of Debbie who this time won their ceaseless
struggle to sit next to me in the reading circle.)

March 17: Julie and her best friend, Paulia, quarreled over a problem
related to a difficulty between the two families while entering the school
grounds in the morning. Characteristically, Julie impulsively and in anger slapped Paulia forcefully in the face. This provoked a battle between the two girls requiring intervention by the yard teacher.

April 4: Jimmy, on courtesy patrol in the hall outside of Julie's third-
grade room, reported to me an incident which had occurred between
him and Julie. When Jimmy attempted to prevent Julie from running
in the hall, she refused to comply and when Jimmy attempted to enforce his command, Julie added insult to injury by defiantly calling him
"stupid."

April 23: By actual count, Julie left her seat to socialize with other
children ten times in the space of one hour this morning—this despite
the fact I ordered her to return to and to remain in her seat each time.
(Little wonder that she seldom completes her seatwork satisfactorily!)

June 3: This morning it was Julie's turn to be in charge of one of the
balls during recess. She agreed to play "four square" with a small group
of children. When Julie was "out" she became angry and upset and
took the ball and ran to an isolated section of the playground. (One of
the playground rules of our school forbids the breaking up of a school
game.)

Ann came to me in tears during afternoon recess because Julie pushed
her out of the line of children waiting to jump rope. (Though Julie
desperately needs friends, the two incidents today illustrate her negative
approach to others which antagonizes her classmates and makes an adequate social adjustment for Julie seem even more remote.)

SUMMARY

Three main areas of appraisal have been explored: infant assessment, assessment of intellectual ability, and assessment of personality.
Despite the fruitless efforts of psychologists to predict future ability

from tests administered to infants, Gesell's methods for measuring rate of general development in infancy have value. The mental testing movement originally developed IQ tests to discern levels of academic ability. Although intelligence tests have been charged with failing to assess a wide range of characteristics, such tests continue to predict adequately a child's level of performance in the school setting, the purpose for which they were originally intended. Four broad techniques for appraising personality were examined: observational methods, projective measures, objective tests, and parental report. For a number of reasons the techniques devised to evaluate personality have not proven as satisfactory as those used for appraising the intellect. Even though each technique falls short of adequate assessment of the dynamic interrelation and interaction among an individual's personality traits, in the actual practice of diagnosing personality a number of the techniques described supplement one another. The result is that a fairly distinct picture of the child's personality structure unfolds.

REFERENCES

Alexander, T. The Adult-Child Interaction Test. *Monogr. soc. Res. Child Develpm.*, 1952, **17**, No. 2 (Serial No. 55).

Allport, G. W. *Pattern and growth in personality.* New York: Holt, 1961.

Anderson, J. E. The limitations of infant and preschool tests in the measurement of intelligence. *J. Psychol.*, 1939, **8**, 351–379.

Bayley, Nancy. *California First-Year Mental Scale.* Berkeley: Univer. Calif. Press, 1933. (a)

Bayley, Nancy. Mental growth during the first three years. A developmental study of sixty-one children by repeated tests. *Genet. Psychol. Monogr.*, 1933, **14**, No. 1. (b)

Burchinal, L., Gardner, B., & Hawkes, G. Children's personality adjustment and the socio-economic status of their families. *J. genet. Psychol.*, 1958, **92**, 149–159.

Cattell, Psyche. *Cattell Infant Intelligence Scale.* New York: Psychol. Corp., 1947.

Doll, E. A. A genetic scale of social maturity. *Am. J. Orthopsychiat.*, 1935, **5**, 180–188.

Doll, E. A. *The measurement of social competence.* Minneapolis: Educ. Test Bur., 1953.

Escalona, Sybille. The use of infant tests for predictive purposes. *Bull. Menninger Clin.*, 1950, **14**, 117–128.

Frank, L. K. Projective methods for the study of personality. *J. Psychol.*, 1939, **8**, 389–413.

Gesell, A. *The first five years of life.* New York: Harper, 1940.

Gesell, A., & Amatruda, Catherine S. *Developmental diagnosis.* New York: Hoeber, 1947.

Gilliland, A. R. The measurement of the mentality of infants. *Child Develpm.*, 1948, **19**, 155–158.

Goodenough, Florence L. *Measurement of intelligence by drawings.* Tarrytown-on-Hudson, N. Y.: World Book, 1926.

Goodenough, Florence L. *Mental testing.* New York: Rinehart, 1949. (a)

Goodenough, Florence L. The appraisal of child personality. *Psychol. Rev.*, 1949, **56**, 123–131. (b)

Griffiths, Ruth. *Griffiths Mental Development Scale.* London: Univer. London Press, 1954.

Haggerty, M. E., Olson, W. C., & Wickman, E. K. Haggerty-Olson-Wickman Behavior Rating Schedules. Yonkers-on-Hudson, N. Y.: World Book, 1930.

Hartshorne, H., & May, M. A. *Studies in the nature of character.* I. *Studies in deceit.* New York: Macmillan, 1928.

Haworth, Mary R., & Normington, Cheryl J. A sexual differentation scale for the D-A-P Test. *J. proj. Tech.*, 1961, **25**, 441–450.

Hoeflin, Ruth, & Kell, Leone. The Kell-Hoeflin Incomplete Sentences Blank: Youth-Parent Relations. *Monogr. soc. Res. Child Develpm.*, 1959, **24**, No. 3.

Hofstaetter, P. R. The changing composition of "intelligence"; a study in T technique. *J. genet. Psychol.*, 1954, **85**, 159–164.

Horowitz, Frances D. The relationship of anxiety, self-concept, and sociometric status among fourth, fifth, and sixth grade children. *J. abnorm. soc. Psychol.*, 1962, **65**, 212–214.

Illingworth, R. S. *The development of the infant and young child.* London: Livingston, 1960.

Knobloch, Hilda, & Pasamanick, B. A developmental questionnaire for infants forty weeks of age: an evaluation. *Monogr. soc. Res. Child Develpm.*, 1955, **22**, No. 2.

Machover, Karen. *Personality projection in the drawing of the human figure.* Springfield, Ill.: Thomas, 1949.

MacRae, J. M. Retests of children given mental tests as infants. *J. genet. Psychol.*, 1955, **87**, 111–119.

Medinnus, G. R. An investigation of school readiness and first grade adjustment. Unpubl. mss., 1961. (a)

Medinnus, G. R. Q-sort descriptions of five-year-old children by their parents. *Child Develpm.*, 1961, **32**, 473–489. (b)

Medinnus, G. R., & Curtis, F. The relation between maternal self-acceptance and child acceptance. *J. consult. Psychol.*, 1963, **27**, 542–544.

Metropolitan Achievement Tests. Yonkers-on-Hudson, N. Y.: World Book, 1959.

Mooney, R. L., & Gordon, L. V. Mooney Problem Check List: 1950 Revision. New York: Psychol. Corp., 1950.

Murphy, Lois B. *Personality in young children.* Vol. 1. *Methods for the study of personality in young children.* New York: Basic Books, 1956.

Osgood, C., Suci, G., & Tannenbaum, P. *The measurement of meaning.* Urbana: Univer. Ill. Press, 1957.

Rafferty, Janet E., Tyler, Bonnie B., & Tyler, F. B. Personality assessment from free play observations. *Child Develpm.*, 1960, **31**, 691–702.

Rogers, C. R. *Measuring personality adjustment in children nine to thirteen years of age.* Teach. Coll., Columbia Univer., Contrib. Educ., 1931.

Rogers, C. R. *Client-centered therapy.* Boston: Houghton Mifflin, 1951.

Smith, L. M. The concurrent validity of six personality and adjustment tests for children. *Psychol. Monogr.*, 1958, 72 (4), 1–30.

Stephenson, W. *The study of behavior.* Chicago: Univer. Chicago Press, 1935.

Stott, L. H., & Ball, Rachel S. Consistency and change in ascendance-submission in the social interaction of children. *Child Develpm.*, 1957, 28, 259–272.

Sullivan, Elizabeth T., Clark, W. W., & Tiegs, E. W. California Short-Form Test of Mental Maturity. Level 2. Monterey, Calif.: Calif. Test Bur., 1963.

Terman, L. M., & Merrill, Maud A. *Measuring intelligence.* Boston: Houghton Mifflin, 1937.

Thorpe, L., Clark, W., & Tiegs, E. California Test of Personality. Primary, Form B. Los Angeles: Calif. Test Bur., 1942.

Tiegs, E. W., & Clark, W. W. California Achievement Tests. Complete Battery. Junior High Level. Form W. Los Angeles: Calif. Test Bur., 1957.

Wechsler, D. *Wechsler Intelligence Scale for Children.* New York: Psychol. Corp., 1949.

chapter 15 ✻ Personality Development

Perhaps no concept in psychology is as important or as elusive as personality. Like intelligence, personality might be thought of as a "hypothetical construct." Psychologists observe an individual's behavior and on the basis of their observations draw inferences about his personality. However, too often personality is more than a descriptive concept; it becomes explanatory.

"Susie stays apart from the other third graders because she has an introverted personality." Thus, the child's behavior has been explained by assuming that it reflects her "basic nature" and by attaching a label to it. Further, she can be linked with other children who are introverts. She has been typed, pigeonholed. Her behavior has been elucidated. This, of course, is one of the perils of employing the concept of personality. Inferences are drawn from selected observations of behavior in which attention is focused on only one aspect or characteristic. The notion of personality is really thought to include all aspects of the individual.

To understand this child more fully necessitates rating her on many different bases. It is not enough to consider just her tendency to remain apart from others in a group situation. This neither explains her behavior nor describes her personality. Nor will a summation of her characteristics constitute a portrait of the individual. The interaction among these characteristics, their organization, and the unique manner in which each modifies and alters the others is what truly matters.

For the purposes of this chapter, personality may be defined as the distinct and unique organization of traits in an individual as reflected in how he reacts to himself and others and in how they react to him, and also in how he meets frustrations and conflicts—that is, in how he adjusts to his environment. The chapter is divided into three general areas: first, a reprise of the antecedents of personality; second, an analysis of the self concept and of self-consistency; and third, a treatment of those phases of personality that appear to be of particular significance in development.

Many attempts have been made to describe stages in personality development. It is not certain whether there are specific, inevitable, well-defined stages, but one assumption concerning their existence is worth attention. This assumes that an individual can move on to the next, more mature stage only after having successfully completed the demands of the previous stage or having satisfactorily met its requirements. For understanding the personality development of children, this is invaluable. It also has far-reaching implications for understanding adult behavior and adjustment.

Erikson (1950) described the following eight stages in personality development, each with its own distinctive goal normally to be attained in that period.

Infancy:	a basic sense of trust
Early childhood:	a sense of autonomy
Play age:	a sense of initiative
School age:	industry and competence
Adolescence:	personal identity
Young adult:	intimacy
Adulthood:	generativity
Mature age:	integrity and acceptance

The advanced stages of psychological maturity cannot be approached unless the goals of the preceding period have been met successfully. For example, a sense of trust is necessary before a child feels sufficiently secure to strive for autonomy. This is a trust in both the reliability of people and the satisfaction of basic physiological and psychological needs. Security gives freedom. The child who is led to mistrust others and his universe may be wedded forever to a need to seek the security he lacks.

In the normal progression to personality adjustment as a mature adult, an individual may be more vulnerable to certain influences during some periods of his life than during others. For example, some say, as noted earlier, that the effects of maternal deprivation are more severe in the second half of the child's first year. Perhaps in general a child cannot move on to a new and higher phase of personality development until he has achieved a certain amount of personality integration at his current level. Perhaps also the appearance of a more mature phase may be blocked or retarded by the interference of some event with the child's present degree of adjustment. The same principles apply as the child grows. Not just the first year or two of his life but the entire period from infancy through adolescence lays the groundwork for adult personality.

PERSONALITY ANTECEDENTS

In a sense, the entire book to this point could be considered as composed of antecedents of personality: maturation, learning, cultural factors, the home and family setting, including parental and sibling influences, the peer society, and finally, aspects of community. It may be argued, however, that the influences that occur earliest in the child's life tend to have the broadest impact on the individual's personality because they are the first incorporated into it and thus they play a part in determining the effects of subsequent experiences.

Because personality is conceived of as the product of interaction between hereditary and environmental factors, let us examine both areas of influence. Since from birth onward, heredity and environment interact, it is impossible even at the age of two to say how much of a child's personality is attributable to one or the other. A child may inherit an irritable temperament from his father, but it is his mother who reacts to it, with resulting consequences for the child's personality.

Innate Predispositional Factors

An infant, as we have noted in a previous chapter, is an active energy system that affects its environment and in turn is affected by it. Flexible and resilient, the infant selects those aspects of the environment to which he responds. Innate characteristics determine both this selectivity and the infant's initial responses to the environment.

Endocrine and Nervous System. Malfunctioning of the endocrine glands produces deviant behavior in only a limited number of individuals. Nevertheless, there is a link between behavior and glandular secretion. An underactive thyroid, for example, causes a low rate of metabolism, resulting in sluggish behavior and lack of endurance. Contrarily, too high a rate of thyroid secretion engenders restlessness and "nervousness."

Hormonal secretion from the gonads, though it can be changed by environmental factors, stems primarily from innate sources. The sex hormones influence a number of behaviors and characteristics. Secondary sex manifestations, such as lower voice pitch, facial hair growth, and growth in musculature appearing in boys at puberty, exert broad influences on personality and adjustment. Further, the rate of sexual maturation, which is largely determined by hereditary forces, bears an important relation to certain personality tendencies at adolescence.

Findings from the California Adolescent Growth Study indicate that the girl who matures early and the boy who matures late both encounter problems of adjustment (Bayley & Tuddenham, 1944). Marked behavioral differences were noted by Jones and Bayley (1950) between boys who matured early and those who matured late. Late maturers persisted in childlike patterns of activity, eager and animated. Their peers considered them restless, talkative, attention-seeking while viewing early maturers as popular, having older friends, a sense of humor about themselves, and good appearance. Quite clearly the rate of maturity relates to several aspects of adolescent personality because of the premium on "maturity" at this age level. Thus, one has an excellent example of the interplay between innate factors—maturity level—and environmental factors—social responses based on values and social expectations—which then affects personality adjustment.

Among infants the differences in the reactive tendencies of their nervous systems influence both their responses to their environments and the manner in which the significant individuals in their environments respond to them. Newborns differ widely in level of activity, irritability, and general emotional excitability—all of which reflect differences in nervous systems. Whether or not these particular characteristics have long-term consistency in the individual, their influence on the child's psychological surroundings and, in turn, on his personality at one point in his development suggests they have some importance. For example, Stewart (1953) concluded from her observations of crying behavior in infants that too much crying tended to generate insecurity in the mother which, in turn, is transmitted back to the offspring.

There is no doubt that emotionality, the physiological portions of emotional experience, has a base in the autonomic nervous system. This is borne out by a study by Gottesman (1960) in which identical twins resembled one another more than fraternal twins, especially with respect to sociability versus withdrawal. It does not mean, however, that differences among adults in emotional behavior are due exclusively to constitutional factors. Environmental factors play a tremendous part. Nevertheless, infants and children differ in the functioning of their autonomic nervous system, thus occasioning differences in emotionality and in the responses of adults (see Wenger, 1947; Jones, 1960).

Finally, any trait or characteristic based on the structure and operation of the nervous system is hereditary in origin. Admittedly, research has hardly scratched the surface in detecting relations between behavior and organic structure. But there seems to be enough evidence to conclude, for example, that intelligence has a physiological source in the central nervous system whereas such a trait as selfishness almost certainly has not.

Body Structure and Physical Abilities. The child's basic physique is primarily a product of heredity. Despite a history of efforts to link type of body to personality and temperament, present evidence indicates only a slight relationship between physical and psychological make-up. Sheldon, the leading protagonist of the body-type theory of personality (Sheldon, Stevens, & Tucker, 1940), devised a scheme for ascertaining the portion of each of three body types in an individual's physique: *endomorphic*—a roundish build weak in bony and muscular development; *mesomorphic*—large bones and muscles with an athletic physique; and *ectomorphic*—long, slender extremities, lacking in muscular development. In addition, three basic types of temperament were described, each associated with one of the body types: with the endomorphic, *viscerotonic*—sociable, relaxed, love of comfort, slow reaction; with the mesomorphic, *somatotonic*—need for activity and action, assertive, courageous, energetic; and with the ectomorphic, *cerebrotonic*—restrained, inhibited, tense, preferring solitude.

The Gluecks found at least twice as many mesomorphic physiques among delinquent boys as among nondelinquents (Glueck & Glueck, 1956). Another investigation observed some differences in IQ test performances of seven-year-old boys grouped into the three categories of body types (Davidson, McInnes, & Parnell, 1957). In addition, more signs of emotional disturbance in the boys were reported by mothers of the ectomorphic group. These findings cannot be discounted, but their explanation may be more important here.

Some physiques more than others permit an individual to perform certain motor and physical behaviors successfully. Competence in the motor area is an important attribute in childhood, especially among boys (see Hardy, 1937; Sanford et al., 1943). The competence of the mesomorph wins favorable reaction from the group. This leads him to solicit further approval in the particular area of activity; thus, an assertiveness induced by social considerations may emanate from the self-confidence he develops. Similarly, a child who is unsuccessful in the motor area will seek rewarding experience elsewhere. Success in the classroom may compensate for failure on the playground.

A second and related factor is social expectation. The stereotypes of the jolly, plump individual, the thin bookworm, and the aggressive mesomorph may not be scientifically derived, but they establish certain expectations of behavior for children of these body types. A father is less likely to spur his ectomorphic son to athletic prowess. Digman (1963) demonstrated that excitability and "outgoingness" were related only minimally to parent attitudes, whereas other traits, such as empathy, and clusters of traits, such as meeting cultural demands, were closely related to them. Possibly excitability and outgoingness result more from genetic factors—perhaps body type—than from strictly social forces.

Attractive appearance has been seen to have some relation to popularity among children (Tryon, 1939; Hardy, 1937). Although popularity may be a result rather than a cause of an individual's personality, the extent to which a child is accepted by his peers, as noted in Chapter 11, exerts some influence on his self-acceptance. This, in turn, affects his subsequent personality development.

Intelligence. To consider intelligence as an innate predispositional factor is not to imply that intellectual functioning is entirely inherited. Indeed, it is an excellent example of the continual interaction of hereditary and environmental factors. Yet it is probable that heredity, by determining an individual's central nervous structure, imposes limits within which environmental influences work.

It is not easy to determine the precise role of intelligence in the development of personality. Despite the conclusion from a survey of 200 studies that no uniform relation exists between intelligence and emotional and personality traits (Lorge, 1940), evidence is at hand showing a tie between intelligence and adjustment. Anderson (1960), in studying prediction of adjustment over a seven-year span, found IQ to be a significant prognosticator of adjustment and concluded: "Our results can be interpreted either as showing how difficult it is to separate out an intelligence factor from the complex of personality characteristics with which we are dealing when we talk about adjustment, or as indicating how important intelligence is in the adjustive process" (p. 64). Through factor analysis of various personality ratings and measures of analysis, Cattell (1945) has shown intelligence to correlate highly with self-control, reliability, industriousness, emotional independence, conscientiousness, and perseverance— all of which are traits of character. Intelligence was less closely associated, however, with basic emotional integration and adjustment.

Several explanations account for the relation of intelligence to adjustment in American society. First, brighter children have brighter parents who handle the emotional problems of childhood more wisely, thus establishing a sounder psychological foundation in childhood. Second, brighter children perceive social expectation more accurately and conform accordingly. Their behavior is rewarded, which leads to good adjustment to the demands made of them. Third, brighter children are more resourceful in meeting social expectations and demands; therefore, they are more likely to be successful. Fourth, a moderate relation exists between intelligence and ingenuity, curiosity, and creativity, traits that abet popularity and adjustment in peer society. Fifth, a closer relation between intelligence and adjustment may be postulated for middle-class than for lower-class children because of middle-class emphasis on academic achievement and educational progress.

Just as intelligence exerts a broad and complex influence on personality development, aspects of personality affect intellectual functioning. In a longitudinal study of mental growth and personality development, children who gained or lost in IQ during elementary-school years were seen to differ significantly in the following personality traits: independence, aggressiveness, self-initiative, problem solving, anticipation, and competitiveness (Sontag, Baker, & Nelson, 1958). And in Terman and Oden's 20-year follow-up (1947) of a group of highly gifted children, comparisons were made between successful and unsuccessful male adults, the measure for success being the extent to which an individual has made use of his superior intellectual ability. The successful received higher ratings on perseverance, self-confidence, integration toward goals, and absence of inferiority feelings, leading to the conclusion that the two groups differed markedly in achievement drive and all-around social adjustment.

To be sure, the interaction between intellect and personality is complex, and a great variance in personality adjustment exists at all levels of intelligence. Certain problems of emotional adjustment are more frequent at the lower intellectual levels, yet highly endowed individuals are not entirely immune from personality difficulties. Thus, it is apparent that even if there is no clear-cut tie between aspects of intellect and personality, intelligence does influence an individual's interactions with other people; it also affects one's adjustment to the demands of the environment.

Environmental Factors

What a child brings to a situation helps to shape the responses of others to him in the situation. This, in turn, determines how he will approach future situations. Let us deal here, then, with the social influences that bear on personality development. These include social expectations for child behavior as well as some cultural differences in expectations for behavior and personality. First, to several nonpsychological factors that have some potential psychological bearing.

Organic Factors. Anything that affects the individual's willingness or ability to respond to his environment is certain to influence his view of himself and his interaction with others. For example, vitamin deficiences may be reflected in such psychological symptoms as depression and irritability. More important perhaps is the lowered vitality of a child suffering from general nutritional deficiency. Illness, injury, and physical handicap undoubtedly impede the child's personality development. Yet research which has sought to find the precise impact of these factors on personality development is largely inconclusive.

To begin with, information concerning the child's personality development prior to illness or injury is seldom available. This limits the extent to which certain aspects of a child's personality may be attributed to them. The use of a control group, of course, would be advantageous, but it is difficult to obtain an adequate one suitably matched with the experimental group. Furthermore, present instruments for assessing personality are largely inadequate in this area of research. The children on whom personality measures were standardized are not comparable with, say, children with physical handicaps. Comparisons are therefore inappropriate. Similar responses by a healthy and a handicapped child on a personality inventory may have quite different meaning for the two.

Prolonged illness reduces the child's contact with the environment and his interaction, which results in decreased stimulation. Coupled with increased bodily concern, this induces the child to withdraw his interest from the world about him and focus it upon himself. Egocentricity, selfishness, and undue concern with oneself follow. Because illness handicaps, feelings of helplessness and dependency are born. These, together with parental resentment, rejection, overconcern, or overprotection, may have long-range effects on the child. Beverly (1936) found, for example, that an overwhelming majority of hospitalized children whom she interviewed answered the question, "Why do children get sick?" with the assertion, "Because they are bad." Indeed such an attitude can pervade the child's concept of himself and his sense of self-worth.

In discussions of the effect of physical injury or handicap on personality the notion of *body image* has often been invoked. An infant gradually becomes aware of his physical self through a variety of physical sensations. At first the distinction between *me* and *not me* is not a sharp one. Then experience furnishes countless clues that assist in the process of self-differentiation. Later, psychological attitudes toward the physical self develop out of the child's social interaction with others so that ultimately the most significant aspects of one's body image are those psychological attitudes that involve evaluation and consequent acceptance or rejection.

Because of the circular nature of an individual's attitude toward himself and the attitude of others toward him, there is not necessarily a close correspondence between the objective aspects of one's physical composition and the psychological attitudes associated with it. In any case, one's image of one's physical self becomes increasingly consistent throughout childhood. For this reason any alteration in one's body requires some adjustments in body image. Perhaps one of the most difficult and yet most imperative adjustments is acceptance of the changed physical condition. This requires acknowledgment of dependency on others when physically handicapped and recognition of the fact that participation and achievement in some areas of life are impossible (Mussen & Newman, 1958). Realization of this avoids needless frustration.

Acceptance. Too frequently physical handicap engenders resentment and frustration in the child. Deviation from normality, especially if it restricts and curtails the child's active participation with his peers, can affect personality development. So can parental nonacceptance of the child and his handicap which is particularly damaging to the child's sense of self-worth. The underlying psychological mechanism of this nonacceptance is complicated. Parents blame themselves for abnormality in their offspring. This was the case, for example, with mothers of children with cleft palate (Tisza, Selverstone, Rosenblum,

& Hanlon, 1958). Actually, any condition in the child which adds to child-care responsibilities often irks the parent. This irksomeness is bound to affect the parent's attitude toward the child. The point is that parental acceptance or rejection, as we have seen earlier in this book, influences the child's attitude toward himself which is a significant factor in personality development.

Similarly, peer acceptance is an important element in self-acceptance, though it is not always clear which causes which. Perhaps the child's lower self-acceptance may generate hostility and resentment which reduce his acceptance by his peers. Sociometric studies have shown that children with speech defects are chosen less often than children without them when play and friendship are the bases for selection (Woods & Carrow, 1959), and that children with defective hearing are not as acceptable among peers as those whose hearing is normal (Elser, 1959).

Case studies spotlight strong differences in the degree to which physical handicaps become psychological burdens among children. What causes these differences? The major factor is doubtless the parent's attitude toward the child—the extent to which they accept him prior to and then with a handicap. Though bodily injury and physical handicap may exacerbate and complicate a prior hostile, nonaccepting parent-child relationship, it is doubtful whether real acceptance of the child for his own sake would be substantially altered by such an occurrence. One five-year-old, severely afflicted with cerebral palsy, was light-hearted, gay, and full of mischief. With much effort and exertion he would manage to propel himself up the ladder of a slide and then slide down, screaming with delight, to land at the bottom, arms and legs twisted appallingly. Every day at five-thirty his father came to fetch him at the Day Care Nursery Center, engulf the child in his arms, and wipe away the boy's uncontrolled saliva as the youngster jabbered on about the day's events. He would never watch his son hit a home run or score a touchdown, but, because of his acceptance of the boy, he would be able to see him grow and develop into a fine, worthwhile young man.

Sociocultural Factors

The differences between cultures are so strong and pervasive that *modal* personality types are often noted by anthropologists. They use the adjective *modal* to signify "common" or "fashionable" as in *a la mode*. This modal type may be essentially paranoid and suspicious as among the Dobuans studied by Fortune (1932), or open and guileless as were some of the Dobuans' neighbors studied by Malinowski

(1922). It has been suggested that there is a modal American personality and that it is changing largely as a result of technological, educational, and economic development within the culture. Within the range of behaviors deemed acceptable by the culture, the specific behavioral pattern of an individual, based on his unique biological composition and social experience, takes form.

Behavior and personality vary among individuals within the culture. Some of this variance results from social class, occupation, racial background, and place of residence. These broad sociological variables, as previously noted, have considerable bearing in the creation of individual differences in personality and behavior. Also contributing to the shaping of an individual's web of responses are various aspects in the family setting.

The biological forces on one side and the social forces on the other fix the limits within which parents and others in intimate association with the child may mold character and personality. Parental personality, attitudes, and behavior all influence the developing child. The development of dependence or independence, of activity level, and of ability to resist stress result, in part, from the child's interaction with his parents.

A host of social influences exists. How these shape the concept of the self and in so doing dispose the individual toward becoming consistent in personality and behavior will be discussed in some detail.

THE SELF CONCEPT

The term *self concept* has many, sometimes conflicting, definitions. For the purpose of this discussion, let it be considered one's attitude toward one's physical self and own behavior. Recent perusals of the self concept (e.g., Hall & Lindzey, 1957; Wylie, 1961; Shlien, 1962) have hit upon two bases for it: one's social roles and the attempts to synthesize them; and second, the body image, "the body as a psychological experience . . . the individual's feelings and attitudes toward his own body" (Fisher & Cleveland, 1958, p. x). In the pages that follow we shall dwell on these two aspects of the self and then turn to the relation of the self concept to behavior.

Role Theory

"All the world's a stage, and every man's a player." The words were Shakespeare's. The idea did not originate with him. Centuries later the scientific study of roles and the use of role theory as an explanatory device had its beginnings in the work of such sociologists as Durkheim and Tonnies. These were first elucidated clearly by Cooley (1902) to be further developed in the social psychology of George H. Mead. Mead did not publish his ideas himself. After his death, his lecture notes were edited by his students so that his ideas have become available in written form (see Strauss, 1956).

Cooley originated the notion of the social or "looking glass" self. To him, man's ideas about himself were reflections of how others saw him. Mead divided personality structure into the *I* and the *me*. The *I* was the part of the self that was partly—perhaps largely—genetic in origin, the continuing part of personality present in every special situation. The *me* was basically social, a reflection of society's demands. Each individual was made up of many *me's*, of as many as he had distinct social roles. The expectations and demands of all social groups of significance to the individual influenced his behavior at all times, but their relative influences shifted with the behavioral situation and the roles it required.

The *me* that is in the forefront at any time depends on the composition of the group toward which behavior is referred. For example, a boy in a Little League game has his teammates as his main *reference group*. They provide him with the most accurate information as to whether he is playing this particular role of baseball player adequately. As he changes roles to son, brother, or pupil, the Little Leaguers lose their power as a reference group while other groups like the family, teachers, and classmates gain in this respect.

Role assignment has much to do with personality. This has been clearly shown at many points throughout this book; individuals have a strong disposition to perform the roles assigned to them, even when the roles are damaging to self-esteem, as in the case of the stutterer, or to adjustment. A wide range of social and biological factors, as well as chance, enters into the roles assigned to an individual. Once assigned, however, the individual tends to respond in terms of the roles. This makes for regular, consistent behavior, as long as the roles are clearly defined and do not clash too sharply. Across those situations the *I* aspect of personality persists. And a good thing, too! One can see that the individual whose behavior is determined only by the demands of the social group would be the ultimate of the *other-directed* person, with no core of personal integrity. To use Freudian terms, this type of person would have an "externalized superego"; a conscience dependent only on the values of the group to which one belongs at the time.

The roles assigned to an individual determine a fair portion of his behavior; when roles are central and significant and yet conflict directly with one another, there is behavioral disturbance. *Romeo and Juliet* is a classic example of role conflict in which romantic love and family honor collide. But it is of little significance today since family honor means less now than it did to individuals in Shakespeare's day —and perhaps the same is true of romantic love. *Crime and Punishment* is more pertinent because Raskolnikov's conflict between conventional upper-middle class values and those of the poverty-stricken, amoral student world is a more immediate one in the contemporary world. The classic primary-group tragedy involving a clash of central roles still exists, and along with it in contemporary industrial society goes the problem of nonexistent roles and a loss of personal identity. The breakdown occurring as a result of ambiguous role definitions has been well described by Dunham (1959) and forms the basis of most contemporary literature. Kafka's heroes, whether on trial for some unnamed crime or for changing overnight into a gigantic cockroach, are the ancestors of Beckett's and Sartre's existential men—individuals without a governing set of roles and values. Whereas having clear and conflicting roles is one basis for tragedy, the tragic nature and emptiness of a life in which one has no roles to play is doubtless greater.

The Body Image

Awareness of the physical self and its separation from the nonself comes about, in part, from body movements, internal changes such as hunger, and such things as laryngeal activity in which the infant feels movement simultaneously with hearing sound (Schilder, 1935). It also comes from observing the effects of one's behavior on the external world (Piaget, 1954). Generally the body image is assumed to be closely tied to physical reality; distortions in it relate to psychological disturbance. In the following case a distorted body image seemed to be the source of some otherwise inexplicable behavior.

Rudy was a man in his early twenties. He was 5' 4" tall and weighed about 135 pounds, and had an athletic body build. He did not seek trouble to any noticeable extent, but certainly did nothing to avoid it. He had had his nose broken twice and his upper front teeth knocked out in fist fights with fellows who outweighed him by about 100 pounds. These fights could have been avoided without "losing face." The writer wondered why Rudy did not do so, and why he continued to get into difficulties of this sort, until one day the writer noticed something. Rudy always stooped when he went through a doorway. Watching Rudy maneuver about made one fact obvious. Rudy thought he was 7' tall, and no number of losses made him the least concerned over someone a mere 6' 2".

Occasionally distortion of body image can be discerned in an individual and explain behavior that appears highly unreasonable and illogical. Hence, body image exists—though not tied as closely to the physical self as is widely assumed.

Attempts to assess body image in a scientific manner and to predict behavior from it have not been successful. Typically, individuals are requested to draw a human figure; it is assumed that they will project into the drawing their own ideas about their physical selves. These drawings are then interpreted. If, for example, the individual draws his figure with hands concealed behind the back, he is believed to disclose a feeling of impotence, of inability to deal with problems. Perhaps the individual feels impotent only in the fine art of drawing hands! Very few individuals represent their own bodies when instructed to draw a person, suggested Swenson (1957). Even when they do, the interpretations of their drawings seem largely based on conjecture (Levy, 1950). Thus, though the body image quite likely exists as a significant part of the self concept and plays an important part in determining behavior, proper techniques for measuring the image do not yet seem to have been developed.

One further point on body image. If body image determined behavior, and especially the self concept, which promotes consistency in behavior, then the demeanor of individuals would become more variable as the physical self changed more rapidly. This is what happens in adolescence; rapid shifts in children's behavior often baffle parents. And, of course, data cited earlier on the relation of physical maturity to social adjustment are themselves suggestive of the impact of the physical self and one's attitudes toward it on adjustment.

The Self Concept and Adjustment

To many interested in psychotherapy (see, e.g., Rogers, 1951; Shlien, 1961), the self concept plays a vital role in adjustment. They say that the fundamental problem of the neurotic is that he is self-rejecting. The objective of their therapy is to cause him to come to terms with himself and adjust his behavior and perception of himself to the point at which he is able to accept himself. Raimy (1948) demonstrated that successful cases in psychotherapy enabled patients to acquire a more favorable view of themselves, whereas unsuccessful cases did not.

The overwhelming evidence from Wylie's (1961) review of the literature on the self suggested that self-acceptance was related to adjustment. A high regard of the self generally meant a high level of adjustment, except in a few cases where high self-esteem worked as adversely as self-rejection. In general, moreover, those individuals who were self-accepting were seen to be accepting of others (e.g., Wylie, 1957). What this means, of course, is that the individual who can accept himself can withstand aggression and disparagement from others; his personal psychological security grants him an objective view of the behavior of others and an understanding of the bases for their behavior. Such an individual can also sustain adversity better than a self-rejecting person. He can return aggression directly toward others, if necessary. He therefore need not develop neurotic defenses or take out his hostility on innocent victims.

Quite obviously it would be to the benefit of the culture to raise children who are self-accepting. From McCurdy's (1957) work on extremely creative individuals as well as from the researches of those directly concerned with the self concept (Maris, 1958), it would appear that individuals who are regarded highly by their parents, who are aware of this regard, and who enjoy a great deal of parental contact are most accepting of themselves. They are best able to face the possible rejection stemming from their own creative efforts, which are considered deviant from the majority standpoint, and are presumably more accepting of others.

Consistency and the Self Concept

Personality presupposes consistency. Without consistent patterns of response, behavior would be chaotic and unpredictable. Since personality refers to persisting continuing, predictable, social aspects of the self, there can be no personality without consistency.

There are many reasons to expect consistency. Man remains the same biological entity throughout life, and many determinants of personality, as we know, are biological in character. To the degree that man's biological composition does not change during lifetime, consistency may be expected. No matter what else may change in the course of development, humans carry around the same physical self, and with it, their own responses and the responses of others to it.

Consistency would also be expected from what is known of the incorporation of social roles into the concept of the self as well as from what is known about identification. Role assignment is sufficient cause to play a social role. The performance of a role leads to increased expectancy on the part of others that the performer will not relinquish it. These firmer and more explicit expectancies impel one to act even more consistently in harmony with them. Since roles even in childhood have some constancy and with age become more so as well as invariable, and sharply defined, *some* consistency is foreseen at all ages, more in later than in earlier years.

A recent psychological theory, Festinger's *theory of cognitive dissonance* (1957), is based on the notion that humans fundamentally need to maintain consonance or consistency among various aspects of the self, and between the self and the outside world. These are some examples of dissonance: an individual believes that his children deserve the best possible education. He regards federal aid to education as creeping socialism. The school district which operates on a skimpy tax base cannot finance an adequate school system. There is a dissonance between two sets of social attitudes; if the individual has enough ability he will recognize the dissonance in himself and attempt to resolve it. The dissonance may occur between two aspects of the self, as in the foregoing illustration, or it may arise between behavior and belief. This is exemplified in the parent who believes that his children should make their own decisions, yet refuses to allow them to do so, because the errors entail grave consequences.

There is evidence that the need for consonance, consistency, or the synthesis of conflicting values increases with age, and among children is also associated with IQ. This need for self-consistency plays a major part in achieving consistent behavior. Yet if people were completely consistent, life would be extremely dull, and change, as in psychotherapy, difficult if not impossible to achieve. To what degree, then, do humans reflect consistency?

Trait Consistency. At one time psychologists studied types, such as introvert versus extrovert. But as research findings failed to support predictions based on type psychology, many personality theorists abandoned types and turned to traits. Admitting that type psychology had not worked out, these theorists assumed that personality was composed of a set of consistent, continuing traits. This assumption was soon subjected to experimental test, and this test, the Hartshorne and May (1928, 1930) study of honesty, had a profound effect on psychology.

The objective of Hartshorne and May was simple: to find out if there were a general and consistent trait of honesty. If there were, individuals should be consistently honest from one situation to the next. Those who lied should also cheat and steal whereas those who were honest in one instance should also be honest in the other two.

Testing a large number of school children in a wide selection of real-life situations involving cheating, stealing, or lying, they interpreted their findings as indicating only a very minor zone of common response to all three areas of honesty. Nor could they predict behavior in one situation from knowledge of the individual's behavior in other situations similarly involving honesty. Their results indicated there was no general trait of honesty. This meant presumably that any assumption of trait consistency was unwarranted and argued against a notion of human consistency altogether. If correct and applicable to broader situations, the Hartshorne and May conclusions would lead to the belief that the study of personality should be abandoned. Actually, this general hypothesis, based on their data, gave the Hartshorne and May study great significance, for it led to a series of investigations and critiques of trait consistency.

From a brief but general interview, MacKinnon (1938) predicted whether college students would be honest on tests modeled after those used by Hartshorne and May. His predictions were more accurate than chance might expect; this corroborated the idea of a general trait of honesty whose existence was rather easily discernible. Furthermore, he had much greater success in predicting honesty than dishonesty. His dishonest subjects fell into two groups: one that appeared basically honest but yielded to temptation and a second that was generally dishonest. For *most* of these individuals, honesty or dishonesty seemed to be the result of a general and consistent trait; for some, their behavior seemed largely determined by the stimulus of the moment. In general, MacKinnon's findings and conclusions presumably contradicted those of Hartshorne and May, perhaps because he used a brighter and older group of subjects, and individual consistency apparently increases with age and IQ (Hartshorne, May, & Shuttleworth, 1930).

Yet even the Hartshorne and May data, though interpreted as showing inconsistency, really represented a substantial degree of consistency. Burton (1963) analyzed the same data and concluded that they disclosed the existence of a moderately general and consistent trait. Other studies (Grinder & McMichael, 1963) also indicate that honesty is sufficiently consistent as a trait for one to predict children's responses on measures of different aspects of conscience development and to anticipate behavior from paper-and-pencil tests.

But investigations of consistency in traits have not been limited to honesty. Murphy (1937) found consistency in sympathetic responses to others among three-year-olds though not among two-year-olds. Kagan and Moss (1960) reported on the stability of passive and dependent behavior in childhood and adulthood. Though part of a longitudinal study to which we shall return presently, their findings supported the notion that much trait consistency existed among different behavioral situations at any time in an individual's life history. They obtained reliable measures of subtle aspects of personality even at preschool ages—and reliability implies consistency. How much consistency will be found depends on the effectiveness of the measuring device, the characteristics of the individuals measured (older and abler persons show greater consistency), and probably on the complexity of the social forces bearing on the trait in question.

Consistency Over Time. To what extent does the individual remain consistent and how much does he change in time? One of the first studies of this question was conducted by Bühler and her students (reported in Murphy, Murphy, & Newcomb, 1937). They divided infants into four types: those easily stimulated by both pleasant and unpleasant stimuli; those easily stimulated by pleasant but not by unpleasant stimuli; those easily stimulated *vice versa;* and those not easily stimulated by either. The results of the study suggested that most children remained in the same category, at least up through middle childhood.

Cited often among studies of consistency and change is Neilon's (1948). After a 15-year interval, she followed up the individuals who had been studied by Shirley (1933; see also Chapter 1) from birth to the age of two. Shirley's personality sketches of the 13 male and 6 female infants she studied were published with pseudonyms attached to each so that neither Neilon nor her associates knew the true names of the children represented by the sketches. Neilon collected rather full and autobiographical sketches of 15 of the original 19 children at the age of 17—ten boys and five girls. She then requested a panel of judges composed of faculty members and graduate students to match the six infant sketches with the five adolescent sketches of girls and the 13 infant sketches with the ten adolescent sketches of boys. Ten judges matched the girls, five the boys. Shirley's original data were then consulted to find out the real names of the children associated with each infant sketch so that the accuracy of the matching could be seen. The judges succeeded in matching the girls to an extent that could be obtained by chance less than once in a million times; with the boys, a somewhat more difficult task, they were correct to an extent that could occur by chance only once in 4000 tries. Although considerable individual difference existed among individual children, one girl being matched correctly by all ten judges and another by none, it was evident that there was much consistency in personality over a period of time; accurate matching occurred so much more often than would be expected by chance.

Several subsequent studies have corroborated the idea that an individual's personality is usually consistent over time. These include Stott's (1957) study of a stability of ascendance and submission in children, in which he found that 82 per cent of a group of 106 youngsters disclosed a consistent pattern in this area from nursery school into adolescence. Escalona and Heider (1959) predicted behavior at the age of five from observation of infants in the first year of life. At five, they found their predictions correct much oftener than by chance but saw that prediction was more accurate in some areas, such as motor skill and sex-role interests, than in others, such as shyness and striving for achievement. Tuddenham (1958), following up individuals studied as adolescents 19 years earlier, observed a significant stability in more than one-third of the traits studied, despite the low reliability of ratings in adolescence and adulthood. The stablest trait for man was aggressive motivation, with a correlation of +.91 between ratings; for women, it was a desire for social prestige, with a correlation of +.81.

The latest and most extensive study of consistency over time was undertaken by Kagan and Moss (1960, 1962) who analyzed the Fels longitudinal data (see Chapter 10). In general, they found that consistency was greater up to the age of ten than thereafter. It seemed likely, as noted in reference to Burks's study of a single pair of identical twins (see Chapter 2), that a person could be "more himself" at later ages when parental pressures played less of a role in shaping behavior. Perhaps the lessening relationship between earlier and later personality, on the one hand, and between adolescent and adult behavior, on the other, stemmed in part from the greater independence from parental influences in later years. Even with this qualification, correlations between childhood and adulthood were generally substantial. Where the correlations were minimal, the shifts in societal pressures seemed most accountable. For example, dependent behavior in females was permissible throughout life, whereas extreme pressures were imposed on males from adolescence onward to become independent. Hence, the high correlation in female and low correlation in male dependency between childhood and adulthood.

PRINCIPAL COMPONENTS OF PERSONALITY IN CHILDREN

Personality seems to gain complexity and consistency as the years pass. It grows more complex because the number and range of its antecedents increase, producing more intricate interactions. It increases in consistency because as physical growth terminates the body image becomes stable and roles played become clearer, more consonant with one another, and more tightly incorporated into the self concept.

Considerable research has been amassed on particular components of personality which seem to be rather central in the personality fabric of childhood, yet relatively independent of one another. These are dependence-independence, aggression, anxiety, conscience development, dominance-submission, and social acceptability. We propose to explore each in some detail, with emphasis on their antecedents.

Dependence-Independence

Dependency is the condition of the human infant. The infant is *instrumentally* dependent on his mother. Because she is associated with the satisfaction of his basic biological needs, the infant also develops a rewarding *emotional* dependence on her (Heathers, 1955b). How then does independent behavior develop? It comes about through maturation and learning. The young child grows increasingly capable of functioning independently.

Moreover, independent behavior is in itself rewarding to the child because of the satisfaction gained from exploring and manipulating the environment and from interacting with peers. Normally, therefore, there is an increase in independent behavior with age (Steth & Conner, 1962). In nursery school, children exhibit less behavior reflecting infantile reliance on adults and a shift toward a more active, assertive dependence on peers (Heathers, 1955a). However, emotional or psychological independence does not invariably accompany physical or instrumental independence. Further, some children manifest greater independence of behavior than others.

A Cultural Phenomenon. The concern of American psychologists over dependence versus independence reflects the importance attached by society to the development of independent behavior. The individual who is able to operate as an independent agent is regarded as a maturer adult. However, anthropologists have shown that American emphasis on early independent training is not shared by all other cultures. Take this illustration, for example, of the attitude and behavior of parents in a New Guinea tribe:

> When the child begins to walk the quiet continuous rhythm of its life changes somewhat. It is now becoming a little heavy for the mother to carry about with her on long trips to the garden, and furthermore it can

be expected to live without suckling for an hour or so. The mother leaves the child in the village with the father, or with some other relative, while she goes to the garden or for firewood. . . . As the child grows older, it is no longer confined so closely to the care of its own parents. Children are lent about. An aunt comes to visit and takes home the four-year-old for a week's stay, handing him on to some other relative for eventual return to his parents. This means that a child learns to think of the world as filled with parents, not merely a place in which all of his safety and happiness depend upon the continuance of his relationship to his own particular parents. . . . There is no insistence at all upon children's growing up rapidly, or acquiring special skills or proficiencies, and there is a corresponding lack of techniques for training them physically. . . . The result is that the child grows up with a sense of emotional security in the care of others, not in its own control over the environment (quoted in Whiting & Child, 1953, from Mead, 1935).

Similarly, a study of child-rearing practices in Puerto Rico (Landy, 1959) found little parental encouragement of independent behavior in the young child. Children are not given regular tasks to perform and little is expected of them. This stems partly from the culture's view of the child. Children are regarded as *sin capacidad*—without capacity.

Symptoms and Causes. What are the earmarks of dependent behavior? Of independent behavior? To Beller (1955) the following behaviors were signs of dependency: seeking help, seeking physical contact, seeking proximity, seeking attention, and seeking recognition. These were the behaviors denoting independence: taking initiative, trying to overcome obstacles in the environment, trying to carry activities to completion, getting satisfaction from work, and trying to do routine tasks by oneself. By and large, dependent behavior is characterized by reliance on someone else for assistance and assurance. A child is said to be dependent when he manifests behavior that, at his age level, should be superseded by independent behavior. The six-year-old who does not dress himself alone, the four-year-old who does not feed himself, the five-year-old who does not play with his peers unattended by his mother all exhibit dependency.

Why does dependent behavior persist? No single explanation accounts for either dependence in children in general or its occurrence in any one child. All explanations, interestingly enough, have focussed on various aspects of the parent-child relationship. An early study (Heathers, 1953) concluded that dependent behavior resulted from maternal overconcern; the mother was not only permissive about dependency behavior but also encouraged it. This view was reached by identifying independent and dependent behavior in children and then applying Fels ratings to the psychological atmosphere of their homes. The homes of the dependent youngsters rated higher on child-centered and babying counts.

Widely held at the present time is the view that dependency increases and is intensified when the parent does not adequately meet the dependency needs of the child. Frustrated through lack of parental warmth, nurture, and affection, the child cannot proceed to greater emotional independence. This notion has its supporting evidence even though the results of various studies are not in full agreement.

In an extensive study of the antecedents of dependency and aggression (Sears, Whiting, Nowlis, & Sears, 1953) the amount of dependent behavior in nursery-school children correlated positively with the severity of their weaning in infancy. However, no such relation was found with respect to toilet training. And even the weaning finding was not supported by data obtained in the Pattern Study (Sears, Maccoby, & Levin, 1957). Conceivably the extent of the frustration of a child's early dependency needs is not adequately assessed through the mother's feeding and toilet-training practices.

Some Conclusions about Dependency Antecedents. To begin with, there is probably a curvilinear relationship within the normal range of dependency behavior between how parents meet or frustrate a child's early dependency needs and the persistence of such needs in the child. If the parent strongly rewards dependent behavior and takes a permissive attitude toward it, preventing or discouraging independence, dependency persists. Similarly, frustration of the infant's needs for dependence might intensify the yearning for dependency. The Pattern Study, for example, found dependency increased in children whose mothers punished them for such behavior. The same thing applied to children of homes where rejection was evident and withdrawal of love was used as a disciplinary technique. Parental conflict and rejection of the child were prominent in the family backgrounds of extremely dependent boys (McCord, McCord, & Verden, 1962). Low parental esteem for one another and for the child pervaded their homes. From this point of view dependent behavior was a manifestation of feelings of insecurity in the parent-child relationship. Gewirtz (1956) noted a high frequency of attention seeking in children when the adult was relatively unavailable. Thus, dependence on adults appeared to increase when the children perceived them as psychologically distant.

Finally, the curvilinear relation between dependency and the extent of frustration by the parent may actually hold for only the broad normal range. If parents or parent-substitutes show a nearly complete absence of nurture, or if parental rejection exists to a pathological degree, the child may develop an intense independence. This is dramatically illustrated by six German-Jewish orphaned refugee children who spent the first two or three years of their lives in a concentration camp. The children had been reared together with a minimum of adult nurture. When transferred to a rehabilitation center, they were excessively distrustful and wary of adults. Their hostility toward adults was replaced by positive feelings only after a long period of time (Freud & Dann, 1951).

Among a group of aggressive adolescent boys, Bandura and Walters (1959) found their fathers to have been rejecting and to have punished early dependent behavior after the affection of their mothers had established a motive for dependency. Thus, anxiety over dependency developed. The aggressive behavior, Bandura and Walters reasoned, was born in the early frustration of their dependency needs. Treatment of this antisocial behavior was hampered by the boys' suspicion and fearfulness of establishing a dependency relationship in therapy.

Although the socialization process is characterized ordinarily by increasing independence in the child, certain parental attitudes impede this development. Stendler (1952) maintained that there were critical periods during the early years when overdependency might result. The first of these occurred toward the end of the first year of life when the child becomes aware of his dependence on his mother. Recognizing her importance, the child tested her to see if he could really depend on her. Separation at this time might produce a child low in ego strength and toleration of frustration. The second critical period appeared between the ages of two and three. At this time the pressure of the culture for independent behavior increases on the child. Disturbances in his relation of dependency with his mother during this period might touch off attempts to cope with the resulting anxiety by developing an extremely strong conscience. To support this notion of a critical period, Stendler (1954) showed that a larger number of discontinuities in personality adjustment turned up in dependent children than in others. Moreover, her data corroborated those of Bandura and Walters in noting the importance of paternal influence in the learning of dependency.

Two further considerations merit brief attention. First, because independence grows out of dependence, the two must not be considered distinct from each other. Several studies (Beller, 1955; Heathers, 1955a) have observed that despite a negative correlation between the amount of independent and dependent behavior shown by nursery-school youngsters, the two are not entirely inversely related. That is, even though some children display generally less dependent behavior than others, some of both kinds of behavior can be seen in all children.

Second, long-term consistency in dependent behavior is of great concern to child psychologists interested in predicting behavior. In their study of the display of passive and dependent behavior in 54 adults, Kagan and Moss (1960) collected information on how much dependency these individuals showed as children between the ages of three and ten. Comparisons of the two sets of data indicated that passive and dependent behaviors remained stable over the years among women but not necessarily among men. Kagan and Moss inferred that passive and dependent behavior was punishable in males while perhaps actually being encouraged in females. More males proportionately than females shifted from high dependency in childhood to independence in adulthood, implying a sex difference in the extent to which pressures for independence are applied in America. Even in adolescence, girls enjoy less independence than boys.

Dependency and Other Behaviors. Is independent or dependent behavior related to other aspects of behavior? Among preschool children a negative connection has been shown between dependence on adults and popularity among peers (McCandless & Marshall, 1957; McCandless, Bilous, & Bennett, 1961). Actually, those children depending most on adults participate least with peers. Thus, dependence on adults presumably hinders a child's interaction with his peers whereas independence seems to be a valued trait even at the preschool level. In adolescence, independence and popularity go together; however, the inverse relation between dependence on adults and popularity is by no means a simple one. Dependent boys were seen in the McCord study (McCord et al., 1962) to display heightened anxiety and internal stress, which perhaps interfered with peer relations.

Independence relates to achievement and motivation for achieving. High-achieving nursery-school children depended less on adults for help and emotional support than did children lower in achievement, according to a study conducted by Crandall, Preston, and Rabson (1960). One might infer that independence as a sign of security enables the child to function autonomously and apply effort toward personal accomplishment and attainment of goals. Furthermore, children who rated high in emotional independence from parents showed increases in IQ during preschool years (Sontag et al., 1958).

Aggressive Behavior

Our culture seems uncertain as to how aggressive behavior should be regarded. During childhood aggression is discouraged; attitudes toward it are highly restrictive. Yet aggressiveness carries a premium in adult society. The ambitious, hard-driving, aggressive male represents the epitome of success in the competitive, free-enterprise system. His quiet, contemplative, introverted opposite is outdistanced in the race to the top. Aggressiveness appears to be approved in covert, sophisticated forms, but frowned upon in the overt, primitive, physical sorts that characterize children's behavior, except in such formalized events as athletic contests and war.

Aggression may be defined as any act or behavior that is intended to harm or injure. Thus defined, it is inimical to friendly, social intercourse. The rights and wishes of others are ignored or abridged. In this sense, aggressive behavior is maladaptive. There is also evidence that the behavior of highly aggressive children is inflexible and stereotyped (Dittmann & Goodrich, 1961). The implication is that children evincing a great amount of aggression have failed to develop inner controls and have not learned more appropriate, adaptable, and acceptable types of behavior.

The social interaction of young children is marked by aggressive, conflict-ridden behavior. Anger, hostility, quarreling, and combativeness are observable frequently in children's relations with each other. It is impossible to determine how early these aggressive feelings appear in the child. However, the infant lashes out very early at the source of events that frustrate, restrict, or irritate him. The child uses any means at his command to eliminate unpleasant and undesirable stimuli. In the young child this usually means crying, screaming, and direct physical attack.

As children grow older overt aggression decreases. Inner controls are learned. More effective and more socially acceptable ways of solving conflicts are developed, and rules governing the rights of property become incorporated. However, at every age there are wide disparities among individuals in the amount of aggressive behavior, and in some children a marked persistence of aggression pervades a great number of behaviors.

Among the notions advanced to explain aggression in children, three stress various aspects of the parent-child relationship. In the first, *frustration-aggression,* any situation, condition, relationship, or experience that produces frustration in an individual is seen to generate aggression. The second notion emphasizes the *parent as a model* for the child; identifying with the parent, the child models his own behavior after the parent's. Third, parental *permisisveness of aggression* is said to increase the child's tendency to behave aggressively. Clearly all three notions are centered in the environment since these stress the child's learning experiences, particularly as they occur in the family setting.

There is also an argument for a biological basis for aggression. Diamond (1957), who examined studies among animals, found strain and sex differences in aggressiveness and concluded that genetic factors were influential in determining aggressive behavior, even though learning experience were important. Reviewing some of the same research, Berkowitz (1962) saw no evidence of an instinctive drive to hostility or aggression in animals. He accounted for the relative rare occurrence of spontaneous aggression by frustration or through prior learning that rewarded aggressive behavior.

Although environmental factors contribute heavily to the appearance of aggressive behavior, it would be a mistake to overlook inherent differences in individuals which might indirectly increase their tendency to react aggressively to environmental events. Certain innate characteristics, then, may determine the kinds of learning experiences to which the child is exposed and these, in turn, influence behavior and personality. Among nursery-school children, Walker (1962) obtained significant correlations between mesomorphic type and clusters of behavioral traits labeled "energetic-active" and "aggressive-assertive." He concluded that "variations in physical energy, in bodily effectiveness for assertive or dominating behavior, and in bodily sensitivity appear as important mediating links between physique structure and general behavior" (p. 79). Whereas no cause-and-effect statements can be drawn from studies showing a relationship between physical factors and personality, it is not possible to ignore entirely the role such factors play in molding responses to the environment.

Frustration-Aggression. Most people experience frustration in the course of a day's events. Goals are blocked. Rewards are not received. Desires remain unfulfilled. Developed by the Yale group (Dollard, Doob, Miller, Mowrer, & Sears, 1939) the frustration-aggression hypothesis holds that aggressive behavior is the typical response to frustration. Support for the hypothesis appears in experimental studies as well as in observation. To mention one briefly (Otis & McCandless, 1955), 63 preschool children were exposed to eight consecutive repetitions of a mildly frustrating situation. Observed and recorded for manifestations of aggressiveness, the children displayed an increase in aggressive conduct from the first four to the last four trials. Quite likely this finding is particularly significant in supporting the Yale group's hypothesis because the frustration was mild and the children were not greatly involved in the situation. Certainly plausible, then, are findings that point out the severe consequences of parental frustrations of the child's emotional needs.

The findings of several parent-child research studies concur in noting a bond between aggressive behavior in children and punishment for aggression. The Pattern Study explained this relationship along the following lines: the child receives some reward in resorting to aggression through the satisfaction realized from hurting others or expressing anger. But when this aggressive behavior incurs punishment, great frustration is felt, which incites the child to further aggression. Moreover, the Pattern Study noted a tendency for severe punishment of aggression toward parents to be one aspect of general strictness in child-rearing.

One study relating parental behaviors to aggressiveness in school children (Eron et al., 1961) found aggressive boys likely to have fathers who severely punished aggressive deportment in the home. That there was no significant correlation between aggression at school and maternal punishment of aggressive behavior at home suggested that fathers, more than mothers, were an important source of frustration in the home, especially for boys.

So much for restrictive and autocratic techniques producing frustration. As we have seen, the young child is totally dependent on his parents. When one or both parents fail him, frustration results. Hostile, aggressive behavior appears. In their book on adolescent aggression, Bandura and Walters (1959) attributed the development of aggressive behavior to disruption of the child's dependency relation with his parents. Their thesis is corroborated by the findings of another study of family correlates of aggression in nondelinquent boys (McCord, McCord, & Howard, 1961). Here, 95 per cent of the aggressive boys come from homes in which at least one parent was emotionally rejecting.

Thus, there seems to be ample evidence for the frustration-aggression hypothesis. It is likely that parents who reject the child's needs for dependence and affection also establish a relatively restrictive home atmosphere which itself is frustrating to the child. Both these behaviors seriously affect the child and his development.

The Parent as a Model. The parent serves as a model for the child. The child adopts his values and imitates his behavior, irrespective of whether such behavior is rewarded or expected. In general, adults set examples for children. Logically, then, it would seem that the more aggressive the adult's behavior, the more aggressive would be the child's. This view is buttressed by several studies (Bandura & Huston, 1961; Bandura, Ross, & Ross, 1961). Preschool children imitated or reproduced the behavior of the conductor of the experiment who was their model. An aggressive model elicited a greater amount of aggressive behavior than a nonaggressive model.

Interestingly enough, boys showed more aggression than girls after exposure to an aggressive *male* model. In the development of aggressive behavior the father played a particularly pivotal role, just as he was a more important source of frustration than the mother. Indeed, a correlation of +.33 was obtained by Eron et al. (1961) between ratings of paternal aggression and child aggressiveness at home. And Winder and Rau (1962) in a study of the parental attitudes of deviant preadolescent boys found parents of the aggressive boys to score higher in aggressiveness than parents of nonaggressive counterparts.

One study pertinent to the notion that parents serve as models for a child's aggression observed that children most closely identified with their parents displayed the most aggression in the doll-play sessions (Levin & Sears, 1956). This was particularly true for boys whose fathers did the punishing. Since boys from homes in which the father was absent showed less aggression in doll play than boys from intact homes (Sears, 1951; Bach, 1946), boys might be thought less likely to act aggressively in the absence of an aggressive male model. In similar manner, more aggression is evident in lower-class children than in those from the middle class (McKee & Leader, 1955) because the lower-class male who serves as the model is seen as typically aggressive, at least in the overt physical mannerisms that might prove most significant.

Permissiveness of Aggression. This notion rests on the fact that aggression is more likely to occur when it is permitted. An increase in doll-play aggression in a permissive situation has been observed from session to session. This has been taken to signify that in a permissive atmosphere, the child's fear of punishment for aggressive behavior diminishes and his inhibitions concerning the show of aggression lessen. The accepting, nonreproachful attitude of the adult is perceived by the child as granting him permission to exhibit aggression.

However, another interpretation is plausible. The amount of session-to-session aggression manifested by pairs of seven-to-ten-year-old boys in a permissive, free-play situation was observed under two conditions (Siegel & Kohn, 1959): the presence of a permissive adult and the absence of any adult. Under the former condition, the typical increase of aggression in playing with dolls was noted from one session to the next. Under the latter condition, however, there was a drop in aggressive behavior from the first session to the second. Thus, when an adult is present the child presumably tends to transfer certain ego functions, such as control of disapproved or punishable behavior, to him. In the absence of the adult the child must exercise his own self-control.

The Fels studies (Baldwin, 1948) indicated that one effect of democracy in the home was to raise the child's activity level. Since there is a connection between sheer level of activity and aggressiveness, this helps to explain the greater aggression noted in children from democratic or permissive homes. Democratic parents incline toward tolerating all child behaviors, including quarreling, activeness, and aggression. In the Pattern Study a slight relationship was seen between aggressive conduct in the child and the mother's permissiveness of aggression. Sears argued that maternal permissiveness signaled the child that aggressive behavior was acceptable; it was not punishable and was expected by the mother to occur. Yet Lynn (1961), in testing the Pattern Study's finding, could not discover such a link between aggression in children and maternal permissiveness of aggressive behavior. However, Lynn did observe a relationship between scores of a mother's extroversion and both her tendency to be permissive and her child's aggression in school. Lynn suggested the existence of a genetic factor since other studies also found a connection between extroversion and aggression.

Weatherly (1962), through ratings of aggression found in TAT stories told by college girls, detected no difference in the amounts of aggressive behavior among girls whose mothers had been low in permitting aggression and those whose mothers had been relatively permissive of aggression in child rearing. However, the former group exhibited a sharp increase in *fantasy* aggression as a result of frustrating, aggression-arousing conditions in childhood. Although maternal permissiveness of aggression may not be highly related to aggression in children, it does increase the likelihood that the child will respond aggressively to various environmental stimuli.

The case for the notion that aggressiveness in children is abetted by a permissive atmosphere in the home is not clear-cut. The idea does not explain the original onset of aggression. Possibly, however, parental reluctance to punish various sorts of child behavior tacitly encourages such behaviors when their exercise is rewarding to the child. Regarding aggression, a child's frustrations are relieved by striking someone interfering with or interrupting his activity. If allowed by parents, the tendency for aggressive behavior to recur in similar situations is reinforced.

Sex Differences. That boys are more aggressive than girls appears early in life and can be observed in a variety of settings and situations. Besides, children themselves perceive boys as the more aggressive of the sexes. Studies of the middle childhood years (Winder & Rau, 1962) and also of adolescence (Eron et al., 1961) show peers nominating boys oftener than girls as deporting themselves aggressively. It is likely that the sources of this greater male aggressiveness are both environmental and biological.

The boy's identification with his father signifies association of himself with a relatively aggressive model for his eventual role. Moreover, at least in America, it is the cultural expectation that boys will display more aggressiveness than girls. Indeed, aggression is tolerated and often urged on boys; their show of aggression is reinforced. And in the Pattern Study mothers appeared to be less permissive of agression in girls than in boys. Following up the five-year-olds of the Pattern Study when they were 12, Sears (1961) rated boys higher in antisocial aggression and girls higher in anxiety over aggression. Apparently the unwillingness to permit aggressive behavior in girls gave them greater anxiety over its exhibition.

Kagan and Moss (1962) in their longitudinal study from childhood to adulthood reported greater long-term stability of aggressive conduct in males than females. Conceivably aggression is allowed in boys during their developmental years, but not in girls; it does not fit the cultural cliché of feminine, lady-like deportment. Whether the frustration-aggression hypothesis applies here is uncertain. The higher activity level of boys may engulf them in more frustrating situations. This might explain Fite's (1940) assertion of a relationship between aggression and level of activity. Then, too, the fact that parents in general and fathers in particular have greater expectations for their sons than for their daughters may produce frustration in boys.

The point was made that biological determinants of aggression cannot be ignored. Activity level rests in part on the nervous system. Greater nervous irritability may be typical of the male. Sex differences in longevity and in incidence of certain illnesses suggest that males may be more susceptible biologically to environmental pressures. Thus, a complex interaction of biological and environmental forces may cause sex differences as well as individual differences in behavior—including aggressive behavior.

Aggression and Popularity. The hostile feelings underlying aggression do not promote positive social exchange. Aggression is likely to incur counteraggression. Not surprisingly, the relation between popularity and aggression throughout childhood and adolescence is negative (Winder & Rau, 1962; Eron et al., 1961). Among lower-class fifth- and sixth-graders, Lesser (1959) gathered Guess Who nominations for five categories of aggressive activity; *provoked physical aggression*—to attack or injure physically upon provocation; *outburst aggression*—to explode in an uncontrolled temper tantrum; *unprovoked physical aggression*—to attack or harm physically without provocation; *verbal aggression*—to attack or damage verbally; and *indirect aggression*—to attack or injure through some other person or object. Between popularity and provoked physical aggression the correlation was positive; the relation of popularity to the other four categories was negative. Most disapproved was indirect aggression, with verbal, unprovoked physical, and outburst aggression following in that order.

Too much aggressive behavior implies some basic maladjustment. Either the child has not learned better ways of responding to environmental forces or his need for aggression is so strong that he cannot behave otherwise. However this may be, it is not looked upon with favor by the child's peers.

Anxiety

This has been called the "age of anxiety." Commemorated in Auden's verse, intoned in Bernstein's music, encapsulated in Robbins's choreography, it has also received a great amount of attention in popular literature as well as in the writings of psychologists, sociologists, and philosophers. Modern man is beset by intense feelings of anxiety which arise from a plethora of causes ranging from the threat of nuclear annihilation to the insecurities flowing from the breakdown of the family as a social unit. The main concern here, however, are the signs, symptoms, and antecedents of anxiety in children.

Psychological Theories. Freud made a distinction between fear and anxiety (see May, 1950). In fear, the individual's concern is drawn to the threat arising from a specific object. Anxiety, on the other hand, may be considered a generalized fear which is a condition within the individual. Freud further distinguished objective anxiety from neurotic anxiety. The former was a reaction to external dangers, a protective, self-preservation mechanism, whereas neurotic anxiety appeared in the absence of any apparent danger and was anticipatory in nature. Freud held that although the capacity for anxiety was innate, its appearance was the result of learning—learning stemming primarily from the child's early emotional relations with the parents. Describing a number of causes of anxiety, Freud stressed the importance in neurotic anxiety of the child's fear of loss of or separation from the mother.

To Rank, best known for his notion of *birth trauma*, anxiety arose from the individual's fear of the endless number of separations which occurred from early childhood onward in the process of acquiring autonomy, independence, and individuality. The beginning of school may be one such threatening experience involving, as it does, a partial disruption of the child's previous closeness with the mother.

Adler, in a sense, equated anxiety with neurotic feelings of inferiority which arose from the child's evaluation of himself as weaker and less competent than others. Basic anxiety, according to Horney, was a product of the child's conflict between dependence on parents and hostile feelings toward them. In general, anxiety arose from any threat to the individual's security. Sullivan thought such threats originated in the infant even before the development of conscious awareness and resulted from his fear of disapproval from the important persons in his interpersonal environment. Because approval, especially from the mother, was of such crucial importance to the child, he tended to mold his behavior to conform to her demands and expectations. Anxiety arose whenever there were tendencies that would bring disapproval from others. These tendencies were therefore repressed. And such repression imposed a restriction on the child's awareness and on his developing sense of the self. As Sullivan saw it, anxiety was antithetical to emotional health which denotes personal awareness and personal growth.

Finally, in his early work with the notion of anxiety, Mowrer saw anxiety as a conditioned form of reaction to pain. Consequently, it was a strong motivating force for behavior since the organism sought to reduce the level of anxiety and reinforced any behavior serving that purpose. Later Mowrer named the origin of anxiety as repressed fears and the guilt associated with them.

Thus, anxiety that arises initially in infancy or early childhood is an outgrowth of the child's relations with his parent. Whereas fear is a response to specific environmental danger, anxiety is a reaction to a pervasive threat to the individual's security. Certain fears are normal and desirable in the growing child. Anxiety, however, is restrictive rather than constructive.

Signs of Anxiety. Two broad types of behaviors indicating anxiety can be discerned in children. In the first, the child avoids a large number of situations and experiences as though each possessed some potential danger. His world becomes restricted as a result; he retreats from life and his conduct becomes rigid and stereotyped. In the second type, the child's demeanor resembles "flight reaction"; he is restless, hyperactive, nervous, and uneasy. In both types, attention to the task at hand, persistence of a constructive nature, and interpersonal relations are all disrupted and impaired. Such children, of course, remain in a state of emotional conflict.

Characteristics of Anxiety. Evolving from the Taylor Manifest Anxiety Scale (Taylor, 1953) for identifying the strength of the anxiety drive in adults, several scales have been devised to assess the characteristics of anxious children. One of these, consisting of 53 items, requires the child to respond either "yes" or "no" to such statements as the following:

> It is hard for me to keep my mind on anything.
> I worry most of the time.
> My feelings get hurt easily.
> Often I feel sick in my stomach.
> I have bad dreams.
> (Castenada, McCandless, & Palermo, 1956, pp. 318–319)

Another test was designed expressly to detect the amount of anxiety experienced by children in a school test situation (Sarason, Davidson, Lighthall, & Waite, 1958a). Subsequent studies have examined various characteristics differentiating children who score high and low on an anxiety scale.

The effects of anxiety on intelligence and learning have received considerable attention. Despite some contradictory results, there has been a consistent negative correlation between anxiety and both intelligence and school achievement at the elementary-school level (McCandless & Castenada, 1956; Feldhusen & Klausmeier, 1962) and also at the senior-high level (Sarason, 1963). Quite likely anxiety impairs a child's intellectual functioning—as though so much of his attention and effort were diverted to coping with his problems that he could not apply himself sufficiently to other tasks. In this sense the child is certainly emotionally handicapped.

Experimental studies on the relation of anxiety to learning have concluded that school children high in anxiety surpass those low in anxiety on simple tasks but prove inferior on complex ones (Castenada, Palermo, & McCandless, 1956). In a complex task requiring a number of competing responses, high drive—in this case, anxiety—impairs performance whereas in a simple task necessitating only a single response, a high degree of motivation facilitates performance. This does not appear to be the case, however, in studies of college students (Buskirk, 1961; Sarason, 1961). From these investigations, the conclusion was reached that anxious subjects did not necessarily perform less well on complex tasks but that their performance was inferior on tasks entailing threats to their feelings of adequacy. This fits the position that anxiety results from any threat to individual security. Clearly, therefore, in a school situation children, particularly anxious ones, function best in a secure, nonthreatening atmosphere.

Research relating anxiety to other personality characteristics falls into a consistent pattern. Highly anxious children are less popular with peers than children of low anxiety (McCandless, Castenada, & Palermo, 1956). They have less positive self concepts (Lipsitt, 1952; Horowitz, 1962); they express more dissatisfaction with themselves and others (Phillips, Hindsman, & Jennings, 1960); and in general they express more negative feelings than less anxious children (Bernard, Zimbardo, & Sarason, 1961). At the middle elementary-school level significant correlations have been obtained between scores on the Children's Manifest Anxiety Test and teacher ratings of adjustment as well as scores of the California Test of Personality (Iscoe & Cochran, 1960). The more anxious children were rated as more maladjusted by their teachers who, in part, defined maladjustment on the basis of restlessness, lack of attention, and inability or unwillingness to "settle down."

In classroom observations, highly anxious boys show less orientation toward tasks than boys of low anxiety; they also display greater insecurity in their relation with their teacher. Among girls, however, the highly anxious are less distractible and evince a stronger need for achievement than those low in anxiety (Sarason, Davidson, Lighthall, & Waite, 1958b). Apparently anxiety operates in different ways with respect to sex. Psychoanalytic writers have argued that boys and girls handle anxiety differently. Girls are said to employ *autoplastic* defenses—defenses involving the individual herself, as in daydreaming—whereas boys handle anxiety through *alloplastic* defenses—defenses in which the individual turns outward toward other persons or objects, as in rebelliousness. Covert versus overt behavior may distinguish between boys and girls in this respect. Consistently, girls score higher on anxiety scales (Castenada, McCandless, & Palermo,

1956), implying that in American society it is easier for females than males to admit they are anxious (Davidson, Sarason, Lighthall, Waite, & Sarnoff, 1958; L'Abate, 1960). Nervousness is a woman's prerogative, whereas it is the male who develops an ulcer.

The idea that anxiety exerts a constricting influence on behavior is buttressed by studies indicating that the more anxious children score higher on scales measuring "rigidity of thinking" (Kitano, 1960). These children also show greater rigidity in their drawings (Fox, Davidson, Lighthall, Waite, & Sarason, 1958) and in their behavior (Smock, 1958). Related to this is the finding that dependency characterizes the behavior of anxious children (Sarason, Davidson, Lighthall, & Waite, 1958b). Since dependency is often a sign of insecurity, anxiety, dependency, and insecurity are interrelated causally. They constrict and restrict the child's behavior and his world.

Parental Antecedents. Not much has been turned up in research thus far regarding parental antecedents of anxiety, perhaps partly because mothers of highly anxious children have taken a highly defensive stance in interviews (Sarason, 1959). They are less frank in their responses and are less willing to divulge information about themselves. Possibly they are themselves anxious and insecure or they may be defensive for reasons of guilt over nonacceptance of the child. Mothers of children low in anxiety indicated that their children were freer to express feelings of anger and aggression (Davidson, 1959).

It may be that parents of children without much anxiety are secure enough in themselves and in their relations with their child to be able to permit him to express negative feelings even if these are directed against the parent. This would certainly fit Horney's notion that anxiety results from the conflict between dependence on parents and feelings of hostility toward them. There is less anxiety when such feelings are expressed. Anxiety begets anxiety.

Conscience Development

Conscience is sometimes defined with tongue in cheek as "that which keeps us from doing what we shouldn't do even when no one is looking." Indeed, this definition lights upon a major element in the idea of conscience: inner controls based on an individual's acceptance of values concerning right and wrong behavior. Yet there are other kinds of control of behavior. Control may be external in origin, resting in the prohibitions and demands of others. In Chapter 7 the distinction was noted between *guilt* and *shame* cultures, the latter controlling behavior by shame—fear of punishment, ridicule, ostracism, retribution—and the former by internalizing society's standards. One other point about conscience: inner controls are learned as are the values to which they relate.

Between the Hartshorne and May (1928) study and the late 1950's, little concern was shown over conscience development in children. Matters of values and conscience were apparently not thought to be appropriate topics for scientific research. Sears (1960) noted that the identification of the child-rearing antecedents of inner controls and sanctions signified "one of the most important problems facing students of personality development today" (p. 97). Miller and Swanson (1960) saw moral standards in terms of inner conflict. Three reasons were advanced for this approach: moral needs, that is, internalized standards, are frequently the cause of conflict within the individual; the manner in which these conflicts are resolved depends on the particular moral values held by the individual; and each individual employs characteristic ways of resolving conflicts, and these are thought of as his "character structure."

Among adults, some are faced more frequently than others with conflicts over moral issues. Such conflicts are likelier, however, to involve a position taken on some moral issue than overt behavior, as in childhood. For example, is racial discrimination in public housing acceptable? Is nuclear war justified? Can unfair business competition be condoned? Most likely the mature adult resolves such issues in a rather consistent manner, and when he does employ defenses such as rationalization to avoid facing the conflict, they are a stable part of his personality. No wonder an understanding of conscience is essential to an understanding of human behavior.

Antecedents. There are three principal elements that affect the development of conscience. First, a culture's values or standards form an important part of the legacy transmitted to a child by his parents. One culture may discourage aggressiveness, another emphasize self-effacement, a third espouse personal recognition. The second factor is the child's intellectual development. The older, more intellectually mature child is better able to perceive what is expected of him; he can understand the reasons for certain restrictions and standards; he is able to generalize a principle and apply it to a variety of situations. More than the younger child, the older one can comprehend some of the abstract concepts behind social issues—unselfishness, equality, justice, truth. Third is the child's relations with his parents. Several research techniques have been used to study parental influences on development of conscience. In the Pattern Study, mothers were asked to indicate signs of conscience in their childhood. Two criteria were used; the child's tendency to "act the parental role," that is, his attempt to teach parental standards to siblings and friends; and the child's behavior following a wrongdoing, that is, his attempts to confess, apologize, or make amends. Evidence of the development of a conscience was rated on the following scale (Sears, Maccoby, & Levin, 1957, p. 381):

1. No evidence. Child hides, denies, does not seem unhappy when naughty.
2. Little evidence of conscience.
3. Moderate conscience development. May not confess directly but looks sheepish; seldom denies.
4. Considerable conscience.
5. Strong conscience. Child feels miserable when naughty; always confesses; never denies; strong need for forgiveness.

The concept employed most frequently to explain the child's internalization of adult standards is identification. Factors producing a strong identification with the parent tend to encourage development of conscience. Kindergarten boys who were highly masculine, presumably because of identification with their fathers, were also high in conscience development (Mussen & Distler, 1960). Research has dealt with two factors, in particular, regarding this antecedent of conscience development: the type of parental discipline and the warmth of the parent-child relationship.

As to disciplinary activity in the home, the Pattern Study indicated that psychological or love-oriented techniques exemplified in praise, isolation, and withdrawal of love aided the development of conscience more than the materialistic or physical methods embodied in tangible rewards, deprivation, and physical punishment. MacKinnon's (1938) investigation of college students found that those who transgressed prohibitions in an experimental setting were likelier to be children of fathers whose disciplinary tactics had been physical rather than psychological. Yet a study of four-year-olds (Burton, Maccoby, & Allinsmith, 1961) on resistance to cheating did not support these findings. In this investigation, scolding and physical punishment were more closely related to resistance to temptation than were psychological punishments or use of reasoning. Direct, physical techniques seemed most effective in the young child, although psychological techniques encouraging identification with the parent took over as the child grew older and gained in cognitive development.

Similar to the distinction between physical and psychological disciplinary methods is the differentiation between techniques of *induction* and of *sensitization* (Aronfreed, 1961). Reasoning with the child, ignoring or rejecting him, and explanation are all inductive techniques. They elicit in the child reactions to his own transgressions, which may become independent of the original source of punishment. For instance, reasoning with a young child and explaining the consequences of an act should encourage him to examine his actions and to accept responsibility for them. Sensitization techniques include physical punishment and scolding. These may simply make the child extremely susceptible to fear of external punishment following transgression and attach importance to the demands and expectations of others. Through use of a story-completion technique among sixth-graders, a relation was found between the child's type of moral response and the mother's disciplinary technique. Children whose mothers used inductive techniques were more prone to include notions of reparation and acceptance in their stories, whereas others whose mothers relied on a technique of sensitization oftener introduced external consequences of transgression in theirs.

In the Pattern Study, love-oriented techniques characterized most middle-class mothers and physical types of discipline, most lower-class mothers. In the Aronfreed study induction was the predominant choice of middle-class mothers and sensitization the major choice of lower-class mothers. The physical types of discipline espoused in lower-class homes, however, neither encourage identification nor produce inner controls.

Turning to warmth, most efforts to link conscience development to specific child-rearing practices, such as the age and severity of toilet training, have not borne fruit (Grinder, 1962; Burton, Maccoby, & Allinsmith, 1961). Perhaps, as noted in the chapters on parental influences on children, the general psychological atmosphere of the home may be more important. In this connection, factors in the home which produce strong identification with parents are also conducive to early development of conscience. In the Pattern Study, the threat to withdraw love, a psychological device, had little effect if the mother was relatively cold and rejecting. Conversely, it proved most effective when the child's relationship with his mother was warm and accepting. Thus, the nonaccepted child has little to lose by diplaying disapproved behavior. To cite the record, only 18 per cent of the rejected children covered in the Pattern Study were judged as having "high conscience," compared with 31 per cent of the accepted group. And in support of the MacKinnon (1938) finding about the import of the kind of discipline practiced by the father, stronger consciences were observed in boys with accepting fathers than boys with fathers who tended to reject them. No such difference was detected, however, in girls.

Two major family qualities are tied to a strong superego in children, that is, to the "presence of an effectively behavior-guiding conscience"—consistency and a combination of mutual trust and approval (Peck, 1958). Logically, a consistent pattern of parental control and expectations provides a clear-cut setting for the development of positive conduct. In addition, an atmosphere of mutual trust inspires the child to absorb his parents' values and standards, which the child accepts for his own.

Development of conscience, then, needs to be understood in order to understand the development of personality. For the manner in which the individual resolves a moral conflict is a stable aspect of his personality. As significant as are the cultural lessons transmitted by parents, the child's own intellectual growth, and also his identification with parents which leads to adoption of their values and to acquisition of inner controls, nothing counts as much as an atmosphere of warmth in the relationship between parents and child. Mutual trust, acceptance, and consistency combined with warmth are likely to assure strong conscience when childhood gives way to adolescence.

Dominant-Submissive Behavior

A hierarchy of behavior ranging all the way from dominance to submissiveness has been seen many times in the social interaction of a wide assortment of organisms including rats, dogs, monkeys, and humans. Implied in this range is the jockeying for position, the maneuvering for power that is virtually an integral part of all social interaction, regardless of species. Here, too, comes into relief the structure of group whose members can be ranked with respect to dominance and submission. Both the struggle and the structure are vividly illustrated by the pecking order of the domestic fowl.

Factor analyses of personality tests and ratings almost invariably find a factor designated ascendance, or dominance, or assertiveness both at child (Cattell & Gruen, 1953; Cattell & Coan, 1957) and adult (Cattell, 1957) levels. In the paragraphs to follow we shall summarize some of the early studies that contributed methodologically to the investigation of ascendant behavior in children and then turn to the antecedents of dominance and submissiveness.

Early Studies. Noteworthy is the Jack (1934) study which sought experimentally to modify behavior. Jack observed four-year-olds in pairs in a room supplied with a sandbox and three types of toys. The following eight types of behavior figured in defining ascendance.

1. Verbal attempts to secure play material
2. Forceful attempts to secure play materials
3. Success in securing material from companion's possession
4. Defense and snatching back of materials taken from one's possession
5. Verbal attempts to direct behavior of companion
6. Companion compliance with direction
7. Forbidding, criticizing, reproving companion
8. Providing pattern of behavior which companion imitates

Concluding that the most significant difference between ascendant and nonascendant children was degree of self-confidence, Jack applied special training materials in her effort to modify the behavior of the five least ascendant youngsters. Later, when she paired them again in the experimental room, the ascendance scores of these particular youngsters showed significant gain.

Page (1936) achieved similar results among three- and four-year-olds. Yet Page noted that teacher ratings of ascendance away from the experimental setting did not change as a result of the modification of the children's behavior through training. Therefore, she questioned whether the results of the training spread to the environment beyond the training room. Though lacking data on long-term effects of training, psychologists find it significant that by increasing a child's self-confidence through developing certain skills and proficiencies in him, they can alter his behavior in a social situation.

Similar modification of behavior was reported by Chittenden (1942). She provided special tutelage to ten preschool children who were most dominating in their relations with other children. Conflicts involving dolls were analyzed, with the social and emotional consequences of certain kinds of behavior emphasized. Tests conducted after the training disclosed that these children had increased their cooperative behavior.

Dominant-Submissive Antecedents. Dominant behavior is observable in children at least as young as three years of age. It is also observable in lower organisms. Conceivably, therefore, constitutional factors predisposing an individual to dominance play a role in such behavior. Nevertheless, this does not eliminate the role of environmental antecedents.

Part of the problem of identifying the antecedents of ascendant behavior results from a confusion in nomenclature. Jack clearly did not differentiate between acceptable and unacceptable kinds of behavior in the types she selected to define ascendance. This distinction largely appeared later. Chittenden (1942) embraced both dominating and cooperative behavior in the term "assertiveness." Anderson (1937, 1939, 1946), it will be recalled, distinguished dominating from integrating behavior. In a similar vein, Parten (1932) described two types of leaders, the bully, who used brute force and bossing, and the diplomat, who used artful and indirect suggestion. Finally, Mummery (1947) spoke of socially acceptable and socially unacceptable behavior.

Various distinctions between socially positive and socially negative types of domination aid in resolving some of the disagreement over parental antecedents of dominating behavior. From some of the Fels studies, Baldwin (1948, 1949) concluded that democracy in the home, especially an actively democratic home, tended to produce an active, aggressive child, likely to be a leader. Children from restrictive, controlled homes tend to be unaggressive and fearful. Baldwin reasoned that freedom in the home encouraged active exploration of the environment and a high degree of social participation.

In agreement with the Fels data, Miles (in Anderson, 1946) noted that parents of adolescent leaders were less restrictive in handling their children. The child enjoyed the freedom to make his own decisions and judgments and to experiment with new opportunities. Yet these findings contradicted those of an investigation by Meyer (1947) who, in rating homes of 29 preschool children on the 30 Fels Parent Behavior Scales, found significant negative correlations between their dominating responses under experimental conditions and such home atmosphere as democracy of policy, readiness of explanation, understanding of child's problems, and rapport with child. The homes of the dominant children were characterized by disciplinary friction and general discord.

Similarly, Radke (1946) reported that children from autocratic homes tended to dominate their companions more readily than children from democratic homes. They were also less considerate of their peers. To Mummery (1954) the chief effect of democracy in the home was perhaps to influence the child's self concept in terms of self-acceptance and self-confidence. Because democratic parents respect the individuality of the child, it is likely that he will show respect for his peers in social situations. If such a child displays assertive behavior it will generally be socially acceptable, integrating, and cooperative in nature.

Leadership Behavior. Although not synonymous with dominating behavior, leadership has much in common with it. Leadership implies the successful use of techniques to guide and direct the behavior of others toward an agreed goal. Dominating behavior, on the other hand, may or may not succeed and may or may not involve a shared goal. Whether children who are dominating in the preschool period assume leadership in elementary-school years is not certain from the scant evidence at hand. Equally sparse is the evidence relating to the transferability of leadership from one group to another although more of this does exist.

Yet leadership is a topic of interest to social psychologists who deal with adult behavior. In general there are two approaches to the subject (Allen, 1952). The *structuralists* regard leadership as a trait or a set of traits. The *functionalists* view it as a function of the situation. The two positions may be synthesized if leadership is seen on the basis of role theory and role expectancy. It is likely that children who later become leaders possess in childhood the earmarks of leadership.

The inclusion of leadership capacities in the child's concept of the self results from the successful use of these characteristics in opportunities to lead. Effective leadership in one situation inspires the child to assert it in others. Through repeated successes the notion of leadership becomes an integral part of the self concept. Furthermore, as others expect the individual to continue to lead, this contributes to further exhibition of leadership demeanor. Reputation occasions the repeated display of specific behaviors in children even if the repute is undeserved.

Having reviewed the available data on the qualities inherent in leaders, Stogdill (1948) listed these characteristics in which leaders surpassed the average members of their groups: intelligence, scholarship, dependability in exercising responsibilities, activity and social participation, socioeconomic status, initiative, persistence, knowing how to get things done, self-confidence, alertness to and insight to situations, cooperativeness, popularity, adaptability, verbal facility, athletic ability, originality, desire to excel, judgment, humor, chronological age, height, weight, appearance, energy, dominance, integrity, and mood control. Those factors associated with leadership, Stogdill (1948, p. 64) concluded, could probably be classified under the following headings.

1. Capacity (intelligence, alertness, verbal facility, originality, judgment).
2. Achievement (scholarship, knowledge, athletic accomplishments).

3. Responsibility (dependability, initiative, persistence, aggressiveness, self-confidence, desire to excel).
4. Participation (activity, sociability, cooperation, adaptability, humor).
5. Status (socio-economic position, popularity).
6. Situation (mental level, status, skills, needs and interests of followers, objectives to be achieved, etc.).

As much as the traits seem to support the structuralist approach to leadership, Stogdill pointed out that the qualities and skills enabling an individual to function as a leader depended on the demands of the group and the situation. In preschool years, mere activity level is enough to determine leadership (Parten, 1932); in late elementary-school years and throughout adolescence, athletic ability and physical prowess are the important requisites for leadership among boys (Partridge, 1934); in college empathy is the key to leadership (Bell & Hall, 1954). Since the functionalists are also correct, "leaders are made as well as born."

Social Acceptance

Social psychologists who contend that Americans place too much emphasis on sociability, adjustment to the group, and "other-directed-ness" support their complaint by pointing to the amount of research on social acceptance in the field of child psychology. Yet there are a number of reasons to believe that a child's degree of acceptance by his peers is of more than fleeting or superficial significance. Children not well accepted by their peers tend to express less positive feelings toward them (Lippitt & Gold, 1959), and it is reasonable to consider positive feelings toward others as one sign of mental health. In the classroom, poor pupil-to-pupil relationships is one indication of an unfavorable climate for learning and for positive group interaction (Spector, 1953).

The second reason for attaching importance to peer relationships is that the adjustment to peers is a good barometer for adjustment in adult life. Roff (1957, 1960, 1961) has been able to predict the adjustment of individuals to military service from comments made about them years before concerning their childhood relations with their peers. Early detection of difficulties in adult adjustment is possible, Roff held, from knowledge of the attitudes and opinions of an individual's associates regarding him. Undoubtedly, a vast number of persons who are not highly accepted by their peers in childhood make an adequate adjustment to adult life. There is a difference, though, between lack of acceptance and active rejection. The Roff data seem to indicate that it was active rejection to which he referred.

Finally, it is important to find the personality correlates of social acceptance because knowledge of them may make it possible to help children develop better relations with their peers. We have seen the negative correlations between social acceptance and aggressiveness, anxiety, and dependence. How can these aspects of personality be altered, modified, or altogether prevented?

Correlates of Social Acceptance. Efforts to isolate the factors bearing on social acceptance go back to the 1920's and the early 1930's. Furfey (1927) noted a tendency among preadolescent boys to elect chums of the same size, age, intelligence, and maturity as themselves. Challman (1932) found preschool children to be similar to their friends in chronological age, sociability, and physical activity. Similarities in mental age, height, extroversion, attractiveness of personality, IQ, and frequency of laughter mattered little in preschool choices of friendship. Lippitt (1941) noted cooperation in routines to be most clearly related to popularity in a group of preschool youngsters. Others correlates of social acceptance in children included socioeconomic status, school achievement, responsibility, cooperativeness, freedom from fears and anxieties, good health, attractiveness of appearance, and empathy. Sex difference is also important since there is an increasing separation by sex in friendship choices throughout the early elementary-school years. Further, girls receive higher social acceptance scores than boys. Table 15-1 lists the traits designated by a group of 13–15-year-old boys as characterizing their most acceptable peers.

In contrast to earlier studies, the more recent ones have tried to single out the antecedents causing different levels of social acceptance. For example, studying family influences on adjustment to peers, Hoffman (1961) noted that children from homes dominated by the mother were experiencing difficulties in their relations with the opposite sex. This was equally true for boys and girls. Influential as was an affectional relationship with the father on the adjustment of both boys and girls to peers, it was especially so for boys. An affectional relationship with the mother augured well for her daughter's adjustment to peers.

The rejected unpopular child is often shy, recessive, socially disinterested, and self-centered. Even if he may be noisy and energetic, his attempts at social acceptance by his agemates go unheeded. This may stem from the fact that the behavior of such children is motivated by strong needs for attention and social approval. Usually they are unable to share, to take turns, and to comply with rules and regula-

TABLE 15-1 * Correlates of Social Acceptance in 13- to 15-Year-Old Boys

Identifying Number	Name	Illustrative Terms
1	Intelligent	Intelligent, keen, bright vs. Dumb, stupid
2	Sociable	Friendly, sociable vs. Unfriendly, too quiet, stiff
3	Minds own business	Minds own business vs. Annoying, pest
4	Plays fair	Good sport, plays fair vs. Poor sport, plays unfair
5	Quiet	Quiet vs. Loud, noisy, overtalkative
6	Witty	Humorous, witty, good joker vs. Not humorous, no sense of humor
7	Athletic	Athletic, ball player vs. Not athletic
8	Helpful	Helpful vs. Not helpful
9	Unconceited	Humble, doesn't show off vs. Conceited, stuck up
10	Good company	Good company, fun to be with vs. No fun, poor company
11	Serious	Serious, not silly vs. Silly, foolish
12	Conscientious	Conscientious, good worker vs. Lazy, listless
13	Masculine	Real man, has guts vs. Sissy, helpless, girlish, fairy
14	Stays out of trouble	Stays out of trouble vs. Always in trouble
15	Talks well	Can talk, talks well vs. Can't talk
16	Honest	Honest, doesn't cheat vs. Dishonest, cheats, lies
17	Clean	Clean, neat vs. Sloppy, dirty
18	Doesn't fight	Doesn't fight vs. Always fighting
19	Kind	Kind, considerate vs. Unkind, not considerate, mean
20	Trustworthy	Trustworthy, keeps his word vs. Unreliable
21	Gets along well with others	Gets along well with others vs. Can't get along
22	Leader	Leader vs. Not a leader

TABLE 15-1 (Continued)

Identifying Number	Name	Illustrative Terms
23	Cheerful	Cheerful vs. Grumpy, complains
24	Cooperative	Cooperative vs. Not cooperative
25	Good scholar	Good scholar, student vs. Poor scholar, student
26	Common interests	Same interests vs. Not same interests
27	Interesting	Interesting vs. Not interesting, dull
28	Good manners	Good manners vs. Poor manners
29	Pleasant, agreeable	Pleasant, agreeable vs. Argues, insults
30	Can take a joke	Can take a joke vs. Can't take a joke
31	Mature	Mature, grownup vs. Immature, babyish
32	Generous	Generous, unselfish vs. Tight, selfish
33	Good-looking	Good-looking, clean cut vs. Ugly
34	Good character	Good character vs. Poor character
35	Understanding	Understanding vs. Not understanding
36	Participates in activities	All around vs. No activities, doesn't take part
37	Calm	Calm, doesn't get excited, easy-going vs. Bad tempered, gets excited
38	Sincere	Sincere, means what he says vs. Insincere
39	Well dressed	Good dresser, sharp clothes vs. Poor dresser
40	Other specific terms used infrequently	
41	General non-specific terms	Swell, good friend vs. No good, real drip

* Feinberg, M. R., Smith, M., & Schmidt, R. An analysis of expressions used by adolescents at varying economic levels to describe accepted and rejected peers. *J. genet. Psychol.*, 1958, **93**, 133–148.

tions, thus disclosing an underlying insecurity. Whether lack of acceptance or unacceptable behavior comes first is hard to ascertain. It is another case of which causes the other. It is likely that both are causes and both are effects: undesirable behavior leads to unpopularity which leads to more undesirable behavior. The importance of therapeutic intervention by a trained adult is obvious.

The following two personality sketches are drawn from a study that investigated the personalities of five popular and five unpopular children. Their contents will add meaning to this discussion of the correlates of social acceptance.

David is about average size for his age, and is quite good-looking. Always neat and clean, but not fussy or overly nice in appearance. Has a happy expression which radiates friendliness and good humor.

David is outstanding in friendliness and social interest. He is "smooth" in inter-personal relationships; carries on a conversation with ease and poise. Shows more initiative than most children in meeting new-comers who enter the room. Goes out of his way to make them feel welcome, and to show them around the building. Never snubs anyone, but still he does not try to establish intimate relationships with those to whom he is not especially attracted. Would never consciously hurt anyone. Is always very courteous in his relations with both teachers and children. Shows more sympathetic concern for others than most children of his age. Sometimes he asks the teacher to allow him to help another child who has difficulty in his school work. Also, he has been observed to pull a larger boy off a smaller one on the playground when his sense of fairness has been violated. As a patrol leader in the halls, he has shown a marked interest in aiding the smallest children. In spite of these characteristics, it must also be stated that David is described as "ego-centric" and "bull-headed" at times. One of his most frequent companions states that he has lots of quarrels with David because "David gets mad if you disagree with him." Also, David does not usually react very well to criticism. He shows some resentment and acts like he considers it unwarranted, but seldom says anything.

David has a number of abilities which bring him group recognition. Is outstanding in dramatics. Often takes leading roles. Always knows his lines perfectly, and helps carry the entire performance. Also sings very well. Is a member of the school choir. Enjoys entertaining others. Likes to be before his public. Sometimes acts as an announcer. Has frequently been elected to class offices. He takes these obligations seriously and performs his duties well. As a patrolman in the sixth grade, he has been especially watchful and has shown marked ability in directing others and in getting them to do the right thing without antagonizing them. Is not bossy or dominating.

In classroom academic work, David is not especially brilliant, but his work is nearly always better than average. He makes good contributions to class discussions. Is very dependable in having his written work in on time. Takes pride in doing good school work and in making good grades. Also, he likes to please the teacher. Although David's application to his academic work is generally steady and conscientious, he seldom shows any initiative or originality. Prefers to be told what to do. Neither does he show much drive in trying to overcome problems that are very difficult. Is inclined to quit, and wait for the teacher to help him.

David conforms well to school regulations, but is not a perfectly behaved child. In the fourth grade he was paddled a number of times for impertinence to the teacher. This trait has not been much in evidence since. He is mischievous at times, both in the classroom and on the playground, but he never does anything of serious proportions and always does things above-board rather than pulling tricks behind the teacher's back. Never sneaking or under-handed. When caught in some kind of mischief, he readily confesses and does not try to shift blame to others (Bonney, 1947, pp. 14–16).

Eugene is a buxom type of boy about average height. His appearance is somewhat marred by blackheads which he frequently picks at. Has a pleasant, but weak facial expression. His ambling gait, poor carriage, and lackadaisical manner cause others to think of him as a boy who has never taken life or its obligations very seriously. Does not appear unhappy, but he gives the impression of being insecure and uncertain of himself.

Eugene's personality structure is primarily that of an effeminate boy. He has never engaged in out-door boyish activities and refuses to play aggressive group games. He participates a little in simpler games like dodge ball or chase, but does not do well in these. Has a "don't care" attitude in respect to all playground activities. He is not uncoordinated or physically weak; he just doesn't identify himself with such things. When left alone at play period, he plays on the teeter-totter, swings, or teases the girls. When forced to participate in a group game such as baseball, he "puts on an act," tries to be cute, does a lot of irrelevant talking, and makes an "out" every time. The other boys laugh at him to his face, and deride him, but he shrugs it all off and pretends not to care. Never fights, never gets angry or argues about a point, and never attacks others. Has a minimum of courage and daring.

Eugene is characterized by emotional instability and immaturity. He is frequently restless in class, does quite a lot of "doodling," jabbers under his breath, and sometimes annoys other children by putting his arm on their desks. Is seriously lacking in persistency of effort. He will work very well at a task which he likes, but not for long. Once he was given an important part in a play, but he never learned his lines, even though he had much help and urging from the teacher. He got some of his lines right, but he improvised so much that the other players had a hard time catching their cues from him. This disgusted the other children. He did, however, show good dramatic sense and entered into the spirit of his part exceptionally well.

Eugene's emotional and social immaturity is emphasized by several other traits. One of these is his strong persistency in wanting his own way in group projects, club meetings, or indoor games. He does not take "no" for an answer from the teacher or the group, but will argue, cajole, or plead for hours to have what he wants. Another evidence of his emotional immaturity is his very naive identification with certain strong, capable boys. One day he told his special reading teacher with obvious elation how he had sat next to one of these admired boys in the picture show the day before. The fact that his sitting next to this boy was purely accidental made his mention of it all the more significant—and pathetic. Additional evidence of Eugene's inadequate social development is found in his excessive eating and in his playing with children much younger than himself. Several investigations have emphasized the relation between excessive eating and social inferiority. Eugene's eating certainly fits the diagnosis of a substitute pleasure for social failure. He frequently brings a mid-morning lunch in addition to eating a big lunch at noon. That there is some degree of unconscious compulsion in his eating is indicated by the fact that several times he said to his sixth grade teacher, "I feel better today; I didn't eat so much."

Eugene has a number of abilities which could be developed into real assets except for his inadequate personality structure. As previously stated, he has unusually good dramatic sense. Also he draws and paints quite well, but he will seldom work at anything long enough to achieve a praise-worthy product. At times he makes interesting and unusual contributions to class discussions. He may come forth with some rare bit of information which he has picked up from the radio or other sources, or he may see unusual, significant relationships in material being discussed in class; but these performances are very irregular (Bonney, 1947, pp. 46–48).

Constancy of Social Acceptance. Several factors indicate the likelihood of relative constancy in social acceptance from one group to another and one time to the next (Northway, 1946). First, Bonney (1943) found that a child's social position in grades two, three, and five was as constant as his intellectual and academic achievement throughout the elementary-school years. Years later, upon interviewing 25 first-grade children throughout the school year, Medinnus (1962) obtained correlations of about +.85 between scores of social acceptance from one interview to the next. Thus, there is certainly short-term constancy in social acceptance. Second, a number of studies concur on the personality characteristics associated with acceptance and nonacceptance. Further, researches into children's friendships report an increasing constancy in friendship choices throughout childhood and adolescence (Horrocks & Thompson, 1946, 1947; Horrocks & Buker, 1951). Prior to school, constancy probably results from the restricted range of choices imposed by limitations in mobility. Later, it may become accounted for by the increasing consistency of personality. In adolescence, friends are chosen on a deeper basis—on aspects of personality that are fairly stable.

That social acceptance is fairly constant while growing up points to its influence on the child's personality and adjustment. As awareness of social position increases with age (Ausubel, Schiff, & Gasser, 1952), a long-term pattern of acceptance and nonacceptance exerts direct and indirect influence on behavior, until knowledge of one's social status becomes an important part of one's self concept.

Modifying Social Acceptance. If social rejection reflects basic maladjustment of personality, raising the level of an individual's social acceptance is not easily accomplished. Because of the role of antecedent parent-child relationships in social acceptance, changes may involve the entire family. But this may be true only of extreme social rejection. For children in the intermediate zone, it may be profitable to concentrate on the self concept. Increasing their self-confidence, self-assurance, and self-esteem is most desirable. Children who manifest unacceptable behaviors usually know that they elicit unfavorable reactions from others but are unable to mend their ways. Feelings of inadequacy interfere with behavior and lead to deeper feelings of inadequacy. Somehow the treadmill must be stopped. And it is likely that modifications in self-feelings and in behavior are best achieved in the early elementary years.

The prime responsibility for assisting the child to more positive and acceptable social relations is the parents'. In the case of the boy, since athletic skill plays so great a role in his acceptability, the father can increase the child's self-confidence by practicing various games with him. This also serves to increase the boy's feeling of parental acceptance. In fact, the child's problems in acceptance by his peers may have their genesis in parental nonacceptance.

The teacher also has a role. An alert, sensitive teacher can do much to create a classroom atmosphere of mutual assistance, mutual understanding, tolerance, and acceptance of others. However, as the child advances through the grades, the teacher becomes less able to estimate his acceptance by peers. Either she judges from criteria differing from those employed by peers or has little knowledge or awareness of children's social interactions. In any event, unless the teacher through use of sociometric techniques tries to identify those children who are not accepted by their peers, help for individual children will be impossible.

SUMMARY

The first part of this chapter recapitulated to a large degree material discussed in earlier parts of the book. It was brought together here in order to be able to deal in one place with references throughout the book to the relation of specific antecedents to that continuing and unique pattern of traits called personality. Differences in personality are evident at birth as a result of hereditary and congenital forces, and these early behavioral tendencies are responded to by the social forces impinging on the child.

The notion of personality implies consistency. Evidence points to the moderate consistency of human behavior, with consistency obtained earlier in some traits than in others, but with younger individuals generally showing less of it than older ones. The existence of the self concept is often posited as a major basis for consistency. The self concept is composed, in part, of the body image—ideas about and acceptance of the physical self. With age and a decreased amount of bodily change, a relatively stable body image develops which, in turn, increases stability of behavior. The self concept also includes social roles. Through reward, people tend to play roles more frequently and with greater degrees of accuracy. If possible, contradictory roles are resolved and an emotional commitment to the roles played is developed. As roles are better defined and better played, consistency increases.

Finally, the chapter examined six areas of personality which appear to be major in childhood and for which considerable information is available. These are: dependence-independence, aggression, anxiety, conscience development, dominance-submission, and social acceptance. With regularity the research in these areas have traced the emergence of these personality characteristics to psychological conditions in the home and to the child's relations with his parents.

REFERENCES

Allen, P. J. The leadership pattern. *Amer. sociol. Rev.*, 1952, **17**, 93–96.
Anderson, H. H. Domination and integration in the social behavior of young children in an experimental play situation. *Genet. Psychol. Monogr.*, 1937, **19**, 341–408.
Anderson, H. H. Domination and social integration in the behavior of kindergarten children and teachers. *Genet. Psychol. Monogr.*, 1939, **21**, 287–385.
Anderson, H. H. Socially integrative behavior. *J. abnorm. soc. Psychol.*, 1946, **41**, 379–384.
Anderson, J. E. Parents' attitudes on child behavior: A report of three studies. *Child Develpm.*, 1946, **17**, 91–97.
Anderson, J. E. The prediction of adjustment over time. In I. Iscoe & H. Stevenson, *Personality development in children.* Austin: Univer. Texas Press, 1960. Pp. 28–72.

Aronfreed, J. The nature, variety and social patterning of moral responses to transgression. *J. abnorm. soc. Psychol.,* 1961, **63,** 223–240.

Ausubel, D. P., Schiff, H. M., & Gasser, E. G. A preliminary study of developmental trends in sociopathy: accuracy of perception of own and others' sociometric status. *Child Develpm.,* 1952, **23,** 111–128.

Bach, G. R. Father-fantasies and father-typing in father-separated children. *Child Develpm.,* 1946, **17,** 63–80.

Baldwin, A. L. Socialization and the parent-child relationship. *Child Develpm.,* 1948, **19,** 127–136.

Baldwin, A. L. The effect of home environment on nursery school behavior. *Child Develpm.,* 1949, **20,** 49–61.

Bandura, A., & Huston, Aletha C. Identification as a process of incidental learning. *J. abnorm. soc. Psychol.,* 1961, **63,** 311–318.

Bandura, A., Ross, Dorothea, & Ross, Sheila A. Transmission of aggression through imitation of aggressive models. *J. abnorm. soc. Psychol.,* 1961, **63,** 575–582.

Bandura, A., & Walters, R. H. *Adolescent aggression.* New York: Ronald, 1959.

Barnard, J., Zimbardo, P., & Sarason, S. Anxiety and verbal behavior in children. *Child Develpm.,* 1961, **32,** 379–392.

Bayley, Nancy, & Tuddenham, R. Adolescent changes in body build. In *Adolescence, 43rd Yrbk, Natl. Soc. Stud. Educ., Part I.* Chicago: Univer. Chicago Press, 1944.

Bell, G. B., & Hall, H. E. The relationship between leadership and latency. *J. abnorm. soc. Psychol.,* 1954, **49,** 156–157.

Beller, E. K. Dependence and independence in young children. *J. genet. Psychol.,* 1955, **87,** 25–35.

Berkowitz, L. *Aggression: a social psychological analysis.* New York: McGraw-Hill, 1962.

Beverly, B. I. The effect of illness on emotional development. *J. Pediat.,* 1936, **8,** 533–544.

Bonney, M. E. The relative stability of social, intellectual, and academic status in grades II to IV, and the interrelationships between these various forms of growth. *J. educ. Psychol.,* 1943, **34,** 88–102.

Bonney, M. E. Popular and unpopular children, a sociometric study. *Sociomet. Monogr.,* No. 9. New York: Beacon House, 1947.

Burton, R. V. The generality of honesty reconsidered. Unpubl. mss. National Inst. Mental Health, Bethesda, Md., 1963.

Burton, R., Maccoby, Eleanor E., & Allinsmith, W. Antecedents of resistance to temptation in four-year-old children. *Child Develpm.,* 1961, **32,** 689–710.

Buskirk, C. V. Performance on complex reasoning tasks as a function of anxiety. *J. abnorm. soc. Psychol.,* 1961, **62,** 201–209.

Castenada, A., McCandless, B., & Palermo, D. The children's form of the Manifest Anxiety Scale. *Child Develpm.,* 1956, **27,** 317–326.

Castenada, A., Palermo, D., & McCandless, B. Complex learning and performance as a function of anxiety in children and task difficulty. *Child Develpm.,* 1956, **27,** 327–332.

Cattell, R. B. Personality traits associated with abilities. I. With intelligence and drawing abilities. *Educ. psychol. Measmt.,* 1945, **5,** 131–146.

Cattell, R. B. *Personality and motivation structure and measurement.* Yonkers-on-Hudson: World Book, 1957.

Cattell, R. B., & Coan, R. A. Child personality structure as revealed in teachers' rating. *J. clin. Psychol.*, 1957, 13, 315–327.

Cattell, R. B., & Gruen, W. The personality structure of 11-year-old children in terms of behavior rating data. *J. clin. Psychol.*, 1953, 9, 256–266.

Challman, R. C. Factors influencing friendships among preschool children. *Child Develpm.*, 1932, 3, 146–158.

Chittenden, Gertude E. An experimental study in measuring and modifying assertive behavior in young children. *Monogr. soc. Res. Child Develpm.*, 1942, 7, No. 1.

Cooley, C. H. *Human nature and the social order.* New York: Scribner, 1902.

Crandall, V., Preston, Anne, & Rabson, Alice. Maternal reactions and the development of independence and achievement behavior in young children. *Child Develpm.*, 1960, 31, 243–251.

Davidson, K. Interviews of parents of high anxious and low anxious children. *Child Develpm.*, 1959, 30, 341–351.

Davidson, K., Sarason, S., Lighthall, F., Waite, R., & Sarnoff, I. Differences between mothers' and fathers' ratings of low anxious and high anxious children. *Child Develpm.*, 1958, 29, 155–160.

Davidson, M. A., McInnes, R. G., & Parnell, R. W. The distribution of personality traits in seven-year-old children: a combined psychological, psychiatric and somatotype study. *Brit. J. educ. Psychol.*, 1957, 27, 48–61.

Diamond, S. *Personality and temperament.* New York: Harper, 1957.

Digman, J. M. Principal dimensions of child personality as inferred from teachers' judgments. *Child Develpm.*, 1963, 34, 43–60.

Dittman, A., & Goodrich, D. A comparison of social behavior in normal and hyperaggressive preadolescent boys. *Child Develpm.*, 1961, 32, 315–327.

Dollard, J., Doob, L. W., Miller, N. E., Mowrer, O. H., & Sears, R. R. *Frustration and aggression.* New Haven, Conn.: Yale Univer. Press, 1939.

Dunham, H. W. *Sociological theory and mental disorder.* Detroit: Wayne Univer. Press, 1959.

Elser, R. The social position of hearing handicapped children in the regular grades. *Except. Child.*, 1959, 25, 305–309.

Erikson, E. H. *Childhood and society.* New York: Norton, 1950.

Eron, L. D., Banta, T. J., Walder, L. O., & Laulicht, J. H. Comparison of data obtained from mothers and fathers on childrearing practices and their relation to child aggression. *Child Develpm.*, 1961, 32, 457–472.

Escalona, Sybille K., & Heider, Grace M. *Prediction and outcome.* New York: Basic Books, 1959.

Feinberg, M., Smith, M., & Schmidt, R. An analysis of expressions used by adolescents at varying economic levels to describe accepted and rejected peers. *J. genet. Psychol.*, 1958, 93, 133–148.

Feldhusen, J., & Klausmeier, H. Anxiety, intelligence, and achievement in children of low, average, and high intelligence. *Child Develpm.*, 1962, 33, 403–409.

Festinger, L. *A theory of cognitive dissonance.* Evanston, Ill.: Row-Peterson, 1957.

Fisher, S., & Cleveland, S. E. *Body image and personality.* Princeton, N. J.: Van Nostrand, 1958.

Fite, M. D. Aggressive behavior in young children and children's attitudes toward aggression. *Genet. Psychol. Monogr.*, 1940, 22, 151–319.

Fortune, R. F. *Sorcerers of Dobu.* New York: Dutton, 1932.

Fox, Cynthia, Davidson, K., Lighthall, F., Waite, R., & Sarason, S. Human figure drawings of high and low anxious children. *Child Develpm.,* 1958, **29,** 297–301.

Freud, Anna, & Dann, S. An experiment in group upbringing. *Psychoanal. Stud. Child,* 1951, **6,** 127–168. Reprinted in W. Martin & C. B. Stendler (Eds.), *Readings in child development.* New York: Harcourt, Brace, 1954.

Furfey, P. H. Some factors influencing the selection of boys' chums. *J. appl. Psychol.,* 1927, **11,** 47–51.

Gewirtz, J. L. A factor analysis of some attention-seeking behaviors of young children. *Child Develpm.,* 1956, **27,** 17–36.

Glueck, S., & Glueck, E. *Physique and delinquency.* New York: Harper, 1956.

Gottesman, I. I. The psychogenics of personality. Unpubl. doctoral dissertation. Univer. Minnesota, 1960.

Grinder, R. E. Parental childrearing practices, conscience, and resistance to temptation of sixth-grade children. *Child Develpm.,* 1962, **33,** 803–820.

Grinder, R. E., & McMichael, R. E. Cultural influence on conscience development: Resistance to temptation and guilt among Samoans and American Caucasians. *J. abnorm. soc. Psychol.,* 1963, **66,** 503–507.

Hall, C. S., & Lindzey, G. *Theories of personality.* New York: Wiley, 1957.

Hardy, M. C. Social recognition at the elementary school age. *J. soc. Psychol.,* 1937, **8,** 365–384.

Hartshorne, H., & May, M. A. *Studies in the nature of character: Vol. 1. Studies in deceit.* New York: Macmillan, 1928.

Hartshorne, H., May, M. A., & Shuttleworth, F. K. *Studies in the nature of character: Vol. 3. Studies in the organization of character.* New York: Macmillan, 1930.

Heathers, G. Emotional dependence and independence in a physical threat situation. *Child Develpm.,* 1953, **24,** 169–179.

Heathers, G. Emotional dependence and independence in nursery school play. *J. genet. Psychol.,* 1955, **87,** 37–57. (a)

Heathers, G. Acquiring dependence and independence: a theoretical orientation. *J. genet. Psychol.,* 1955, **87,** 277–291. (b)

Hoffman, Lois W. The father's role in the family and the child's peer-group adjustment. *Merrill-Palmer Quart.,* 1961, **7,** 97–105.

Horowitz, Frances D. The relationship of anxiety, self-concept, and sociometric status among fourth, fifth, and sixth grade children. *J. abnorm. soc. Psychol.,* 1962, **65,** 212–214.

Horrocks, J. E., & Buker, M. E. A study of the friendship fluctuations of preadolescents. *J. genet. Psychol.,* 1951, **78,** 131–144.

Horrocks, J. E., & Thompson, G. G. A study of the friendship fluctuations of rural boys and girls. *J. genet. Psychol.,* 1946, **69,** 189–198.

Iscoe, I., & Cochran, I. Some correlates of manifest anxiety in children. *J. consult. Psychol.,* 1960, **24,** 97.

Jack, Lois. An experimental study of ascendant behavior in preschool children. In Lois Jack, Elizabeth M. Manwell, Ida G. Mengert, et al. Behavior of the preschool child. *Univ. Ia. Stud. Child Welf.,* 1934, **9,** 7–65.

Jones, H. E. The longitudinal method in the study of personality. In I. Iscoe & H. Stevenson (Eds.), *Personality development in children.* Austin: Univ. Texas Press, 1960. Pp. 3–27.

Jones, Mary C., & Bayley, Nancy. Physical maturing among boys as related to behavior. *J. educ. Psychol.,* 1950, **41,** 129–148.

Kagan, J., & Moss, H. A. The stability of passive and dependent behavior from childhood through adulthood. *Child Develpm.*, 1960, **31**, 577–591.

Kagan, J., & Moss, H. A. *Birth to maturity*. New York: Wiley, 1962.

Kitano, H. Validity of the Children's Manifest Anxiety Scale and the Modified Revised California Inventory. *Child Develpm.*, 1960, **31**, 67–72.

Koch, Helen L. Popularity in preschool children: some related factors and a technique for its measurement. *Child Develpm.*, 1933, **4**, 164–175.

L'Abate, L. Personality correlates of manifest anxiety in children. *J. consult. Psychol.*, 1960, **24**, 342–348.

Landy, D. *Tropical childhood*. Chapel Hill: Univer. N. Car. Press, 1959.

Lesser, G. S. The relationships between various forms of aggression and popularity among lower-class children. *J. educ. Psychol.*, 1959, **50**, 20–25.

Levin, H., & Sears, R. R. Identification with parents as a determinant of doll play aggression. *Child Develpm.*, 1956, **27**, 135–153.

Levy, S. Figure drawing as a projective test. In L. E. Abt & L. Bellak (Eds.), *Projective psychology*. New York: Knopf, 1950.

Lippitt, Rosemary. Popularity among preschool children. *Child Develpm.*, 1941, **12**, 305–332.

Lippitt, Rosemary, & Gold, M. Classroom social structure as a mental health problem. *J. soc. Issues*, 1959, **15** (1), 40–49.

Lipsitt, L. A Self-Concept Scale for Children and its relationship to the children's form of the Manifest Anxiety Scale. *Child Develpm.*, 1958, **29**, 463–472.

Lorge, I. Intelligence and personality as revealed in questionnaires and inventories. *39th Yrbk, Natl. Soc. Stud. Educ.*, 1940, Part II. Pp. 275–281.

Lynn, R. Personality characteristics of the mothers of aggressive and non-aggressive children. *J. genet. Psychol.*, 1961, **99**, 159–164.

McCandless, B. R., Bilous, Carolyn B., & Bennett, Hannah Lou. Peer popularity and dependence on adults in preschool-age socialization. *Child Develpm.*, 1961, **32**, 511–518.

McCandless, B., & Castenada, A. Anxiety in children, school achievement, and intelligence. *Child Develpm.*, 1956, **27**, 379–382.

McCandless, B., Castenada, A., & Palermo, D. Anxiety in children and social status. *Child Develpm.*, 1956, **27**, 385–391.

McCord, W., McCord, Joan, & Howard, A. Familial correlates of aggression in nondelinquent male children. *J. abnorm. soc. Psychol.*, 1961, **62**, 79–93.

McCord, W., McCord, Joan, & Verden, P. Familial and behavioral correlates of dependency in male children. *Child Develpm.*, 1962, **33**, 313–326.

McCurdy, H. G. The childhood pattern of genius. *J. Elisha Mitchell Sci. Society*, 1957, **73**, 448–462. Also in R. A. King (Ed.), *Readings for an introduction to psychology*. New York: McGraw-Hill, 1961. Pp. 269–278.

McKee, J. P., & Leader, Florence B. The relationship of socio-economic status and aggression to the competitive behavior of preschool children. *Child Develpm.*, 1955, **26**, 135–142.

MacKinnon, D. Violations of prohibitions. In H. A. Murray et al., *Explorations in personality*. New York: Oxford Univer. Press, 1938.

Malinowski, B. *Argonauts of the western Pacific*. New York: Dutton, 1922.

Maris, M. Personal adjustment, assumed similarity to parents, and inferred parental evaluations of the self. *J. consult. Psychol.*, 1958, **22**, 481–485.

Marshall, Helen R., & McCandless, B. R. Relationships between dependence on adults and social acceptance by peers. *Child Develpm.*, 1957, **28**, 413–419.

May, R. *The meaning of anxiety.* New York: Ronald, 1950.

Mead, Margaret. *Sex and temperament in three primitive societies.* New York: Morrow, 1935.

Medinnus, G. R. An examination of several correlates of sociometric status in a first grade group. *J. genet. Psychol.,* 1962, **101,** 3–13.

Meyer, Charlene T. The assertive behavior of children as related to parent behavior. *J. Home Econ.,* 1947, **7,** 77–80.

Miller, D. R., & Swanson, G. E. *Inner conflict and defense.* New York: Holt, 1960.

Mummery, Dorothy V. An analytical study of ascendant behavior of preschool children. *Child Develpm.,* 1947, **18,** 40–81.

Mummery, Dorothy V. Family backgrounds of assertive and nonassertive children. *Child Develpm.,* 1954, **25,** 63–80.

Murphy, G., Murphy, Lois B., & Newcomb, T. M. *Experimental social psychology.* (Rev. ed.) New York: Harper, 1937.

Murphy, Lois B. *Social behavior and child personality.* New York: Columbia Univer. Press, 1937.

Mussen, P., & Distler, L. Child-rearing antecedents of masculine identification in kindergarten boys. *Child Develpm.,* 1960, **31,** 89–100.

Mussen, P., & Newman, D. Handicap: motivation, and adjustment in physically disabled children. *Except. Child.,* 1958, **24,** 255–260, 277–279.

Neilon, Patricia. Shirley's babies after fifteen years: A personality study. *J. genet. Psychol.,* 1948, **73,** 175–186.

Northway, M. L. Sociometry and some challenging problems of social relationships. *Sociometry,* 1946, **9,** 187–198.

Otis, Nancy B., & McCandless, B. R. Responses to repeated frustrations of young children differentiated according to need area. *J. abnorm. soc. Psychol.,* 1955, **50,** 349–353.

Page, Marjorie. The modification of ascendant behavior in preschool children. *Univ. Ia. Stud. Child Welf.,* 1936, **12,** No. 3, p. 69.

Parten, Mildred B. Leadership among preschool children. *J. abnorm. soc. Psychol.,* 1932, **27,** 430–440.

Partridge, E. D. Leadership among adolescent boys. *Teach. Coll. Contr. Educ.,* 1934, No. 608.

Peck, R. F. Family patterns correlated with adolescent personality structure. *J. abnorm. soc. Psychol.,* 1958, **57,** 347–350.

Phillips, B., Hindsman, E., & Jennings, E. Influence of intelligence on anxiety and perception of self and others. *Child Develpm.,* 1960, **31,** 41–46.

Piaget, J. *The construction of reality in the young child.* New York: Basic Books, 1954.

Radke, Marion J. The relation of parental authority to children's behavior and attitudes. *Univ. Minn. Child Welf. Monogr.,* 1946, No. 22.

Raimy, V. C. Self reference in counseling interviews. *J. consult. Psychol.,* 1948, **12,** 153–163.

Roff, M. Preservice personality problems and subsequent adjustments to military service: The prediction of psychoneurotic reactions. *USAF Sch. Aviat. Med. Rep.,* 1957, No. 57–136.

Roff, M. Relations between certain preservice factors and psychoneurosis during military duty. *Armed Forces med. J.,* 1960, **11,** 152–160.

Roff, M. Childhood social interactions and young adult bad conduct. *J. abnorm. soc. Psychol.,* 1961, **63,** 333–337.

Rogers, C. R. *Client-centered therapy.* Boston: Houghton Mifflin, 1951.

Sanford, R. N., Adkins, M. M., Miller, R. B., Cobb, E. A., et al. Physique, personality and scholarship: a cooperative study of school children. *Soc. Res. Child Develpm. Monogr.,* 1943, **8**, No. 1.

Sarason, I. The effects of anxiety and threat on the solution of a difficult task. *J. abnorm. soc. Psychol.,* 1961, **62**, 165–168.

Sarason, I. Test anxiety and intellectual performance. *J. abnorm. soc. Psychol.,* 1963, **66**, 73–75.

Sarason, S., Davidson, K., Lighthall, F., & Waite, R. A Test Anxiety Scale for Children. *Child Develpm.,* 1958, **29**, 105–113. (a)

Sarason, S., Davidson, K., Lighthall, F., & Waite, R. Classroom observations of high and low anxious children. *Child Develpm.,* 1958, **29**, 287–295. (b)

Schilder, P. *The image and appearance of the human body.* London: Kegan, Paul, 1935.

Sears, Pauline S. Doll play aggression in normal young children: influence of sex, age, sibling status, father's absence. *Psychol. Monogr.,* 1951, **65**, No. 6.

Sears, R. R. The growth of conscience. In I. Iscoe & H. W. Stevenson (Eds.), *Personality development in children.* Austin: Univer. Texas Press, 1960. Pp. 92–111.

Sears, R. R. Relation of early socialization experiences to aggression in middle childhood. *J. abnorm. soc. Psychol.,* 1961, **63**, 466–492.

Sears, R. R., Maccoby, Eleanor E., & Levin, H. *Patterns of child rearing.* Evanston, Ill.: Row, Peterson, 1957.

Sears, R. R., Whiting, J. W. M., Nowlis, V., & Sears, Pauline S. Some child-rearing antecedents of aggression and dependency in young children. *Genet. Psychol. Monogr.,* 1953, **47**, 135–234.

Sheldon, W. H., Stevens, S. S., & Tucker, W. B. *The varieties of human physique.* New York: Harper, 1940.

Shirley, Mary M. *The first two years: A study of twenty-five babies. Vol. 3. Personality manifestations.* Minneapolis: Univer. Minn. Press, 1933.

Shlien, J. A client-centered approach to schizophrenia: first approximation. In A. Burton (Ed.), *Psychotherapy of the psychoses.* New York: Basic Books, 1961.

Shlien, J. The self concept in relation to behavior: Theoretical and empirical research. *Relig. Educ.,* 1962, **17**, Research Supplement. Pp. S111–S127.

Siegel, Alberta A., & Kohn, Lynette G. Permissiveness, permission, and aggression: the effect of adult presence or absence on aggression in children's play. *Child Develpm.,* 1959, **30**, 131–141.

Smock, C. Perceptual rigidity and closure phenomenon as a function of manifest anxiety in children. *Child Develpm.,* 1958, **29**, 237–247.

Sontag, L. W., Baker, C. T., & Nelson, V. L. Mental growth and personality development: a longitudinal study. *Monogr. soc. Res. Child Develpm.,* 1958, **23**, No. 68.

Spector, S. I. Climate and social acceptability. *J. educ. Sociol.,* 1953, **27**, 108–114.

Stendler, Celia B. Critical periods in socialization and over-dependency. *Child Develpm.,* 1952, **23**, 3–12.

Stendler, Celia B. Possible causes of over-dependency in young children. *Child Develpm.,* 1954, **25**, 125–146.

Steth, Marjorie, & Connor, Ruth. Dependency and helpfulness in young children. *Child Develpm.,* 1962, **33**, 15–20.

Stewart, Ann. Excessive crying in infants—a family disease. In M. Senn (Ed.), *Sixth conference on problems of infancy and childhood.* New York: Josiah Macy, Jr., Foundation, 1953. Pp. 138–160.

Stogdill, R. M. Personal factors associated with leadership: A survey of the literature. *J. Psychol.,* 1948, **25,** 35–71.

Stott, L. H. Stability in ascendance-submission. *Merrill-Palmer Quart.,* 1957, **3,** 145–159.

Strauss, A. (Ed.). *The social psychology of George Herbert Mead.* Chicago: Univer. Chicago Press, 1956.

Swensen, C. H., Jr. Empirical evaluations of human figure drawings. *Psychol. Bull.,* 1957, **54,** 431–466.

Taylor, Janet A. A personality scale of manifest anxiety. *J. abnorm. soc. Psychol.,* 1953, **48,** 285–290.

Terman, L. M., & Oden, Melita H. *The gifted child grows up.* Stanford, Calif.: Stanford Univer. Press, 1947.

Thompson, G. G., & Horrocks, J. E. A study of the friendship fluctuations of urban boys and girls. *J. genet. Psychol.,* 1947, **70,** 53–63.

Tisza, Veronica B., Selverstone, Betty, Rosenblum, Gershen, & Hanlon, Nancy. Psychiatric observations of children with cleft palate. *Amer. J. Orthopsychiat.,* 1958, **28,** 416–423.

Tryon, Caroline M. Evaluation of adolescent personality by adolescents. *Monogr. soc. Res. Child Develpm.,* 1939, **4,** No. 4, p. 88.

Tuddenham, R. D. Studies in reputation. III. Correlates of popularity among elementary school children. *J. educ. Psychol.,* 1951, **42,** 257–276.

Tuddenham, R. D. The constancy of personality ratings over two decades. *Genet. Psychol. Monogr.,* 1958, **60,** 3–29.

Walker, R. N. Body build and behavior in young children: I. Body build and nursery school teachers' ratings. *Soc. Res. Child Develpm. Monogr.,* 1962, **27,** No. 3.

Weatherly, D. Maternal permissiveness toward aggression and subsequent fantasy aggression. *J. abnorm. soc. Psychol.,* 1962, **65,** 1–5.

Wenger, M. A. Preliminary study of the significance of measures of autonomic balance. *Psychosom. Med.,* 1947, **9,** 301–309.

Whiting, J. W. M., & Child, I. *Child training and personality.* New Haven, Conn.: Yale Univer. Press, 1953.

Winder, C. L., & Rau, Lucy. Parental attitudes associated with social deviance in preadolescent boys. *J. abnorm. soc. Psychol.,* 1962, **64,** 418–424.

Woods, Sister Frances Jerome, & Carrow, Sister Mary Arthur. The choice-rejection status of speech-defective children. *Except. Child.,* 1959, **25,** 279–283.

Wylie, Ruth C. Some relationships between defensiveness and self-concept discrepancies. *J. Pers.,* 1957, **25,** 600–616.

Wylie, Ruth C. *The self concept: A critical survey of pertinent literature.* Lincoln: Univer. Nebr. Press, 1961.

chapter 16 ✳ Disturbances in Development

Like true love, the course of development never runs smooth. As development progresses psychological problems often emerge. Disturbances set in motion problem behavior. How such behavior is caused, how it is diagnosed, how it is treated, and the probability of its cure constitute the substance of this chapter. These subjects will be considered under four general headings: causes, diagnosis, treatment techniques, and prognosis.

CAUSES OF BEHAVIORAL PROBLEMS

Only rarely does one find a disturbed individual with one specific form of maladjustment and no other symptoms. Oftener a patient will have a dominant set of problems accompanied by other less well developed signs of disturbance. So, too, with causation. Seldom can one say about any one problem of any one patient that this and only this aspect of his background produced the disturbance. Far more frequently a variety of factors contribute to the production of a given kind of problem.

A fine illustration of the diversity of factors that may be seen in the background of an individual appears in the autobiography of Carryl Chessman (1955), a robber who was convicted and executed for kidnapping. Chessman attributed his long record of crime to having been reared in a Los Angeles slum and to overcompensation for being a small, picked-on child. Although he placed no emphasis on the fact, Chessman did have a severe attack of encephalitis as a child, a disease which frequently produces undesirable behavioral changes in its victims. Thus, all those who believe in sociological forces, feelings of inferiority, or organic factors as the prime cause of problem behavior are satisfied by Chessman's explanation of his deviant behavior. In addition, certain aspects of his family relationship support a Freudian interpretation of his conduct.

Although numerous forces combine to produce many behavioral problems, the effect of any one force differs from behavior to behavior. Hence the statement that "Problem A has much more of an innate physiological component, and is less influenced by the social milieu of the patient, than Problem B." The relative import of the several forces believed to cause specific problem disorders can be, but seldom has been, determined.

Genetic Factors

Many problem behaviors relate to *affective,* or emotional, maladjustment. The individual may "feel too much" and be devastated by events that bring no concern to others. Or he may "feel too little" and not have much attachment for others, in which case he is not greatly affected by social approval or disapproval and shows incompetence at learning social roles. The disturbed, fearful, neurotic youngster and the psychopathic delinquent have one thing in common: neither is influenced by the attitudes of others toward them nor by inner guilt in the same manner as better adjusted children. As seen earlier, emotionality and emotional stability have a fairly substantial genetic base. In this broad sense, genetic forces may underlie many varieties of problem behavior.

More specifically, the role of heredity is evident in many cases of schizophrenia. If one of a pair of siblings becomes schizophrenic, the chances are roughly one in seven that the other will become so. For fraternal twins the probability is the same. For stepbrothers and sisters growing up in the same home, the probability is approximately one in 50. Among identical twins, it is seven in eight. Although these findings by Kallman (summarized in Garrison, 1947) have been subjected to criticism (e.g., Pastore, 1949), the critique has not seemed to have sufficient validity to damage their value seriously.

Many studies, including Gottesman's (1960) conclusion that individual differences in tendencies to approach or withdraw have a large genetic component, imply that heredity plays a significant role both in psychotic disturbances and in behavior problems falling closer to cultural norms.

Congenital Factors

It is difficult to separate the effects of hereditary from congenital factors since symptoms become apparent at birth or some time after it. For instance, a controversy raged over the question of whether *mongolism,* a type of mental defect, resulted from defective germ plasm or from conditions in the uterus.

The most thorough study thus far of the connection between congenital factors and problem behavior was undertaken by a group headed by Pasamanick. The group's subjects were 363 white and 108 Negro children who had been referred to a division of special services in the Baltimore Department of Education because of behavioral disturbances (Pasamanick, Rogers, & Lilienfeld, 1956). Their disorders were described as hyperactivity, confusion, and disorganization. During their pregnancies, the mothers of these children had had a higher proportion of complications than mothers of a corresponding group of white and Negro control children. The pregnancy complications most closely associated with behavioral disorders were maternal *toxemia,* a pathological condition resulting from poison in the blood, and maternal hypertension. It seemed likely that these complications produced *anoxia,* a shortage of oxygen supply for the tissues, and that this, in turn, gave rise to brain injury. As Kawi & Pasamanick (1959) noted, there was within the uterus a continual maldevelopment "with a lethal component consisting of abortions, still births, and neonatal deaths, and a sublethal component consisting of cerebral palsy, epilepsy, mental deficiency, and behavior disorders in children."

Postnatal Physical Factors

After presenting his parents with 12 years of no untoward problems, a young boy developed a number of symptoms. He refused to go to school, saying it gave him a headache. He demanded to be allowed to sleep with his parents because he had dizzy spells in bed. In addition, there were a number of other hypochondriac complaints. His parents took him to a private clinic where a clinical psychologist and psychiatrist concurred that the youngster would benefit from therapy. Treatment had commenced when the parents decided to play it safe and consult a physician specializing in diagnosis. After learning of the symptoms, the internist measured the electrical potentials of the boy's brain by electroencephalograph and concluded that the youth had a brain tumor. Surgery confirmed the internist's diagnosis; a benign tumor was found and removed. The case illustrates the importance of being fully aware of the patient's physical condition before diagnosis.

Brain injury suffered in the uterus, at birth, or after birth appears to produce deviant behavior as well as mental deficiency, as Kawi and Pasamanick observed. Since brain injury results not only from tumors but also from diseases, such as encephalitis and meningitis, and from physical damage, it is a factor of relevance in the study of behavioral problems. On the other hand, it is the favored cause in diagnoses made by parents. *All* children have bad falls and high fevers; hence, parents with a problem child can always assuage their guilt by blaming a fall or a fever, rather than their own behavior. Although brain injury may be a valid cause and must be considered a possibility during diagnosis, unsubstantiated parental statements of injury or pressures to attribute the problem to it call for a wary attitude in the diagnostician.

The influence of biological factors in postnatal life is reinforced by Hebb's (1949, p. 262) citation of evidence which shows neurotic or psychotic behavior to have been associated, at least on occasion, with various physical diseases. Inherited, congenital, or postnatal, physical conditions are obviously related to behavior disorders. For this reason it is not redundant to point up again the necessity of determining the physical state of the youngster who is referred to a social agency or clinic as a "problem child."

Family Factors

Ever since Freud's day, it has been believed that the basis of pathology lies in the family setting. Contemporary theory attributes pathology in the child to the behavior of the parents, especially that of the mother. It is rather surprising to find parental guilt and responsibility increasingly emphasized at the same time that the person with the problem, whether child or adult, is absolved of responsibility. Although, in many cases, parental deviations contribute to problem behavior in their children, these parental behaviors should be judged on the same basis as the child's problems—as being caused.

Further defense of the parents lies in the fact that the cause-and-effect relationship between parental behavior and child problems is often unclear. For example, "three-month colic," a term used by parents to describe a disorder in which the infant howls, in apparent agony, for roughly 20 out of every 24 hours in its first three months of life and then suddenly ceases without reason, illustrates the difficulties of attributing cause and effect to parental influences on child behavior problems. Lakin (1957) found that mothers of colicky infants, in contrast to mothers of noncolicky infants, were less accepting of the female role, felt less adequate, were less happy with their husbands and with their parents, and were less motherly in their attitudes. He concluded that these attributes of mothers produced the colic in their infants. However, could it not be that having an infant cry for 20 out of 24 hours for a few months might have produced the differences in attitude?

Similarly, several studies (e.g., Heilbrun, 1960; Kohn & Clausen, 1956) have shown mothers of schizophrenics to be both harsher and more overprotective than mothers of normal children. Aside from the obviously important fact that these judgments usually occur *after* the schizophrenic onset, there is still the matter of cause and effect. Fish (1959) produced evidence to corroborate Bender's (1947) contention that certain characteristic deviations of behavior were observable at or shortly after birth in a child who would later become schizophrenic. Other evidence indicates that a child who will later succumb to schizophrenia suffers no more traumatic experience than normal siblings, but will more probably react pathologically to any change in the environment and *invite a special response* from parents which further impairs an innately weak capacity to resist stress (Prout & White, 1956). Although it is unpopular to attribute pathological behavior to hereditary factors, genetic sources cannot be easily dismissed.

In some behavioral problems, however, parental pathology seems clearly to be the primary cause, as illustrated in this case reported by Bender (1952, pp. 214–216).

> Morris was a 10 year old boy. When he came to us he was a pathetic child. He had a neurological condition especially in his legs which made them feeble and produced chorea-like movements. Before admission it was said that at times the movements were so severe that he had to be carried about, and on occasion they became so intense that they were thought to be epileptic fits. This diagnosis seemed reasonable especially since his mother had epilepsy and was being cared for in an institution for epileptic patients. Morris had been living in an orphan home which was thought to be inadequate to care for a boy with such difficult problems. Morris had had some very unhappy experiences. Even before his

mother had been separated from him, she would often become psychotic and at such times she would chase Morris with a knife and threaten to cut off his feet, saying his feet were not any good and were making him have fits like hers. He told us that on one occasion he hid under the bed just in time to avoid losing his feet.

When he came to the hospital his legs were weak, clumsy, and awkward. There was definite evidence of a slight choreiform disability and poor muscular development, especially in the left leg. There was however never any indication of epilepsy. Morris was very self-conscious of his disability and tried to conceal it by clowning. He tried to play the role of Charlie Chaplin. But among the children he felt very inferior and could not compete in their active play and fights.

When asked to draw pictures of a man, he drew a one-legged man and called it Joe Palooka. When he was given the miniature toys which we used for psychotherapeutic work, he always had his soldiers riding to battle in trucks, because he said they did not want to walk. During the weeks that he spent with us he was given active orthopedic treatment and physiotherapy for his legs, psychotherapy by play technique, as well as group work in the art class. We could follow the progress of his improvement in his art work. Soon his men had two legs instead of one, although at first they were still always riding in carts. Later, they were walking on the ground, and soon they were climbing ladders. Finally when Morris was ready for discharge we got the picture where a man is walking a tight rope between two buildings. When Morris left he was not secure on his feet and in his ability to compete with other boys in active play. He was placed in a boarding home and arrangements were made for further orthopedic care and psychotherapy which utilized his ability to express himself in art. He joined a boys' club where he participated in an art class and a class in jujitsu. His physical condition, posture and gait improved steadily. At 15 he returned to the home of his father's family, together with his father, while his mother was still in the institution. With his growing motor coordination and interest in sports he developed good social success despite his limited intellectual endowment. (See Figure 16-1.)

As Ackerman (1958) pointed out, the parent often produces a kind of pathology in the child that fills certain parental needs. A clear illustration of this "secondary" gain by the parent is seen in cases in which the parent has a dislike for authority figures, yet cannot bring this dislike out into the open. By providing subtle reinforcement, the parent produces a rebellious child. It does not take much talent or imagination on the part of the youngster to recognize a green light when a parent laughs and says, "Oh, you shouldn't have hit the high school principal in the nose." Verbal protest notwithstanding, the parent finds hitting an authority figure to be a rather pleasant prospect.

In other instances, parents produce deviation by providing the child with a deviant behavior model. Roebuck and Johnson (1964) show

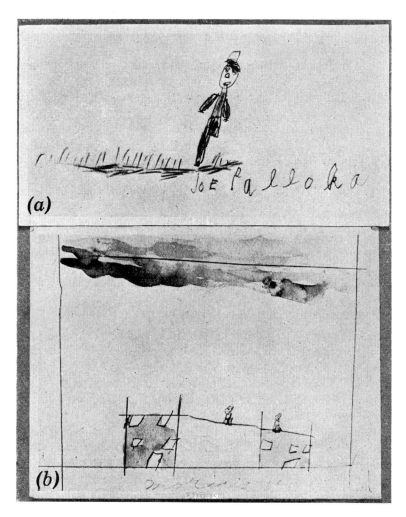

FIGURE 16-1 (a) Joe Palooka, by Morris (crayon). (b) Tight-rope walker, by Morris (pencil and water color). (Bender, 1952, p. 215.)

that individuals who as youths and adults have operated as "con men" have learned from parents a life style centered on deceit. As one con man related:

> I learned from my mother that "front" and how you carry yourself is the main thing with the marks (suckers). She'd buy $10 worth of groceries and while I held them walk up to the man and give him a rubber check for $50. She talked fast, smooth, and bold. You know, like

she had a million. Of course she always dressed the part. She had such a way about her that the clerks in stores where she stole dresses were afraid to question her though they had a good idea she had their "rags" under her coat. She always said, "son if you get in the life (life in the underworld) get a soft hustle. No rough stuff."

This is clearly an example of imitation and direct social learning, not so much of one type of criminality but a way of life predicated on cheating. Another life style learned in much the same manner is that of hypochondria. Observing a parent using a certain style of response to life, the child sees that the behavior pays and adopts it as his own.

One further aspect of the family situation: this is the role of the parent as diagnostician. The only common element in all behavioral problems is that they are so diagnosed by someone. Every clinician sees many children whose behavior is representative of children in general, yet who are viewed as relatively severe problems by parents or, less often, by teachers. Other children seen as "holy terrors" by the world at large are angels to their parents. In this respect, an item on the "Lie" scale of a well-known personality test rests on the fact that nearly all adults confess to having indulged in petty theft at some time during childhood; thus, in a statistical sense this behavior is normal. The same thing may be said for the findings of the Kinsey reports (1948, 1953) in which most children admitted to indulging in many varieties of sexual behavior at some time in development prior to reaching maturity. Yet if these behaviors are detected by parents and made to symbolize an evil nature, the child may well accept the parental diagnosis of being evil or delinquent and live up to the role thus assigned him.

A final illustration of a problem created primarily by diagnosis is found in feeding. Clinical psychologists are familiar with the maternal complaint: "He hasn't eaten anything for two days and he never does more than pick at his food. I'm afraid he'll become ill if he doesn't eat more." The starving child who usually accompanies her to the consultation nearly always turns out to be highly active, healthy, and obviously well nourished. The mother's diagnosis, though clearly having no foundation in reality, is certainly of great concern to her.

The high frequency of feeding problems (25 per cent of all children are diagnosed as feeding problems by someone, usually parents, according to Kanner [1957]) is associated with aspects of the culture as well as of the mother-child relationship. Most of the world goes to bed hungry whereas Americans, as a nation, have more than enough. Because of this affluence, food is urged on children and its consumption is heavily emphasized. Advertising and other social forces make a fetish of nutrition in what is perhaps the best-fed society of all. This becomes an area of parental concern when many children shift from having a remarkable appetite (in the parent's view) for the first few years of life to a much reduced food intake at three and after as growth rate slows down and a high peak of metabolic efficiency is attained. The parent is concerned; the child feels it. The parent assigns the role of feeding problem to the child and the child accepts it. Since feeding problems occur only in food-rich societies, it seems likely that they do not originate with the child but with parental responses to the child's eating habits.

The problem in all these examples is more in diagnosis than in child behavior. Yet once the diagnosis has been made, the child is treated as a pariah, often acquiesces in the "problem child" role, and becomes a genuine problem. The child judged doomed to perdition begins to think that he might as well live up to the reputation. The child diagnosed a stutterer stutters; the child considered a dullard may become a nonachiever (see Lecky, 1945), and the one deemed a feeding problem may verily become one (see Kanner, 1957, pp. 470–477). Adults should, therefore, exercise extreme caution in diagnosis.

Sociological Factors

Sociologists have argued that most delinquents are psychologically "normal" but that they come from slum areas in which certain operative forces dispose the individual to become involved in illegal behaviors. Among children from depressed and criminal slum environments, it hardly seems necessary to seek strictly psychological forces to account for delinquency.

The subcultural delinquent is perhaps the commonest sociological problem. However, there are also others. Research in progress (Johnson, 1964) suggests that, far oftener than one would expect by chance, the neurotic or the severely withdrawn type of child is reared within the confines of a highly emotional fundamentalist group. Mowrer (1960) has held that the emotionally disturbed individual is guilty of misdeeds and that therapists err in absolving him of guilt. True as this may be, the Johnson research indicates that the anxious, neurotic, withdrawn child is much harsher in self-judgment than the normal child.

Extreme concern over personal sin and depravity lead to behavioral sequels such as compulsive acts, extremely scrupulous demeanor, and withdrawal. Though in many ways this kind of problem child occupies the opposite behavioral extreme from the majority of slum-reared delinquents, the bases of their problems are similar. In both cases, the deviation is not so much the result of the child's own physical or psychic make-up, or of parental behavior and attitudes, as it is a product of the larger social milieu.

Thus, the causes for any type of behavior problem are multiple, often interacting with one another. Yet careful study of prior conditions leading to problem behavior will, for many types of problems, yield discrete categories, as we shall presently observe, each with its own major cause and each with its own treatment.

DIAGNOSIS

The term *diagnosis* comes from the Greek and means to "know one from another." As the term itself indicates, the task of the diagnostician is to observe the symptomatic behavior closely and to establish the particular type of disorder most probably associated with the evident symptoms. Psychotherapists have not succeeded well in fulfilling this task. Sometimes they believe the challenge to be insurmountable. Yet medical doctors have faced and largely mastered the same problem.

Differential Diagnosis in Medicine

There are a number of varieties of fever, just as there are a number of varieties of mental deficiency and, probably, of schizophrenia. Fever, mental retardation, and schizophrenia have one thing in common: each has a single dominant symptom—high temperature, inability to learn adequately, and dissociation, respectively. Beneath the surface similarity of high temperature, the physicians observing closely, discerned secondary symptoms which allowed them to differentiate types of fever within the broad phenotype of fever. Malaria began with chills accompanied by blueness of the skin and cyclical vomiting, then showed high fever followed by normal or subnormal temperature until the next paroxysm. Typhoid showed some similarity to malaria in early symptoms, since chills are common to them. Unlike malaria, however, typhoid also produces early symptoms of tiredness and loss of appetite; as the disease advances, there are pains in the limbs and severe headaches. The cyclical quality of malaria is missing. Later, in typhoid, lethargy increases, pulse rate rises slightly, and temperature climbs higher. There is nervousness and delirium, and a rash on the chest and abdomen. Recovery is gradual.

A third fever, yellow fever, resembles typhoid in many respects, since early symptoms of both include severe headaches. However, victims of yellow fever feel pain in the back and neck rather than in the limbs, and the pulse rate drops rather than rises. In its early stages, yellow fever also resembles malaria; vomiting is a symptom of each. But jaundice accompanies yellow fever compared with the blueness of malaria.

By observing *all* the symptoms, one can detect a specific configuration that accompanies each disorder and allows for a clear differential diagnosis—a "telling one from the other." This diagnosis *could not* be arrived at through observation of only the dominant symptom, fever, nor through observing most of the individual secondary symptoms. One can differentiate these fevers from one another and note the effectiveness of specific treatment techniques on each. Since no treatment suffices for all of them, any treatment is necessarily a failure in most cases until the subspecies of fever are distinguished so that one of them susceptible to a particular type of treatment can be singled out from the rest. Causes can now be discovered and steps taken for prevention as well as cure. The same point applies, as we shall see, to psychological problems.

Differential Diagnosis in Disturbance

The problems of psychotherapy can be solved only through use of the technique that has proven so successful for physical medicine. The big catch-all categorizations, such as mental retardation, schizophrenia, character disorder, and delinquency, are as useless as the notion of treating *all* fevers with a single technique. At the outset of this book the search for subtle phenotypical differences among individuals superficially similar in being defective was seen to lead to isolation of one variety of deficiency from all other varieties. Discovery of the cause, the genotype, and of the potential cure followed the phenotypical differentiation. Let us apply this procedure to behavioral problems.

Two groups of theories exist about the major causes of juvenile delinquency. Sociological theories stress the notion that a delinquent is usually a normal, well-integrated member of a subculture which accepts values judged to be delinquent by the majority culture. Psychological theories consider personal maladjustment as the basis for the delinquency. There has been little or no effort to fragmentize the broad category, delinquent, into various subtypes in order to determine the relative seriousness of each—how many remain delinquent and later become criminals, to what degree deviant behaviors are dangerous to others—or to learn whether specific varieties of delinquency respond better to one kind of treatment than another.

Johnson (1950) noted a phenotypical difference of some apparent significance among delinquents: solitary delinquents seemed to differ considerably from those who acted in concert with others. Further research (Randolph, Richardson, & Johnson, 1961) found that the simple division of delinquents into those who committed their delinquencies alone and those who did not was sufficient to uncover two distinct groups on the basis of background, however gross and simple this phenotypical classification might be. Solitary performers usually come from an ostensibly normal, middle-class environment. They are of average ability and disclose a very high degree of pathology in their responses to personality tests; they are *psychological* delinquents. Social delinquents generally come from lower-class homes in high-delinquency areas. They are usually dull to normal in ability and show few pathological signs on a standardized personality inventory; these are *sociological* delinquents.

The division is certainly a crude categorization, but far better than none at all. Solitary delinquents evince a much higher degree of *recidivism*—that is, a stronger tendency to be delinquent or criminal again in the future—indicating that the solitary delinquent is a more serious problem. The psychological nature of the solitary delinquent's problems points to the advisability of psychotherapy as a technique for treatment. Since the social delinquent's problems appear to be largely the product of a deviant environment, direct manipulation of the setting, such as some form of placement outside the home, might serve more effectively as an ameliorating approach.

Another area in need of more adequate differential diagnosis is the separation of schizophrenia from mental deficiency in children and also, within the schizophrenic-type disturbances in childhood, the separation of various subtypes. Each of these types would be expected to have a distinctly different basis, a differing rate of spontaneous recovery without specific treatment, a differing accessibility to treatment, and would perhaps require a unique form of treatment. Without subdividing schizophrenia but separating it from mental deficiency, Schachter, Meyer, and Loomis (1962) characterized the schizophrenic child as follows:

1. Prolonged withdrawal reaction (physical, social and/or emotional).
2. Consistently and characteristically bizarre motility patterns.
3. Prolonged, seriously disturbed sleep patterns.
4. Extraordinary resistance to change.

5. Speech (where present) characterized by pronominal reversal, immediate or delayed cholalia, failure to be used for conventional communication, and bizarre associations.
6. Cataclysmic panic reactions.
7. Low spontaneity, affective flatness and/or inappropriateness.
8. Persistent marked negativism.
9. Absence of demonstrable organic brain damage.

They characterized the mentally defective child, on the other hand, in this manner:

1. Reasonably symmetrical general retardation in emotional and intellectual development to patterns more typical of younger children.
2. Speech development slow and appropriate to younger age period.
3. Absence of marked social withdrawal, negativism, bizarreness, or other evidence of psychosis.
4. Absence of demonstrable organic brain damage.

In a free-play situation, the mentally retarded children resembled a control group in their responses to people and the schizophrenics in their responses to objects. In contrast, the schizophrenics showed a grave impairment in responses to things and people. As might be expected, the schizophrenic children displayed more variability in performance on intelligence tests.

Differential diagnosis of mentally defective and of schizophrenic children is clearly possible. Although the two generally resemble one another in inability to benefit much from training and in being somewhat unresponsive, they differ in many ways. First, unlike most severely retarded children, schizophrenics have no apparent abnormalities of physical development. Second, they display a great deal of variability in level of ability; a ten-year-old may function like a ten-year-old in some test situations and like a two-year-old in others. Third, they exhibit movements typical of schizophrenics—whirling, walking in circles, and others perseverative motor habits. They are less interested in people than are more genuinely defective children. Yet there is a fair amount of misdiagnosis, with children who are schizophrenic, or, perhaps, schizophrenic *and* retarded, placed in mentally retarded programs, even though a number of easily observable symptoms might be used correctly to differentiate the two groups.

Thus, despite the possibilities for relatively accurate differential diagnosis, it is not always made. Clearly schizophrenic or schizoid children do not benefit as a rule from placement in mentally retarded educational programs and those programs suffer from their presence. Only through precise differentiation of two superficially similar problem groups can the genotype of each be ascertained and the most suitable treatment method be applied.

TREATMENT

Differential treatment must be preceded by differential diagnosis. Diagnoses, of course, are made by many people and those of parents and teachers are markedly different from those of clinicians with respect to the seriousness of behavioral problems. Even when parents or teachers recognize a bona fide problem, the evidence suggests that neither knows where to obtain help (e.g., Stendler, 1949). This section, therefore, describes various types of therapists and then considers various forms of therapy.

Quacks: How to Avoid Them

Charlatans, frauds, quacks, and crackpots abound in the field of diagnosing psychological disturbance and providing treatment for it. The ground is fertile for even bad seeds. First of all, legitimate therapists fall into several professional categories, leading often to abrasive relations which may erupt as open conflicts. The clinical psychologist seeks recognition for his speciality and sometimes believes himself better qualified to handle psychological problems than the psychiatrist, the psychoanalyst, and a more recent addition, the psychiatric social worker. Each professional in turn, considers himself uniquely prepared for the practice of certain therapeutic techniques. The division of the treatment field accompanied by the fact that practioners in one area are not often competent to judge the qualifications of those in other fields—or perhaps think of all members of rival areas as incompetents—makes it easy for the quack to obtain a foothold.

A second reason for the prevalence of quacks is that many forms of therapy are in use and the relative efficacy of any one kind is hard to evaluate. With any luck at all, a quack who sets himself up as a therapist will find that at least half of his patients will improve since there is evidence that, on the average, at least 50 per cent of neurotic individuals with no organic antecedent get well even without treatment (see Eysenck, 1961, pp. 697–725, especially 704–705). That people often get well by themselves, have a *spontaneous remission,* works to the advantage of all therapists, including quacks.

Quacks fall into two main categories: commercial types in the business of therapy for money alone and single-minded crackpots who believe they have *the* answer to all of the world's ills but are being persecuted by better educated but jealous contemporaries. Both generally have college degrees of a sort, often from unaccredited institutions. Brophy and Durfee (1960) listed the various mail-order degrees purporting to qualify one for the practice of psychotherapy. In one of these diploma mills, they noted, four doctoral degrees—PsD, MsD, DD, and PhD—could be acquired in 20 months for $250. At this price, any quack could afford a doctor's degree. Some were not even graduates of elementary school.

The *American Psychologist,* the "trade" journal of psychology, has published various studies (David, 1954; David & Springfield, 1958) dealing with individuals who advertised themselves to be psychologists. Forty-four per cent of all individuals listed as psychologists in 1957 phone directories were not members of the American Psychological Association. Not all legitimate psychologists belong to the APA. Yet the high proportion of non-APA members, plus the fact that not all APA members are qualified to engage in therapy, suggests that perhaps one-third of all those calling themselves psychologists and offering treatment lack professional competence. Moreover, since it is possible in many states for any medical doctor to call himself a psychiatrist or psychoanalyst without having passed through the requisite training, it seems likely that the proportion of incompetents may be as high here as among those calling themselves psychologists. The choice of a therapist is thus made doubly difficult: first, one must avoid quacks and second, one must choose the legitimate therapist whose potentialities for achieving success in a given case are highest.

The second problem is woefully short of information. For the first, some cues may be useful. The legitimate therapist, whether MD or PhD, is limited, if he belongs to a professional organization, in his size and format of advertising. He does not promise a cure—or if he does, he is ethically bound to let the rest of the world know his secret discovery. He never violates confidences by naming former patients to impress a prospective patient with their social prominence. His degrees are from known, accredited institutions and he does not balk if asked about his qualifications. His ideas may differ from those of the world in general and even of his colleagues, but he works to perfect them in the open, scholarly marketplace of ideas, the professional journals; he does not cloak his methods in secrecy.

One can generally avoid quacks through obtaining information regarding available legitimate professional help. The National Association for Mental Health in New York City publishes a directory of out-patient psychiatric clinics. The American Board of Psychological Services in St. Louis publishes a similar directory of psychological services. City or county medical associations can provide information regarding competent therapists. Many school systems now have their own staff psychologists and counselors. Numerous cities and counties have mental-health clinics, child-guidance centers, or family services where free or inexpensive treatment is obtainable.

Legitimate Therapists

Individuals engaged in legitimate mental-healing endeavors fall into five major categories. Their natures are as follows:

1. *Psychologists.* Generally they have a Doctor of Philosophy (PhD) degree although a number of psychologists engaged in therapy have only the Master's (MA or MS) degree. Therapy is largely "client-centered" and nondirective. It is based on the notion that therapists are not all-knowing, and that theories aimed at *explaining* all psychological disturbances are far from perfect. The therapist can help the patient best by *not* telling the patient what to do or what is wrong, but by being supportive and making the patient feel secure, and by planning the situation so that the patient has an opportunity to gain insight into his problems and thus, for the most part, heal himself (Rogers, 1951). Not being MDs, psychologists cannot administer drugs or perform certain other useful functions. Of the various types of therapists they are generally the best trained in experimental design and in diagnostic testing.

2. *Psychiatrists.* These individuals are—or should be—MDs with a great deal of special training acquired during postdoctoral residency. Many psychiatrists use some form of physical treatment, ranging from electro-convulsive shock (ECS) to tranquilizing drugs. Most of the remainder follow some form of psychoanalytic theory. Therapy is usually more directive than among psychologists. Organic psychiatrists deal oftener with the treatment of psychotics; "talking therapists" deal largely with treatment of neurotics.

3. *Psychoanalysts.* The psychoanalytic category consists mainly of MDs plus occasional PhDs, known as lay analysts. The basic qualification for becoming an analyst is to have been analyzed oneself; otherwise one's own neurotic problems become intertwined with those of the patient. Second, the analyst generally undertakes a training analysis in which he analyzes a patient under the supervision of an experienced psychoanalyst. Although splintered into many schools of thought, most analysts share the idea that they know the cause of the difficulty and that their task is to get the

patient to recall those incidents occuring in childhood that precipitated his problem. Thus, analytic therapy is generally more directive than the psychologist's.

4. *Psychiatric Social Workers.* The social worker began as the individual on the clinic's team who wrote up the patient's case history. He then branched out into therapy, especially group therapy, where a number of individuals interact with the therapist *and* with one another in the therapeutic setting. Special training was initiated, culminating in the psychiatric social worker's generally acquiring a Master of Social Work (MSW) degree. Until recently most psychiatric social workers were apparently oriented toward the psychoanalytic technique, but increasing numbers of them have begun to swing to a nondirective approach in therapy.

5. *Pediatricians.* Unlike the other four, the pediatrician finds the diagnosis and treatment of behavioral problems an insignificant portion of his average professional duties. An MD with specialized training in children's physical diseases, the pediatrician sometimes but not invariably receives some training in the diagnosis and treatment of behavior problems. Even though often quite naive in this area, he is called on by parents to produce answers regarding psychological maladjustment on the basis of extremely scanty data. He does this of necessity, but in many instances, unfortunately, he begins to believe that he does know the answers.

The first four groups of therapists work full time at the practice of therapy. Although they sometimes battle among themselves over their respective roles in therapy, they generally compose their differences in a clinical setting and establish excellent working conditions with one another.

Forms of Psychotherapy

However psychotherapists may differ from each other in professional affiliation, they all are confronted by the same problem: how to change the patient's behavior, the behavior of the people interacting most closely with the patient, or both. The therapist's approach to this task depends on his conception of the role he can play and of the nature of problem behavior.

Directive therapists, more frequently the psychiatrists and psychoanalysts, generally believe they *know* the basis of a given problem behavior. Whether their core of belief revolves around the Rankian birth trauma or Freudian Oedipus complex, they know the cause of the behavior. Their assignment is to *direct* the patient's flow of thoughts and associations in such a way that the patient also becomes aware of the cause. Once there is conscious awareness, the patient need not expend psychic energy in repressing feelings and can function normally.

The nondirective or "client"-centered therapist, usually a psychologist, does not claim to know the cause of the disorder. But he believes that in a supportive relationship with the patient, he can reflect back to the patient the latter's own comments and behavior in a way that will cause him to develop insight into his problems. By understanding his problems, he will thus solve them.

Basically, there are three not mutually exclusive views of the nature of problem behavior. The first, more prevalent among the directive therapists, is that problem behavior results from exposure to universal human situations, such as the Oedipal situation. Exposed to a universal problem, the child reacts to it in an atypical fashion because the situation is itself in some manner atypical or because he is weak in psychic strength.

A second view of problem behavior, held by both many directive and nondirective therapists, is that problem behavior results from specific rather than universal problems. Maternal rejection would fit the case. A third view, not too fully defined but gaining support, is that problem behavior is primarily a result of the problem child having learned maladaptive social roles, perhaps as an outgrowth of universal or specific familial problems. Therapists favoring the first two views would be inclined to base treatment on discussion or conversation with patients or in interpretative or cathartic play situations. Those leaning to the third view would stress the learning of new social roles and therefore build therapy around new models for behavior, either in play or in other settings.

Nondirective Play Therapy. Play is the child's commonest activity and much treatment of children centers on play therapy. Although some play therapists are directive (see Kanner, 1957, p. 231), more commonly play therapy is quite nondirective. Axline's (1947) description of the theoretical basis and techniques of nondirective play therapy is classic. Like that of many contemporary therapists, her position was that the basis for problem behavior was in the environment, usually the home, of the child and that the child's play often revealed the cause of the problem. Furthermore, the child, in a nondirective atmosphere, could resolve his problems. The therapist reflected back to the child the child's own statements so that the child could understand himself better. Play provided catharsis, an outpouring of feeling; this in itself was important. Finally, though the therapist was not essentially concerned with the learning of adequate social roles, this learning undoubtedly occurred, especially in a group play-therapy situation.

Here is an example of play therapy. The patient lived in an orphanage, was somewhat better than of average ability, but was doing poorly in school. She was rather unattractive and aggressive toward both children and adults. Inexperienced in play therapy, the therapist had read extensive background material.

First Contact—Individual. When Emma appeared for the first interview, she was told that she could come for forty-five minutes every Tuesday to play with the toys if she wanted to come. It was also explained that she could play with these toys in any way that she wanted to. The limitations were mentioned at this first meeting: She must stay inside the play area that had been marked off with chairs; she could not damage the walls or furniture; she could not take any of the toys out of the room. Otherwise she could do or say anything that she wanted to do or say while in the room with the therapist and the therapist would not tell anyone what she did do or say.

Emma stared at the therapist. Then she smiled her twisted smile and walked over to the drawing paper, picked up a piece of it and the crayons, brought them over to the table at which the therapist was sitting, sat down across from her and began to draw. She seemed very tense, and she certainly was silent. Not one word or glance in the direction of the therapist was forthcoming until the picture was finished. Then she glanced quickly at the therapist and looked away again.

Emma: This is my house. This where I live at 7 Blank Street with my father and mother sister. I have a sister older than me.

Therapist: Does your sister live here too?

Emma: Yes.

(Emma got up from the table, walked over to the bench where the paper dolls were, and brought them to the table where she had been drawing. Without a word she began to cut out the dolls—the father doll first, then the little girl, then the big girl, and lastly the mother doll. She began to cast more glances in the direction of the therapist. When she finished cutting out the family, she looked up and grinned. Then she cut out an evening dress for the mother.)

Emma (whispering): Is this *her* dress?

Therapist: Yes, that is the mother's dress.

(Emma continued cutting out dresses. She seemed completely absorbed with the task.)

Therapist: You like to play with the paper dolls.

Emma (making a face at the therapist): No, not very well.

Therapist: Would you rather play with something else?

Emma: I would rather color, but you don't have a color book.

Therapist: You wish I had a coloring book so you could color in it.

Emma: Yes.

(Emma continued to cut out dresses for each paper doll with the exception of the father. She picked him up and stared at him. Then quickly she piled them in a neat pile and put them away. She went back to the bench where the toys were laid out and looked at them. She turned suddenly and looked at the therapist.)

Emma (shortly): May I have a drink? (She pointed to the nursing bottle.)

Therapist: You may do anything with the toys that you want to do.

(Emma picked up the nursing bottle and drank from it, keeping her back turned to the therapist. Then she picked up the baby's rattle and shook it. Next she played quietly with the soldiers on the horses. She kept her back to the therapist all the time and so the therapist was unable to see what she was doing with the soldiers, but there seemed to be some kind of a quiet battle going on between the two soldiers. First one, then the other was knocked down. She muttered something that the therapist could not understand. She seemed very upset about something. She scowled, glanced back at the therapist, picked up the bottle again and began to drink from it, glanced back at the therapist, drank from the bottle, glanced at the therapist.)

Therapist: You like to drink from the bottle.

(Emma immediately put the bottle down. She picked up the gun, took it out of the holster, whispered "Bang!" and put it back. Then she took the train out of the box and put it together. She pushed it along the bench for about two inches and then very suddenly crammed it back into the box. Then, still keeping her back to the therapist, she stood there and rubbed her hand along the edge of the bench.)

Therapist: Our time together is over for today, Emma.

(Emma came over to the table and stared at the therapist. The therapist smiled at her. Emma moistened her lips and smiled back with her lips only.)

Therapist: Do you want to say something, Emma?

Emma (whispering): Yes.

Therapist: What do you want to say? (Emma twisted her hands together, made faces at the therapist.)

Emma (whispering): I want to come back.

Therapist: You may come here by yourself every Tuesday, Emma. And you may come with a group tomorrow if you want to. (Then Emma really smiled. She walked over to the door.)

Therapist: Good-bye, Emma.

(No answer. Emma opened the door, went outside, looked back in, whispered "Good-bye!" and was gone.)

Comments. The picture which Emma drew during this first interview was a very conventional type of drawing, consisting of a square brown house, with three windows and a door. There were blue, red, and purple curtains at the windows. There was a big tree beside the house. A bit of blue sky was across the top of the picture, and a smiling blue sun with yellow lines radiating from it was in the left-hand corner. There were five bluebirds flying in the sky. This is mentioned in such detail because, as time passed, the art work produced by this child became more and more expressive. This first picture seemed a typical, formal type of picture. It also seems significant that she volunteered the information that she lived in this house with her father and mother and sister, although the child has been in the Orphans' Home for nearly three years. However, it is a part of her history that the mother is continually writing to the children and telling them that she is going to take them out of the Home. The mother has called them up many times and told them to get their things packed and she will come after them and take them away. The children get ready to go and the mother does not appear. The social worker had attempted to stop this practice, but had been unsuccessful up to the time of this report. Occasionally the mother does arrive for a brief visit, but seldom takes the children off the grounds with her.

The therapist's first response seems to be a very poor one. Emma had just expressed the crux of her problem—the broken home. The therapist responds with a question that takes the center of interest away from Emma and places it upon the sister. Quite naturally, Emma retreats. When Emma plays with the paper dolls, and contradicts the therapist when she suggests that Emma likes to play with paper dolls, the uneasy therapist tries to push Emma along with "Would you rather play with something else?" Emma names something that is not there. It would have been better in each instance if the therapist had followed along with the child.

The choice of uncut paper dolls for play-therapy material seems to be a poor choice, but in this case it seemed like good introductory material. The order in which she cut out the dolls is noteworthy. The fact that she cut out clothes for all except the father might be significant. At least it seems so in the light of what followed in later sessions when she played with the family of dolls.

Response by the therapist seems a bit meager in this interview, but it was a case of the therapist's not being quite sure of what to say and thinking that silence would be the best course to follow. Looking back over the interview, it seems that the therapist might have recognized the desire to drink from the bottle when Emma said, "May I have a drink?" rather than generalize on the permissiveness of the situation. When Emma apparently resented the comment from the therapist a little later to the effect that Emma did like to drink from the nursing bottle, the therapist might have recognized her resentment. Again, when Emma very quietly shot the therapist for her intrusion, the therapist might have recognized Emma's desire to shoot her. She might also have recognized the child's desire to come back again, rather than emphasizing the permissiveness of the situation (Axline, 1947, pp. 274–278).

Nothing highly dramatic happened during this session, yet the therapist gained some insight into Emma's problems. Emma achieved catharsis. Fourteen sessions with the child were reported, some individual, some group therapy. Although no one session produced remarkable change, Emma's feelings toward herself, other children, and adults became far more realistic and more positive as therapy progressed.

Activity Group Therapy. Many individuals in each of the social sciences believe that most maladaptive behaviors stem from the defining and playing of social roles. Seen thus, the problem in therapy is to eliminate the disturbed individual's maladaptive roles and to build in new behaviors. The old, maladaptive behavior may have arisen from any number of sources—Oedipal problems, parent pathology, social learning. The immediate challenge is to develop a new concept of the self, new social roles, and new patterns of behavior consonant with new self concept and the new set of roles.

Slavson approached this problem with a new therapeutic technique which he called *activity group therapy.* Probably most useful in the 6–13 age range, the technique is employed in conjunction with other types of therapy, such as analytic therapy for parents. Although it has a number of additional benefits, one important aspect of this form of therapy is the learning of social roles. Six to eight boys or girls form the therapy group. These youngsters are chosen carefully to balance one another. A passive, effeminate boy will be counterbalanced by a boy who has made a good masculine identification and who has problems in the other direction—who may be an aggressive delinquent. Each is influenced by the other and learns a more adequate set of roles. Slavson offered the following comments:

> Appropriate and meaningful identifications and participation with others correct the sexual confusion from which many children who come for treatment suffer. Boys who because of a solely or predominantly feminine environment or an unsuccessful sibling rivalry with sisters reject a masculine role, or are ambivalent or confused about it, establish male identification by participating without fear or conflict in masculine activities. They perceptibly assume boys' attitudes and characteristics, and those who had been isolated, lonely, or stigmatized as a result soon find friends and playmates and become better adjusted in their social environment. Similarly, girls whose home environment was equally unfavorable, can accept their feminine role with greater equanimity because of such intimate group association.
>
> The infantilized child finds in these groups an educational and maturing environment. Here protection and controls that he habitually sought and expected from his parents are not forthcoming. He must learn to stand on his own feet. His dependence trends are not nurtured or encouraged, and the operational field for his life is appropriate for his age and increased powers. Such a child may at first play like a baby, lie on the floor or a table on his abdomen, read the funnies, or suck his thumb, but he soon gives up these anachronistic acts because of the examples set by the others in the group, who act more maturely and more responsibly. The immature child may attach himself briefly to another on whom he leans for support in his upward climb, and having

received this sustenance, he may soon begin to work and act on his own more appropriately (Slavson, 1952, p. 287).

Psychodrama. Another form of therapy aimed directly at the learning of social roles is Moreno's (1946) *psychodrama.* This is based in part on the ideas that individuals develop problems because they wish to play roles—that is, behave—in ways that they have had no opportunity to learn, and that practice in playing these roles in an artificial or theatrical environment may be transferred to behavior in real life. Patients write plays and perform roles in them and in the plays of others. They gain experience in playing varied roles, especially those roles that they find to be highly important to them yet beyond their capabilities.

Therapeutic Group Work. This form of therapy is aimed at providing the patient with adequate behavioral models. Once given adequate models, the patient can learn to make more adequate social responses. As Konopka (1955, p. 23) wrote:

> The assumption underlying therapeutic group work is that the ego-building devices which have been employed regularly by social group workers with relatively stable individuals, when used with appropriate modifications, have utility for personality disturbances. This type of social group work practice is distinguished from others by several features, one of the most prominent being "intensified individualization and less emphasis on group goal."

The individual in need of therapeutic assistance is placed in a group that is not too demanding, yet challenges him to model behavior after the normal members. Take this example: for seven years Gloria had been in psychotherapy for school phobia, having dropped out of school in the fourth grade following the death of two grandparents and having attended school only occasionally from that time onward. She was tutored at home by two competent teachers. She would not leave home except in the company of her mother and had only two casual acquaintances of her own age. It was decided to create a social group, to meet at Gloria's home, because—

1. Gloria was at a crucial stage. The adolescent years offered a chance for change that might not come again. There was the possibility of either indeepndence and establishment of a separate identity on the one hand or of an isolated and inactive adulthood on the other.
2. Individual therapy had reached an impasse.
3. Gloria had expressed a yearning for contact with girls her own age.
4. It appeared that because Gloria had kept up to her grade through tutoring and had interests and skills appropriate to her age and sex, she would have a basis for a beginning relationship with her peers.
   (Garland, Kolodny, & Waldfogel, 1962, pp. 659–696)

Understandably, Gloria was unwilling to allow the social worker to seek members for the group by making prospects aware of her condition.

The worker encouraged Gloria in her efforts to obtain members and she did manage to bring in one very popular girl. When she could not find any other members, however, she was able to allow the worker to secure members from school and agreed that the worker would discuss the group's purpose with them. With the help of the school guidance office four other girls were drawn into the group. All of the girls selected had experienced some difficulty in making friends at school and were generally dissatisfied with their level of academic and social achievement. On the other hand, they were all interested in social contacts and had a normal range of adolescent interests. These girls represented, for the most part, desirable but not unattainable ego models for Gloria. During the club's first year, meetings were held in Gloria's home. The familiar crafts activities, which demanded little in the way of close interacting, her mother's presence as hostess, and the home setting all contributed to Gloria's ability to assume the role of a member with a minimum of discomfort. This experience was not without its painful aspects, however, as Gloria's mode of life was soon challenged by pressure from the other members, who began to ask for trips around the community. Gloria found this suggestion extremely frightening, as it entailed separation from her mother. Her differences with the other members on this matter culminated in an angry exchange at one meeting, with Gloria tearfully telling the others that they didn't care for her and could go without her. The leader allowed this challenge to Gloria's adjustment to materialize and did not inhibit the expression of hostile feelings. She then helped the girls to work out a compromise. They decided to go to a movie, but Gloria's mother was to be permitted to attend. While not disrupting Gloria's tie with her mother this would permit the group to move out of the emotional and physical confinement of the home. This activity was carried out, although not without a prominent display of trepidation on Gloria's and her mother's part, and was followed at the end of the year by a trip farther away from the community. On this occasion all of the mothers were invited, which legitimized the presence of parents at a club activity and deemphasized the difference between Gloria and the other girls (Garland et al., p. 696).

This small step led to a larger one. Gloria began to attend one class a day in a regular school setting. The class was taught by her favorite tutor but her mother had to accompany her.

At about this time Gloria's parents felt secure enough to take a trip together for a week. Gloria stayed with a neighbor and the group worker maintained individual contact with her during her parents' absence. She had her first date during the spring, her teacher having introduced her to a boy who had also had anxieties about attending school. With constant support from the group worker in the form of discussion of proposed activities, Gloria was able to accompany the group without her mother on cook-outs, for bowling, and to restaurants.

. . . At the start of the third year Gloria was able to respond to the demands of the school that she attend classes full time.

As the year went along Gloria was able to meet the demands of the school and the group and even brought in a new member who, she explained, "needed help in making friends." She was still anxious any time she left home without her mother but continued to move out in her contacts with others. Upon graduation from high school she applied to a local college some ten miles from her home. She was accepted and is currently attending this college as a day student (Garland et al., pp. 697–698).

For Gloria, whose fear of separation resulted in increasing social isolation at a time when peer relationships are crucial, the group experience afforded (1) a protective vehicle for non-destructive exposure to a wider social world, (2) a series of gratifying social experiences which reinforced her desire and ability to search further for peer contacts, and (3) a range of alternative ego models and adaptive patterns to experiment with in the process of constructing an adult identity (Garland et al., p. 699).

Thus, one sees a range from the more or less incidental learning of social roles in Axline's nondirective play therapy to the Garland et al. situation where the learning of social roles through imitation is central. It seems reasonable to regard investigation and amelioration of the bases of maladaptive behavior as well as the building of normal response habits as highly significant aspects of the therapeutic process.

Therapy with children, coupled with treatment of parents, is aimed at rehabilitating the family so that stresses are reduced and the child is better able to deal with the pressures that remain. The alternative is to remove the child from the family—in a sense, to give up—and to place him in an institution or foster home. Sometimes this may be necessary, and it may be effective. But as long as the culture holds the family to be of crucial value in growing up, society is limited to psychiatric, psychoanalytic, or psychological treatment. Thus, at the present time, in treating a child who remains in the family setting, the child almost certainly participates in some kind of therapy.

PROGNOSIS

As noted in the previous chapter, humans show a good deal of consistency in their behavior. This consistency is undoubtedly related to the fact that, for any given individual, certain behaviors lead to reward or positive reinforcement. This reinforcement may come from the self or from others who reward the individual's consistency because it makes behavior more orderly and predictable. Reinforcement may also take the form of "secondary gain" as, for instance, when an individual thinks to himself, "I feel less tense now that I've stolen a car."

So long as behaviors judged by society as deviant and maladaptive reward the specific individual, it is unlikely that change will occur. The therapeutic process, by rewarding a new class of behaviors, by extinguishing an old set through nonreinforcement, or by both, endeavors to reduce deviant behavior. Quite likely changes in age alone, without therapeutic assistance, produce new demands on the individual which reduce the rewards of certain deviant behaviors and increase the rewards of others. In considering prognosis—the probability of recovery—one attempts to distinguish from the problems that persist over time, despite therapeutic aid and the shifts that accompany age, those problem behaviors that are easily extinguishable through therapy or that disappear of their own accord as the patient grows older.

Looming large on the list of clinical referrals are problem behaviors that result largely from adult misunderstanding of child behavior —from judging normal acts to be atypical and deviant. These problems do not become problems until diagnosed. Next come the genuine problems that will decrease in severity or even disappear in most cases without any treatment whatsoever. Then there are the problems that are severe but transient and those that are mild but long-term. Finally, there are the severe, persisting problems which do not yield easily to treatment.

Physicians have long distinguished between chronic and transient disorders. Perhaps psychologists need to follow the example of medical practice. As long as therapists are in short supply, it would be of great value to have normative data on the duration and degree of debilitation of various problem disorders. Lacking this information, one cannot make a judicious use of therapy time. Without knowledge of how frequently various problems disappear by themselves, it is not possible even to evaluate the effects of therapy.

Acting Out and Withdrawn Behaviors

So broad a division of behavioral problems into acting out and withdrawal behaviors may not serve much purpose in permitting one to predict specific disorders. Yet the relative seriousness of each of these two broad categories warrants consideration, especially since the subject has aroused considerable controversy.

In one of the first studies aimed at finding the views of various individuals toward the seriousness of problems, Wickman (1928) found teachers and clinicians differing widely in their judgments of problem severity (see Chapter 12). From the rather large collection of problem behaviors rated, those judged as among the most serious by one group were often considered as among the least serious by the other. Although later studies (e.g., Beilin, 1959) have shown teachers and clinicians to be more in agreement nowadays than in Wickman's time, some of the differences he noted remain (Ritholz, 1959). The Ritholz study further demonstrated that parents and even children themselves agreed with the teachers. Whereas clinicians consider psychological conditions resulting in withdrawn behavior as the most serious, teachers, parents, and children are more concerned with actual conduct, generally aggressive in character.

In general the clinicians' assessment of problem seriousness appears correct, though incorrect in some particulars. The entire cluster of traits composing "withdrawal" seems to be a poor sign in prognosis. From among 73 children referred to a clinic, Brown (1960) took 20 who were doing well and an equal number who were doing poorly and compared them in symptoms exhibited at the time of original referral to the clinic. The worst cases manifested greater withdrawal in every respect. The best, on the other hand, oftener showed inhibition and caution—behaviors that have come to be associated with withdrawal. Whereas it might be argued that inhibited, cautious behavior will predict withdrawal, this is not true. These symptoms more accurately reflect a lesser frequency of the discharge of tension through total and diffuse motor behavior. Withdrawn behavior does appear to be quite serious, as clinicians maintain, but the clinicians seem wrong, in part, in their analyses of its constituent traits.

In the Wickman study, clinicians rated shyness as a rather serious problem. Some of them may have believed shyness itself to be pathological. Many more probably rated it as a serious problem because they believed that the shy, introverted individual was prone to schizophrenic disorders. This is questionable. The idea that the shy introvert is more susceptible to schizophrenia than the more extroverted individual is doubtful; both older (Ackerson, 1931) and more recent (Michael, Morris, & Soroker, 1957) studies indicate that shyness has a strong tendency to vanish of its own accord as an individual ages, and that it in no way is able to predict later schizophrenia. The withdrawn child who *can* relate to others, but does not do so, is withdrawn in a very different sense from the child who does not relate to others because of a general confusion and inability to respond. The latter kind of withdrawn behavior is more serious than acting out behaviors.

In any broad category of behavior, certain subtypes have good prognosis and others are less promising of successful recovery. Table 16-1 lists behaviors ranging from simple problems of habit formation to relatively severe disorders. Accompanying them is evidence concerning their probability of remission—that is, recovery—in most cases, without treatment.

Only when it is known that individuals can recover by themselves from a number of problems can the effectiveness of therapy be determined. Some studies suggest that therapy is of little value (e.g., Levitt, Bieser, & Robertson, 1959; Robins & O'Neal, 1958). Other studies claim high rates of remission (e.g., Rexford, Schleifer, & Van Amerongen, 1956; Cunningham, Westerman, & Fischhoff, 1956). Either is hard to evaluate without knowing the frequency with which various problems arose among the children studied, the rate of spontaneous remission of these problems, and the type of therapy used.

SUMMARY

Hereditary, physiological, familial, and sociological factors all operate in the production of problem behavior. Their respective contributions vary from one disorder to the next. Moreover, as skill is developed in differentiating between superficially similar disorders, specific single causes may be found in the background of each of the subtypes of disorder composing a broad phenotypical category.

Clinicians differ from other individuals in their judgments of the seriousness of various disorders. Although perhaps incorrect about specifics, the clinicians seem generally correct in their assessment of problem severity. Unlike others who deal with children, the clinician uses systematic observation and is committed to scientific rules of evidence. Thus, he is potentially capable of developing adequate diagnostic and therapeutic techniques.

In diagnosis, so far, emphasis on broad phenotypical categories has impeded the development of effective treatment methods. Differential diagnosis, based on observation of variation within the phenotype, leads to discovery of various genotypes and permits development of specific treatment aimed at one genotypical variety of problem.

As far as most problem behaviors are concerned, there is only one

TABLE 16-1   Behavior Problems and Their Probability of Remission

Investigator	High Probability of Remission	Low Probability of Remission
McFarlane, Allen & Honzik, 1955 (an extensive longitudinal study)	Timidity Specific fears Tantrums Speech problems Enuresis Bad dreams Restlessness in sleep Poor appetite, "finicky" eating Thumb sucking Destructiveness Excessive demanding of attention Excessive activity Lying Masturbation	Excessive modesty Excessive dependence Oversensitiveness Nail biting Jealousy Somberness
Ackerson, 1931 (an extensive cross-sectional study)	Restlessness Shyness Distractibility Fearfulness Tantrums Finicky eating habits Negativism Cruelty to younger children	Depression Seclusiveness Unresponsiveness Oversensitiveness Daydreaming Sullenness Egocentricity Emotional lability Boastfulness Irritability Selfishness
Johnson, 1950	Social delinquent	Solitary delinquent
Michael, Morris, & Soroker, 1957	Shyness	
Bender, 1947		Childhood schizophrenia
Kanner & Eisenberg, 1955	Autism, if child verbal by age 5	Autism, if child still mute at age 5
Berkowitz, 1955	"Predelinquent" behavior (76% had no record as delinquents)	
Griffiths, 1952	Upper- and lower-class "delinquency-related" behaviors	Middle-class "delinquency-related" behaviors

general approach to treatment of children—some form of play therapy. The value of even this form is not entirely certain. Fortunately, many problem behaviors disappear without treatment. Despite the present lack of knowledge of problem behavior and its treatment, there is reason to hope that present skills in treatment can be greatly improved.

REFERENCES

Ackerman, N. W. *The psychodynamics of family life.* New York: Basic Books, 1958.

Ackerson, L. *Children's behavior problems. I. Incidence, genetic, and intellectual factors.* Chicago: Univer. Chicago Press, 1931.

Axline, Virginia M. *Play therapy.* Boston: Houghton Mifflin, 1947.

Beilin, H. Teacher's and clinician's attitudes toward behavior problems of children: a reappraisal. *Child Develpm.,* 1959, **30,** 9–25.

Bender, Lauretta R. Childhood schizophrenia; clinical study of one hundred schizophrenic children. *Amer. J. Orthopsychiat.,* 1947, **17,** 40–56.

Bender, Lauretta R. *Child psychiatric techniques.* Springfield, Ill.: Thomas, 1952.

Berkowitz, B. The Juvenile Aid Bureau of the New York City Police. *Nerv. Child,* 1955, **11,** 42–48.

Brophy, A. L., & Durfee, R. A. Mail order training in psychotherapy. *Amer. Psychologist,* 1960, **15,** 356–360.

Brown, Janet L. Prognosis from presenting symptoms of preschool children with atypical development. *Amer. J. Orthopsychiat.,* 1960, **30,** 382–390.

Chessman, C. *Cell 2455, death row.* New York: Pocket Books, 1955.

Cunningham, J. M., Westerman, Hester H., & Fischhoff, J. A follow up study of patients seen in a psychiatric clinic for children. *Amer. J. Orthopsychiat.,* 1956, **26,** 602–611.

David, H. P. Phones, phonies, and psychologists. *Amer. Psychologist,* 1954, **9,** 237–240.

David, H. P., & Springfield, F. B. Phones, phonies and psychologists: II. Four years later. *Amer. Psychologist,* 1958, **13,** 61–64.

Eysenck, H. J. *Handbook of abnormal psychology.* New York: Basic Books, 1961.

Fish, Barbara. Longitudinal observations of biological deviations in a schizophrenic infant. *Amer. J. Psychiat.,* 1959, **116,** 25–31.

Garland, J. A., Kolodny, R. L., & Waldfogel, S. Social group work as adjunctive treatment for the emotionally disturbed adolescent: The experience of a specialized group work department. *Amer. J. Orthopsychiat.,* 1962, **32,** 691–706.

Garrison, M. The genetics of schizophrenia. *J. abnorm. soc. Psychol.,* 1947, **42,** 122–124.

Gottesman, I. I. Heritability of personality: A demonstration. *Psychol. Monogr.,* 1963, **77,** Whole No. 572.

Griffiths, W. *Behavior difficulties of children as perceived and judged by parents, teachers, and children themselves.* Minneapolis: Univer. Minn. Press, 1952.

Hebb, D. O. *The organization of behavior.* New York: Wiley, 1949.

Heilbrun, A. B., Jr. Perceptual distortion and schizophrenia. *Amer. J. Orthopsychiat.*, 1960, **30**, 412–418.

Johnson, R. C. Causal factors in the delinquency of fifty Denver boys. Unpubl. M.A. thesis, Denver Univer., 1950.

Johnson, R. C. A comparison of the moral judgments of normal and neurotic children. In preparation (1964).

Kanner, L. *Child psychiatry.* Springfield, Ill.: Thomas, 1957.

Kanner, L., & Eisenberg, L. Notes on the follow-up studies of autistic children. In P. H. Hoch & J. Zubin (Eds.), *Psychopathology of childhood.* New York: Grune & Stratton, 1955.

Kawi, A. A., & Pasamanick, B. Prenatal and paranatal factors in the development of childhood reading disorders. *Monogr. soc. Res. Child Develpm.*, 1959, **24**, No. 4.

Kinsey, A. C., Pomeroy, W. B., & Martin, C. E., *Sexual behavior in the human male.* Philadelphia: Saunders, 1948.

Kinsey, A. C., Pomeroy, W. B., Martin, C. E., & Gebhard, P. H. *Sexual behavior in the human female.* Philadelphia: Saunders, 1953.

Kohn, M. L., & Clausen, J. A. Parental authority behavior and schizophrenia. *Amer. J. Orthopsychiat.*, 1956, **26**, 297–313.

Konopka, Gisela. The generic and the specific in group work practice in the psychiatric setting. In H. B. Trecker (Ed.), *Group work in the psychiatric setting.* New York: Whiteside & Morrow, 1955.

Lakin, M. Personality factors in mothers of excessively crying (colicky) infants. *Monogr. soc. Res. Child Develpm.*, 1957, **22**, No. 1.

Lecky, P. *Self consistency, a theory of personality.* New York: Island Press, 1945.

Levitt, E. E., Bieser, Helen, & Robertson, R. A follow-up evaluation of cases treated at a community child guidance clinic. *Amer. J. Orthopsychiat.*, 1959, **29**, 337–346.

MacFarlane, Jean W., Allen, Lucile, & Honzik, Marjorie. *A developmental study of behavior problems of normal children between 21 months and 14 years.* Berkeley: Univer. Calif. Press, 1955.

Michael, Carmen M., Morris, D. P., & Soroker, Eleanor. Follow-up studies of shy, withdrawn children. II. Relative incidence of schizophrenia. *Amer. J. Orthopsychiat.*, 1957, **27**, 331–337.

Moreno, J. L. *Psychodrama.* New York: Beacon House, 1946.

Mowrer, O. H. "Sin," the lesser of two evils. *Amer. Psychologist*, 1960, **15**, 301–304.

Pasamanick, B., Rogers, Martha, & Lelienfeld, A. Pregnancy experience and the development of behavior disorder in children. *Amer. J. Psychiat.*, 1956, **112**, 613–617.

Pastore, N. Genetics of schizophrenia. *Psychol. Bull.*, 1949, **46**, 285–302.

Prout, C. T., & White, Mary A. The schizophrenic's sibling. *J. nerv. ment. Dis.*, 1956, **123**, 162–170.

Randolph, Mary H., Richardson, H., & Johnson, R. C. A comparison of social and solitary male delinquents. *J. consult. Psychol.*, 1961, **25**, 293–295.

Rexford, E. N., Schleifer, M., & Van Amerongen, Suzanne T. A follow-up of a psychiatric study of 57 antisocial young children. *Ment. Hyg.*, 1956, **40**, 196–214.

Ritholz, Sophie. *Children's behavior.* New York: Bookman, 1959.

Robins, L. N., & O'Neal, Patricia. The marital history of former problem children. *Soc. Probl.*, 1958, **5**, 347–358.

Roebuck, J. B., & Johnson, R. C. The short con man. *Crime and Delinq.*, 1964, **10**, 235–248.

Rogers, C. R. *Client centered therapy.* Boston: Houghton Mifflin, 1951.

Schachter, Frances F., Meyer, Lucile R., & Loomis, E. A., Jr. Childhood schizophrenia and mental retardation: differential diagnosis before and after one year of psychotherapy. *Amer. J. Orthopsychiat.*, 1962, **32**, 584–594.

Slavson, S. R. *Child psychotherapy.* New York: Columbia Univer. Press, 1952.

Stendler, Celia B. How well do elementary school teachers understand child behavior? *J. educ. Psychol.*, 1949, **40**, 489–498.

Wickman, E. K. *Children's behavior and teacher's attitudes.* New York: Commonwealth Fund, 1928.

chapter 17 ✳ Summing Up

The aim of science is to understand natural phenomena. The scientist assumes that the universe is orderly and that natural phenomena, ultimately, are predictable and lawful. Understanding and prediction come from the use of the scientific method. The scientific method is merely a set of "rules" by which scientists attempt to eliminate bias from their observations and thus view nature as it is, not as they wish it to be.

Systematic observation of unbiased samples of the phenomenon under investigation is the key to an accurate understanding of the universe. Experiments are the form of observation most commonly used in science, since in experiments uncontrolled or unknown sources of variance are reduced to a minimum. Further, experiments, far more than naturalistic observation, may be directed to highly specific problems whose solution may provide the information needed to decide which of two or more conflicting theories is the most accurate portrayal of the relations between natural phenomena.

On the negative side, an emphasis on experimentation may cause the neglect, for the most part, of those natural phenomena that do not readily fit within conventional experimental design. This is illustrated in the psychology of learning; there is a plethora of experiments dealing with forms of learning common to all species but few dealing with those complex forms of cognition that set mankind apart from other species.

We observe, systematically and without bias. From this observation we attempt to understand, predict, and, at times, control the phenomena with which we deal. In psychology, especially in child psychology, there are grave ethical problems involved in scientifically controlling behavior. It seems reasonable to believe that the level of development of a science should be judged by the degree to which that science allows understanding and predictions.

This book has attempted to provide information about the known and the predictable in child psychology. In general, although at a lesser stage of development than the physical or biological sciences, child psychology has much to be proud of. It has steadily increased the rigor of its methods of investigation and the accuracy of its predictions. From the scattered anecdotes and unsupported folk beliefs of a century ago, and from the scanty array of methods and information available at the turn of the century, it has developed adequate research methods, a vast store of facts, and a few theories useful for knitting together at least some of the facts in an orderly fashion. Child psychology appears to be at the stage where theories, more accurate and inclusive than those now available, can be evolved and proved valuable rather than merely blinding people to those natural events for which they cannot account.

The child psychologist has to deal with two major questions. First, in what ways are humans all alike, and why? Second, within this framework of similarity, how do individual differences arise? These are the two problems that this book has attempted to deal with as best possible in the light of imperfect knowledge.

Two sets of forces work upon mankind, those that are biological-genetic, and those that are social. The biological-genetic forces are chiefly influential in producing a basic similarity between all humans; they also serve to produce a biological core of individual difference which is further increased by each individual's unique set of social experiences. Social forces also produce similarity between humans. We share the characteristic of growing up within some primary group, of being cared for by one or more parents or parent-surrogates; we all must face the challenge of moving from a position of dependence to one of comparative independence. Further similarity results from being brought up within one specific culture, with its own pattern of relieving social stresses. However alike humans may be, as a result of the similarity in the way they are socialized, it is their unique social environment which greatly enlarges their individual differences that are hereditary in nature.

Humans are alike. We are bipedal, with stereoscopic vision and with sensitive hands, free to manipulate objects in the environment. We follow the same general course of growth and maturation. We share with all other animals certain ways of learning, such as operant and respondent learning, but are different from all nonprimates in other areas, such as in the ease of formation of learning sets. We are like one another, but unlike all other organisms, in the ease with which we deal with abstract concepts, delayed reactions, and complex and creative problem solving. This human uniqueness appears to be the result of the fact that only humans are capable of symbolic behavior. Language is again an inherited ability, causing humans to share a broad social heritage, built up across generations, and to show similarity in social and intellectual responses to the world. We are manipulative, curious, and arousal seeking. Within this framework of similarity individual differences occur.

We are different. Genetic inheritance makes individuals differ from one another in obvious ways, as in eye color, skin color, size, and physical attractiveness, and in less obvious but more significant ways, as in intelligence and in activity level. Certain innate differences are present, and these differences are enhanced by the environment.

The contemporary American child grows up in a rich, urban, industrial society in which there is little need for early economic productivity. This society is becoming milder in its approach to child rearing, although it may still be considered relatively harsh in some areas if judged by crosscultural standards. The child is less subject to parental pressures and more subject to the influences of such agents of socialization as his peers and the school. Although parental influences are probably somewhat less pervasive than previously at any given time in the child's early life, the period of dependency on parents has lengthened considerably.

Within these areas of similarity within the culture, forces producing diversity operate. The sex of the child, his ordinal position, the characteristics of his siblings, and the economic well-being and marital adjustment of the parents are all important factors producing differences in the way the child is treated within the family—and thus, in causing variation in personality, adjustment, and behavior, both in childhood and in later years. These sociological factors within the family setting, interacting with the child's innate characteristics and with parental personalities, attitudes toward child rearing, and behaviors, help make each child unique. The family, and especially the parents, plays the major role of shaping the child and producing that complex set of traits called personality.

Other agents of socialization also operate on the child. Certainly, for most individuals, agemates play an important role in socialization. Although the peer group is often viewed as a "bad" influence, it has a number of useful functions. It conveys information and value, provides the child with a source of identification and, perhaps most important of all, serves as a buffer and a normalizer of deviant parent attitudes.

The school is a second extrafamilial grouping that has considerable influence on the development of the child. Both information and values are transmitted. By exposing all children to a relatively uniform set of experiences, the school helps to produce a more homogenerous culture—one that is in some ways increasingly oriented toward a middle-class value system based on a belief in hard work, delayed gratification, and social mobility. The educational system engenders a drive for mobility and provides the formal education necessary for its achievement.

The community, religious institutions, and mass media of communication also have some influence on the socialization process. However, the effect of these last social forces appears to be less than is commonly believed. Further, the effects of the so-called "good" forces such as school books and religious instruction are not all good, nor are the effects of movies, television, and comics as uniformly pernicious as is often assumed. The effects are ambiguous and generally rather minor. Some few children, however, are deeply influenced by such things as community setting or television. These children appear to be young people whose parents have largely abdicated the responsibility of providing values and security, or are individuals with a fair degree of psychological disturbance, or both.

Although genetic inheritance sets the limits within which individuals vary from one another, it also produces a substantial portion of the resulting variation. Upon this genetic variation multifarious environmental forces act to make each of us unique. The complex and interactive play of environmental and hereditary forces, plus the interaction between the many environmental factors themselves, combine to produce the individual. Family and friends, community and school, and books and comic books are only a small sampling of the social influences encountered by a child. Influences may be short-term or long-range, gradual and mild, or sudden and traumatic. Further, the child is not merely a weak and passive recipient of stimulation but is a vigorous and active organism that determines, to a considerable extent, the kind of stimulation it is to receive and the degree of impact that stimuli will have in changing behavior.

From these crosscurrents of stimulation the 'child broadens his sphere of activity. The child develops a personality—a unique set of traits. He develops a self concept—a set of ideas concerning the physical self and a set of self-expectations concerning behavior; this makes him relatively consistent and predictable in behavior. He tends to respond in ways consistent with this self concept and thus develops a more rigid and clearly delineated set of social roles with age.

The human, born weak, small, and totally dependent, masters his developmental tasks and emerges as a tough and strong organism, resistant to stress and capable of self-repair and of manipulating the environment to shape it closer to his heart's desire—social, yet independent; unique, yet part of the whole stream of human life.

We have attempted to map the course of child development. The problems faced in understanding and predicting child behavior are complex and although some questions, such as the influence of maturation on physical development, have been largely answered, others, such as the bases of personality deviation in childhood, are far from solution. We believe that all scientific problems are potentially solvable, and hope that at least some of the *terra incognito* of child psychology will be mapped by students who have read this book.

> Science as a tight little defence against the universe doesn't appeal to me; as an adventure, a continuing exploration, it does. For it is my faith that the universe is real, inexhaustibly rich, and capable of opening out endlessly for inquiring minds; and that we psychologists have barely begun to realize what capacity for experience and action there is in human beings. . . .
>
> *Harold McCurdy*

✻ NAME INDEX

✳ SUBJECT INDEX